The Economics of the Welfare State

The Economics of the Welfare State

Second Edition

Nicholas Barr

Stanford University Press
Stanford, California
1993

Stanford University Press
Stanford, California
© 1987, 1993 Nicholas Barr
Originating publisher: Weidenfeld and
    Nicolson, The Orion Publishing Group, London
First published in the U.S.A. by
    Stanford University Press, 1987
Second edition published 1993
Printed in Great Britain
Cloth ISBN 0–8047–2206–4
Paper ISBN 0–8047–2205–6
LC 93–83252
This book is printed on acid-free paper

For
My Mother and Father

Justice is the first virtue of all social institutions, as truth is of systems of thought. A theory however elegant and economic must be rejected or revised if it is untrue; likewise laws and institutions no matter how efficient and well-arranged must be reformed or abolished if they are unjust. [John Rawls, 1971.]

Let us remember that it [*laissez-faire*] is a *practical rule*, and not a doctrine of science; a rule in the main sound, but like most other sound rules, liable to numerous exceptions; above all, a rule which must never for a moment be allowed to stand in the way of any promising proposal of social or industrial reform. [J. E. Cairnes, 1873.]

Contents

x *Contents*

Tables

Figures

Preface to the Second Edition

The friendly reception the first edition received was very gratifying, and I regret that it has taken so long till the appearance of the second. Much has happened in the intervening years both in Britain and elsewhere, particularly in the formerly Communist countries (one reason why the second edition has not appeared till now is that I spent two years with the World Bank working on the design of social safety nets in central and eastern Europe and the former Soviet Union).

The demise of Marxism faces those countries with the problem of the appropriate division of responsibility between the state and the private sector – the central theme of this book. The economic argument and strategic policy conclusions remain the same as in the first edition: that the welfare state (i.e. income support, health care, education and housing), quite apart from its distributional and other objectives, has a major efficiency role. To the extent that this is so, it is no longer public involvement *per se* which is controversial, but only its precise form and the choice of its distributional objectives. It is therefore not surprising, as discussed in Chapter 15, that the welfare state weathered the storm of the 1980s in Britain and America intact and, in many ways, strengthened.

Throughout the book, the main arguments are contrasted with those arising from different perspectives, especially from socialists and from libertarians like Hayek and Friedman. The debate with the latter is particularly fruitful. The difference between their views and a liberal defence of the welfare state rests less on ideology than on economic theory. Specifically, information problems, which are largely left out of account in most libertarian writing, are crucial to establishing the welfare state's efficiency role.

Though the book is written specifically for economics specialists, the needs of a diverse readership are kept in mind. The early theoretical chapters (3–6) assume a working knowledge of intermediate microeconomic theory. To help readers with little economics, each of these chapters has a non-technical appendix, with the aid of which the rest of the book should, for the most part, be intelligible. Algebra is used where necessary to pin down some important concepts precisely, but the results are always explained verbally so that the equations can be skipped by those who are prepared to take their conclusions on trust. This book is thus accessible to readers in related academic areas (e.g. social administration, public policy and political economy) and to professionals in such fields as medicine and education. Familiarity with British institutions is not essential; they are described in separate sections which can be consulted as desired. The important arguments do not depend on institutional knowledge and should therefore make sense to readers in (or from) other countries. The principles developed are applicable to all industrialised economies and, to a large extent, also to transition economies. Where possible, examples and parallels from other countries are given.

Though the main thrust of the argument has not changed, there are a number of significant changes from the first edition. Chapter 1 contains a new section on the objectives of the welfare state. The theoretical discussion is strengthened by new sections in Chapter 4 on public choice and government failure, and on the boundary between the market and the state, and in Chapter 5 by a new section on social insurance, and by extended discussion of the problems caused by asymmetric information.

Policy analysis includes discussion of three major UK developments: the 1988 social security reforms; reform of the National Health Service in the aftermath of the 1989 White Paper; and changes to school and university education under the 1988 Education Reform Act. In addition, the analysis of targeting in Chapter 10 has been extended, and there is a new section assessing the arguments for child benefit. Chapters 12 and 13 on health care and education have been completely reorganised. Chapters 12, 13 and 14 now discuss health care, education and housing, respectively, and all have a common structure. Alongside discussion of ongoing reforms, the chapters include additional material on international comparison of health care systems and a new section on the reform of higher education, including discussion of student loan schemes. The References have been brought up to date, and expanded to include more international material.

Readers in a hurry can find the major arguments in Chapters 1 and 15, plus the concluding sections of Chapter 4 (economic theory), Chapter 11 (cash benefits), and Chapters 12, 13 and 14 (health care, education and housing, respectively). Readers in less of a hurry may want to look at a number of other books and articles which are, in many ways, companion volumes. My colleague, Howard Glennerster's (1992) book sets out the detailed finances of the welfare state. Barr and Whynes (1993) invites a range of authors to cover the welfare state from a variety of different perspectives. Barr (1992) sets the arguments in a broader OECD context.

My thanks are due to all the colleagues and friends who helped with the first edition. My specific thanks for help with this revision (without implicating them in errors which remain) are to Howard Glennerster and John Hills, to Alan Thompson for guiding me through the morass of UK cash benefit institutions, and to Martin and Peggy Baer for letting me share their rural idyll for a good part of the writing. My greatest debt is to Gill, for her support and encouragement, and for tolerating the sound of the nocturnal keyboard in hotels throughout central and eastern Europe.

Nicholas Barr
November 1992

Part 1
Concepts

Chapter 1
Introduction

[The duties of the state are] ... first ... that of protecting the society
from the violence and invasion of other independent societies; ...
second ... that of protecting, as far as possible, every member of the
society from the injustice or oppression of every other member of it;
... third ... that of erecting and maintaining those publick institutions
and those publick works which, though they may be in the highest degree
advantageous to a great society, are of such a nature, that the profit
could never repay the expence to any individual or small number of
individuals. [Adam Smith, 1776.]

1 The Approach

1.1 The Central Argument

One of the wellsprings of this book was the exuberant insistence of various
of my students and colleagues that economics appeared largely irrelevant
to major issues of social policy. They had a point, and this book is an attempt
to remedy their grievances and to assert the importance of economics. To
help with the former I try to relate economic theory to different notions of
social justice and to the historical development of the welfare state. In
attempting the latter, two results stand out. First, the welfare state is not a
subject apart, but one which fits very naturally into the framework of
economic analysis. Second, the theoretical arguments support the existence
of the welfare state not only for the familiar equity reasons but also very
much in efficiency terms. This, it turns out, is an area in which economic
theory is capable of strong results which can justify the general idea of the
welfare state to a surprising extent without resort to ideology.

Given the size of the subject, this book of necessity is an attempt to paint
a broad canvas in the hope that readers, even if they do not accept all the
answers, will at least be directed to the right battleground. The book
addresses two broad questions: what theoretical arguments can justify the
existence of the various parts of the welfare state in a modern industrialised

economy; and, given these arguments of principle, how sensible (or otherwise) are the specific arrangements in Britain and in other countries?

The approach is best illustrated by two questions which permeate throughout:

1. What are the *aims* of policy?
2. By what *methods* are those aims best achieved?

Question 1 is very broad ranging. There is general agreement that the major aims of policy in Western societies include *efficiency* in the use of resources; their distribution in accordance with *equity* or *justice*; and the preservation of *individual freedom*. These aims, however, can be defined in different ways, and may be accorded different weights. To a utilitarian,[1] the aim of policy is to maximise total welfare; to Rawls the aim is social justice, defined in a particular way; libertarians make their main aim individual freedom, and socialists their prime concern equality. Beveridge's goal was the conquest of what he called the five giants of Want, Disease, Ignorance, Squalor and Idleness. Harold Macmillan once remarked that a just society should contain both a safety net and a ladder. The answer to question 1 is explicitly normative and largely ideological. The objectives of the welfare state are discussed in more detail in section 2.2.

In contrast, it is argued that once question 1 has been answered, question 2 is not *ideological* but *technical*, i.e. it raises a *positive* issue. Whether a given aim should be pursued by market allocation or by public provision depends on which of these methods more nearly achieves the chosen aim. Market allocation is neither 'good' nor 'bad' – it is useful in some instances (e.g. private markets for food in Britain are effective in achieving the aim that people should not starve); but in others (it is argued in Chapter 12 that health care is one) the market mechanism works less well, and a system with substantial state intervention can be argued to be more efficient and just. Similarly, public provision is neither good nor bad, but useful in some cases, less so in others. One of the questions throughout is which method is the more useful in different areas of the welfare state.

The distinction between aims and methods is fundamental, and bears reinforcement. Consider two central questions which all societies face:

- How much redistribution (of income, wealth, power, etc.) should there be?
- How should the economy best be run (i.e. the market system, central planning, or a mixed economy)?

The first question is clearly ideological and normative; it is an aims question and so properly the subject of political debate. But *once that question has been answered*, the second question is very largely one of method (i.e. a

[1] Utilitarianism and other theories of society, including those of Rawls and libertarian and socialist writers, are discussed in Chapter 3.

positive issue) and more properly the subject of technical than political discussion. This approach is explained in detail in Chapters 3 and 4, and summarised in the concluding section of Chapter 4.

1.2 Organisation of the Book

Part 1 sets the scene, starting in Chapter 2 with a discussion of the historical development of the welfare state in Britain, including some comparison with other countries, particularly the USA. The next three chapters are the theoretical heart of the book: Chapter 3 discusses various definitions of social justice and their different implications for the welfare state; Chapter 4 sets out the economic theory of state intervention and Chapter 5 the theory of insurance. Chapter 6 discusses problems of definition and measurement. To help readers who are diffident about their theoretical background, each of the conceptual chapters (3, 4, 5 and 6) has a non-technical Appendix which summarises the essential material; and technical terms are explained in the Glossary.

Three major threads are developed in Part 1 which run through the rest of the book: the social welfare maximisation problem; alternative definitions of social justice; and measurement problems. The social welfare maximisation problem (set out in Chapter 4) is the conventional starting point for economic theory. An important theorem states that under appropriate assumptions a competitive market equilibrium will allocate resources efficiently. It is argued that, where these conditions hold, the role of the state, if any, is limited to income redistribution; conversely, where these conditions fail, there may be efficiency grounds for intervention in a variety of forms. The second major theme is social justice. The definition chosen will determine the weights assigned to different individuals, with major implications for the form and extent of intervention, e.g. whether people with no income should be supported at subsistence, or at some higher level. The third thread, discussed in Chapter 6, concerns problems of definition and measurement. Many variables are hard to define and, once defined, hard to measure. A crucial and recurrent difficulty is that utility (see the Glossary) is not measurable. This makes it hard both to measure living standards and to compare them. Costs or benefits may also be hard to measure.

As far as possible each chapter in Parts 2 and 3 has a similar layout to clarify the structure of the argument. Each chapter discusses in turn: the *aims* of policy; the *methods* by which they might be achieved, i.e. the theoretical arguments about intervention for reasons of efficiency and social justice; *assessment* in the light of this theoretical discussion of the appropriateness (or otherwise) of the British and other systems, including discussion of the empirical literature; and *reform*.

Part 2 analyses cash transfers. Chapter 7 briefly describes the finances of the welfare state. Chapter 8 looks at unemployment, sickness and disability benefits, Chapter 9 at retirement pensions and Chapter 10 at non-contributory benefits, in each case starting with the theory and then assessing the practice. Chapter 11 considers a variety of reform strategies. Part 3 discusses provision in kind. Chapter 12 looks at health care, analysing the theoretical arguments for public production and allocation, assessing the effectiveness of the UK national health service in comparison with systems in other countries, and discussing alternative ways in which health care might be organised. Chapters 13 and 14 cover similar ground for education and housing, respectively.

The conclusions of the book are summarised in Chapter 15. Readers in a hurry can get an idea of the book's approach and its main conclusions by reading Chapter 15 and the concluding sections of Chapters 4 (economic and political theory), 11 (income support), and 12, 13 and 14 (health care, education and housing, respectively).

2   The Welfare State: Definition and Objectives

2.1   Defining the Welfare State

We shall see in Chapter 6 that important concepts like poverty and equality of opportunity are hard, if not impossible, to define in principle, and even harder to measure. The concept of the welfare state similarly defies precise definition, and no attempt is made to offer one (see the Further Reading). Even Richard Titmuss (1958) ducked the problem – that book is called *Essays on 'The Welfare State'* (his quotes). As he later put it, 'I am no more enamoured today of the indefinable abstraction "The Welfare State" than I was some twenty years ago when ... the term acquired an international as well as a national popularity' (1968, p. 124). Three areas of complication stand out.

Welfare derives from many sources in addition to state activity: individual welfare derives not only, nor necessarily primarily, from state institutions, but from at least four sources.

- *The labour market* is arguably the most important, first through *wage income*. Full employment is a major component of welfare broadly defined. High levels of employment and rising labour productivity over the post-war period were at least as much an equalising force as redistribution. In addition to wage income, firms (individually or on an industry-wide basis, voluntarily or under legal compulsion) provide *occupational welfare* in the face of sickness, injury and retirement.
- *Private provision* includes voluntary private insurance and individual saving.

- *Voluntary welfare* arises both within the family and outside, where people give time free or at a below-market price, or make voluntary charitable donations in other forms.
- *The state* intervenes by providing cash benefits and benefits in kind. In addition, it contributes through various tax concessions to the finance of occupational and private provision.

Modes of delivery are also diverse. Though a service may be *funded* by the state, it does not follow that it must necessarily be publicly *produced*. The state can produce a service itself and supply it to recipients at no charge (e.g. health care under the National Health Service); or it can pay for individuals to consume goods produced in the private sector (e.g. free drugs under the National Health Service); or it can give individuals money (either explicitly or in the form of tax relief) to make their own purchases (e.g. tax relief in some countries for private medical insurance premiums). The issue of 'privatisation', as we shall see in Chapter 4:6, is much more complex than is recognised in most public discussion.

The boundaries of the welfare state are not well defined: though the state's role should not be exaggerated, neither should it be understated. Some typically excluded expenditure (e.g. public health and environmental policies) is very similar in purpose to activities which are included.

Welfare is thus a mosaic, with diversity both in its source and in the manner of its delivery. Nevertheless the state, through various levels of government, is much the most important single agency involved in Britain, and in most industrialised countries (for a survey of the welfare state in ten OECD countries, see Barr (1992)). Throughout the book the term 'welfare state' is used as a shorthand for the state's activities in four broad areas: cash benefits; health care; education; and food, housing and other welfare services (Lampman, 1984, Ch. 1).

In broad terms the welfare state today comprises cash benefits and benefits in kind. The latter embrace a wide range of activities, including education, medical care and more general forms of care for the infirm, the mentally and physically handicapped, and children in need of protection. Cash benefits have two major components.

1. *Social insurance* is awarded without an income or wealth test (see the Glossary), generally on the basis of (a) previous contributions and (b) the occurrence of a specified contingency, such as unemployment or being above a specified age.

2. *Non-contributory benefits* are of two sorts. '*Universal*' benefits are awarded on the basis of a specified contingency, without either a contributions or an income test. There is no convenient shorthand for this type of benefit: such benefits are often referred to (Gordon, 1988, p. 37) as 'universal' and, reluctantly, I shall follow that usage. Major examples in Britain are child benefit and the National Health Service (discussed in

Chapters 10 and 12, respectively). *Social assistance* is awarded on the basis of an income test. It is generally a benefit of last resort, designed to help individuals and families who are in poverty, whether as an exceptional emergency, or because they are not covered by social insurance, or as a supplement to social insurance.

In practice the British welfare state can be taken to comprise, at a minimum, the publicly provided benefits (representing about 23.5 per cent of gross domestic product) shown in Figure 1.1, together with the contributions which pay for them. Cash benefits follow the pattern described above. National insurance is payable to people with an adequate con-tributions record; benefits cover, *inter alia*, unemployment, sickness (short- and long-term) and retirement, of which the last (not far short of 20 per cent of social spending) is much the largest. Non-contributory benefits include child benefit (a weekly cash payment to the parent or guardian of every child), and income support (paid on the basis of a means test to those with little or no other income). The major benefits in kind are the National Health Service (23.5 per cent of total social spending), education (approximately 21.6 per cent), and housing (6 per cent, plus substantial additional expenditure on cash assistance with housing costs).

2.2 The Objectives of the Welfare State

The objectives of social institutions, as in any other area of economic policy, are efficiency, equity and administrative feasibility. In this context, however, it is useful to adopt a more detailed categorisation.

Efficiency has at least three aspects.

1. *Macro efficiency*: the efficient fraction of GDP should be devoted to the totality of welfare-state institutions, e.g. policy should seek to avoid distortions which lead to cost explosions.

2. *Micro efficiency*: policy should ensure the efficient division of total welfare-state resources between the different cash benefits, different types of medical treatment, and different kinds of education.

3. *Incentives*: where institutions are publicly funded, their finance and the construction of benefits should minimise adverse effects (a) on labour supply and employment, and (b) on saving.

Supporting living standards, the second strategic aim, has at least three components.

4. *Poverty relief*: no individual/household should fall below a minimum standard of living. As discussed in Chapter 6, there is no analytically satisfactory way of defining a poverty line, so that the definition of the minimum standard is largely normative. Once the poverty line has been decided, the effectiveness of the system is measured by statistics relating to

Figure 1.1 *Overview of the welfare state, UK, 1992/3 (est.)*

Sources: UK (1992j, Table 2.1); UK (1992e, Table 1); UK (1992c, Table 1); UK (1992d, Tables 1 and 2); UK (1992b, Figure 82); UK (1992f, Introductory Table and Table 9.4); UK (1992g, Figure 1.03 and Appendix 3); UK (1992h, Tables 1.1 and 12.2).

Notes: [a] Estimated figure.
  [b] Includes current and capital spending and debt interest.
  [c] Figure greater than sum of its parts because expenditure in Northern Ireland and on administration has been included.
  [d] Includes widows' benefit.
  [e] Invalidity benefit and industrial disablement and death benefits.
  [f] Excludes statutory sick pay.
  [g] Attendance allowance, invalid care allowance, severe disablement allowance, mobility allowance, disability living allowance and disability working allowance.

how many people are below the poverty line ('headcount' measures), by *how much* ('poverty gap' measures), and for *how long* (i.e. life-cycle and intergenerational matters) (see Atkinson, 1987b; Foster, 1984).

5. *Insurance*: no one should face an unexpected and unacceptably large drop in their living standard. This is a major objective of unemployment benefits and most health-related benefits. Its success is measured by the replacement ratio, which shows a person's income when on benefit in comparison with his or her previous income.

6. *Income smoothing*: institutions should enable individuals to reallocate consumption over their lifetime. As discussed in Chapter 9, individuals can redistribute from themselves at one stage in the life cycle to themselves at another (an actuarial private pension scheme); or such redistribution could be notional (an unfunded state pension scheme which embodies an inter-generational social contract (Samuelson, 1958)). Alternatively, there could be tax-funded provision, with no pretence of individual contributions, to groups whose stage in the life cycle suggests that they are likely to be financially constrained (e.g. benefits for families with young children).

Objectives 5 and 6 are different aspects of the broader aim of *economic security*. Objective 5 concerns unexpected reductions in living standards (i.e. it is mainly an insurance objective); objective 6 concerns predictable falls in income (i.e. it is more a savings objective). Both objectives therefore have an efficiency as well as an equity dimension.

The reduction of inequality, in contrast, is almost entirely an equity issue.

7. *Vertical equity*: the system should redistribute towards individuals/families with lower incomes. This aim is contentious. All income-tested benefits contribute to it to a greater or lesser extent; so, second, do non-means-tested benefits whose recipients disproportionately have lower incomes (e.g. the UK flat-rate pension). A third form of redistribution arises where the benefit formula favours lower-income individuals. 'Free' provision of a tax-funded service (e.g. health care in Britain) is also generally redistributive.

The success or otherwise of benefits in reducing inequality is assessed by inspection over time of aggregate inequality measures, though with all the caveats noted in Chapter 6.

8. *Horizontal equity*: differences in benefits should take account of age, family size, etc., and differences in medical treatment should reflect only factors which are regarded as relevant (e.g. whether or not the patient has dependants), but not irrelevant factors like race.

Social integration   So far the objectives have been conventional economic ones. Some commentators include broader social goals.

9. *Dignity*: cash benefits and health care should be delivered so as to preserve individual dignity and without unnecessary stigma (Meade, 1978,

p. 269). Beveridge emphasised the importance of contributions in this context:

The popularity of compulsory social insurance today is established, and for good reason; by compulsory insurance, ... the individual can feel assured that [his] needs will be met ...; by paying ... a contribution, he can feel that he is getting security not as a charity but as a right. [Beveridge Report (UK, 1942), para. 296.]

10. *Social solidarity*: cash benefits and health care should foster social solidarity, a frequently stated goal in mainland Europe. So far as possible, benefits should depend on criteria which are unrelated to socioeconomic status. Retirement pensions are an example; so is medical care in many countries. Additionally, benefits should be high enough and health care good enough to allow recipients to participate fully in the life of the society in which they live – an aim which relates closely to the objective of poverty relief.

Administrative feasibility has two aspects.

11. *Intelligibility*: the system should be simple, easy to understand and as cheap to administer as possible.

12. *Absence of abuse*: benefits should be as little open to abuse as possible.

Problems of definition and measurement abound. Efficiency objectives 1–3 have precise analytical definitions, but measurement problems, particularly the incidence of taxes, contributions and benefits, make it difficult to assess how far they are achieved. How do we define a poverty line in objective 4; and how large a drop in living standard is 'unacceptable' (objective 5)? The appropriate extent of vertical redistribution and a workable definition of horizontal equity (objectives 7 and 8) have occupied economists, philosophers and political theorists almost since the dawn of time, and have plagued policy-makers at least since the British Poor Law Act of 1601. Even 'equality' is difficult to define unambiguously (Okun, 1975, Ch. 3), especially in the context of benefits in kind like health care (Le Grand, 1982, Ch. 2). Concepts like 'dignity', 'stigma' and 'social solidarity' (objectives 9 and 10) are hard to define and raise major measurement problems. Writers like Hayek (1976) argue in addition that the term 'social solidarity' is devoid of meaning, and that its pursuit is both pointless and dangerous. These problems are discussed in some detail in Chapters 3–6.

Even were these problems assumed away, a second set of difficulties arises, in that some objectives are inherently in conflict and others may be. The trade-off between efficiency and distributional objectives, and between horizontal equity and administrative simplicity, are no less intractable for their familiarity. Other objectives conflict almost by definition. Income smoothing implies that an individual with higher earnings should receive higher benefits, which sits uneasily with the requirement that benefits should redistribute towards those with lower incomes, and with the objective that benefits should contribute to social solidarity. On one interpretation of equity everyone should receive benefits proportional to their past contributions, but that, again, conflicts both with redistribution towards lower incomes and with social solidarity. The choice of objectives and of priorities between them is a fundamental normative issue.

Further Reading

The diversity of sources of welfare is discussed by Glennerster (1992, Ch. 1). Titmuss (1958) and Briggs (1961a) attempt to define the welfare state; see also Esping-Anderson (1990). On the idea of welfare see Robson (1976), Pinker (1979) and Higgins (1981).

Chapter 2
The Historical Background

The principle of *laissez-faire* may be safely trusted to in some things but in many more it is wholly inapplicable; and to appeal to it on all occasions savours more of the policy of a parrot than of a statesman or a philosopher. [J. R. McCulloch, 1848.]

The poverty of the poor is the chief cause of that weakness and inefficiency which are the cause of their poverty. [Alfred Marshall, 1885.]

1 Early Days

1.1 Poor Relief

The British welfare state is neither the outcome of the Second World War nor simply the creation of the post-war Labour government. Its roots are ancient and complex. Christian charity to relieve poverty has gradually (though even today not wholly) been taken over by state action. And state activity has grown over the years from small scale to large; from local to central; from permissive to mandatory; and from piecemeal to complex and interrelated. From this tangle, however, four events stand out: the *Poor Law Act* of 1601 and the *Poor Law Amendment Act* of 1834 were the main legislative bases of poverty relief before the twentieth century; the *Liberal reforms* of 1906–14 represented a substantial departure from *laissez-faire* capitalism and so can be argued to form the basis of the welfare state; and the *post-war legislation* of 1944–8 set the scene for the welfare state as we know it today.

It should be clear that the question 'how did the welfare state come about?' is vast, so discussion is limited in two important ways. No attempt is made at complete coverage; the story is confined for the most part to the British experience, with only a sideways glance at other countries, notably the USA. The question is also controversial; I shall sketch out the major areas of historical dispute, but make no attempt at resolving them. The chapter is organised chronologically, discussing *seriatim* the period up to the end of the nineteenth century (section 1); the Liberal reforms of 1906–14 (section 2); British developments between the two World Wars (section 3); inter-war poverty relief in the USA (section 4); the Second World War and its immediate aftermath in Britain (section 5); and developments since 1948 in Britain and the USA (section 6). Section 7 draws the threads together by considering the forces which created the welfare state.

Among the early motives for public poor relief in Britain were the fear of social disorder and chronic labour shortages in the years after the Black Death of 1348–9. As a result, the state attempted, *inter alia*, to control wages and labour mobility in the Statute of Labourers 1351 and the Poor Law Act 1388. Tudor legislation grew away from this repressive and not very effective regime:

In 1576 the concept of 'setting the poor on work' was enshrined in statute law where it was to remain for something like three and a half centuries. If the able-bodied required assistance they had to work for it, and in the 1576 Poor Relief Act JPs were instructed to provide a stock of raw materials on which beggars could work in return for the relief they received. [Fraser, 1984, p. 32.]

The 1601 Poor Law Act, built on the 1576 Act, adopted a twofold approach: each parish was required to assume responsibility for its poor; and different treatment was prescribed for three categories of pauper. The 'impotent poor' (the old and the sick) were to be accommodated in 'almshouses'; the able-bodied were to be given work in a 'house of correction' (not at first a residential workhouse); and those who refused to work were to be punished in this 'house of correction'. The idea was that paupers not able to work should be cared for and the able-bodied should be given work; neither regime was intended to be punitive.

This arrangement worked moderately well for nearly two hundred years; but eventually its institutions, locally financed and adapted to a pre-industrial economy, came under pressure from population growth, increased social mobility, industrialisation and economic fluctuations. By 1795 food shortages and inflation resulting from war and bad harvests had spread poverty from the unemployed to those in work, giving rise to various local initatives, notably the Speenhamland system which supplemented wages with an 'allowance' based on the price of bread. The novelty of these changes was that they extended aid to people in work. Poor relief, whether under the Poor Law *per se* or under a local variant, carried less social stigma than it was later to acquire.

These arrangements soon came under attack. Bentham believed that they caused moral degeneracy among recipients. Malthus argued that poor relief would cause excessive population growth, and Ricardo that it would depress wages and thereby exacerbate poverty. Possibly more important than these theoretical arguments was the escalating cost of relief, partly due to rising prices (especially of bread), and also because of rising unemployment as soldiers returned from the Napoleonic wars. As a result the costs (which were met from local revenues) rose sharply.

The Poor Law Report and the Poor Law Amendment Act 1834 were consequences of this philosophical and financial climate. A Royal Commission was set up in 1832; its report, which was *laissez-faire* in tone (see the Glossary), was written by Nassau Senior and Edwin Chadwick, a former secretary to Bentham. The intellectual background to the report, and particularly the position of the Classical economists on the Poor Law, is often misunderstood. It is true that Malthus and Ricardo, worried by population growth and shocked by the earlier effect of the Poor Law, advocated its gradual repeal. But it is *not* the case that Nassau Senior (who was, according to Robbins, more in the mainstream of Classical thought) was against poor relief. In Senior's view, 'the great test which must be applied to any project of state action in regard to relief is the question *whether it has any tendency to increase that which it is proposed to diminish*' (Robbins, 1977, p. 128, his emphasis). Thus, he supported public provision for orphans, the blind and the disabled, including provision of medical treatment and hospitals. He was not in favour of abolishing relief for the able-bodied and their dependants, but insisted on the principle of 'less eligibility', i.e. that relief should be limited to an amount and administered in a manner which left the recipient worse off than the employed.

The Poor Law Report was entirely consistent with this approach when it argued that the new system should contain three elements (often referred to as 'the Principles of 1834'): the notion of less eligibility, the workhouse test, and administrative centralisation. Less eligibility was the central doctrine of 1834. It was not intended to apply to the old or sick, but only to the able-bodied whose indigence, it was argued, would be encouraged by higher benefits.[1] The workhouse test (i.e. relief conditional upon living in the workhouse) was not a principle, but simply a means of enforcing less eligibility. As far as possible, the workhouse would provide a standard of living lower than that of the lowest worker. Additional restrictions were imposed, including the strict segregation of husbands, wives and children. The purpose of centralisation was to avoid local corruption and incompetence; to ensure uniformity; to enhance cost-effectiveness; and to promote labour mobility. The difference between the 1601 Poor Law and the Principles of 1834 is important. The former was intended to give work to the able-bodied without stigma; the latter discouraged claims for relief by making its receipt highly unpleasant and also stigmatising.

---

[1] Readers may note more than a passing similarity between these arguments of 150 years ago, and the more recent debates discussed in sections 6 and 7. Some commentators argue that part of the Poor Law spirit persists, e.g. the decline in unemployment benefit relative to other benefits in Britain in the 1980s can be interpreted as a case of less eligibility.

The Poor Law Amendment Act followed quickly in the wake of the Poor Law Report. Despite controversy among historians it is now clear that, though the intention of the Act was largely (though in important respects not fully) to implement the recommendations of the report, the effect of the Act in practice was less than appeared in principle. The Poor Law Commission (in whom the powers of central government were vested) was never able to bend local administration of the Poor Law to its will, particularly in respect of enforcing the workhouse test. But in other respects, it is argued, the implementation of the Act had more unpleasant effects than was intended by its architects (see Bowley, 1937, Pt II, Ch. 2). Many people were forced to accept the harsh conditions of the workhouse, and many others endured appalling privation to avoid it. Because of its very cruelty, however, the system became over time a force for change, and thus the 1834 Act may be seen as one of the roots of later developments.

1.2 Other Early Social Legislation

Notwithstanding the philosophical underpinnings of the Principles of 1834, *laissez-faire* was increasingly eroded over the nineteenth century, in three areas in particular: factory legislation, education, and public health. The first Factory Act, passed in 1802, protected women and children by limiting hours and regulating working conditions. Althorp's Factory Act of 1833 tightened the rules and, probably of greater long-run importance, appointed four inspectors to enforce its provisions. The latter was implicit acknowledgement of the right of the state to regulate certain social conditions.

The role of the state in education started more gradually (Fraser, 1984, Ch. 4; West, 1970). Most schools in the early nineteenth century were charitable and reflected the prevailing ethos of social deference, Christian morality and voluntarism. The Sunday school movement had an important role in teaching reading, often with the Bible as the only text. State intervention started in 1833 with a grant to Protestant schools for school building, i.e. as financial help for voluntarism, and from 1847 a grant was paid for a limited scheme of teacher training. As government involvement grew, a Royal Commission was established, though its recommendations were largely superseded by the Education Act 1870, which gave every child the right (at least in principle) to some form of schooling. School Boards were empowered (but not compelled) to provide elementary education, financed by a mixture of central and local revenues. The resulting system was a compromise in which the new board schools coexisted with the voluntary sector. Later developments made elementary school attendance compulsory between five and ten (Mundella's Education Act 1880) and virtually free (the Fee Grant Act 1891).

Thus a process of gradual accretion over the nineteenth century led to a system of primary education which was compulsory and largely publicly funded. Of the many explanations of these changes one in particular is a recurring theme – the *national efficiency* argument, which justified state involvement in education on the grounds that it made labour more productive, thus contributing to economic growth. It is also argued that the 1870 Act was encouraged by the extension of the franchise in 1867, creating a need to educate the growing electorate.

The third breach in *laissez-faire* was in public health (Fraser, 1984, Ch. 3; Finer, 1952, Chs 5, 7 and 8). In the first half of the nineteenth century, urbanisation (largely the result of the industrial revolution) and population growth caused cities to grow rapidly, leading to a housing shortage and, connected with it, a sanitation problem. The poor in particular were afflicted by typhus and tuberculosis; and a series of cholera epidemics, being waterborne, attacked everyone, including the middle classes with their ready access to water supplies.

This was the problem. The solution again involves Edwin Chadwick, whose *Report on the Sanitary Conditions of the Labouring Population of Great Britain* (UK, 1842) was remarkable for the high quality of its statistical analysis. Chadwick originally advocated sewage disposal as a public enterprise on the grounds that ill-health, by causing poverty, added to the cost of the Poor Law. The report, however, included wider grounds for intervention. Its main recommendation (though based on a faulty theory of the transmission of cholera) was that sewage should be separated from other water through the use of glazed pipes. The report met considerable opposition, both technical and based on financial, ideological and political arguments. As a result legislation was delayed, and initially ineffective. After several false starts, the Public Health Act 1875 established clear duties for local authorities, and remained the basis of most public health activities until 1936.

This, then, was the situation in the 1870s. The state was slowly becoming involved in increasing areas of social and economic life; but though the Classical economists supported much of the new legislation, the prevailing doctrine was still largely *laissez-faire*.

2 The Liberal Reforms[2]

2.1 The Origins of the Reforms

The third major development was the period of the Liberal reforms between 1906 and 1914. Historians have debated at length this burst of activity so

---

[2] This section draws on Hay (1975). See also the Further Reading.

much at variance with the ideology of the nineteenth-century Liberal Party. Hay (1975) distinguishes three influences in particular which historians regard as underlying the reforms: pressure from below; changed attitudes to welfare provision; and institutional influences.

Pressure from below   There is a measure of agreement that working-class political pressure was one of the origins of the reforms, though the relationship is far from simple. If reform was so popular, why was it not a major election issue; and why the long lag between electoral reform in 1867 and social reform in 1906–14? Pelling deals with the problem by denying the premise, arguing that working-class pressure was negligible:

The members of the working class as a whole, cynical about the character of society as they knew it, were yet fearful of change which would more likely be for the worse than for the better. They advanced into the twentieth century with little expectation of social improvement being engineered by political means, and none at all of the 'welfare state' as we know it today. [1979, p. 18.]

Hobsbawm (1964) argues that it was only unorganised workers who opposed reform. Nor was working-class pressure necessarily important for all the reforms.

Changing attitudes to welfare provision among the political élite arose *inter alia* out of the national efficiency issue. The argument at its simplest was that economic growth depended on a healthy, educated workforce. In dramatic contrast with the Principles of 1834, a speaker in Parliamentary debate could argue:

The future of the Empire, the triumph of social progress and the freedom of the British race depend not so much upon the strengthening of the Army as upon fortifying the children of the State for the battle of life. [*Hansard* (Commons), 18 April 1905, col. 539, quoted by Bruce, 1972, pp. 152–3.]

The influence of the national efficiency arguments is debated. At a minimum they made social reform politically respectable.

A second reason for greater acceptance of intervention was a changed attitude towards poverty. The social surveys of Booth (1902) and Rowntree (1901) and the study of the health of Boer War recruits yielded much empirical information. The effects of these data on attitudes were complex; they suggested that poverty was more widespread than had been believed, and that not all poverty, even among the able-bodied, was due to moral defect. They also raised doubts about the effectiveness of private philanthropy.[3]

A third influence was the rise of collectivism. The 'Old Liberalism', which was opposed to state intervention, had twofold roots in the 'natural rights'

---

[3] For the view that poverty was 'discovered' much earlier, see Himmelfarb (1984).

individualist philosophy of writers like Spencer (1884) and in utilitarianism.[4] Between 1860 and 1900, however, several philosophers, though in no sense advocating collectivism, suggested that the traditional definition of individual freedom as *absence of coercion* was too narrow. It was argued (e.g. Hobson, 1909, Pt II, Ch. II) that 'positive freedom' should include not only economic freedom but also a measure of *economic security*. It followed that the state, in advancing individual freedom, should adopt an active role in social reform. This was the 'New Liberalism' (see Freeden, 1978).

In the context of these changing ideas the German example became important. Between 1883 and 1889, largely as a counter to socialist agitation, the German government under Bismarck had created a broad system of social insurance, under which compulsory contributions gave entitlement to a system of guaranteed benefits, thereby removing the threat of the means test and poor house. The scheme was investigated by Lloyd George, and had a major influence on the shape of the National Insurance Act 1911 (discussed below).

Institutional influences on the reforms included pressure groups such as the Friendly Societies, which represented the idea of working-class self-help. It is also argued that bureaucracies like the civil service exerted an independent influence. McDonagh (1960) describes a process whereby, as awareness of a problem grew, a body of experts would be set up to investigate. As a result of its findings awareness of the problem increased, and so did the volume of resources devoted to combatting it. Experts thus contributed not only to the *manner* in which social problems were tackled, but also to the *range* of issues regarded as the proper province of public policy.

The reforms were central rather than local mainly because of the reluctance of central government (despite several official inquiries) to reform local authority finance in the light of regional inequalities, and the failure of local revenues to rise in step with expenditure.[5] Finally, the reforms were outside the Poor Law partly because the latter was financed locally; partly to sidestep the long-established vested interests of local Poor Law institutions; and partly because of popular hostility towards the old system.

2.2 The New Measures

Whatever their causes (about which historians continue to argue) and motives (discussed below), the reforms of 1906–14 were substantial by any standards and particularly so in the context of the times. The new measures concerned children, pensions, unemployment, health and fiscal policy.

---

[4] The important distinction between a natural rights and a utilitarian defence of individual freedom is discussed at length in Chapter 3, which also discusses the ideas of collectivist writers.
[5] The owner of my borrowed copy of Hay has written 'so what's new?' in the margin.

Children   The Education (Provision of Meals) Act 1906 permitted (but did not compel) local authorities to provide school meals for needy children; the Education (Administrative Provisions) Act 1907 introduced medical inspection of school children; and the Children Act 1908 made it a punishable offence for parents to neglect their children. The motives for these Acts were partly humanitarian and partly on national efficiency grounds.

Pensions   The Old Age Pensions Act 1908

introduced a new principle into social policy. Hitherto relief had been provided ... from *local* funds and only after a test of destitution. Now for the first time payments were to be made, as of right, from *national* funds ... within strict limits of age and means, but with no test of actual destitution. [Bruce, 1972, p. 178, his emphasis.]

The Act introduced a non-contributory pension of five shillings (25 pence) per week for people over 70 whose income was below £31 per year, though it excluded previous recipients of Poor Law relief, and some people on moral grounds.[6]

Unemployment and minimum wages   Various earlier proposals to resolve the growing problem of unemployment had met with little success (see Harris, 1972). Any acceptable solution had to meet four criteria (Hay, 1975, pp. 50–1). It had to 'make the minimum alterations in the normal workings of the labour market to satisfy individualists, economists and industrialists.' Second, 'it ... had to be largely self-financing in order to avoid unacceptable increases in direct taxation or the reintroduction of tariffs.' It had to be separate from the Poor Law to avoid the need to discriminate between the 'deserving' and 'undeserving' poor. Lastly, it had to be sufficiently attractive to head off any socialist threat. The resulting package had three elements: voluntary labour exchanges would assist the normal working of the labour market; there was to be a limited scheme of unemployment insurance; and a Development Fund would finance counter-cyclical public works expenditure, mainly by local authorities.

The scheme of unemployment insurance was limited: it applied only to a narrow range of industries; only workers earning less than £160 per year were covered; and benefits were low to discourage deliberate unemployment. A variety of other industrial legislation, including the Trades Disputes Act and the Workmen's Compensation Act in 1906, and the Trade Boards Act 1909, gave the government limited power to set minimum wages. It was recognised that unemployment and sickness were interrelated, so the National Insurance Act 1911 also contained health insurance. The combined

---

[6] History is full of small anomalies. An additional reason for the pensions legislation, according to Pelling (1979, p. 11), was '[a] loosening of the Treasury's purse strings [because of] the temporary lull in the naval building race, which was due to the destruction of Russian battleships in the Russo-Japanese War ... Thus in a sense it was Admiral Togo, the victor of Tsushima, who laid the groundwork of Old Age Pensions and deserves to be remembered as the architect of the British Welfare State.'

package was financed by a weekly contribution of 9d, of which 4d was paid by the worker, the rest by the employer.

Health Whereas unemployment insurance, according to Hay, was largely the result of working-class pressure, health insurance arose more from considerations of national efficiency. Prior to 1911 there were voluntary hospitals for those who could afford to subscribe to them; for others Poor Law hospitals offered free and (for the most part) non-stigmatising health care (Abel Smith, 1964, Ch. 15). The 1911 Act did little to change these arrangements. Cover was extended only to the breadwinner, who was entitled to a sickness (i.e. cash) benefit, free medical treatment and drugs from a panel doctor, and access to a sanatorium.

Fiscal policy The fiscal controversies of the period concerned tariffs (which are not the issue here), and progressive income tax. The traditional economic argument was that taxation should be based on the principle of 'equal sacrifice' (implying a poll tax), or of 'equi-proportional sacrifice' (implying a proportional tax). Both approaches ruled out redistribution through the tax system. By the turn of the century, however, there was limited support for redistribution through tax-financed public expenditure. Edgeworth justified progressive taxation by appeal to the 'least aggregate sacrifice' principle under which *marginal* rather than *total* sacrifice was to be equalised. Equal marginal sacrifice plus the assumption of diminishing marginal utility of income together imply progressive taxation.

A different line of argument by people like Hobson (1908) was that monopoly elements resulted in a sub-optimal income distribution, leading to underconsumption. By thus attributing unemployment to under-consumption which could be remedied by income redistribution Hobson foreshadowed Keynes some thirty years before the publication of *The General Theory*. Others, notably socialists, saw progressive taxation as an issue of social justice, a subject to which we return in Chapter 3.

A brief assessment In assessing the reforms two hotly debated issues arise: what was their motive (discussed in section 7.1); and were they particularly radical? It can be argued (Marsh, 1980, p. 17) that the virtually simultaneous introduction of old age pensions, unemployment insurance, sickness benefits and progressive taxation, supported by the interventionist philosophy of the New Liberalism, constituted a fundamental break with earlier economic and political doctrines.

However, a closer look at the individual programmes gives a less clear answer. The pension scheme, albeit non-contributory, was to some extent means-tested, and applied only to individuals over 70 who had never received poor relief and were not excluded on moral grounds. Its main purpose, it can be argued, was to improve national competitiveness by weeding out inefficient labour (the national efficiency argument again).

Unemployment insurance was based in part on a weekly employee contribution of 4d (i.e. lump-sum and therefore regressive), and applied only
to a few relatively skilled workers in some industries. Sickness benefits were
financed by the same contribution, with similar coverage; and the health
care benefits applied only to the breadwinner. It can be argued, therefore,
that the reforms were relatively minor and with limited coverage; and that
only the pension scheme was substantially redistributive from rich to poor.
The New Liberalism, from this viewpoint, was not very new; it still accepted
capitalism unquestioningly, and in that sense was only a reinterpretation of
the Old Liberalism. As we shall see in section 4, strikingly similar issues
arise in considering the novelty (or otherwise) of the 1935 US Social Security
Act.

Nor, in conclusion, were the Liberal reforms in any way unique. Germany,
as we have seen, had introduced social insurance in the 1880s, motivated
in part by fears of social unrest. New Zealand introduced non-contributory
pensions in 1898, *inter alia* for reasons of national efficiency, in the face of
increased international competition on an economy highly dependent on its
exports. By 1908 Denmark, Ireland, Austria, Czechoslovakia and Australia
also had social legislation of some sort (Pechman *et al.*, 1968, Appendix C;
and for more general international comparison Kaim-Caudle, 1973). The
Liberal reforms, though one of the earlier examples of nationally organised
income support, were not the first; nor did they represent a major dis-
continuity either with previous arrangements or with developments in other
countries.

3 The First World War and the Inter-War Period in Britain

3.1 Housing

In contrast with the eventful years between 1906 and 1914 the period
thereafter was largely a time of stagnation in social policy, with the
important exception of housing. There were also major changes in unemployment insurance (section 3.2). In housing, probably more than any other
part of the welfare state, past policies, notably during and after the First
World War, have a crucial bearing on more recent institutions. Before 1914,
virtually all housing was provided by the private market. By and large the
system worked well for those who could afford it; but for the lowest income
groups, particularly in large cities, it led to overcrowding and squalor
(Gauldie, 1974). In a strictly technical sense the housing market cleared,
but policy-makers found the result unacceptable both for reasons of public
health and public order, and for more charitable motives. Early legislation
had little effect, mainly because it imposed no *duty* on local authorities to
remedy poor housing. Though working-class housing conditions continued

to cause concern in the latter part of the nineteenth century, the response was limited mainly to philanthropic efforts (see Merrett, 1979).

By 1918, however, for at least three reasons, housing had become a problem for which existing methods were no longer regarded as adequate. First, there was an acute housing shortage because of falling supply (due to the cessation of building during the First World War, and the deterioration of older property) and rising demand (because people were living longer and marrying earlier, and mobility among young people was increasing). Second, this shortage was regarded as politically too sensitive to be left to private charity and discretionary local action. In 1918 large numbers of soldiers were demobilised, and there were fears of social unrest (the Russian Revolution having occurred in the previous year). Lloyd George's promise in November 1918 'to make Britain a fit country for heroes to live in' was seen as a commitment on which it would have been politically dangerous to renege.

The third reason why housing was thought to warrant government action was because intervention had already occurred, through the imposition of rent control in 1915 as an emergency wartime measure. As we shall see in Chapter 14, rent control is rather like smoking – if one never starts one can do without, but once started it is hard to give up. By 1918 many people were unable to pay the market price of housing, which had risen sharply because of the shortage; at least as important, controlled rents had already assumed an aura of 'fair' rents.

Since immediate decontrol was politically impossible, the government chose to assume some responsibility for people dependent on renting at the lower end of the market, through direct provision of housing at rents equivalent to controlled rents.

The resulting Housing and Town Planning Act 1919 (the Addison Act) contained three provisions: local authorities were invested with the *duty* of remedying housing deficiencies in their areas; house building was to meet *general* needs rather than concentrating only on slum clearance; and the operation received a central government subsidy which underwrote the entire cost of house building in excess of the product of a penny rate.[7] In contrast with nineteenth-century thought, the Act embodied three new principles – central supervision, compulsion and subsidy. It had three long-term effects: the acceptance of the idea of housing as a legitimate area of government intervention, in the sense of public production as opposed merely to regulation; the provision of accommodation at a subsidised rent implied a view of housing as a social service; and the service was to be delivered by local authorities. The Act, together with rent control, laid a foundation for housing policy which has lasted almost to the present.

---

[7] I.e. the revenue raised by increasing local rates (property taxes) by 1d in the pound.

The Addison Act met with some success. However, generous subsidies, when the capacity of the building industry was already stretched by private-sector demand, led inevitably to soaring costs; and when the post-war boom faltered, the resulting public spending cuts (the so-called 'Geddes axe') halted expenditure under the Act. Chamberlain's Housing Act 1923 reduced the subsidy and laid the burden of excessive costs on local revenues. But the subsidy was too small to help the worst-off, and the scheme was used mainly by private builders for moderately priced houses for the middle class and the more affluent section of the working class. The hope that a process of 'filtering up' would free cheaper housing for the less well-off remained unfulfilled, partly because controlled rents reduced housing mobility (a recurring theme). The Labour government of 1924 recognised that the subsidies were failing to reach the people who needed them most (another recurring theme). The Wheatley Act 1924 increased the subsidy on condition that it was used for houses to be let at controlled rents subsidised from local revenues. This stimulated local authority building, and the Wheatley and Chamberlain schemes operated side by side, finally coming to an end in 1933 when it was felt that the housing shortage had been resolved.

To sum up, the First World War and its aftermath saw the introduction of rent control and the provision of subsidised housing by local authorities. But not everyone shared in the gains. Though the overall size of the housing stock increased, there remained a shortage of accommodation at rents the poor could afford. In particular, much local authority housing remained beyond the reach of poorer workers,[8] who still relied largely on the private sector, a fact recognised by the 1938 Housing Act which continued rent control on smaller houses. It can be argued that the continuation of rent control perpetuated the initial shortage; there remained little incentive for the private sector to provide rented accommodation for the less well-off. And the continuing story of local authority housing (Chapter 14) is one of considerable subsidy, uneconomic rents and long waiting lists.

3.2 Unemployment Insurance

From 1920 to 1940 unemployment never fell below one million and reached a peak of over three million, in the face of which unemployment insurance *qua* insurance virtually collapsed. The story in many other countries involves similar problems, similar debates and, in broad terms, similar solutions (Kaim-Caudle, 1973). The case of the USA is taken up in section 4.

Developments in the 1920s   The Unemployment Insurance Act 1920 extended the 1911 Act to more workers, and also paid an allowance for

---

[8] Though in the 1930s some poorer people obtained local authority housing as a result of slum clearance.

dependants. It was introduced hastily in the face of rising unemployment after the war, not least among demobilised soldiers. The Act was doomed to failure since rising unemployment inevitably undermined the insurance aspect of the scheme. This led to continual juggling with contribution and benefit levels, and to a series of devices which sought to preserve the fiction of insurance while in reality paying benefits not financed by contributions, thereby violating the insurance principle. The payment of such benefits out of the insurance fund was partly because the locally financed Poor Law could not cope with mass unemployment and, equally important, because the unemployed strenuously resisted the Poor Law. The realisation grew only slowly that insurance has problems even with short-term unemployment, and is totally inadequate in the face of long-term or mass unemployment (a central topic of Chapters 5 and 8).

As a result of the report of the Blanesburgh Committee, two benefits were introduced in 1927. *Standard* benefit was paid as an insurance benefit of indefinite duration to anyone who had made *any* contributions. *Transitional* benefit was payable as of right to those who did not satisfy even the minimal requirements of the insurance scheme, provided that they were 'genuinely seeking work'. Both benefits were paid from the insurance fund. Transitional benefit protected the unemployed from the Poor Law, which was reorganised in 1929, when the powers of the Guardians were transferred to Public Assistance Committees (PACs) run by local authorities.

In 1930 the Labour government changed the regulations for transitional benefit in two ways: they made the benefit a charge on the Consolidated Fund (i.e. general government revenues) rather than the insurance fund; and they relaxed the 'genuinely seeking work' clause. As a result, the numbers receiving transitional benefit doubled within two months, at a cost of £19 million in its first year, just as the economic crisis came to a head.

The 1931 crisis and the benefit cuts By the late 1920s one strand of policy was concerned with how unemployment benefits should be arranged and financed; another concentrated on the economic crisis more generally, and particularly on how unemployment could be reduced. Economic radicals, most obviously Keynes, with support from the Liberal Party and from various politicians in other parties, favoured expansionary public works expenditure. Economic conservatives like Ramsay MacDonald and his Chancellor Philip Snowden followed the traditional orthodoxy, supporting expenditure cuts, a balanced budget and lower government borrowing.[9] In the 1931 crisis the economic conservatives dominated. The decision to preserve the gold standard by stringent fiscal and monetary policy, particularly a cut in unemployment benefit, split the Labour cabinet and led to the formation of a National Government under Ramsay MacDonald. In the face of expenditure cuts, unemployment and controversy mounted.

[9] The parallel with the situation fifty years later is striking.

The rapid escalation of benefit payments at a time of economic crisis led to immediate action. Benefits were cut by 10 per cent from 17s (85 pence) to 15s 3d (76 pence) in 1931. Standard benefit was limited to 26 weeks, and the administration of transitional benefit (renamed transitional payment) was transferred to the local PACs, though still paid from central funds.

It is a matter of controversy whether *real* benefits fell, since prices had also declined. Between 1921 and 1931 the overall price of consumer goods fell by about 28 per cent, and those of food, clothing and fuel and light by even more. Compared with 1927 (when standard and transitional benefits were introduced) the price of consumer goods fell by 8 per cent, though the price of housing increased by 2 per cent (Feinstein, 1972, Tables 61 and 62). Possibly of greater importance as an explanation of the anger engendered by the cuts was the manner of their implementation. The role of the PACs in this context was crucial, and had ramifications for the relief of poverty which survive to the present. Eligibility for benefit was tightened, though with regional variation which was itself a further cause of anger. The interpretation of the 'genuinely seeking work' condition became more harsh. Additionally, from 1931, in sharp contrast with arrangements after 1927, the PACs administered transitional payment on the basis of the stringent Poor Law *household* means test, which 'like the workhouse before it, was destined to leave an indelible mark on popular culture ... long after its official demise ... Receipt of transitional payment through the PACs in effect put the unemployed right back on to the Poor Law' (Fraser, 1984, p. 194).

It is often not appreciated that the desperate plight of many of the unemployed in the 1930s was not typical of the country as a whole. The unemployment rate varied widely between regions, and long-term unemployment was concentrated in a limited number of decaying areas. While the unemployed suffered, living standards rose substantially for those in regular work.

The Unemployment Act 1934 was based on the report of the Holman Gregory Royal Commission in 1932, whose main recommendation was the complete separation of unemployment insurance proper from measures to support the long-term unemployed. The Act, consequently, was divided into two parts. Part I extended compulsory insurance to more workers; restored benefits to their level prior to the 1931 cut; organised contributions on the basis of one-third each from worker, employer and government; and established an independent committee to run the scheme, with responsibility only for those receiving *insurance* benefits. Part II dealt with unemployment assistance for people with no insurance cover, or whose cover had expired. Benefits were paid from general government funds, and run on a *national* basis by the newly established Unemployment Assistance Board. Payment was on the basis of need, in the light of family circumstances. The principle of less eligibility was finally laid to rest. Sixteen years after the end of the First World War, Britain had a system of unemployment relief which worked reasonably smoothly.

The social measures of the 1906–14 period were inadequate for the mass unemployment of the inter-war years. The Widows, Orphans and Age Contributory Pensions Act 1925 (extended by a further Act in 1929) introduced the first national scheme of contributory pensions; the 1911 health insurance scheme was enlarged; and there was action on housing. For the most part this legislation was a product of the 1920s. In the 1930s the welfare state was in abeyance, and new measures were little more than crisis management. The main lesson for the future was that *laissez-faire* capitalism could not solve the problem of unemployment – in this area, too, state intervention was necessary. When intervention came, in the form of rearmament and war production, the unemployment problem disappeared – an unhappy way of ending an unhappy period in British social policy.

4 Inter-War Poverty Relief in the USA

4.1 The Roots of the 'New Deal'

It is instructive at this stage briefly[10] to discuss contemporaneous events in the USA, where government involvement in income support (at least at the federal level) began late by international comparison. There was no American equivalent of the Liberal reforms, nor any analogue to the broadening of the British welfare system during and after the First World War. Until 1935 it was accepted that except in times of disaster no able-bodied person need be without work. Public assistance was regarded as charity, and its receipt generally carried social stigma. Until the 1930s such aid as existed came mainly from state and local government, though private schemes also had a limited role. By 1929 approximately 75 per cent of all relief derived from public funds, mostly local. *Until 1933 the federal government paid no grants and organised no programmes for relief or insurance, except for its own employees.* Emergency appropriations were made occasionally in the face of local disasters, but *no federal relief had ever been granted to the unemployed.*

Eligibility requirements and benefit levels varied widely by locality. Common among eligibility rules were taking the 'pauper's oath', disenfranchisement (in fourteen states), residency requirements, and the condition that recipients live in almshouses (US National Resources and Planning Board, 1942, pp. 26–8). In states where relief was granted to

[10] For additional detail, see the Further Reading.

people outside almshouses, payments were very low; and many localities gave benefits only in kind.

A detailed explanation of why these arrangements changed sharply in the 1930s lies outside the scope of this chapter and is, in any case, a matter of controversy. I shall do no more than set out the main questions. First, why did income support at a national level begin in the USA later than in almost any other industrialised country[11] and, moreover, at a level which by international standards was low?[12] The arguments are complex (for an overview see Higgins, 1981, Ch. 4). Most writers concentrate on one or more of three sets of factors: the influence of ideology (see section 7.1); the cultural and political heterogeneity of the USA (Gronbjerg *et al.*, 1978; Katznelson, 1978); and the influence of pressure groups (Menscher, 1967; Derthick, 1979; Weaver, 1982, Ch. 4).

A second question is why the 1930s legislation took the shape it did. To a minor extent it was influenced by the experience of other countries, notably Britain, Germany, France, Sweden and Canada. Considerably more important was the desire to head off more radical proposals. Douglas (1925) advocated a system of family allowances for dependants. The Townsend Plan in the early 1930s called for a monthly pension of $150 for everyone over sixty. Simultaneously, Huey Long was pursuing his populist campaign to 'share our wealth'. The Social Security Act 1935 was in part 'a compromise measure to blunt the political appeal of the enormously expensive and essentially unworkable Townsend Plan' (Pechman *et al.*, 1968, p. 32).

Why, finally, did reform occur when it did? Well before the 1930s, pressures for change were emerging out of various long-run developments, notably technological innovation, the decline of the family farm and decreasing average household size (see Wilensky and Lebeaux, 1965, pp. 341–8). However, the crisis of the 1930s brought developments to a head. As unemployment mounted after 1929, local expenditure on relief rapidly outstripped declining tax revenues; and emergency assistance by states ran into similar problems, so that federal participation became inevitable. Under Title I of the Emergency Relief and Construction Act 1932, $300 million in federal funds was made available for loans to states to help in their relief efforts.[13]

---

[11] By 1930, 27 countries had public schemes of poverty relief of some sort. Among industrialised countries only Norway, Japan and Switzerland started later than the USA (Pechman *et al.*, 1968, Appendix C).

[12] Why, to use a concept first developed by Wilensky and Lebeaux (1965) and subsequently adopted by other writers (see Higgins, 1981, pp. 41–5), did the USA adopt a *residual* model of welfare? We return to this issue in section 7.1.

[13] Repayment of these loans was eventually waived.

4.2 The Social Security Act 1935

Between 1933 and 1935 the federal government played an increasing financial and administrative role. The Civilian Conservation Corps, the Public Works Administration, and the Federal Civil Works Administration organised public works; the Federal Surplus Relief Corporation distributed surplus commodities to the needy; and the Federal Emergency Relief Administration supervised federal grants to states for unemployment relief. This last had the greatest impact, both at the time and through its influence on subsequent legislation. The use of federal funds gave federal government a measure of influence over the state programmes, in particular on benefit levels and administration, and these features were carried over into the permanent legislation.[14]

The 1935 Social Security Act created what, for the USA, was a broad-ranging scheme. It established two major insurance schemes and three major forms of assistance, administered by a new Social Security Board whose powers and duties were set out in Title VII of the Act.[15]

Federal Old Age Benefits (Title II) were financed by contributions from employees and employers under Title VIII and, as originally envisaged, were to be run largely on actuarial lines with respect to both benefit levels and financing (as we shall see shortly, neither resolve was effected).

Federal assistance to states for unemployment compensation was granted under Title III, financed by taxes levied on employers under Title IX. Unlike the pension scheme, which was federal, unemployment insurance was organised by states, which had wide discretion over the precise form of their arrangements. Though the scheme (being insurance) provided no benefits for individuals currently out of work, this was much the most controversial part of the Act, many employers being bitterly opposed to any form of unemployment compensation. Nevertheless, by 1937 all the states and territories had such a scheme.

Old Age Assistance (Title I) provided for means-tested cash payments to the elderly through federal grants to states with approved schemes. It was envisaged that costs would decline as the insurance benefits under Title II became payable. By 1940, 51 jurisdictions offered Old Age Assistance.[16]

Aid to the Blind (Title X) provided federal grants to approved state plans of aid to the needy blind. By 1940, 43 states qualified for federal funds.

Aid to Dependent Children (Title IV) paid federal grants to states giving cash assistance to families with needy children 'under the age of 16 [or under the age of 18 if found by the State agency to be regularly attending

---

[14] For further details of the emergency programmes, see US Federal Emergency Relief Administration (1942), and US National Resources and Planning Board (1942, pp. 26–7).

[15] For the wording of the Act itself, see Social Security Act, 14 August 1935, ch. 531, 49 Statutes at Large 620, or for an edited version, Stevens (1970, pp. 167–80).

[16] The 48 continental states, plus Washington DC, Alaska and Hawaii.

school] ... deprived of parental support or care by reason of the death, continued absence from the home, or physical incapacity of a parent'.[17] By 1949, 42 jurisdictions had schemes of this sort which qualified for federal funds.[18]

The 1939 amendments   to the Social Security Act stressed its welfare objectives and broadened its scope. The strict actuarial principles of the 1935 legislation were diluted; insurance benefits became payable to dependants of aged recipients, and to widows and children of workers covered by the scheme; payments were to begin in 1940 rather than 1942; benefits were tied to average earnings over a minimum period, thus breaking the link with lifetime contributions; and the earnings test prescribed by the 1935 Act was slightly liberalised before the first benefits were paid.[19] The financial basis of the scheme also changed. The intention of accumulating an actuarial fund was abandoned, and benefits for the elderly and their dependants paid almost entirely out of current contributions (i.e. the scheme was organised on a 'pay-as-you-go' rather than a 'funded' basis, an issue discussed at length in Chapter 9).

A brief assessment   To a greater extent than the Liberal reforms, the Social Security Act can be criticised as in certain respects timid. The Act, admittedly, was an improvement on earlier arrangements: the range of benefits was broader, the age requirements for retirement more liberal, and the eligibility restrictions on residence and citizenship less stringent; and benefits were paid in cash, this being a condition of the federal contribution to state schemes.

In important respects, however, 'the ... Act may be reasonably regarded as a conservative legislative solution to a difficult and explosive problem' (Pechman *et al.*, 1968, p. 32). First, though the federal government ensured some uniformity, state programmes still varied widely in terms of benefit levels and eligibility requirements. Second, the insurance arrangements were severely constrained: in 1940 only about 60 per cent of workers were covered; benefits were intended originally to bear a fairly simple relationship to contributions, thus ruling out any substantial redistribution (though this aspect was relaxed somewhat by the 1939 amendments); and the insurance benefits were subject to an earnings test. Third, the assistance measures were categorical, i.e. they granted aid only to individuals falling into one of the three categories, aged, blind, or dependent child, since it was felt that only these groups should ever require assistance during times of high employment.

---

[17] Social Security Act 1935, Title IV, section 406(a). Phrase in brackets added by an amendment in 1939.

[18] A further eight states (Alaska, Connecticut, Illinois, Kentucky, Mississippi, Nevada, South Dakota and Texas) operated schemes without federal funds (US National Resources and Planning Board, 1942, p. 83).

[19] These changes were based on recommendations in US Advisory Council on Social Security (1938), which contains valuable background information. For details of the legislative history, see Myers (1965, Ch. 4) or, more briefly, Pechman *et al.* (1968, Appendix B).

It is possible, in conclusion, to argue that the historical importance of the original Social Security Act lies less in its precise legislative content, which was in many ways rather conservative, than in the way it gradually brought about public acceptance of income support as a permanent institution, and in the way in which the federal government, through carefully designed subsidies to states, was able to encourage an element of uniformity in state programmes.

5 The Second World War and its Aftermath

5.1 Wartime Activity

Policy The final climacteric in the development of the welfare state occurred in the years 1940–8. The Second World War was a total war; *everyone's* life was affected, and this, it is argued, led to important changes in attitude. The totality of the war effort forced the British government to adopt powers (e.g. rationing and the direction of labour) on a scale hitherto unknown. It also reduced social distinctions; unlike the divisive unemployment of the 1930s, food shortages and bombs affected all social classes (though not all areas) equally. The pressure of common problems prompted the adoption of common solutions. Attitudes were changed also by increased awareness of social problems as social classes mingled during the war. In the armed services men who would otherwise have led separate lives were thrown together. Evacuation, too,

was part of the process by which British society came to know itself, as the unkempt, ill-clothed, undernourished and often incontinent children of bombed cities acted as messengers carrying the evidence of the deprivation of urban working-class life into rural homes. [Fraser, 1984, p. 210.]

As well as planning for the future, there was some action on social policy as a direct result of the war, including action on school meals, the transformation of the Unemployment Assistance Board, and dramatic changes in the organisation of health care. As a result of wartime food shortages, school meals and school milk, previously a form of charity, became a normal feature of school life. The needs of wartime diversified the activities of the Unemployment Assistance Board (renamed the Assistance Board). In particular, wartime inflation adversely affected pensioners, and legislation in 1940 allowed the Board to pay supplementary pensions on the basis of need. By 1941 it dealt with ten pensioners to every one unemployed person. It also helped others who fell outside the traditional categories – victims of bombing, evacuees, dependants of prisoners of war, etc. As a direct result of the war, the Assistance Board became a generalised relief agency and so foreshadowed the National Assistance Board of 1948.

From 1939 onwards there were two sorts of hospital patient. Some received emergency treatment which was free, and financed and organised nationally. Others had to take their turn, as previously, in a voluntary or municipal hospital. Payment in the latter two cases was generally through membership of a contributory scheme to a voluntary hospital, or via a means test (Abel Smith, 1964, Ch. 26). Initially only military personnel fell into the emergency category, but wartime exigencies extended the services to an ever-widening group of people. This served as an example of large-scale, state-financed health care and also exposed the deficiencies of the old system.

Planning for the post-war period   The Beveridge Report (UK, 1942) has pride of place on the planning front. It was based on three assumptions: that a scheme of family allowances would be set up; that there would be a comprehensive health care service; and that the state would maintain full employment. The report envisaged a scheme of social insurance which would be

all-embracing in scope of persons and of needs ... Every person ... will pay a single security contribution by a stamp on a single insurance document each week ... Unemployment benefit, disability benefit [and] retirement pensions after a transitional period ... will be at the same rate irrespective of previous earnings. [UK, 1942, pp. 9–10.]

Benefits were to be paid also for maternity, and to widows and orphans. Coverage was to be compulsory and (in contrast with the 1935 US Social Security Act) universal in respect of individuals and risk. Flat-rate contributions would give entitlement to flat-rate, subsistence benefits; there would be no means test; and the scheme was to be administered nationally.

The 1944 White Paper, *Social Insurance* (UK, 1944c), accepted most of these recommendations, and became the basis of the National Insurance Act 1946. In the same year two other major White Papers were published. *A National Health Service* (UK, 1944a) envisaged 'a comprehensive service covering every branch of medical and allied activity' providing free treatment on a universal basis, financed out of general taxation. *Employment Policy* (UK, 1944b) was very much a Keynesian document. It committed the government to 'the maintenance of a high and stable level of employment', brought about, where necessary, by counter-cyclical deficit spending. The economic radicals of 1931 had finally come into their own.

The true novelty of the Beveridge proposals, with hindsight, was their replacement of the old, haphazard and piecemeal methods by a coherent *strategy* embracing not only social insurance, but also family allowances; national assistance paid out of central government revenues; the National Health Service; and (possibly crucially) a presumption of high employment.

The major piece of social legislation during the war was the Education Act 1944, based on Butler's 1943 White Paper (UK, 1943), which set the foundation for post-war education. It created a comprehensive national system of what the Act called primary, secondary and further education. Primary and secondary education were to be free up to school-leaving age, which was to be raised to 15 in 1945[20] and to 16 as soon as possible thereafter. An accommodation was made with the voluntary church schools which were, in certain respects, integrated into the state system.

5.2 Policies 1946–48

The 1945 Labour government was armed with a large Parliamentary majority and a stack of White Papers, many of which had met with Conservative approval during the wartime coalition. Under the Family Allowance Act 1945 a payment of 5 shillings (25 pence) was made for the second and subsequent children in each family. The benefit was universal and paid out of general tax revenues.

The National Health Service Act 1946, based on the 1944 White Paper, established a national system of comprehensive health care available universally at no charge. The system was financed from general taxation, except for a small proportion from national insurance contributions. The detailed arrangements (Abel Smith, 1964, Chs 27–9) involved considerable discussion with the medical profession.

The National Insurance Act 1946 was based on the 1944 White Paper, which in turn followed closely the recommendations of the Beveridge Report. All insured persons were required to buy a weekly stamp (to which the employer also contributed), whose cost varied by age, sex, and marital and employment status. An employed person was eligible for flat-rate benefit under seven heads, including unemployment, maternity, sickness, widowhood, retirement and a death grant to cover funeral costs. Beveridge had envisaged that it would take twenty years to build up entitlement to a full retirement pension, but in the event the Labour government implemented full pensions from October 1946.

Alongside the National Insurance Act was the National Insurance (Industrial Injuries) Act 1946, which entitled those injured at work to various benefits (usually at a higher rate than sickness benefit), financed by an identifiable component of the national insurance contribution. Because the scheme was compulsory it was possible to pool risks across industries with higher and lower accident rates (see Chapter 5:4.1).

The National Assistance Act 1948 established a safety net for those whose needs were not covered (or not fully covered) by insurance. The Act, like the other major Acts, was universal in approach. The old Assistance Board

[20] The school-leaving age had been set at 14 under Fisher's Education Act 1918.

became the National Assistance Board, administering means-tested benefits to those not in full-time work, whose income was below subsistence. In doing so it assumed the residual functions of the local Public Assistance Committees left over from the Poor Law, which were explicitly repealed by the Act.

The legislation of 1944–8 was, on the whole, successful. If the welfare state has any official birthday it is 5 July 1948, when the provisions of the National Insurance, Industrial Injuries, National Assistance and National Health Service Acts came simultaneously into effect, family allowances and higher pensions having been implemented in 1946. With unemployment below 250,000 the insurance fund made a surplus of £95 million in its first year, but the National Health Service cost more than anticipated.

There is considerable debate about the importance, or lack of it, of the Second World War in bringing about this legislation. Some writers (Marshall, 1975; Titmuss, 1958, Ch. 4) regard the war as a *sine qua non* for subsequent events, others (Glennerster, 1990) as merely one of a long chain of formative influences.

The greatest achievement of the 1945–51 Government lay . . . in the firm rounding-off of half a century's constructive work of welfare, and the final shaping of the Welfare State on the lines first laid early in the century on the basis of nineteenth-century experience and investigation. [Bruce, 1972, p. 25.]

6   Recent Developments in Britain and the USA

This section reviews and briefly compares post-war developments in the UK and USA, concentrating mainly on cash benefits. Discussion of health care, education and housing is deferred to the relevant chapters. For fuller assessment of the post-war development of the welfare state, see Glennerster (1990).

Income support in the UK   National insurance contributions continued broadly unchanged through the 1950s apart from periodic adjustments as prices and incomes rose. This regime came under pressure. An implication of a self-balancing fund is that total contributions must match total benefits. Since contributions (being flat-rate) could not exceed the reach of a low-paid worker, benefits, too, had to be low. This constraint was gradually relaxed, motivated initially by the view that the flat-rate retirement pension was inadequate. From 1961, therefore, most employees were required to pay an additional, earnings-related pension contribution.

The 1975 Social Security Act introduced a fundamental change. It abolished the weekly stamp for most insured persons, and replaced it from April 1975 with an earnings-related contribution for all employed persons. In October 1985 a system of graduated contributions was introduced, i.e.

the contribution rate was reduced for individuals with lower earnings. One of the effects of the changes was to enable the insurance system to redistribute from rich to poor (see Chapters 8 and 9).

National insurance benefits remained unchanged in broad outline for nearly twenty years. The National Insurance Act 1966 introduced an earnings-related supplement to unemployment and sickness benefit for some employed people. This was abolished in 1982, and sickness benefits reformed in 1983. The National Insurance Act 1971 introduced invalidity benefits for the long-term sick. On the pensions front, as we have seen, a supplementary contribution was levied from 1961, and the resulting increment to pensions became payable gradually in subsequent years. This was a minor change compared with the Social Security Pensions Act 1975, which was one of the most important pieces of social legislation since 1948. During the later 1960s and early 1970s there had been much political wrangling over a series of proposed pension reforms, and the 1975 Act was in certain respects a blend of these proposals. In a wide-ranging overhaul it considerably extended earnings-related pensions and, for the first time, gave a statutory basis for the indexation of benefits.

The system of family support advocated by Beveridge remained largely intact until the late 1970s. It had two strands: a taxable family allowance for the second and subsequent child in any family; and an income tax allowance for all children. The resulting system was complex and did not give the greatest benefit to the poorest families (such interrelations between the tax and benefit systems will be a recurring theme). To avoid these difficulties the Child Benefit Act 1975 (a remarkable year for social legislation) abolished family allowances and child tax allowances, and replaced them, with full effect from April 1979, by *child benefit*, a weekly, tax-free cash payment in respect of *all* children in the family, with an additional payment for single parents (see Chapter 10).

Assistance benefits are also discussed in Chapter 10. The National Assistance Board was abolished in 1966, and a Supplementary Benefits Commission with wide discretionary powers established. There was a large increase over the years in the number of recipients. As a result of the 1985 review (see below), the benefit was overhauled and renamed income support.

The 1960s saw the 'rediscovery' of poverty (Abel Smith and Townsend, 1965), including poverty among working families, who were normally not eligible for supplementary benefit. One response was the introduction in 1971 of family income supplement, a cash benefit for working families with children. The scheme's success was limited by problems with take-up (i.e. potentially eligible families not applying), and (again) anomalous interactions between the tax and benefit structures. At certain income levels, for instance, a family was eligible for family income supplement, but also liable for income tax. As a result of the 1985 review (see below), the scheme was replaced by a broadly similar benefit, family credit.

More generally, the years after 1960 saw a proliferation of cash assistance benefits. Some directly paralleled the insurance scheme (e.g. pensions for people too old to have an adequate post-1948 contributions record); others were means tested; and the relation between different benefits, and between benefits generally and the tax system, became complex and muddled, raising problems of the 'poverty trap' discussed in detail in Chapter 10:3. By the early 1970s there were over fifty benefits outside national insurance (UK, 1973, pp. 47–8).

The results of what was intended as a fundamental review were published as a Green Paper (UK, 1985b) and in a White Paper later in the same year (UK, 1985h). The bulk of the proposed changes, however, were incremental. The review focused on two areas in particular: pensions, and the various income-tested benefits. Though some thought was given to making pensions, except the basic pension, a matter for the private sector, the eventual outcome was slightly to reduce the national insurance pension for individuals retiring after the turn of the century (see Chapter 9:5). The main changes to income-tested benefits were measures to reduce the likelihood of poor families losing more in benefit than they gained in extra earnings (see Chapter 10:3).

A final development was the increasing regulatory role of the state in respect of occupational benefits. Two examples were the conditions imposed on private employers who wished to 'contract out' of the post-1975 pension arrangements (Chapter 9:1), and the requirement that employers administer benefits for short-term sickness after 1983 (Chapter 8:1.2).

Developments in the USA in the 1940s lay outside the social security system. The Full Employment Act 1946, which represented a considerable departure from previous policies, imposed on federal government the (implicitly Keynesian) responsibility for the maintenance of full employment. In the years after 1950 the insurance scheme was steadily broadened to the point where, together with various related programmes, virtually all workers and their dependants were covered. The parallel extension of risks covered is conveniently summarised by the changing name of the scheme: the 1935 Act concentrated on Old Age Insurance (OAI); survivor benefits were added in 1939 (OASI), disablement benefits in 1956 (OASDI), and various health benefits for the elderly and the poor in 1965 (OASDHI).[21]

The system of earnings-related contributions established by the 1935 Act remained broadly unchanged over the years. The benefit regime was liberalised in several respects: there were proportionately larger increases for lower-income workers (increasing the scheme's redistributive impact);

[21] These were amendments, respectively, to Title II of the Social Security Acts of 1939 and 1956; for details, see Stevens (1970, pp. 247–9 and 506 *et seq.*). Health care for the aged ('medicare') and the poor ('medicaid') was introduced as Titles XVIII (Health Insurance for the Aged) and XIX (Grants to States for Medical Assistance Programs) in the Social Security Act Amendments 1965 (30 July 1965, 79 Statutes at Large 286). For details, see Stevens (1970, pp. 758–75).

benefits for survivors and dependants were raised relative to those for the insured person (increasing the support given to families); and the rules about the age of retirement were relaxed.

There was considerably less change in the system of assistance benefits. A new benefit, Aid to the Permanently and Totally Disabled, was established in 1950; and Aid to Dependent Children (renamed Aid to Families with Dependent Children) was liberalised in various ways in the 1960s. Of particular note, states were given the option after 1962 of paying benefit not only where the father was absent or disabled, but also where he was unemployed.

Health care for recipients of assistance (so-called 'medicaid') was introduced in 1965, at the same time as its inclusion for the elderly under the main insurance scheme ('medicare'). As we shall see in Chapter 12:4.1, this had major implications for the aggregate cost of health care.

Two events over the post-war period are of particular note: the 'welfare explosion' in the 1960s and 1970s; and the 'rediscovery' of poverty. The welfare explosion was a dramatic expansion in the size and cost of Aid to Families with Dependent Children. The increase was particularly great in the states with the largest cities, especially in New York (where numbers rose from 462,000 in 1963 to 951,000 five years later) and California (where numbers rose from 375,000 to 901,000).

Governor Reagan complained last night that California's 'permissive' welfare system is encouraging teenaged girls to become pregnant and subsidising hippie communes at poor folks' expense. 'The Age of Aquarius smells a little fishy,' he told a sympathetic audience of conservative Republicans. [*San Francisco Chronicle*, 14 September 1970, p. 37.]

The phenomenon evoked considerable concern, particularly because it coincided with a period of low unemployment and sustained economic growth (see Gordon, 1969; Barr and Hall, 1981).

Poverty became a major political issue during the 1960s for the first time in thirty years, not simply as a defensive response to the escalating numbers receiving assistance but also for more positive reasons, at least during President Johnson's 'War on Poverty' (see, for instance, US, 1969). With hindsight, however, the response to the crisis was long on words but muted in action. There was a measure of support for major reform, and a number of experiments with negative income tax took place (see Chapter 11:2.2), but changes *ex post* were small. President Nixon's Family Assistance Program proposed the abolition of existing assistance schemes and their replacement by a universal system of income supplementation. The McGovern 'Demogrant' advocated what was essentially a large-scale negative income tax. Nothing came of either proposal, partly because of the complexity of the issue, but largely because of a lack of political will in the face of their substantial cost.

The conclusion on the 1960s is that little had changed. Assistance programmes were still categorical, and still varied widely across states. The insurance system had been broadened considerably, but poverty persisted. The view of Wilensky and Lebeaux (1965, pp. xvi–xvii) remained (and remains) true:

[The] United States is more reluctant than any rich democratic country to make a welfare effort appropriate to its affluence. Our support of national welfare programs is halting; our administration of services for the less privileged is mean. We move toward the welfare state but we do it with ill grace, carping and complaining all the way.

Comparative issues   Four strategic issues are the subject of much of the rest of the book: the role of employment; the importance of social insurance; the relation between the benefit and tax systems; and the continued and substantial reliance on means-tested benefits. A high level of employment was seen in both countries as the primary method of income support. The UK government committed itself to such policies in its wartime White Paper (UK, 1944b). The US analogue was the Full Employment Act 1946. The retreat from these commitments in the 1980s is discussed briefly in Chapter 15:2.2.

Social insurance was the major line of defence. The coverage of the 1946 National Insurance Act was broader in three important ways than the Social Security Act as amended in 1939: it dealt with contingencies such as sickness, maternity and burial costs, which were not covered by US legislation; its coverage was virtually universal with respect to individuals; and, as its name implied, it was a *national* scheme (so, too, were assistance payments). In contrast, the US system (apart from federal retirement and disability insurance and, later, health insurance for the elderly) was organised by states, with wide variations in benefit levels and eligibility requirements.

The original intention of both Acts was to emulate private, actuarial insurance as closely as possible, both generally, and particularly in the way pensions were to be paid out of an accumulated fund. But political pressures and favourable demographic and economic trends resulted instead in pensions paid largely out of current contributions, starting in 1940 (USA) and 1946 (UK); and over the years political pressure led to further erosion of actuarial principles, as the coverage of both schemes was broadened and the relation between contributions and benefits relaxed. The overall result, in a British context, was considerable erosion of the Beveridge strategy. The extent to which such benefits are (or should be, or can be) true insurance is one of the main topics of Chapters 5, 8 and 9.

Tax expenditures (see Chapter 7:1.1) served in both countries to buttress social insurance. Parallel to public pensions, for instance, was the tax relief granted to private schemes. Both methods provide income support for the elderly, though often with very different distributional consequences. That tax expenditures should properly be included in any assessment of income support has long been recognised in the academic literature (for early analyses, see Surrey (1948, 1958) and Titmuss (1956)), though awareness of the issue by politicians has come more slowly. Income tax is relevant also because of the increasing overlap between taxpayers and benefit recipients. Some social insurance benefits are taxable, an issue of acute relevance today when (in sharp contrast with the 1930s and 1940s) most adults are liable for income tax. The overlap is crucial also in connection with income-tested benefits, as we shall see in Chapters 10 and 11.

Reliance on means-tested benefits continued in both countries (and in many others) on a substantial scale despite the existence of wide-ranging social insurance and tax expenditures, and notwithstanding Beveridge's expectation that the assistance measures would become residual. This was partly because in Britain many of the insurance benefits were below the subsistence level established by national assistance (thus violating what Beveridge regarded as an essential ingredient of his proposals), and partly because of problems with take-up (see the Glossary). As a result, means-tested assistance continued in both cash (e.g. income support, Aid to Families with Dependent Children) and kind (e.g. free medical prescriptions in the UK, 'medicaid' and food stamps in the USA).

The persistence of these benefits, and the large numbers of people involved, demonstrate that insurance and related measures were only partially successful in abolishing 'want'.[22] Studies in both countries (Abel Smith and Townsend, 1965; US, 1969) revealed continuing and widespread poverty, partly due to factors outside the direct scope of income support (e.g. racial discrimination). But poverty was also found among the elderly and the unemployed, to whom social insurance was directly relevant.

Finally, as we have seen, there were two substantial differences. There remained a complete absence in the USA of any analogue of child benefit, notwithstanding the many countries which had such arrangements (France introduced the first scheme before the First World War).[23] Nor was there anything remotely resembling the UK National Health Service. This remains true in the early 1990s.

[22] This is not to imply that income testing is *necessarily* a sign of a failing system of income support. For an interesting account of the Australian system, which deliberately relies on substantial income testing of most benefits, see Aaron (1984), and for a summary of social security institutions worldwide, US Department of Health and Human Services (1989).

[23] For a review and international comparison of family allowances, see Bradshaw *et al.* (forthcoming) and Kamerman and Kahn (1991).

7 Concluding Issues: from the Past to the Present

7.1 Interpreting the Forces Creating the Welfare State

Given the variety of influences on the welfare state, it is not surprising that
there is controversy over their relative importance. The key issue is whether
the dominant factor was ideology or the nature of the industrial process.
The ideological debate concentrates on the motives underlying social legislation. A *liberal* (as defined in Chapter 3:1) interpretation of history
attributes the development of the welfare state to the quest for social justice,
and sees the events described earlier as progress along a road towards the
good society. Fraser (1984, p. 157) writes of Lloyd George's 1909 'People's
Budget' that '[here] was the essence of the novel approach: financial policy
geared to the social needs of the people; the budget as a tool of social
policy'.

Marxists, *per contra*, did not see the welfare state as arising out of a
concatenation of disparate events, and certainly not as the result of a quest
for social justice. They argue that the primary motive of social legislation
was the protection and preservation of the capitalist system. The welfare
state, according to this view, fills two roles: it helps to meet the needs of
the capitalist industrial system for a healthy, educated workforce; and it is
the 'ransom' paid by the ruling élite to contain social unrest. To a Marxist,
the Liberal reforms were very limited and intended mainly to preserve the
existing economic system. Unemployment, sickness and health benefits
under the 1911 National Insurance Act applied only to limited classes of
worker; and some historians argue that one of the main motives of the
1908 Pension Act (the only substantially redistributive measure) was to
weed out of the workforce older men and women whose presence was
reducing Britain's industrial efficiency in the face of international competition. These different views of the welfare state are discussed in more
detail in Chapter 3:5.3.

Ideology, then, can be argued to have fostered the development of the
welfare state either in the quest for social justice or as 'capitalist conspiracy'.
But is ideology actually very important? The *theory of convergence* (see the
Further Reading) is based on detailed studies of how welfare states (under
whatever name) have arisen in different countries. The theory is based on
two propositions: first, that all countries, *whatever their dominant ideology*,
have over time developed similar industrial structures (this is the so-called
'logic of industrialism'); and, second, that a welfare state in one form or
another is an inevitable concomitant of this industrial structure. The theory
therefore bases its argument on technological determinism. At its strongest,
it asserts that the dominant force in the development of the welfare state is
industrialism and, by implication, that ideology is largely irrelevant.

Ideology or technological determinism? I make no serious attempt to judge the two theories – but a few remarks are in order. The world is a complicated place, and I have a profound suspicion of almost any unicausal explanation of anything: marriages are rarely due *only* to love (or only to money); inflation is rarely caused *only* by monetary phenomena; and the Second World War was not caused only by Hitler, nor only by the Treaty of Versailles. So simply on *a priori* grounds it can be questioned whether either ideology (liberal or Marxist) or industrialism has a monopoly of truth. Most industrial countries face similar problems of unemployment and pockets of poverty, so it is not surprising that many have adopted broadly similar solutions; the logic of industrialism clearly has some validity. Similarly, the technical problems with private markets discussed in Chapters 4 and 5 afflict all industrialised countries.

But ideology also appears to play a part, if only in determining whether a country adopts a *residual* or an *institutional* model of welfare. The former accords welfare a role only when market or family structures break down; the latter regards it as an integral part of modern industrial society (Wilensky and Lebeaux, 1965, pp. 138–9; Higgins, 1981, pp. 41–5). Thus a 'capitalist' country like the USA has (and has always had) a system of income support and social services which is small relative to its population and national income (though it has a wide-ranging system of publicly provided education). A 'socialist' country like Sweden has a highly articulated welfare state; Denmark and New Zealand (which were not highly industrialised) were among the first countries with a public system of old age pensions; and Saskatchewan was the first Canadian province to have publicly organised health insurance.

It is clear, in conclusion, that the forces which created the British (or any other) welfare state are diverse and complex. The question 'how did it come about?' has no easy answer.

7.2 What Was Created?

The nature of what was created, as we have just seen, is a matter of controversy. Is the welfare state a step in the direction of the good society (discussed in detail in Chapter 3:3), an expensive and demeaning road towards totalitarianism (Chapter 3:2), or a cynical device to prop up the capitalist system (Chapter 3:4.2 and 3:5.3)? Setting these issues to one side, the successes of the post-1948 arrangements are twofold and clear. There is, first, a comprehensive system of income support which has since been extended in a variety of ways. The insurance arrangements are underpinned by a broad safety net in the form of income support (i.e. means-tested social assistance), which is organised nationally and for which *everyone* is potentially eligible. Many other countries have considerably less comprehensive systems. The second major success has been the National Health Service [which] has brought to all the most obvious and immediate benefits. To many it *is* the Welfare State, and every survey ... has shown how much it is ... valued and taken for granted as part and parcel of British life. Serious defects and deficiencies there still are ... [but] critics, seeing no visible alternative ... devote their attention to improvement rather than to abolition. [Bruce, 1972, p. 330.]

The failures are also fairly clear. It is striking how many current and prospective problems have their roots or their parallels in the past. The inter-war difficulties with unemployment insurance raised questions about the extent to which unemployment is an insurable risk (see Chapters 5 and 8); the introduction of state pensions in 1908 was motivated in part by demographic problems (Chapter 9); the present antipathy to means testing (Chapters 10 and 11) is strongly influenced by the folk memory of the stringent household means test between the wars; the post-war distributional complexities arising out of the interaction between family allowances and child tax allowances will emerge in many guises; the housing measures during and after the First World War are a direct contributory cause of current difficulties with housing (Chapter 14); and similarly, the exploding costs of medical care in the USA (Chapter 12:4.1) stem in part (though far from wholly) from the introduction of 'medicare' and 'medicaid' in 1965.

Over and above these problems is the fact, despite the relative success of the cash benefit system, that poverty remains. In part this is because the poverty line has moved up as living standards and expectations have risen; but for many the issue is not just one of *relative* poverty, but of uncertainty and harsh discomfort (Mack and Lansley, 1985).

For some, the most important problem of all is the attack on the welfare state in the 1980s. The 'welfare consensus' on both sides of the Atlantic has been threatened (Higgins, 1981, pp. 150–7), though the roots of the attack, at least in America, go back further (Wilensky and Lebeaux, 1965, pp. xxxii–xxxvii). Public expenditure generally, and social spending in particular, have come under close scrutiny. Policy in the UK in the early 1980s included a reduction in unemployment benefit relative to other benefits, less generous indexation, and expenditure cuts in education and housing. The British government declared that a report suggesting large-scale dismantling of the welfare state was a 'dead duck'. However, in the words of a prominent member of the British poverty lobby, 'Dead ducks ... have a habit of being served in individual pieces' (Lister, 1983, p. 3).

The change in attitude is highlighted by the contrast between the 1944 employment White Paper (UK, 1944b), committing the government to counter-cyclical demand management, and a mid-1980s White Paper on the subject (UK, 1985a), which argued that unemployment should be tackled by reducing inflation, through wage restraint and through job training. The high summer of 1948 has passed. And though no one has a monopoly of wisdom, to some commentators at least, the Principles of 1834 (section 1.1) come rather readily to mind, thereby completing a historical circle.

Further Reading

Good general texts on the historical development of the British welfare state are Bruce (1972), Fraser (1984), Marshall (1975) and Thane (1982). For a shorter account, see Glennerster (1990). Contemporary discussion of the 'New Liberalism' can be found in Hobson (1909); for recent analysis of economic and political thought at the time, see Robbins (1977) and Freeden (1978). For a brief introduction to early poor relief, see Rose (1972); on the principle of *laissez-faire*, Taylor (1972); and on the Liberal reforms, Hay (1975) (brief) or Gilbert (1973) (compendious). The early debates on unemployment are detailed in Harris (1972) and a history of health care prior to 1948 in Abel Smith (1964). A brief official historical account is given in UK (1985d, Ch. 3).

The origins of the modern welfare state are discussed explicitly by Harris (1977) (a magisterial biography of Beveridge) and Titmuss (1958) (who stresses the influence of the Second World War). The Beveridge proposals are contained in UK (1942) and those for the National Health Service in UK (1944a). Detailed historical statistics for the UK from 1855 to 1965 can be found in Feinstein (1972). For the modern institutions, see Tolley (1991). Glennerster (1990) assesses the post-war development of the British welfare state. For a detailed account of the British welfare state since the mid-1970s, see Hills (1990).

For contemporary accounts of US developments in the 1930s, see Douglas (1939), US Federal Emergency Relief Administration (1942) and US National Resources and Planning Board (1942). For retrospective analysis, see Altmeyer (1966), Schottland (1963) or Witte (1962); and for later debates, Tobin (1968) and US (1969) (a remarkable document). Details of US legislation are given in Stevens (1970).

For differing interpretations of the origins of the welfare state, including discussion of the theory of convergence, see Higgins (1981, Ch. 4) and Mishra (1981, Ch. 3) for a summary; and for specific views, Wilensky and Lebeaux (1965) and Rimlinger (1971). A more general international comparison is given in Kaim-Caudle (1973). For a compendious summary of institutions internationally, see US Department of Health and Human Services (1989).

Chapter 3
Political Theory: Social Justice and the State[1]

The fundamental issue [of the welfare state] is not economic. It is moral
... The issue is the responsibility of people to manage their own affairs
... Is it not the case that while adults manage incomes children receive
pocket money? The operation of the welfare state tends to reduce the
status of adults to that of children. [Lord Bauer, 1983.]

[The] major evil [of paternalistic programs] is their effect on the fabric of
our society. They weaken the family; reduce the incentive to work, save
and innovate; reduce the accumulation of capital; and limit our freedom.
These are the fundamental standards by which they should be judged.
[Milton Friedman, 1980.]

Traditional socialism was largely concerned with the evils of traditional
capitalism, and with the need for its overthrow. But today traditional
capitalism has been reformed and modified almost out of existence, and
it is with a quite different form of society that socialists must now
concern themselves. [Anthony Crosland, 1956.]

1 Theories of Society

A society is a co-operative venture for the mutual advantage of its members.
It generally contains both an identity of interests and conflicts of interest
between individuals and groups. The institutions of any society (e.g. its
constitution, laws and social processes) have a profound influence on a
person's 'life chances'. The purpose of a theory of society is to offer
principles which enable us to choose between different social arrangements.
In analysing the welfare state it is helpful to distinguish three broad types
of theory: libertarian; liberal; and collectivist.

Libertarians (discussed in section 2) are in many ways the direct descendants

[1] Readers with a limited background in political theory can find the gist of the argument in the Appendix
to this chapter.

of the 'Old Liberalism' of the nineteenth century (Chapter 2:1.1 and 2:2.1) although, as we shall see, there are important differences between 'natural rights' and 'empirical' libertarians. The former (e.g. Nozick) argue that state intervention is *morally wrong* except in very limited circumstances. The latter, including writers like Hayek and Friedman, are the modern inheritors of the Classical liberal tradition;[2] they argue against state intervention not on moral grounds, but because it will *reduce total welfare*. Both groups analyse society in terms of its individual members (as opposed to the group or social class); give heavy weight to individual freedom; and strongly support private property and the market mechanism. As a result, the state's role *vis-à-vis* taxation and redistribution is severely circumscribed.

Liberal theories (section 3) are the modern inheritors of the 'New Liberalism' (Chapter 2:2.1). They find their philosophy in utilitarianism (section 3.1) and in writers like Rawls (section 3.2); their policy advocates in people like Beveridge, Keynes and Galbraith; and their practitioners in politicians like Harold Macmillan and John Kennedy. The theory has three crucial features. First, societies are analysed in terms of their individual members. Second, 'private property in the means of production, distribution and exchange [is] a contingent matter rather than an essential part of the doctrine' (Barry, 1973, p. 166), i.e. the treatment of private property is explicitly regarded not as an end in itself, but as a means towards the achievement of policy goals. Finally, liberal theories contain 'a principle of distribution which could, suitably interpreted and with certain factual assumptions, have egalitarian implications' (ibid.), i.e. in certain circumstances income redistribution is an appropriate function of the state. This book, as Chapter 4 will amplify, is firmly in the liberal tradition.

Collectivist theories, too, are varied. *Marxist* theory (section 4.2) draws its philosophy from Marx and its policies from writers like Laski, Strachey and Miliband. The theory sees industrial society as consisting of social classes, defined narrowly in terms of their relation to the means of production. Private property has only a limited role, and the allocation and distribution of resources in accordance with individual need is a primary concern of the state. *Fabian socialists* (section 4.1) present an intermediate case. They derive their philosophy from writers like Tawney, and find their policy advocates in, for example, Crosland and Titmuss, and their practitioners in politicians like Clement Attlee. Though sharing to some extent the egalitarian aims of Marxists, their analysis and methods have much in common with liberal thinking.

---

[2] There is a confusing ambiguity in the use of the word 'liberal'. In the nineteenth century it was used as a label for *laissez-faire* thinkers like Bentham and Nassau Senior (Chapter 2:1.1); and today a writer like Friedman, in calling himself a liberal, is using the term in the same way. I shall, throughout, refer to such writers as libertarians, and use the term 'liberal' in the sense described below.

In practice the theories blur into each other like the colours of the rainbow – but it is useful for exposition to talk about them as separate entities, especially when contrasting their implications for policy (section 5). Nevertheless, their differences and similarities are complex, and involve subtleties well beyond the scope of one brief chapter. The purpose here is limited to sketching the ideological debate only in outline. Knowledgeable readers will, I hope, be forgiving.

2 Libertarian Views

It is necessary to return briefly to nineteenth-century debates (Chapter 2:1.1 and 2:2.1). The ideology of *laissez-faire* derived from two quite distinct sets of philosophical arguments. When modern writers like Hayek and Friedman advocate free markets and private property, they follow Hume (1770), Smith (1776), Bentham (1789) and Mill (1863) in doing so on a *utilitarian* or *empirical* basis, out of a belief that such institutions maximise total welfare. Nozick, in contrast, follows Spencer (1884) by defending private property on *moral* grounds, as a *natural right* (see Robbins, 1978, pp. 46 *et seq.*). Though not completely watertight, the distinction between the two views (exemplified by the first two quotes at the head of the chapter) is crucial to debates about policy (section 5), and so merits closer attention.

Natural rights libertarians   To Nozick (1974) everyone has the right to distribute the rewards of his own labour. He calls this *justice in holdings*, which has three elements. A person is entitled to a holding if he has acquired it (a) through earnings (so-called justice in acquisition), or (b) through the inheritance of wealth which was itself justly acquired (justice in transfer). Holdings which fall under neither principle cannot be justified, hence, (c) government may redistribute holdings acquired illegally (the principle of rectification).

These propositions support the libertarian predilection for a minimalist or 'nightwatchman' state with strictly circumscribed powers: the state can provide one and only one public good, viz. the defence of our person and property, including the enforcement of contracts; but other than correcting past wrongs it has no legitimate distributional role. Nozick regards taxation as theft (since it extracts from people money (legitimately acquired) which they would otherwise have allocated in other ways), and also as slavery, in that people are forced to spend part of their time working for government.

Empirical libertarians   Hayek's theory has three strands: the primacy of individual freedom; the value of the market mechanism; and the assertion that the pursuit of social justice is not only fruitless (because there is no such thing) but actively harmful because it can (and, he argues, will) end up destroying individual liberty. Freedom to Hayek (1960, Ch. 1) and other libertarians is defined narrowly as absence of coercion or restraint; it includes political liberty, free speech and economic freedom. Coercion is legitimate only in strictly limited cases, such as the protection of individual liberty (ibid., Ch. 9). Individualism is the corollary of freedom, and the two are interdependent;[3] the pursuit of equality will reduce or destroy them (Hayek, 1944).

To Hayek the market is beneficial because it is efficient, and because it protects individual freedom.

[It is] a procedure which has greatly improved the chances of all to have their wants satisfied, but at the price of all individuals . . . incurring the risk of unmerited failure. With the acceptance of this procedure the *recompense of different groups and individuals becomes exempt from deliberate control.* It is the only procedure yet discovered in which information widely dispersed among millions of men can be effectively utilised for the benefit of all – and used by assuring to all an individual liberty desirable for itself on ethical grounds. [Hayek, 1976, pp. 70–1, my emphasis.]

These advantages arise, according to Hayek, only if prices and wages are allowed to act as signals to individuals as to where to direct their efforts. An individual's reward will be that which induces him to act in the common good; it will often bear no relation to either his individual merit or his need.

Hayek's view of social justice contrasts sharply with that of Rawls. According to Hayek, a given circumstance (e.g. winning the pools, or dying young) can be regarded as good or bad; but it can be described as just or unjust 'only in so far as we hold someone responsible for bringing it about or allowing it to come about' (ibid., p. 31). Thus something is just or unjust *only if it has been caused by the action or inaction of an individual or individuals.* The market, in contrast (ibid., pp. 64–5), is an impersonal force like 'Nature', akin to an economic game with winners and losers, whose outcome can be good or bad, but never just or unjust. To Hayek, therefore, the whole notion of social justice is 'a quasi-religious superstition of the kind which we should respectfully leave in peace so long as it merely makes those happy who hold it' (ibid., p. 66). However, 'the striving for [social justice] will . . . lead to the destruction of the indispensable environment in which the traditional moral values alone can flourish, namely personal freedom' (ibid., p. 67). The reason is that

the more dependent the position of individuals . . . is seen to become on the actions of government, the more they will insist that the governments aim at some recognisable scheme of distributive justice; and the more governments try to realise some preconceived pattern of desirable distribution, the more they must subject the position of the different individuals . . . to their control. *So long as the*

[3] See particularly the explanation of individualism in Hayek (1944, p. 44).

belief in 'social justice' governs political action, this process must progressively approach nearer and nearer to a totalitarian system. [ibid., p. 68, my emphasis.]

Friedman's views are broadly of the same stripe. His primary value is individual freedom. Hence

the scope of government must be limited. Its major function must be to protect our freedom both from the enemies outside our gates and from our fellow-citizens: to preserve law and order, to enforce private contracts, to foster competitive markets. Beyond this major function, government may enable us at times to accomplish jointly what we would find it more difficult . . . to accomplish severally. However, any such use of government is fraught with danger. We should not and cannot avoid using government this way. But there should be a clear and large balance of advantages before we do. [1962, pp. 2–3.]

To Friedman and Hayek the state has no distributional role, other than for certain public goods and for strictly limited measures to alleviate destitution.

3   Liberal Theories of Society

3.1 Utilitarianism

The utilitarian arguments which form the basis of much of this book derive from the 'New Liberalism' of the early twentieth century (Chapter 2:2.1), which was itself firmly rooted in the nineteenth-century Classical tradition. Thus modern utilitarians have common intellectual roots with empirical libertarians.

The utilitarian aim is to distribute goods so as to maximise the total utility[4] of the members of society. 'Goods' are interpreted broadly to include goods and services, rights, freedoms and political power. Maximising total welfare has two aspects: goods must be produced and allocated *efficiently* (discussed in Chapter 4); and they must be distributed in accordance with *equity* (though not necessarily equally). The equitable distribution is shown in Figure 3.1. Total income to be distributed is AB. Individual A's marginal utility (read from left to right) is shown by the line aa, and is assumed to diminish as his income rises. Individual B's marginal utility, which declines from right to left, is shown by the line bb. Total utility is maximised when income is shared equally; A's income is AC, and B's is BC.

[4] Synonymously, to maximise total happiness or total welfare.

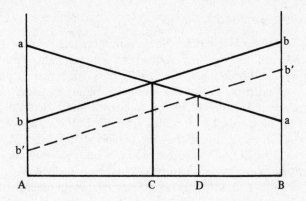

Figure 3.1 *The optimal distribution of income under utilitarianism*

Utilitarianism can therefore justify redistributive activity by the state in pursuit of an egalitarian outcome; but this result depends crucially on two conditions. First, A and B must have identical marginal utility of income functions.[5] If B's marginal utility is shown by *b'b'*, then the distribution which maximises total welfare is unequal, since A now has an income of *AD*. Second, utilitarianism can fully specify the optimal distribution only where the utility of A and B can be measured cardinally.[6]

Various criticisms have been made of this approach. It is asked whether utility is capable of precise definition; whether interpersonal comparison of utility has any meaning; and whose utility counts (e.g. future generations, animals, etc.). These questions are set to one side to focus on the fundamental criticism, namely that utilitarianism can *sanction injustice* by justifying harm to the least well-off if this maximises total utility. 'The trouble with [utilitarianism] is that maximising the sum of individual utilities is supremely unconcerned with the interpersonal distribution of that sum' (Sen, 1973, p. 16).

Formally, suppose that individual B in Figure 3.1 derives less pleasure from life than A because he has major health problems. His marginal utility is shown by the line *b'b'*, and the optimal distribution of goods by point *D*. Thus B should receive *less* income than A because of his health problems. This outcome is criticised as being unjust.

[5] Strictly, several other (technical) conditions are necessary, e.g. that the underlying social welfare function is symmetric and concave (see Chapter 6:1.2). For further discussion of Paretian utilitarianism and its underlying assumptions, see Rowley and Peacock (1975, Ch. 1).
[6] For the definition of cardinal utility, see the Glossary.

3.2 Rawls on Social Justice

Rawls in some ways is Nozick's liberal counterpart. Nozick is a natural rights defender of liberty. For Rawls the natural right, and hence the prime aim of institutions, is *social justice*: thus 'each person possesses an inviolability founded on justice that even the welfare of society as a whole cannot override' (1972, p. 2). Justice, to Rawls, has a twofold purpose: it is desirable for its own sake on moral grounds; but also, and importantly, institutions will survive only if they are perceived to be just. Rawls argues that there exists a definition of justice which is both *general* (i.e. not specific to any particular culture) and can be derived by a process which everyone can agree is fair. The resulting principles deal with the distribution of what Rawls calls 'primary goods', i.e. economic goods, and also position, · opportunity, skill, liberty and self-respect.

The original position is Rawls' starting point. He assumes that each person has goals which are facilitated by the possession of these primary goods, and invites us to contemplate a group of rational individuals, each concerned only with his own self-interest, coming together to negotiate the principles of justice. They are free agents in the negotiation, but they must abide by the resulting principles. Rawls thus uses the convention of a *social contract*.

In this situation no discussion between interested parties will yield principles of justice which command universal acceptance. Rawls therefore abstracts the negotiators from their own society by placing them behind a *veil of ignorance*. They are assumed to be well-informed about the general facts of the world – psychology, economics, sociology, etc. – but each is *deprived of all knowledge about himself*, i.e. of his natural characteristics or endowments, his position in society, and the country or historical period into which he is born. The negotiators seek to advance their own interests, but are unable to distinguish them from anyone else's.

The role of the veil of ignorance is best illustrated by example. To distance ourselves from personal interests we (i.e. citizens through our elected representatives) may decide that aircraft hijackers' demands should never be met, even if innocent lives are lost. We do this in order to save even more lives in the long run; and we establish this doctrine in advance of the event (i.e. behind the veil of ignorance) because if it were our personal loved ones who were kidnapped we would be likely to do anything to save them, irrespective of the possible consequences for others in the future.

The negotiators can consider any principle of justice, e.g. the just action is that which is in the interests of the stronger; or that which ennobles the species; or that which maximises total utility. According to Rawls, the rational negotiator will reject all these definitions because under each he might systematically be underprivileged. The only rational choice is to select principles in terms of what Rawls calls the 'maximin rule' which maximises the position of the least well-off individual or group. The negotiators do this because 'for all they know they may turn out to be the least privileged inhabitants of a country like South Africa' (McCreadie, 1976, p. 117).

The original position, together with the veil of ignorance, plays two distinct roles. First, it is an analytical device, which 'reduc[es] a relatively complex problem, the social choice of the principles of justice, to a more manageable problem, the rational individual choice of principles' (Daniels, 1975, p. xix). Second, and possibly of greater importance, Rawls sees the procedure of rational, self-interested negotiation behind the veil of ignorance as a *moral justification* of the resulting principles – they will be seen to be fair, he argues, because they are selected in a manner which is both rational and fair, hence his term 'justice as fairness'.

The principles of justice which follow are those which Rawls claims would be chosen rationally and unanimously by the negotiators. Because of the veil of ignorance, they will choose to maximise liberty for everyone. Hence:

The first principle (the 'liberty principle'): 'Each person is to have an equal right to the most extensive basic liberty compatible with a similar liberty for others' (Rawls, 1972, p. 60).

The negotiators then turn to the distribution of the other primary goods. Each will reject any principle of distribution which could leave him disadvantaged or exploited.

The negotiators may consider a principle that mandates a thoroughly equal distribution of goods ... But they will soon come to realise that they stand to benefit by the introduction of certain inequalities in the distribution of advantages. For example, giving a rural [doctor] an airplane would make him relatively advantaged, but even – and perhaps especially – the least advantaged among the rural populace stand to benefit as a result, and thus should sanction such inequality. [Gorovitz, 1975, p. 281.]

Hence:

The second principle (the 'difference principle'): 'Social and economic inequalities are to be arranged so that they are both (a) to the greatest benefit of the least advantaged and (b) attached to offices and positions open to all under conditions of fair equality of opportunity' (Rawls, 1972, p. 83).

The possibility of a conflict between the two principles is ruled out by a *priority principle*, which gives the first principle absolute priority over the second. A reduction in the liberty of, for example, the least well-off cannot be justified even if it is to their economic advantage. In addition, in the second principle he gives priority to part (b) over part (a). Subject to these priorities the two principles can be regarded, more simply, as a special case of a more general conception of justice, in which 'all social primary goods – liberty and opportunity, income and wealth ... are to be distributed equally unless an unequal distribution of any or all of these goods is to the advantage of the least favoured' (ibid., p. 303). At its simplest, the distribution of goods between individuals A and B in Figure 3.1 should be that shown by point *C* unless any other distribution benefits the less advantaged of the two. If goods are not so distributed, then any policy which improves the position of the less well-off would be an improvement according to Rawls.[7,8]

Rawls and utilitarianism   Rawls is an explicit opponent of utilitarianism. He regards it as illogical (inasmuch as it would be rejected by rational negotiators in the original position) and as unjust (in that it can sanction injustice in the interests of maximising total welfare). The two theories can have very different implications. Suppose a given policy change makes at least one person better-off without making anyone else worse-off. This is an increase in Pareto efficiency,[9] and hence desirable to utilitarians even if the individual thus benefited were rich. Rawls' difference principle, in contrast, would oppose the policy unless it were also (though not necessarily only) to the advantage of the least well-off. Thus an efficient answer in Paretian terms will not always be a just answer in a Rawlsian sense (though, as argued in Chapter 4:2.2, it may be possible to find a distribution which is both just in a Rawlsian sense *and* Pareto efficient).

Criticisms of Rawls' theory   are summarised only briefly. It has been argued that the veil of ignorance would be immobilising, i.e. the negotiators would be unable to make any decisions at all. According to Nisbet (1974, p. 112),

[the negotiators] don't know much of anything – anything, that is, that we are justified by contemporary psychology in deeming requisite to thought and knowledge of any kind whatever. Nevertheless, Professor Rawls is shortly going to put his happy primitives through feats of cerebration that even the gods might envy. Out of the minds of his homunculi, these epistemological zombies who don't know their names, families, races, generation or societies of origin, are going to come principles of justice and society so vast in implication as to throw all present human societies into a philosopher's limbo.

Miller (1976) (discussed shortly in more detail) similarly argues that removing *all* cultural knowledge will immobilise the negotiators; but failure to do so, though permitting them to make a decision, will result in a culture-bound definition of justice.

Criticisms of the first principle concern Rawls' definition of liberty and his assertion of its primacy. It is argued[10] that Rawls' list of liberties may be too narrow; that the principle of toleration (e.g. of diversity of goals)

---

[7] Under the lexical extension of the difference principle any policy should benefit the worst-off individual; if he/she is indifferent, it should benefit the next worse-off, and so on. Rawls thus admits a policy which benefits *only* the best-off, provided that everyone else is indifferent to it.

[8] Formally, a utilitarian social welfare function (see Chapter 4:1) does not constrain the way individuals are weighted; a Rawlsian social welfare function gives infinite weight to the least-advantaged individual/group.

[9] See Chapter 4:2.1 and the Appendix to Chapter 4, paras 2–4.

[10] See Daniels (1975, pp. xxviii-xxix) and the chapters therein by Hart, Scanlon, Daniels and Fisk.

inherent in Rawls' definition of liberty may reflect class bias; and that some issues are left unresolved, e.g. what liberty should be accorded racists? Additionally, Barry (1973, p. 6) and Hart in Daniels (1975, p. xxx) dispute the priority given to liberty. Poor people might well be willing to trade some liberty for greater social or economic advantage. The second principle is criticised for its crucial dependence on maximin which, it is argued (Letwin, 1983, pp. 22–9; Arrow, 1973a), is the optimal outcome only under very restrictive assumptions. It is also criticised by Marxists as being incompatible with any substantial degree of class conflict.

Finally, some writers argue that Rawls has developed not a *general* theory of justice, but a liberal theory. Rawls set out to find an 'Archimedean point' from which a culture-free definition of justice could be derived, but

in the end the 'Archimedean point' for judging the basic structure of society that Rawls seeks eludes him. Every political theory, and every theory of justice, expresses a particular political and moral perspective. Rawls' achievement, which is considerable, is indeed to have produced *a* theory of justice – a theory of liberal democratic justice. [Lukes (1972) quoted by Daniels, 1975, p. xvi.]

Miller's analysis of social justice   Miller (1976) argues that a completely general theory of justice is logically impossible, and that in this respect Rawls was bound to fail. According to Miller, social justice has three distinct elements:

- *Rights*, e.g. political liberty, equality before the law.
- *Deserts*, i.e. the recognition of each person's actions and qualities.
- *Needs*, i.e. the prerequisites for fulfilling individual plans of life.

The 'deserts' aspect implies, *ceteris paribus*, that someone who works longer hours should receive more pay, and the 'needs' aspect that an individual incapable of work should not be allowed to starve. Though admitting the difficulty of precise theoretical definition, Miller argues that each element is a logically distinct principle embodying a particular type of moral claim.

It is easy to see that rights and deserts can be reconciled (e.g. a man should have the right to keep all his income if he has earned it legally); similarly, rights and needs can be compatible (e.g. a man should be entitled to health care if he is ill). But conflict can arise between desert and need: if I am rich and healthy and you are poor and ill, then either I am taxed (and do not receive my deserts) to pay for your medical treatment, or you receive no treatment (hence your need is not met) so as to protect my deserts.

The essence of Miller's argument is that the definition of social justice depends crucially on the type of society being discussed. In a pure market economy, justice will be defined in terms of rights and the requital of deserts. A collectivist defines justice as distribution according to need.

Miller thus argues that the different principles of justice are connected to wider views of society. He criticises utilitarians and Rawls, first, because they take no explicit account of the conflicting claims of rights, deserts and needs, but blur them into a single, indistinct whole. Second, Miller criticises the view implicit in Rawls that there is a single conception of justice upon which everyone's definition will converge, arguing instead that justice comprises conflicting principles, the relative weights attached to which may vary sharply between different societies.

The whole enterprise of constructing a theory of justice on the basis of choice hypothetically made by individuals abstracted from society is mistaken, because these abstract ciphers lack the prerequisites for developing conceptions of justice. [Miller, 1976, p. 341].

Or if they do manage to make choices, it must be in terms of culturally acquired attitudes. In short, the negotiators in the original position will be immobilised unless they have some knowledge of the nature of the society for which they are choosing rules of justice. Finally,

Rawls individuals are given the attitudes and beliefs of men in modern market societies, and it is therefore not surprising that the conception of justice they ... adopt should approximate to the conception ... dominant in those societies. [ibid., p. 342.]

Hence, he argues, Rawls fails to develop a *general* theory of social justice; such generality is not possible.

4 Collectivist Views

4.1 Fabian Socialism

Collectivist writers agree on the importance of equality. They regard resources as available for collective use, and consequently favour government action; but historically they have disagreed about whether socialist goals could be achieved within a market order. Some writers advocate a mixed economy which blends private enterprise and state intervention; Marxists (discussed in section 4.2) argue that this is not possible; that capitalism is inherently unjust; and that socialism is possible only where the state controls the allocation and distribution of most resources.

Socialist aims vary widely, but three are central – equality, freedom and fraternity. Equality is a variant of the vertical equity aim discussed in Chapter 1:2.2, and fraternity of the social solidarity aim. It is recognised that these aims can clash; and different writers accord them different weight; but together they make up the socialist definition of justice. In Miller's terms the dominant themes are rights and needs, with deserts (though not entirely left out) assigned a smaller role.

There is a measure of agreement (Tawney, 1953 and 1964; Crosland,

1956; and, for a counter-view, Donnison, 1972) that the crucial element of justice is equality, which to socialists is an active concept. Equality of opportunity on its own may be insufficient (Laski, 1967, Ch. 4; Tawney, 1964), since substantial inequality of outcome may persist. Positive equalising measures are needed, though not necessarily complete equality of outcome.

Such emphasis on equality bears closely on Miller's concept of need. Weale points out that 'in some political arguments ... the assumption is made that to distribute according to need is to satisfy the claims of equality' (1978, p. 67), but suggests (Ch. 5) that the relationship is rather more complicated. For present purposes we need only note that equality and meeting need are closely related concepts, though not logically equivalent.

The socialist concept of freedom is broad. It embraces the free exercise of individual choice (which is possible only if there is no poverty and no substantial inequality of wealth and power), and extends from legal and political relations to economic security. Thus individuals should have some power in relation to their conditions of work, including stability of employment, and should not be subject to the arbitrary power of others. In sharp contrast with libertarian views,

the socialist believes that freedom is the product of government action rather than government inaction. Only government action through law, economic, social and fiscal policy can redistribute freedom so that its exercise can become a reality for all. [George and Wilding, 1976, p. 66.]

The third major value is fraternity. To a socialist this

means co-operation rather than competition, an emphasis on duties rather than rights, on the good of the community rather than on the wants of the individual, on altruism rather than self-help. [ibid., p. 66.]

Altruism (e.g. Titmuss, 1970) is a recurring theme in later chapters.

Socialist criticism of the free market   starts with the motive given to individuals to pursue personal advantage rather than the general good (see Tawney, 1921), and denies the libertarian assertion that the former brings about the latter. Second, the market is undemocratic, inasmuch as some decisions with widespread effects are taken by a small power élite, and others are left to the arbitrary distributional effects of market forces. Third, the market is unjust because it distributes rewards which are unrelated to individual need or merit, and because the costs of economic change are distributed arbitrarily. Fourth, the free market is not self-regulating; in particular, left to itself, it is unable to maintain full employment. Lastly, the market has not been able to abolish poverty, let alone inequality. In sum,

production is carried on wastefully and without adequate plan. The commodities and services necessary to the life of the community are never so distributed as to relate to need or to produce a result which maximises their social utility. We build picture palaces when we need houses. We spend on battleships what is wanted for schools . . . We have, in fact, both the wrong commodities produced, and those produced distributed without regard to social urgency. [Laski, 1967, p. 175.][11]

Socialists are in general agreement over the failings of the free market, and in their choice of aims, but they part company over the best way of achieving them. Though the distinction is far from watertight, and is disputed by some writers, it is useful for exposition to contrast the 'fundamentalists' (largely Marxists), who reject capitalism and its associated pattern of economic and social relations, with the 'revisionists', who hold that the ills of society can be corrected within a broadly capitalist framework.

Revisionists see two great changes in the capitalist system: first, government today has a large role to play in economic life as well as in other areas; second, the classical entrepreneur has largely disappeared, the ownership of modern corporations being both diffuse and largely separate from the people who manage them. It is argued in consequence (see the quote by Crosland at the head of the chapter) that capitalism has been 'tamed', and that the resulting mixed economy, with an active role for government in the distribution of goods, income and power, is fully compatible with socialist objectives.

4.2 Marxists

This is not a Marxist book and I am no Marxist writer, so this section seeks only to sketch out as much Marxist thought as is necessary to contrast it with other theories (see the Further Reading). In considering the Marxist view of capitalism we need to turn our minds to three things: the contrast between the Marxist approach and that of conventional economic analysis; its analysis of the exploitation of labour; and its view of the role of government in supporting capitalism.

The Marxist approach differs substantially from that of the classical political economists like Smith (1776) and Ricardo (1817), for whom the production of commodities was largely independent of the society in question. This approach has continued to dominate economic thinking. It is argued that conventional economic theory is applicable to the USA, to Britain, to Sweden, and to the former Communist countries; and such economic analysis is seen as almost entirely separate from political and social arrangements. Thus to Sweezy (1942, p. 5), 'economic theorising is primarily a process of constructing and interrelating concepts from which all specifically

---

[11] Having read this paragraph, it is instructive to re-read the quote from Hayek (1976, pp. 70–1) in section 2, on the virtues of the market.

social content has been drained off'. A key part of Marx's thought, in contrast, is that the economic, political and social structure of a society is determined largely by its dominant *mode of production*. It is argued that the capitalist mode of production will result not only in a particular form of economic organisation, but also (and inevitably) in a particular and inequitable structure of social class and political power.

The exploitation of labour under capitalism is a central tenet of Marxist thought. Conventional economic theory sees individuals as selling their labour services (more or less) freely in a (more or less) competitive market; the wage is established when the demand for labour equals its supply, which, under competitive conditions, results in a wage rate equal to the marginal product of labour. Capital, similarly, receives its marginal product, which, under competitive conditions and in the long run, is equal to the 'normal' rate of profit plus any premium for risk. Under certain conditions[12] these payments to factors exhaust the product leaving no surplus; thus, it is argued, there is no exploitation. In a Marxist analysis of the labour market this *apparently* free exchange of labour services (called *labour power*) for the wage is seen as a key feature of the capitalist mode of production. But for most people the sale of their labour power is their only means of subsistence, since other methods (e.g. the cultivation of common land) are largely blocked. Thus,

in the capitalist mode of production the worker is *forced* to sell his/her labour power because he/she has no substantial savings or independent access to the means of production ... Hence the relations of production are *enforced* through the institution of the labour market. [Ginsburg, 1979, p. 21, my emphasis.]

Because of this compulsion, the capitalist is able to extract *surplus value* from the labour he employs.

Marx's argument is complex, but in essence exploitation arose because the capitalist was obliged to pay only a weekly wage sufficient to support the worker and his family at around subsistence, but could then extract as much output as possible by imposing long working hours. The surplus value is the difference between the value of a worker's output and his wage and is, according to Marx, much greater than that necessary to yield a 'normal' rate of profit. This view, suitably modified to account for wages above subsistence, is held by Marxists today (see Robinson and Eatwell, 1973, pp. 28–9). Individuals whose only source of income is the sale of their labour thus have less power than the (fewer) people with more choice (e.g. because they own wealth and/or have independent access to the means of production). Marx argued that this inequality of power is inevitable in a

---

[12] Euler's theorem states that paying all factors their marginal product will lead to product exhaustion under constant returns to scale. This can occur *either* where the production function exhibits constant returns to scale at all levels of output *or* at the point of minimum long-run average cost.

capitalist society, and consequently the more powerful few are able to exploit labour by extracting its surplus value, hence enjoying a disproportionate share of output.

Because of its exploitative nature, Marx's attitude to capitalism 'was one of total rejection rather than reform and much of his intellectual effort went into proving that the capitalist system was both unworkable and inhuman' (Mishra, 1981, p. 69). The heart of the argument is that the capitalist mode of production causes conflict between one class (the large, poor, exploited working class) and another (the small ruling class, which derives power from wealth and/or political influence), and that conflict between these classes is inherent and inevitable.

The role of government in a capitalist society   Given this position, it is necessary to ask why capitalism has survived despite the numerical superiority of the working class. The first reason, according to Marxists, relates to *economic* power, which is concentrated in a small number of hands. The second is the distribution of *political* power. The ruling class dominates government decisions, Marxists argue, both because of its economic power and because members of the economic élite share a common education and social class with the political élite. Accordingly, government in a capitalist society always favours the ruling élite (Miliband, 1969, Chs 4–6). Third, there is the power of the ruling class over *ideas*. The arguments are complex and the details controversial (see Strachey, 1936; Miliband, 1969, Ch. 8). From this prop to capitalism derives the Marxist emphasis on 'consciousness raising'.

All three factors constitute the Marxist explanation of the continuance of capitalism despite class conflict. But there is disagreement whether the resulting structure supports capitalists by furthering the interests *only* of the ruling class, or whether the state, rather more broadly, supports the entire capitalist *system*, with some benefits also for the working class. Gough (1979, pp. 13–14) criticises some Marxist writers for ignoring the effects of class conflict; he argues that in order to protect the capitalist system in the face of working-class pressure, the state has extended the benefits of the welfare state, with gains not only for the ruling élite, but for workers as well.

The Marxist state   The next step is to outline the Marxist definition of a just society and the role of government necessary for its achievement. Marxists share the socialist triad of liberty, equality and fraternity, though with some differences in interpretation and in their relative weights. Liberty is a much more active concept than the mere absence of coercion. It cannot exist where economic or political power is distributed unequally, nor where the actions of the state are biased (Laski, 1967, Ch. 4; Miliband, 1969, Ch. 7); freedom, moreover, includes a substantial measure of equality and economic security. To a Marxist, therefore, freedom and equality are two essential and intermingled aspects of social justice. This contrasts very sharply with the liberal perspective, in which the potential conflict between freedom and equality creates the central problem of political economy.

Equality to a Marxist does not necessarily imply complete equalisation. According to Laski (1967, p. 157), 'the urgent claims of all must be met before we can meet the particular needs of some'. Once this basic condition has been met, differences in rewards should depend on effort or ability. It can therefore be argued that the Marxist aim is one not of equality, but of meeting need, which, as we have seen (Weale, 1978), is a related but logically distinct objective. In Miller's terms, the Marxist definition of justice is based largely on needs, with rights somewhat secondary and with a small place for deserts.

Finally, we turn to the methods advocated by Marxists for the achievement of these aims. It is clear that their view of society, particularly the emphasis on economic equality and analysis of class conflict, implies a highly active role for government. They stress the importance of nationalising the means of production, both because profits though produced socially generally accrue to a few large shareholders, and because private ownership of productive resources is incompatible with the Marxist definition of freedom. Though not a panacea, nationalisation is regarded as essential to the achievement of Marxist aims, including industrial democracy, which is seen as a necessary concomitant of political democracy. An additional purpose is to ensure that industry is run for social rather than private benefit.

A Marxist society, therefore, would combine public ownership and government planning with wide-scale participation by workers in decisions affecting their lives. Libertarians argue that there is too much planning in the welfare state, Marxists that there is not enough – planning, they argue, far from reducing individual freedom, enhances it. It is logical that each side should reach the conclusion it does – planning reduces freedom defined by libertarians as the absence of coercion, but (if successful) enhances freedom defined by socialists to include some guarantee of economic security.

5 Implications for the Role of the State

5.1 Theoretical Issues

This section compares the theories, and discusses their implications for policy generally (section 5.2) and the welfare state in particular (section 5.3).

Criticisms of liberalism by libertarians centre largely on the definition of individual freedom. The liberal concept includes economic security, so that social justice embraces needs as well as rights and deserts. Libertarians criticise the inclusion of needs (at any rate above subsistence) because the resulting institutions (e.g. taxation) abridge natural rights (Nozick); are part of a slippery slope towards totalitarianism (Hayek); and reduce economic efficiency. Several counter-arguments are possible. The first concerns Hayek's argument that it is not possible to define social justice. As we shall see in Chapter 6, many concepts, including poverty and inequality, are hard, if not impossible, to define; but this does *not* imply that no such phenomenon exists. Defenders of Rawls would argue, in addition, that the priority of the liberty principle is explicit protection against the Hayekian slippery slope; and also that redistribution does not violate individual rights where it was agreed behind the veil of ignorance, as part of the social contract.[13]

Criticisms of liberalism by collectivists   arise, first, because of the greater collectivist emphasis on needs. Additionally, collectivists adopt a broader definition of freedom. As a case in point, Daniels (1975) criticises Rawls' liberty principle, because it underestimates the effect of economic inequality on political liberties; as a result the two principles may be incompatible. Marxists also criticise liberal theories because they leave out class conflict.

Criticisms of libertarianism   There is no opposition by liberals to markets *per se*. But they attack the libertarian emphasis on *free* markets, which can distribute resources unjustly by failing to meet individual need. More specifically, Hayek (1976, pp. 64–5) has a view of markets as a game with winners and losers; but it can be argued that it is a game without rules, like a boxing tournament in which participants are not divided into different classes by weight. To liberals this violates the assumption of equal power on which, *inter alia*, the advantages of a market system depend (see Chapter 4:3.2). Collectivists criticise the libertarian definition of freedom as too narrow, and regard equality and economic security as inseparable aspects of freedom (contrast Hayek, 1944, Ch. 9, and Laski, 1967, p. 520). In addition, Marxists reject the market system entirely.

Criticisms of collectivism   Natural rights libertarians, in consequence, entirely reject collectivist views, since attempts to redistribute resources equally or in accordance with need are regarded as violations of individual freedom. Empirical libertarians and liberals criticise collectivist views not

---

[13] There is at times an opacity about Hayek's arguments about social justice. He states (1976, p. xi) that '[eventually] I perceived that the Emperor had no clothes on, that is, that the term "social justice" was entirely empty and meaningless ... The more I tried to give it definite meaning the more it fell apart.' Yet, in discussing Rawls he observes that 'the differences between us seemed more verbal than substantial' (p. xiii). Later, he argues 'that the recognition that in such combinations as "social", "economic" [or] "distributive" ... justice the term "justice" is wholly empty should not lead us to throw the baby out with the bath water' (p. 100), since if *distributions* cannot be just, *institutions* can. On the latter point Hayek claims that he and Rawls are in agreement.

because they include meeting need as one of their objectives, but because they give it pride of place.

A different line of criticism is that collectivism (particularly when combined with central planning and state ownership of the means of production) is inefficient, as shown, for instance, by the poor post-war economic performance of countries in central and eastern Europe. The major purpose of the late 1980s revolution throughout the region was to replace central planning by a market system, with the explicit objectives of improved efficiency and increased individual freedom. It is important, however, not to misinterpret these events. It can be argued that collectivism defined, as by Marxists, in terms of its *methods* (e.g. state ownership and control) has been discredited. Fabian socialism, however, is defined in terms of its *aims*, e.g. the pursuit of more or less egalitarian goals. This form of socialism, which blurs into a liberal analysis, remains firmly on the agenda.

5.2 Policy Implications

Private property is inviolate only to natural rights libertarians like Nozick (1974, Ch. 7), for whom justice in holdings implies total freedom for the individual to allocate as he chooses those resources which he has justly acquired. To Marxists, resources are available collectively to be distributed according to need, hence their emphasis on public ownership, and the view that 'property is theft' (see Laski, 1967, Chs 5 and 9).

To liberals, private property and public ownership are a pragmatic matter, and government should be free to adopt whichever mix of the two is most helpful in achieving its aims. Rawls maintains that his two principles are compatible with either private or public ownership of resources, or with a mixed economy. Empirical libertarians, as we shall see shortly, accord private property a major but not overriding role; and Fabian socialists allow it a more important role than is the case with Marxists.

Taxation to Nozick means that an individual will work (say) three days a week for himself, and two days working compulsorily for the government; to Nozick, therefore, it is taxation, not private property, which is a form of theft. It is, however, mistaken to attribute this view to all libertarians. The necessity of taxation was always acknowledged by the Classical liberals (Robbins, 1978, Ch. 2), albeit with some reluctance because of the consequent interference with liberty. The modern inheritors of this position like Hayek and Friedman concede the necessity of some taxation for the provision of public goods (narrowly defined) and for poverty relief (generally at subsistence).

To collectivist writers (Tawney, 1964, pp. 135–6) taxation for any social purpose is entirely legitimate. Liberals, also, regard taxation as an appropriate means towards policy objectives, though they are concerned about its disincentive effects particularly on labour supply and capital formation, and more generally with selecting an optimal trade-off between efficiency and social justice (Atkinson and Stiglitz, 1980, Lectures 12–14).

Redistribution   Distributive justice is not a problem for everyone. To Marxists, resources are available for collective allocation on the basis of need, which is given clear priority. Natural rights libertarians like Nozick concentrate entirely on rights and deserts. Resources are produced by *individuals*, who thereby acquire the right to allocate them; the question of *societal* allocation does not arise. Distributive justice is therefore removed entirely from the agenda.

Other groups have difficulties with distribution precisely because they are concerned with both desert and need. Empirical libertarians may oppose progressive taxation; but they do not take an absolute line against redistribution in that they accept public action to relieve destitution. Utilitarians favour redistributive activity which increases total welfare, but are concerned about the trade-off with efficiency. Rawls, too, is not a complete egalitarian, since privilege is acceptable where it improves the position of the least well-off.

Public production   raises similar arguments. Libertarians countenance provision by the state of at most a limited class of public goods such as law and order, and even those only if no method of private supply can be found (Hayek, 1960, p. 223; Friedman, 1962, Ch. 2). In complete opposition, Marxists regard it as a function of the state to supply all basic goods and services, and to distribute them in accordance with individual need. To liberals the issue of public versus market production and allocation is a pragmatic question of which method is more effective – which is the subject of most of this book.

5.3 Attitudes Towards the Welfare State

The welfare state is a complicated set of institutions, so it is not surprising that attitudes towards it are complicated and often confused.

Natural rights libertarians   like Nozick regard a welfare state of any sort as an anathema, seeing its pursuit of the spurious (or immoral) goal of equality as an unacceptable violation of individual liberty.

Empirical libertarians   like Hayek and Friedman require careful discussion. Let us return to the distinction (Chapter 2:7.1) between an institutional welfare state, which pursues substantially redistributive goals, and a residual welfare state. The former is strongly opposed by all libertarians as a coercive agency, stifling freedom and individualism, and courting the risk of totalitarianism through the amalgamation of economic and political power under collective planning, in contrast with their separation in a market system. A welfare state of this sort is also seen as creating inefficiency in several ways: it wastes resources because at a zero or subsidised price demand is excessive; resources are used inefficiently because government monopoly is insulated from competition; and the necessary taxation will have costs in terms of efficiency and economic growth.

A residual welfare state has much more limited aims. It is recognised that a free society based on private property and competitive markets is likely to distribute income unequally. Limited state activity may therefore be appropriate to relieve destitution and to provide certain public goods. Empirical libertarians consider this rather austere welfare state as essential to their conception of a civilised society. It is therefore not inconsistent when they attack existing social arrangements in the strongest terms (see Hayek, 1960, and the quote from Friedman at the head of this chapter), but support more limited welfare institutions (see Friedman, 1962, Chs 6 and 12; Willetts, 1992, Ch. X).

Liberals and Fabian socialists tend unambiguously to support the welfare state. To Beveridge (1944, p. 254) it was necessary 'to use the powers of the State, sofar as may be necessary without any limit whatsoever, in order to avoid the five giant evils'.[14] For most socialist writers, however, the welfare state is not a complete solution to society's ills, but only a step along the way.

[W]hile socialists see the welfare state as only the limited and partial achievement of some socialist goals, they are, nevertheless, optimistic about its influence. They see it not as dampening down the political forces making for further social change, but rather as a powerful ally ... In brief, they see the welfare state as ... a stepping stone toward socialism. [George and Wilding, 1976, p. 84.]

It is not surprising that liberals and socialists share some common ground. Robson (1976, p. 17), citing Hobhouse, writes:

The liberal ... stands for emancipation, and is the inheritor of a long tradition of those who have fought for liberty, who have struggled against government and its laws or against society because they crushed human development ... The socialist stands for solidarity of society, for mutual responsibility and the duty of the strong to aid the weak ... On this analysis the ideals of the liberal and socialist were seen as complementary rather than conflicting.

Marxists have tended to disagree strongly among themselves. Is the welfare state (a) *only* an instrument of capitalist oppression, or does it (b) *also* represent a progressive outcome of working-class pressure? Under the first view, the welfare state is at best irrelevant, a 'ransom' paid by the dominant class, and an institution dealing with symptoms rather than causes of

[14] Want, disease, ignorance, squalor and idleness – see the discussion in Chapter 1:1.1.

economic and social problems; at worst, the welfare state is actively malign, in that it has sustained the capitalist system.

[S]ocial control ... has to do with the maintenance of order and the reduction of social conflict and tension. From the viewpoint of the ruling classes this often means reducing the workers' hostility towards the capitalist regime ... [Mishra, 1981, p. 82.]

This, according to some Marxists, is the major purpose of the welfare state.

Other Marxist writers see the welfare state as serving the interests of the capitalist class *and* those of workers. A central insight (Gintis and Bowles, 1982) is the contradictory position of the welfare state in a modern capitalist economy; the former is based on rights (e.g. of citizenship) and needs, the latter recognises claims on resources based on deserts (e.g. through the ownership of property). Thus Gough (1979) sees the state not as a neutral umpire, nor as acting *merely* in the interests of the capitalist class (as opposed to the capitalist *system*), but as responding to pressure: from the working class to meet needs and extend rights; and from capital to foster capital accumulation. Ginsburg, too, recognises the importance of class conflict in the development of the welfare state, but argues that though the demands of the working class have produced important material gains, 'those demands have been processed and responded to in such a form that, far from posing a threat to capital, they have deepened its acceptance and extended its survival' (1979, p. 19).

The welfare state thus has contradictory functions.

It simultaneously embodies tendencies to enhance social welfare, to develop the powers of individuals, to exert social control over the blind play of market forces; and tendencies to repress and control people, to adapt them to the requirements of the capitalist economy. [Gough, 1979, p. 12.]

As a result it is not surprising that some Marxists have ambivalent attitudes. Is the welfare state an

agency of repression, or a system for enlarging human needs and mitigating the rigours of the free-market economy? An aid to capitalist accumulation and profits or a 'social wage' to be defended and enlarged like the money in your pay packet? Capitalist fraud or working-class victory? [ibid., p. 11.]

Whether the welfare state contributes to justice is clearly a matter of perspective, and hence susceptible of no definitive answer. Miller (1976, pp. 343–4) admits that

readers with a yearning for Rawlsian 'moral geometry' may ... find this [conclusion] disappointing. Can there be no ... arguments of universal validity that hold good across social and historical barriers? This is indeed a pleasant prospect, but since there seems little hope of it being realised, I conclude that we shall have to make do with more modest results.

It is, nevertheless, instructive to conclude with a few words on who can usefully talk with whom, and about what. It is not possible to enter debate with natural rights defenders of free markets and the nightwatchman state, save by disputing their values, nor with Marxists, to whom the evils of the market system are axiomatic. But dialogue *is* possible between empirical libertarians, liberals and Fabian socialists, and would (I suspect) be particularly fruitful between the first two. Writers like Hayek and Friedman share common roots in nineteenth-century Classical liberalism with the largely utilitarian arguments of this book. Their position rests less on an ethical than on a theoretical and empirical view about the institutions likely to maximise total utility. The distinction is vital. The issues dividing a liberal defence of the welfare state from the views of empirical libertarians are not moral but largely factual. The main thrust of the argument is that technical problems with markets as both a theoretical and an empirical matter are much more pervasive than Hayek and Friedman allow. These are the grounds of the debate; the theoretical heart of the argument is the subject of Chapter 4.

Further Reading

Libertarian ideas are set out by Nozick (1974) (a natural rights defence), Hayek (1944, 1960, 1976) and Friedman (1962, 1980). The intellectual roots of these ideas are discussed by Robbins (1978). For a libertarian critique of egalitarianism, see the essays in Letwin (1983).

The liberal approach is analysed by Barry (1973) and Miller (1976). For an introduction to Rawls (1972), see Gorovitz (1975) (one of the best teaching articles I have read, and one to which readers are most warmly referred). For more detailed commentary, see the contributions in Daniels (1975), and Sen (1992, Ch. 5); for liberal critiques Barry (1973) and Miller (1976); and for cogent libertarian criticism Nisbet (1974). McCreadie (1976) offers an interesting application to the UK National Health Service.

A simple introduction to socialist thought (and also to the other theories of society) is given by George and Wilding (1976), and discussion in greater depth by Laski (1967), Miliband (1969), Crosland (1956) and Tawney (1964) (a defence of equality).

The classic exposition of Marxist economic theory is Sweezy (1942). For a simple introduction, see Robinson and Eatwell (1973) and Fine (1975); and for more complete discussion, Mandel (1976), Harrison (1978) and Desai (1979). Marxist attitudes to the welfare state are discussed by Gough (1979), Ginsburg (1979) and Mishra (1981).

Appendix: Non-Technical Summary of Chapter 3

1. Chapter 3 discusses various theories of society – libertarianism, utilitarianism, Rawlsian arguments and socialism. In practice the theories blur into each other like the colours of the rainbow – but it is useful for exposition to talk about them as separate entities.

LIBERTARIAN THEORIES

2. To libertarians (section 2), as their name implies, the primary aim of institutions is individual liberty, and the best method of achieving its economic dimension is through the operation of private markets. *Natural rights libertarians* like Nozick (1974) defend a minimal (or 'nightwatchman') state on ethical grounds; *empirical libertarians* like Hayek and Friedman out of a belief that such a regime will maximise total welfare. For natural rights libertarians the state has no legitimate distributional role at all; to empirical libertarians its distributional activities are strictly circumscribed.

3. Hayek argues in addition that the pursuit of social justice is not only fruitless because there is no such thing, but also dangerous because it will destroy the market order which is both efficient and the only guarantee of personal freedom. According to Hayek (1976) a given circumstance is just or unjust only if it has been caused by the action/inaction of a *named* individual or individuals. The outcome of impersonal forces ('Nature') can be good or bad, but never just or unjust. The market is seen as an impersonal force, akin to an economic game with winners and losers, and so the market-determined distribution of goods can be neither just nor unjust. The notion of social justice therefore has no meaning. Its quest, however, is dangerous, according to Hayek, because once governments start to interfere with the market-determined distribution a process is set in motion which progressively approaches totalitarianism.

LIBERAL THEORIES

4. Liberal theories (section 3), e.g. utilitarianism and writers like Rawls, contrast with libertarian views first by allowing the state a greater distributional role, and second through a weaker presumption that the free market is necessarily the best means of production and distribution. The treatment of property rights is not an end in itself, as with libertarians, but a means towards the achievement of stated policy aims. In certain circumstances this can justify a mixed economy.

5. The utilitarian aim is to distribute goods so as to maximise the total utility of society's members (section 3.1). Where individuals have identical marginal utility of income functions this occurs when income is shared

equally (Figure 3.1). Utilitarianism thus enables statements to be about the optimal distribution of goods (which in certain circumstances can be egalitarian), and so legitimates a redistributive role for the state.

6. This approach is criticised by Rawls and others because it can justify harm to the least well-off individual or group, if this raises total utility.

7. Rawls, in contrast, makes justice the primary aim of policy (section 3.2) (for a very clear introduction, see Gorovitz (1975)). Rawls defines social justice in terms of two principles, the first dealing with the distribution of liberty, the second with that of other goods. Taken together they imply that all goods (interpreted broadly to include liberty and opportunity) should be distributed equally unless an unequal distribution is to the advantage of the least well-off individual or group. No policy should be undertaken, according to Rawls, unless it benefits also (though not necessarily only) the least well-off. Again, there is a legitimate, and generally egalitarian, redistributive role for the state.

8. The theories of utilitarians and Rawls can have different policy implications. Suppose a given policy change makes at least one person better-off without making anyone worse-off. This is a Pareto improvement (see Chapter 4:2.1); hence utilitarians would regard the policy as desirable even if the individual thus benefited were rich. Rawls' principles of justice would oppose the policy unless it were also to the advantage of the least well-off. Thus an efficient answer in a Paretian sense is not always just in a Rawlsian sense (see Chapter 4:2.2).

SOCIALIST THEORIES

9. The main socialist aims are equality, freedom and fraternity. These values can conflict, and different writers accord them different weight. But there is general agreement about the importance of equality, which is closely related (though not logically equivalent) to the further socialist aim of meeting need.

10. Despite agreement about their aims, and in their diagnosis of the failings of the free market, socialists are divided over how best to achieve them, most fundamentally over the role, if any, of the market system.

11. Some socialists (section 4.1) argue that institutional changes, not least the enlarged role of government in economic life, have greatly reduced the evils of capitalism and made it possible to harness the market system to socialist goals. Adherents of this view accept a role for private property and the market mechanism, though modified in both cases by state intervention – i.e. like liberals they feel that their aims are likely to be best achieved by some sort of mixed economy.

12. Other socialists, e.g. Marxists (section 4.2), argue that private ownership and the market system are inherently in conflict with socialist aims. In particular they regard the market as exploitative and therefore incompatible with equality. Marxists therefore reject capitalism outright, whether or not it makes up part of a mixed economy, and give the state a primary role in production and allocation, as well as in distribution and redistribution.

ATTITUDES TOWARDS THE WELFARE STATE

13. The appropriate role of the state depends crucially on the underlying theory of society (sections 5.1 and 5.2), as also do attitudes towards the welfare state (section 5.3).

14. Natural rights libertarians reject all but minimal intervention and are unambiguously hostile to the welfare state, which they regard as a coercive agency which stifles freedom and individualism, and encourages waste and inefficiency in pursuit of the spurious and dangerous goal of social justice.

15. Empirical libertarians have a broadly similar attitude towards a large-scale welfare state with substantial redistributive goals. They do, however, recognise that a free society based on private property and competitive markets is likely to distribute income unequally, and are therefore prepared to support an austere welfare state whose primary aim is the relief of destitution.

16. The main support for the welfare state comes from liberals and some socialists, in the latter case unreservedly, because it is seen as an equalising force. For liberals its existence is a contingent question: they support the institutions of the welfare state where (and only where) they contribute more than alternative arrangements to the achievement of society's aims. In such cases their support is unreserved.

17. Marxists are generally hostile to the welfare state, though with some controversy. 'Hardline' commentators regard it as an actively malign agency which serves *only* (or mainly) as an instrument of social control, to protect the continued existence of the capitalist system. Other writers argue that, though the welfare state is indeed a 'ransom' paid by the dominant class, it *also* represents a genuine improvement in working-class conditions.

18. Finally, who can talk with whom, and about what? No debate is possible between liberals and natural rights libertarians on the one hand, or Marxists on the other. Debate *is*, however, possible between liberals and libertarians like Hayek and Friedman, who argue less from a moral position than from an empirical view about the institutions likely to maximise total utility. The main thrust of this book is that technical problems with markets, as both a theoretical and an empirical matter, are much more pervasive

than Hayek and Friedman allow. In other words, the issues which separate a liberal defence of the welfare state from the views of empirical libertarians are at least as much factual as ideological.

Chapter 4
Economic Theory 1: State Intervention[1]

Every individual ... generally ... neither intends to promote the public interest, nor knows by how much he is promoting it. By preferring the support of domestic to that of foreign industry he intends only his own security; and by directing that industry in such a manner as its produce may be of the greatest value, he intends only his own gain, and he is in this, as in many other cases, led by an invisible hand to promote an end which was no part of his intention. [Adam Smith, 1776.]

[The] market needs a place, and the market needs to be kept in its place. It must be given enough scope to accomplish the many things it does well. It limits the power of bureaucracy, ... responds reliably to the signals transmitted by consumers and producers ... Most important, the prizes in the market place provide the incentives for work effort and productive contribution ... For such reasons I cheered the market; but I could not give it more than two cheers. The tyranny of the dollar yardstick restrained my enthusiasm. [Arthur Okun, 1975.]

1 The Formal Structure of the Problem

We now change gear sharply and move from the world of political philosophy to economic theory. The main aim is to develop a framework which (a) explains and (b) justifies (or fails to justify) the fact that the state produces and/or allocates some goods like health care and education, but leaves others like food for the most part to the private market. The main issues concern economic efficiency and social justice. Section 1 sets out the formal structure of the problem. Section 2 shows that the efficiency aim is common to all theories of society, but that redistributive goals depend crucially on what definition of social justice is chosen. The next step (section 3) is to consider the circumstances in which the market will allocate efficiently, and appropriate forms of intervention in their absence. The

[1] Non-technical readers can find the gist of the argument in the Appendix to this chapter.

pursuit of social justice (section 4) raises such questions as: why does redistribution occur; should it be voluntary; should it be in cash or in kind; and what role (if any) should the state adopt to bring about equal access to goods and services, or to foster equality of opportunity or outcome? One set of counter-arguments to government intervention comes from the 'government failure' analysis, discussed briefly in section 5. As a precursor to policy discussion in later chapters, section 6 sets out the logic of what has come to be known as 'privatisation'. Section 7 pulls together the major threads running through Chapters 3 and 4 by discussing the appropriate boundary between the market and the state, setting out the main theoretical argument of the book, and establishing the areas of debate with its opponents, particularly libertarian writers like Hayek and Friedman.

The conventional starting point for economic theory is the social welfare maximisation problem. The aim of policy is to maximise social welfare subject to the three basic constraints of tastes, technology and resources,[2] i.e.

Maximise: $\quad W = W(U^A, U^B) \quad$ Social welfare function $\qquad$ (4.1)

Subject to: $\quad \left.\begin{array}{l} U^A = U^A(X^A, Y^A) \\ U^B = U^B(X^B, Y^B) \end{array}\right\}$ Tastes $\qquad\qquad\qquad\quad$ (4.2)
(4.3)

$\qquad\qquad\quad \left.\begin{array}{l} X = X(K^X, L^X) \\ Y = Y(K^Y, L^Y) \end{array}\right\}$ Technology $\qquad\qquad$ (4.4)
(4.5)

$\qquad\qquad\quad \left.\begin{array}{l} K^X + K^Y = \bar{K} \\ L^X + L^Y = \bar{L} \end{array}\right\}$ Resources $\qquad\qquad$ (4.6)
(4.7)

The aim in equation (4.1) is to maximise social welfare, W, as a function of the utilities of individuals A and B, U^A and U^B (i.e. the problem is a joint maximisation of efficiency and social justice). The constraints of tastes, technology and resources are shown by equations (4.2) to (4.7). The utilities of individuals A and B are constrained by their consumption of goods X and Y (equations (4.2) and (4.3)); and consumption is constrained by equations (4.4) and (4.5), which show the production functions for X and Y in terms of the inputs of capital, K and labour, L; the inputs used to produce X and Y are constrained by the total availability of capital and labour, $\bar{K}$ and $\bar{L}$ (equations (4.6) and (4.7)).

The problem as formulated relates to a *first-best economy*. This implies one of two situations: either there is no impediment to efficiency, and also an optimal distribution of endowments; or it is possible for government to counter problems of inefficiency or maldistribution with first-best policies

---

[2] This formulation is taken from Layard and Walters (1978, Ch. 1).

(e.g. through lump-sum taxation). An important theorem discussed in section 3 establishes the (first-best) assumptions under which a competitive market will allocate resources efficiently; and it is argued that where these conditions hold, the state has no role except (possibly) a distributional one.

The conditions, however, are stringent, as is the assumption that lump-sum taxation is feasible. A *second-best economy* faces additional constraint(s) due, for instance, to technical problems or to social institutions. Imperfect information is a recurring theme, e.g. if U^A is not well-defined with respect to X^A. As a result, unrestricted markets may be inefficient or inequitable, and intervention may improve matters. Another problem concerns externalities. If U^A depends on, say, X^B we have a consumption externality which constitutes a constraint additional to those in equations (4.2) to (4.7). This may justify intervention in one of a number of forms. We return to these issues in sections 3 and 4.[3]

2 Why Economic Efficiency is One of the Aims of Policy

2.1 The Concept of Economic Efficiency[4]

Since the concept of efficiency is fundamental to the whole book, this brief and very elementary introduction is included in the main body of the chapter rather than relegated to the Appendix. Technical readers should proceed directly to section 2.2.

Broadly speaking, economic efficiency[5] is about making the best use of limited resources given people's tastes. It concerns both the production and allocation of goods. This involves the choice of an *output bundle*

$$X^* = (X_1, X_2, \ldots, X_n) \qquad (4.8)$$

(where X_i is the output of the ith good) with the property that any deviations from these quantities will make at least one person worse off. The intuition of this efficient output bundle is shown at its simplest in a partial equilibrium framework in Figure 4.1. The optimal quantity of any good, *ceteris paribus*, is that at which the value placed by society on the marginal unit equals its marginal social cost.[6]

---

[3] For a compendious survey of the literature on first- and second-best analysis within the social welfare maximisation framework, see Atkinson and Stiglitz (1980, Lectures 11–14) and the references therein; and for a wide-ranging collection of articles, Atkinson (1983b).

[4] Non-technical readers should consult (in ascending order of difficulty) the relevant chapters (see the following footnotes) in Le Grand *et al.* (1992), Baumol and Blinder (1991, Ch. 29) or Laidler and Estrin (1989, Ch. 26).

[5] Referred to synonymously as Pareto efficiency, Pareto optimality or allocative efficiency.

[6] For a clear and simple exposition, see Le Grand *et al.* (1992, Ch. 1) or Baumol and Blinder (1991, Ch. 26).

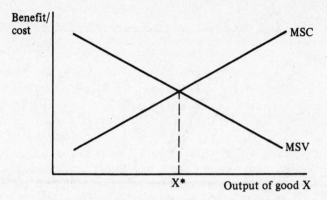

Figure 4.1 *Pareto optimal output: the simple case*

For a general equilibrium three conditions must hold simultaneously.

1. *Efficiency in production*: factor proportions should be optimal so as to obtain the maximum output from given inputs – i.e. production is at a point on the transformation curve Y_0X_0 in Figure 4.2, which shows the maximum quantities of the two goods which can be produced with available resources. Formally, this requires the marginal rate of factor substitution to be equal in the production of all goods.

2. *Efficiency in product mix*: the output bundle should be optimal given existing production technology and consumer tastes. Formally, production is not at *any* point on the transformation curve in Figure 4.2, but at the specific point *a*, at which the ratio of marginal production costs (i.e. the

Figure 4.2 *A simple general equilibrium representation of Pareto optimal output*

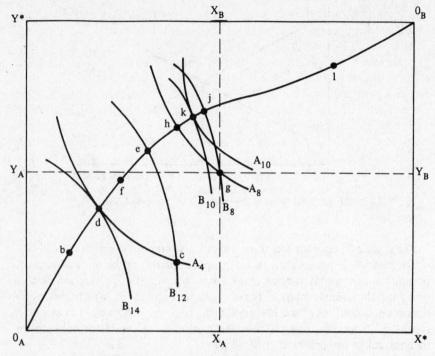

Figure 4.3 *The Edgeworth box (distribution)*

slope of the transformation curve) is equal to the ratio of marginal rates of substitution in consumption (i.e. the slope of the 'social' indifference curve, *I-I*).

3. *Efficiency in consumption*: the resulting output should be allocated so as to maximise utility – in formal terms, the marginal rate of substitution must be equal for all individuals.[7]

The meaning of the third condition is analysed further in the Edgeworth box in Figure 4.3. The size of the box shows the total output to be divided between individuals A and B, $O_A X^*$ of good X and $O_A Y^*$ of good Y, where the quantities X^* and Y^* are those in Figure 4.2 (hence fulfilling efficiency in production and in product mix). The output allocated to A is measured from the origin O_A, and that to B from O_B; at point *g* the two individuals share output equally. The contract curve, represented by the line $O_A O_B$, shows those combinations of X and Y at which the marginal rate of substitution between the two goods is the same for both individuals. Any movement away from the contract curve makes at least one person worse off. Hence any point on the contract curve constitutes an efficient allocation.

The concept of a *Pareto improvement* is important for the analysis which follows. Suppose the initial allocation is shown by point *c*; then individual

[7] See, in ascending order of formality, Laidler and Estrin (1989, Ch. 26) or Varian (1984, Ch. 5).

A on indifference curve A_4 is 'poor' and B on indifference curve B_{12} 'rich'. If trade moves the allocation to point d, then B is better-off (he has moved to the higher indifference curve B_{14}) and A is no worse-off; this is a Pareto improvement. Similarly, a move to the allocation shown by e makes A better off without harming B; and a move to an intermediate allocation like f benefits both parties. Thus any move from the distribution shown by c to any distribution on the contract curve between d and e, including points d and e themselves, increases efficiency and constitutes a Pareto improvement.[8]

A different concept, *administrative efficiency*, is illustrated in Figure 4.2.[9] We have seen that point b is not economically efficient, since the dotted 'social' indifference curve passing through b lies below I-I; but b is administratively efficient, in that movement from b to a, increasing the output of Y, is possible only by reducing the output of X. Point c, in contrast, is both economically and administratively inefficient, since a movement from c to a increases the output of *both* X and Y. Thus all points inside the transformation curve are administratively inefficient; all points on the transformation curve are administratively efficient, but only point a is economically efficient. Similarly, only points on the contract curve in Figure 4.3 are efficient. The next question is which of these allocations is socially optimal.

2.2 The Relevance of Efficiency to Different Theories of Society

The relationship between efficiency and social welfare at its simplest can be illustrated in terms of Figure 4.3.[10,11] We have seen that a move from point c to a point like e is a Pareto improvement. The next step is to show that this is not just a utilitarian result. In each case two questions are considered: (a) given an initial sub-optimal allocation, what constitutes a welfare improvement; and (b) what is the optimal distribution of goods, i.e. what allocation is both efficient and socially just? Two results are established: economic efficiency, in the sense of a movement to an appropriate subset of the contract curve, is an important aim under *all* the definitions of social justice discussed in Chapter 3; and in a first-best economy no distribution can be socially just unless it is also efficient.

The fixed factor case assumes an Edgeworth box of given size, and also

---

[8] For an amusing and informative example taken from a prisoner of war camp, see Radford (1945).

[9] Also synonymously called non-economic efficiency, non-allocative efficiency, X-efficiency or engineering efficiency.

[10] The issue can be approached also via a utility possibility frontier, which can be derived as a simple transformation of the contract curve in Figure 4.3; see Brown and Jackson (1990, Ch. 1), and, for fuller treatment, Atkinson and Stiglitz (1980, Lecture 11.2).

[11] These can be murky waters. This section (and Barr, 1985, from which it largely derives) abstract from a number of potential problems; for a critique of the whole welfarist approach, see Sen (1979, 1992).

that the conditions for efficiency in production and in product mix hold. This is equivalent to discussing a first-best solution.

Libertarianism:[12] welfare is increased by any Pareto improvement, which to writers like Nozick is the only source of welfare gain. Thus a movement from *c* in Figure 4.3 to any point on the contract curve between points *d* and *e* (including the end points) increases welfare.

Natural rights libertarians have little to say about the optimal distribution of goods. If the initial distribution is at *c* then any point on the contract curve between *d* and *e* is optimal, provided that *c* accords with Nozick's idea of justice in holdings, and that the movement from *c* to the contract curve is the result of individual utility maximisation through voluntary trading in a competitive market system. More generally, depending on the initial distribution, *any* point on the contract curve can be an optimum. Empirical libertarians like Hayek and Friedman support this conclusion, save that they accept redistributive activity up to (but not beyond) a guarantee of subsistence – i.e. they would have nothing to say about movements along the contract curve between points *b* and *l*, if these show subsistence for individuals A and B, respectively.

Utilitarians aim to maximise total utility. Again, any Pareto improvement, such as a move from *c* to the contract curve between (and including) points *d* and *e*, will increase welfare.

Is any point on the contract curve superior to any other, i.e. do movements *along* the contract curve raise welfare? The utilitarian answer, which is often misunderstood, depends on whether utility is ordinally or cardinally measurable (see the Glossary). When utility is cardinally measurable and A and B have identical marginal utility of income functions (as in Figure 3.1), welfare is maximised by starting from an equal distribution of goods, shown by point *g* in Figure 4.3. From this egalitarian endowment Pareto improvement is possible; under the stated assumptions total utility will be highest at point *k*. Individuals A and B are on indifference curves A_{10} and B_{10}, respectively; each enjoys ten units of utility (because utility is cardinally measurable); and (because marginal utility of income declines) total utility is lower at all other points on the contract curve. In these circumstances a move *along* the contract curve from a point like *e* towards *k* constitutes a utilitarian welfare improvement.

This egalitarian outcome, however, depends on A and B having identical marginal utility of income functions. If A is a gloomy guy and B is a cheerful chappie, social welfare is maximised at a point like *d*, and with roles reversed at a point like *l*. The same logic applies when utility is measurable only ordinally but here, though we know that the optimum distribution is at a point like *k* (or *d* or *l*), we cannot say which point

---

[12] The libertarian theory of society is discussed in Chapter 3:2. Utilitarianism, Rawls and socialism are discussed in Chapter 3, sections 3.1, 3.2 and 4, respectively, and in the Appendix to Chapter 3.

because we cannot compare the utility of the two individuals. The latter conclusion, it is important to note, is fundamentally different from the libertarian argument that there is no ethical difference between points on the curve like *d, k* and *l.*

Rawls' aim is to distribute resources in accordance with social justice. Starting again from point *c*, a movement to *e* is a Rawlsian improvement (RI) because it benefits the less advantaged individual A. But a movement from *c* to *d*, though a Pareto improvement (PI) is *not* RI because it violates Rawls' principle that matters are to be arranged to the benefit of the least advantaged. A movement from *c* to a point between *d* and *e* is RI (and PI), because it benefits A at least to some extent. In addition, a movement from *c* to points between (and including) *e* and *k*, though it is not PI (since individual B is made worse-off), is RI because it benefits the less advantaged A. Hence a movement from *c* to the contract curve between *d* and *e*, *including* points *d* and *e*, is PI; RI excludes point *d*[13] and includes points between *e* and *k*. The conclusion is that if we are off the contract curve at a point like *c*, there will always be a subset of the contract curve which is RI. Thus, in a first-best economy *all Rawlsian socially just distributions lie on the contract curve.*

According to Rawls, goods should be distributed equally, unless any other distribution benefits the least well-off. Hence the just distribution is generally point *g*, and the optimum outcome point *k*, i.e. a single, known and (generally) egalitarian point. Any movement along the contract curve towards *k* is an unambiguous improvement.

Socialism: under one interpretation resources are to be shared equally. A movement from *c* to *e* raises the welfare of (poor) individual A, thereby reducing relative inequality. Such a move is a socialist improvement (SI). But a movement from *c* to *d* helps only (rich) individual B. If output is fixed (i.e. ruling out the case where B uses the extra resources to bring about economic growth to the advantage of A), this increases relative inequality and is therefore not SI. A movement from *c* to an intermediate point like *f* is arguable. I shall define (though others may disagree) SI to refer to any movement which increases individual A's *relative share* of output, thereby reducing inequality. Suppose *f* is the point on the contract curve at which A's relative share is the same as at *c*. We can then interpret as SI a movement from *c* to any point on the contract curve between (and including) *e* and *k*, and arguably also to any point between *e* and *f* (excluding point *f* itself). *SI is thus a subset of RI*, and all first-best solutions which are just in a socialist sense lie on the contract curve; and, like Rawls, socialists will favour any movement along the contract curve towards *k.*

Relaxing the fixed factor supply assumption complicates matters because of the resulting need, in the absence of lump-sum taxation, to analyse policies

[13] Unless the lexical extension to the difference principle applies (see Chapter 3, footnote 7).

in a second-best economy. It is a standard proposition (Atkinson and Stiglitz, 1980, p. 343) that lump-sum transfers, being based on characteristics exogenous to the taxpayer, can bring about any desired distribution of income or goods without efficiency loss. Taxes related to income, however, (including any indirect tax whose payment rises with income) are not lump-sum, and generally cause inefficiency, *inter alia* through their effect on individual labour supply. But attempts to achieve social justice (such as a movement from e to k in Figure 4.3) generally require redistribution; and this involves taxation which, by the definition of its aim, must be income-related. As a result, any practicable system of taxation may restrict factor supply, reduce output and cause inefficiency in production and/or product mix. Thus there may be a trade-off between efficiency and equity.

This trade-off is analysed formally in the optimal taxation literature[14] in terms of the social welfare maximisation framework set out in section 1. The distribution which jointly optimises efficiency and social justice depends on two sets of factors: the efficiency costs of redistribution (mainly a technical matter depending, *inter alia*, on the compensated elasticity of factor supply); and the relative weights attached to efficiency and equity (which is primarily an ideological issue).

When account is taken of the efficiency impact of redistribution it may not be possible, for instance, to move from point c to point e. The only feasible possibilities might be:

● A movement to a point like b, which is efficient and leaves total production unaffected, but which, in most theories of society, is less just than the distribution shown by c; or
● A movement to a distribution less unequal than b. In this case redistributive taxation will cause efficiency losses, generally by reducing output (i.e. attempts to move from c towards e will shrink the size of the box in Figure 4.3).

In the face of this trade-off there will be different views about the desirability of an increase in efficiency, which will not be seen as a welfare gain if its equity cost is 'too' high. To some libertarians equity has a zero weight; a movement from c to b will therefore increase both efficiency and welfare. To utilitarians the weight given to social justice is an open question. A given efficiency gain may or may not increase welfare; and the utilitarian optimum will not necessarily be efficient (i.e. utilitarians are prepared to sacrifice some efficiency in the interests of greater justice). Rawlsians and socialists give social justice a higher weight, and will therefore generally accept a higher efficiency cost to achieve a just distribution. Note, however, that no theory of society gives social justice complete priority. Even a

---

[14] See Atkinson and Stiglitz, 1980, Lecture 11; or, for a simple introduction, Stiglitz (1988, Ch. 20), Brown and Jackson (1990, Ch. 13), or Cullis and Jones (1992, Chs 16 and 17).

Marxist would resist the pursuit of distributional objectives if the resulting efficiency costs reduced output to zero.

Conclusions focus particularly on the relationship between efficiency and social welfare. The overall conclusion is that the analysis of this chapter is general in its application.

Conclusion 1: the meaning of efficiency (e.g. a movement from point c to a point on the contract curve) is the same in all theories of society.

Conclusion 2: welfare improvements: welfare is increased under all the theories of society by a movement from a point like c to an appropriate subset of the contract curve. Additionally, a movement from c to a point between e and f (excluding f) is SI *and* RI *and* PI. *Efficiency gains of this sort raise social welfare under all the theories of society discussed in Chapter 3.*[15] Where such a movement is feasible, this conclusion is valid whether factor supply is fixed or variable.

Conclusion 3: the optimal distribution in a first-best economy: for any of the theories of society discussed earlier *all first-best socially just distributions are also Pareto efficient*. Efficiency in this case is a necessary condition for social justice.

Conclusion 4: the optimal distribution in a second-best economy: in this case an increase in efficiency may be possible only at the expense of social justice. Whether such an efficiency gain raises social welfare depends on the relative weights accorded efficiency and equity, weights which will generally vary with different theories of society. Thus, the second-best optimum distribution may be a point which is not Pareto efficient.

3 Intervention for Reasons of Efficiency

3.1 Types of Intervention

Discussion so far has concerned the *aims* of policy. The next step is to consider *methods*. This section discusses the circumstances in which market allocation is efficient and, if not, the types of intervention which might be justified. The analysis here (and for most of the book) looks mainly at static efficiency, though in later chapters issues of economic growth (i.e. dynamic efficiency) are discussed where relevant.

The state can intervene in four ways: regulation, finance and public production, which all involve direct interference in the market mechanism; and income transfers, which may have indirect effects.

---

[15] Note that this does *not* imply that the definition of efficiency is value free. Pareto efficiency is generally considered to embrace two value judgements: (a) social welfare is increased if one person is made better-off and nobody worse-off, and (b) individuals are the best judge of their own welfare; see Le Grand (1984), and Rowley and Peacock (1975, Ch. 1). The assertion here is that a subset of Pareto improvements, though not value free, is consistent with all the theories of society discussed in Chapter 3.

Regulation The state interferes with the free market through large numbers of regulations. Some (e.g. concerning alcohol sales or shop opening hours) have more to do with social values than economics. But many are directly relevant to the efficient and/or equitable operation of markets, especially where knowledge is imperfect. Regulation of *quality* is concerned mainly with the supply side, e.g. hygiene laws relating to the production and sale of food and drugs; laws forbidding unqualified people to practise medicine; and consumer protection legislation generally. Regulation of *quantity* more often affects individual demand, e.g. the requirement to attend school; mandatory automobile insurance; and compulsory social insurance contributions. Examples of *price* regulation include minimum wages and rent control.

Finance involves subsidies (or taxes) applied to the *prices* of specific commodities or affecting the *incomes* of individuals. Price subsidies affect economic activity by changing the slope of the budget constraint facing individuals and firms. They can be partial (e.g. for public transport or local authority housing) or total (e.g. free drugs for the elderly in Britain, and under medicare in the USA). Similarly, prices can be affected by a variety of taxes (e.g. on pollution or congestion). Income subsidies raise different issues which are discussed shortly.

Production Though regulation and finance modify market outcomes, they leave the basic mechanism intact. Alternatively, the state can take over the supply side by producing goods and services itself; in such cases the state owns the capital inputs (e.g. school buildings and equipment) and employs the necessary labour (e.g. teachers). Other (more or less pure) examples are national defence and (in Britain) most health care. It is important to be clear that finance and production are entirely separate forms of intervention, both intellectually and in practice. The distinction is of considerable relevance to the issue of 'privatisation', discussed in section 6.

Income transfers can be tied to specific types of expenditure (e.g. education vouchers or housing benefit) or untied (e.g. social security benefits). First-best transfers take the form of a lump sum, and therefore affect economic activity by changing the incomes of individuals, with no extra-market effect on product or factor prices. As we saw in section 2.2, however, redistributive transfers in practice are not of this sort, and so cannot be regarded in efficiency terms as wholly neutral.

3.2 Efficiency Arguments for Intervention

This section is in some respects the theoretical heart of the book. The so-called *Invisible Hand theorem* asserts that the market clearing set of outputs, X_M, will be the efficient output bundle X^* in equation (4.8) if and only if a number of assumptions hold. These (henceforth collectively called the *standard assumptions*) concern perfect competition, the absence of market failures and, crucially, perfect information, which are discussed in turn. The Invisible Hand theorem asserts that a market allocation will automatically be efficient if and only if the standard assumptions *all* hold. In this case there is no justification for intervention on efficiency grounds. But if one or more of the assumptions fails, the resulting market equilibrium will generally be inefficient, and state intervention in one of the forms described above may be appropriate.

PERFECT COMPETITION

Perfect competition must hold in product and factor markets, and also (and importantly) in capital markets. The assumption has two essential features: economic agents must be price-takers; and they must have equal power.

Price taking implies a large number of individuals and firms, with no entry barriers in any market. The assumption can fail, e.g. in the presence of monopoly, monopsony or oligopoly, and appropriate intervention can increase efficiency. It is a standard proposition (Hirshleifer, 1980, pp. 348 *et seq.*) that a monopolist can be given an incentive to produce the efficient output either through the imposition of a maximum price (i.e. *regulation*) or via an appropriate *price subsidy* (with or without the addition of a lump-sum tax). Where imperfect competition takes the form of oligopoly, other forms of regulation may be appropriate (e.g. the Monopolies and Mergers Commission in the UK and anti-trust legislation in the USA).

Equal power is not violated if some individuals have higher incomes than others and so have more 'dollar votes'. In all other respects agents must have equal power – there can be no discrimination. The assumption is frequently breached, and hard to correct. In some areas (e.g. safety legis-lation in factories) the state intervenes through *regulation*. Others, such as having friends in high places (which socialists regard as a major cause of inequality), have no easy solution; nor does outright discrimination, e.g. by race or sex. Legislation (i.e. regulation) in these areas has met with only limited success.

NO MARKET FAILURES

This assumption can be violated in three major ways: public goods, external effects, and increasing returns to scale, which are discussed in more detail in the Appendix.

Pure public goods exhibit three technical characteristics, non-rivalness in consumption, non-excludability and non-rejectability, which together imply that the market is likely to produce inefficiently, if at all. Once a public good is produced, non-excludability makes it impossible to prevent people from using it, hence it is not possible to levy charges (this is the *free-rider* problem); in such cases the market may fail entirely. Non-rivalness implies that the marginal cost of an extra user (though *not* of an extra unit of output) is zero. The efficient price should therefore be based on individual marginal valuations of the good, i.e. on perfect price discrimination; where this is not possible, the market is likely to be inefficient. If a public good is to be provided at all, the appropriate form of intervention is generally *public production*.[16]

External effects are a closely related phenomenon. They arise when an act of agent A imposes costs or confers benefits on agent B for which no compensation from A to B, or payment from B to A, takes place. Formally, a technological externality arises when A's utility function or production function is interrelated with B's. It is a standard proposition[17] that in the presence of an external cost the market clearing output will generally exceed the efficient output, and vice versa for an external benefit. The market itself can sometimes solve the problem, either (Meade, 1952) through merger of the activities of the relevant parties, or (Coase, 1960) where property rights are well-defined, through negotiation between the parties concerned. This, however, is not always possible, for instance where property rights are not enforceable (e.g. air pollution), or where transactions costs are high because large numbers of people are involved (e.g. traffic congestion). In such cases, intervention may be warranted in one of two generic forms: *regulation*, or an appropriate Pigovian *tax or subsidy*. The choice of method depends on a complex of factors. Taxation/subsidy is the usual solution if the intention is marginally to change levels of consumption or production. But regulation may be useful where the aim is to enforce at least a minimum level of some activity (e.g. compulsory automobile insurance); or to restrict it below some maximum (e.g. mandatory pollution controls); or where measurement problems prevent assessment of the appropriate tax/subsidy.[18]

Increasing returns to scale at all levels of output imply that average cost will exceed marginal cost, as in Figure 4.4. The consequent long-run losses will drive competitive firms from the industry, which will either become monopolised or (if even a monopolist makes losses) will cease to exist at all. Intervention can take one of two forms. The industry could remain private, buttressed by an appropriate lump-sum subsidy, $(AC_0 - P_0)X_0$ in

[16] For further details, see Baumol and Blinder (1991, Ch. 29); Brown and Jackson (1990, Ch. 3); Stiglitz (1988, Ch. 5); or Musgrave and Musgrave (1989, Chs 4 and 5). The classic exposition of the theory of public goods is Samuelson (1954).

[17] For discussion of the welfare effects of externalities, see in ascending order of difficulty, Le Grand *et al.* (1992, Ch. 2), Stiglitz (1988, Ch. 8), and Varian (1984, Ch. 7.3).

[18] For discussion in the context of environmental issues, see Baumol and Oates (1979).

Figure 4.4 *The loss resulting from marginal cost pricing under increasing returns to scale*

Figure 4.4;[19] or it could be nationalised and similarly subsidised. The appropriate intervention, therefore, is *subsidy or public production* or both.

PERFECT INFORMATION

The analysis of imperfect competition and market failures has two note-worthy features: for the most part it has a long pedigree in the economic literature; and it justifies regulation and subsidy but (with the exception of public goods) gives no efficiency argument for public production. Two conclusions follow (see Barr (1992, section III (A)) for fuller discussion): when applied to the welfare state, these traditional arguments give little justification, at least in utilitarian terms, for large-scale, publicly organised welfare-state services; and, to the extent that they support welfare-state institutions at all, they justify only a *residual* welfare state.[20]

A more recent body of theory focuses on the extent to which consumers and firms are well-informed. Simple theory implicitly assumes that consumers know about what goods are available and about their nature. The assumption can fail, *inter alia*, in two important ways: economic agents may have imperfect knowledge of the *quality* of goods and/or their *prices*. The literature thus has two strands. The first analyses the effects of imperfect information about quality: consumers might be badly informed (e.g. about the quality of an automobile); so might producers (e.g. about the riskiness of an applicant for insurance). The resulting literature investigates such topics as 'lemons' and signalling. The second strand, imperfect information

---

[19] Though the taxation necessary to finance the subsidy would itself be distortionary unless levied on a lump-sum basis.

[20] The distinction between a residual and an institutional welfare state is set out in Chapter 2:7.1.

about prices, embraces search theory and reservation wages.[21]

As set out in detail in later chapters, it is this literature, particularly the first strand, which provides the analytical key to the economics of the welfare state. Complete information requires at least three types of knowledge: about the quality and nature of the product; about prices; and about the future.

Quality   The assumption that economic agents have perfect knowledge about the nature of the product (including factors) implies that individuals have well-defined indifference maps, and firms, similarly, well-defined isoquants. This is plausible for some goods, e.g. food, but less so for technically complex commodities. When the assumption fails, the market itself can sometimes solve the problem by supplying the information necessary for rational decisions. When I buy a house I do not know whether it is structurally sound, but I can buy the information by hiring the services of a surveyor. More generally, information is available from a large number of specialist publications. In such cases intervention is unnecessary.

Other types of information failure may justify regulation. Consumers usually have sufficient knowledge about the characteristics of food to choose a reasonably balanced diet, but may be imperfectly informed about the conditions in which the food was prepared. The state therefore intervenes with hygiene laws (i.e. *regulation*), whose effect is to improve consumer information, thereby increasing efficiency.

Where the information failure is small, regulation may suffice. Where information is seriously deficient, however, market outcomes *may* be less efficient than some sort of administrative solution. Markets are generally more efficient (a) the better is consumer information, (b) the more cheaply and effectively it can be improved (e.g. computer magazines, hygiene laws for food), (c) the easier it is for consumers to understand available information, (d) the lower are the costs of choosing badly, and (e) the more diverse are consumer tastes. Commodities which conform well with these criteria are food and such consumer durables as hi-fi, personal computers and automobiles. As discussed later, health care conforms less well: consumer information is often poor; people generally require individual information, so that the process will not be cheap (violating (b)); much of the information is highly technical (violating (c)); and the costs of mistaken choice can be high. In these circumstances, there may be a justification for *public production and allocation*.

Price   Rational choice requires also that agents are perfectly informed about prices, i.e. that they face a well-defined budget constraint. This is plausible for commodities like clothes, less so for things like car repairs. Where the assumption fails, the market, again, may supply the necessary information,

---

[21] The quality literature has its roots in classic articles by Arrow (1963) and Akerlof (1970) (see Stiglitz (1987) for a survey). For a survey of the literature on imperfect price information, see Mortensen (1986).

e.g a house or a piece of jewellery can be professionally valued. In such cases the services of the valuer improve knowledge about prices, and so increase efficiency. Where the market does not resolve the problem, state intervention via *regulation* may be necessary, for instance a requirement to issue price lists.

It should be noted that rational choice depends on both indifference/ isoquant map and budget constraint; hence perfect information is needed about the nature of the product *and* about prices – neither on its own is sufficient. The two together have a critical efficiency role: it is conventionally argued, not least by writers like Hayek and Friedman, that the advantages of competition are the maximisation of consumer choice (i.e. consumer sovereignty) and the minimisation of cost. Without perfect information, however, agents are unable to exercise their consumer sovereignty rationally; nor can they tell whether competitive cost reductions are associated with an unacceptable reduction in quality. An important conclusion follows – that *the efficiency advantages of perfect competition are contingent on perfect information.*

The future Intertemporal utility maximisation requires perfect information also about the future. I know that I will need food this week and again next week, and shop accordingly; but I do not know how much furniture I will consume over the next ten years nor how many cars, because I do not know whether my house will catch fire or my car be involved in an accident. In such cases, the market solution is to offer insurance, which gives me certainty since any losses I suffer will be made good by the insurance company. However, as discussed in Chapter 5, technical problems (due largely to information failures in insurance markets) can make private insurance inefficient or impossible. In these circumstances *public production* might be appropriate.

It is important to be clear about what has been said, and what not said, about the size of the public sector. Discussion has concerned the circumstances in which goods and services are produced more efficiently in either sector. But the size of the public sector depends not only on these supply-side considerations, but also on demand. If there are only two goods, food (produced privately) and education (produced publicly), the optimal size of the public sector will depend on preferences over food and education, and will vary over time and across countries, depending *inter alia* on tastes.

3.3 Examples of Intervention on Efficiency Grounds

By and large the market for food conforms with the standard assumptions. People generally have sufficient information to buy a balanced diet; food prices are well-known; and most people know roughly how much they will need over a given period. Food production and (especially) distribution are competitive; and there are no major market failures. A possible violation is ignorance about the conditions under which food is produced, so the state intervenes with hygiene regulations. Such regulation enhances consumer information, leaving the private market to operate efficiently. There are no serious advocates of a national food service.

With health care, in sharp contrast, most of the assumptions fail (as discussed in detail in Chapter 12:3.1). Consumer information can be highly imperfect, since much medical treatment is complex and technical. In addition, knowledge of prices is scant. Nobody knows how much health care they will need and, as shown in Chapters 5 and 12, there are major technical (again, largely information) problems with private medical insurance. It is also argued that health care is not competitive. Finally, some medical care can generate externalities. What type of intervention is then appropriate? Information failures and the lack of competition justify regulation; the externality, coupled with major insurance problems, may justify public funding; and a strong (though not overriding) argument for public production and allocation arises out of the serious problems with both consumer information and private insurance.

It is instructive to apply these arguments also to past or present public enterprises well outside the welfare state, like railways, electricity, telephones, steel, coal and airlines.

4 Intervention for Reasons of Social Justice

4.1 Why Does Redistribution Occur?

Different definitions of social justice (or equity) were discussed in Chapter 3. The main questions in this section are different, namely: why does redistribution occur; should it be in cash or kind; and is there enough redistribution?

Coerced redistribution   According to writers like Downs (1957) and Tullock (1970),[22] the 'poor', acting as individuals or as part of a coalition, use their voting power to enforce redistribution from the 'rich'. Downs assumes that politicians seek office for reasons of income, status and power, and therefore choose policies which maximise the votes they receive at the next election; and that citizens vote for the party whose programme promises them the highest expected utility. Since the income distribution in most countries contains relatively few people with high incomes and many with lower incomes, governments maximise votes by redistributing from the rich, thereby gaining the (many more) votes of those with lower incomes.

[22] See also Buchanan and Tullock (1962), and for a non-technical introduction, Tullock (1976).

The logic of the argument is that the system will redistribute towards equality. That equality is not reached is attributed to three countervailing pressures: fear of the efficiency losses (especially the labour supply disincentive) of high taxation; the fact that the rich generally have more power and can to some extent protect themselves; and the fact that the poor might want some inequality to remain, in the hope that they might some day themselves be rich.

Tullock assumes that policy is based on the wishes of the majority, and discusses how different income groups might form voting coalitions. In particular, he notes that any coalition of at least 51 per cent of the electorate must contain not only the very poor but also many in the middle-income group. His theory therefore offers an explanation of the commonly observed phenomenon (Le Grand, 1982) that public expenditure on the poor is often lower than on the middle-income group (which tends, for example, to make more intensive use of the educational system). There is a direct relationship between these arguments and the 'government failure' analysis discussed in section 5.

Voluntary redistribution According to Downs and Tullock redistribution is motivated by selfishness and enforced by political coercion. Hochman and Rodgers (1969), in contrast, recognise the possibility of generous (or even altruistic) motives. Their theory seeks to explain both voluntary giving, and the fact that people with high incomes may vote for political parties which propose to tax them more heavily to finance redistributive policies. At the heart of this approach lies the notion that individual welfares are interdependent.

The simplest explanation of *voluntary* redistribution is a breakdown in the assumption of no externalities. Assume a two-person world with representative 'rich' and 'poor' individuals, R and P. If R is concerned with P's utility as well as with his own, both may gain by a gift from R to P. Where redistribution makes some people better-off without making anyone worse-off, transfers from rich to poor may be justified on quasi efficiency grounds.[23]

Formal analysis: in the simplest case R and P each has a utility function which is dependent only on his own income. Thus

$$U^R = f(Y^R) \tag{4.9}$$

and

$$U^P = f(Y^P) \tag{4.10}$$

where U^R and U^P are the utilities of the rich and the poor man, respectively,

---

[23] For a fuller exposition, see Hochman and Rodgers (1969); also the comments in Meyer and Shipley (1970), Musgrave (1970) and Goldfarb (1970); and the reply in Hochman and Rodgers (1970). A similar approach treats the size distribution of income as a public good; see Thurow (1971).

and Y^R and Y^P their incomes. But now suppose that R's utility depends not only on his own income, but also on P's. Then,

$$U^R = f(Y^R, Y^P), f_1 > 0, f_2 \geqslant 0 \qquad (4.11)$$

where f_1 and f_2 are the partial derivatives of U^R with respect to Y^R and Y^P, respectively. There is an externality in as much as, *ceteris paribus*, R's utility rises with P's income.[24] In this situation redistribution from rich to poor can be rational: it will raise P's utility (because his income goes up) and also R's utility (because of the increase in P's income) so long as

$$\frac{\partial U^R}{\partial Y^P} - \frac{\partial U^R}{\partial Y^R} > 0 \qquad (4.12)$$

where the first term shows the increase in R's utility as a result of the increase in P's income, and the second the reduction in R's utility because of the reduction in his own income. Voluntary redistribution from R to P will be rational so long as the first term exceeds the second.

Criticisms of voluntarism: this approach leaves no distributional role for the state through compulsory taxation unless voluntarism can be shown to be sub-optimal. Two such arguments have been proposed. The first concerns the problem of free-riders, which can arise when the model is extended from the two-person case to the *n*-person. Suppose that it is not the income of specific *individual* poor people which affects the utility of the rich, but the *overall* distribution, which then displays all the characteristics of a public good.

Each individual in society faces the same income distribution. No one can be deprived of the benefits flowing from any particular income distribution. My consumption of whatever benefits occur is not rival with your consumption. In short, the income distribution meets all the tests of a pure public good. Exclusion is impossible; consumption is non-rival; each individual must consume the same quantity. The same problems also occur. *Each individual has a vested interest in disguising his preferences concerning his desired income to avoid paying his optimal share of the necessary transfer payments.* [Thurow, 1971, pp. 328–9, my emphasis.]

Hence,

It can be argued that private charity is insufficient because the benefits from it accrue to people other than those who make the gifts ... [We] might ... be willing to contribute to the relief of poverty, *provided* everyone else did. [Friedman, 1962, p. 191, his emphasis.]

Thus it may be rational for the rich to vote for redistributive taxation,

---

[24] In formal terms we are relaxing the assumption that the social welfare function is additive – see Chapter 6:1.2.

which is compulsory and so avoids free riding.[25,26] I shall refer to this as 'voluntary compulsion'. Since it is, up to a point, imposed by the rich upon themselves, this is a very different argument from the 'coercion via the ballot box' of Downs and Tullock.

A second and completely separate criticism of voluntarism is that, if redistribution were *only* that which the rich volunteered, it might be sub-optimal even in the absence of free-riders. Suppose the initial situation is shown by point *d* in Figure 4.3, and the social welfare maximising distribution by point *k* (as for Rawls or a socialist). The rich might be prepared through voluntarism to move the distribution from *d* to *f*, or through compulsory taxation to *e*. But if the income externality is 'exhausted' at *e* then a movement to *k*, though possibly raising *total* utility, would reduce the utility of the rich. In such a case voluntary transfers would be insufficient to bring about the egalitarian distribution advocated, for example, by Rawls.

It follows, in conclusion, that voluntary redistribution *alone* will be sub-optimal unless one believes *both* that free riding is not a problem *and* that the optimal amount of redistribution is that which the rich wish to volunteer.

4.2 Should Redistribution Be in Cash or Kind?

What, if any, are the arguments for redistribution in kind (i.e. transferring commodities directly to the poor at zero or non-market prices)? We have seen that if the standard assumptions all hold, markets will allocate efficiently, in which case equity aims are generally best pursued through cash transfers (though subject to the caveat that redistributive taxation is itself a potential source of inefficiency). This suggests that the use of in-kind transfers for distributional purposes is appropriate only where they are also justified on *efficiency* grounds. I shall argue that this proposition is generally valid, with the exception of one counter-argument, again based on voting, which suggests that in some circumstances it may be politically easier to redistribute in kind (e.g. to give the poor free education rather than the money to buy it).

Formal analysis: in equation (4.11), the utility of the rich person depends both on his own income, and that of the poor man. But suppose the externality is caused not by P's *income* but by his *consumption*. Then,

$$U^R = f(Y^R, C^P) \tag{4.13}$$

where C^P is P's consumption. However, not all increases in C^P will necessarily

---

[25] Attempts have been made to defend voluntarism against the free-rider argument. As yet the issue is unsettled. See Sugden (1982, 1984), and subsequent discussion by Collard (1983) and Sugden (1983a). For a simple introduction to the literature, see Sugden (1983b) and Jones and Posnett (1993).

[26] Many charitable organisations now attempt to reduce free riding by assigning a specific, named family to the giver.

raise the utility of the rich – consumption of alcohol by the poor might fail to do so. It is necessary to disaggregate so that,

$$C^P = G^P + B^P \tag{4.14}$$

where G^P is 'good' consumption by the poor (children's clothing, basic food), and B^P is 'bad' consumption (whisky, welfare Cadillacs), where 'good' and 'bad' are defined by the rich.

From equations (4.13) and (4.14) we have

$$U^R = f(Y^R, G^P, B^P) \quad f_1 > 0, f_2 \geqslant 0, f_3 \leqslant 0 \tag{4.15}$$

where f_1, f_2 and f_3 are the partial derivatives of U^R with respect to Y^R, G^P and B^P, respectively. R's utility increases with his own income, and with 'good' consumption by P, but decreases with P's 'bad' consumption. In this situation, transfers of 'good' consumption take place as long as

$$\frac{\partial U^R}{\partial G^P} - \frac{\partial U^R}{\partial Y^R} > 0 \tag{4.16}$$

where the first term shows the increase in R's utility resulting from the increase in P's 'good' consumption, and the second is the decrease in R's utility because of the decrease in his own income.

Merit goods are defined as commodities in respect of which the state overrides consumer sovereignty, e.g. school education is compulsory, irrespective of the wishes of parents or children.[27] If the standard assumptions hold, there is no efficiency justification for merit goods. Figure 4.5 shows how their existence can be explained by a consumption externality. Suppose individual P initially faces the budget constraint Y_P-Y_P and maximises utility by choosing point *a*. Now compare a cash transfer with a compulsory in-kind transfer. Suppose that the cash transfer shifts P's budget constraint outward to Y_1 Y_1 so that he maximises utility at point *b*. Alternatively, a compulsory transfer of Y_P-Y_2 units of education shifts P's budget constraint to Y_2 Y_2, and utility is maximised at *c*. Given the choice, a rational poor person will favour the in-kind transfer, since *c* is on a higher indifference curve than *b*.

Now consider matters from the viewpoint of individual R. It is clear that the in-kind transfer is the more costly (i.e. measuring along the horizontal axis, the in-kind transfer consists of Y_P-Y_2 units of education, whereas the cash transfer buys only Y_P-Y_1 units). However, though R gives up more *income* to finance the in-kind transfer, he might give up less *utility*. In the presence of a consumption externality, an income transfer can reduce the utility of the rich both *per se* and because it might be used by the poor to finance 'bad' consumption. Transfers in kind, though costing more in financial terms, have the advantage, from R's point of view, that they are

---

[27] For further discussion, see Musgrave and Musgrave (1989, Ch. 4), and Barr (1992, section III (A)).

Figure 4.5 *Redistribution in cash and kind*

entirely 'good' consumption. If f_2 in equation (4.15) is large and positive, and f_3 large and negative, then R too might prefer the in-kind transfer.

In this case social welfare might be higher with in-kind transfers, despite the absence of any efficiency reasons for public production or allocation, simply because both rich and poor prefer it that way. This runs counter to the conventional argument that cash transfers are usually more efficient.

4.3 Horizontal Equity

Discussion thus far has concentrated on *vertical equity*, i.e. the redistribution of income or consumption from rich to poor. Social justice also involves *horizontal equity*, which concerns goals like minimum standards for certain goods and services, or equal access to them, and equality of opportunity.[28]

Minimum standards are a form of regulation, and can therefore be justified only by the failure of one or more of the standard assumptions. This can occur in three ways. Where agents have imperfect information they are generally unable to make rational choices; a case can be made on this basis for minimum standards in schools and hospitals. Second, if agents have unequal power they might not be able to enforce their decisions; this justifies, for example, regulations about safety standards at work. Finally, there may be externalities. If my house has inadequate sewage disposal the

[28] For the place of horizontal equity in the social welfare maximisation framework of section 1, see King (1983).

resulting public health hazard is an argument for appropriate building codes.[29]

If the standard assumptions hold, however, consumers are able to make rational choices, and to enforce them, provided they have sufficient income to do so. In such cases, concern with the quality of consumption should manifest itself in income transfers rather than minimum standards except, possibly, in the presence of consumption externalities. The latter, however, is a dangerous argument, since minimum standards imposed on the poor 'for their own good' (i.e. 'good' consumption) may end up harming the poor if pitched at a higher level than is justified in efficiency terms (see Chapter 14:5.2 for the case of housing standards).

Equal access Where the standard assumptions hold, the only cause of unequal access is shortage of income, for which the appropriate remedy is generally cash redistribution. But action to ensure equal access may be justified in particular by the failure of the assumptions of perfect information and equal power.[30] A case in point is 'know-how', inequality of which is a major cause of inequality generally. Know-how includes understanding the value of education; knowing your entitlements under the National Health Service; knowing your legal rights; and also, more generally, your social and professional contacts. In the face of such inequality the state can intervene through regulation (e.g. legislation against discrimination); through subsidy (e.g. legal aid for people with low incomes); or through public production (e.g. the provision of compulsory, free education, which is supposed to be of an equal standard for all).

Equality of opportunity is closely related to equal access. We return to the issue in some detail in Chapter 6:3.1.

The horizontal equity argument should not be overstated. Where the standard assumptions hold, any problems of unacceptable standards or unequal access are generally *income distribution problems*. If so, minimum standards and institutional action to ensure equal access may be inappropriate; the state can best ensure equal access to consumption of an acceptable standard through income transfers which, in this case, serve both efficiency and social justice.

4.4 Is There Enough Redistribution?

We saw in section 2.2 that social justice is concerned with movements

---

[29] In the light of these theoretical arguments it is noteworthy that much early social legislation in Britain was concerned with factory conditions and public health – see Chapter 2:1.2.

[30] For a powerful theoretical analysis of how the failure of the equal power assumption leads to discrimination against women, see Apps (1981).

along the contract curve towards the optimal distribution. What is that distribution; and have we achieved it?

Libertarians[31] see the optimal distribution as the result of competitive market forces on legally acquired endowments. They support the relief of destitution through voluntary charity, which writers like Nozick regard as the only legitimate method, all redistributive taxation being coercive. It follows from earlier discussion that if the free-rider problem is non-trivial, voluntary giving will be sub-optimal even in libertarian terms. Empirical libertarians like Hayek and Friedman allow taxation to bring incomes up to (but not beyond) subsistence if voluntary giving fails to do so, not least because of the free-rider problem, which Friedman explicitly accepts (see the quote in section 4.1). However, as discussed in the next section, most libertarians argue that benefits are too high, and therefore that we have *too much* redistribution.

Utilitarians are unsure which distribution maximises social welfare because of the impossibility of measuring utility cardinally. They are therefore unclear whether there has been too much redistribution or not enough.

Rawls argues unequivocally that goods should be distributed equally unless any other distribution is to the advantage of the least well-off. This is not the actual situation, and therefore there has been too little redistribution. Rawls disagrees with the Downs/Tullock argument that democratic politics have resulted in excessive redistribution, arguing that voting and other political activity in practice takes place *outside* the veil of ignorance. Negotiation is therefore hindered by special pleading, particularly because the rich generally have greater power. The resulting distribution is nowhere near the Rawlsian optimum. Socialists, too, are clear that their goal of equality has not been reached.

5 Public Choice and Government Failure

The argument Inman (1987) and Mueller (1989) survey the public choice literature, of which this section is a very brief account. There are four explanations of the extent of and growth in government activity. The role of government (a) in dealing with market failures and (b) as redistributor of income and wealth has been the major focus of this chapter and the previous one. The literature analyses in addition (c) the response of government to the electorate in the form of coalitions of voters or through pressure groups, and (d) the role of bureaucrats. The government failure arguments point to the latter two as important distorting influences.

The influence of the electorate operates in various ways. The coercion-

[31] See footnote 12.

via-the-ballot-box arguments were discussed in section 4. Writers like Buchanan and Tullock (1962) and Tullock (1970, 1971) argue that most transfers from the rich are captured by the middle class through their electoral power as median voters or acting as interest groups.[32] Other arguments stress the broader role of interest groups on redistributive transfers (e.g. the poverty lobby). Interest groups use their lobbying power to bring about redistribution also through regulation. It is argued that regulators are frequently 'captured' by those whom they are supposed to regulate (Stigler, 1971; Posner, 1975; Pelzmann, 1976). According to this view, regulation (e.g. of the medical profession) is an entry barrier which allows the extraction of monopoly rent.

Distortions can arise also within government. Public-sector institutions may in part be run for the benefit of the bureaucrats who run them (Niskanen, 1971). Such 'organisational slack', it is argued, occurs because politicians are not able fully to monitor the actions of their utility-maximising officials.

For one or more of these reasons, it is argued, the size of the public sector may be inefficiently large; or its composition may be distorted to meet the needs of the bureaucracy, powerful interest groups, voters in marginal constituencies, etc.

Assessment These insights, however, should not be overstated. Even within a strict utilitarian framework, as discussed in section 4, writers like Friedman (1962) and Hochman and Rodgers (1969) explain tax-financed redistribution in ways which do not rely on electoral coercion. Interest groups may enhance efficiency (Becker, 1983, 1985). Regulation *may* result in monopoly rents (e.g. doctors in some countries) but, as discussed in section 3.2, it also serves to protect imperfectly informed consumers (e.g. regulation of medical training).

The power of bureaucrats can be overstated and their motivation misunderstood (Dunleavy, 1985). Organisational slack should not be exaggerated: pay increases or enlarged departments can be monitored; voters may be able to vote with their feet against high local taxation (Tiebout, 1956); and bureaucratic utility maximisation can just as easily lead to *less* government (Treasury officials under Margaret Thatcher won favour by cutting expenditure). In addition, organisational slack may be more pronounced where the state regulates private activity than with public production: as discussed in Chapter 12:4.1, countries where private, fee-for-service medical care is publicly funded find it more difficult to contain costs than those with public production.

Nor do the government failure arguments necessarily apply equally everywhere. Tullock's (1971) claim that benefits go disproportionately to the middle class may be more true of the USA than elsewhere. In Germany

---

[32] For fuller discussion of public choice and the median voter theorem, see Stiglitz (1988, Ch. 6).

and Sweden, for instance, the lowest-income quintile in the mid-1980s received net transfers of about 10 per cent of GDP.

Choosing the borderline between the market and the state is discussed further in section 7.1

6 From Theory Towards Policy: The Issue of Privatisation

The concept of privatisation is considerably more complicated than most participants in policy debate realise. It is important to be clear that *finance* and *public production* (discussed in section 3.1) are entirely separate forms of intervention, both conceptually and in practice. A good can be financed publicly or privately, and it can be produced in either sector; thus there are four cases. A commodity like food is generally financed and produced in the private sector (Box 1 of Table 4.1); at the other extreme, most school education is produced publicly and paid out of tax revenues (Box 4). Two intermediate cases are frequently overlooked. In Britain, until recently, goods like electricity and domestic gas were produced in the public sector but, with some exceptions, were financed by charges on the private sector (Box 2). Other goods are produced privately but sold to the public sector, including part of university output and many of the material inputs to the National Health Service, e.g. drugs, blankets. Those who favour privatisation have at the back of their minds a movement from Box 4 to Box 1. But, more generally, it can be defined as any movement up and/or to the left in Table 4.1.

This analysis, unfortunately, is too oversimplified to be much use for our purposes. Markets in reality are virtually never purely private: food is subject to regulation about quality, and its price is distorted *inter alia* by agricultural subsidies; and it may be purchased out of transfer income (e.g. social security benefits), or provided without charge (e.g. free school meals). Nor are there many pure cases of free public provision, e.g. charges are levied under the National Health Service for prescriptions and dentistry.

To clarify the situation, even keeping matters as simple as possible, it is necessary to distinguish not only (a) in which sector *production* takes place and (b) which sector *finances* it, but also the influence of *regulation* on decisions about production and consumption, in particular on (c) the total quantity produced of any good and (d) how much each individual consumer will receive. These are illustrated in Table 4.2, though the analysis is still far from exhaustive. The first part shows different examples of private production. Line 1 (which corresponds to Box 1 in Table 4.1) shows the pure private case, e.g. food purchased out of non-transfer income. Production is private, and total supply determined by producers; individuals decide how much to consume, and pay for it themselves. Line 2 is identical except that

Table 4.1   *An overview of public and private provision*[a]

		PRODUCTION	
		Private	Public
FINANCE	Private	(1) Food	(2) Domestic gas (formerly in the UK) Electricity (formerly in the UK) Her Majesty's Stationery Office
			PRIVATISATION
	Public	NHS inputs (eg drugs, blankets, etc) Universities (in the UK) Education vouchers Military equipment (3)	Health care under the NHS Primary and secondary education National defence (4)

NOTE: [a]The examples in boxes 1–4 are only approximate.

individual consumption is financed by the state. The simplest case is food purchased out of transfer income; other examples are food stamps, medicare and medicaid in the USA. Line 3 illustrates a private market subject to regulation. In line 3(a) the individual consumption decision is made by the state (mandatory automobile insurance); in line 3(b) the state puts a ceiling on total production, though allocation to individuals remains private (very roughly the case of health care in Canada). Line 4 illustrates private production modified by both regulation and finance (i.e. roughly Box 3 in Table 4.1). In line 4(a) production decisions are wholly private (e.g. education vouchers). Line 4(b) shows the case where allocation and finance are wholly public, but production itself takes place in the private sector (National Health Service inputs like blankets and X-ray machines, certain types of military equipment).

The second half of the table looks at public production. In line 5(a) output is produced in the public sector but allocated and financed privately (electricity and domestic gas until recently, Her Majesty's Stationery Office);

Table 4.2 *Public and private provision: a more complete view*[a]

TYPE OF ALLOCATION	PRODUCTION (1)	REGULATION		FINANCE (4)	EXAMPLES
		Decision about Total Production (2)	Decision about Individual Consumption (3)		
(1) Pure private (= Box 1 in Table 4.1)	PRIVATE	PRIVATE	PRIVATE	PRIVATE	food purchased out of non-transfer income
(2) Private market plus state finance (income subsidy)	Private	Private	Private	Public	all consumption of privately produced goods purchased out of transfer income: food stamps; medicare & medicaid (USA)
(3) Private market plus regulation					
(a) regulation of individual consumption	Private	Private	Public	Private	mandatory car insurance;
(b) regulation of total supply	Private	Public	Private	Private	health care (Canada, approx)
(4) Private production, state regulation and finance (= Box 3 in Table 4.1)					
(a) supply wholly private	Private	Private	Public	Public	education vouchers
(b) total supply determined by state	Private	Public	Public	Public	inputs for NHS & national defence
(5) Public production, private allocation and finance (= Box 2 in Table 4.1)					
(a) · total supply determined by private demand	Public	Private	Private	Private	gas, electricity (formerly in UK)
(b) supply wholly public	Public	Public	Private	Private	NHS pay beds
(6) Public apart from private finance	Public	Public	Public	Private	national insurance (UK), health care insurance (Canada approx)
(7) Public apart from private consumption decision	Public	Public	Private	Public	secondary education after age 16
(8) Pure public (= Box 4 in Table 4.1)	PUBLIC	PUBLIC	PUBLIC	PUBLIC	NHS, national defence

NOTE: [a]The examples are only approximate.

in line 5(b) supply is determined publicly, but demand decisions and finance are private (pay beds in Health Service hospitals). These cases approximate Box 2 in Table 4.1. Line 6 illustrates public production and allocation with private finance, e.g. social insurance. Line 7 illustrates public production and finance, though the individual consumption decision is private, e.g. secondary education after minimum school leaving age. The case of pure public production is shown in line 8 (i.e. Box 4 in Table 4.1); examples include (as approximations) compulsory school education, the National Health Service and national defence.

We can now see what privatisation means. Libertarians favour private production under column (1), producer and consumer sovereignty under columns (2) and (3) and private finance under column (4). They would therefore choose line 1 or, failing that, the private market underwritten by income transfers, shown in line 2. Privatisation can therefore be seen as an upward movement in the table from a lower line to a higher.

The issues   How, then, should specific proposals for privatisation be analysed? It was argued in section 3 that regulation, finance or public production may increase efficiency where the standard assumptions fail. Conversely, where they all hold there are no efficiency grounds for intervention in private markets, and distributional objectives are generally best approached through income transfers.

The issues raised by the privatisation debate (see the Further Reading) fall naturally into this framework. It is necessary, in the case of any particular activity, to consider the extent to which it conforms with the standard assumptions. And in this context information problems assume considerable importance. Because of technological change over the century, the optimal scale of many types of industry is large; and in any large organisation information (i.e. management) problems are likely to arise whether the industry is public or private. It is therefore not surprising that 'the fundamental problems concerned with the control of public utilities are very similar, irrespective of whether they are in the public or private sectors' (Webb, 1984, p. 99).

Whatever the answers about privatisation (and they are rarely clear-cut) the technical dimension of the analysis should not be obscured by ideology,[33] an observation which leads naturally to the final part of the chapter.

---

[33] As an example of how ideology can bias logic, note the tendency for proponents of free markets to regard 'managers' as 'good' and 'administrators' as 'bad' ('bureaucrats' being a term of abuse for everyone). In many respects, however, managers, administrators and bureaucrats all do broadly the same job and face similar problems. Calling them by different names with differing emotive connotations does little to advance the argument.

7 Conclusion: Economic and Political Theory

7.1 Drawing the Borderlines between Government and Markets

This section brings together the analysis of Chapters 3 and 4. The efficiency arguments for intervention were set out in section 3, and the government failure counter-argument in section 5. The important contribution of the public choice literature is the idea that analysis of government should treat its activities as endogenous. It does not, however, follow that the social-welfare outcome of the political market place is necessarily inferior to that of conventional markets. Markets can be efficient or inefficient; so can governments. A counterpoint to government failure is market failure and, in the welfare-state context, particularly information failures.

Inman's (1987) survey concluded:

Markets fail. They fail for the fundamental reason that the institution of market trading cannot enforce cooperative behavior on self-seeking, utility-maximising agents, and cooperative behavior between agents is often required for beneficial trading. In each instance of market failure ... agents were asked to reveal information about their benefits or costs from trades with no guarantee that that information would not be used against them. Without that guarantee, information is concealed, trades collapse, and the market institution fails. [p. 672.]

While democratic processes do not generally guarantee an efficient allocation of social resources, *we cannot go the next step and conclude that collectively-decided allocations ... are inferior to individually-decided market allocations.* [p. 727, my emphasis.]

[N]either the institution of markets, or voluntary trading, nor the institution of government, or collectively decided and enforced trading, stands as *the* unarguably preferred means for allocating societal resources. Each institution has its strengths and its weaknesses. [p. 753, his emphasis.]

The 'New Right' properly criticises a naive predisposition towards state intervention at the slightest sign of problems in private markets; but to argue that public-sector inefficiency *automatically* implies that private markets raise social welfare is to make the same mistake. Decisions about the borderline between market and state involve judgement, so that different interpretations are possible. Le Grand (1987b), with echoes of Tullock (1971) (though from a very different perspective), argues that the British welfare state has been 'captured' by the middle class, and goes on to suggest that this is a matter for ambivalence. It is 'bad' because the welfare state's major benefits should go to the poor; but it is 'good' because it keeps the articulate middle class as consumers of the welfare state, thus creating pressure to maintain standards. The arguments above suggest that we should not be ambivalent: as subsequent chapters explain, many parts of the welfare state are a response to pervasive technical problems in private markets, and therefore serve not only the distributional and other objectives listed in Chapter 1:2.2 (poverty relief, vertical and horizontal equity, dignity and social solidarity), but also efficiency objectives such as income smoothing and the protection of accustomed living standards in the face of uninsurable risks and capital market imperfections. As such, the welfare state exists quite properly both for lower-income groups *and* for the middle class. In the Wilensky and Lebeaux sense discussed in Chapter 2:7.1, there is an *efficiency* case for a universal welfare state.

7.2 Achieving Policy Aims: A Liberal View

The vital distinction between the *aims* of policy and the *methods* available to achieve them should by now be clear. Aims include social justice and economic efficiency: the definition of social justice will vary with different theories of society (Chapter 3); economic efficiency has broadly the same meaning in all theories of society (section 2). Methods embrace income transfers and direct intervention in the market through regulation, finance and public production. The resulting form of economic organisation, at one extreme, is the free market (with or without redistribution) and, at the other, central planning and public production of all basic goods and services (with or without charges). In between are different types of mixed economy involving both private markets (with or without intervention in the form of regulation and finance) and public production.

The central argument of this book is that the proper place of ideology is in the choice of aims, particularly in the definition of social justice and in its trade-off with economic efficiency; but *once these aims have been agreed* the choice of method should be regarded as a *technical* issue rather than an ideological one. Whether a particular good or service is provided publicly or privately should be decided on the basis of which method more nearly achieves the chosen policy objectives; and government intervention, similarly, should take place not on the basis of doctrinaire views about methods, but only if the achievement of policy aims is thereby enhanced. In the sense that the issue of market versus state provision is a contingent matter rather than an item of dogma, this book is firmly in the liberal tradition.[34]

How, then, should we choose between different methods? The analysis of section 3 suggests:

Proposition 1: efficiency: where one or more of the standard assumptions fails, state intervention in the form of regulation, finance or public production may increase economic efficiency. If none of the assumptions fails, efficiency is generally best achieved without intervention.

---

[34] For a classic defence of the mixed economy on broadly similar grounds, see Okun (1975).

Proposition 2: social justice: assume that there is no consumption externality in the utility functions of the rich (section 4.2). Then:

(a) Only efficiency arguments can justify intervention other than cash
redistribution. If no such efficiency justification exists, the interests of social
justice are likely to be served best by *income* transfers.

(b) But if there exist arguments which suggest that efficiency will be
furthered by public production and allocation of any good or service, then
social justice can be enhanced by *in-kind* transfers (e.g. redistribution via
free education or health care).

There are three possible exceptions to Proposition 2. The first is the
consumption externality argument, which offers a justification of sorts for
transfers in kind even where there are no efficiency grounds for public
production or allocation. The second concerns the role of giving. There is
no technical argument against having a market for babies. But most societies
rule this out on ethical grounds. It is argued, for instance, that health care
might more appropriately be regarded as a gift than a purchase, and Titmuss
(1970) makes a cogent argument for blood to be treated in this way.

The optimal taxation literature offers the third exception (see Bos, 1984).
The taxation necessary to finance income transfers may reduce labour
supply; if so, a given distributional objective *may* be possible at lower
efficiency cost by subsidising the *prices* of goods consumed by the poor.
The result requires (a) that such goods are consumed only (or mainly) by
the poor, and (b) that their consumption is not strongly complementary to
leisure.

From a purely theoretical viewpoint, this suggests that the two propositions can be criticised for their 'piecemeal' approach, i.e. for discussing
conformity with the standard assumptions in a given area while implicitly
assuming that they hold in all other areas. This ignores second-best considerations (Lipsey and Lancaster, 1956). Several defences are possible.
First, in a limited number of cases the approach is *theoretically* valid (Davis
and Whinston, 1965). Second, the measurement problems involved in
applying the approach to policy are intractable, so that 'the rules of first-
best optimality, coupled with the caveat of second-best ... constitute part
of the fund of guidelines from which good, if not perfect, policy might be
formulated' (Winch, 1971). Third, none of the areas covered by the welfare
state conforms closely with the two conditions in the previous paragraph.

Finally, I want to nail a wholly fallacious line of argument. In one form it
runs, 'we must have a National Health Service because otherwise the poor
could not afford adequate health care' – an argument which does the cause
of its proponents little service. The fallacy is that if inability to pay were
the *only* difficulty, there would not be a *market allocation problem* with
health care but an *income distribution problem*, which could be solved by

income transfers, as currently with food. The justification for the National Health Service, as argued in Chapter 12, lies not in Proposition 2(a) (which applies to food) but in Proposition 2(b).

Even more woolly is the assertion that, 'we must have a National Health Service because everybody has a right to health care'. The fallacy lies in the word 'because'. It is just as plausible to argue that everybody has a right to good nutrition, yet there are few advocates of a national food service. The statement confuses aims with methods. There is wide acceptance of the value judgement that people have a right to adequate nutrition and health care. These are *aims*; but the existence of these rights does not, *per se*, have any implications for the best method of achieving them. As we shall see, there are good reasons why Britain has a National Health Service but not a national food service – entitlement to food and health care, however, is not one of them.

7.3 The Debate with Libertarians

Propositions 1 and 2 would meet with general agreement from liberals and Fabian socialists. Marxists would reject them for the reasons discussed in Chapter 3:5. They accept the idea of social justice, but argue that too little has been done to achieve it. The efficiency arguments embodied in Proposition 1 are in large measure rejected on the grounds that the market system, though possibly in some respects efficient, is the fundamental *cause* of the failure to achieve social justice.

The debate with empirical libertarians like Hayek and Friedman is in many ways the most interesting and, given current policy concerns, the most relevant. The less interesting part of the argument is ideological. Libertarians reject almost in their entirety the social justice arguments of section 4, and in consequence reject Proposition 2. Hayek argues (Chapter 3:2) that there is no such thing as social justice, and that its quest risks eventual totalitarianism. Libertarians argue, largely for the government failure reasons set out in section 5, that there is too much redistribution, and that redistribution in kind is even more dangerous than transfers in cash. Taken as an ideological view little counter-argument is possible, save to assert a different set of values.

The debate over efficiency is much more important. As we saw in Chapter 3:2 empirical libertarians are the direct descendants of Classical liberalism (compare the views in Friedman (1962, Ch. 2) on the role of the state with those of Adam Smith quoted at the head of Chapter 1). Writers like Hayek and Friedman therefore admit a limited role for the state in the presence of market failures like externalities and public goods; and both accept a very restricted welfare state. Beyond this, however, both would resist the efficiency arguments of section 3. State intervention, it is argued, is often the *cause* of imperfect information rather than its result (e.g. if there were a competitive market for health care, people would acquire better information, in part because market institutions would arise to supply it). They support intervention to break monopolies or near-monopolies in product and (particularly) factor markets, and argue that domestic monopolies of tradeable goods need not be a problem if there are no barriers to foreign trade. As a result they argue that state intervention is excessive.

In sum, libertarians like Hayek and Friedman accept the analytical framework of section 3, but interpret facts differently. To that extent the debate is empirical. But it is also (and importantly) theoretical. What is not in dispute is the aim of maximising social welfare, nor the existence of imperfections in the form of monopolies, externalities, public goods and increasing returns to scale. The critical difference, as suggested in section 3, is that the analysis of Hayek and Friedman takes little account of information problems. These afflict consumers of increasingly complex products, and managers of increasingly large-scale enterprises, and they include technical – again largely information – problems in insurance markets (Chapter 5). The existence of information problems, more than any other theoretical consideration, suggests that a properly designed welfare state is much more than an instrument of social justice. It also has a major efficiency role.

Further Reading

The most comprehensive treatment of the subject matter of this chapter is Atkinson and Stiglitz (1980, Lectures 11–18) or, at a less technical level, Stiglitz (1988, Chs 3 and 4). For a gentler introduction to the economic theory of markets and welfare economics, see Le Grand *et al.* (1992, Chs 1 and 2) or Baumol and Blinder (1991, Ch. 29) (elementary); Laidler and Estrin (1989, Chs 26 and 27; Stiglitz, (1988, Chs 3 and 4); Brown and Jackson (1990, Chs 2–4); Musgrave and Musgrave (1989, Chs 4 and 5) (intermediate, non-mathematical); and Varian (1984, Chs 5–8) (somewhat more advanced). For a lucid, non-technical discussion of efficiency, equity and their trade-off see Okun (1975) (a classic and strongly recommended defence of the mixed economy). References to the literature on information problems are given in the Further Reading at the end of Chapter 5.

For a simple introduction to the theory of externalities, see Le Grand *et al.* (1992, Ch. 2) and Baumol and Blinder (1991, Ch. 29); and for fuller discussion of market failures, Musgrave and Musgrave (1989, Chs 4 and 5) and Stiglitz (1988, Chs 4, 5 and 8). A complete technical account of the optimal taxation literature and the trade-off between efficiency and equity is given by Atkinson and Stiglitz (1980, Lectures 11–18); for less technical discussion, see Brown and Jackson (1990, Ch. 14).

Different definitions of equity are discussed in Chapter 3; for an excellent brief summary, see also Le Grand (1984). A non-technical introduction to the theory of coerced redistribution through the ballot box is given by Tullock (1976), and in more complete form by Downs (1957) and Tullock (1970). The theory of voluntary (Pareto optimal) redistribution is developed by Hochman and Rodgers (1969); see also Thurow (1971). For general discussion of the economics of charity, see Sugden (1983b) (a simple introduction), and for a more complete treatment Sugden (1982, 1984) and the discussion in Collard (1983) and Sugden (1983a). The literature on the economics of charity is surveyed by Jones and Posnett (1993) and the references therein.

The large literature on public choice is surveyed by Inman (1987) and Mueller (1989).

Minford (1984b) favours radical privatisation. For argument about privatisation in the context of the welfare state, and public enterprise generally, see the contributions in Le Grand and Robinson (1984) and Steel and Heald (1984). More general discussion is contained in Beesley and Littlechild (1983) and Peacock (1984). The relative efficiency of public and private enterprise is discussed by Caves and Christensen (1980) and Pryke (1982). For an analysis of UK government policy, see Kay and Thompson (1986), the comment by Brittan (1986), and Kay *et al.* (1986). Le Grand and Estrin (1989) discuss the relationship between the market system and the achievement of socialist objectives.

Appendix: Non-Technical Summary of Chapter 4

1. Chapter 4 sets out the economic theory of state intervention, with particular emphasis on why intervention might foster efficiency and/or social justice (also referred to as equity).

THE CONCEPT OF ECONOMIC EFFICIENCY

2. The efficient (or Pareto optimal) output of any good (section 2.1) is the quantity which maximises the excess of benefits over costs. This is the output X^* in Figure 4.1 at which the value placed by society on the marginal unit of output equals its marginal social cost (for an excellent exposition, see Le Grand *et al.*, 1992, pp. 9–14).

3. A Pareto improvement (i.e. an increase in efficiency) takes place if any change in production or distribution makes one person better-off without making anyone else worse-off.

4. Section 2.2 shows that an increase in efficiency can raise welfare under any of the theories of society discussed in Chapter 3. The aim of efficiency is therefore common to all these ideologies, though the weight attached to it will vary when its achievement conflicts with distributional goals.

INTERVENTION FOR REASONS OF EFFICIENCY

5. The state can intervene in four ways (section 3.1). **Regulation** mainly concerns the quality of supply (e.g. hygiene laws relating to food, minimum building standards) and regulation of individual demand (e.g. the legal requirement to attend school, compulsory membership of national insurance). **Finance** can involve subsidies (or taxes) which change the price of specific commodities. Subsidies can be partial (e.g. local authority housing) or total (e.g. free drugs under the National Health Service). **Public production** covers national defence, education and (in Britain) most health care. These three types of intervention all involve direct interference in the market mechanism. **Income transfers** do not do so directly, but enable recipients to buy goods of their choice at market prices, e.g. elderly people receive a retirement pension with which they buy food.

6. **The Invisible Hand theorem** asserts that markets are automatically efficient if and only if a number of assumptions hold (section 3.2). These conditions (collectively called the standard assumptions) are discussed in paragraphs 7–16 below, which, together with paragraphs 22–6, summarise the theoretical heart of the book. The conditions relate to perfect information, perfect competition and the absence of market failures.

7. **Perfect information** implies, first, that consumers and firms should be

well-informed about the nature of the product, and also about prices. This is plausible for some goods (e.g. food and clothing), less so for others (e.g. health care). Where the assumption fails, several solutions are possible: the market itself may develop institutions to supply information (e.g. professional valuers, consumer magazines); or the state may respond with regulations (e.g. hygiene laws in the case of food); where information problems are serious the market might be so inefficient that public production might be a better answer.

8. Individuals need perfect information also about the future, so as to make rational choices over time. This is broadly true of food (since I know that I will need to eat tomorrow, next week, next month); it is not true with motor cars, because I do not know whether my car will be involved in an accident. The market can frequently cope with this sort of uncertainty through the mechanism of insurance (the main topic of Chapter 5). But private insurance can be inefficient or impossible for technical reasons; some risks (e.g. unemployment) are not insurable, largely because of information problems in insurance markets. In such cases public production may increase efficiency.

9. **Perfect competition** must apply in all input and output markets and also to capital markets (i.e. access to borrowing). Two conditions must hold: individuals must be price-takers; and they must have equal power.

10. Price taking implies free entry and exit into/from an industry with a large number of consumers and firms, none of whom individually is able to influence market prices. Where the assumption fails (e.g. in the case of a monopoly) intervention generally involves regulation (e.g. a price ceiling) or an appropriate mix of taxation and subsidy.

11. Equal power is violated by any difference (apart from differences in individual incomes) in the ability of individuals to choose their consumption. The assumption rules out all forms of discrimination; where it fails, solutions (to the extent that they exist) are usually based on regulation.

12. **Market failures** arise in three forms: public goods, external effects and increasing returns to scale.

13. **Public goods** in their pure form exhibit three technical characteristics: non-rivalness in consumption; non-excludability; and non-rejectability. Private (i.e. 'normal') goods are rival in consumption in the sense that if I buy a cheese sandwich there will be one sandwich less available for everyone else; excludability means that I can be prevented from consuming the cheese sandwich until I have paid for it; and rejectability implies that I do not have to eat it unless I wish to. Not all goods display these characteristics, the classic example being national defence. If the Royal Air Force is circling over Britain, the arrival of an additional person does not reduce the amount

of defence available to everyone else (non-rivalness in consumption); nor is it possible to exclude the new arrival by saying that the bombs will be allowed to fall on him until he has paid his taxes (non-excludability); nor is the individual able to reject the defence on the grounds of pacifist beliefs (non-rejectability). Similar considerations apply wholly or in part to roads, public parks and television broadcast signals.

14. In discussing public goods, an important distinction should be noted. For a private good the marginal cost associated with an *extra unit of output* and the marginal cost of an *extra user* are one and the same thing – if it costs £1 to produce an extra cheese sandwich, it also costs £1 to provide for an extra cheese-sandwich-consumer. But this identity does not hold for public goods – the marginal cost of, for example, an extra hour's broadcasting is positive and generally large, whereas the marginal cost of an extra viewer is zero. This has important implications. If a public good is provided at all, non-excludability makes it impossible to charge for it (this is the **free-rider** problem); in such cases the market will generally fail entirely. Non-rivalness implies that the marginal cost of an extra user (though *not* of an extra unit of output) is zero, and therefore the efficient price should be based not on costs, but on the value placed by each individual on an extra unit of consumption. Since this is impractical, the market is likely to produce an inefficient output. Thus the market is either inefficient or fails altogether; if the good is to be provided at all, it will generally have to be publicly produced.

15. **External effects** arise when an act of individual A imposes costs or confers benefits on individual B, for which no compensation from A to B or payment from B to A takes place, or, more formally, when A's utility or production function is interrelated with B's. The effect of externalities is to create a divergence between private and social costs and benefits. As a result, the market output in the presence of an external cost will generally exceed the efficient output, X^* in Figure 4.1, and vice versa for an external benefit. On occasion the market can resolve this inefficiency itself. Coase (1960) shows that, where the law assigns unambiguous and enforceable property rights, the externality problem may be solved by negotiation between the parties concerned. But this is not always possible, for instance where property rights are not enforceable (e.g. air pollution) or where large numbers of people are involved (e.g. traffic congestion). In this case intervention may be justified either through regulation (e.g. mandatory filtering equipment) or via an appropriate tax (sometimes referred to as a Pigovian tax) on the activity generating the external cost (see Le Grand *et al.*, 1992, Ch. 2; Baumol and Blinder, 1991, Ch. 29).

16. **Increasing returns to scale** arise when doubling all inputs leads to more than twice the output. If a production function exhibits increasing returns

to scale at all levels of output, average cost will always exceed marginal cost, as in Figure 4.4. It follows that at an output of X_0 the marginal cost price P_0 is less than average cost, AC_0. Hence competitive pricing results in an inherent loss, shown by the shaded area. If firms in a competitive industry make long-run losses, they will leave the industry, which will either become monopolised or, if even a monopolist is unable to make a profit, cease to exist. The result, therefore, is a sub-optimal output or a failure by the market to produce at all. Two solutions are possible: paying firms a lump-sum subsidy equal to the loss associated with competitive pricing; or nationalising the industry and paying an identical subsidy. The appropriate intervention is therefore subsidy or public production, or both.

17. The market will allocate efficiently only when *all* the assumptions in paragraphs 7–16 hold, in which case no intervention on efficiency grounds is necessary. Where one or more of the assumptions fails it is necessary in each case to consider which type of intervention (regulation, finance or public production) is most likely to improve efficiency.

INTERVENTION FOR REASONS OF SOCIAL JUSTICE

18. Section 4.1 sets out two broad explanations of why redistribution occurs. To libertarians it is enforced on the rich by the voting power of the poor. Utilitarians argue that the rich may *choose* out of altruistic motives to vote for political parties which propose to tax them more heavily to finance redistributive policies.

19. In certain circumstances it may be politically easier to make direct in-kind transfers, e.g. education. The formal analysis (based on the idea of a consumption externality) is shown by the voting model in section 4.2. Suppose the utility (see the Glossary) of a representative rich individual, R, rises with his own consumption, and also with the consumption of a representative poor man, P. In particular, suppose that R's utility rises with 'good' consumption by P (e.g. education), but falls with P's 'bad' consumption (e.g. whisky), where 'good' and 'bad' are defined by R. In this circumstance it might be rational for R to offer P an education costing (say) £1000, but to offer a cash transfer of only £200 (since P might spend the latter in part on 'bad' consumption). Faced with these offers, P might prefer the in-kind transfer to the lower cash sum (see Figure 4.5) – i.e. both rich and poor might vote for compulsory in-kind transfers.

PRIVATISATION

20. The term 'privatisation' is considerably more complicated than most of its users realise (section 6). As a first approximation, commodities like food are *produced* and *financed* privately whereas, at the opposite extreme, most education is produced in the public sector and paid for out of tax revenues.

But intermediate cases are possible (Table 4.1). Some goods are publicly produced, but are financed by user charges (e.g. electricity until recently); others are paid from tax revenues but produced in the private sector (e.g. drugs supplied free under the National Health Service).

21. Matters become considerably more complicated when regulation is included. It is then necessary to distinguish not only the sector in which (a) production and (b) finance take place, but also who decides (c) how much in total of any good will be produced and (d) how much each individual consumer will receive. Some of these cases are set out in Table 4.2.

ACHIEVING THE AIMS OF POLICY

22. Section 7 draws together the main arguments of Chapters 3 and 4 by repeating the distinction between the *aims* of policy and the *methods* available to achieve them. Aims embrace social justice and economic efficiency; methods include income transfers and direct interference in the market through regulation, subsidy or public production.

23. The central argument of this book is that the proper place of ideology is in the choice of aims, particularly the definition of social justice and its trade-off with economic efficiency; but once these aims have been agreed, the choice of method should be regarded as a *technical* issue, not an ideological one. Whether a commodity like health care is produced publicly or privately should be decided on the basis of which method more nearly achieves previously agreed aims. A rationale for choosing between the different methods is given in section 7.2 in the form of two propositions.

24. **Proposition 1: efficiency:** where one or more of the standard assumptions fails, state intervention in the form of regulation, finance or public production may increase economic efficiency. If none of the assumptions fails, the efficiency aim is generally achieved best by the market with no intervention.

25. **Proposition 2: social justice:** subject to minor qualifications it is possible to argue:
(a) Only efficiency arguments can justify intervention other than cash redistribution. If no such efficiency justification exists, the interests of social justice are best served by *income* transfers.
(b) But if there exist arguments which suggest that efficiency will be furthered by public production and allocation of any good or service, then social justice can be enhanced by *in-kind* transfers (e.g. redistribution in the form of free education or health care).

26. The two propositions make the issue of market versus state production

and allocation a contingent matter, placing this book firmly in the liberal tradition (as defined in Chapter 3:1). The debate between this book and libertarian writers like Hayek and Friedman is joined in section 7.3.

Chapter 5
Economic Theory 2: Insurance[1]

Insurance, *n*. An ingenious modern game of chance in which the player
is permitted to enjoy the comfortable conviction that he is beating the
man who keeps the table. [Ambrose Bierce, 1842–1914.]

1 Introduction

The term 'insurance' is used by different people to mean different things.
Two meanings above all should be distinguished. Insurance can be defined
(a) as a device which offers individuals *protection against risk*, and/or (b) as
an *actuarial mechanism* (as defined in equation 5.12, below) which the
private sector can organise. The first defines insurance in terms of its
objective, the second in terms of a method by which that objective might
be pursued. Even where institutions are not insurance in the sense of (b),
they might still be regarded as insurance in that they offer protection against
risk.

It is possible to insure against a wide variety of common mishaps like
burglary, death or car accidents; against losses caused by bad weather; and
for holiday deposits lost through illness. It is even possible to buy life
insurance for one's dog or cat. On the face of it this is all a bit curious,
since the published accounts of insurance companies show that they usually
make a profit. A representative individual thus receives less in benefit in the
long run than he pays in contributions.

This gives rise to two questions: why do people insure voluntarily, e.g.
against burglary; and under what conditions will the private market provide
insurance? These questions concerning, respectively, the demand and supply
sides of the insurance market are discussed in sections 2 and 3. It is also
important to consider the circumstances in which a market equilibrium will
exist, and will be efficient (section 4.1).

[1] Non-technical readers can find the gist of the argument in the Appendix to this chapter.

The analysis of insurance markets pre-dates interest in the economics of information, but many of the problems which arise are examples of a more general class of information problem (see the Further Reading). The parallels will be noted as we proceed.

2 The Demand for Insurance

2.1 Individual Demand

Why might a rational individual choose to insure when the expected payout is less than his premium payments? The answer, if he is risk-averse, is that uncertainty *per se* causes disutility; hence certainty is a commodity yielding positive marginal utility, for which he will pay a positive price. The formal argument starts with the definition of a risk-averse individual as someone with diminishing marginal utility of income, as shown in Figure 5.1.[2] Suppose there is a 'bad' outcome, y_1, yielding utility $U(y_1)$, and a 'good' outcome, y_2, yielding utility $U(y_2)$, occurring with probabilities p_1 and p_2, respectively. The individual's expected income and expected utility are:

$$\text{Expected income:} \quad E(y) = \bar{y} = p_1 y_1 + p_2 y_2 \tag{5.1}$$

$$\text{Expected utility:} \quad E(U) = \bar{U} = p_1 U(y_1) + p_2 U(y_2) \tag{5.2}$$

If $p_1 = p_2 = 1/2$, expected income, $\bar{y}$, is midway between y_1 and y_2 (if $y_1 = £100$, and $y_2 = £1000$, then $\bar{y} = £550$); and expected utility, $\bar{U}$, is midway between $U(y_1)$ and $U(y_2)$.

It is important to realise that a risk-averse individual can obtain the utility $\bar{U}$ in two entirely different ways. First, it could be obtained as the *expected* utility from an uncertain income of y, or y_2. Note that the individual never receives $\bar{y}$; each year he receives *either* y_1 *or* y_2, with corresponding utilities $U(y_1)$ and $U(y_2)$; the expected (or average) outcome is $\bar{y}$. Second, he could obtain $\bar{U}$ from a *certain* income y^*, as shown directly by the utility function in Figure 5.1. A rational individual will therefore be indifferent between an income y^* with certainty and an expected income $\bar{y}$ arising from uncertain outcomes y_1 and y_2. The total value of certainty (including consumer surplus) is thus

$$V = \bar{y} - y^* \tag{5.3}$$

and a rational individual will pay a net price, φ, so long as:

$$\varphi < V \tag{5.4}$$

The net price of insurance, φ, should be carefully distinguished from the gross premium. The difference is shown in Table 5.1, where the insurance

---

[2] A good, simple introduction is Laidler and Estrin (1989, Ch. 7); see also the Further Reading.

Figure 5.1 *The demand for insurance by a risk-averse individual*

company charges an annual premium of £550, and compensates for up to £900 of lost income. In a 'good' year the individual has an income of £1000, and pays a gross premium of £550, leaving a net income of £450. In a 'bad' year his income is £100; he pays a premium of £550 but receives compensation of £900. Thus the effect of insurance is to guarantee a net income of £450.

Table 5.1 *Gross and net insurance premiums, and net income in good and bad years*

	Good year	Bad year
(1) Income	£1000	£100
(2) Insurance premium	£550	£550
(3) Insurance benefit	–	£900
(4) Net income ((1) − (2) + (3))	£450	£450
(5) Net premium ((2) − (4))	£100	£100

The net premium, φ, is the difference between the gross premium and the average payout. The latter is the individual's expected loss

$$E(L) = pL \tag{5.5}$$

defined as the size of the loss, L, times the probability, p, that it will occur. Thus the net price of insurance is

$$\varphi = \pi - pL \tag{5.6}$$

where π is the gross premium. In the example, the individual's expected loss is £450; so £450 of the gross premium can be regarded as a form of saving to cover his own losses over the long run. The *net* price of insurance is £100, which the individual will pay so long as it does not exceed the value to him of certainty, V, in equation (5.3). We return to the calculation of insurance premiums in section 3.1.

2.2 The Nature of the Product: Insurance as a Mechanism for Pooling Risk

The twin intellectual bases of insurance are the law of large numbers and gains from trade. Under the former, *individuals* may face uncertainty, but society can face approximate certainty, e.g. I do not know whether I will die this year, but the death rate for men aged 30 to 50 is known and stable. It is the relative certainty about the *aggregate* probability resulting from the law of large numbers which opens up to individuals the possibility of exploiting gains from trade by agreeing to pool risks.

This can be shown formally.[3] Suppose each individual's income is a random variable y with mean, μ, and variance, var(y); there are N such individuals with incomes $y_1, y_2 \ldots y_N$, respectively. We assume:

- All individuals face the same probability distribution of outcomes.
- y, μ and var(y) for each individual are independent of those for every other individual (e.g. fire hazard or burglary, but not crop failure). In the absence of insurance, the variance (i.e. risk) facing the ith individual is var(y_i). Now suppose all N individuals put their income into a pool agreeing that each will receive

$$\bar{y} = \frac{1}{N}(y_1 + y_2 + \ldots + y_N) \tag{5.7}$$

This pooling is a form of insurance. The variance for society is

$$\text{var}(y_1 + y_2 + \ldots + y_N) = N \, \text{var}(y)$$

since all incomes are independent and have the same variance. But the variance for the *individual* is smaller. He receives the average income, $\bar{y}$ in equation (5.7) and

$$\text{var}(\bar{y}) = \text{var} \left(\frac{y_1}{N} + \frac{y_2}{N} + \ldots + \frac{y_N}{N} \right)$$

$$= N \, \text{var} \left(\frac{y}{N} \right)$$

$$= \frac{\text{var}(y)}{N} \to 0, \text{ as } N \to \infty \tag{5.8}$$

[3] This presentation is drawn from Layard and Walters (1978, Ch. 13).

Equation (5.8) shows that, if N identically distributed and independent incomes are pooled, the variance of average income (and hence the risk to the individual) tends to zero as N tends to infinity. By 'trading' (i.e. pooling) individuals can acquire certainty.

2.3 An Example: Annuities

Annuities (i.e. an annual income stream) are another form of pooling. An individual could buy an income of £y per year for n years by paying a lump sum, A, equal to its present value: i.e.

$$A = y + \frac{y}{1+r} + \frac{y}{(1+r)^2} + \dots + \frac{y}{(1+r)^{n-1}} \tag{5.9}$$

where r is the rate of interest.[4] More generally, the capital cost of a given income stream is

$$A = f(y, n, r) \tag{5.10}$$

Consider someone with £50,000 accumulated in pension contributions over his working life. He could finance his retirement (12 years on average, for a 65-year-old man in Britain) by consuming this lump sum at a rate of, say, £5000 per year; but he thereby risks outliving his savings. He can avoid this uncertainty by buying an annuity, which is a form of insurance in which he exchanges £50,000 and an uncertain lifespan for an annual income of £y, with certainty and for life. He is, in effect, making a bet with the insurance company: if he hands over the lump sum and immediately drops dead he loses (because he receives back less than the lump sum), but if he lives to 98, he wins. This arrangement is exactly analogous to income pooling. All retired persons put their lump sums into a pool and draw the average income; those who live longer draw more than those who die younger, but the fund can pay for the long-lived because it is based on average life expectancy. The process is technically feasible and has low transactions costs because the aggregate distribution of age at death is known and stable.

How large is the annuity? Equation (5.10) can be rewritten as

$$y = g(A, n, r) \tag{5.11}$$

which shows that the annual payment, £y, for a given lump sum, A, depends on the insurance company's view of n (the applicant's life expectancy) and r (its expected interest rate).

Life expectancy The insurance company will pay a lower annual income

---

[4] For further detail, see Brown and Jackson (1990, Ch. 8), Cullis and Jones (1992, Ch. 6), Stiglitz (1988, Ch. 10), or Musgrave and Musgrave (1989, Ch. 9). For a complete treatment of cost–benefit analysis, including discussion of the discount rate, see Mishan (1982).

the longer it expects to pay benefit. This depends on four broad factors.

Age: the younger a person, the longer, on average, he has to live and the smaller the annuity he is offered in respect of a given lump sum.

Sex: on average women live longer than men. Thus, other things being equal, a woman will receive a smaller annuity than a man. In practice, many pension schemes pool across men and women for annuity calculations; this raises important equity issues (see Chapter 9:4.2).

Health: we should expect an insurance company to be interested in an individual's health. But since it is easier to detect health problems than to prove their absence, there is usually more interest in an applicant's health for life insurance than for annuity purposes, the more so because in the case of annuities early death is to the company's advantage. Insurance companies therefore usually pool across health for annuities, but not for life insurance.

Marital status: where an annuity is payable also to a surviving spouse, the age difference between husband and wife becomes relevant. If I retire at 65, and my wife is considerably younger, she is likely to outlive me by many years, in which case the payout period, n, is longer, and the annuity correspondingly smaller. However, where schemes are compulsory (e.g. a pension scheme for school teachers), insurance companies usually pool across men aged 65 irrespective of the age of their wives. This is feasible because for the *group* the average age difference is predictable.[5]

The rate of interest   If changes in the price level are not to affect the real value of an annuity, it is necessary to base calculations on the real rate of interest (i.e. the excess of the nominal interest rate over the rate of inflation).

Suppose an individual has accumulated a lump sum of £50,000, and the insurance company expects him to live for 12 years ($n = 12$) and anticipates a real rate of interest of 1 per cent ($r = 0.01$). The actuarial value of an annuity is obtained by substituting these values into equation (5.11) to obtain a value for y. The subject of annuities in the context of pension finance is a major topic in Chapter 9.

3 The Supply Side

3.1 The Supply of Insurance

This part of the chapter discusses the price at which the private market will supply insurance, and then turns to a number of technical problems.

The actuarial premium   Suppose that I insure the contents of my house for £1000, when the probability of being burgled is 1 per cent. From equation

---

[5] The fact that such schemes are compulsory is important, an aspect discussed in more detail in sections 3.2 and 4.2, below.

(5.5) my expected loss is the product of the insured loss, L, and the probability, p, that the loss will occur. The insurance company knows that on average it will have to pay out £10 per year (i.e. 1 per cent of £1000). The actuarial premium, π, is then defined as:

$$\pi = pL + T \qquad (5.12)$$

where pL is the individual's expected loss, and T the insurance company's transactions costs, including administrative costs (e.g. sending an expert to assess the damage) and normal profit. π is the price at which insurance will be supplied in a competitive market.

Conditions for private insurance The actuarial premium in equation (5.12) rests on a number of conditions on the probability, p. Some are strictly technical; others bring us directly back to the issue of perfect information. Problems under either head can make private insurance inefficient or impossible.

Private insurance requires, first, that the probability of the insured event for any individual is *independent* of that for anyone else. This condition is necessary because insurance depends on the existence in a given period of a predictable number of winners and losers. If, in the extreme, individual probabilities are completely related, then if one person suffered a loss so would everyone else; actuarial insurance cannot cope with such *common* (as opposed to individual) shocks. An important example (discussed in Chapter 9:3) concerns inflation, which, if it affects any one member of an actuarial pension scheme, will affect all.

The second condition is that the relevant probability must be less than one. If not, equation (5.12) simplifies to:

$$\pi = L + T > L \qquad (5.13)$$

and the actuarial premium exceeds the insured loss. I might, for example, have to pay a premium of £1500 to insure against potential burglary losses of £1000. Private insurance will not be offered because there will be no demand for it. In economic terms there is no possibility of spreading risk, and hence no gains from trade. This problem can arise for the chronically or congenitally sick, where the probability of ill-health is equal to one unless insurance is taken out before the condition is diagnosed. Medical insurance policies usually exclude treatment for pre-existing conditions precisely because the probability of needing treatment is too high to insure. Similarly, it may be difficult to buy insurance against burglary in high-risk areas.

We have seen (Chapter 4:3.2) that market efficiency requires perfect information on the part of consumers and firms. Firms may face information problems in a number of ways: employers may not be well-informed about the quality of labour, nor lending institutions about the degree of riskiness of prospective borrowers. A particular class of information problem concerns insurance markets.

The relevant probability (condition 3) must be *known or estimable*. Where the assumption fails, the carrier (i.e. the insurance company) is unable to calculate a premium from equation (5.12), making private insurance impossible. For that reason, private markets are generally unable to offer insurance against future inflation, *inter alia* because the probability distribution of different levels of future price change cannot be estimated.

Further problems are caused by asymmetric information, where the supplier of insurance has less information than the customer. Thus (conditions 4 and 5), there should be *no adverse selection*, and *no moral hazard*. The former arises where the purchaser is able to conceal from the carrier the fact that he is a high risk, e.g. in medical insurance, where it may be possible for people to conceal facts about their health. Moral hazard (slightly to oversimplify) occurs where the customer can costlessly manipulate the probability of the insured event without the supplier's knowledge. In the context of unemployment insurance (Chapter 8:2.2), for instance, a problem arises if individuals can affect either the likelihood or the duration of unemployment. Another example is pregnancy, which can be influenced by individual action, and may be the result of choice. In the latter case (chapter 12:3.1), the probability cannot be regarded as wholly exogenous, and private medical insurance may exclude the costs of a normal pregnancy (though the extra costs of complications are often covered because the probability of *complications* is exogenous).

Adverse selection and moral hazard are central parts of efficiency arguments about the welfare state, and so merit further discussion.

3.2 Asymmetric Information[6]

Adverse selection is a manifestation in insurance markets of the more general concept of 'lemons' (Akerlof, 1970). The purchaser of insurance may have a much better idea than the supplier of whether he is a 'lemon' (i.e. a poor risk). Akerlof's competitive analysis was extended by Rothschild and Stiglitz (1976) to cover strategic behaviour by firms. The Rothschild–Stiglitz argument is important.[7] They start by assuming the simplest case: risk-averse individuals, constant marginal utility of income, actuarial insurance and no administrative costs. Point A in Figure 5.2 shows the income of an uninsured individual when working and when unable to work because of

[6] The literature starts from Arrow (1963), followed by Akerlof (1970), Pauly (1974), Rothschild and Stiglitz (1976) and Wilson (1977); for a recent overview, see Laffont (1989, Chs 8, 10 and 11) or, less formally, Kreps (1990, Chs 16 and 17).

[7] For further discussion see, in ascending order of difficulty, Atkinson (1989, Ch. 7) reprinted in Barr and Whynes (1993, Ch. 2), Kreps (1990, Ch. 17) and Laffont (1989, Ch. 10).

illness. Under the stated assumptions, a rational individual will choose to insure fully. With full insurance, income (net of the insurance premium) will be the same when ill as when working, i.e. at a point on the 45-degree line.

Suppose that there are two groups of people, low-risk with a probability of illness p_L, and high-risk with a probability P_H. Suppose, initially, that the insurance company can distinguish the riskiness of individual applicants. The premiums are thus:

$$\pi_L = p_L L + T \tag{5.14}$$

$$\pi_H = p_H L + T \tag{5.15}$$

Low-risk individuals, paying a premium of π_L, can trade from A on favourable terms; they give up relatively little income in premiums when working and receive generous benefits when ill. They will be able to buy any insurance contract along the line AC_L and, under the stated assumptions, will choose the contract (i.e. a pair of incomes when at work and ill, respectively) shown by point C_L. High-risk individuals face the less-favourable terms shown by the line AC_H, and will choose point C_H.

Where the insurance company cannot distinguish high- from low-risk individuals, it must charge a premium based on average risk:

$$\pi = [ap_H + (1-a)p_L] \, L + T \tag{5.16}$$

where p_H and p_L are the (now unobserved) probabilities of high- and low-risk individuals, respectively, and a and $(1 - a)$ the proportions of high- and low-risk individuals buying insurance. The locus of potential insurance contracts is shown by the line AD in Figure 5.2.

If low risks buy less cover and high risks more at an average premium, π, the resulting policies are less efficient than would exist if individually tailored policies, π_L and π_H, were possible. The resulting problems are best shown by considering the contract shown by B. Any contract in the shaded area above B would (a) be preferred by the low-risk group, and (b) would still be profitable. Thus the *pooling equilibrium* (i.e. a common premium for all applicants) at B is not stable; if any company offered such a contract, another company could bid away the low-risk group by offering a policy in the shaded area above B. The same argument applies for any other contract along AD.

Suppose instead that the insurance company tried to have separate policies for the two groups. It cannot verify the riskiness of each individual; it might, however, be able to use *self-selection*, by offering carefully designed policies which face customers with incentives such that their market behaviour reveals their true probability (see Salop and Salop (1976) and Ravallion (1991) for analysis of such self-selection in different contexts). Thus the policy offered to the low-risk group along AD must lie to the left of point

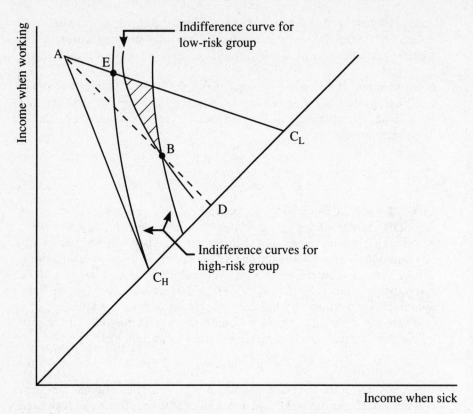

Figure 5.2 *Effects of adverse selection on a competitive equilibrium*

E (anywhere to the right would attract high-risk applicants). However, as Figure 5.2 is drawn, low-risk individuals would prefer the pooling contract shown by *B* to any contract between *A* and *E*. In such a case no *separating equilibrium* exists. Even if it did, it would still be inefficient because it does not allow low-risk individuals to buy complete cover.

Adverse selection thus causes two sets of problems: a pooling equilibrium is unstable, either because low risks drop out or because of competitive behaviour by insurers; and a separating equilibrium, if it exists at all, is inefficient because it prevents low-risk individuals from buying complete cover. In the face of adverse selection, the market is either inefficient or fails entirely, the ultimate outcome depending on the precise behaviour of insurer and insured (see Hellwig, 1987).

One solution (or partial solution) is to restrict the range of choice the insured is allowed: a particularly relevant possibility is to make membership compulsory to prevent low risks opting out of a pooling equilibrium (i.e. seeking to move into the shaded area above point *B*). If preferences are sufficiently similar, the welfare loss from compulsion may be minimal (see discussion in a different context by Weitzman (1977)).

Moral hazard At its strongest, the no moral hazard condition requires that both the probability, *p*, and the insured loss, *L*, should be exogenous to the individual. Slightly less stringently, moral hazard can be avoided so long as individuals can influence *p* or *L* only at a cost to themselves greater than the expected gain from so doing. Where the assumption fails, customers can affect the carrier's liability without its knowledge (another example of asymmetric information).

Pauly's (1974) analysis of moral hazard remains a landmark. He considers the case of individual expenditure on a preventive activity, *z*, which can reduce the probability of the insured event. From a social point of view, the efficient level of *z* is that at which its marginal cost is equal to the marginal reduction in insured losses. But if losses are fully insured and the insurance company cannot monitor individual preventive activity, the private incentive is to spend little or nothing on it. At its simplest, my extra spending on *z* reduces my premium by only an infinitely small amount: the main beneficiaries are other insured people who now pay slightly lower premiums. As a result of this type of externality, Pauly argues, individuals face private incentives to underinvest in preventive activities. Moral hazard thus causes inefficiency in the form of excessive purchase of insurance cover.

Pauly's analysis is sensitive to one strong assumption, namely that all losses, *including* non-material losses, are insurable. If that assumption is relaxed, there are several possible outcomes, of which Pauly's is only one. To show the effects of uninsurable psychic losses, it is useful to distinguish which of *p* or *L* is endogenous. There are four cases.

1. *Endogenous p_i, but only at substantial psychic cost*: an example is suicide. In this case the problem of moral hazard is more apparent than real. It is possible to influence the probability of dying, but generally only at a very high cost in utility terms to the individual concerned. People do not commit suicide *only* to make their legatees rich. (It is true that someone intending to commit suicide *for other reasons* might do so; but that is a problem of adverse selection, to deal with which most policies have a clause excluding cover during the first year of the policy). Individuals cannot insure against the psychic cost to themselves of death. Insurance is thus incomplete; in consequence there is little or no overinsurance. Moral hazard in such cases is not a problem.

2. *Endogenous p_i, with no substantial psychic cost*: people might drive less carefully if they are insured, or buy fewer fire extinguishers, since insurance reduces the cost to the insured individual of those unwelcome events. In

this case, the Pauly result holds: moral hazard does not make insurance impossible but causes inefficiency, in that people take less care than if they had to bear the full loss themselves.

3. *Endogenous p_i, with substantial psychic gains*: this is the case of voluntary pregnancy or elective health care (e.g. a hair transplant). Here the insured outcome is not an undesired exogenous event but a deliberate act of consumer *choice*. Individuals can control at small cost the probability, p, in equation (5.12), and the insurance company can calculate neither the expected loss nor the actuarial premium. This is a far cry from an insurable risk; such activities are generally uninsurable for individuals.

The problem can sometimes be sidestepped where insurance is compulsory. A woman will not become pregnant just because the medical costs are covered by insurance; but if she intended to have a child, she would take out insurance before doing so (so that the problem is one of adverse selection as well as moral hazard). But where all workers in (say) the steel industry are compelled to join a particular medical insurance scheme, the insurer can impose a pooling solution, based on the expected number of births per 1000 families. In contrast, if insurance were voluntary, a disproportionate number of intending parents might join.

4. *Endogenous L at zero or low cost* (the so-called *third-party payment problem*): here it is not the probability, p_i, which is endogenous but the size of the insured loss. To see intuitively what is going on, contrast behaviour in a conventional restaurant with that in an 'all you can eat for £9.95' restaurant. In the case of medical care, for instance, if an insurance company pays all medical costs, neither patient nor doctor is constrained by the patient's ability to pay. The marginal private cost of health care is zero for both doctor and patient, even though social cost is positive. The results of this form of moral hazard are twofold: because of the divergence between private and social costs, consumption of health care (and consequently the insurance payout) is larger than is efficient (Chapter 12:3.1); and there is an upward bias in insurance premiums.

Similarly, suppose automobile insurance pays for all car repairs. I then have an incentive to drive recklessly (i.e. p is endogenous), and also to have my car repaired lavishly (e.g. a respray where touching up the paintwork would suffice). The result of this type of moral hazard, as with case 2 above, is inefficiency in the form of overconsumption.

Moral hazard thus causes a fundamental problem: the more complete the cover and the lower the psychic loss from the insured event, the less individuals have to bear the consequences of their actions and the less, therefore, the incentive to behave as they would if they had to bear their losses themselves. A number of devices try to reduce the problem, either through regulation or through the use of incentives. *Inspection* (a form of regulation) is frequently used for damage claims (e.g. for house contents or automobile repairs); in this case the carrier inspects the damage and pays benefit only in respect of what it regards as the true insured loss. Incentive mechanisms seek to share the cost between the individual and the insurer (see Shavell, 1979): frequent claimants (e.g. accident-prone car drivers) pay *higher premiums*; *deductibles* make the insured person pay the first £X of any claim; with *coinsurance*, the insured person pays x per cent of any claim. None of these, however, faces the individual with the full marginal financial cost of making good the loss.

In analytical terms, adverse selection and moral hazard are both examples of information failure. Neither problem would arise if the insurance company could 'get inside the head' of insured persons (i.e. could read their thoughts), and hence could verify their risk status, or whether they were manipulating the relevant probability (i.e. behaving differently from the way they would behave in the absence of insurance).

4 The Insurance Market as a Whole: Private and Social Insurance

4.1 The Existence and Efficiency of Private Insurance Markets

The existence of private insurance markets requires three conditions.
   1. There must be positive demand. From equation (5.3) this requires that

$$V = \bar{y} - y^* > 0$$

This condition holds only if some individuals are risk-averse.
   2. It must be technically possible to supply insurance, i.e. none of the problems discussed previously must make private insurance impossible.
   3. It must be possible for insurance to be supplied at a price which the individual is prepared to pay. Equation (5.6) defines the net premium as

$$\varphi = \pi - pL$$

Thus, from equation (5.4), a market for insurance exists only if

$$V \geqslant \varphi - pL$$

i.e. (from equations (5.3) and (5.12)) only if

$$\bar{y} - y^* \geqslant T \tag{5.17}$$

Thus insurance can be supplied at an acceptable price only where the individual's risk aversion (represented by the difference between $\bar{y}$ and y^*) is sufficient to cover the carrier's administrative costs and normal profit.

   These three conditions hold for the examples of private insurance in section 1. Consider the case of the vicar who wants to insure against the loss to the parish if it rains on the day of the church fête. Since he wants to insure, it follows that he is risk-averse, hence the demand condition holds. Nor are there technical problems on the supply side; the probability of rain on a given day is known and less than one; there is no adverse selection (since the vicar cannot hide rainfall statistics from the insurance company) and no moral hazard (since he cannot influence the weather). Finally, administrative costs are low, since it is easy to establish whether or not the weather was bad, and so insurance can be provided at a low net price.

Efficiency It was argued in Chapter 4 that an unrestricted private market allocates resources efficiently only if the standard assumptions hold. These assumptions apply equally to insurance.

Perfect information is relevant to those who buy insurance, and to the companies supplying it. Because of the multiplicity of insurance policies, individuals do not usually have perfect information; but, as in similar cases, the market has developed institutions – insurance brokers – to provide it. Suppliers must have perfect information about the overall probability of an insured event; and information must be symmetric.

Perfect competition provides consumers with their desired type and mix of insurance, and ensures that suppliers make no long-run excess profits.

No market failures: the relevant market failure is externalities. These can arise in the presence of adverse selection, one of whose effects is to impose external costs on low-risk individuals. A further cause of externalities is the third-party payment problem, which will generally create a divergence between private and social costs.

Where these assumptions fail, private insurance (a) may be inefficient, and (b) may not be supplied at all. Both types of problem are acutely relevant to unemployment insurance (Chapter 8:2.2), to the protection of pensions against inflation (Chapter 9:3.1) and to medical insurance (Chapter 12:3.1).

Premium differentials A question which arises from the earlier discussion of adverse selection is whether efficiency requires that differences in individual probabilities should *always* result in different premiums. Suppose I am burgled more often than my brother. This could be because I am unlucky (a *random* difference), or because I live in London, which has a high crime rate, and he lives in the country (a *systematic* difference).

To define more precisely what we mean by random and systematic differences suppose that individual probabilities can vary randomly, i.e.

$$\pi = \bar{p} + \varepsilon_i \tag{5.18}$$

where π, the probability of the ith individual being burgled, comprises a 'true' or average probability, $\bar{p}$, and a random component, ε. If ε is truly random, and hence has a zero mean, the average probability, $\bar{p}$, is simply the mean of the observed probabilities, p_i. Thus, over N individuals

$$p = \frac{1}{N} \Sigma \bar{p}_i \qquad (5.19)$$

Now consider two groups of individuals: p_{11}, p_{12}, ..., p_{1M} are the probabilities facing the M individuals in group 1, and p_{21}, p_{22}, ..., p_{2N} those of the N people in group 2. From (5.19) we can calculate the average probability for individuals in group 1, $\bar{p}_1$, and similarly for group 2. We can then say:

1. If $\bar{p}_1 = \bar{p}_2$ any difference in probabilities between individuals in the two groups is random.

2. If $\bar{p}_1$ is significantly greater than $\bar{p}_2$ differences in the probabilities are *systematic*. It is then appropriate to talk of high- and low-risk individuals, with average probabilities p_H ($= \bar{p}_1$) and p_L ($= \bar{p}_2$), respectively.

We can sum up:

Conclusion 1: the efficient price of insurance should not reflect random differences in probabilities.

Conclusion 2: but where the decision to insure is voluntary, efficiency requires that suppliers should seek to discover who is high and who low risk, and charge premiums accordingly, as in equations (5.14) and (5.15).

In contrast, where insurance is compulsory, it might be possible to pool high and low risks and charge everyone the average premium (equation (5.16)), since low-risk people cannot choose not to insure. Such a pooling solution raises important issues, so it is instructive to consider some examples.

The 1946 National Insurance Act (Chapter 2:5) applied pooling explicitly both to individuals and to risks. All employed men of working age paid the same lump-sum contribution to buy entitlement, *inter alia*, to the same unemployment benefit, even though some groups (e.g. doctors) were much less likely to be unemployed than others (e.g. construction workers). All individuals paid an average premium as in equation (5.16); and because contributions were compulsory it was not possible for overcharged low-risk individuals to opt out. Analytically, the low-risk group paid an actuarial premium (equation (5.14)) plus an unavoidable lump-sum tax, and the high-risk group paid an actuarial premium shown by equation (5.15) and received a lump-sum transfer. Thus a system which charges a compulsory average premium irrespective of risk can alleviate problems of adverse selection; it might, however, cause secondary inefficiency, e.g. charging everyone the same premium for industrial injury insurance might lead to inefficient expansion of risky industries.

Another example (Chapter 9:4.2) is the pooling of men and women in pension schemes, despite the fact that on average women live longer. Again, the broken link between premiums and individual probabilities causes little inefficiency in insurance markets *per se*, though it might have an efficiency impact on the relative wages of men and women and/or on the relative size of the male and female workforce. In contrast, automobile insurance is also compulsory, but there is no pooling across groups – people with worse accident records generally pay higher premiums. We can therefore add:

Conclusion 3: if insurance is compulsory, charging all categories of risk the same premium causes little inefficiency in *insurance* markets, though it might cause secondary inefficiency in related activities.

Fallacious equity arguments appear in a number of guises. The first is that insurance is inequitable because it redistributes from those who do not make claims to those who do. This assertion merits little discussion. The whole point of insurance is that people do not know whether they will need to claim (i.e. whether the 'good' or the 'bad' outcome will occur). A rational risk-averter increases his utility by choosing a lower income with certainty (y^* in Figure 5.1), in preference to the higher expected income, $\bar{y}$. Insurance can bring about this increase in utility precisely because the individual is a net contributor in a 'good' year and a net beneficiary in a 'bad' year.

A second fallacious argument is that 'private insurance is inequitable because the poor cannot afford adequate cover.' This proposition can be attacked in a number of ways. First, if the *only* difficulty is that the poor cannot afford enough, then the problem is one not of market allocation but of income distribution, and can be solved by cash redistribution. Second, who decides what level of cover is 'adequate'? Public provision on these grounds can be justified only where there are efficiency problems with private insurance, or if the poor have imperfect information. The arguments developed earlier, in particular the two propositions in Chapter 4:7.2, apply equally to insurance.

4.2 Social Insurance

Arrow argues that where markets fail, other institutions may arise to mitigate the resulting problems, sometimes through public production and sometimes through private institutions using non-competitive allocation mechanisms: '[T]he failure of the market to insure against uncertainties has created many social institutions in which the usual assumptions of the market are to some extent contradicted' (Arrow, 1963, p. 967). In other words, as discussed in the first paragraph of this chapter, institutions (public or private) may arise which are insurance in the sense of protecting against risk, even if they are not insurance in a narrow actuarial sense.

The Arrow arguments and their subsequent elaboration contrast with the position of writers like Nozick (1974), who argue that what matters is not the outcome, or end-state, but the process by which it is reached; even if compulsory public provision could be shown to make everyone better off it should, according to such a view, be rejected. The conclusions of the Arrow arguments are also in strongest possible contrast with Hayek (1945). Both writers started from the assumption of asymmetric information. To

Hayek the fact that different people knew different things is an argument *in favour* of markets: he argued (analogous to the existence of skill differences) that the market makes beneficial use of such differences by allowing gains from trade to be exploited. Arrow showed that the market is an inefficient device for mediating certain important classes of differences in knowledge between people. Nor is the Arrow view idiosyncratic. The Rothschild and Stiglitz (1976) and similar arguments were discussed in section 3.2. Lucas, in discussing unemployment, reached an identical conclusion:

Since, ... with private information, competitively determined arrangements will fall short of complete pooling, this class of models also raises the issue of *social insurance*: pooling arrangements that are not actuarially sound, and hence require support from compulsory taxation. The main elements of Kenneth Arrow's analysis of medical insurance are readily transferable to this employment context' (1987, p. 62, his emphasis).

Information failures provide both a theoretical *justification of*, and hence also an *explanation for*, a welfare state which is much more than a safety net. A central argument in later chapters is that private insurance cannot cover contingencies such as unemployment, inflation and important medical risks. It is useful to anticipate that discussion by considering one response, social insurance.

Membership of most social insurance schemes is compulsory, thus preventing low risks from opting out (though partial opting out may be allowed, e.g. for earnings-related retirement pensions). Compulsion makes possible the three generic forms of organisation described in Chapter 1:2.1, all of which are insurance in the sense of offering protection, but which diverge increasingly from insurance in conventional actuarial terms.

Social insurance (i.e. contingency-based benefits with a contributions test) can take two broad forms. *Quasi-actuarial contributions* are related to the average risk (e.g. the flat-rate weekly contribution of the British scheme between 1948 and 1975); this is a pure pooling equilibrium. *Income-related contributions* break the link with individual risk; the contribution in this case looks like an earmarked tax.

'Universal' benefits abandon the attempt to mimic private insurance. Tax-financed benefits are awarded on the basis of specified contingencies without a contributions or income test (the flat-rate retirement pension in some countries, health care *inter alia* in some countries including the UK).

Social assistance benefits are awarded on the basis of specified contingencies and an income test.

Administration can be by the state at central level (as mostly in Britain) or at a lower level (as for most programmes in the USA, and for health care in Australia, Canada and Sweden). Alternatively, administration can be hived off to private-sector institutions such as friendly societies or trades unions (as with unemployment compensation in Sweden and medical care in Germany); in such cases the private sector is acting, in effect, as an agent of the state.

The social insurance arrangements just described are based on private institutions: benefits are conditioned on an implicit or explicit contributions record and on the occurrence of a specified event, frequently related to employment status, in that one of their major purposes is to replace lost earnings.

Social insurance, however, differs from private insurance in at least two important respects. First, because membership is generally compulsory, it is *possible* (though not essential) to break the link between premium and individual risk; a pooling solution is therefore an option. Second, the contract is usually less specific than private insurance: protection can be given against risks which the private market cannot insure (Chapter 8 argues that unemployment is one example); and the risks can change over time. Atkinson (1989, p. 117) points out that

[actuarial] insurance is against a well-defined contingency, about which individuals can form probabilities. [However,] much of the function of social insurance is to provide for contingencies which are unforeseen ... [I]t is hard to imagine that individuals could have taken out insurance to cover such events as the 1974 fuel price rise, the development of new surgical techniques, or the breakdown of the extended family. A looser form of contract, as with social insurance, may in this respect have significant advantages.

Social insurance, in various guises, will appear repeatedly in later chapters.

Further Reading

The economics of uncertainty is set out in simple form in Laidler and Estrin (1989, Ch. 7), and in slightly more detail and somewhat more formally in Varian (1984, Ch. 3). For discussion in the context of cash benefits, see Stiglitz (1988, Ch. 12).

On information problems more generally, see Kreps (1990, Chs 16, 17 and 18) and Varian (1984, Ch. 8) for an overview. The classic articles are by Arrow (1963) (who discusses medical insurance), on adverse selection by Akerlof (1970) and Rothschild and Stiglitz (1976), and on moral hazard by Pauly (1974). For surveys of the literature on imperfect information about quality, see Stiglitz (1987), and on imperfect information about price, Mortensen (1986).

Appendix: Non-Technical Summary of Chapter 5

1. Chapter 5 discusses the demand and supply of insurance, and some problems which can arise on the supply side of a private insurance market.

2. The term 'insurance' is used by different people to mean different things. Two meanings above all should be distinguished. Insurance can be defined (a) as a device which offers individuals *protection against risk*, and/or (b) as an *actuarial mechanism* (as defined in equation (5.12), below) which the private sector can organise. The first defines insurance in terms of its purpose, the second in terms of a method by which that purpose might be pursued. Even where institutions are not insurance in the sense of (b), they might still be regarded as insurance in that they offer protection against risk.

THE DEMAND AND SUPPLY OF INSURANCE

3. Uncertainty reduces the utility of an individual who is risk-averse; hence certainty has a positive marginal value, and a risk-averse individual will be prepared to pay a positive price for it. When I take out insurance the commodity I am buying is certainty (e.g. that if my car is stolen it will be replaced). The formal argument is presented in section 2.1.

4. The supply of insurance is discussed in section 3.1. Suppose that the probability, p, of being burgled is 1 per cent; and that if I am burgled my loss, L, will be £1000. On average, therefore, I can expect a loss of £1000 once every 100 years. In annual terms my expected loss is $p \times L = 1\% \times £1000 = £10$, i.e. the insurance company knows that on average it will have to pay me £10 per year. Formally, an **actuarial premium**, π, is defined as

$$\pi = pL + T \qquad (5.12)$$

where pL is the expected loss of the individual buying insurance, and T is the insurance company's administrative costs and normal profit. π is the price at which insurance will be supplied in a competitive market.

TECHNICAL PROBLEMS ON THE SUPPLY SIDE

5. Private insurance will be inefficient or non-existent unless the probability, p, in equation (5.12) meets five conditions (sections 3.1 and 3.2). First, the probability of a given individual being, for example, burgled must be **independent** of the probability of anyone else being burgled. What this means (roughly speaking) is that insurance depends for its financial viability on the existence in any year of a predictable number of winners and losers.

6. Second, p must be **less than one**. If $p = 1$ it is certain that my car will be stolen; hence there is no possibility of spreading risks, and the insurance premium will equal or exceed the cost of a new car. This problem can arise for the chronically or congenitally ill, for whom the probability of ill-health equals one unless insurance is taken out *before* the condition is diagnosed.

7. A third condition is that p must be **known or estimable**. If it is not, insurance companies will be unable to calculate an actuarial premium, and private insurance will be impossible. Thus the private market is generally unable to supply insurance against future inflation because the probability of different levels of future price increases cannot be estimated.

8. Fourth, there must be **no adverse selection**, which arises when a purchaser is able to conceal from the insurance company the fact that he is a poor risk. If the insurance company cannot distinguish high- and low-risk customers it will have to charge everyone the same premium, based on the average risk. As a result, low-risk individuals will face an inefficiently high premium and may choose not to insure even though, at an actuarial premium, it would be efficient for them to do so. This problem arises particularly in the case of medical insurance for the elderly.

9. Finally, there must be **no moral hazard**. The problem can arise in two ways: first, where the customer is able costlessly to manipulate the probability p in equation (5.12) that the insured event will occur; and second, where the customer can manipulate the size of the loss, L. The latter difficulty is conventionally called the **third-party payment problem**.

10. There are numerous ways in which consumers can manipulate the relevant probability. The chances of developing appendicitis are beyond individual control, and so medical insurance for this sort of complaint is generally possible. In contrast, the probability of becoming pregnant, and visits to one's family doctor, can both be influenced by individual actions and are therefore generally not well-covered by private medical insurance. Where the problem is serious, the supplier is unable to calculate the actuarial premium, and private insurance may be impossible.

11. The third-party payment problem does not make insurance impossible, but causes overconsumption. The problem is particularly relevant to health care. If an individual's insurance pays all medical costs, then health care is 'free' to the patient. Similarly, on the supply side, the doctor knows that the insurance company will pay his charges; he is therefore not constrained by the patient's ability to pay. As a result, both doctor and patient can act as though the cost of health care were zero. This is inefficient: it causes overconsumption and creates upward pressure on insurance premiums.

12. The problems discussed in paragraphs 5–11 can cause inefficiency, and

may make private insurance impossible. Both difficulties are relevant to unemployment insurance (Chapter 8:2.2), to the protection of pensions against inflation (Chapter 9:3.1) and to medical insurance (Chapter 12:3.1).

Chapter 6
Problems of Definition and Measurement[1]

To criticise inequality and to desire equality is not ... to cherish the romantic illusion that men are equal in character and intelligence. It is to hold that, while their natural endowments differ profoundly, it is the mark of a civilised society to aim at eliminating such inequalities as have their source, not in individual differences, but in its own organization. [R. H. Tawney, 1964.]

Common prosperity cannot and never will mean absolute egalitarianism or that all members of society become better off simultaneously at the same speed ... Such thinking would lead to common poverty. [People's Republic of China, Central Committee's Decision on Reform of the Economic System, 1984.]

1 Measuring Welfare

1.1 Individual Welfare

Measurement problems are a recurring theme. They are illustrated here in the context of poverty (section 2) and inequality (sections 3 and 4). Two sets of issues are discussed: how do we define poverty and inequality; and how do we measure them in principle and in practice? A useful starting point is to consider the definition and measurement of welfare for individuals and for society as a whole.

DEFINING INDIVIDUAL INCOME

Wealth and income The theoretical concept of income is complex and the literature vast (see the Further Reading). For present purposes it is possible to simplify matters by considering income as the flow deriving from a stock of wealth. Individual wealth can arise, broadly, in three forms. *Physical wealth* consists of consumer durables like houses, machines (e.g. cars,

[1] Non-technical readers may omit sections 1.2, 4.1 and 4.2. The gist of the argument is in the Appendix to this chapter.

television sets), Picassos and Persian rugs. *Financial wealth* includes shares, government bonds and bank accounts.[2] *Human capital* is wealth embodied in individuals as a result of skill and training, and has two quite separate sources: it is the result of past investment in education and training (which is what most people mean when they talk of human capital); it also arises from 'natural talent'. The latter requires explanation. Obvious examples are Shakespeare and Mozart, whom most of us could not emulate however much training we had. The concept, however, is much broader. The talent of, for example, a road sweeper consists mainly of muscle and an ability to put up with simple routine; and a major item under this head is the ability to walk, dress, wash oneself, etc. (which forms of human capital are denied to individuals with serious health problems).

Each type of wealth yields a flow of income. Physical wealth produces non-money income in the form of a flow of services, e.g. housing, or televisual services, but can also yield money income (e.g. a house to a landlord, or an automobile to a taxi driver). Financial wealth yields money income, e.g. the annual flow of interest from a £1000 bank account. Human capital produces income in several forms. Suppose an individual divides his time between 'work' and 'leisure'.[3] When he is working, his human capital yields money income (i.e. wages), and non-money income like job satisfaction (which can be positive or negative); and when not working, he receives non-money income through the enjoyment of leisure (again positive or negative), and also in the form of own production (household chores, gardening, etc.).

Full income, Y_F, consists of the flow of services from *all* individual wealth, i.e. money income, Y_M, plus all forms of non-money income, Y_N. In short,

$$Y_F = Y_M + Y_N \tag{6.1}$$

where money income comprises wage and non-wage money income (e.g. dividends and interest),[4] and non-money income includes job satisfaction, the flow of services from physical wealth, the value of own production and, importantly, the enjoyment of leisure.[5] For given prices, full income thus defined is a measure of an individual's *opportunity set*. The word 'opportunity' is crucial. The opportunity set measures the individual's potential power to consume goods (including leisure) whether or not *ex post* he chooses to do so (for the central importance of choice in assessing individual

---

[2] It is legitimate to include both physical and financial wealth for *individuals*. But for society as a whole, care is needed to avoid double counting, which would arise if, for example, Ford factories and Ford shares were both included in the definition of wealth.

[3] The distinction between work and leisure is in many respects suspect (see, for instance, Apps, 1981). But it does no harm to retain the distinction for present purposes, and makes the exposition clearer.

[4] This definition leaves unanswered the difficult question of whether, and to what extent, capital gains should be included in income. See Prest and Barr (1985, Ch. 13, section 4).

[5] For the importance of leisure in the definition of income, see Atkinson and Stiglitz (1980, pp. 260–1).

welfare, see Le Grand, 1984). Full income is thus a form of generalised budget constraint, and so a natural variable in terms of which to measure poverty and inequality.

The logic of the theoretical argument is completed by observing that if we assume given prices and identical tastes, there is a one:one correspondence between an individual's full income as defined in equation (6.1) and his utility. Whether or not we adopt the stringent assumption of identical tastes, it is possible by defining full income as the return to *all* forms of individual wealth to construct a measure of individual consumption opportunities which makes theoretical sense.

The Haig–Simons definition   The next step is to see how this theoretical approach might be put into practice. The classic definition of individual income is by Simons (1938, p. 50), also called the Haig–Simons definition:

Personal income may be defined as the algebraic sum of (1) the market value of rights exercised in consumption and (2) the change in the value of the store of property rights between the beginning and the end of the period.

More simply, 'income in a given period is the amount a person could have spent while maintaining his wealth intact' (Atkinson, 1983a, p. 39). The word 'could' is important. My income is increased if my *potential* to consume is raised, whether or not I actually choose to consume more.

The Haig–Simons definition has twofold importance: it indicates how income might be measured in practice; and it is comprehensive (and therefore theoretically sound) because it includes the following types of income which are omitted from conventional definitions, e.g. for tax purposes.

Non-pecuniary benefits from work include the consumption of work-related goods. Where such 'fringe benefits' are marketable (e.g. a chauffeur-driven car) they can be valued fairly easily. But problems arise where benefits are non-marketable and/or a mixture of 'work' and 'leisure'. Is a business trip abroad pure work, or leisure in disguise, or a mixture of the two? And how should 'enjoyment' of the trip be valued? The measurement of job satisfaction raises obvious problems. All these non-pecuniary benefits are part of 'rights exercised in consumption', and their market value forms part of the Haig–Simons definition.

Own production includes goods I have produced for myself (e.g. building an extension to my house) which could in principle be part of market production, and also the consumption of unpaid services produced by others within the household sector, e.g. cooking, cleaning, child minding.[6] Both forms of activity give rights over consumption, and their market value is properly included in the Haig–Simons definition. Income under this head

---

[6] In formal terms these two sorts of activity correspond to production for own consumption and production for trade within the household sector (see Apps, 1981).

also includes leisure, whose value to an individual is not less than the earnings thereby forgone, £*X*.

Imputed rent is the market value of the services of consumer durables, notably owner-occupied houses, whose importance has already been stressed.

Capital gains and losses, according to Haig–Simons, are part of income since they constitute a change in the value of the store of property rights. An individual with a £1000 asset which appreciates over the period to £1100 would be able (assuming no inflation) to spend an extra £100 without reducing his wealth. Thus capital gains should be included as part of income *in the period in which they accrue*, whether or not they are realised; and capital losses should be deducted from income as they accrue.

MEASURING INDIVIDUAL INCOME

The next step is to consider how a theoretically sound definition of income might in practice be measured. This raises three sets of problems.

How do we measure income? A version of Haig–Simons which might be workable is the sum of wage income, non-wage money income, fringe benefits, imputed rent and realised capital gains. But this measure deviates from full income as defined in equation (6.1) through the omission of job satisfaction, extra-market production and forgone income taken as leisure, and also because capital gains are not measured as they accrue. Further problems arise in attributing to individuals the benefits of publicly provided goods and services (e.g. education, roads).

Because non-money income is largely unmeasurable, it is necessary to focus on money income. This would not matter if money income were a good proxy for full income, but in practice the proportion of income arising in non-money form varies widely and unsystematically across individuals. Non-observability of parts of full income prevents a complete characterisation of the individual opportunity set, and forces us to use the unreliable yardstick of money income. The notion of full income is useful less as a guide to policy than as an explanation of why conventional definitions of poverty and inequality in terms of money income have only limited validity as measures of individual welfare.

The income unit, i.e. whose income is being measured? This raises the two separate questions of how to define an income unit, and how to compare units of different sizes. The latter issue of 'adult equivalents' is discussed in section 3.3. On the first, consider a household consisting of a man, a woman and two children, whose only source of income is £15,000, earned by the man. Regarded as a family, two adults and two children share an income of £15,000; no one is poor; nor is there necessarily substantial inequality. But if the man is regarded as a separate unit (as for income tax purposes), then the woman and child have no income; they will be counted as poor; and there will be substantial measured inequality. The narrower the definition of the income unit, the greater are measured poverty and inequality.

The problem is more intractable than it seems. At its heart lies another measurement problem – the impossibility of measuring income flows *within* a household. In the example just discussed, the real focus of interest is the extent to which income is shared; since this is unobservable we note instead the observable but not strictly relevant fact that the man and woman are married, and thereby infer (rightly or wrongly) that income is shared.[7]

Over what time period is income measured?   Problems arise here because income does not in practice flow continuously. Consider a salesman who earns £400 per week in commission but receives no wage; during the year he works 50 weeks, earning £20,000, and in the remaining two weeks, because of illness, earns nothing. If income is measured over a year he is not poor, but on a weekly basis he is poor for two weeks. For some purposes (e.g. setting a level for student support) it might be appropriate to use a long-run notion like permanent income. In other circumstances the answer might be different. If a student with no family to help him and no job with which to support himself applied for assistance during the summer vacation, it would not be very helpful to refuse benefit because he had a high expected lifetime income. In cases of immediate need, the relevant definition of income is usually short-run.[8]

1.2 Social Welfare

Similar arguments apply at an aggregate level. A comprehensive measure of national income would include both money and non-money income as the following speech by Robert Kennedy illustrates:[9]

We cannot measure ... national achievement by the gross national product. For the gross national product includes air pollution and advertising for cigarettes, and ambulances to clear our highways of carnage ... It swells with equipment for the police to put down riots in our cities; and though it is not diminished by the damage these riots do, still it goes up as slums are rebuilt on their ashes ... And if the gross national product includes all this, there is much that it does not comprehend. It does not allow for the health of our families, the quality of their education or the joy of their play ... It allows neither for the justice in our courts, nor for the justice of our dealings with each other ... It measures everything, in short, except that which makes life worthwhile.

---

[7] Further discussion of defining income and income units is contained in the literature on the taxation of husband and wife. See Barr (1980), Hurley (1985) and UK (1986a).

[8] For further discussion, see Atkinson (1983a, Ch. 3.2).

[9] See Newfield (1978, pp. 59–60). The speech was made in Detroit in May 1967.

More formally, the *social welfare function* in equation (4.1) is the explicit relation between aggregate welfare and the welfare of the individuals who make up society. If U^i, the utility of the ith individual, depends on his income (appropriately defined), y^i, then social welfare, W, can be expressed as

$$W = W\left(U^1(y^1),\ U^2(y^2),\ \ldots,\ U^n(y^n)\right) \tag{6.2}$$

or, more simply, as

$$W = W(y^1,\ y^2,\ \ldots,\ y^n) \tag{6.3}$$

Thus $y^1, \ldots, y^n$ measure the welfare individually of each of the n members of society; these are aggregated into a measure of social welfare through the function W. Social welfare functions are categorised in terms of their properties (see Cowell, 1977, pp. 41–50), an explanation of which is a necessary prelude to the discussion of aggregate inequality in section 4.

Property 1: Non-decreasing Formally, let social welfare in state A be $W_A = W(y^1, y^2, \ldots, y^{iA}, \ldots, y^n)$ and in state B, $W_B = W(y^1, y^2, \ldots, y^{iB}, \ldots, y^n)$. In other words, the distribution in states A and B differs only because the ith individual has a higher income in state B than in state A. Then a social welfare function is non-decreasing if and only if

$$W_B \geqslant W_A \text{ if } y^{iB} \geqslant y^{iA} \tag{6.4}$$

Non-decreasing implies that if any individual's income rises, social welfare cannot decrease.

Property 2: Symmetric A social welfare function is symmetric if

$$W(y^1, y^2, \ldots, y^n) = W(y^2, y^1, \ldots, y^n) = \ldots$$
$$= W(y^n, \ldots, y^2, y^1) \tag{6.5}$$

Social welfare depends on the distribution of income, but not on who gets which income, i.e. social welfare is unchanged if two people 'swap' incomes. This is equivalent to assuming that all individuals have identical utility functions.

Property 3: Additive A social welfare function is additive if

$$W(y^1, y^2, \ldots, y^n) = \sum_{i=1}^n U^i(y^i) = U^1(y^1) + U^2(y^2) + \ldots + U^n(y^n) \tag{6.6}$$

This is the utilitarian social welfare function, under which social welfare is the sum of the utilities experienced individually by members of society. Additivity implies that a person's utility will be independent of everyone else's income – a strong assumption which rules out the possibility of welfare interdependence discussed in Chapter 4:4.1. It also rests uneasily with the relative definition of poverty discussed shortly.

These three properties taken together have important implications. If a social welfare function is non-decreasing, symmetrical and additive it has the general form

$$W = \sum_{i=1}^{n} U(y^i) = U(y^1) + U(y^2) + \ldots + U(y^n) \tag{6.7}$$

where: (a) (in contrast with equation (6.6)) U is the same for each individual (a consequence of symmetry); and (b) $U(y^i)$ increases with y^i (because the social welfare function is non-decreasing).

Equation (6.7) makes it possible to use $U(y^i)$ as an index of social welfare. If there is an increase in the income of the ith individual, the increase in social welfare will be

$$U'(y^i) = \frac{dU(y^i)}{dy^i} \geqslant 0 \tag{6.8}$$

The welfare index $U(y^i)$ is *not* an ordinary utility function. It shows the social marginal valuation or *welfare weight* of changes in the ith person's income. To show why $U'(y^i)$ is the welfare weight, consider a tax/transfer scheme which leads to a series of (small) changes in individual incomes, Δy^1, Δy^2, ..., Δy^n. The resulting change in social welfare is the total differential ΔW; and if the social welfare function takes the simple form of equation (6.7), then

$$W = U'(y^1)\Delta y^1 + U'(y^2)\Delta y^2 + \ldots + U'(y^n)\Delta y^n \tag{6.9}$$

and the terms $U'(y^i)$ act as a system of weights when summing the effects of the scheme on social welfare. The next step is to discuss what value the weights might take. This brings us to:

Property 4: Concave   A social welfare function is concave if the welfare weight always decreases as y^i increases, i.e. concavity implies diminishing social marginal utility of income. A £1 increase in income raises social welfare more if it goes to a poor than to a rich man; thus a small redistribution from rich to poor raises social welfare. For some purposes it is useful to know how concave a social welfare function is, i.e. how rapidly the welfare weight falls as an individual's income rises. Thus:

Property 5: Constant relative inequality aversion   A social welfare function has constant relative inequality aversion (or constant elasticity) if the utility index $U(y^i)$ has the specific form

$$U(y^i) = \frac{1}{1-\varepsilon} y^{i(1-\varepsilon)} \tag{6.10}$$

where ε is a non-negative *inequality aversion parameter*. The welfare index in equation (6.10) has the property that the proportional decrease in the welfare weight for a given proportional increase in income is the same at all income levels. A 1 per cent increase in an individual's income reduces his welfare weight by ε per cent whatever his income (i.e. the 1 per cent increase can be from £100 to £101 or from £10,000 to £10,100). The larger is ε, the more rapid is the decline in the welfare weight as income rises, hence the name 'inequality aversion parameter'. We return to these issues in more detail in section 4.2.

2 Poverty

2.1 Defining Poverty

This section discusses various attempts to define poverty (section 2.1); makes the important distinction between poverty and inequality (section 2.2); and considers the measurement of poverty (section 2.3).

Indicators of poverty Attempts to construct an objective (i.e. value-free) poverty line face a series of largely intractable problems. Individual consumption opportunities should be measured in terms of full (i.e. money plus non-money) income. Since this is not possible it is necessary to turn to more measurable indicators. Three approaches have commonly been used: actual consumption of a specific bundle of goods; total expenditure; and total money income. Each has its difficulties, of which the following is the barest of summaries (for further discussion, see Atkinson, 1987b, and 1989, Ch. 1). The first approach requires a definition of the appropriate consumption bundle; and when that difficult task has been accomplished leads to a multi-dimensional (and hence complex) definition of poverty. The expenditure measure requires adjustment for inefficient spending.

Money income is a flawed measure of individual welfare, and is one of the major causes of the somewhat unhappy intellectual state of analytical definitions of poverty.[10] Three problems were discussed in section 1.1: the unsystematic relation beween money income and full income; the definition of the income unit; and the time period over which income is measured. None has an unambiguous answer, so any definition of poverty in terms of money income is somewhat arbitrary, a point reinforced in section 3.2.

All three measures – consumption, expenditure and income – face an additional and major problem. They all look only at *ex post* magnitudes, without regard to the (possibly crucial) influence of choice *ex ante* (see the definition of the individual opportunity set in equation (6.1) and the discussion in subsequent paragraphs). I may eat no meat and have low expenditure and income, and so be poor according to all three measures.

---

[10] See Townsend (1979); and for a trenchant critique, Piachaud (1981). See also the Further Reading.

But if by choice I am a vegetarian ascetic, then my opportunity set (i.e. my *potential* living standard) may exceed the poverty line.

Defining a Poverty Line would raise major difficulties even if all problems with measurable indicators had been solved. In particular, should poverty be regarded as an absolute or a relative concept? With an *absolute* definition a person is poor if his money income is too low to keep him alive and healthy. Early studies (see the Further Reading) attempted to define poverty 'objectively' by reference to basic nutritional requirements. There are serious objections to this approach. People have different nutritional requirements even in the absence of special medical diets, so that no universally applicable standard is possible; nor is it reasonable to expect people to fill these requirements at minimum cost. Philosophically, the idea of an absolute poverty line stems from times when it was natural to think in subsistence terms; but this can be argued to be out of place, at least in industrialised countries, when people live well above subsistence, and where the concept of deprivation is applied to emotional and cultural standards as well as to physical ones.

Under a *relative* definition, with deceptive simplicity, a person is regarded as poor if he or she feels poor. The definition of poverty will vary by time and place according to prevailing living standards; and whether or not a person feels poor will depend in part on what he sees around him (see Runciman, 1972). It can be argued (though there is no way in which the hypothesis can be tested) that riots in America's inner cities are caused not only by the poverty of black residents, but also by the contrast implied by television advertisements for gleaming kitchens and automatic garage door openers, aimed at middle-class whites living only five miles away.

An absolute poverty line will remain fixed at subsistence; with a relative definition it will tend to rise with living standards generally. In the latter case it is argued (Townsend, 1979) that a person is poor if he or she cannot participate in 'normal' life (this is known as a participation poverty standard). Thus a person without access to television is culturally deprived, and a poverty budget should include at any rate a black-and-white television set. Similarly, it might be argued that a child is deprived if he or she does not have access to a computer.

A different line of argument for real increases in the poverty line is that over time incomes rise; hence the demand for inferior goods falls, and they tend to disappear from the market.

The paradox of affluence is that [it] actually creates, as a by-product, a new poverty ... [M]ore people have cars, so that buses carry fewer passengers at higher fares, and services are cut ... The more people who have central heating, the harder and dearer it becomes, as the number of coal merchants dwindles for the others to buy coal. [*Sunday Times*, 19 September, 1982.]

In such cases it is necessary to raise the poverty line so that people can buy the next cheapest substitute (for further discussion, see Sen, 1983).

Formally, an absolute definition of poverty is more appropriate the greater the extent to which the utility of rich and poor depend only on their own incomes, and a relative definition is more appropriate the greater the extent of income externalities. Suppose the relevant utility functions are

$$U^R = f(Y^R) \tag{6.11}$$

$$U^P = f(Y^P) \tag{6.12}$$

where U^R and U^P are the utilities of a representative rich and poor person, respectively, and Y^R and Y^P their incomes. This is the case implied by an additive social welfare function (equation (6.6)), and an absolute definition of poverty might be appropriate. But if the utility functions are

$$U^R = f(Y^R,\ Y^P)\quad f_1 > 0, f_2 > 0 \tag{6.13}$$

$$U^P = f(Y^R,\ Y^P)\quad f_1 < 0, f_2 > 0 \tag{6.14}$$

(where f_1 and f_2 are the partial derivatives of utility with respect to Y^R and Y^P, respectively), we have an income externality of the type discussed in Chapter 4:4.1, and both rich and poor might prefer a poverty line which rose over time.

To conclude, the definition of poverty, like the definition of a just distribution, is less a matter of positive economics than of social convention and of the underlying notion of social justice (embodied formally in the welfare weights of the social welfare function). A definition of poverty in terms of money income may be widely accepted, but analytically it is inevitably somewhat arbitrary.

2.2 Poverty and Inequality

Absolute poverty and inequality are separate concepts which should not be confused. Absolute poverty refers to a standard of living below some benchmark. The undotted income distribution in Figure 6.1 shows a substantial number of poor people (i.e. the area A), a large number of middle incomes and few high incomes. Inequality is concerned not with the absolute living standard of the poor, but with the *differences* between income groups; the dotted distribution shows more inequality (but less absolute poverty) than the undotted one. Various measures of this dispersion are discussed in section 4.

Figure 6.1 *Poverty and inequality*

The difference between poverty and inequality is illustrated more fully in Table 6.1, which shows the average income in two societies of the poor (the lowest two-thirds of incomes), the rich (the top third), and the average income of rich and poor together. In society 1 the poor have an average income of £6000, which is one-third of the average income of the rich, £18,000. In society 2 (which is identical in all respects except income) the average income of the poor, £9000, is one-quarter of the average income of the rich, £36,000. In society 2 the poor have a higher standard of living than in society 1 (i.e. there is less absolute poverty), but are further behind both the average income and the standard of living of the rich (i.e. there is more inequality).

Table 6.1 *Poverty and inequality in two different societies*

	Society 1	Society 2
Average income of the poor ($\frac{2}{3}$ of population)	£6000 ($\frac{1}{3}$ income of rich)	£9000 ($\frac{1}{4}$ income of rich)
Average income of the rich ($\frac{1}{3}$ of population)	£18,000	£36,000
Average income of rich and poor together	£10,000	£18,000

It is instructive to ask which society the poor would choose. Suppose a representative poor person has the utility function shown by equation (6.12); his utility depends on his own income, and his rational choice is society 2. In contrast, with equation (6.14), his utility increases with his own income but decreases as that of the representative rich person rises. If the externality (shown by f_1) is sufficiently strong, it will be rational for a poor person to choose society 1, in which the difference between rich and poor is smaller.

The distinction between poverty and inequality is important because it might not be possible to reduce *both*. A supply-side argument is that poverty can be alleviated by reducing the taxation of the rich, thereby encouraging economic growth and making possible further redistribution from rich to poor (i.e. reducing the top rates of tax might change society 1 into society 2). The relevance of this argument (whose truth is ultimately an empirical question) is its implicit assumption that the real enemy is absolute poverty rather than inequality, i.e. it assumes an individual utility function of the form of equation (6.12). In consequence, policy design is concerned with poverty relief (objective 4 in Chapter 1:2.2), but not with inequality reduction (objective 7).

In contrast, it was stated at a Labour Party Conference in the early 1970s that any subsequent Labour government would introduce a wealth tax to 'squeeze the rich until the pips squeak.' Such a statement implicitly assumes that inequality rather than poverty is the main enemy, i.e. that the utility of the poor is shown by equation (6.14). But if the argument of the previous paragraph is true, then any attack on inequality might aggravate absolute poverty through the effect of higher taxation in reducing economic growth and hence the size of the tax base (i.e. attacking inequality might convert society 2 into society 1). The policy conclusion is not that attacks on inequality *will* increase absolute poverty, but that they might, making it important to be clear about the relative weights given to the objectives of poverty relief and inequality reduction.

2.3 Measuring Poverty

Empirical definitions of the poverty line We have seen that poverty is hard to define without a measure of full income. But policy-makers cannot refuse to establish a poverty line on the grounds that there exists a conceptual impasse; and it is possible to infer roughly what the state thinks by looking at what it does. First, is poverty regarded as absolute or relative? With an absolute definition, the poverty line, as represented, for instance, by the level of social assistance (i.e. 'welfare') in the UK, would have about the same real value today as in 1948 when the Beveridge arrangements came into effect, i.e. the benefit would have been uprated in line with price changes. In fact, at least until the early 1980s, benefits kept pace with changes in pre-tax average earnings,[11] so in practice poverty has been treated as a relative concept. As an example, between 1948 and 1982 nominal, pre-tax average earnings rose some twentyfold, and so did the major long-term social assistance benefit.

---

[11] Since the real burden of taxation rose substantially over the post-war period, this implies that the real level of benefits *rose* relative to *post-tax* average earnings.

Turning to the other questions posed earlier, the definition of the income unit for benefit purposes is fairly broad. Couples in the UK pay income tax on an individual basis; in contrast, the incomes of individuals living together are usually aggregated for the purposes of benefit assessment, irrespective of marital status.[12] In comparing families of different sizes, the poverty line has been set at about 20 per cent of pre-tax average earnings for a single person, at around 30 per cent for a married couple, and at 40–45 per cent for a family of four. Thus the implied adult equivalents (see section 3.3) for a single individual, a couple and a family of four are 100, 150 and about 200, respectively. Finally, the time period over which income is measured for awarding cash benefits is frequently short. For some benefits it is necessary only to show that one has no current income; for others evidence of the previous five weeks' income is required.

These are the state's answers to the various definitional questions (for further detail, see Barr, 1981). They are valid to the extent that over the years they have acquired the force of social convention; but they should not be regarded as having any particular intellectual merit.

Measuring the extent of poverty raises two major questions: how much poverty is there; and who are the poor? Since it is not possible to define poverty even for an individual, it is not surprising that the first question has no unambiguous answer. The simplest measure of aggregate poverty is the *head count*. Suppose that the poverty line is set at £X per week. One can then ask how many people are poor in terms of that definition. Even this simple question cannot be answered readily. It is not possible to use the number of recipients of social assistance as an estimate of the poor population. Not everyone who is eligible for benefit receives it; and recipients are an unknown proportion of those potentially eligible, so that it is not possible to scale up the number of recipients into an estimate of the poor population.[13] On this definition, the number of poor people in Britain is larger than the number receiving income support (5.1 million[14] in 1992/3), but without additional information we do not know how much greater. As a result, estimates have to be constructed from sample surveys, which suggest that in the late 1980s there were close to 10 million poor people in Britain (Barr and Coulter, 1990, Table 7.10 (d); see also Piachaud, 1993).

The head count, even were an accurate figure to be obtained, gives at best a partial picture. It fails to indicate by how much people fall below the poverty line. Even worse, a transfer of £100 from someone well below the poverty line to someone only £50 below *reduces* poverty as measured by the head count. In part because of this deficiency, a second measure, the

---

[12] The treatment of cohabitation has always generated considerable heat and not very much light. For general discussion of the choice of income unit, see Fiegehen and Lansley (1976).

[13] The issue of these so-called 'take-up rates' is discussed in Chapter 10:3.

[14] This figure refers to the number of *recipients*. When account is taken of their dependants the total number supported wholly or in part by income support is about 70 per cent higher.

poverty gap is sometimes used. This considers the total shortfall from the poverty line, divided by the poverty line or by total income. The former gives an approximate measure of the average depth of poverty, the latter of the relative cost of relieving it. Both approaches have been criticised (see the discussion in Atkinson, forthcoming).

Foster (1984) proposes a poverty gap which gives greater weight to larger shortfalls. He suggests a measure

$$P_a = (1 - Y/P)^a \qquad (6.15)$$

where Y = family income and P = the poverty line. The value $a = 0$ gives the head count; $a = 1$ gives an unweighted poverty gap; $a = 2$ gives a higher weight to greater shortfalls.

A further dimension of poverty is its *duration*. If most people experience poverty only as a short-term phenomenon, the problem is smaller than if large numbers suffer near permanent poverty. In practice, long-term poverty is substantial, and compounded by the extent to which it is transmitted across generations. Atkinson *et al.* (1983) found that nearly half of their sample of poor people came from poor parents (see also Atkinson, 1989, Chs 4 and 5).

Empirical evidence The fact that a definitive aggregate measure of poverty is not possible does not mean that empirical work is not useful, merely that considerable care is needed in interpreting results. So this bare summary should be regarded as no more than indicative, and subject to qualifications (for which see the studies themselves). Poverty has been extensively studied in individual countries.[15] Problems are compounded when attempting to make comparisons across countries, mainly because the definitions of income and income recipients are frequently inconsistent. In addition, the fact that country A has less measured poverty than country B could be due to A's more generous benefits *or* to differences in the level and distribution of pre-transfer income.

These various problems have been addressed over the 1980s by the availability of microdata (i.e. data on individuals) from the Luxembourg Income Study (LIS) which covers various OECD countries, with data on central and eastern Europe and the former Soviet Union being added. Microdata have the two overriding advantages of comparability and completeness: it is possible to choose income units, income definitions and equivalence scales, facilitating systematic comparison; and the data include income from all sources, including private pensions and savings. The disadvantage is that such data are available only with a lag.

The broad conclusion of Smeeding *et al.* (1990, Table 3.5), based on LIS

---

[15] On poverty in the UK, see Beckerman (1979), Mack and Lansley (1985) and Atkinson (1989, Ch. 3); and for a review of evidence between 1974 and 1985, Barr and Coulter (1990). On the USA, see Haveman (1987), Levy (1988) and Sawhill (1988). Atkinson (1991) reviews evidence in various OECD countries.

data, was that the head count of post-transfer poverty among a sample of OECD countries[16] in the early 1980s was highest in the USA, and was also relatively high in Australia and Canada. Income poverty was least in Sweden and Germany. Income transfers in Sweden removed from poverty over 80 per cent of the pre-transfer poor; the comparable figure for the USA was 22.6 per cent. Pre-transfer poverty was generally highest amongst the elderly and single-parent families. The Swedish pension system was spectacularly successful in pulling almost all elderly people out of poverty. In the USA, 20 per cent of elderly people and half of all individuals in single-parent families remained poor after all transfers, in part because there is no automatic relation between the poverty line (which is federal) and benefit levels (which are usually set by states).

There are two regularities: state pensions have a major effect in reducing poverty; and the poor are disproportionately people who are elderly, unemployed or with health problems, or in single-parent families, large families and non-white racial minorities. Discussion of empirical evidence is resumed in Chapter 10:3.4.

3 Inequality 1: Individuals and Families

3.1 Defining Equality and Inequality

Different definitions of equality   This section discusses equality (as with poverty it turns out that no wholly satisfactory definition is possible), and then turns to inequality between individuals (section 3.2) and families (section 3.3). The first question is: equality of what? In principle the answer is easy – individuals are equal if they face identical opportunity sets. But full income cannot be measured, so matters in practice are more complex. Le Grand (1982, pp. 14–15) distinguishes five possible definitions. The simplest, *equality of final income*, implies that individuals are equal if they have the same level of money income plus income in kind. But complications arise in measuring income in kind. Should there be *equality of public expenditure* (i.e. expenditure on, say, health care is the same for everybody); or *equality of use* (e.g. everyone is allocated the same quantity of health care); or *equality of cost* (e.g. everyone faces the same cost of using the National Health Service, which implies that people visiting their doctor should be compensated for any lost earnings); or *equality of outcome* (e.g. health care is allocated so that, as far as possible, everyone enjoys equally good health)? All have valid claims as definitions of equality; all are different. (For further discussion, see Le Grand, 1991a, especially Ch. 5; Sen, 1992.)

Similar problems arise when we try to define 'equality of opportunity'.

---

[16] Canada, Germany, Sweden, UK and USA.

An individual's income according to Atkinson and Stiglitz (1980, p. 267) depends on three sets of factors: his *endowments* (e.g. of human capital or inherited wealth); his *tastes* with respect to work and leisure, consumption and saving, risk, etc.; and his *luck*, inasmuch as the outcome of choices is often stochastic. Thus two individuals with identical tastes and opportunity sets may experience very different outcomes – 'some people work for a firm that goes bankrupt; some people invest early in Rank Xerox' (ibid.).

Equality of opportunity is best approached in several steps.

First step: equality of opportunity exists if

$$Y_F = K \text{ for all } i \qquad i = 1, 2, \ldots, N \tag{6.16}$$

where Y_F is full income as defined in equation (6.1), and includes a time dimension. Equation (6.16) states that full income should be the same for all N individuals in society. The obvious problem is that no account is taken of the stochastic element in individual income. Equality of opportunity implies that people should have an equal *chance*, i.e. it is an expected value not an absolute value which should be equal. Hence:

Second step: equal opportunity can be said to exist if

$$E(Y_F) = K \text{ for all } i \tag{6.17}$$

Here equality of opportunity requires only that expected income should be the same for all individuals. This is an adequate definition of equality of opportunity in terms of *full* income, which captures all aspects of the individual opportunity set. In practice, however, measurement problems force us to use money income, which varies not only with the individual opportunity set, but also with individual tastes; and differences in income for the latter reason (as we shall see in section 3.2) need not imply inequality. Hence, if Y is money income:

Third step: equal opportunity exists if

$$E(Y \mid T_i) = K_i \text{ for all } D_i \tag{6.18}$$

Equation (6.18) requires explanation. Some characteristics may affect money income without causing inequality; these include age, and any differences in individual choice which are the result of differences in tastes, and so are referred to as T (taste) characteristics. But if money income varies systematically with other characteristics (social class, race, sex, parental money income), we would regard society as unequal. These are the D (discrimination) characteristics. Equation (6.18) states that equality of opportunity exists if the expected value of money income is the same for all individuals with given T characteristics, but must be invariant to their D characteristics.

At first glance equation (6.18) seems to offer a workable (and possibly even a measurable) definition of equality of opportunity. But it contains two strategic difficulties concerning (a) the definition of *Y*, and (b) the distinction between the *T* and *D* characteristics. The use of money income as an indicator of welfare raises problems even if we control for age and tastes. There are two difficulties. First, equality of opportunity must apply both to cash income and to income in kind. We have seen that Le Grand distinguishes various definitions of equality (of public expenditure, of use, of cost and of outcome); each has a claim as a definition of equality yet, when discussing distribution in kind, each can be different. Equation (6.18) is no longer unambiguous. Second, defining inequality narrowly in terms of material well-being conceals its social and political dimensions (Runciman, 1972, Ch. 3). These aspects can be analysed in economic terms as violations of the perfect information and equal power assumptions (Chapter 4:3.2), but they stand in their own right as independent sources of inequality.

Even if full income were measurable, there would remain the problem of distinguishing a *T* from a *D* characteristic. There is general agreement that social class, race and sex are *D* characteristics; and it can be argued that laziness or a long time horizon are *T* characteristics. But what about 'natural ability'? If ability is entirely exogenous (i.e. 'innate') one might argue that differences in ability are the luck of the draw, giving rise to the stochastic element of *Y*. Society might choose to take no action where people do well out of their gifts (e.g. the state does not confiscate the high incomes of musicians or athletes), but may compensate those who have done badly (e.g. someone born with a congenital health problem). A completely different case arises if ability is at least partly endogenous, e.g. induced by differences in the quality of education. Ability is then in part a *D* characteristic, and positive discrimination might be justified.

Thus people can be unequal for two entirely different reasons. Where incomes differ because of discrimination, one can argue that society is unfair, and appropriate remedial action might involve trying to change the structure of society (see the quote by Tawney at the head of the chapter). In contrast, inequality of money income can arise purely because of random differences in people's luck (i.e. 'life' can be unfair). This is captured by the stochastic element in equation (6.18). Bad luck may require remedial action, but does not imply that society is unfair.

The last word should go to Okun (1975, p. 76, reprinted in Atkinson, 1980), who summarises the problem with customary eloquence and a plea for action.

The concept of equality of opportunity is far more elusive than that of equality of income ... [It] is rooted in the notion of a fair race where people are even at the starting line. But ... it is hard to find the starting line. Differences in natural abilities are generally accepted as relevant characteristics that are being tested in the race rather than as unfair headstarts and handicaps. At the other extreme, success that depends on whom you know rather than what you know is a clear case of inequality of opportunity. And it seems particularly unfair when the real issue is whom your father knows.

The inheritance of natural abilities is on one side of the line of unequal opportunity, and the advantages of a family position are clearly on the other. But much of the territory is unsettled.

3.2 Measuring Inequality Between Individuals

Inequality between individuals is best approached by considering A and B, with money incomes of £20,000 and £10,000, respectively, and asking why they might in fact be *equal*. There are three reasons why differences in money income might have no bearing on an individual's opportunity set, and so be irrelevant to issues of equality.

Different choices can cause differences in money incomes in two ways. A and B have *different tastes about money income* if they have different leisure preferences. Suppose A likes champagne and foreign travel, and B likes walking across the hills with his dog. A (with money-intensive consumption preferences) might choose to work longer hours; and B might work fewer hours (i.e. enjoy more leisure) and/or choose work with more job satisfaction (i.e. higher non-money income). Both A and B are maximising their utility, and there is no case for regarding them as unequal simply because one has higher money income. Second, there can be *differences in acquired skills*: suppose A has chosen to forgo income early in life in order to acquire skills, while B has not. A's higher income is a return to his investment in human capital. Again there is no reason to suppose that there is any inequality provided (and the proviso is crucial) that A and B had the *same opportunity*, including access to information, to acquire skills (for further discussion, see Le Grand, 1984).

Age   Suppose A earns twice as much as B because he is 40 years old and highly skilled, whereas B is 20 years old and an apprentice. Suppose, further, that when B is 40 he will earn as much as A does now. In this case, the difference in money income is simply a life-cycle effect, and no long-term issue of inequality arises.[17]

The time dimension   If A and B have fluctuating incomes, A might earn

---

[17] The need to control for age is particularly important in analysing the distribution of wealth. Consider an equal society, in which everyone has identical earnings, of which 5 per cent are saved to finance his/her retirement. The resulting wealth distribution would be highly unequal, since young people would have no wealth (because they had not yet started to save); people aged 98 would have very little wealth (because they had spent all their savings); and people aged 64 would have substantial wealth (because they had been saving all their working lives and had yet to start dissaving).

£20,000 and B £10,000 this year, with the positions reversed next year. Taking the two years together, there is no inequality. More generally, inequality is greater if it is perpetuated across generations, i.e. if a rich person systematically has rich descendants and a poor person poor ones (see the Further Reading).

It is possible also to ask the question in reverse. Suppose A and B each has money income of £15,000. That does not necessarily mean that they are equal. They might face different price levels; more importantly, A might have a larger family than B and so, it might be argued, has a lower standard of living. This raises issues of how to compare families of different sizes.

The conclusion is that money income is a misleading indicator of inequality. *This does not imply that there is no inequality in society – just that money income is bad at measuring it.*

3.3 Measuring Inequality Between Families

If it is not possible to compare the living standards of two individuals, we are likely to make even less headway with families of different sizes. Families with the same standard of living are said to have 'equivalent' incomes, from which can be derived equivalence scales which say, for instance, that a family consisting of a man, woman and two children has an 'adult equivalent' of 2.5, i.e. the family needs 2.5 times the income of a single person to have an 'equivalent' standard of living. Putting the issue a different way, suppose A has a money income of £10,000 and is married; if he and his wife then have a child, what increase in their money income is necessary to leave them as well-off as before?

The problem inherent in the question is illustrated by the following two arguments. The *per capita money income argument* states that if a couple has a child, then per capita income in the household falls, and the couple will need a higher money income to maintain their standard of living. The *utility argument*, along revealed preference lines, asserts that a couple will have a child by choice only if it raises their utility; thus where two people with perfect information (admittedly a strong assumption) have a child by choice, their utility is increased, and they can maintain a given standard of living with a *lower* money income.[18]

It follows that the question as posed (i.e. if a couple have a child, by how much must their money income be increased to leave them as well-off as before?) implies an assumption that parents' living standards depend only on their consumption level, ruling out the possibility that they might derive utility from the child. This should be borne in mind when considering the

---

[18] Some couples are prepared to pay large amounts to adoption agencies or for medical treatment to cure infertility.

conventional analysis of adult equivalents, typified by McClements (1977 and 1978, Ch. 3), which accepts this stringent assumption rather uncritically.[19]

Figure 6.2, taken from McClements (1978, p. 47), illustrates the conventional approach. Consider two couples, A (with one child) and B (with no child) under the following assumptions:

1. Each family consumes two commodities, food and housing.

2. A child eats 50 per cent of the food eaten by a couple but needs no more housing (this is unrealistic but highlights the analysis).

3. Utility depends *only* on the consumption of food and housing (as we have seen, this is a highly restrictive assumption).

4. If a couple have a child, their indifference map does not change; hence neither does their consumption pattern except in response to a change in relative prices (this is another restrictive assumption).

Figure 6.2 *The cost of maintaining an 'equivalent' standard of living for different families*

Childless couple B face the budget constraint Y_0-Y_0 with the unbroken indifference curve, and maximise utility at point a (F_1, H_1). Because of assumption 2, at the same level of housing, H_1, couple A with one child

---

[19] For a simple introduction, see Atkinson (1983a, Ch. 3.3). The literature on adult equivalents is large – see the Further Reading.

need F_3 ($= 1.5F_1$) of food to achieve the same standard of living as couple B. This is shown by point b (F_3, H_1) on the dotted indifference curve. With the given relative prices couple A can reach the living standard shown by this indifference curve at point c, at a lower cost than at b.

Given the earlier assumptions, the following incomes are equivalent:

Couple B (childless): $Y^B = P_F F_1 + P_H H_1$

Couple A: $Y^A = P_F F_2 + P_H H_2$ (6.19)

                              $< 1.5 P_F F_1 + P_H H_1$

where Y^A and Y^B are the money incomes of couples A and B, respectively, and P_H and P_F the prices of housing and food. It is not necessary to compensate a couple fully for the extra food consumed by their child because, under the stated assumptions, raising food standards for the couple with a child costs 1.5 times as much as a similar increase for the childless couple, whereas a given increase in housing standards costs the same for each couple. This is equivalent to a 50 per cent increase in food prices for the couple with a child, and leads to a substitution of (now relatively cheaper) housing.

These conclusions rest crucially on two assumptions: not only the minor assumption that a child will eat half as much as a couple but, more importantly, the assumption that the couple derives no utility from the child and does not change its consumption pattern. The first requires that the indifference curve for the couple with a child must lie outside that for the childless couple to maintain a given standard of living, and the second constrains the movement to a 50 per cent vertical upward shift. The two assumptions together ensure that the equivalent money income will always be higher for the couple with a child. This might be realistic for a low-income family; but the utility argument might well be more plausible for families well above the poverty line.

4 Inequality 2: Aggregate Measures

4.1 The Descriptive Approach

This section discusses the measurement of inequality in society as a whole, starting with simple representations of the income distribution, and proceeding to more complex measures and a brief review of empirical studies. The aim is to construct a scalar representation of income differences within a given population. Ideally it would take on values between zero (if everyone had the same income) and one (if one person had all the income). This would enable us to answer questions like: how much inequality is there in Britain today; is it less than ten years ago; is it less than in the USA? Any such overall measure of inequality rests on two ingredients:

● What is the unit defined to be equal or unequal, e.g. the individual, family or household? Here we talk only of 'individuals' and abstract from issues of household size and definition.
● Inequality of what, e.g. income, wealth, power? The literature generally looks at 'income', which usually means money income.

An inequality measure combines knowledge of the 'incomes' of 'individuals', though we shall see that its usefulness is qualified both by conceptual difficulties and by measurement problems (e.g. the use of household money income).

The frequency distribution and associated measures   The simplest starting point is the *frequency distribution*, which shows the number of income recipients at each level of income. It can be represented as a continuous function as in Figure 6.1, or as a histogram. The frequency distribution has the advantage of being simple and easy to interpret, especially in the middle-income ranges. But it is weak at the tails; the left-hand tail should include negative incomes (e.g. business losses), and the right-hand tail has been severely truncated.

A simple yet dramatic way of representing the income distribution is *Pen's parade*,[20] in which each person (i.e. income recipient) marches past the onlooker. The parade takes an hour and each person's height corresponds to his/her pre-tax income (a person with average income having average height). This representation is vivid; it shows up the tails well; and we can see not only the distribution, but also who is where in it. It does not, however, lend itself readily to quantification.

Several measures of inequality based on the frequency distribution are discussed in detail by Sen (1973, Ch. 2) and Cowell (1977, Ch. 2). This section discusses only the most important. A natural way of trying to capture aggregate inequality is by a summary measure of dispersion like the *variance*,

$$V = \frac{1}{n} \sum_{i=1}^{n} (y_i - \mu)^2 \qquad (6.20)$$

where y_i is the money income of the ith individual and μ is average income, and where there are n income recipients. The advantage of the variance is that it considers the whole distribution, and that measured inequality is reduced by any redistribution which brings an individual's income closer to the mean. Its main disadvantage is its sensitivity to the absolute level of income; if all incomes double (or are expressed in dollars at an exchange rate of $2 = £1$), inequality does not change but V quadruples.

[20] See Pen (1971), reprinted in Atkinson (1980, pp. 47–55) for an entertaining and non-technical description of the income distribution.

This problem is avoided by the *coefficient of variation* defined as

$$C = \frac{V^{0.5}}{\mu} \qquad (6.21)$$

which is the variance normalised on average income. The advantage of C is its independence of scale. But it has a number of difficulties, not least that it is neutral to the income level at which transfers take place, i.e. transferring £100 from an individual with an income of £1,000 to one with an income of £500 has the same effect on C as a £100 transfer from a person with an income of £1 million to one with £999,500.

If we want to give greater weight to transfers to lower incomes, one procedure is to take some transformation such as the logarithm which staggers income levels. The *variance of the logarithm of income* has the added advantage of scale independence (if income, say, doubles, this simply adds a constant to all logarithms of income, which cancel when calculating deviations from the mean). For this reason the variance of the logarithm of income

$$H = \frac{1}{n} \sum_{i=1}^{n} (\log y_i - \log \mu)^2 = \frac{1}{n} \sum_{i=1}^{n} \log \left(\frac{y_i}{\mu} \right)^2 \qquad (6.22)$$

has often been proposed as an inequality measure. H has the advantages that it is invariant to the absolute level of income, is sensitive to income transfers at all income levels, but gives greater weight to transfers to lower incomes. There are also disadvantages. The measure (in common with V and C) considers only differences of income from the mean; and it squares those differences. Both procedures are somewhat arbitrary. In addition, the logarithmic transformation increasingly contracts higher incomes so that, as a measure of social welfare, H may not be concave at higher income levels, i.e. H can rise in the face of some transfers from rich to poor.[21]

The Lorenz curve was devised explicitly as a representation of inequality. Though the approach is old (Lorenz, 1905), it is a powerful device, intimately connected with an important theorem by Atkinson discussed in section 4.2. In Figure 6.3 the horizontal axis shows the percentage of income recipients (individuals or households), the vertical axis the share of total income. The Lorenz curve is shown by the line OaB. Each point shows the share of total income received by the *lowest x* per cent of income recipients; thus point a shows that the bottom 40 per cent of individuals receive 17 per cent of income.

It should be clear that the Lorenz curve will coincide with the diagonal O-B if income is distributed completely equally (because only then will the lowest 50 per cent of individuals receive 50 per cent of total income, and

---

[21] Concavity and other properties of social welfare functions are discussed in section 1.2.

so on); and the greater the degree of inequality, the further the curve will lie from the diagonal. If the Lorenz curve for the UK lies entirely inside that for the Netherlands (Figure 6.4A) we can say that income inequality is lower in the UK; but where the curves cross (Figure 6.4B) an ambiguity arises. Lorenz curves thus give only a partial ordering of outcomes.[22]

Figure 6.3 *The Lorenz curve*

The Gini coefficient is based on the Lorenz curve; diagrammatically it is the ratio of the shaded area in Figure 6.3 to the triangle *OAB*. If incomes are distributed completely equally it will be zero; and if one person has all the income it will be unity. Formally, the Gini coefficient is defined as half of the arithmetic average of the absolute differences between *all* pairs of incomes, the total then being normalised on mean income:

[22] For an interesting attempt at least partly to resolve the ambiguity, see Shorrocks (1983). He constructs a 'generalised Lorenz curve' by scaling up the conventional Lorenz curve by the mean of the income distribution. While the measure is often successful at resolving ambiguity, it does so only because of strong assumptions about the weight given to absolute living standards. Weakening these assumptions greatly reduces the ambiguity-resolving power of the construct.

$$G = \frac{1}{2n^2\mu} \sum_{i=1}^{n} \sum_{j=1}^{n} |y^i - y^j| \qquad (6.23)$$

This can also be written (Sen, 1973, p. 31) as

$$G = 1 + \frac{1}{n} - \frac{2}{n^2\mu}(y^1 + 2y^2 + \ldots + ny^n) \qquad (6.24)$$

for $y^1 \geqslant y^2 \geqslant \ldots \geqslant y^n$

Figure 6.4 A and B *Lorenz curves for the UK, the Netherlands and West Germany* (Source: Atkinson (1970), non-mathematical summary in Atkinson (1980, p. 41).)

The Gini coefficient has several advantages. It is independent of the absolute level of income (like C and H); it avoids the arbitrary squaring procedure of V, C and H; and it compares each income not with the mean (like V, C and H), but with each other income, as equation (6.23) makes clear. Its disadvantages are twofold. It gives ambiguous results when comparing distributions for which the Lorenz curves cross. The second disadvantage is more subtle, and we return to it later. Formulation (6.24) shows that the Gini coefficient is a weighted sum of people's incomes, with the weights determined solely by the person's *rank-order* in the distribution. Thus y^1 (the highest income) enters the term in brackets with a relative weight of 1, y^2 (the second highest income) with a relative weight of 2, and so on. This is an entirely arbitrary social welfare function.

General critique of the descriptive measures To set the scene for subsequent discussion, it is helpful to bring out four sets of criticisms which apply to all the descriptive measures.

1. They lack generality. V, C and H all incorporate the arbitrary procedures of squaring differences from the mean.

2. They all incorporate an *implicit* and *arbitrary* social welfare function

with built-in welfare weights. With V and C a given transfer from a relatively higher to a relatively lower income always has the same effect; the implied social welfare function values all reductions in inequality equally, even if redistribution is from a millionaire to a semi-millionaire. For H the implied social welfare function embodies weights derived from the logarithm function, which again might not be one's chosen weights. The social welfare function underlying the Gini coefficient, as equation (6.24) shows, embraces weights based on rank-order.

3. At best the descriptive measures give only a partial ordering of outcomes. This is obviously true of intersecting Lorenz curves and hence of the Gini coefficient. The same problem arises with the other measures.[23]

4. In addition to these conceptual difficulties, all the measurement problems discussed earlier apply to measures of inequality as much as to measures of poverty.

4.2 Explicitly Normative Inequality Measures

Normative measures start explicitly from a social welfare function. This section discusses an important theorem by Atkinson, its implications, and the Atkinson inequality measure and its interpretation.[24]

The Atkinson theorem on Lorenz ranking is remarkable for its generality.[25] Assume:

1. States A and B have income distributions given by $(y^{1A}, y^{2A}, \ldots, y^{nA})$ and $(y^{1B}, y^{2B}, \ldots, y^{nB})$, respectively.

2. Total income is the same in states A and B.

3. W is a social welfare function which is non-decreasing, symmetric, additive and concave (see section 1.2).

Then: the Lorenz curve for B lies wholly inside the Lorenz curve for A *if and only if* $W_B > W_A$ for *every* social welfare function with the four properties listed in assumption 3.

To amplify, the theorem tells us:

1. If the Lorenz curve for B lies wholly inside that for A, then: (a) welfare in state B is higher than in state A; we can say this *without knowing what the social welfare function is*; (b) the income distribution is unambiguously more equal in state B; (c) the Gini coefficient compares distributions unambiguously; and (d) all the conventional summary measures (e.g. V, C and H) give the same result.

---

[23] For trenchant criticism of virtually all summary measures, see Wiles (1974, especially pp. 7–12). He advocates the semi-decile ratio (i.e. the ratio of the average income of someone in the top 5 per cent of incomes to the corresponding average for the lowest 5 per cent) as the least bad summary statistic.

[24] Other approaches, by Dalton (1920) and Theil (1967) are discussed by Sen (1973, Ch. 2) and Cowell (1977, Ch. 3).

[25] For a simple introduction, see Atkinson (1983a, pp. 54–9). See also the Further Reading.

2. Conversely, if social welfare is higher in state B, then we know that Lorenz curve B must lie strictly inside Lorenz curve A.

3. As a corollary, if Lorenz curves cross: (a) we cannot say whether inequality is greater in state A or B; (b) the Gini coefficient gives an ambiguous comparison; and (c) different inequality measures give different results.

These conclusions link the (descriptive) Lorenz curve to the explicitly normative world of the social welfare function. But the result is still not sufficient, both because not all Lorenz curves are non-intersecting, and because we still want a *numerical* measure of inequality. Atkinson approaches the issue by considering the Lorenz curves in Figure 6.4. The theorem enables us to say unambiguously that the distribution of income is less unequal in the UK than in the Netherlands. Figure 6.4B shows that the share of lower incomes is higher in West Germany than in the UK, but at higher incomes there is less inequality in the UK. By inspection, the area between the Lorenz curve and the diagonal is greater for West Germany than the UK, so that the Gini coefficient will show that the UK is *less* unequal than West Germany. But a measure which gives greater weight to lower incomes will show that the UK is *more* unequal.

Atkinson draws two major conclusions:

1. Where Lorenz curves cross it is necessary to compare one income group with another. Thus the degree of inequality cannot in general be compared without introducing values about the distribution, in the form of welfare weights for different income levels. This should be done *explicitly* via a social welfare function, in contrast with descriptive measures, which all embody implicit but unstated weights.

2. Only where Lorenz curves do not intersect is it possible (subject to assumption 3 of the theorem) to avoid the necessity of explicit welfare weights; in this case all the descriptive measures will agree.

The Atkinson inequality measure considers distributional values explicitly. It is based on a social welfare function with the five properties discussed in section 1.2, i.e. non-decreasing, symmetric, additive, concave and with constant relative inequality aversion, ε, as in equation (6.10), as an explicit representation of distributional values. The Atkinson measure is given by

$$A = 1 - \left[\sum_{i=1}^{n} \left(\frac{y^i}{\mu} \right)^{1-\varepsilon} f(y^i) \right]^{1/(1-\varepsilon)} \qquad \varepsilon \neq 1 \qquad (6.25)$$

where y^i is the income of individuals in the ith income range (N ranges altogether), $f(y^i)$ is the proportion of the population with incomes in the ith range, and μ is mean income. A will be zero *either* if $y^i = \mu$ for all i (i.e. if income is equally distributed), *or* if $\varepsilon = 0$ (i.e. if policy is concerned only with the absolute level of income, not its distribution). The greater the deviation of y^i from μ and/or the higher the value of ε the greater the value of A.

There is a natural connection between ε and the theories of society discussed in Chapter 3. If $\varepsilon = 0$ society is indifferent to inequality, and A is zero. If $\varepsilon = \infty$ society is concerned only with the position of the lowest individual or income group, as advocated by Rawls. Socialists, too, would choose a high value. Utilitarians set no *a priori* limits, but choose the value which maximises total welfare. In general the place of ε between the two extremes determines the importance of redistribution from richer to poorer. It should be clear from equation (6.25) that the deviation of y^i from μ is weighted by the exponent $(1 - \varepsilon)$, rather than the arbitrary squaring formula of V, C and H.

The meaning of ε is shown by Atkinson's 'mental experiment', subsequently elaborated as Okun's 'leaky bucket'. Consider taking £100 from a rich man and giving a proportion £x to a poor man, the rest leaking away in efficiency losses (disincentives, administration). How far can x fall (i.e. how leaky can the bucket be) before we no longer regard the redistribution as desirable? The answer determines ε.[26] The higher is ε, the lower x can be (i.e. the more egalitarian the view, the more 'leakiness' is tolerable): if $\varepsilon = 1$ it is fair to take £100 from a rich person and give £50 to a poor person; if $\varepsilon = 2$ it is sufficient if the poor man receives £25.

The Atkinson measure can be interpreted both as an inequality measure *and* as an index of the potential welfare gains from redistribution. Consider the proportion of present total income necessary to achieve the same level of welfare if it were equally distributed. If $A = 0.3$, we can say that if income were equally distributed we should need only $100\% - 30\% = 70\%$ of present national income to achieve the same level of social welfare. Alternatively, the gain from redistributing to equality is equivalent to raising national income by 30 per cent. The welfare gain is higher (a) the greater the value of ε, and (b) the more unequal the pre-existing distribution.

Table 6.2 *Values of the Atkinson inequality measure for the UK, the Netherlands and West Germany*

Value of ε	UK	Netherlands	West Germany
0.5	0.12	0.15	0.17
1.0	0.24	0.29	0.29
1.5	0.34	0.42	0.38
2.0	0.43	0.52	0.45
3.0	0.55	0.66	0.54

Source: Atkinson (1970), non-mathematical summary in Atkinson (1980, p. 42).

[26] ε is determined from the formula $1/x = 2\varepsilon$; see Atkinson (1983a, p. 58).

Table 6.2 (taken from Atkinson, 1970) shows the value of A for the UK, the Netherlands and West Germany. Measured inequality is greater the higher is ε; consequently the welfare gains from redistribution to complete equality in the UK rise from 12 per cent of national income when $\varepsilon = 0.5$ to 43 per cent when $\varepsilon = 2$. The table also shows that inequality in the Netherlands is unambiguously greater than in the UK for all values of ε, as shown by the non-intersecting Lorenz curves in Figure 6.4A. West Germany is more unequal than the UK for $\varepsilon < 3$; but when inequality aversion is high, West Germany is less unequal because of its greater equality at lower incomes.

The Atkinson measure thus has powerful advantages. Conventional measures like the Gini coefficient obscure the fact that a complete ranking of states is possible only where the form of the social welfare function is specified, and the social welfare functions implicit in conventional measures are often arbitrary, if not unacceptable. The Atkinson measure avoids both difficulties – a complete ranking of states is possible, though precise knowledge of the social welfare function is unnecessary.

The main criticism of the measure is not operational but philosophical, namely its basis on an additive, individualistic social welfare function, i.e. on the assumption that social welfare is a (more or less) simple sum of individual utilities. Writers like Sen (1973, pp. 47–53, and 1979) criticise this feature, and argue that the social valuation of the welfare of individuals should allow for the sort of welfare interdependence discussed in Chapter 4:4.1.

4.3 Inequality: Some Empirical Results

Problems with empirical work on the distribution of income are ubiquitous.

1. Virtually all studies are based on the current money income of households or tax units. This procedure raises serious difficulties for all inequality measures:
   (a) It fails to include non-money income (section 1.1) and is therefore inherently a poor measure of individual opportunity sets. Additionally, cross-country comparisons may omit certain dimensions of inequality, e.g. differences in political freedom.
   (b) It fails to exclude differences in money income which have no bearing on inequality, e.g. life-cycle factors and individual choice (section 3.2).
   (c) Adjustments for differences in the size and composition of different households, where they are attempted at all, face the problems described in section 3.3.

2. Summary measures of inequality raise the following conceptual problems:

(a) Conventional measures are subject to the criticisms set out at the end of section 4.1.
(b) The Atkinson measure is based on the assumption of additivity.
(c) Trends over time need to be interpreted in the light of structural change. For example, an increase in the size of a poor group, e.g. students or old people, will appear to increase inequality even though the position of each student or pensioner is unchanged.
3. Data problems:
(a) Information on income by type or level of income, or type of recipient, might be scant.
(b) The definition of income might change over time, or be incompatible with those of other countries.
(c) Estimation is generally based on income classes, and so neglects dispersion within each class; the use of more disaggregated data generally increases measured inequality.

Empirical evidence   The absence of any definitive measure of inequality does not mean (nor should it) that empirical work is useless, merely that it should be interpreted with all the earlier caveats in mind. Soltow (1968), in a study of long-run changes in the UK, drew Lorenz curves for 1688, 1801–3 and 1867, which showed that inequality decreased for lower incomes, but increased for higher incomes. It follows that whether inequality increased or decreased depends on the relative weights attached to higher and lower incomes (the Gini coefficients for the three periods were 55 per cent, 56 per cent and 52 per cent, respectively). The Lorenz curve for 1962/3 was strictly inside the other three: the Gini coefficient was 34 per cent. From this and other evidence Soltow tentatively concluded that overall inequality did not change in the eighteenth and nineteenth centuries, that only since about the First World War has there been a decrease in inequality, and that the decrease since then has been substantial. These findings have not been without their critics (see the Further Reading).

The size distribution of money income in the UK in the 1960s was investigated by Nicholson (1974, pp. 78–82), and that for the post-war period as a whole by the Royal Commission on the Distribution of Income and Wealth (UK, 1979a, Ch. 2, reprinted in part in Atkinson, 1980, pp. 71–8). The Royal Commission found that between 1949 and 1977 the share of the top 1 per cent fell from 6.4 per cent of after-tax income to 3.5 per cent, and of the top 10 per cent from 27.1 per cent to 22 per cent. But this was balanced by the increased share of the other groups in the top half of the distribution. As a result, the income share of the bottom 50 per cent rose very little, from 26.5 per cent to 27.6 per cent; and the top 10 per cent in 1976/7 received almost as much income after tax as the bottom 50 per cent. The impression of a decline in inequality is misleading. The fall in the Gini coefficient from 35.5 per cent in 1949 to 31.5 per cent in 1976/7 was mainly because of reduced inequality at the top of the distribution. Atkinson (1980, p. 45) sounds yet another warning about summary measures; the Gini coefficient fell from 35.5 per cent in 1949 to 33.9 per cent in 1970/1, but the share of the bottom 50 per cent *fell* slightly from 26.5 per cent to 26.1 per cent (on the same problem see Wiles, 1974, pp. 7–12).

Inequality can occur also through access to goods in kind, as we saw in section 3.1. Le Grand (1982) analyses the use made by different income groups of health care, education and housing, and concludes that the UK institutions for alleviating inequality are less successful than is sometimes supposed. We return to this issue in greater detail in Chapter 7:4.2 and Chapters 12, 13 and 14.

The LIS data discussed in section 2.3 have also been used to estimate inequality across countries (Buhmann *et al.*, 1988; O'Higgins *et al.*, 1990). Equality was higher in Sweden and Germany, and lower in Australia and the USA. Different assumptions and different inequality measures sometimes give different results, but one result was invariant: Sweden had the most equal post-tax-and-transfer distribution, and the USA the least equal. That result owes more to the redistributive nature of the Swedish tax/transfer system than to the distribution of pre-transfer earnings: in Sweden and Germany the lowest quintile received net transfers equal to some 10 per cent of GDP, more than twice the transfer in the USA.

Problems are even more complex in countries like those in central and eastern Europe where prices were often not market prices (e.g. subsidised food), and much income was received in kind (e.g. free holidays). An attempt at least partially to navigate these shoals can be found in Wiles (1974).

Empirical studies of the distribution of wealth (see the Further Reading) also face serious difficulties. Some are conceptual, e.g. what should be included in personal wealth. Others are measurement problems, e.g. the valuation of estates at death. Many are problems of both concept and measurement, e.g. whether accrued pension rights should be included as part of personal wealth and, if so, how they should be valued; or how the distribution of estates at death might be grossed up to give a picture of the wealth holdings of the living.

Further Reading

For an overview of the problems of defining and measuring income, poverty and inequality, see Atkinson (1983a) (compendious and non-mathematical) and Sen (1992); and for wide-ranging collections of recent contributions, Atkinson (1980, 1989).

The classic works on defining and measuring income are Fisher (1930, pp. 3–35), Simons (1938, pp. 41–58), Hicks (1946, pp. 171–81) and Kaldor (1955, pp. 54–78).

The classic historical studies of poverty are by Booth (1902) and Rowntree (1901); for follow-up studies see Rowntree (1941) and Rowntree and Lavers (1951); for an assessment, Briggs (1961b); and for reworking and updating, Atkinson *et al.* (1983). For more recent discussion of the definition and measurement of poverty, see Fiegehen and Lansley (1976), Fiegehen *et al.* (1977), Townsend (1979), Piachaud (1981) (a critique of Townsend), Sen (1983), Piachaud (1987) and Atkinson (1987b and 1989, Chs 1 and 2). Orshansky (1965) discusses the calculation of a poverty line for the USA.

For recent attempts to quantify poverty in the UK, see Beckerman (1979), Mack and Lansley (1985), and Atkinson (1989, Ch. 3); and for a review of evidence between 1974 and 1985, Barr and Coulter (1990). On the USA, see Danziger, Haveman and Plotnick (1984); Haveman (1987); Levy (1988); and Sawhill (1988). Atkinson (1991) reviews evidence in various OECD countries. For international comparison, see Smeeding *et al.* (1990).

The meaning of 'equality' is discussed by Okun (1975, Ch. 3) and Le Grand (1982, 1984, 1991a, Ch. 5). On the theory of the intergenerational transmission of inequality see Bowles (1973); Arrow (1971) examines the impact of job discrimination; more general aspects of the inheritance of inequality are discussed by Meade (1974), and in a US context by Brittain (1977, 1978) (the articles by Bowles, Arrow and Meade are reprinted in Atkinson (1980)). For a simple introduction to the literature on adult equivalents, see Atkinson (1983a, Ch. 3), and McClements (1978, Ch. 3). For further detail, see Muellbauer (1977, 1979, 1980). A study based on US data is given in Lazear and Michael (1980). The literature is surveyed by Nicholson (1976) and Deaton and Muellbauer (1980).

Aggregate inequality is illuminated in Pen (1971) (reprinted in Atkinson, 1980), and discussed more generally by Atkinson (1983b). Sen (1973, Ch. 2) and Cowell (1977, Ch. 2) discuss aggregate inequality measures (the latter contains a useful introduction to social welfare functions). The classic article on the Atkinson inequality measure is Atkinson (1970), reprinted with a non-mathematical summary in Atkinson (1980, pp. 23–43) (for a simple introduction, see Atkinson (1983a, pp. 54–9)). For the 'leaky bucket' experiment, see Okun (1975, pp. 91–100) (another piece of vintage Okun to which the reader is warmly recommended); and for a witty and highly critical review of most inequality measures, Wiles (1974).

Lydall (1979) discusses the difficulties of empirical work. Empirical analysis of the UK income distribution over the long run is given by Soltow (1968) (for a critique, see Williamson (1980) and Lindert and Williamson (1982, 1983)). For international comparisons, see Buhmann *et al.* (1988) and O'Higgins *et al.* (1990).

Estimates of the distribution of wealth are given in Atkinson (1974), Atkinson and Harrison (1978), and Brittain (1978) (a study of the USA); Harrison (1979) looks at the distribution of wealth in ten countries.

Appendix: Non-Technical Summary of Chapter 6

1. Chapter 6 discusses problems which arise in defining and measuring the key concepts of income, poverty and inequality.

INCOME

2. The only theoretically sound definition of individual income (section 1.1) is **full income**, Y_F, which consists of money income, Y_M, plus all non-money income, Y_N (e.g. job satisfaction, the value of own production, and the enjoyment of leisure), i.e.

$$Y_F = Y_M + Y_N \tag{6.1}$$

The inclusion of non-money income, including the enjoyment of leisure, is crucial. Full income defined this way is a broad measure of an individual's *potential* consumption, i.e. of his power to consume goods (including leisure) if he so chooses. As such it is a form of generalised budget constraint.

3. The measurement of income (section 1.1) is bedevilled by several sets of problems. First, money income is used as a proxy for full income because it is not possible to measure most forms of non-money income. The fact that there is no systematic relation between Y_M and Y_N makes money income an unreliable yardstick of consumption opportunities, and therein lies the origin of many of the problems of defining and measuring poverty and inequality. A second difficulty concerns the definition of the unit whose income we are measuring, e.g. whom does the income unit include, and how should the incomes of families of different sizes be treated? Finally, over what time period should income be measured? The conclusion is that a theoretically sound definition of income faces intractable measurement problems.

POVERTY

4. In principle poverty should be defined in terms of full income. Its measurement therefore faces all the problems described in para. 3. But even if these were solved it would still be necessary to decide whether poverty, however measured, should be defined in absolute or relative terms (section 2.1). **Absolute poverty** means that a person's money income is too low to keep him alive and healthy. Early studies hoped in this way to measure poverty 'objectively', an approach now out of favour, at least in developed economies. **Relative poverty** implies that a person is poor if his/her standard

of living deviates substantially from the average of the society in which he lives, i.e. if he cannot participate in 'normal' life.

5. Poverty (in an absolute sense) and inequality are two entirely separate concepts (section 2.2). Absolute poverty relates to a standard of living below some benchmark, inequality to the *difference* between the incomes of poor and non-poor. The distinction is important because policies aimed at one might aggravate the other. It is therefore necessary to be clear whether poverty relief or inequality reduction is the major objective.

INEQUALITY

6. **Equality of opportunity** (section 3.1) would be hard to define even if full income could be measured. The main problem is to decide which causes of income differences reflect inequality. Systematic differences due to race, sex or social class are generally regarded as examples of inequality. But ambiguity can arise when differences are due to 'natural ability', depending on whether or not it is influenced by differences in the quality of education. Equality of opportunity does not, however, rule out random differences in income (i.e. luck).

7. These problems are compounded because in practice it is necessary to use money income as a proxy for individual welfare. Differences in money income can overstate inequality between individuals A and B for at least three reasons (section 3.2): they may have different tastes and hence have made different choices (e.g. about leisure); they may be at different stages in their life cycle (e.g. A fully trained, B an apprentice); and the difference in their incomes may be the result of random fluctuations. Other factors can understate inequality. None of this implies that there is no inequality in society – just that money income is bad at measuring it.

8. Further problems arise when comparing the incomes of families of different sizes (section 3.3). One argument is that if a couple has a child, per capita household income will fall; it follows that larger households need higher money income than smaller households to maintain an 'equivalent' standard of living. Alternatively, if a couple has a child by choice, it can be argued that, though per capita money income falls, the couple's *utility* rises because otherwise they would not have had the child. In the latter case a larger household does not necessarily need a higher money income to maintain a given living standard. Again, the problem arises because it is not possible to measure full income; and again there is no practical solution.

9. Section 4 discusses measures of the overall degree of inequality in society. These measures, to the extent that they are valid, enable us to compare inequality in Britain today with inequality ten years ago, or with inequality in the USA.

10. A widely used measure is the **Lorenz curve** (section 4.1). In Figure 6.3 the horizontal axis shows the percentage of individuals/households, the vertical axis the percentage of total income. The Lorenz curve is shown by the line *OaB*. Each point on the curve shows the share of total income received by the *lowest x* per cent of individuals. Thus point *a* shows that the bottom 40 per cent of individuals receive 17 per cent of income. If income is distributed completely equally, the Lorenz curve will coincide with the diagonal (i.e. the lowest 50 per cent of individuals receive 50 per cent of income, and so on). Thus the greater the degree of inequality, the further the Lorenz curve will be from the diagonal, and vice versa. The **Gini coefficient** is an inequality measure based on the Lorenz curve; diagrammatically it is the ratio of the shaded area in Figure 6.3 to the triangle *OAB*. It follows that the Gini coefficient will vary between zero (if income is distributed completely equally) and one (if one person has all the income).

11. The use of the Gini coefficient as a measure of inequality is subject to a variety of criticisms (section 4.3). First, it is based on the current money income of individuals or households: this omits all non-money income (paras 2 and 3); it fails to exclude differences in money income which have no bearing on inequality, e.g. life-cycle factors and individual choice (para. 7); and it faces difficulties over differences in household size (para. 8). Second, the data on money income are not always accurate, complete or consistent over time or across countries. Finally, the Gini coefficient raises a number of conceptual problems. These are discussed in section 4.2 together with the Atkinson inequality measure, which treats inequality in a more sophisticated way, and hence avoids some of the problems of the Gini coefficient.

12. The main message of paragraph 11 for non-technical readers is that the Gini coefficient, though widely used and useful in some circumstances, is in no way definitive as a measure of overall inequality.

Part 2
Cash Benefits

Chapter 7
Financing the Welfare State

Taxes, after all, are the dues that we pay for the privileges of membership in an organised society. [Franklin D. Roosevelt, 1936.]

Thrift should be the guiding principle in our government expenditure. [Mao Tse-tung, 1893–1976.]

1 The Structure of the UK Government Accounts

1.1 Conceptual Issues

This chapter discusses the finances of the welfare state, and is somewhat more institutional than the rest of the book. The subject is vast, and the account here is no more than a very brief summary of the ground covered in detail by Glennerster's (1992) companion volume. National insurance and other cash benefits are discussed in section 2, and the rest of the welfare state, mainly the National Health Service, education and housing, in section 3. Section 4 considers a number of important methodological issues. This section describes the structure of UK[1] government accounts, as a backdrop to which it is necessary to mention a number of conceptual points.

The boundaries of the public sector have to be established, *inter alia* between the government sector and public corporations, and between government on the one hand and companies and the personal sector on the other. The task is more complex than is apparent (Prest and Barr, 1985, Ch. 8). It is not possible to define such boundaries unambiguously; careful judgement is needed; and any definition, however carefully constructed, will be open to criticism.

Levels of government activity The most obvious distinction is between

---

[1] Hitherto the terms 'Britain' and 'the UK' have been used interchangeably. Henceforth (particularly when talking about statistical data) they will be used more precisely, viz. Britain (or Great Britain) consists of England, with Wales and Scotland (Act of Union with Scotland 1706). The United Kingdom (UK) is Great Britain and Northern Ireland (Act of Union with Ireland 1800; Government of Ireland Act 1920).

central and local government. For instance, total spending by central and local government is *not* the simple sum of their respective expenditures. Part of central expenditure is a grant to local authorities, which then forms part of local spending. In producing overall public-sector accounts it is necessary to avoid double counting, so that care is needed in Table 7.1 in showing central government grants to local authorities.

Government activity on current, capital and financial account   It is necessary to distinguish receipts on current account (mainly from taxes on income and expenditure); receipts on capital account (e.g. from capital taxation and the sale of capital assets); and financial receipts (mainly the revenue from government borrowing). Similar distinctions arise on the expenditure side.

Types of government expenditure   It is vital to distinguish absorption of goods and services from transfer payments. To illustrate, public spending on education comprises:

1. Absorption of goods and services, which includes (a) current expenditure (i.e. public consumption in the form of teachers' salaries, etc.); and (b) capital expenditure (i.e. public investment, such as the costs of building new schools).

2. Transfer payments, which include (a) current grants to the personal sector (e.g. student maintenance grants); and (b) capital grants to the private sector (e.g. contributions to the cost of university building).[2]

Chapter 4:3.1 set out the four generic forms of state intervention – regulation, finance, public production and income transfers. Government absorption of goods and services (as in 1 above) corresponds with public production. Transfer payments take two very different forms. The first is explicit transfers, as in 2 above, including all state cash benefits. Second there are:

Tax expenditures, i.e. implicit public expenditure in the form of tax reliefs. Cash assistance to help poor tenants with their rent is an explicit transfer, mortgage interest tax relief for owner-occupiers an implicit transfer. Both serve similar purposes, i.e. assisting with accommodation costs, and both ultimately make up part of private-sector spending. Tax relief for private pensions is similarly a form of transfer.[3] But tax expenditures do not appear in conventional public spending figures; and their distributional implications have been criticised. Both issues assume special relevance in the context of pensions (Chapter 9) and housing (Chapter 14) (for detailed discussion, see the Further Reading).

---

[2] These are transfer payments from the viewpoint of government because universities are regarded as part of the private sector.

[3] Though valuation problems may arise – see UK Board of Inland Revenue (1983).

1.2 Government Revenue and Expenditure

The revenue proposals of government are set out each year in the Budget, and more formally in the *Financial Statement and Budget Report* and the Finance Bill. The details of the central government accounts need no repetition here, save to note the long-standing principle of British public finance, that in general all central government revenues, whatever their source, are paid into the *Consolidated Fund*, from which all central government expenditure is made. The only major exception is the *National Insurance Fund*, discussed in section 2.2.

The income of a local authority derives from two main sources: grants from central government (i.e. from the Consolidated Fund), whose complexities lie well outside the scope of this book; and local taxation. For present purposes the most important aspect of local finance is the size of the central government grant (nearly four times local revenues in 1992/3), which raises major issues for the relationship between central and local government, particularly in the light of tight control by central government of the revenue-raising powers of local government (see the Further Reading).

Table 7.1 gives an overview of the income and expenditure of government. The three main blocks of revenue relate to central government, national insurance contributions and local government. Central government revenue in 1992/3 was £176.9 billion, mainly from current taxation. Taxes on income, administered by the Inland Revenue, raised £80.4 billion, nearly three-quarters from income tax, making it the largest single revenue source. Taxes on expenditure, mostly administered by Customs and Excise, raised £67.4 billion. In addition to tax revenues, central government also received £8 billion, *inter alia* from rents, dividends and interest.[4] National insurance contributions (£38.7 billion) are discussed in more detail in section 2.

Local government receipts were £14.2 billion, mainly from the community charge (the only tax levied by local authorities) of £8.4 billion.[5] Rents, mainly from local authority housing, and dividends and interest raised another £3.5 billion. In addition, there are central government grants (£54.8 billion in 1992/3). To avoid double counting, these intra-governmental transfers are omitted from the totals.

Total current and capital receipts were £229.8 billion, to which are added financial receipts (i.e. public-sector borrowing) of £28.7 billion, bringing the total revenue of all levels of government to £258.5 billion.

The spending proposals of government are set out each year in a series of departmental reviews (UK, 1992b, c, d, e, f, g, h, j) and debated by Parliament. There has been much discussion over the years about the

---

[4] This £8 billion does *not* include proceeds from the sale of assets, which appear as a negative item on the *expenditure* side in the government accounts; for criticism, see Barr (1986).

[5] Known colloquially as Poll Tax (for assessment, see Cullis *et al.* (1991), Smith (1991) and Wilson (1991)). The tax was highly controversial and was replaced by Council Tax in 1993.

Table 7.1 *Income and expenditure of central and local government, UK, 1992/93 (est.) (£ billion)*

REVENUE	(1)	(2)	(3)	(4)
CENTRAL GOVERNMENT				
Taxes on income				
Income tax	59.6			
Corporation tax	16.8			
Other	4.0			
		80.4		
Taxes on expenditure				
VAT	40.0			
Taxes on alcohol, tobacco and hydrocarbon oils	23.7			
Other	3.7			
		67.4		
National non-domestic rates, etc.		14.1		
Other taxes and royalties		7.8		
Total central government tax revenue			169.7	
Other central government revenue			7.2	
TOTAL CENTRAL GOVERNMENT REVENUE				176.9
NATIONAL INSURANCE CONTRIBUTIONS				38.7
LOCAL GOVERNMENT				
Community charge	8.4			
Rents, dividends and interest	3.5			
Other	2.3			
(Grants from central government)				
Current	(54.8)			
Capital	(7.1)			
TOTAL LOCAL GOVERNMENT REVENUE				14.2
TOTAL GENERAL GOVERNMENT RECEIPTS				229.8
GENERAL GOVERNMENT BORROWING REQUIREMENT				28.7
GENERAL GOVERNMENT RECEIPTS AND BORROWING				258.5

Sources: UK (1992a, Tables 1.2 and 6.7); and UK (1992j, Tables 3.1, 3.3, 5.5 and 5.11).
Notes: [a] Social security comprises expenditure on all contributory and non-contributory cash benefits.
[b] See Table 7.5 for a breakdown of this total.

EXPENDITURE	Central government	Central government transfers to local government	Total
	(1)	(2)	(3)
SPENDING BY PROGRAMME			
Defence	24.2	–	24.2
Social security[a]	66.0	4.6	70.6[b,c]
Health	27.9	0.2	28.1[d,e]
Education and science	4.9	3.1	8.0[f,e]
DOE – Housing	2.8	4.9	7.7[g,e]
DOE – Local government	0.3	30.8	31.1
Scotland	6.4	6.1	12.5
Wales	2.8	3.0	5.8
Northern Ireland	7.0	–	7.0
Other departments	26.5	5.7	32.2
Financing requirements of nationalised industries	3.4		3.4
Central privatisation proceeds	– 8.0	–	– 8.0
Reserve	4.0	–	4.0

PLANNING TOTAL	168.1	58.5	226.6
LOCAL GOVERNMENT OWN EXPENDITURE			9.5
CENTRAL GOVERNMENT DEBT INTEREST			17.6
NATIONAL ACCOUNTS ADJUSTMENTS			4.7
GENERAL GOVERNMENT EXPENDITURE			258.5

[c] Excludes expenditure in Northern Ireland.
[d] See Table 12.1 for a breakdown of this total.
[e] Excludes expenditure in Scotland, Wales and Northern Ireland.
[f] See Table 13.1 for a breakdown of this total.
[g] See Table 14.1 for a breakdown of this total.

planning of public spending and its control (see the Further Reading), in part because of the increased costs of the welfare state. The departmental reviews in their current format give a detailed breakdown of public spending,[6] and are the source of the expenditure side of Table 7.1 and many of the later tables.

The 1992/3 planning total for expenditure was £226.6 billion, £168 billion (74 per cent) by central government, to which must be added local government own expenditure (£9.5 billion), and £17.6 billion interest on the national debt. Total expenditure in national account terms was £258.5 billion. Much the largest programme was social security (£70.6 billion), mainly by central government, almost entirely on national insurance and other cash benefits.[7] Defence spending was £24.2 billion, and health £28.1 billion, also mainly by central government.[8] Spending under several of these heads was in reality somewhat higher, since expenditure on, for example, education in Scotland, Wales and Northern Ireland is included in the totals for those countries.

One point to emerge immediately is the sheer size of the welfare state, however defined (and it consists at a minimum of cash benefits, health, education and housing). In Table 7.2 these are divided into social services (approximating to the last three) and current grants to the personal sector (approximating cash payments). Figures are given also for defence and debt interest in current and constant prices in 1920, 1948 and 1992/3. There is always room for differences in judgement about the definition of the welfare state; and the price index is subject to the usual caveats; the figures should therefore be regarded as no more than indicative (for further discussion, see Heald, 1983, Ch. 2). Several broad results emerge:

1. The welfare state has assumed an increasing proportion of public spending; in 1920 it absorbed about 28 per cent of total government expenditure, only marginally greater than debt interest payments and about 1.75 times defence spending; the picture had not changed greatly by 1948; but by 1992/3 the welfare state made up nearly 60 per cent of public spending, nearly seven times defence spending.

2. Government spending doubled as a percentage of gross national product, from about 21 per cent in 1920 to nearly 41 per cent in 1992/3.

3. A consequence is the sharp increase in the welfare state as a percentage

---

[6] The departmental reviews, and their predecessors, the Public Expenditure White Papers, have been the subject of considerable criticism. Since 1980 planning has been in 'cash' terms, i.e. departments are allocated a specific sum, irrespective of subsequent price changes. This makes planning of expenditure easier, but creates great difficulties for *volume* planning (i.e. for resource allocation) – see Glennerster (1992, Ch. 4).

[7] As explained in the Glossary, there is an ambiguity in the use of the term 'social security'. In the USA it generally refers only to retirement benefits; in British usage it refers to *all* contributory and non-contributory cash benefits; in mainland Europe the term refers to all cash benefits and health care. The term will be avoided where possible. Where its use is inevitable it will be used in the British sense.

[8] Disaggregated figures are given in Tables 7.5 (cash benefits), 12.1 (health), 13.1 (education) and 14.1 (housing).

of gross national product, from under 6 per cent in 1920 to 10 per cent in 1948, and to 23.5 per cent in 1992/3.

4. In real terms (1948 prices), expenditure on the welfare state rose from £420 million in 1920 to £1,195 million in 1948 and to £8,374 million in 1992/3, representing a 15-fold increase since 1920, and a 7-fold real increase since 1948. The resulting expenditure, however, is still well below the European average as a proportion of national income (see Barr, 1992, Table 1).

2 Cash Benefits

2.1 Individual National Insurance Contributions

Current arrangements are the outcome of various changes since 1948 (Chapter 2:6). There are three types of contributor for national insurance purposes: employed persons, the self-employed and the non-employed, as summarised in Table 7.3.[9]

Employed persons Class 1 contributions are paid by both employee and employer. There is a *lower earnings limit* (£54 per week in 1992/3), which is set at about the level of the basic retirement pension (Chapter 9:1), and an *upper earnings limit* (£405 per week in 1992/3), which is set at about $7\frac{1}{2}$ times the lower earnings limit. The employee contribution is 9 per cent of earnings up to the upper earnings limit, with various exceptions: an individual with weekly earnings below the lower earnings limit paid a reduced rate of 2 per cent (Table 7.3); and individuals contracted out of the state earnings-related pension scheme (Chapter 9:1) paid contributions at a rate of 7 per cent.

A full contribution year requires a total contribution of at least that due on 52 times the lower earnings limit. An individual receiving unemployment benefit or sickness benefit, if he or she would otherwise fall below this minimum, is given a *credit*, i.e. no contribution is paid, but future benefits are awarded as though the appropriate percentage contribution had been made on earnings equal to the lower earnings limit. Formerly, a married woman could opt out of most of her contribution (thereby losing entitlement to most benefits), but this option is no longer available.

Unlike income tax and the other types of national insurance contribution, the income limit for Class 1 contributions is a *weekly* exemption. Thus, someone earning £53.50 in some weeks and £54.10 in others would pay contributions in weeks where earnings were £54.10, even if his average for the year was under £54. These contributions are not refundable, in sharp contrast with the operation of income tax in similar circumstances. Uneasy relationships like this have generated pressure for an integrated system of

[9] For compendious details of these institutions, see Tolley (1991, Ch. 3).

Table 7.2 *Gross national product and spending by central and local government, UK, 1920, 1948 and 1992/93*

Item	1920				1948				1992/93			
	£m current prices	£m 1948 prices	% of government spending	% of GNP	£m current prices	£m 1948 prices	% of government spending	% of GNP	£m current prices	£m 1948 prices	% of government spending	% of GNP
	(1)	(2)	(3)	(4)	(5)	(6)	(7)	(8)	(9)	(10)	(11)	(12)
Defence (military and civil)	186	234	16	3.3	743	743	19	6.3	24,200	1362	9	3.8
Social services (current expenditure on goods and services)	169	420	28	5.9	541	1195	31	10.1	75,900	8374	58	23.6
Current grants to the personal sector	165				654				72,900			
Debt interest	320	402	27	5.6	553	553	14	4.7	17,600	990	7	2.8
Total government current spending	1182	1485	100	20.8	3862	3862	100	32.6	258,500	14,547	100	41.0
GROSS NATIONAL PRODUCT (market prices)	5688	7146	—	100	11,837	11,837	—	100	631,000	35,509	—	100

Sources: Feinstein (1972, Tables 12, 13, 33, 35 and 61); *National Income and Expenditure* (1957, Tables 1, 36 and 39); *Monthly Digest of Statistics*, various issues; and Table 7.1.

Table 7.3 *National insurance contribution rates 1992/93*

CLASS 1 (employed earners)	Not contracted out (1)	Contracted out (2)
Employee contribution (on all earnings, where total weekly earnings are):		
First £54.00	2%	2%
£54.00–£405.00	9%	7%
Employer contribution		
£54.00–£89.00	4.6%	0.8%
£90.00–£134.99	6.6%	2.8%
£135.00–£189.99	8.6%	4.8%
£190.00–£405.00	10.4%	6.6%
Over £405.00	10.4%	6.6%

CLASS 2 (self-employed, flat-rate)	
Self-employed persons with profits in excess of £3030 per year	Flat-rate contribution of £5.35 per week

CLASS 3 (voluntary contributions by non-employed persons)	
Non-employed persons	Flat-rate contribution of £5.25 per week

CLASS 4 (self-employed, earnings-related)	
Self-employed persons with profits in excess of £4450 per year	6.3% of profits between £6120 and £21,060 per year[a]

Note: [a] Half of the Class 4 contribution is deductible for income tax purposes.

income tax and national insurance contributions (Chapter 11:3.2).

The basic employer Class 1 contribution in 1992/3 was 10.4 per cent of the employee's gross weekly earnings with no upper limit. For lower earnings the employer contribution was payable at a lower percentage rate (Table 7.3); and a lower contribution was payable in respect of contracted-out employees.

Both employee and employer Class 1 contributions are collected together with income tax. They help to pay for national insurance benefits; and part of the contribution is channelled to the National Health Service.

The self-employed pay both Class 2 and Class 4 contributions. The Class 2 contribution is flat-rate (£5.35 in 1992/3), paid in the form of a weekly stamp. Class 4 contributions are a percentage (6.3 per cent in 1992/3) of a self-employed person's profits between certain limits, collected by the Inland Revenue as part of the individual's income tax assessment. Half of the contribution is deductible for income tax purposes. Class 2 and 4 contributions do not entitle a self-employed person to the full range of benefits available to an employee. There is no unemployment benefit, no earnings-related retirement pension, and no entitlement to redundancy pay.

A person who is both employed and self-employed is potentially liable to pay Class 1, Class 2 and Class 4 contributions, subject to an annual ceiling on total contributions (see Tolley, 1991, Ch. 3).

The non-employed, broadly, are not current members of the labour force, e.g. students or married women who are not employed or self-employed. To maintain an unbroken contributions record, such a person is permitted (but not compelled) to pay a flat-rate Class 3 contribution (£5.25 per week in 1992/3).[10] The payment of Class 3 contributions gives no right to immediate benefit, but may protect future entitlement.

2.2 The National Insurance Fund

National insurance benefits are paid from the National Insurance Fund, and all other central government benefits from the Consolidated Fund. The distinction is important for operational purposes and for understanding the structure of government accounts, but has rather less economic significance.

Revenue   On the revenue side the relation between the two funds is straightforward. The income of the National Insurance Fund (Table 7.4) derives mainly from the contributions of the various classes of insured persons. Virtually all other central government revenues go into the Consolidated Fund. There used to be a transfer from the Consolidated Fund to the National Insurance Fund, a practice which has now ceased.

In 1992/3 total net contributions were £32.3 billion, the great bulk from Class 1 contributions. The interest item (£725 million in 1992/3) is earned on current revenue and on the accumulated surplus (nearly £9 billion at the start of 1992/3) shown at the bottom of the table. At various times there has been debate about the proper role of the Fund, though a surplus of some sort is desirable for a number of reasons: to bridge short-term imbalances (the end-year balance represents about twelve weeks' outgoings); to cushion a growing increase in contribution rates to finance pensions; and to assist with public-sector borrowing (which last aspect has drawn a certain amount of political fire). Whether the Fund should be organised on actuarial lines (i.e. have a reserve sufficient to pay all expected future liabilities) is a major topic in Chapter 9.

[10] An exception is a woman (or in certain circumstances a man) staying at home to look after young children; she is normally able to avoid breaks in her contributions record without paying Class 3 contributions because she receives home responsibility protection; see Chapter 9:1.

Table 7.4 *Account of the National Insurance Fund, Great Britain, 1992/93 (est.)* *(£ million)*

REVENUE AND EXPENDITURE		
REVENUE		
Total gross contributions	33,408	
Less employers' recoveries in respect of statutory sick pay and statutory maternity pay	1109	
Total net contributions		32,299
Interest receipts		725
Other[a]		1288
TOTAL REVENUE		34,312
EXPENDITURE		
Benefits		35,727
Transfer to Northern Ireland		190
Administration, etc.		1245
TOTAL EXPENDITURE		37,162
BALANCE OF FUND		
Balance at beginning of year		8990
Excess of receipts over payments		− 2850
Balance at end of year		6140

Source: UK (1991).
Note: [a] Includes £1092 million transfer from the Consolidated Fund in respect of statutory sick pay and statutory maternity pay.

Two general points should be noted. First (Table 7.1), total gross contributions in 1992/3 were £38.7 billion; hence revenue of the National Insurance Fund was nearly 22 per cent of central government revenue from all other sources, and larger than any other revenue source except income tax. In effect there is a third estate alongside the Inland Revenue and Customs and Excise. Second, this revenue does not go through the normal budgetary process of central government. Although administered by the Department of Social Security, the accounts of the National Insurance Fund are kept separate from the general accounts. Changes in the rates of contribution or benefit may be announced in Parliament separately from the Budget, and are debated on separate occasions (though national insurance has not been immune from attempts to contain public spending).

Expenditure On the expenditure side matters are less tidy. In principle benefits from the National Insurance Fund (e.g. for unemployment) are paid only to individuals with an appropriate contributions record, while similar benefits paid from the Consolidated Fund are awarded on the basis of other criteria, such as low income or number of children (e.g. child benefit). In practice, however, there are many linkages and interactions because many individuals receive benefits from both sources, so that it is often necessary to discuss them together.

Expenditure on cash benefits is set out in Table 7.5. Much the largest is the retirement pension (£27 billion in 1992/3, nearly three-quarters of all contributory benefits). This does not include pensions outside the scope of national insurance (listed in the second half of the table), such as war pensions and pensions for people who retired too soon after 1948 to be entitled to a national insurance pension. The remaining insurance benefits cover unemployment, sickness (i.e. relatively short-run health problems), invalidity (i.e. long-term and permanent health problems) and widowhood. Total spending on the insurance benefits was £36.6 billion.

Expenditure on non-contributory benefits in 1992/3 was £26 billion, of which nearly three-quarters was on income support (£13 billion) and child benefit (£6 billion). Income support is payable to individuals/families whose income after receipt of all other benefits is still below the poverty line; it thus constitutes the final 'safety net' on the cash side of the welfare state. Child benefit is a tax-free cash payment in respect of each child, payable weekly to (usually) the mother; an additional sum is payable to single parents. Both benefits are discussed in Chapter 10.

3 Benefits in Kind

This section surveys very briefly the finances of the National Health Service, of the state educational system, and of local authority housing (for details, see Glennerster (1992) and the Further Reading). As we shall see in Chapter 12, the original intention of the National Health Service that all health care should be free has largely been realised. Medical attention is generally free, with the exception of certain items (e.g. prescriptions) for which charges, generally below full cost, apply to some people. About 15 per cent of National Health Service expenditure is financed by national insurance contributions, and 4 per cent from the charges just mentioned (UK, 1992c, Figure 1). The remaining 80 per cent comes from general taxation. Table 7.1 shows that total spending in England in 1992/3 was £28.1 billion (for further detail see Table 12.1). The National Health Service, clearly, is not a contributory scheme, and any assessment of its finances must discuss the tax system as a whole (see section 4).

State education (discussed in Chapter 13) is supplied largely without charge. Historically it was both produced and financed locally. Table 7.1 shows that spending on education and related activities in England was £8 billion by central government, with considerable spending also by local

Table 7.5 *Cash benefits, UK, 1992/93 (est.) (£ million)*

CONTRIBUTORY BENEFITS (i.e. those paid from the National Insurance Fund)		
Retirement pensions (including lump-sum payments)	27,002	
Widows' benefit, etc.	1006	
Unemployment benefit	1455	
Sickness benefit	1010	
Invalidity benefit	5695	
Maternity allowance and statutory maternity pay	406	
Guardian's allowance	2	
		36,576
NON-CONTRIBUTORY BENEFITS (i.e. those paid from the Consolidated Fund)		
Non-contributory retirement pension	45	
War pensions	815	
Attendance allowance and invalid care allowance	1503	
Severe disablement allowance	636	
Mobility allowance	101	
Disability living and disability working allowance	2002	
Industrial injury benefit	677	
Income support	13,017	
Child benefit and one-parent benefit	5977	
Family credit	850	
Independent living fund and Motability	80	
Housing benefit	99	
Expenditure from the social fund	203	
		26,005
ADMINISTRATION		
Contributory benefits (including costs of collecting contributions)	1182	
Non-contributory benefits	2202	
		3384
TOTAL CENTRAL GOVERNMENT SPENDING		65,964
TOTAL CENTRAL GOVERNMENT GRANTS TO LOCAL AUTHORITIES		4590
TOTAL DEPARTMENT OF SOCIAL SECURITY		70,554
NORTHERN IRISH EXPENDITURE		2327
TOTAL SOCIAL SECURITY BENEFITS		72,881

Sources: UK (1992e, Table 1); UK (1992h, Table 1.1).

authorities (for further detail see Table 13.1). However, because of central government grants this implies that the greater part of educational finance derives indirectly from the Consolidated Fund. I shall abstract from most of the central versus local debates as they apply to education (and the

National Health Service and local authority housing) and discuss education for the most part as a non-contributory scheme financed from general taxation, and differing from the National Health Service only to the extent that there is a larger role for local government (see the Further Reading).

Table 7.1 shows that net expenditure on housing in England in 1992/3 was £7.7 billion, with substantial involvement by both central and local government (see Table 14.1 for further detail). This figure *understates* public involvement in housing: first, it is a net figure, and therefore excludes capital receipts from the sale of housing and land; second, it omits other forms of housing expenditure, e.g. housing benefit, which appear as part of spending on cash benefits; third, the tax relief for owner-occupiers, like all tax expenditures, is an invisible item in government accounts (they serve simply to reduce the revenue from income tax in Table 7.1). The importance of tax expenditures in any systematic analysis of public spending is emphasised by their scale. Mortgage interest tax relief in 1991/2 amounted to £6.1 billion (see Table 14.2), considerably more than total direct expenditure (and even larger if capital gains tax relief is included). Housing expenditure thus broadly defined is set out in Table 14.2.

In 1988 about 25 per cent of households lived in local authority housing (Hills, 1991, Table 1.2). For Britain as a whole, local authority rents never covered current housing costs, the shortfall (which declined in the 1980s) coming from local taxation and a central subsidy. Thus local authority housing is financed partly out of 'contributions' (i.e. rents), partly out of local taxation and partly from the Consolidated Fund. The system, which aroused considerable controversy over the years, is assessed in Chapter 14.

4 Assessing the Welfare State

4.1 Incidence Considerations

Assessing the efficiency and redistributive impacts of the welfare state is a vast undertaking which raises both methodological and measurement problems (see Atkinson and Stiglitz, 1980, Lecture 9), and one on which little more than a start has been made. This section limits itself to outlining some of the issues of principle, leaving more detailed discussion to later chapters. Two aspects assume special relevance: the notion of tax incidence; and the importance of considering benefits and taxes together.

The simple tax incidence argument is illustrated in Figure 7.1, which analyses the partial equilibrium incidence of a housing subsidy. Suppose the housing market is in equilibrium at price, P_0 and quantity, X_0. A specific rent subsidy shifts the supply curve vertically downwards to *S-subsidy*; this reduces the price paid by the tenant from P_0 to P_1 (i.e. only a small reduction), and increases the price received by the landlord substantially from P_0 to P_2. The result is that if landlords are rich and tenants poor (not that this is necessarily the case), then a seemingly redistributive housing subsidy might of itself be regressive. Similarly, suppose that labour is supplied inelastically to the market (empirically plausible for primary workers).[11] A reduction in income tax or the national insurance contribution can be analysed as a labour subsidy, and Figure 7.1 shows how the subsidy reduces unit wage costs to the employer from P_0 to P_1 (since P_1 is on the demand curve for labour), and increases the wage received by the employee from P_0 to P_2 (since P_2 is on the labour supply curve). In this case the tax reduction benefits mainly the employee. But the result is reversed where labour supply is elastic.

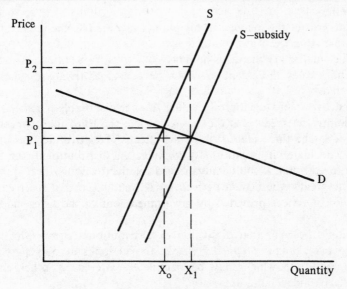

Figure 7.1 *Partial equilibrium incidence of a subsidy*

The general equilibrium incidence argument   However, to be sure of the efficiency of any policy or of its redistributive effects, it is necessary also to see how the *general* equilibrium of production, consumption and distribution is affected. There has been some work on applied general equilibrium analysis (see the Further Reading), though none yet on the impact of the welfare state.

The discussion of incidence concentrates on the effect, *ceteris paribus*, of tax/expenditure changes on the relative position of different income groups. The crucial words are *ceteris paribus* and the *relative* position of individuals

---

[11] The primary labour force consists of 'breadwinners', i.e. people who would normally be in the labour force full-time. It consists traditionally of men aged 18 to 65 and unmarried women aged 18 to 60. The secondary labour force consists of people who are not *necessarily* full-time members of the labour force, e.g. people under 18, people past retiring age and married women.

or groups (see Prest and Barr, 1985, pp. 101–5). The *ceteris paribus* condition is important because we are trying to separate the distributional effect of a given change in tax (or expenditure) from any other change in the system. This makes it necessary in principle to introduce a countervailing tax which (a) is distributionally neutral and (b) keeps the budget balance unchanged. It should be clear that this procedure is fraught with difficulty.

Assuming that this can be done by one means or another, the effect of a tax change on the relative position of different income groups will depend on several sets of factors. Suppose individual A sells factor m, which is used to make good x, and B sells factor n, which is used to make good y; and suppose that a tax change raises the relative price of x. Individual A is then better-off:

1. The greater the increase in his pre-tax income (i.e. the greater the rise in the relative price of m).
2. The smaller are the taxes he pays.
3. The greater the extent to which he consumes (relatively cheaper) y rather than x.

The first two items together determine A's net disposable income, and are often jointly referred to as the 'sources' side; the third item concerns the 'uses' side. The three factors show the effect on relative incomes of a tax change considered in isolation. To complete the distributional picture, it is crucial to add that A will be advantaged relative to B also:

4. The greater the benefit derived by A (relative to that received by B) from goods/services provided by government out of the taxes paid by A and B.

It should be clear that discussion of distributional effects which limits itself to tax changes *simpliciter* (i.e. 2 above) looks at only part of the picture, and one which may be completely altered by other changes, particularly under 3 and 4.

4.2 Redistribution: A Preliminary Discussion

The meaning of progressivity is illustrated by an individual's average tax rate, i.e. his tax bill as a proportion of his total income. A tax is progressive if the average rate is higher for someone with a higher income. Suppose that an individual can earn £3500 tax-free per year, and pays tax at a marginal rate of 25 per cent on anything above this. Someone earning £3500 pays no tax; someone earning £7,000 pays £825 ($12\frac{1}{2}$ per cent of his income); and someone with £15,000 pays £2875 in tax (19.2 per cent of his income). Thus the tax (which is a stylised version of the UK system) is progressive, even though most people face the same marginal rate of 25 per cent.[12]

---

[12] Whether the degree of progression is the *right* one is an entirely different question.

In assessing the progressivity of a tax it is necessary, in addition to its formal structure, to know the number of people affected, and also the extent to which the formal tax rates apply in practice. Thus a tax of 25 per cent on income up to £30,000 and 100 per cent thereafter may sound highly progressive, but if nobody has income in excess of £30,000 then in practice the tax is proportional. On the second point, a tax is less progressive than it appears if the highest rates are never applied, i.e. if tax avoidance or evasion[13] are proportionately more frequent at higher incomes.

Considering taxes and benefits together The discussion in section 4.1 suggests two implications. First, in assessing the finance of the welfare state it may be necessary to consider simultaneously a variety of taxes contributing to the Consolidated Fund, the National Insurance Fund and local revenues. Suppose a government tries to help the poor by increasing the employer national insurance contribution relative to the employee contribution. The discussion underlying Figure 7.1 suggests that it is of no analytical consequence whether a tax is imposed on the buyer or seller. In the case of national insurance, it is therefore (except in the very short term) the combined employer and employee contribution which matters; any attempt to increase one and reduce the other is little more than window dressing.

Second, it is frequently the *overall* system which is important. The issue is complex (see Prest (1968), Peacock and Shannon (1968), and the Further Reading), but for present purposes the crucial point is that taxation and expenditure should be considered together. At its simplest, a scheme which uses a proportional tax to subsidise mink coats will usually be regressive; the same tax used to finance poor relief is progressive.

In principle the logic is simple. Consider a commodity (e.g. health care) which is publicly supplied without charge, and financed by a specific contribution. This arrangement is redistributive from rich to poor *if (rich) individual A pays more in contributions than (poor) B, if each consumes the same quantity; it is also progressive if A consumes twice as much as B, but pays more than twice as much in contributions.*

In practice matters are more complicated because it is hard to identify precisely which contributions/taxes have paid for the commodity, i.e. which tax(es) would be reduced or abolished if it were no longer publicly supplied. It might be argued that health care is redistributive so long as A (who consumes twice as much as B) pays more than twice as much in taxes. But this implicitly assumes that health care is financed by a proportionate share of all taxes. The definition in the previous paragraph must therefore be qualified: health care is financed progressively if A consumes twice as much as B, but pays more than twice as much in whatever taxes are used to finance it.

---

[13] Tax avoidance is legal (e.g. reducing one's tax liability via a mortgage); tax evasion is illegal (e.g. concealing part of one's income).

Redistributive implications These various aspects must be borne in mind in considering the extent to which the welfare state is financed progressively. This is done for unemployment and sick pay in Chapter 8:3.2, for pensions in Chapter 9:5.2 and for the major non-contributory benefits in Chapter 10:3.4. It is concluded that these benefits all redistribute from rich to poor to a greater or lesser extent, particularly in recent years, when a variety of changes in contribution conditions have corrected earlier perverse redistributive effects. Cash benefits in 1986 reduced the Gini coefficient by about 11.5 per cent (Barr and Coulter, 1990, Table 7.11).

The redistributive effects of the National Health Service and the educational system are discussed in Chapters 12:4.3 and 13:4.3, and of local authority housing in Chapter 14:4. It was traditionally thought that all three systems redistributed from rich to poor, but Le Grand (1982) argues the contrary. The core of his argument is that though these benefits are financed progressively, in that the rich pay more towards them in taxes and contributions than the poor, they are used even more progressively so that the overall result can be regressive. For example, if the rich pay twice as much in taxes as the poor to finance education, but use it proportionately ten times as much, then it is not the rich who subsidise the poor, but the other way round. We return to these arguments in Chapters 12, 13 and 14.

Thus there is a limited presumption that at least the cash side of the welfare state is progressive. But any such view is rendered somewhat tentative by incidence considerations; by conceptual difficulties (e.g. the validity of the Gini coefficient); and by measurement and data problems.

Further Reading

Glennerster (1992) covers the ground of this chapter in much greater detail. For a historical perspective, see Peacock and Wiseman (1967).

Conceptual problems with government accounts are discussed in Prest and Barr (1985, Chs 8 and 9). On the concept and measurement of tax expenditures see McDaniel and Surrey (1984), Surrey and McDaniel (1985) and, in a UK context, Willis and Hardwick (1978).

For data on public spending, see *The Government's Expenditure Plans*, and for taxation the Financial Statement and Budget Report. For general data, see *National Income and Expenditure* (the 'Blue Book'). All are published annually by HMSO.

On the planning and control of public expenditure see Glennerster (1992, Ch. 4). More general issues of the growth of taxation and expenditure are discussed by Heald (1983).

The institutions of national insurance contributions (and other state benefits) are described in Tolley (1991), published annually. On the finances of the National Health Service, personal social services and education see Glennerster (1992, Chs 10, 11 and 12); and of housing, ibid., Ch. 13, and Hills (1991).

The theory of tax incidence is set out in Brown and Jackson (1990, Chs 11 and

12), Cullis and Jones (1992, Ch. 7), Musgrave and Musgrave (1989, Chs 14–16) and Stiglitz (1988, Ch. 17). For empirical studies, see Aaron and Pechman (1981) and Pechman (1985). The pioneering work on applied general equilibrium analysis is Harberger (1962); for later developments, see Piggott and Whalley (1985 and 1986).

For methodological discussion of the distribution of public expenditure, see Prest (1968), Peacock and Shannon (1968), O'Higgins (1980), Stephenson (1980) and Le Grand (1987b). For empirical analysis of redistribution (and its pitfalls), see Nicholson (1974), Le Grand (1982), and Barr and Coulter (1990) for the UK; and for the USA, Danziger, Haveman and Plotnick (1984).

Chapter 8
Contributory Benefits 1: Unemployment, Sickness and Disability

The plan covers all citizens without upper income limit, but has regard to their different ways of life; it is a plan all-embracing in scope of persons and of needs. [The Beveridge Report, 1942.]

1 Introduction and Institutions

1.1 The Issues

Aims and methods   Historically the main aim of cash benefits was *poverty relief* (objective 4 in Chapter 1:2.2), in particular the prevention of absolute poverty (see the Glossary). Motives were controversial, ranging from altruism to capitalist oppression (Chapters 2:7.1, 3:5.3 and 4:4.1), but with widespread agreement about the aim itself. Increasingly over the twentieth century other aims have been recognised. *Insurance* (objective 5) is concerned with protection in the face of stochastic contingencies like unemployment or ill-health). *Income smoothing* (objective 6) relates to life-cycle effects connected with retirement or the presence of dependent children. The objective of *inequality reduction* is more controversial, particularly the aim of redistribution from rich to poor. Other aims discussed in Chapter 1:2.2 concern various aspects of *efficiency* and *ease of administration*. All these aims recur repeatedly in the following chapters.

More specifically, unemployment benefit and sickness benefit both contribute to the insurance objective. If the benefit formula is weighted towards the lower paid, they also contribute to poverty relief and to vertical redistribution. One of the major purposes of explicit social insurance contributions is to give recipients an entitlement to benefit, thereby fostering social solidarity. If properly constructed, the benefits minimise adverse labour-supply effects, thereby contributing to the incentives objective. In addition, in that unemployment is uninsurable in private markets (a major argument in this chapter), state-organised unemployment compensation contributes to the micro-efficiency objective.

The methods available for income protection vary enormously, but schemes can usefully be classified into three types – private, public and mixed. Pure private arrangements include the voluntary purchase of actuarial insurance and voluntary charity. Mixed schemes involve public participation in private arrangements through regulation (e.g. minimum standards for private insurance) and/or through finance. The latter frequently takes the form of tax expenditures (Chapter 7:1.1), e.g. tax relief for private pension contributions. Public schemes embrace the forms of institution discussed in Chapter 1:2.1. *Social insurance* is awarded on the basis of a contributions record and the occurrence of a specified contingency, such as unemployment or being above a specified age. *Social assistance* is financed from taxation and awarded on the basis of a means test. *'Universal' benefits* are awarded on the basis of a specified contingency (e.g. having dependent children), without either a contribution or an income test.

Which method is preferred depends in part on how the aims of cash benefits are interpreted, which in turn depends on political perspective. Libertarians make a sharp distinction between two forms of income transfer: under actuarial insurance an individual provides for his *own* benefits through his previous contributions; under a non-contributory scheme, his benefits are paid by *others*. In the former case an individual may legitimately choose any desired benefit provided he pays an actuarial premium; in the latter, the aim of cash transfers should be to prevent *absolute* poverty, i.e. benefits should be at subsistence. To a libertarian the preferred methods for achieving these aims are voluntary private insurance and private charity, respectively. Socialists see income transfers as contributing to their egalitarian aims, and therefore favour publicly organised transfers to prevent *relative* poverty and to reduce inequality.

Liberals take an intermediate line. We saw in Chapter 6:2.1 that poverty cannot be defined analytically, so its definition is largely ideological. The alleviation of poverty, however defined, can be via insurance (private or public, voluntary or compulsory); through cash transfers out of tax revenues; via private charity; or through whatever mix of these approaches best meets stated aims. The pros and cons of these methods are the subject of Part 2 of the book. This chapter looks at social insurance. Retirement pensions raise a number of separate issues which are discussed in Chapter 9. Chapter 10 looks at non-contributory benefits, and Chapter 11 discusses possible reform strategies.

Questions about national insurance are of two sorts. The first (section 2) is whether it should be national (i.e. publicly provided). This in turn raises questions about the circumstances in which people insure voluntarily, and those where it might be appropriate for the state to make insurance compulsory and/or to provide insurance itself. The second issue (section 3) is the effectiveness of the existing system, including its effects on work effort and saving. Where necessary, different benefits are discussed separately. The major conclusions about cash benefits are set out at the end of Chapter 11.

Non-economic arguments Three types of argument are commonly adduced to justify publicly provided cash transfers. The first is that 'the state has a duty to protect its less fortunate members', or that 'everyone has a right to protection from catastrophic income loss'. Both value judgements are widely accepted. Both, however, beg the crucial question of *how* individuals are most effectively helped. It is precisely this issue which is the main subject of this chapter and the next. The second type of argument is that 'without national insurance the poor could not afford adequate cover'. The weakness of this position was discussed in Chapter 4:7.2. If there are no technical problems with private insurance, the market can supply it efficiently. In such cases, distributive aims are generally best achieved through cash transfers.

A third argument is that 'it is immoral for insurance companies to profit from people's misfortunes'. This is tenable as a value judgement. But it has been argued (Chapter 4:7.2) that the question of public versus private production and allocation is less a moral issue than a technical one. Hence insurance against income loss should be publicly provided if that is more efficient and/or just; but where private insurance is more efficient, equity aims can generally be achieved through income transfers. We do not, after all, say that food should be publicly provided because it is immoral for food manufacturers to exploit the fact that without it people would starve.

1.2 Institutions

In institutional terms, national insurance refers to benefits payable to individuals with the necessary contributions record; in economic terms it is an insurance scheme against income loss due to events like unemployment, ill-health or old age. The development of the Beveridge system after 1948 was discussed in Chapter 2:6 and contribution arrangements in Chapter 7:2.1. This section summarises current benefit institutions (for detailed discussion see Tolley (1991) and the Further Reading).

Unemployment benefit is paid at a flat rate (£43.10 per week in 1992/3 for someone with a full contributions record), and is included in taxable income. Claimants must be willing and able to work, and actively seeking work. Benefit is payable for up to one year, at which time, if not earlier, the individual may become eligible for income support (Chapter 10:1). Where entitlement to the insurance benefit is exhausted, individuals must work for at least 13 weeks at a minimum of 16 hours per week to qualify for further benefit.

Statutory sick pay Compensation for sickness operated similarly until 1983, when the Social Security and Housing Benefits Act 1982 transferred to employers the administration of short-term sickness benefits (for details of the debate, see Prest (1983)). Under the scheme, as subsequently amended, employees are eligible for statutory sick pay for up to 28 weeks in a tax year, which covers the vast majority of health-related absences. Benefits, which are subject to income tax and national insurance contributions, are partly earnings-related, at weekly rates (in 1992/3) of £45.30 and £52.50, depending on previous earnings. Various groups are excluded, *inter alia* those below the lower earnings limit, the self-employed, and people over pensionable age. In addition, benefit is not payable in respect of the first three days of absence. A medical certificate is required only where sickness lasts more than seven days; for shorter absences a system of self-certification operates.

Statutory sickness payments are made by employers, who simply deduct such disbursements from their monthly return of national insurance contributions. The benefit is, in effect, paid from the National Insurance Fund.[1] Far from privatising sick pay (as had originally been intended), the main effects of the changes were the transfer of administration from the social insurance authorities to employers, and also the greater administrative ease of subjecting such benefit to tax and national insurance contributions. The finance of statutory sick pay remains firmly in the public sector, though most administration is hived off to employers.

Sickness benefit applies to individuals not covered by statutory sick pay. The benefit is flat-rate, tax-free and payable for up to 28 weeks. Once entitlement to statutory sick pay or sickness benefit runs out after 28 weeks, recipients are eligible for invalidity benefit (discussed below).

The contribution conditions for unemployment and sickness benefit are complex. To qualify for full benefit, an individual must have paid at least the minimum contribution (Chapter 7:2.1) in the complete tax year preceding the calendar year in which the interruption of employment occurred. Where contributions fall short of this minimum but exceed half, benefit is paid on a sliding scale. In sharp contrast, there is no contribution condition for statutory sick pay.

Invalidity benefit, introduced in 1971, pays a tax-free pension, which replaces statutory sick pay or sickness benefit after 28 weeks. An additional payment, **invalidity allowance**, is made where incapacity began more than five years before pensionable age.

Disability living allowance and disability working allowance came into effect in April 1992, replacing a number of previous benefits (for further details,

[1] Formally, it appears as a negative item in the *revenue* of the National Insurance Fund (see Table 7.4). The only obvious advantage of such an accounting fiction is the apparent reduction in public spending which thereby results. Tax expenditures have a similar effect; see Barr (1986).

see Tolley (1991, Ch. 12)). Disability allowance has two components: the care component, payable at one of three weekly rates, is awarded to individuals who are physically or mentally disabled to the point where they are unable to care for themselves; the mobility component offers assistance to individuals who are unable or virtually unable to walk. The benefit is awarded only to individuals who have met the necessary conditions for at least three months, and who are expected to continue to do so for at least six more months. Eligible individuals can receive either or both the care and mobility components.

The disability working allowance is an income-tested benefit, in some ways analogous to family credit (see Chapter 10:1). It is awarded to individuals (a) whose disability (physical or mental) puts them at a disadvantage in finding a job, or restricts their earning potential, (b) who are working for at least 16 hours a week, and (c) whose income does not exceed a prescribed amount.

From Table 7.5, the total cost of these benefits in 1992/3 was £1.5 billion for unemployment benefit, £1.0 billion for sickness benefit, and £5.7 billion for invalidity benefit. These three benefits, together with retirement and widows' pensions, make up nearly 99 per cent of direct national insurance disbursements. The remainder comprise a wide variety of smaller benefits, the rates of some of which are shown in Table 8.1.

Statutory maternity pay, the main maternity benefit, is analogous to statutory sick pay. Benefit, which is taxable, is paid for up to 18 weeks at a higher and a lower rate depending on length of service. Payments are made by employers, who deduct outgoings from their monthly national insurance contribution receipts.

Industrial injury benefit applies to all employed earners. *Statutory sick pay/sickness benefit* is payable without contribution condition for up to 28 weeks of absence from work. *Industrial disablement benefit*, in contrast, is payable (a) for the entire duration, temporary or permanent, of any loss of faculty, and (b) whether or not the person is unable to work. Benefit is payable when statutory sick pay/sickness benefit ceases, or from three days after the accident if there is no incapacity for work. Various additional payments can be made where injury is exceptionally severe (see Tolley, 1991, Ch. 13).

Child's special allowance and guardian's allowance both specifically concern children. The first is payable to a woman who is divorced and has not remarried, upon the death of her former husband, where she has a child to whose support he previously contributed. The allowance (£10.85 per week in 1992/3) is paid for each child, in addition to child benefit. Guardian's allowance may be paid where the parents (at least one of whom satisfied a

Table 8.1 *Main national insurance benefit rates, 1992/93*

RETIREMENT PENSION	
Basic state retirement pension	
Single person	£54.15[T] per week
Married couple	£86.70[T]
State earnings-related pension	earnings-related
Non-contributory retirement pension	
Single person	£32.55[T]
Married woman	£19.45[T]
INVALIDITY PENSION	
Invalidity pension	£54.15
Invalidity allowance (in addition to invalidity pension)	£3.60–£11.55[a]
WIDOW'S PENSION	
Widow's payment (lump-sum)	£1000.00[T]
Widowed mother's allowance	£54.15[T]
Widow's pension	£54.15[T]
UNEMPLOYMENT BENEFIT	
Single person (under pension age)	£43.10[T]
Married couple (under pension age)	£69.30[T]
SICK PAY	
Sickness benefit	
Single person (under pension age)	£41.20
Married couple	£66.70
Statutory sick pay	
Lower rate	£45.30
Higher rate	£52.50
DISABILITY BENEFITS	
Disability living allowance	
Care component	£11.55–£43.35
Mobility component	£11.55–£30.30
Disability working allowance	
Single person	£42.40
Couple or lone parents	£58.80
INDUSTRIAL INJURIES BENEFIT	
Disablement pension (100 per cent rate)	£88.40
Widow's pension	
Spouse who is disabled, elderly or looking after children	£54.15[T]
Otherwise	£16.25[T]
MATERNITY BENEFITS	
Maternity allowance	£42.25
Statutory maternity pay	
First 6 weeks	90% of earnings
Thereafter	£46.30
MISCELLANEOUS BENEFITS	
Child's special allowance (in addition to child benefit)	£10.85
Guardian's allowance (in addition to child benefit)	£10.85

Source: Tolley (1991, pp. SP1–12).

Notes: [a] Benefit is tax-free except when paid as an addition to retirement pension.

     [T] Benefit chargeable to income tax.

nationality or residence condition) of a child are dead, to anyone who looks after a child as part of his or her family.

Increases for dependants   The level of many of these benefits may be increased if the beneficiary has dependants (adult or child) whom he or she supports. In the latter case, child benefit is normally payable in addition.

The level of almost all benefits is reviewed regularly. Most are uprated according to statutory formula; some are increased on an *ad hoc* basis; most are increased annually. A rare exception was the death grant, whose original intention was to pay the cost of a simple funeral. The benefit was was set at £20 in 1949 but, notwithstanding occasional increases, its real value was eroded by inflation. The benefit was abolished in 1987; funeral costs may now be paid, at least in part, by an income-related payment out of the social fund (Chapter 10:1). The 'cradle to grave' claim is less realistic than once it was.

2 Theoretical Arguments for State Intervention

2.1 Efficiency 1: Regulation

Are efficiency and social justice assisted by state involvement in insurance markets? In particular, would individuals in a private market buy the *socially* efficient quantity of insurance against the causes of income loss covered by national insurance? This breaks down into three separate questions: (a) why do people insure at all; (b) why does the state make membership of national insurance compulsory; (c) why does the state provide such insurance itself?

The first question was answered in Chapter 5 – a rational risk-averse individual will insure voluntarily so long as the value of certainty exceeds the net cost of insurance. Why, second, is membership of national insurance compulsory? The standard argument for voluntarism is that it is efficient for an individual to make his own decision so long as he bears fully the costs of so doing. If I do not insure my Picasso, society regards this as my prerogative. Similarly, it might be argued that I should be free not to insure against income loss because of unemployment or ill-health. If I then lose my job and starve that is my fault.

The flaw in the voluntarism argument in this case is that it overlooks the external costs which non-insurance can impose on others. Suppose someone chooses not to insure, and then loses his job. If society bails him out by paying a non-contributory benefit, the external cost falls upon the taxpayer. Alternatively, if he is given no help he starves, which imposes costs on others in a variety of ways. First, non-insurance may bring about not only his own starvation, but also that of his dependants. There are also broader costs, including the excess of the individual's lost output over his consumption; any resulting increase in crime; and the financial costs of disposing of his body, or the health hazards if it were left where it fell. Additionally, though more arguably, it is possible to specify a psychic externality, where people do not like the idea of a society which allows people to starve. If so, the individual's death from starvation imposes external costs by reducing the utility of others directly.[2]

Where an activity causes an external cost, one form of intervention is a Pigovian tax.[3] Here, however, the aim is not marginally to influence consumption decisions through marginal price changes, but to prevent non-insurance. Making insurance compulsory (i.e. regulation) is likely to be a more effective way of achieving this.

In sum, the major efficiency argument for compulsory membership (which applies equally to the smaller national insurance benefits) is that uninsured losses due to unemployment, illness or industrial injury may impose costs on others, including dependants like spouses and children. There is an analogy with automobile insurance, which is also compulsory in most countries. But, quite correctly on efficiency grounds, compulsion is limited to insurance to cover the damage I might inflict on *others*. I can choose whether to take out insurance to cover damage to my *own* car or person.

2.2 Efficiency 2: Public Provision

To continue the analogy, the state makes car insurance compulsory, but does not supply insurance itself. Why, then, does it provide national insurance? This question brings us back to the discussion in Chapter 5:4.1 of the circumstances in which private insurance markets are efficient. In particular, we need to look at the supply conditions, namely that the probability of the insured event must be: independent across individuals, less than one, known or estimable, known equally to all parties (i.e. no adverse selection) and exogenous (i.e. no moral hazard). Efficiency arguments about the appropriateness of public provision hinge on whether these five assumptions hold in the cases of the risks covered by national insurance.

Unemployment insurance We need to consider each assumption separately.

1. Whether individual probabilities of becoming or remaining unemployed are independent is a matter of high controversy. Simple Keynesian theory suggests that unemployment reduces demand and contributes to further unemployment. Those who believe in a natural rate of unemployment deny

[2] Some activities impose unambiguous external costs, e.g. air pollution. In other cases a given activity by individual A may or may not impose costs on B, depending on B's utility function. Whether or not my late night trumpet playing is a cost to my neighbour depends *inter alia* on his taste in music. It might similarly be argued that the psychic cost imposed on society by my starvation would not arise if members of society had different utility functions. These issues are addressed by Sen (1970).

[3] See, in ascending order of completeness, the Glossary, the Appendix to Chapter 4, para. 15 and/or Chapter 4:3.2.

this conclusion except in the short run. Individual probabilities may be partly correlated, though this problem alone is unlikely to make private insurance impossible.

2. The overall probability of being unemployed is less than one, though for some sectors of the labour force, such as unskilled young people, it may be too high for private insurance to be viable. Individuals returning to the labour force after a long break in employment, and unemployed school-leavers cause additional problems.

3. The average probability of being unemployed is well-known – it is simply the aggregate unemployment rate. There is also considerable knowledge of the probability of unemployment for sub-groups of the labour force.

4. Adverse selection: a private insurance company could in principle ask about an applicant's previous employment record. This is not a complete solution, however: the process is costly; verification is not always possible; and not everyone has a past employment record.

5. Much the greatest problem with private unemployment insurance is moral hazard. The insured individual may be able to influence the probability of being unemployed in two ways. First, he can influence the *stock* of unemployment by bringing about his own redundancy ('I'll work for you this week for nothing if you'll then make me redundant'). Second, and of much greater importance, he can influence the *duration* of unemployment.

A key question is how costly (financial and psychic) it is for an individual to remain unemployed. Since psychic costs are unobservable, it is not possible to distinguish two cases:

- The psychic cost to the individual is high (case 1 in Chapter 5:3.2), and unemployment is due to a lack of jobs.
- The cost is low (case 3), and the individual remains unemployed to some extent by choice.

The first is an insurable risk; the second is not – the insurer is imperfectly informed and, as discussed shortly, the problem is worse for unemployment than for most other risks.

As we shall see (section 3.1) the relationship between the level of benefits and the level and duration of unemployment is hotly disputed. It should be noted, however, that to say that individuals with insurance devote more time to job search is not *necessarily* to imply inefficiency. In principle, the efficient duration of unemployment for the ith individual, x_i, is that period which he would rationally choose if he had to finance his unemployment from accumulated savings or by borrowing in a perfect capital market. Inefficiency arises when an individual chooses to be unemployed for longer than x_i because insurance has reduced the marginal cost to him of so doing. It was for this reason that Beveridge insisted on full employment, because 'the only satisfactory test of unemployment is an offer of work' (UK, 1942, p. 163).

We saw in Chapter 5:3.1 that an actuarial premium is calculated as

$$\pi_i = p_i L + T \tag{8.1}$$

where p_i is the probability of the ith individual becoming or remaining unemployed, L is the unemployment benefit, and T the carrier's transactions cost. Moral hazard of the sort described above means that p_i can be manipulated by the insured individual, making it impossible for the insurance company to calculate a premium.

The theory is borne out by empirical evidence. There are no private policies I can buy to top up the (relatively low, flat-rate) UK state unemployment benefit (the analogue for sick pay appears regularly in my junk mail). Nor, for such white-collar schemes, is it possible to argue that private schemes have been driven out by the existence of a state scheme. It is true that unemployment benefit in Sweden is organised by trade unions (Bjorklund and Holmlund, 1989); but the system (a) is heavily regulated, and is buttressed (b) by a complementary public insurance scheme and (c) by income-tested unemployment assistance.

A second source of support for the impossibility of *general* private unemployment insurance arises from an attempt by Beenstock and Brasse (1986) to show the opposite. They discuss a number of private-sector examples. Mortgage protection policies, offered *inter alia* in Britain and the USA, which make mortgage repayments during unemployment, illustrate the point. Such policies have three salient characteristics. They are open, by and large, only to the best risks: owner-occupiers tend to be in more secure jobs, and so have a lower-than-average probability of *entering* unemployment; they are also more mobile (since owner-occupiers are generally less affected than renters by housing market rigidities), reducing the probability of *remaining* unemployed. Second, such policies can typically be started only at the time the mortgage is taken out, on the grounds that few people will seek to buy a house if they know their job is at risk; this reduces adverse selection. Third, owner-occupiers tend to have higher-than-average earnings, and so face lower replacement rates, thus minimising moral hazard. Mortgage protection policies are therefore limited to the best risks, impose restrictions which minimise adverse selection, and sidestep the worst problems of moral hazard. Such policies are genuinely private insurance, but they offer no basis whatever on which to generalise.

Thus unemployment is not a risk which accords well with the model of actuarial insurance, so it should not be surprising that earlier schemes under the 1911 National Insurance Act and during the 1920s ran into trouble (Chapter 2:2.2 and 2:3.2). The theoretical conclusion, supported by empirical evidence, is twofold:

1. If income support is to exist for the unemployed, it will have to be

publicly provided. This outcome can be supported on *efficiency* grounds because of information problems in insurance markets, problems of which no mention is made in Hayek's (1960, Ch. 19) attack on publicly provided benefits. The libertarian predilection for private markets and voluntarism in this instance is untenable.

2. The resulting institutions do not look actuarial. The argument in Chapter 5:4.2 suggested that no other result is possible.

Sick pay insurance[4] Asking the same questions about sick pay insurance, the individual probabilities of absence from work because of ill-health are unrelated, except during a major epidemic (i.e. the likelihood of my missing work for health reasons is independent of your state of health). Except for the chronically ill, the probability of absence is less than one, and can be estimated. There is no major problem of adverse selection, since a private insurance company could ask about an applicant's previous health and absenteeism. Nor is there a serious problem of moral hazard. The probability of missing work is broadly exogenous, since making oneself genuinely ill is costly, and pretended illness can, at least up to a point, be policed by requiring claimants to provide a doctor's certificate.

Thus there is no substantial technical difficulty with private sick pay insurance, and such institutions exist in many countries. The only efficiency justification for public provision is through a two-step argument:

1. There are economies of scale to be derived from running unemployment and sick pay insurance jointly. It is administratively cheaper to collect both contributions simultaneously; and, if a claimant is genuinely unemployed *or* ill, it avoids the need to decide which of the two is applicable.

2. Unemployment benefits must be publicly provided for technical reasons.

Given 2 it follows from 1 that there are at least administrative savings to be made by running a public sick pay scheme alongside unemployment insurance.

The smaller national insurance benefits Voluntary maternity insurance may face problems of adverse selection (i.e. only women intending to become pregnant would insure), making private supply impossible. However, as we saw in Chapter 5:4.1, compulsion can sidestep the problem. Thus, if maternity insurance is compulsory, it would not necessarily have to be publicly provided.

Similar arguments apply to the child's special allowance and guardian's allowance, which are payable when one or both parents are dead, and also to increases for dependants more generally. What we are talking about here is a form of life insurance, with which the private market is well able to cope. If private insurance is feasible for the individual, it is also feasible for

---

[4] Discussion here is concerned with income replacement during health-related absence from work, *not* with insurance against the cost of medical treatment, which is discussed in Chapter 12.

his/her dependants (e.g. we saw in Chapter 5:2.3 how an annuity can cover a spouse).

In the case of industrial injury insurance, again, there is no strong efficiency argument for public provision. The probability of injury is independent across individuals, less than one, and can be estimated. Nor do serious problems arise with adverse selection or moral hazard (for instance, it would not generally pay an individual deliberately to injure himself). It is true that some occupations are riskier than others, but this simply means that private insurance would require higher premiums for riskier occupations.

In all these cases, there is an overwhelming case for compulsion but not for public provision. Counter-arguments to the latter position are that there might be administrative economies if all social benefits were organised together; and there might be administrative difficulties in enforcing compulsion if supply were private. The issue of public versus private pensions is deferred to Chapter 9:3.1

Two other arguments have been put forward at various times to explain or justify public provision of national insurance. Marxists argue (Chapter 3:5.3) that such institutions are a form of social control, whose main aim is to prevent social unrest. This argument may *explain* the existence of national insurance, but it does not necessarily *justify* it. In particular, it does not establish why we have publicly organised social insurance rather than, say, simple cash transfers. It is sometimes also argued, along Keynesian lines, that national insurance generally, and unemployment benefit in particular, is a built-in stabiliser. But asserting that this is a consequence (albeit a beneficial one), again, does not necessarily *justify* national insurance.

2.3 Social Justice

What are the equity arguments for publicly provided insurance? Horizontal equity is concerned with such goals as minimum standards for certain commodities and/or equal access to them. It was argued in Chapter 4:4.3 that these occur automatically where the assumptions of perfect information and equal power hold, in which case horizontal equity grounds for intervention are limited. This line of argument lends little support to public provision of national insurance. Individuals can acquire information about different insurance policies, as they do currently for car insurance with the advice, if necessary, of insurance brokers and the various automobile associations. Should protection be necessary there is a case for regulation of standards, as for food; but analogously this is not an argument for public provision.

It is true that power is not distributed equally among individuals. This can be a major problem for health care and education, but is unlikely to be serious in this case. Where insurance markets are competitive what matters is not whether individuals have more or less power, but whether they are able to pay an actuarial premium. In the case of car insurance, premiums are generally related to age and previous driving record, but there is no evidence of a systematic relationship between premiums and social class. Similarly, there is no reason to expect substantial discrimination with unemployment and sick pay insurance.

Vertical equity concerns redistribution from rich to poor. The standard argument, that 'the state must provide insurance, because otherwise the poor would not be able to afford adequate cover' is false (section 1.1). A somewhat more subtle variant is that actuarial insurance cannot redistribute from rich to poor, only from 'lucky' to 'unlucky', and therefore insurance should be publicly provided to redistribute income. Again, the key argument in Chapter 4:7.2 suggests that without efficiency reasons for provision, distributive goals should be pursued through income transfers except, possibly, in the presence of consumption externalities (Chapter 4:4.2). In this case, the rich may want the poor to consume insurance, and so impose it as a merit good; and the poor may feel less stigmatised by receiving 'insurance benefit' than 'welfare'. Both reasons offer an explanation (though not necessarily a justification) of public provision for reasons of vertical equity.

Finally, it can be argued (Chapters 4:7.2 and 5:4.1) that to the extent that there are *efficiency* grounds for making membership of national insurance compulsory, it is not inappropriate to finance the scheme so as to redistribute from rich to poor. We return to this issue in the next section.

3 Assessment of the National Insurance System

3.1 Efficiency and Incentives

ARGUMENTS OF PRINCIPLE

This part of the chapter briefly assesses the UK system in the light of earlier theoretical argument (for fuller discussion of the UK, see Barr and Coulter (1990), and, for international comparison, Barr (1992)). Most of the issues are empirical, but we start with a number of issues of principle: should national insurance be national (i.e. publicly provided); does the state provide the optimal quantity of insurance; and are the resulting institutions insurance?

Should it be national? The efficiency arguments rest on externalities, justifying compulsion, and technical (mainly information) failures on the supply side of the insurance market, justifying provision of the major benefits, though with a somewhat weaker argument for sick pay than for the other schemes. If we ignore consumption externalities, the main equity arguments are (a) that the poor may feel less stigmatised by insurance, and (b) that if insurance is publicly provided for efficiency reasons, it can then be used as a redistributive device. These arguments are compelling. Some areas could, indeed, be returned to the private sector, as considered for short-term sick pay (Prest, 1983). However, unemployment is an uninsurable risk and, as argued in Chapter 9, so is inflation, with major efficiency implications for public involvement with pensions. Since unemployment benefits and retirement pensions comprise 78 per cent of national insurance expenditure, if we ask 'Should national insurance be national?' the short answer is yes.

Does the state provide the optimum quantity of insurance? Where insurance is compulsory and publicly provided, inefficiency arises if the state, through misperception of individual preferences or for other reasons, constructs a larger or smaller than optimal scheme. In a first-best world, the ith individual (assumed rational and risk-averse) will choose to insure against a loss L_i for which he pays the actuarial premium shown in equation (8.1). All N individuals make this utility-maximising decision, resulting in a vector of optimal insurance purchases

$$(L_1, L_2, \ldots, L_N) \tag{8.2}$$

The L_i vary across individuals depending *inter alia* on their risk-aversion.

Will national insurance offer these optimal quantities? The answer must be no, because the insurance offered will be some sort of average which does not cater for differences in individual tastes. Even so, national insurance is likely to be less inefficient than the free market outcome, partly because risks like unemployment are uninsurable, and because individuals can buy additional insurance against risks like sickness and disability. What can be said (albeit arguably) is that there is no solid evidence to suggest that the cover offered by national insurance, plus voluntary private arrangements, differs *substantially* from the notional optimum in equation (8.2).

Is it insurance? On the face of it, national insurance does not look very much like insurance, for at least three reasons.

1. Contributions are not related to individual risk. In the scheme envisaged by Beveridge, contributions were geared to the *average* risk, as shown in equation (5.16), and adverse selection avoided by making membership compulsory. This principle was violated because retirement pensions from 1946 onwards were not actuarial (see Chapter 9); because from 1975 contributions by the employed (Class 1) and self-employed (Class 4) were related not to average risk but to the contributor's income; and because of the existence of credits for the unemployed, and for a parent who stays at home to look after young children or the disabled. In the latter two cases,

compulsion avoids the worst of the efficiency losses associated with adverse selection.

2. The scheme is not financed on actuarial lines. As discussed in Chapter 9, state pensions, unlike most private schemes, generally make no provision for future liabilities.

3. Entitlement to benefit does not depend only on the occurrence of the insured event. Benefits (but not contributions) are higher where the contributor has dependants; contributions and benefits taken together are redistributive from rich to poor; and until 1989 pensions in the first five years after normal retirement age were subject to an earnings test (i.e. the pension was rapidly withdrawn for individuals with more than small earnings). Elsewhere, additional restrictions may be imposed, e.g. 'workfare' in various American states requires recipients of unemployment and related benefits to undertake work or training.

The conclusion is that national insurance is insurance in the sense that it offers protection against risk, but not insurance in which premiums bear an actuarial relationship to individual risk. In the sense discussed in Chapter 5:4.2, the mechanism is social insurance rather than actuarial insurance. For the reasons given in section 2.2, no other result is possible.

It is important to be clear that social insurance does not *have* to be redistributive from rich to poor. Its precise form will depend on the objectives of policy. It is perfectly possible to have social insurance arrangements which closely mimic actuarial arrangements (e.g. the original Beveridge scheme, or a scheme in which both contributions and benefits are strictly proportional to individual earnings). Over the years there has been much confusion about the purposes of social insurance. There are good reasons for thinking of it both as a technical instrument for dealing with market failure *and* as a redistributive device. But the two cases are argued on very different grounds and should be carefully distinguished.

INCENTIVE ISSUES

In discussing the incentive effects of social insurance two questions predominate: is the system itself a contributory cause of unemployment; and does it reduce the rate of saving and capital accumulation (the latter issue being particularly relevant in the case of pensions)?

Are unemployment benefits a contributory cause of unemployment? The discussion of moral hazard in section 2.2 has already hinted at this issue. With a high replacement rate (i.e. the ratio of income when unemployed to post-tax-and-transfer income in work) the low paid may be scarcely worse-off (and possibly, in the short run, better-off) when out of work. It is estimated (UK, 1992e, Figure 19) that about 595,000 workers face replacement rates of 70 per cent and over. This it is argued (Minford *et al.*, 1985) creates an 'unemployment trap', whereby an unemployed individual has no financial incentive to seek work (this should be contrasted with the 'poverty trap' (Chapter 10:3.2), under which an individual doing at least some work is given no incentive to work longer hours).

The logic of the disincentive argument is appealingly straightforward. Simple theory suggests that higher replacement rates tend to reduce work effort which is financially motivated. This view, it is claimed, is supported empirically by the sharp rise after 1966 (when the earnings-related supplement to unemployment benefit was introduced) in both replacement rate and the number of unemployed individuals. Reality, however, is less simple: people may not work solely for monetary gain; the replacement rate is far from easy to measure (Hemming, 1984, pp. 97–107); only one in six of the unemployed met the contribution conditions for the earnings-related supplement, which therefore had a much smaller impact on replacement rates than was commonly supposed (Atkinson and Flemming, 1978); and the UK replacement rate is low by international standards.

The quantitative literature is large, complex and controversial (for surveys, see Atkinson (1987a) and Johnson and Layard (1986)). Early studies used aggregate time-series data (Maki and Spindler (1975) for the UK; Grubel and Maki (1976) for the USA), and found that benefits exerted a substantial upward effect on the level of unemployment. The advantage of the time-series approach is its apparent ability to analyse the effects of a policy change. But in practice it is difficult to separate these effects from other influences on unemployment, not least because aggregate data necessitate such devices as representative individuals, replacement rates based on average benefit levels and average tax rates, and so on, which obscure most of the variation between individuals.

Cross-section data have the great advantage of being a much richer source of information on the large differences between individuals, making it possible to estimate the determinants of unemployment with greater precision than the aggregate data allow. The general conclusion of the cross-section studies (see the Further Reading) is that, though the duration of unemployment is likely to be slightly longer at higher replacement rates, the magnitude of the effect is not large.

This consensus, however, conceals a rich collection of difficulties, both of principle and of measurement. The major methodological problem with cross-section analysis is its attempt to extrapolate from individual behaviour to the aggregate economy, a procedure which is valid only where individual responses are not interdependent. Suppose that as someone with a high replacement rate I am very choosy about accepting a new job. If everyone else's behaviour is independent of mine this will increase unemployment. But if behaviour is interdependent, my choosiness simply means that someone else takes the job I have rejected. In this case the replacement rate determines *who* is unemployed, but not total unemployment. Cross-section analysis does not enable us, as an empirical matter, to distinguish the two cases.

The treatment of benefits also raises substantial problems. Institutional complexities, in particular the interaction of the tax and benefit systems, make it difficult to estimate benefits accurately. One approach is to estimate the individual's potential entitlement; the difficulty here is that the sample may not contain sufficient information (e.g. past contribution records) to make this procedure accurate. Alternatively, it is possible to use actual benefit receipts. This avoids complexity, but causes statistical difficulties where unobserved individual characteristics influence *both* the level of benefit *and* the probability of accepting a particular job offer, e.g. if I am lazy (unobserved) I may have a poor employment record and consequently receive less benefit *and* be less keen to accept a new job. In view of these difficulties it is not surprising that the precision of the estimates (as measured, for instance, by the statistical significance of estimated coefficients) is often low even by cross-section standards.

Recent work (Atkinson and Micklewright, 1991; Layard *et al.*, 1991) has emphasised cross-country data, making it possible to include institutional differences as explanations of why unemployment was more persistent over the 1980s in most European countries than in the USA and Japan. Particular emphasis is placed on three aspects of the labour market. First are aspects of the benefit structure additional to the replacement rate, such as the maximum duration of benefit, the proportion of the unemployed receiving benefit, and the stringency with which the 'actively seeking work' condition is enforced. Second are active labour market policies, such as placement and counselling services, training and job creation (see Flanagan (1987) for an account of Swedish policy). Third is the structure of the labour market, including the power of trade unions and the extent of centralised wage bargaining. The conclusion is that, though the replacement rate has an effect, labour supply is influenced more by other aspects of the benefit structure, in particular the maximum duration for which benefit can be received.

The general conclusion, which applies equally to cross-section and time-series studies, is that they lack robustness with respect to the definition of variables, the choice of sample and time period, and the specification of the estimated equation. The simplicity of the original argument disappears the deeper one digs – and the more we learn, the greater the complications of which we are made aware. In short, the hypothesis that unemployment benefits exert a substantial upward effect on the level of unemployment receives little empirical support.

Disability benefits and labour supply are also a controversial relationship. Some writers (Parsons, 1980; Halpern and Hausman, 1986) conclude that disability payments substantially reduce US labour force participation. But the Parsons results are not robust, and are criticised in a number of respects by Haveman and Wolfe (1984) (see also Haveman *et al.*, 1984), who conclude that the effect, though statistically significant, is small.

Pensions and labour supply may also be related if pensions induce early retirement. In addition, it is argued that publicly provided pensions financed out of tax revenues may reduce savings, capital accumulation and economic growth. These issues are discussed in Chapter 9:5.

3.2 Equity Issues

Horizontal equity It can be argued that national insurance gives everyone equal access to income support. One of the major themes of the Beveridge Report was that national insurance should be comprehensive, unified and compulsory. This aim has been achieved in that there is no evidence of discrimination in the payment of benefits, nor of substantial mal-administration.

However, not all groups receive equal coverage, despite Beveridge's intention to the contrary. Fifty years ago most single-parent families resulted from widowhood, which therefore received extensive coverage, especially where there were young children. It is argued that this group (which today comprises only one in six single-parent families in Britain) is treated generously relative to families separated by other causes, such as divorce. The difficulty (and the prominence of the latter group among the poor) arises largely because benefits are conditioned on cause (e.g. widowhood) rather than outcome (i.e. being a single parent).

Disability benefits have also been criticised. Again, individuals facing similar problems do not necessarily receive similar benefits. Under plausible assumptions a single man could receive twice as much if 100 per cent disabled in an industrial accident than with identical disabilities from a non-industrial cause (Hemming, 1984, p. 119). The topic of compensation generally was discussed by a Royal Commission (UK, 1978b), but institutions remain piecemeal despite pressure for a system of unified income support for all forms of disability, irrespective of cause (for discussion, see Sainsbury (1986) and Oliver (1989)).

There is also criticism that the relative treatment of men and women can be inequitable (e.g. for certain benefits it is the husband in a two-parent family who must apply).

Vertical equity raises two sets of questions. First, how redistributive is national insurance? The major difficulties include conceptual problems (Chapter 7:4) and many of the measurement problems discussed in Chapter 6. A definitive answer would require general equilibrium analysis of the joint incidence of contributions and benefits. No such work exists, so we must be content with more rough-and-ready answers. National insurance contributions for most people rise disproportionately with income for all except the highest earners (Table 7.3). The state pension is redistributive from rich to poor (Chapter 9:5.2). Unemployment benefits are also redistributive, inasmuch as those with lower incomes pay smaller contributions, generally for fewer weeks, and receive unemployment benefit more frequently than someone with a higher income. Sick pay is redistributive to the extent that claims are more common among the lower paid. In 1986 the combined effect of unemployment benefit and sick pay was to reduce the Gini coefficient by 2.1 per cent (Barr and Coulter, 1990, Tables 7.11 and 7.12).

Another aspect is whether benefits are pitched at the right level. This raises two further questions. First, and largely an efficiency matter, is whether the level of benefit is that which would have been chosen voluntarily by a hypothetically perfectly informed, rational individual. This is the issue, discussed earlier, of whether national insurance provides the optimal quantity of insurance. Second, we need to consider the level of insurance benefits relative to the poverty line. Since poverty cannot be defined in any wholly satisfactory way (Chapter 6:2.1) the poverty line, as manifested, for instance, by the level of income support (Chapter 10:1) has status only as a social convention. If this is regarded as an appropriate poverty line, it follows that the main national insurance benefits, which are generally below the income support level, are too low. We return to the subject in Chapter 10:3.1.

Further Reading

A compendious and up-to-date account of institutions (including legal sources) is published annually by Tolley (1991). For a simple introduction to income support generally, see International Labour Office (1984a). For wide-ranging international comparison, see Gordon (1988).

On the theory of insurance see the Further Reading at the end of Chapter 5, and on unemployment/sickness insurance Creedy and Disney (1985, Chs 6–8). The application to social insurance is discussed by Stiglitz (1988, Ch. 13).

Barr (1992) applies the arguments in this chapter in a survey of ten OECD countries.

A good general reference on the economics of labour supply is Brown (1983) or (more advanced) Ashenfelter and Layard (1986). For empirical analysis of the causes of unemployment, see Minford *et al.* (1985); see also Nickell's (1984) critique of an earlier version and Minford's (1984a) reply.

Incentive issues more broadly are surveyed by Danziger *et al.* (1981), Atkinson (1987a), Johnson and Layard (1986) and Atkinson and Micklewright (1991). The incentive effects of pensions are surveyed by Aaron (1982), Aaron and Burtless (1984), Kotlikoff (1989a) and Lazear (1986a). For a useful *tour d'horizon*, see the

AEA symposium papers by Gramlich (1989), Kotlikoff (1989b) and Summers (1989).

A general discussion of disability benefits is contained in Walker and Townsend (1981). The main empirical studies of labour supply effects are by Parsons (1980), Halpern and Hausman (1986) and (critical of Parsons) Haveman and Wolfe (1984). For a brief survey, see Atkinson (1987a).

For a (somewhat depressing) account of the difficulties of reforming the system even in a relatively minor way, see Prest (1983).

On the distributional impact of national insurance see Barr and Coulter (1990), Smeeding *et al.* (1990) (an international comparison) and the Further Reading at the end of Chapter 7.

Chapter 9
Contributory Benefits 2: Retirement Pensions

'You are old, Father William,' the young man said,
'And your pension has almost run out;
And yet you insist that funding is safe
It's no wonder you're all up the spout.'

'In my youth,' Father William replied to his son,
'They told me my savings would grow;
But, now that I'm perfectly sure I have none,
I'd prefer you to Pay as I Go.'

[With apologies to Lewis Carroll]

1 Introduction and Institutions

Pensions contribute to many of the objectives in Chapter 1:2.2. Retirement pensions, in that they enable individuals to redistribute from themselves to themselves over the life cycle, contribute to income smoothing. Invalidity and widows' pensions contribute to the insurance objective. Pensions also contribute to the relief of poverty, particularly long-term poverty, and may also contribute to vertical redistribution. Like other social insurance benefits, they may also contribute to social solidarity. The relative terms on which men and women receive pensions (e.g. whether there is a common retirement age) raise important issues of horizontal equity.

The questions which arise broadly parallel those of Chapter 8. Section 2 discusses different methods of organising pensions, and their pros and cons; the efficiency and equity arguments for state intervention, and the effects of different types of intervention are analysed in sections 3 and 4; and national insurance pensions and related benefits are assessed in section 5.

The 1975 Social Security Pensions Act was one of the most important pieces of social security legislation since the National Insurance Act 1946 (Chapter 2:5), and is the basis of the current arrangements described here. A number of proposed reforms, introduced by the Social Security Act 1986 and affecting people retiring after the end of the century, are discussed in section 5.1 (for references on current and future institutions, see the Further Reading).

The contributions side was discussed in Chapter 7:2.1. To qualify for a full pension an individual must generally have contributed to the current (i.e. 1975) scheme for at least 20 years, and to the current scheme or its predecessor (i.e. the 1948 scheme) for at least 49 years (men) or 44 years (women). Where this requirement is not met, pension is awarded on a sliding scale. In contrast with previous legislation, *home responsibility protection* ensures that years spent by a parent at home looking after children or a disabled dependant will not usually result in loss of pension. Thus a woman who drops out of the labour force for 15 years to look after children has to work for only 29 years (i.e. 44 *minus* 15) to qualify for a full pension.

On the benefits side, the major provisions of the 1975 Act may be summarised as follows, noting subsequent amendments, and in particular a number of important changes (motivated by cost containment) which are to be phased in for individuals retiring after 2000.

1. The weekly pension consists of two components, the *basic component* (which is flat-rate) and the *earnings-related*[1] component.

2. The basic component for a single person is set at about one-quarter of national average earnings; the lower earnings limit (Chapter 7:2.1) for national insurance contributions is set at about the level of the basic pension.[2] For earnings below this level the basic component is reduced pound for pound with earnings.

3. The earnings-related component for a person with a full contributions record is currently calculated as 25 pence of pension per pound of pensionable earnings between the lower earnings limit and a ceiling equal to the upper earnings limit. The figure of 25 pence per pound will decline gradually for individuals retiring after 2000; for those retiring in or after 2010 the figure will be 20 per cent.

4. The pension is based on the individual's best 20 years, thus improving pensions by omitting years in which earnings were low. For individuals retiring after 2000, the calculation will be based on the individual's entire contribution record.

5. The same pension formula applies to men and women, though pensionable age is 65 for men and 60 for women.[3]

6. For individuals retiring before 2000, each year of contribution gives entitlement to earnings-related pension equal to $1\frac{1}{4}$ per cent of the excess of earnings (or the ceiling, whichever is the lower) over the lower earnings

[1] Also referred to as the state earnings-related pension scheme (SERPS).
[2] The actual calculations are done on an annual basis, but achieve the same effect as the (simpler) weekly description in the text.
[3] This age differential is under increasing pressure – see section 5.2.

limit. Thus, a person who has contributed for 20 years will receive an earnings-related pension of 25 per cent (i.e. $20 \times 1\frac{1}{4}$ per cent) of the relevant earnings, in addition to the flat-rate pension.

7. A man receives an increase in his pension if he is married unless his wife has a pension in her own right, in which case she receives the full pension to which she is entitled on the basis of her earnings. Where a couple have two contribution records, the surviving spouse receives the basic pension plus both earnings-related components, up to the maximum which could have been earned by a single person. After 2000, the surviving spouse will inherit only half of his/her partner's earnings-related pension.

8. From 1975 the basic component was uprated each year in line with the increase in average earnings or the increase in prices, whichever was the greater. This caused a number of problems, and legislation in 1980 changed the formula so that the *mandatory* uprating reflected only price increases. The earnings-related component is protected in two ways. First, the earnings on which the pension is calculated are revalued each year in line with the general movement of earnings, so that the earnings-related pension, when first awarded, reflects the 20 years of highest *real* earnings. Second, the earnings-related component, once in payment, is uprated each year in line with price increases.

9. The pensions of people who work beyond pensionable age are increased by $7\frac{1}{2}$ per cent (in real terms) for each year by which pension is deferred. This has important implications, to which we return in section 5.2.

10. Membership of the flat-rate scheme is compulsory. It is possible to contract out of the earnings-related component by belonging to an occupational (i.e. private) scheme which offers a *guaranteed minimum pension*. Such schemes must meet stringent conditions but, broadly, should pay at least the pension offered by the state scheme to someone with an identical earnings record. In sharp contrast with any past arrangements, the state will index in line with price changes greater than 3 per cent per year the guaranteed minimum pension paid under approved private schemes. The important issues this raises are discussed in section 3. As discussed shortly, the 1986 Social Security Act significantly liberalised conditions for contracting out.

Let us take a specific example of the scheme at maturity (but assuming 1992 data for simplicity). Suppose someone retires with a full contribution record, and with average earnings over his best 20 years of £300 per week. If he were single he would receive a basic pension of £54.15 per week, plus one-quarter of the excess of his average earnings (£300) over the lower earnings limit (£54). His earnings-related pension would therefore be £61.50 per week and the total pension £115.65.

Many individuals and couples receiving a national insurance pension are also eligible for income support (Chapter 10:1), including automatic entitlement to benefits like housing benefit. One of the main purposes of the 1975 scheme was to reduce the numbers receiving both retirement pension and means-tested social assistance. Historically this has been a serious problem; in 1991–2 out of 8.6 million pensioners some 15 per cent also received income support (UK, 1992e, Table 7).

Widowhood Provision for widows (and in restricted circumstances for widowers) takes three forms. *Widowed mother's allowance*, subject to contribution conditions, is payable to a widow with at least one qualifying child. *Widow's pension* is payable to a widow over 40 after the termination of her widowed mother's allowance (for widows between 40 and 50, the pension is payable at a reduced rate). Widows who qualify for neither benefit receive a tax-free lump sum of £1000 in 1992/3.

All the pensions discussed so far depend on a contributions record. In addition, there is a **non-contributory retirement pension**, primarily for people who retired too soon after 1948 to have made adequate contributions. Anyone who is 80 or over and not receiving a national insurance pension, or receiving one at a low rate, may qualify for a non-contributory pension. As its name implies it is not a national insurance benefit, and is paid out of the Consolidated Fund.

Private pension schemes vary widely: some are contributory, others not; some cover all workers in an occupation, others only senior personnel (so-called 'top-hat' schemes); some, but by no means all, meet the conditions for contracting out of the state scheme; there are various arrangements for transferring pension rights to a new job; virtually no scheme promises anything close to complete indexation. Private pensions in industrialised countries are typified by four characteristics. Almost all are *funded*.[4] They are *supplemental*, in that they replace only part of the state pension. They are *constrained* in two ways: individual choice is generally limited; and the conduct of pension companies is regulated to protect consumers. Finally, virtually all private pension schemes are *subsidised* through tax expenditures (Chapter 7:1.1), though with serious valuation problems (UK Board of Inland Revenue, 1983).

Given this variety, no attempt is made to discuss private schemes in detail.[5] Until 1988 the great majority of schemes were *occupational pensions* (i.e. organised by employers) offering pensions on a defined benefit basis.[6] The coverage of occupational schemes has grown substantially over the years. Since 1988, under changes introduced by the 1986 Social Security Act, employers have been able to opt out of SERPS by guaranteeing a level of contribution rather than of benefit. In addition, since 1988 employees

---

[4] I.e. paying benefits out of a previously accumulated fund, as explained in detail in section 2.
[5] For an analysis of private pension schemes in the UK, see Hannah (1986) and in the USA, Munnell (1982) and Aaron *et al.* (1989). For international comparison, see Gordon (1988, Ch. 8).
[6] As discussed in section 2, defined benefit schemes pay benefits related to previous earnings, as opposed to defined contribution schemes, in which benefits depend on previous contributions.

have had the right to have a *personal pension*, rather than remain in their employer's scheme or fully in the state scheme. Such individuals can either join a private scheme of their choice, run by a financial institution or, even more individually, may manage their own pension portfolio.

2 Methods of Organising Pensions

The economics of pension schemes can be confusing because writers easily become bemused by its *financial* aspects (i.e. analysis of insurance companies' portfolios of financial assets). I shall try to simplify matters by concentrating on the essential *economic* issues (i.e. the production and consumption of goods and services).

From an individual viewpoint, the economic function of pensions is to redistribute consumption over time. By contributing to a pension scheme an individual consumes today less than he produces, so as to continue to consume when he has retired and is no longer producing. In principle, an individual can transfer consumption over time in two ways, and in *only* two ways: he can store current production; or he can acquire a claim to future production.

One way of ensuring future consumption is to set aside part of current production for future use, e.g. by digging a hole in one's back garden and adding to its contents each year tins of baked beans, shoe laces and soap powder. Though this is the only way Robinson Crusoe could guarantee consumption in retirement, the method in practice has major inefficiencies. Storing current production is costly in terms of the potential return to savings forgone, and also because storage costs for many commodities are high. A second problem is uncertainty, e.g. about what quantities to store, what new goods might become available, and how one's tastes might change. Third, some services can be transferred over time by storing the physical wealth which generates them (e.g. it is possible to store housing services by being an owner-occupier); but it is not possible, even in principle, to store services deriving from human capital, medical services being a particularly important example. Organising pensions by storing current production on a large scale is therefore a non-starter.

The alternative is for individuals to exchange current production for a claim on future output. There are two broad ways in which I might do this: by saving part of my wages each week I could build up a pile of *money* which I would exchange for goods produced by younger people after my retirement; or I could obtain a *promise* that I would be given goods produced by others after my retirement. The promise could be from my son ('Don't worry, dad, I'll look after you when you're old'), or from government – '[The Government's] policy on pensions is to secure better benefits for all pensioners, present and future . . .' (UK, 1974, p. iii). The two most common ways of organising pensions broadly parallel these two sorts of claim on future production. So-called *funded* schemes follow the first; *Pay-As-You-Go* or unfunded schemes the second.[7]

Funded and Pay-As-You-Go schemes   In a funded scheme (frequently organised in the private sector by insurance companies), contributions are invested in a variety of financial assets, the return on which is credited to its members. When an individual retires, the pension fund will be holding all his/her past contributions, together with the interest and dividends earned on them. This usually amounts to a large lump sum which is converted into an annuity (Chapter 5:2.3). The annuity is then the individual's pension. Funding, therefore, is simply a method of accumulating money, which is exchanged for goods at some later date. Most occupational schemes are of this type.

Funded schemes in practice take many forms, of which two in particular should be distinguished. Under a *defined contribution* scheme, the contribution rate is fixed, so that the individual's pension (given his life expectancy) is determined *only* by the size of the lump sum accumulated during working life. The individual therefore bears two sorts of risk: that of unanticipated changes in the rate of return to pension assets during his working life; and that of unanticipated inflation after retirement. As explained in Chapter 5:2.3, insurance can protect the individual against the risks associated with longevity; however, the individual bears the entire risk associated with varying real rates of return to pension assets.

Under a *defined benefit* scheme, usually run at a firm or industry level, the firm promises to pay an annuity at retirement; the size of the annuity depends on the employee's wage in his/her final year (or final few years) of work and upon length of service (a typical formula is one-eightieth of final salary per year of service, up to a maximum of 40 years). Thus the annuity is, in effect, wage indexed until retirement (though as discussed later, not typically indexed thereafter). The employee contribution is generally a fraction of his/her salary. Thus, the employer's contribution becomes the endogenous variable. In a defined benefit scheme, it is the firm or industry which bears the risk in the face of unanticipated changes in the real rate of return to pension assets.

Funded schemes of whatever sort have two major implications: they always have sufficient reserves to pay all outstanding financial liabilities

---

[7] There are other ways of organising pensions. The so-called *book* method makes advance provision for pensions on the company's balance sheet in the same way as provision is made for other deferred liabilities (e.g. future tax payments). Money is not transferred out of the company (as with funded schemes) but is retained for use by the company. At the same time a reserve is set up in the balance sheet to reflect the estimated liability. In *cash* terms there is little difference between book reserving and Pay-As-You-Go. Funding and Pay-As-You-Go are thus the two generic methods of organising pensions, and discussion is confined to them.

(since an individual's entitlement is simply his past contributions plus the interest earned on them); and a representative individual, or a generation as a whole, gets out of a funded scheme no more than he has put in, i.e. with funding, a generation is constrained by its own past savings. Other implications emerge throughout the chapter.

Pay-As-You-Go (PAYG) schemes are usually run by the state. They are contractarian in nature, based on the fact that the state has no need to accumulate funds in anticipation of future pension claims, but can tax the working population to pay the pensions of the retired generation. Almost all state pension schemes today are PAYG, the only major exceptions in the OECD countries being the earnings-related component of the state pension in Sweden and Japan (see Rosa, 1982; Gordon, 1988).

From an economic viewpoint PAYG can be looked at in several ways. As an individual contributor, my claim to a pension is based on a promise from the state that if I pay contributions now I will be given a pension in the future. The terms of the promise are fairly precise; they were set out in some detail in section 1. From an aggregate viewpoint, the state is simply raising taxes from one group of individuals and transferring the revenues thereby derived to another. State-run PAYG schemes, from this perspective, appear little different from explicit income transfers.

The major implication of the PAYG system is that it relaxes the constraint that the benefits received by any generation must be matched by its own contributions. Samuelson (1958) showed that with a PAYG scheme it is possible in principle for *every* generation to receive more in pensions than it paid in contributions, provided that real income rises steadily; this is likely when there is technological progress and/or steady population growth.

Preliminary comparison   PAYG schemes have three advantages: they are generally able to protect pensions in payment against inflation; they can generally increase the real value of pensions in line with economic growth; and full pension rights can be built up quickly, since pensions are paid not by one's own previous contributions, but by those of the current workforce. These points are illustrated in Table 9.1. In period 1 the total income of the workforce is £1000, so that a contribution rate of 10 per cent yields £100. Suppose by period 2 prices and earnings have risen by 100 per cent (column 2). A contribution of 10 per cent now yields £200, which has a purchasing power of £100 at the old price level, and so maintains the real value of pensions in the face of inflation. Alternatively, suppose (column 3) that economic growth raises earnings to £2000, while prices stay at their original level. In this case the 10 per cent contribution rate has a *real* yield of £200, and so it is possible to double the real value of pensions.

Against these undoubted advantages must be offset the major problem that PAYG is sensitive to any change in the age structure of the population

Table 9.1 *Financing a Pay-As-You-Go pension scheme in the presence of inflation and growth*

	Period 1 (1)	Period 2 (Inflation) (2)	Period 2 (Growth) (3)
(1) Total income of workforce	£1000	£2000	£2000
(2) Price index	100	200	100
(3) Pension contribution rate	10%	10%	10%
(4) Available for pensions	£100	£200	£200
(5) Real value of pensions (= (line (4)/line (2)) × 100)	£100	£100	£200

which reduces the workforce relative to the number of dependants. The crucial variable is the so-called dependency ratio,

$$\frac{P}{W} \tag{9.1}$$

where P is the number of pensioners and W the number of workers. Influences like increased longevity raise the number of pensioners, and longer education reduces the size of the workforce. Lowering the retirement age simultaneously reduces the workforce and increases the number of pensioners. Finally, as we shall see, any large 'bulge' in the birth rate can cause serious difficulties.

Another claimed disadvantage of PAYG finance is that it makes pensioners dependent on the future workforce. This is true. But, as we shall see in section 3.2, the same is true of funded schemes. In both cases pensioners are dependent on future generations, since both schemes build pensions round claims on future production rather than by storing current production.

The disadvantages of funded schemes tend to mirror the advantages of PAYG. Starting with inflation, it is important to distinguish (a) pensions in build-up, when contributions are still being paid, and (b) pensions in payment. Funded schemes can generally cope with inflation during the build-up of pension rights, and with a given rate of *anticipated* inflation once the pension is in payment. But they do not cope well with unanticipated post-retirement inflation. The reason is straightforward. A pensioner under a funded scheme builds up over his working life a capital sum, which he exchanges upon retirement for an annuity. From equation (5.11) the size of the annuity depends not only on the lump sum, but also on the *real* rate of interest facing the insurance company (i.e. the excess of the nominal interest rate over the rate of inflation). Where inflation is correctly anticipated, nominal interest rates, and hence also the nominal annuity payment, can be adjusted to take account of inflation. But where post-retirement inflation is higher than expected, a pure funded scheme is generally unable to index benefits. Up to a point it is possible to hedge against inflation in any one country by having an internationally diversified portfolio of pension assets. But private schemes are unable to cope with common inflation shocks, e.g. private pensioners in the UK suffered a drastic reduction in the real value of their pensions during the years of high inflation in the mid-1970s in the aftermath of the first oil shock.[8]

It should be noted that the relative ability of PAYG and funding to cope with inflation is due less to the method of finance *per se*, than to the fact that in many instances only the state can guarantee indexed amounts. Funded schemes may be able to cope with inflation if their assets are indexed by the state, e.g. where the state sells indexed gilts or where it underwrites directly the indexation component once funded pensions are in payment.[9] However, the part of the return which compensates for inflation is paid out of current tax revenues, i.e. on a PAYG basis. More generally, any receipts of funded schemes deriving from current tax revenues, whether the return to indexed bonds or the tax advantages they currently enjoy, constitute a PAYG element in such schemes.

In principle, an individual can insure against uncertainty. We saw in Chapter 5 how private insurance works in the case of burglary, which suggests the possibility that individuals insure against inflation. This is one of the issues considered in section 3.1; it turns out that such an escape route is generally not possible without state intervention.

For similar reasons it is not possible for funded schemes substantially to increase the real value of pensions in line with economic growth which occurs after a pensioner's retirement. Finally, it takes a long time to build up full pension rights in a funded scheme, because it takes an individual many years to build up a lump sum sufficiently large to generate an annuity which will support him fully in retirement.

Against these disadvantages, it is often claimed that funding has the major advantage of being insensitive to changes in the dependency ratio. The argument is that a funded scheme always has sufficient resources to pay the pensions of its members, since the present value of a representative pension stream exactly equals past contributions plus interest. It is true that a funded scheme will have sufficient resources to pay all *money* claims against it; but it does *not* follow that funding, on that account, offers pensioners better protection against demographic change. This controversial topic is addressed in detail in sections 3.2 and 5.1.

[8] 'Lady Spencer Churchill; Why She and Others Like Her Deserve All the Help They Can Get', *The Times*, 24 February 1977.

[9] As discussed in section 1, the latter is the current situation in the UK in respect of the guaranteed minimum pension received by individuals who have contracted out of the state earnings-related pension scheme. The UK government also sells indexed bonds (see footnote 22).

3 Efficiency Arguments for State Intervention

3.1 Public Versus Private Provision

Section 3.1 discusses efficiency aspects of public versus private provision, and section 3.2 looks at the PAYG versus funding controversy. Social justice is considered in section 4.

Efficiency requires that individuals buy the *socially* efficient *real* level of pension. The theoretical conditions under which private insurance markets achieve this result were discussed in Chapter 5:4.1. The three major policy issues are why people insure at all, why the state makes membership of a pension scheme compulsory, and why it provides retirement pensions itself.

We know that a rational, risk-averse individual will pay pension contributions (i.e. buy insurance) so long as their net cost does not exceed the value to him of the certainty he thereby derives (Chapter 5:2.1). Membership is compulsory because of the external costs which arise if an individual does not buy pension rights (Chapter 8:2.1). The issue of public provision is more complicated. The private market provides pensions efficiently only if the standard assumptions of perfect information, perfect competition and no market failures hold. On the demand side it is not unreasonable to postulate well-informed consumers, not because individuals are necessarily able to acquire it themselves, but because they could purchase it from an insurance broker. On the supply side it is necessary to consider separately the five technical conditions (Chapter 5:3) which must hold if the private market is to supply insurance efficiently.

The probability of living to a given age for pensioner A is independent of that for pensioner B; and the probability is known and less than one. Data on mortality rates are reliable in all industrialised countries. Nor is there any problem of adverse selection – by and large people do not know when they are going to die. Moral hazard is not a problem either; suicide is costly to the individual, and works in the insurance company's favour.

The initial conclusion, therefore, is that there is no technical problem with private pension provision. This, however, overlooks inflation. An individual can purchase a future consumption bundle which is efficient in terms of quantity and quality only if he is able to guarantee the *real* value of his future pension. This can occur without intervention only if the private market can supply insurance against unanticipated inflation. Such insurance is not possible for two reasons. First, the probability of pensioner A experiencing a given rate of inflation is *not* independent of that for pensioner B – the rate of inflation facing one pensioner will (by and large) face them all. There is no possibility of winners compensating losers and so insurance is impossible. In addition, the probability distribution of different future levels of inflation is neither known nor estimable.[10]

---

[10] Inflation is not a problem for car repairs, for example, because automobile insurance, unlike pensions, is financed by *current* premiums.

Inflation is therefore an uninsurable risk. Thus pensioners cannot insure each other. To what extent might they be able to find protection through some other mechanism, e.g. by buying assets whose value keeps pace with inflation? That would be possible without intervention if real rates of return were independent of inflation. As an empirical matter, this is not the case. The dependence is partly the result of distortions elsewhere (e.g. non-indexed tax systems) which could in principle be corrected. However, where an inflationary shock represents other adverse movements in the economy, no private agency can offer a complete hedge against inflation. Bodie (1989) argues that short-term deposit accounts are the best (albeit incomplete) hedge since short-term interest rates are revised frequently; Zeckhauser and Patel (1987) find that buying futures contracts on government bonds eliminates only about one-third of the risk of unanticipated inflation.

Thus inflation is an uninsurable risk; and private-sector hedges offer incomplete protection. Though there is controversy as to why there are no private-sector financial instruments offering a risk-free real return, the empirical conclusion is clear. Bodie's survey points out (1990, p. 36) that 'virtually no private pension plans in the US offer automatic inflation protection after retirement'. Gordon's cross-national conclusion is that 'indexing of pension benefits after retirement ... presents serious difficulties in funded employer pension plans' (1988, p. 169).

The conclusion is that, if pensions are to be protected against inflation, such protection must come from government. Thus there is an efficiency argument, at a minimum, for state intervention to assist private schemes with the costs of unanticipated inflation once pensions are in payment. The state is able to offer such a guarantee because it can use current tax revenues on a PAYG basis. This will introduce a PAYG element even into the purest funded scheme. It should be clear that an indemnity against inflation, if publicly provided, is not true insurance (because it cannot be), but a form of tax/transfer. Since efficiency requires individuals to make decisions about the real value of the pension they purchase, and since the appropriate guarantees against inflation can be given only by the state on a PAYG basis, there is a cast-iron efficiency argument for at least some public involvement with pensions. Whether this should stop at the provision of inflation indemnities for private markets, or whether the state should step in to provide pensions itself on either a PAYG or a mixed funded/PAYG basis, is an open issue upon which most of the rest of the chapter has a bearing.

3.2 Funding Versus Pay-As-You-Go: Theoretical Arguments

The demographic problem Having established the case for at least some public involvement, the next question is whether any state scheme should be funded or PAYG and, in particular, what are the relative merits of the two methods in the face of demographic change. This issue is analysed by Barr (1979), on which this section draws heavily (see also Falkingham, 1989).[11] The problem has become important, as shown in Figure 9.1, because of the peak in the birth rate in the 1940s, and the secondary bulge of the mid-1960s. These cohorts of 'bulge' babies will retire between 2010 and 2030, and will have to be supported in old age by the much smaller succeeding generations. Specifically, in 1985 there were 2.3 national insurance contributors for each pensioner; the projected figure for 2035 is 1.6 (UK, 1985h, para. 1.12; see also the Further Reading).

The problem is compounded by the increases in the earnings-related pension under the 1975 Act (see section 1). Even with the reforms discussed in section 5.1, a worker with an average contributions record will receive a pension almost twice the current flat-rate benefit.

Number
of
births

Figure 9.1 *Live births per 1000 population, 1940–84*
(Source: *Annual Abstract of Statistics*, various years.)

The demographic problem is not confined to Britain. A startlingly similar pattern exists in the USA (see Munnell, in Pechman (1983, pp. 84–5)) and in most of the EC countries, including Belgium, Denmark, Germany, Italy and the Netherlands, and also in Australia, New Zealand and Japan.[12]

---

[11] The analysis is similar in spirit to Samuelson (1958).

[12] This is a remarkable fact. Why should countries as different as Denmark (Protestant and highly industrialised) have a pattern of birth rates very similar to Italy (Catholic and with some largely unindustrialised parts)? Australia, which escaped much of the recession of the 1970s, nevertheless has a declining birth rate. And Japan faces exactly the same problem despite large differences in religion, social organisation and patterns of industry. No one has yet given a satisfactory explanation of this striking similarity. For further discussion and quantification of the increasing cost of pensions, see Barr (1992, Table 4) and OECD (1988).

Much of the industrialised world thus faces the potentially explosive problem of an ageing population with heavy retirements after about 2010.

The widely held (but false) view that funded schemes are inherently 'safer' than PAYG is an example of the fallacy of composition.[13] For *individuals* the economic function of a pension scheme is to transfer consumption over time. But (ruling out the case where current output is stored in holes in people's gardens) this is not possible for society as a whole; the consumption of pensioners as a group is produced by the next generation of workers. From an *aggregate* viewpoint, the economic function of pension schemes is to divide total output between workers and pensioners, i.e. to reduce the consumption of workers so that sufficient output remains for pensioners. Once this point is understood it becomes clear why PAYG and funded schemes, which are both simply ways of dividing output between workers and pensioners, should not fare very differently in the face of demographic change.

The simple model highlights the argument under strong assumptions. These simplify the analysis without substantially altering the conclusion. They are:

1. Output per head remains constant over time, and is the same whether pensions are funded or PAYG.
2. The number of workers remains constant.
3. Wages are fixed in real terms, pensions in nominal terms.[14]
4. There is no trade with other countries.

The simplest case is illustrated by the first column of Table 9.2. There are 10 workers who produce an output of 1000. Assume that there are no taxes, so that the workers receive the whole of their output; and assume that each unit costs £1. Now suppose that workers use 900 units of output for current consumption, and set the remaining 100 units aside for their retirement. Pension provision can take two forms. Workers can sell 100 units of output for £100 to the current generation of pensioners, who are able to buy it with their own past savings. The current generation of workers saves the money, and uses it when it retires to buy the non-consumption of the then workforce. This, at its simplest, is how funded schemes operate.[15] Alternatively, in a PAYG world, 100 units of output are transferred from workers to current pensioners via a 10 per cent tax on the workforce, so

---

[13] It is a fallacy of composition to assume that because something is true for an individual it will *necessarily* be true on aggregate. For instance, if I stand on my seat in the theatre I will get a better view, but if everybody does so nobody will get a better view.

[14] This assumption, like the others, is relaxed later. But empirically it is not much of an exaggeration for occupational pensions.

[15] In practice things can be more complicated: contributions can come from employers and the government as well as from workers; and contributions may not be entirely at the expense of workers' consumption. These factors complicate the analysis but do not change the logic of the underlying argument.

that it can afford to consume only 900. When the current workforce retires it in turn receives 100 units of output.

Table 9.2 *Output and consumption with workforces of different sizes*

	Period 1 (1)	Period 2 (Constant productivity) (2)	Period 2 (Doubled productivity) (3)
Size of workforce	10	5	5
Total output = total income of the workforce	1000	500	1000
Workers' consumption	900	450	900
Workers' non-consumption	100	50	100

Note: Output is measured in physical units.

Under the stated assumptions both schemes can continue indefinitely and both lead to the same three conclusions: (a) pensioners can consume only what workers produce but do not consume; (b) pensioners always depend on succeeding generations to provide the labour to produce the goods which they consume; and (c) under the stated assumptions PAYG and funding lead to identical results.

The effects of a decline in the workforce The previous assumptions stand, except that the labour force halves. This case is shown in the second column of Table 9.2. With output per worker unchanged (by assumption) output has halved to 500, and workers' consumption to 450, leaving 50 units of output for pensions. Under PAYG, the 10 per cent tax mentioned above leads to exactly this result. With a funded scheme matters are more complicated. The current generation of pensioners is taken to be the previous workforce of 10 in column 1, which has accumulated sufficient funds to buy an output of 100 at the initial price of £1 per unit. If the savings habits of workers do not change, total expenditure will be £450 by workers on current consumption, plus £100 by pensioners out of accumulated funds. The total of £550 is greater than the value at current prices of output of 500. While pensioners get their £100 in *money* safely transferred to their retirement, they will not necessarily receive 100 units of *consumption*.

In economic terms, if there is a large accumulation of pension funds when the workforce is declining, the high level of spending by pensioners out of their accumulated savings will reduce the rate of saving in the economy, and possibly lead to aggregate dissaving. Net pensioner consumption (i.e. the excess of pensioner consumption over any pensioner production) is greater than saving by workers (i.e. the excess of workers' production over their consumption at current prices); and at full employment this causes demand inflation, which erodes the purchasing power of pensioners' accumulated funds, and hence their consumption. The precise mechanism of this inflationary process is spelled out in Barr (1979), which shows that if the labour force halves then, under the stated assumptions, output will halve, the price level double, and pensioner consumption halve. In the extreme, it does me no good to accumulate a huge fund if on the day I retire the last of the workforce boards ship for Australia – I will have plenty of pound notes, but no mechanism for transforming them into consumption.[16]

Relaxing the assumptions Suppose first that workers' wages are not necessarily indexed, nor pensions necessarily fixed in money terms. If the labour force halves (the other assumptions remaining in force), output will halve (column 2 of Table 9.2). This output can be divided between workers and pensioners in different ways; but their joint demand is constrained by total supply. The relative shares of the two groups will depend on such factors as their political and bargaining strengths, i.e. whether pensioners are more powerful lobbying for current tax revenues (PAYG) or as the owners of capital. There is no difference of principle between the two methods, only a practical issue.

Suppose, next, that productivity doubles, but is unaffected by the method of pension finance. If the other assumptions still hold, a smaller workforce of 5 can now produce the same output as previously produced by 10 (column 3). Workers can consume 900, leaving 100 for pensioners. The system is in equilibrium, in this case because supply has adjusted. In a world of funding, the growth in output makes possible sufficient extra saving by the smaller workforce to match dissaving by the larger group of pensioners. Under PAYG, a tax at an unchanged rate of 10 per cent enables government to transfer to pensioners the 100 units of output promised to them.

Relaxing the demographic assumptions is straightforward. Suppose that the decline in the working-age population is entirely offset by increases in the labour force participation of women, and in the retirement age. In this case, column 1 of Table 9.2 applies in period 2, notwithstanding demographic change. The problem is entirely resolved, again on the supply side, for both types of pension scheme, for the same reason as in the previous paragraph. A similar conclusion arises from any combination of increased productivity and labour force participation which prevents output from falling.

Finally, it is in principle possible to maintain the consumption of both workers and pensioners with goods produced abroad, provided the country has sufficient overseas assets to do so. This could be done with publicly owned stocks of foreign currency (PAYG) or with foreign assets accumulated by pension funds.

Two conclusions emerge.

1. If changes in productivity and labour force participation are inde-

---

[16] Australia would be unlikely to allow me to buy Australian goods with pounds in this situation.

pendent of the method of finance, then relaxing the assumptions does not change the previous results. In particular, it remains the case that funding and PAYG are not substantially different in their ability to cope with demographic change. This should not be surprising. The task of both schemes is to reduce workers' consumption; PAYG does this by taxing workers, funding by forcing (or allowing) them to save. The only difference is that PAYG makes explicit the notion that pensions involve current resources.

2. The crucial variable is *output*. A decline in the labour force causes problems for any pension scheme only if it causes a fall in output; the problem is solved to the extent that this can be prevented.

The choice between PAYG and funding in the face of demographic change is therefore relevant only to the extent that funding (as is sometimes argued) systematically causes output to be higher. This is a matter of considerable controversy both theoretically and empirically, and is the main topic of section 5.1.

Other aspects This section digresses briefly to a number of other issues dividing the proponents of PAYG and funding, mainly to make clear that they have little or nothing to do with the central issue of paying for pensions. The main arguments are that funded schemes are safer, give more freedom and impose greater financial discipline.

The question of safety, as we have seen, turns on whether pensioners as a group are better able to fight for their share of national output as recipients of current tax revenues or as the owners of capital. The PAYG mechanism makes clear both the quarrel over output shares and the dependence of pensioners on the next generation of workers. Funding hides both issues, but does not remove them. It is, indeed, possible for the state to break promises made earlier under a PAYG scheme. But funded schemes are equally vulnerable and equally political (consider the reaction to proposals to reduce the tax advantages currently granted to pension funds).[17] As a practical matter the flat-rate component of the national insurance retirement pension has more than doubled in *real* terms since 1948. Funded benefits have usually failed to keep up with inflation (see the quotes from Bodie and Gordon in section 3.1).

A related, libertarian-type argument asserts that taxes in a PAYG world curtail individual liberty. The counter-argument is that the issue of freedom is raised not by PAYG versus funding but by compulsion versus voluntarism. A compulsory funded scheme would give no more freedom than current arrangements.

---

[17] While on the subject, it should not be imagined that storing current output at the bottom of one's garden gives complete protection against *all* contingencies. The state can always expropriate such output either explicitly, or by a tax on individual wealth or, more subtly, by engineering inflation and imposing a non-indexed capital gains tax on an accruals basis. In similar vein, funded schemes run a potential risk of state direction of their investment portfolios, a besetting problem in Latin America (see Mesa-Lago, 1990).

A final argument is that funding imposes greater financial discipline. With PAYG, the state makes promises now, but may not have to pay anything till later (e.g. increases under the 1975 Act are not fully payable until 1998). The immediate revenue charge is negligible relative to the annual value of the potential future liability, which, it is argued, may lead to irresponsible pension promises (this is an example of the government failure arguments set out in Chapter 4:5). With funding, promises of higher future benefits must be matched by increased contributions immediately, thereby, it is argued, guarding against government failure. Though factually true, these are not necessarily arguments against PAYG. Many would regard as one of the great advantages of PAYG its ability to increase benefits rapidly should there be the political will to do so. The argument that PAYG is 'unsound' because it is open to abuse can be applied equally to automobiles or pain-killing drugs.

A related view is that PAYG is dangerous because it can be used profligately to redistribute income. To some, however, the ability to redistribute income is one of the great *advantages* of PAYG. Which argument one adopts depends largely on views about social justice.

4 Social Justice

4.1 Public Versus Private Provision

This section, which closely parallels Chapter 8:2.3, considers the equity arguments for public organisation of pensions. Horizontal equity concerns goals like a guaranteed minimum standard of some commodities, or equal access to them. These occur without intervention (Chapter 4:4.3) where individuals have perfect information and equal power, a line of argument which lends little support to public provision of pensions. If individuals did not have perfect information, they would generally be able to buy it. At most there is a case for regulation of minimum standards. The fact that individuals do not have equal power lends further support to minimum standards but, again, there is no argument for public provision.

I have already discussed in Chapter 8:2.3 and elsewhere the weakness of the vertical equity argument that the state should provide pensions because otherwise the poor could not afford them. The earlier conclusions apply equally here – that public provision solely to foster redistribution is justified only by a consumption externality, where the rich confer pensions on the poor as a merit good.

Consumption externalities apart, equity reasons for public provision must appeal to efficiency arguments. These arise out of the inability of the private market to offer protection against inflation, giving an efficiency justification for public provision at least of the indexation component of pensions, and possibly (depending on the outcome of the funding versus PAYG debate) of the entire pension. As discussed in Chapter 4:7.2, once a commodity is publicly provided on *efficiency* grounds, it is not inappropriate to finance it redistributively. In addition, the fact that membership is compulsory, by imposing a pooling solution, avoids the worst problems of adverse selection (Chapter 5:4.1); in consequence, premiums based on income rather than individual risk need cause no major inefficiency. These efficiency arguments for compulsion and public provision, taken together, suggest that using publicly organised pensions for distributional purposes does not necessarily cause substantial efficiency losses.

4.2 The Redistributive Effects of Pensions

A pension scheme, depending on its precise construction, can redistribute from young to old, from rich to poor, and from men to women. It is necessary to consider PAYG and funded schemes, and in each case to ask three questions: is such redistribution possible; is it inevitable; and to what extent does it occur in practice?

Redistribution from young to old PAYG finance enables a generation as a whole to receive more than the sum of its past contributions. Thus redistribution from the young workforce to the retired generation is *possible*. But it is not *inevitable*, since a PAYG scheme could be organised to pay actuarial benefits. *In practice*, as we shall see in section 5.2, there has been substantial redistribution from young to old in many countries over the past 40 years.

With funded schemes it is necessary to consider separately the cases of stable and unstable price levels. In a world with no inflation, the funded benefits of any generation are constrained by its past contributions, rendering redistribution from young to old impossible. The effect of unanticipated inflation is to bring about unintended redistribution from old to young (and vice versa for unanticipated price deflation).

Redistribution from rich to poor can, and usually does, occur with PAYG pensions. In many state schemes there is *formula redistribution*, in that individual B with half the income of individual A will generally pay half the contribution, but receive a pension which is more than half of A's. The UK system was described in section 1. In the USA, though the formula has changed from time to time, it has always been explicitly redistributive (Aaron *et al.*, 1989, Table 2.4). In 1988 the US pension for a single person retiring at the normal retirement age was 90 per cent of the first $319 of relevant earnings, 32 per cent between $319 and $1921, and 15 per cent thereafter. The same general feature is true in the systems of most industrialised countries (Barr, 1992, section V).

The effect of formula redistribution is partially offset by *differential mortality*, to the extent that the rich live longer than the poor. But redistribution is not inevitable – it is possible to organise a PAYG scheme in which pensions are proportional to contributions.

It might be possible to devise a (compulsory) funded scheme which redistributed from rich to poor. But where membership is voluntary, the present value of the annuity received by a representative individual must equal the lump sum accumulated over his working years. This implies, *ceteris paribus*, that pensions must be proportional to contributions, thus ruling out systematic redistribution.

Redistribution from men to women   The following are all statements of fact referring to the UK:

1. The normal retiring age for men is 65, at which age a man has a life expectancy of 77. The average man is thus retired for 12 years.

2. The normal retiring age for women is 60, at which age women have a life expectancy of 80, so that the average woman is retired for 20 years.

3. It is therefore $20/12 = 1\frac{2}{3}$ times as expensive to provide a given weekly pension for a woman as for a man.

4. If men and women pay equal contributions and receive equal weekly benefits, then redistribution takes place from men to women. Since women live longer than men, abolishing the differential retirement age would reduce the subsidy but would not eliminate it.

Redistribution from men to women occurs for these reasons in both funded and PAYG schemes. The phenomenon is widespread, but is particularly strong in the UK, which is an outlier in international terms in having a lower retiring age for women (a subject to which we return in section 5.2). Two issues arise: is such redistribution inevitable; and is it desirable? On the first point, one could devise a scheme (PAYG or funded) in which women received benefits related to their longevity. A woman could receive a lower weekly/monthly pension than a man with an identical contributions record, i.e. a definition of equity as a pension stream of equal present value. Alternatively, women could pay a higher contribution and receive the same weekly/monthly pension as men, i.e. equity consists of women receiving a pension stream with a higher present value, matched by a larger contributions stream. Thus there are two definitions of equity: equal present value; or equal weekly value. Either is defensible; but they are different, hence the equity problem.

Redistribution from men to women in pensions, though not inevitable, is almost universal, partly from a belief that any differential is a form of discrimination. A decision by the US Supreme Court (1978) declared differential pensions unconstitutional even if calculated actuarially (i.e. on the basis of equation (5.11)).[18] Nor is such redistribution necessarily

---

[18] Though tenable on equity grounds, the decision was based on a total failure to understand the nature of insurance.

undesirable. Analytically, it occurs because women pay the same premiums as men despite being (from the insurer's viewpoint) worse risks because they live longer. As we saw in Chapter 5:4.1, efficiency generally requires that premiums should be proportional to risk; where insurance is compulsory, however, low-risk individuals are not able to opt out, and charging the same premium for all categories of risk does not cause adverse selection. It is possible that secondary inefficiency might arise, e.g. the possible distortion of labour supply decisions which non-actuarial contributions might cause. To the extent that this is not a substantial problem, the decision whether all classes of risk should pay the same premium can be made mainly on equity grounds. Thus some compulsory schemes do not match premium with risk (unemployment benefits), while others do (automobile insurance).[19]

5 Assessment of National Insurance Retirement Pensions

5.1 Efficiency and Incentives

BACKGROUND QUESTIONS

This section asks whether the national insurance pension scheme is efficient and equitable, starting with the *a priori* questions of Chapter 8:3.1: should pensions be national (i.e. publicly provided), are they optimal in quantity and type, and are they insurance?

Should pensions be national? The efficiency arguments for state pensions rest on externalities, justifying compulsion, and technical failures in the insurance market, justifying public provision at a minimum of protection against inflation. There is no serious argument that it should be compulsory for people to belong to a pension scheme, at least up to some minimum level, nor that economic efficiency requires choices about future consumption levels. Decisions about pensions are therefore more efficient if inflation can be ignored; but only the state can offer inflation insurance (i.e. indexation). Thus there is an uncontentious role for public provision at least of indexed assets for use by private, funded schemes.[20] The efficiency argument for public provision of the whole pension is less clear-cut.[21]

Does the state provide the optimal quantity and type of pension? Only tentative answers are possible. But inflation raises far more serious problems

---

[19] More controversially, women have been required to pay higher medical insurance premiums than men of the same age ('Weaker Sex Should Pay More for Health Insurance, Judge Rules', *The Times*, 16 August 1985, p. 3).

[20] The role of the state *vis-à-vis* indexation is generally accepted even by writers who oppose public provision of any pension above a basic minimum; see, for instance, Morgan (1984, p. 74).

[21] For comprehensive discussion of these issues, see the reports of an Australian Committee on the subject (National Superannuation Committee of Inquiry, 1976, 1977).

for pensions than for unemployment and sickness insurance, and so requires separate discussion. The state has long been active in indexing pensions. Barr (1981) shows that from 1948 to 1975 the basic pension was in practice indexed to average pre-tax earnings though there was no legal requirement for this. Since 1975 annual uprating at least in line with price changes has been mandatory; and the government has indemnified certain private, funded schemes against inflation (section 1). In addition, since 1981 there have been a number of issues of state indexed bonds for use *inter alia* by private pension funds.[22]

It can be argued that the increasing role of the state in indexing public and private pensions has contributed to the relative certainty with which individuals can plan for the future, and has therefore increased efficiency, albeit imperfectly because the state scheme makes no allowance for different degrees of risk aversion between individuals. But there have been a number of problems of implementation, not least in the years between 1975 and 1980, when the indexation formula gave an unintended upward bias to the real value of the basic flat-rate pension (a similar problem arose in the USA). For this and other reasons some writers (see Hemming and Kay, 1982a, p. 46) argue that the pension system is larger than would voluntarily be chosen.

Are pensions insurance? Chapter 8:3.1 pointed out that national insurance contributions are not geared to risk; that the scheme is not funded; and that rights to benefit are not determined solely by the occurrence of the insured event. In addition, as we shall see in section 5.2, the scheme redistributes to the poor, and offers credits for people at home looking after young children, and for the unemployed. These arrangements are a considerable departure from the Beveridge scheme, whose lump-sum contributions and benefits ruled out redistribution from rich to poor (assuming, for example, equal life expectancy); and since the original proposals were for a funded scheme, they would also have ruled out redistribution from young to old.

The result is social insurance, as defined in Chapter 5:4.2. Pensions are insurance in the sense of offering protection against risk, but not in the sense of an actuarial mechanism. No other result is possible (Chapter 8:2.1). As discussed in Chapter 8:3.1, social insurance, though it *enables* redistribution from rich to poor, does not *require* it. The extent to which social insurance is redistributive therefore depends on the relative weights attached to the different objectives in Chapter 1:2.2.

---

[22] To give a simplified example, an ordinary 10-year government bond sold in 1993 for £100 would pay, say, £10 interest per year and repay the £100 loan in 2003. A similar indexed bond would make a lower interest payment each year, but would repay in 2003 not £100, but the initial sum indexed for changes in the price level. If prices had doubled over the period, the bond holder would receive £200 plus interest (also indexed) in 2003.

INCENTIVE ISSUES

The literature on the incentive effects of pensions is large and controversial (see the Further Reading at the end of Chapter 8). Two issues predominate: does PAYG restrict saving and output growth; and do pensions reduce labour supply?

Pensions, saving and economic growth It is often regarded as self-evident that saving, and hence economic growth, will be higher with funding than under PAYG. But this assertion requires at least three major qualifications. First, it is only while a fund is building up that saving might be higher. It should be clear from column 1 of Table 9.2 that in the long run workers save 100 and pensioners dissave 100, so that net saving is zero.

The second qualification is that opinion is very divided as to whether funding increases saving even during the build-up phase. The issue was discussed long ago by Sydney and Beatrice Webb in the context of the 1908 Old Age Pensions Act (Chapter 2:2.2). They reported that 'some of our witnesses ... have taken the view ... that such non-contributory pensions would be likely to discourage thrift and saving' (Webb and Webb, 1909, p. 334). Current debate was reopened by Feldstein (1974 and 1979). He argued that PAYG financing, particularly if pensions are higher than actuarially justified, reduces saving; but that any inducement to early retirement (discussed below) would tend to increase savings to pay for a longer retirement after a shorter working life. The issue is therefore theoretically indeterminate. His empirical work, based on time-series data, concluded that the US social security (i.e. pension) scheme (which is PAYG) reduced personal saving by about 50 per cent, thereby reducing the capital stock by 38 per cent below what it would have been in the absence of the social security system.

Aaron (1982) sets out three theoretical models of the determinants of saving: the life-cycle model (which rules out bequests); the multigenerational model (which allows bequests); and the short-horizon model (which relaxes the assumption that individuals make rational lifetime plans based on (more or less) full information). Barro (1974 and 1978) criticises Feldstein's use of a life-cycle model, in which an increase in PAYG benefits *must* in theory reduce savings, and points out that in a multigenerational model increased benefits could instead increase bequests (and hence not reduce savings). Aaron (1982, p. 28) summarises the theoretical debate by observing

that a person determined to find a respected theoretical argument to support a preconception will find one, and that a person without preconceptions will find a bewildering diversity of answers in economic theory about whether social security [i.e. pensions] is more likely to raise or to lower consumption or labor supply.

To get by this theoretical impasse, one turns with hope to the empirical research ... As will become clear, most of these hopes remain unfulfilled.

Feldstein's empirical work was also criticised: additional variables such as the unemployment rate or a measure of permanent income tended to reduce the effect on saving, and to destroy its statistical significance; and the results were highly sensitive to the time-period over which the relation was estimated. The results were finally discredited by Leimer and Lesnoy (1982) who found an error in some of Feldstein's data. They also pointed out that the results are very sensitive to the way in which people are assumed to form expectations. Subsequent work (Auerbach *et al.*, 1989; Auerbach and Kotlikoff, 1990) uses a 75-period life-cycle general equilibrium model to simulate the effects of demographic change under different pension regimes. The results highlight the key role of expectations and their impact on retirement behaviour. Since the formation of expectations is unmeasurable, the issue remains unresolved.

The third qualification is that an increase in saving does not *necessarily* raise output. There are not one, but three links in the argument that future output will be higher with funding than with PAYG: (a) funding leads to a higher rate of saving in the build-up period than PAYG; (b) this higher saving is translated into more/higher-quality investment than would otherwise occur; and (c) this investment leads to an increase in output. The last two links need not hold, and so converting the national insurance scheme on to a funded basis may not improve matters. According to Rosa (1982, p. 212) the experiences of Sweden and Japan in running state funded schemes

offer powerful evidence that this option may only invite squandering capital funds in wasteful, low-yield investments [which] should give pause to anyone proposing similar accumulations elsewhere.

The Government Actuary makes the same point in a more agnostic way, by admitting that he is 'not in a position to judge whether ... pension fund money is more capable than other money of being deployed in accordance with the long-term national interest' (UK, 1978a, para. 25). All three links have to hold before it can be asserted that funding will lead to greater increases in output than PAYG. At best the assertion is not proven.

Pensions and labour supply   The question here is whether pensions (either PAYG or funded) reduce aggregate labour supply. The problems are similar to those which beset empirical analysis of the labour supply effects of unemployment benefits (Chapter 8:3.1). On the contributions side, the theoretical analysis of taxation on work effort is generally accepted (see Atkinson and Stiglitz, 1980, pp. 23–61; or Brown, 1983). The effect of national insurance contributions is to drive a wedge between gross and net money wages. If workers discount future benefits entirely, contributions have the same effect as an income tax; at the other extreme, where future benefits bear an actuarial relationship to contributions, and are perceived to do so, national insurance contributions are not a tax but simply the price of insurance which, like any other price, has little if any distortionary effect on labour supply.

The impact of future benefits, on the other hand, is harder to analyse. They are payable only in certain contingencies, can be changed by legislation, and will depend on, for example, marital status; and it is not possible to borrow against future benefits, which must therefore be weighted by the probability that each type of benefit will be received at some given future date. The weighted benefits must then be discounted to present value using the market rate of interest or, for people who cannot borrow as much as they wish, at a personal rate of time preference. Similar problems arise (see section 5.2) in valuing pension rights considered as part of personal wealth.

As a result, modelling the effect of pensions on labour supply is complex. Some studies conclude that pensions (both public and private) reduce labour supply (for the UK, Zabalza and Piachaud (1981); for the USA, Boskin (1977), Boskin and Hurd (1978) and Diamond and Hausman (1984)). Others argue that pensions have little or no effect on work effort (Gordon and Blinder, 1980; Hamermesh, 1984; and Burtless and Moffitt, 1984). Up to a point the conflicting results can be explained *inter alia* by differences in model specification, different treatment of benefits and taxes, and different choice of samples (see Atkinson, 1987a). To a considerable extent, however, the issue is not only unresolved, but may remain so. A study by Mitchell and Fields (1981) used a single body of survey data in four different (and plausible) ways, and found that the US social security scheme induced workers to retire earlier, or later, or left the retirement decision unaffected.

Though pensions may not affect overall labour supply, employer pension schemes can affect individual decisions: pension design may reduce shirking (Lazear, 1986b); vesting rules (which specify the length of service before a worker gains title to any pension benefits) reduce labour turnover (Wise, 1986); and benefit provisions can encourage older workers to retire early (Stock and Wise, 1988).

It is important to be clear that the issue of labour supply, though highly significant, is entirely separate from the PAYG versus funding controversy. Though different methods of organising pensions may influence the rate of saving, it is most unlikely that the method of finance *per se* affects work effort. Individuals will base labour supply decisions on the size of their future pensions, on the terms on which they can buy them, and on the range of choice they are allowed; decisions might be affected by uncertainty, but a rational person is unlikely to care whether his income in retirement derives from tax revenues or from a pension fund. The issue of PAYG and funding is relevant to labour supply only to the extent that perceptions about certainty might differ between the two methods; and if pensions (of whatever sort) do induce retirement, the simplest solution is to raise the retirement age and/or to give greater financial incentives to defer retirement.

DEALING WITH FUTURE PROBLEMS

Possible policies in the face of the demographic problem We saw earlier that the Eurotoddlers of the 1950s and 1960s will cause a sharp rise in the dependency rate when they retire in the years after 2010. Any solution to the declining population of working age must reduce demand and/or increase supply. This implies one (or more) of three outcomes. Demand can be reduced (a) by increasing contributions, thereby reducing the average consumption of workers, and/or (b) by reducing benefits, thereby reducing the average consumption of pensioners.

Alternatively, on the supply side, both workers and pensioners can have the consumption they currently expect, so long as (c) output rises sufficiently to maintain average consumption per head (hence the emphasis in section 3.2 on the key role of output). In theory, this involves either or both of two strategies. *Increased output per worker* can arise from increases in the quantity and quality of capital, and from increases in the quality of labour. *Increased numbers of workers* can arise from increased labour force participation by those of working age; from an increase in the retirement age; and/or by importing labour (e.g. 'guestworkers').

In practice, supply-side policies in the face of a declining workforce should therefore include some or all of the following.

1. Policies to increase the capital stock and its quality, e.g. robots (which have the added advantage of not requiring pensions). We must be clear, strange though the idea may sound at present, that we are talking about an era of potential labour *shortage*, hence the importance of labour-saving capital.

2. Increased investment in labour through education and training.

3. Increasing labour force participation by reducing the unemployment rate and by encouraging more married women to join the labour force (e.g. by providing more child day-care facilities).

4. Raising the retirement age. A two-year increase for men from 65 to 67 with no increase in pensions is an implicit reduction in benefits of about 15 per cent, but with the advantage that it works not by reducing living standards in retirement, but by reducing the average duration of retirement. A policy of this sort has already been announced in the USA for the years after 2000. In Britain it would also be possible (and desirable – see section 5.2) to abolish the anomalous differential retirement age of men and women.

5. Importing labour through immigration. It has been suggested that a uniquely British solution would be to absorb the (mostly young) population of Hong Kong in 1997, when the colony's lease returns to China. Similarly, German reunification has enabled west Germany to absorb workers from the (younger) east German population.

To what extent is funding a solution? Funding is clearly irrelevant to policies 2–5, which can all be pursued by *direct* methods. If funding makes any difference, it can only be if it (a) leads successively to an increase in saving, in investment and in output (i.e. policy 1), *and* (b) does so more effectively than any other method of garnering resources and channelling them into productive investment. The stringency of these conditions should be clear from earlier discussion. The evidence on (a), both theoretically and empirically, is mixed, inconclusive and highly controversial, and that on (b) is unlikely to be less so. The funding versus PAYG controversy can therefore be argued rather to miss the point by concentrating on a method of increasing output which is both indirect (viz. the three steps in (a)) and debatable. Since the issue is one of economic growth, it seems easier and more reliable to adopt direct methods of effecting policies 1–5.

We saw in Chapter 5:2.2 that it is possible to insure against individual risks (e.g. life expectancy), but not against aggregate risk (i.e. common shocks which affect everyone). Funding and PAYG both offer individuals a measure of certainty about their future, but neither method (indeed, no method) can insure against common shocks. The future is full of uncertainties (about rates of inflation, output growth, birth rates and the like), which affect pension schemes just as they affect most other institutions. Thus it should not be surprising that there is little to choose between PAYG and funding in this respect. To imagine that funded schemes are substantially better in the face of aggregate uncertainty is to fall for crude mythology.

The 1985 review In response to widespread concern (Hemming and Kay, 1982b) over the prospective cost of the state earnings-related pension scheme (SERPS), the results of 'the most fundamental examination of our social security system since the Second World War' (UK, 1985b, Preface) were published as a Green Paper and later as a White Paper (UK, 1985h). The Green and White Papers gave a valuable insight into the government's objectives:

- '[T]he social security system must be capable of meeting genuine need' (UK, 1985b, para. 1.12), i.e. the objective of poverty relief.
- [T]he social security system must be consistent with the Government's overall objectives for the economy' (ibid.) (the macroeconomic efficiency objective).
- [T]he social security system must be simple to understand and easy to administer' (ibid.).

These objectives are consistent with private, non-redistributive, actuarial pensions. It is therefore not surprising that the Green Paper proposed the abolition of SERPS and its replacement, for the most part, by occupational pensions. The proposal was hotly opposed, not least by the pensions industry, worried that it might be expected to offer pensions not only to salaried professionals in stable jobs but also to the less-well-off. The White Paper was more circumspect, retaining SERPS but reducing benefits in later years, as described in section 1. The earnings-related component will be reduced to 20p (rather than 25p) per pound of earnings between the lower and upper earnings limit, the change to be phased in for those retiring after 2000. The calculation will be based on lifetime average earnings (not the best 20 years), with safeguards for those currently eligible for home responsibility protection. The surviving spouse will inherit up to half, rather than all, his/her partner's earnings-related pension. These changes increase the importance of the basic, flat-rate pension, and hence increase the redistributive tilt in the state pension scheme.

Occupational schemes were changed in several ways. The 1986 Social Security Act gave added protection to people leaving a scheme early and/or transferring to a new scheme (i.e. as an aid to labour mobility, occupational pensions were required to have 'portable' benefits). As an explicit cost-saving measure, occupational schemes contracted out of the state scheme were made responsible for indexing the guaranteed minimum pension (section 1) in respect of the first 3 per cent of inflation each year.

Contracting out was liberalised in two important ways. First, as discussed in section 1, employer schemes after 1988 are required only to provide a defined level of contribution, not a defined level of benefit. As discussed in section 2, this faces the pensioner with the risk of variable returns to pension assets. Second, individuals were allowed to opt out of both the state scheme and employer schemes and, instead, to have a defined-contribution personal pension. Such individual pensions have two effects: because they are defined-contribution schemes, they face the individual with the risk of unanticipated inflation during contribution years (see section 2); and, because they are based strictly on individual contributions, they also imply that a woman will receive a lower weekly pension than a man with an indentical con-tributions record. Individual pensions thus greatly extend the actuarial element in earnings-related pensions. Major issues concerning the future development of private pensions are discussed in UK Pension Law Review Committee (1992).

The Green Paper proposal to abolish SERPS was an attempt to move earnings-related pensions from the less actuarial stance of the 1975 legis-lation towards stricter actuarial principles. In the end, the White Paper represented a smaller move in an actuarial direction. The changes after 2000 reduce the weight put on equity objectives. For instance, the calculation of benefits over a whole working life rather than over the best 20 years works to the disadvantage of individuals with fluctuating incomes, par-ticularly those individuals (mainly women) who have spells in and out of the labour force. However, though the redistributive element in the state scheme was reduced, the move towards actuarial principles was only partial.

Whether such a move is good or bad depends on the answers to two questions: first, and ideological, is whether one believes that pensions should be redistributive: second, and largely technical, is whether or not one regards a move towards funding as an effective response to demographic prospects.

The details of any scheme are liable to criticism. However, if the SERPS promises are regarded as too generous, then the strategy of making the promise less generous is more sensible than the earlier proposal to scrap SERPS and rely on private, funded schemes. The arrangements described in section 1 were the result of nearly two decades of debate (Chapter 2:6), with a considerable measure of all-party support for the final outcome. Little has changed since the original legislation in 1975, save that the scheme has turned out to be more costly than predicted, given likely demographic trends and their effect on output. The proposed changes should reduce the most acute cost (i.e. demand-side) pressures, particularly if buttressed by supply-side policies 1–5, listed above (for assessment of the changes, see Dilnot and Disney (1989) and Disney and Whitehouse (1991); for more wide-ranging reform proposals, see Johnson and Falkingham (forthcoming). In the USA, similar changes, in the form of future increases in contribution rates and in the retirement age, have already been announced (for discussion, see Aaron *et al.* (1989)).

5.2 Equity Issues

The discussion in Chapter 8:3.2 of equity aspects of national insurance applies equally to pensions. This section concentrates on a number of other issues.

Redistribution from young to old The real purchasing power of the basic state pension in the UK increased by 225 per cent between 1948 and 1990, and far exceeds that to which pensioners are actuarially entitled. In the USA many retirees receive a social security pension at least twice their actuarial entitlement (Rosen, 1982, pp. 152–3). Whether this is more equitable than a funded scheme with no such redistributive possibilities is a matter of judgement.

Redistribution from men to women can occur in both funded and PAYG schemes as a consequence of differential life expectancy (section 4.2). This type of redistribution is particularly strong in Britain, which is unusual in having a lower retirement age for women. The differential started in 1940, when the retirement age for women was reduced to 60, partly because of a campaign by women's organisations.[23] The measure accorded well with

---

[23] The Old Age Pensions Act 1908 established a common retirement age of 70. It was reduced to 65 under the Old Age and Widows and Orphans Contributory Pensions Act 1925. For details of the events leading to the change in 1940, see Thane (1982, p. 245).

prevailing and earlier views about the role of married women, 'the great bulk of whom are fortunately in this country free at all ages to devote their attention to the care of their household' (General Report of the 1911 Census (p. 161), quoted by Hunt (1981)).

The redistribution arising from the differential retirement age is inequitable for at least two reasons. First is the anomaly whereby a woman who retires at 65 will receive a higher pension than a 65-year-old man with an identical contributions record, because she has worked beyond her normal retirement age.[24] Second is the discrimination against women who would prefer to work longer. This is likely to change in the near future (see UK Department of Social Security, 1991)).[25]

Were this indefensible anomaly to be removed, the transfer from men to women would be reduced but not eliminated. What, if anything, could or should be done about it? The argument that the transfer to women's pensions is justified because women are discriminated against in the labour market is weak because it suggests that two wrongs make a right. A more honest argument for the transfer is its retention as an explicit equity objective. As we have seen (section 4.1) this is defensible, since compulsory membership means that the subsidy will not cause inefficiency in insurance markets through adverse selection. This being the case, it can be argued as a matter of general policy that one should recognise the fact of a transfer from men to women, but having recognised it, should leave it at that.

Redistribution from rich to poor The system of benefits (section 1) and contributions (Chapter 7:2.1) together imply considerable formula redistribution (see section 4.2). At its simplest, from Table 7.3, someone with weekly earnings of £60 pays a contribution of £5.40, and someone earning £300 pays £27.00. If each received only the basic pension, the 'poor' person would receive five times as much pension per pound of contribution. Because of the earnings-related component, the effect is not as strong as the example suggests; but *ceteris paribus* there is still redistribution from rich to poor.

Other factors, however, work in the opposite direction. First, there is differential mortality, in that the better-off have a greater life expectancy (and hence collect their pensions longer) and, a related phenomenon, tend to stay in education longer (and hence start to pay contributions later). Second, it is disproportionately the better-off who contract out of the state

[24] The real pension is increased by $7\frac{1}{2}$ per cent for each year of work beyond normal retiring age (section 1); thus a woman retiring at 65 receives a pension $37\frac{1}{2}$ per cent higher than that of an identical 65-year-old man.

[25] The possibility of a common retirement age of 60 can be ruled out because of its cost. It has been estimated, even with the current dependency ratio, that common retirement at 60 would raise the cost of the national insurance retirement pension by about 40 per cent, i.e. by some 2 per cent of GDP. In any case, many people would retire later out of choice. In the USA political pressure led to the Age Discrimination in Employment Act 1978, which enables (but does not compel) broad classes of people to defer retirement until the age of 70.

scheme, and this, too, significantly reduces its redistributive impact.[26]

The overall redistributive effect is therefore complex and results are far from definitive. Nicholson (1974, Table 3.3) found that in 1970 the national insurance retirement pension reduced the Gini coefficient in Britain by 3.6 per cent. The subsequent introduction of earnings-related contributions (and *a fortiori* with graduated contributions) strengthened this effect. In 1986 national insurance pensions reduced the Gini coefficient by nearly 10 per cent (Barr and Coulter, 1990, Tables 7.11 and 7.12). Similar features are found in the pension schemes of many other countries (see the Further Reading).

Other aspects   Redistribution also takes place between households of different sizes. From Table 8.1, the basic pension for a married couple is 60 per cent higher than for a single person making the same contribution; in the USA the situation is broadly comparable (Rosen, 1982, p. 153).

Finally, note should be taken of the important relation between accrued pension rights and the distribution of personal wealth. Because pension rights are distributed more equally than most other forms of non-human wealth, the overall wealth distribution is more equal when they are included. The size of the effect, however, is controversial, depending on (a) precisely which types of pension wealth are included (e.g. how should national insurance pension rights be treated?), and (b) the valuation placed on entitlements to a future income stream. The latter problem is particularly intractable.[27]

5.3 Conclusion

Empirical investigation suggests that funding is likely to make little difference, if any, to growth rates. The funding solution is indirect in its mechanism, controversial in its outcome, and likely in any case to have only a second-order effect. It would, therefore, be highly dangerous to imagine that simply by embracing funding the demographic problem would be solved. In addition, efficiency arguments of principle point strongly towards a public role at least for indexation. The efficiency case for substantial public, PAYG involvement is therefore strong. Such an argument accepts that it is appropriate for people to use the state as a collective institution for saving and insurance where it is able to perform these

[26] Contracting out raises other important issues, including its impact on finances. The extent to which reliance on private-sector earnings-related pensions will save the state money in the long run depends on a complex of factors, including the size of the current revenue loss to the state in terms of lower contribution receipts; the rate of economic growth; and the cost on public funds of indexing the guaranteed minimum pension paid by private schemes. See Creedy (1982, Ch. 6), Creedy and Disney (1985, Ch. 4) and Hemming (1984, pp. 131–5).

[27] The valuation problems involved were discussed briefly in section 5.1. See also UK (1975, pp. 665–75) for the problems of valuing an indexed pension, and UK (1979a, Ch. 4).

functions more cheaply and efficiently than any private alternative. This does not mean that PAYG schemes have never made profligate promises. But the efficiency case for state involvement is, at its very least, a counterblast to the government failure arguments in Chapter 4:5.

Aaron (1982) contrasts the absence of conclusive evidence that PAYG schemes have deleterious efficiency effects, with the strong evidence that their equity impact is beneficial, in that they have greatly improved the economic status of the elderly. He concludes that decisions about the future of state pensions should therefore be made mainly on equity grounds.

Further Reading

Details of UK institutions are set out in Tolley (1991) (comprehensive, and includes references to the legislation) (published annually). Systems abroad are discussed by Lynes (1986) (France), Aaron *et al.* (1989) (USA), Gordon (1988), Holzmann (1988) and Rosa (1982). The large literature is surveyed by Hurd (1990). For general discussion, see Johnson and Falkingham (1992).

For an introduction to the theoretical issues underlying pension finance, see Samuelson (1958); for the prospective demographic picture, Ermisch (1980 and 1983) and UK (1985h, para. 1.12); for policy, Falkingham (1989); and for international discussion of policy, Gordon (1988) and Rosa (1982).

The incentive effects of pensions concern (a) saving and economic growth and (b) labour supply. For surveys, see the Further Reading at the end of Chapter 8.

Discussion of the prospective costs of the UK state earnings-related pension is contained in Hemming and Kay (1982b) and UK (1985d, Ch. 2). For assessment of the 1986 reforms, see Dilnot and Disney (1989), and for a more wide-ranging reform proposal, Johnson and Falkingham (forthcoming).

The distributional effects of national insurance pensions are discussed by Barr and Coulter (1990). For US analysis, see Aaron (1982, Ch. 6), Danziger, van der Gaag, Smolensky and Taussig (1984) and Aaron *et al.* (1989). See also the Further Reading at the end of Chapter 7.

The literature on the distribution of wealth is surveyed in Atkinson (1980, Part 4) and (1983b, Chs 7 and 8). Specific discussion of pension rights as part of wealth is contained in UK (1979a, Ch. 4) and UK (1975, pp. 665–75).

Chapter 10
Non-Contributory Benefits

Poverty is a great enemy to human happiness; it certainly destroys
liberty, and it makes some virtues impracticable, and others extremely
difficult. [Samuel Johnson, 1709–94.]

1 Introduction and Institutions

Non-contributory benefits are many and diverse. Their only common feature
is that they are all paid from general taxation rather than the National
Insurance Fund. The main schemes listed in Table 7.5 are buttressed by
many smaller benefits. They differ widely: some are administered centrally,
some locally; some are mandatory, others discretionary; some take the form
of cash grants for specific purposes (higher education awards for students),
others serve to reduce the price of specific commodities (rent subsidies),
others make certain goods available without charge (free medical
prescriptions). In many cases the distinction between benefits in cash and
kind becomes blurred, though for the purposes of this book, it is not
necessary to dwell on them.

As discussed in Chapter 1:2.1, non-contributory benefits are of two sorts:
means-tested (i.e. awarded only where income/wealth falls below a prescribed
limit), and universal (i.e. awarded without a contributions or income test
on the basis of other criteria), a key example of the latter being child
benefit. The two sorts of benefit have various of the aims set out in Chapter
1:2.2. The major objective of means-tested benefits is poverty relief; such
benefits also contribute to vertical redistribution. The key objectives of child
benefit are poverty relief and income smoothing in the face of life-cycle
effects. To the extent that the benefit is financed out of progressive taxation,
it also contributes to vertical redistribution. If the benefit is awarded to all
families without an income test, it assists social solidarity.

This chapter starts by summarising the institutions of four of the most
important of these benefits in the UK (for details, see the Further Reading):
income support, housing benefit and family credit are all means-tested; and

child benefit is universal. Section 2 considers the arguments for state intervention; section 3 assesses means-tested benefits and child benefit, respectively, including a brief survey of empirical evidence.

Income support (formerly supplementary benefit) is the final safety net, when family income from all other sources falls below a specified minimum. Expenditure is large (£13 billion in 1992/3 – Table 7.5), exceeding that on any other benefit except the national insurance pension. The numbers involved are also large: in 1992/3 there were 5.1 million recipients of whom two-thirds were pensioners or unemployed (UK, 1992e, Tables 6 and 7). The scheme has changed in various ways since 1948 (Chapter 2:6) and its details are complex. Where a benefit is intended to supplement people's incomes there are bound to be complications in its interactions with other income sources. Discussion here is restricted to the simplest cases.

Income support is calculated by setting requirements against resources. If the latter are less than the former, the difference is paid as benefit. Additionally, income support acts as a 'passport' to other benefits, including housing benefit, free prescriptions and dental treatment, and free school meals. The scheme is usefully discussed under three heads: eligibility; benefits for those with no income or capital; and the treatment of income.

Eligibility: anyone aged 18 or over (in limited cases, 16 or over) who is not in full-time work may be eligible, whether or not he or she has a national insurance record or is receiving national insurance benefit. For those under pensionable age the benefit officer has the power to make the benefit conditional on registering for work, though this rule is not applied to the sick, to single parents of children under 16, to blind people not used to working outside the home, and to certain other groups.

Benefits for those with no income or capital are of two sorts: income support itself, which offers benefit on a weekly basis, and the social fund, from which single payments are made. The determination of income support in any particular case rests on two considerations: how much benefit is awarded to a family with no other income; and how this award is affected by any income the family has, corresponding to the requirements and resources aspects of the benefit.

Requirements are calculated according to scales of applicable amounts laid down by law, which vary according to the numbers and ages of dependants. Some of the applicable amounts for 1992/3 are shown in Table 10.1. Higher rates of benefit are payable for families, single parents, disabled and elderly individuals, and for carers.

The social fund offers assistance additional to the applicable amounts. There are four types of single payment: budgeting loans (repayable through reduced weekly benefit) to enable income support claimants to meet immediate lump-sum needs; crisis loans (also repayable) to meet urgent needs; community care grants (non-repayable) for people facing exceptional problems; and automatic grants for income support recipients for maternity, funerals and in exceptionally severe weather (payments of this type are generally not repayable, save that payments made for funerals may be repayable from the estate of the deceased). As the names imply, the first two forms of payments are (interest-free) loans; the latter two, grants.

Table 10.1 *Income support rates, 1992/93 (partial listing)*

	£s per week
PERSONAL ALLOWANCES	
Couple (one or both over 18)	66.60
Single householder (25 or over)	42.45
Lone parent (18 or over)	42.45
Dependent children	23.85
16–17	25.55
11–15	21.40[a]
Under 11	14.55[a]
PREMIUMS	
Family	9.70
Lone parent	4.75
Pensioner	
Single	14.70–20.77
Couple	22.35–29.55
Disability	
Single	17.80
Couple	25.55
Severe disability	
One person who qualifies	32.55
Couple (both qualify)	65.10
Disabled child	17.80
Carer	11.55

Source: Tolley (1991, pp. SP1–12).
Note: [a] Child benefit and child benefit increase are, in effect, deducted from these rates.

The treatment of income and capital: the resources element calculates income for the purposes of income support, the underlying principle being that all income is included unless it is specifically 'disregarded'. Though the regulations for disregards are complex (Tolley, 1991, Ch. 4), the following income is *ignored* for the purposes of establishing entitlement: £5 per week for each claimant; or up to £10 per week for a couple; or £15 per week for elderly or disabled recipients; or £25 per week for a single parent. Certain other types of income may be disregarded; and a variety of other disregards relate to such income as education maintenance allowances, and benefits like mobility allowance.

Disregards apart, *all* income is included in family resources, in particular:

most national insurance benefits including retirement and unemployment and sickness benefit; industrial injury benefit; and child benefit. For income support purposes the relevant magnitude is 'net' earnings after tax and national insurance contributions, and after allowing for limited work expenses, including fares. The ability to deduct these expenses contrasts sharply with the rules applicable for income tax purposes.

Complications arise in defining the types of income which are disregarded or included; in the interactions when claimants or their families have several different sources of income; and in the calculation of work expenses. In addition, any capital owned by the individual or family may affect entitlement. The value of an owner-occupied house is ignored entirely. Other capital, including savings, redundancy payments and some tax rebates, is ignored if it does not exceed an upper limit (£3000 in 1992/3). For recipients with savings between £3000 and £8000, benefit is reduced by an imputed amount (so-called 'tariff income'). Individuals with more than £8000 (in 1992/3) in savings are not normally eligible for benefit.

A family's benefit is calculated as the difference between its requirements and its resources. If requirements are estimated at £100 and resources at £40 per week, benefit will normally be £60. At the margin an extra pound of earnings therefore costs £1 of benefit, in economic terms a 100 per cent implicit tax rate. Thus the implicit tax on disregarded income is 0 per cent; on most other income, including most national insurance benefits, it is 100 per cent. Income support can therefore be thought of as 'topping up' family income from whatever source to bring it up to a basic minimum.

Housing benefit was introduced in 1983 under the Social Security and Housing Benefit Act 1982 to replace earlier arrangements, and revised in 1988 in the wake of the 1985 social security review. It is administered by local authorities, and provides means-tested assistance with rent and local taxation for tenants. Total spending on housing benefit in 1992/3 was £8.6 billion, comprising £3.7 billion in rent rebates, £2.5 billion in rent allowances, and £1.5 billion in assisting poor people with their local tax bills (UK, 1992e, Table 3).

For individuals in receipt of income support (so-called 'certificated' cases) the Department of Social Security automatically notifies the relevant local authority of the claimant's circumstances, and benefit is normally equal to the full amount of eligible rent. Individuals not in receipt of income support are eligible for 'standard housing benefit', whose value depends on the claimant's gross income (including that of his/her spouse), household size and the amount of rent. Where family income exceeds a specified limit, 65 per cent of 'excess' income is subtracted from the eligible rent in calculating benefit (see the Further Reading).

Family credit is payable to a low-income family with at least one dependent child, and where at least one adult in the family is engaged in full-time paid work. The maximum credit depends on family size. There is an adult credit (£41.00 in 1992/3), plus an additional, age-related credit per child, which are paid in full to families whose net income is below a prescribed amount (£66.60 in 1992/3). Benefit is reduced by 70 per cent of the excess of family net income over the prescribed amount. An award will normally be made for 26 weeks, and once made will not be affected by any increase in income during the period. Recipient families are automatically entitled to the same variety of additional benefits as those receiving income support. Benefit is administered by the central Department of Social Security.

Child benefit is not a national insurance benefit, though, like most cash benefits, it is administered by the Department of Social Security. The current scheme replaced child tax allowances and family allowances from 1979 (Chapter 2:6), and cost £6 billion in 1992/3 (Table 7.5). Child benefit consists of a tax-free weekly payment (£9.65 for the first child and £7.80 for each subsequent child in 1992/3), where a child for these purposes is under 16, or under 19 if in full-time education. The benefit is payable to the person responsible for a child, either someone with whom the child is living, or someone who contributes to the support of a child living elsewhere. When a child lives with both parents the mother has title to the benefit.

Some single parents are eligible also for **one-parent benefit**, payable in 1992/3 at a rate of £5.85 per week for the first or only child. In principle all single parents are eligible, except those who already receive certain long-term national insurance benefits.

In contrast with the former combination of child tax allowances and family allowances, child benefit is administratively much less cumbersome, and is worth the same to everyone whatever their income. The benefit is part of a gradual trend towards standardising support for children. Schemes of this sort exist in many countries – for surveys, see Kamerman and Kahn (1991) and Bradshaw *et al.* (forthcoming).

Other schemes range over educational benefits (e.g. free school meals, clothing grants); health benefits (free prescriptions, free welfare milk and vitamins); benefits for the disabled and handicapped; employment and job-training benefits; help for the elderly (e.g. meals on wheels); legal aid; and help for the homeless. There are at least 50 schemes of this sort (see the Further Reading).

2 Theoretical Arguments for State Intervention

Efficiency and Social Justice

Non-contributory benefits cover three broad categories of people. First are those whose national insurance (despite compulsory membership) leaves them in poverty. An unemployed person receiving full unemployment benefit might still be below the poverty line, especially if he/she has a large family. Such a person is eligible also for income support. Second are those without national insurance cover because they have exhausted their entitlement or because they never had any (e.g. a school-leaver, or a recently divorced woman with no recent contributions). Such individuals have to rely on income support and, where relevant, child benefit. Finally, there are those whose reason for poverty is not covered by national insurance, e.g. the parent of a large family in full-time, low-paid work, who has to rely on child benefit and family credit.

None of these categories can readily be dealt with by private insurance; and none except the first can be helped by raising national insurance benefits or by extending their coverage. Much poverty is associated with children and/or high housing costs, neither of which is an insurable risk. Two conclusions emerge: *private* insurance is not possible in most of these cases; nor is extending *national* insurance a complete answer.

The state could, of course, do nothing, and let people face the risk of starvation, but even ignoring equity arguments this would have a variety of *efficiency* costs including social unrest/crime among those facing starvation; the death by starvation of dependants including children (the future labour force); and the fact that malnutrition causes poor health, thereby raising health care costs and lowering the capacity of adults to work and of children to absorb education. These costs (cf. the nineteenth-century national efficiency arguments in Chapter 2:2.1) give efficiency grounds for publicly provided income support.

From the viewpoint of social justice, libertarians incline towards private charity where poverty is caused by a non-insurable risk. As discussed in Chapter 4:4.1, however, various difficulties, including the free-rider problem, might cause voluntary giving to be inefficiently low even by libertarian standards. Thus writers like Friedman and Hayek do not oppose subsistence payments out of public funds, though they favour every inducement to encourage people to work (the modern incarnation of 'less eligibility' (Chapter 2:1.1)). Socialists, in contrast, argue for generous benefits paid on the basis of need, to advance their egalitarian objectives.

Thus there are solid arguments of both efficiency and social justice for public provision of subsistence benefits on a non-insurance basis. By how much they should be higher than subsistence is a matter of judgement.

Criteria for assessing redistributive schemes   How effective are non-contributory benefits in achieving the objectives listed at the start of the chapter? This question was tackled for national insurance benefits (and will be for health care, education and housing) in terms of their efficiency and equity. But for redistributive schemes the argument is illuminated by three somewhat different criteria which cut across the efficiency/equity distinction.

The level of benefits: does the scheme give recipients a socially acceptable standard of living, i.e. does it achieve the poverty relief objective? This involves, first, *money benefits*: does the scheme pay enough to enable the purchase of an adequate consumption bundle? Second, the issue of *stigma*: for any given level of money support a person's living standard (in utility terms) is reduced to the extent that he/she feels stigmatised by receiving benefit.

Targeting: in Weisbrod's (1969) terminology, targeting efficiency has two aspects. *Vertical efficiency* is concerned with avoiding leakages, i.e. benefits should go *only* to those who need them. This reduces the cost of the scheme, but may involve high implicit tax rates and the poverty trap (see the Glossary). *Horizontal efficiency* is concerned with avoiding gaps, i.e. benefits should go to *all* the poor. Failure can arise either because *eligibility rules* prevent some needy groups from applying, or because *take-up* is less than 100 per cent. In the latter case, on the demand side, eligible claimants may not apply, either for lack of information or because of stigma; on the supply side an eligible person may apply but be refused, either in error or because of discrimination.

The cost criterion embraces the benefits themselves and also the cost of administration.

These three criteria interact in important ways which emerge in subsequent discussion. Cost constrains the freedom to have high benefits. There is an important interaction between cost and the level of benefit: as we shall see, increasing, say, income support by x per cent is likely to increase cost by much more than x per cent. A further interaction is between cost and targeting: again it transpires that reducing the rate at which benefits are withdrawn as family income rises disproportionately affects costs.

3 Assessment of Non-Contributory Benefits

3.1 Income Support

Level Are benefits high enough to relieve poverty? With an absolute definition (Chapter 6:2.1) the answer is generally yes, in that nobody starves,[1] and also because between 1948 and 1980 real benefits rose in line

---

[1] But there has been increasing concern in recent years about the incidence of hypothermia among the elderly. For discussion of whether the level of supplementary benefit is too low, see Cooke and Baldwin (1984), and Barr and Coulter (1990).

with pre-tax average earnings (Chapter 6:2.3). With a relative definition, no unambiguous answer is possible.

There has been considerable criticism of the social fund (see Berthoud (1991) and Huby and Walker (1991) for assessments): it works within a fixed budget; most of the payments are loans rather than grants; and most awards involve at least some local discretion. Though the last aspect is, up to a point, inevitable in a scheme designed to meet exceptional needs, the former two are not. As a result, it is argued, the social fund fails in a significant number of cases to meet the poverty relief objective, in that take-up is well below 100 per cent.

Targeting is concerned both with horizontal efficiency (the avoidance of gaps) and with vertical efficiency (the minimisation of leakages) (see Atkinson, forthcoming; Nichols and Zeckhauser, 1982; Blackorby and Donaldson, 1988; Besley and Kanbur, 1991).

Horizontal efficiency: the eligibility rules for income support are broad, reflecting its status as benefit of last resort. France has no comparable scheme, neither does the USA for non-aged adults without children. Income support from that point of view does well.

However, a sizeable proportion of eligible recipients do not receive benefit (i.e. take-up is incomplete). On the demand side an unknown number do not apply. On the supply side, not all eligible applicants are awarded benefit, for instance if a benefit officer attributes to the regulations a harsher interpretation than was intended, or is unaware of certain entitlements. Such difficulties cannot entirely be avoided, but there is little evidence of systematic discrimination in the enforcement of rules (e.g. by race) in the award of benefit.[2]

More generally, three sets of theories seek to explain incomplete take-up: ignorance, inconvenience and stigma. It is not surprising that many people are ignorant of their entitlement under the benefit system (Berthoud, 1984). Attempts to improve take-up through publicity campaigns, however, have only limited success (Spicker, 1986); in part this is because ignorance is not the only cause of incomplete take-up.

Inconvenience is concerned with the cost to the applicant of making a claim, including the time spent filling in long and complex forms, and the need to answer potentially embarrassing questions about income and family circumstances. Some writers[3] argue that the imposition of such costs may be both deliberate and rational as a device for attempting to avoid the worst problems of adverse selection and moral hazard. The underlying

---

[2] Two qualifications are necessary. First, the rules themselves might be discriminatory (e.g. towards women). Second, it is claimed that some racial discrimination in the award of benefits has occurred (CPAG, 1984). For evidence of systematic racial discrimination in some US cities in awarding benefits under Aid to Families with Dependent Children in the 1960s, see Barr and Hall (1975).

[3] Nichols and Zeckhauser (1982); Blackorby and Donaldson (1988); for more general discussion, see also Ravallion (1991).

argument is that the imposition of costs on claimants assists the operation of self-targeting (see the discussion of self-selection in the context of adverse selection in Chapter 5:3.2).

Stigma in its pure form arises if individuals feel that if they receive certain benefits they will be labelled as belonging to a socially rejected group. Hence there is a psychological cost to claiming benefit additional to the convenience costs just discussed. This is all the more the case in the UK, given the strong folk memory of the stringent household means test between the wars (Chapter 2:3.2).

Vertical efficiency concerns the extent to which benefit is withheld from those who do not need it. Viewed narrowly, income support scores well. Once a recipient family has used up its small disregard (section 1), it normally loses £1 of benefit for every pound of additional net earnings, which, in effect, imposes a 100 per cent implicit tax rate on earnings. This targets benefits very tightly indeed.

Figure 10.1 shows in stylised form the combination of leisure and income available to a recipient of income support with an initial endowment at *b* of 24 hours of leisure. The line *ab* shows his/her earning opportunities. Suppose a scheme is now introduced under which income is not allowed to fall below *Oc*. This is shown by the line *cde*. An individual choosing 24 hours of leisure will receive an income of *Oc* = *be*. If he works, the first £5 (say) of net earnings is disregarded, and spendable income rises above the income support level, as shown by the line *eg*. But once his disregards are exhausted, he loses benefit pound for pound with earnings, and so his spendable income is fixed, as shown by the dotted line *fg*. This is equivalent to an implicit marginal tax of 100 per cent, in the sense that all extra earnings are 'taxed away' by the loss of benefit: it is impossible for recipients to raise their net disposable income; it also removes all financial incentive to work. Where people work solely to earn money, the budget constraint collapses to the two segments *af* and *ge*. No-one who works only for money will choose a point on the segment *fg* (since at point *g* the individual has the same income as at *f*, but more leisure). If a person receives £100 in income support, which he loses pound for pound with earnings above £5, then *fg* covers earnings from £5 to at least £105. This strong potential labour supply disincentive is the price of targeting benefit tightly on those in need (i.e. vertical efficiency through means testing is inherently in conflict with labour supply incentives).

The labour supply disincentive is one of the major economic criticisms of income support. An individual who works only for money will choose either to be on the segment *af* (i.e. earning enough to be off income support), or at a point on the line *ge* (i.e. earning under £5 per week). By its very construction, income support almost forces people into one of two extreme categories, of being fully self-sufficient or almost completely dependent on the state, a conjecture supported by US evidence (Barr and Hall, 1981).

Figure 10.1 *Stylised representation of the budget constraint under income support*

There is no real provision for people who, though not self-sufficient, are able at least partly to support themselves. Such people are rarely apparent because the system almost forces them into full dependence. The very fact of targeting benefits tightly brings about one of the worst features of income support – its tendency to be strongly divisive between the self-supporting and the dependent. The qualitative direction of the disincentive is clear; but there is controversy about its empirical magnitude, to which we return in section 3.4.

Cost In 1992/3 the number of recipients was 5.1 million (and over 8 million when account is taken of dependants); in addition, the long-term benefit rate has more or less kept pace with pre-tax average earnings. For both reasons costs have risen sharply over the years; and as the amount handed over to the poor has increased, so have administrative costs. When national insurance was introduced in 1948 it was thought that eventually everyone would be self-supporting through work or insurance, and that national assistance (as it was then called) would dwindle. But over time the number of recipients grew, as did the complications.

Expenditure on income support in 1992/3 was £13 billion to which must be added estimated administrative costs, which in 1990/1 were 15.2 per cent of benefit expenditure; the comparable figure for the national insurance retirement pension was 1.6 per cent (UK, 1992e, Figures 27 and 28). Put another way, the administration of supplementary benefit/income support absorbed 42 per cent of the administrative costs of all cash benefits, for a benefit which absorbed only 16 per cent of benefit spending (ibid.). In

1988/9 each loan out of the social fund cost about £50 to administer (Berthoud, 1991). Are these benefits affordable? The answer must be yes, since they are actually paid. But the possibility of enhancing the scheme is clearly limited.

The scope for improvement is reduced by interactions between the three criteria. First, could benefits be increased? Suppose a family of given size receives £100 per week, which is reduced pound for pound with earnings (disregards are ignored for simplicity). Doubling benefit from £100 to £200 would roughly double the cost of benefits to existing recipients (i.e. by assumption those earning less than £100 per week); but in addition, more people (by assumption those earning between £100 and £200) would become eligible. Another possible improvement would be to reduce the rate at which benefits are withdrawn as earnings rise. This would increase the transfer receipts of families with other income; and it might reduce stigma, inasmuch as means testing (the main cause of stigma) could be reduced. Unfortunately, the room for manoeuvre in this direction is also limited. Returning to the example above, with a 100 per cent implicit tax rate only those earning below £100 are eligible; with a 50 per cent rate anyone earning below £200 is eligible. Halving the tax rate, like doubling the benefit level, raises costs both by increasing benefits to existing recipients and by increasing the number of potential beneficiaries (see Levy (1979) for empirical verification in a US context). The increase in costs associated with either change is accentuated by the shape of Britain's income distribution. The number of people with incomes between 1 and 1.5 times the income support level is large, correspondingly reducing the scope for increasing benefits.

3.2 Other Income-Related Benefits

HOW THE POVERTY TRAP ARISES

The poverty trap can arise also for people not in receipt of income support, who lose benefit under a variety of other schemes. In March 1988 a person earning an extra pound could lose 27 pence in income tax, 9 pence in national insurance contributions, 50 pence in family income supplement (the predecessor of family credit), and 23 pence in various forms of assistance with housing costs, giving a total marginal tax rate of 109 per cent (see, for instance, Atkinson *et al.*, 1989).

When discussing the measurement of poverty (Chapter 6:2.3), the three important questions concerned how many people were poor (the 'head count'), by how much they fell below the poverty line (the 'poverty gap'), and for how long they remained there. In the case of the poverty trap, analogously, we need to ask how high are implicit tax rates; how many people do they affect; and for how long do they apply or not apply?

How high are implicit tax rates? The empirical literature is discussed in section 3.4; many individuals/families face marginal rates of close to (and in limited cases exceeding) 100 per cent. The ill-effects of such tax rates are twofold. First, low-income families cannot raise their net income. In early 1986 (Dilnot and Stark, 1986, Table 1), four-person families with pre-transfer earnings between £70 and £145 per week all had spendable income, after taxes and benefits, of between £117 and £122 (cf. the range of hours *fg* in Figure 10.1). The second ill-effect is that high tax rates bring about a strong substitution effect against work effort, and so are potentially a major labour supply disincentive.

A complete analysis, however, must take account of several complications. The first is the complexity of the benefit formulae. The more benefits are introduced, the greater the variation in implicit tax rates. At the point at which entitlement to free school meals was lost, the tax rate in 1982 could reach nearly 300 per cent, i.e. an extra pound of earnings could cost nearly £3 in taxes and lost benefit (UK, 1983b, p. 201). In addition, the interactions between different benefits in calculating entitlement to each is complex. The structure of implicit tax rates facing any particular family will depend both on its size and composition, and on the precise mix of benefits it receives.

This brings us to a second set of complications. It is not enough to analyse the case of a 'typical' family. To assess the impact of the poverty trap we also need to know *how many* families face such rates, i.e. how many families of different sizes and types there are at each income level; which benefits they actually receive (the take-up question); and which margin we are discussing, that for the primary or a secondary earner. The empirical literature is discussed in section 3.4.

MITIGATING FACTORS

The third complication concerns the *length of time* over which people face or do not face these tax rates. Here, fortunately, there are mitigating factors, the most important of which are the existence of fixed period awards, and the fact that most benefits are uprated annually.

The logic of fixed period awards Family credit (and hence also the benefits to which it is a 'passport', such as free school meals and free prescriptions) is granted on the basis of five weeks' pay slips, and the award is made for six months, during which the authorities need not be informed of any increases in family income. A family which is awarded £30 a week receives a book of 26 vouchers for £30 each, which can be cashed week by week.

The main reason why benefit is awarded for six months is the administrative convenience of not having to reassess a family each time its income changes. This administrative practice has a substantial impact on implicit tax rates. Any increase in earnings which occurs during an award period does not result in any immediate loss of benefit, and so the marginal tax rate is zero, at least in the short run. And even if an increase in earnings is permanent, so that benefits at some future date are assessed on the basis of a higher income, any loss of benefit which occurs not at the time of the increase in earnings, but only later, is likely at least partly to be discounted, and hence to be less of a disincentive.

A conventional presentation of the poverty trap shows that a family earning an extra pound could lose up to, say, 95 pence in benefit. This figure must now be reinterpreted. It is certainly the case that family A will receive 95 pence less benefit than family B if its earnings are one pound higher. Thus the high implicit tax rates apply cross-sectionally. Our interest, however, is the impact on family A's benefits of an increase in its earnings. This is a time-series question, and from this perspective the poverty trap is mitigated in two ways: because of fixed period awards an increase in earnings may cause no loss of benefit, at least in the short run; in addition, benefits will generally have been uprated by the end of the award period, taking much of the sting out of reassessment. The moral of the story is the important economic impact of administrative practice.

Formal analysis The effect of fixed period awards in reducing the perceived tax effect of the withdrawal of benefits is of sufficient importance to merit more formal analysis (non-technical readers can skip the equations). Consider the value of an income stream of £1 per year subject to a tax rate, t. In perpetuity this is worth

$$P = \int_0^\infty (1-t)e^{-rv}\, dv = \frac{1-t}{r} \tag{10.1}$$

where $v = $ time, and r can be interpreted either as the rate of interest or as a marginal rate of time preference (both interpretations will be discussed).

If no tax is imposed until the end of the current award period (here till the end of year 1), then the present value of the income stream is P (from equation (10.1)) plus the value of the first year's tax remission, t.

$$P' = P + t = \frac{1-t+rt}{r} = \frac{1-t(1-r)}{r} \tag{10.2}$$

Comparing equation (10.2) with (10.1) shows that the effect of not levying any tax for the first year is to 'write-down' the effect of the tax by a factor $(1-r)$, i.e. the effective burden of the tax is only $(1-r)$ times the nominal burden. Interpreted as a rate of interest, the tax not paid in the first year (£t) can be invested to yield £rt in each successive year, to pay part of each year's tax bill. Interpreted as a rate of time preference, the more heavily the future is discounted, the lower is the perceived burden of the tax.

Equation (10.2) applies strictly only when tax is unpaid for a full year. More generally, suppose that earnings increase when a fraction k,

$0 < k < 1$, of the year has already passed. Then only £$(1-k)$ is earned during the current award period, and the present value of the income stream if fully taxed is

$$P_k = \int_k^\infty (1-t)e^{-rv}\ \mathrm{d}v = \frac{1-t}{r}e^{rk} \tag{10.3}$$

But if no tax is levied till the end of the first period then the present value of the income stream is P_k plus the value of the first year's tax remission:

$$P'_k = P_k + \int_k^1 te^{-rv}\ \mathrm{d}v \tag{10.4}$$

Evaluating and simplifying

$$P'_k = \frac{e^{-rk}}{r} - \frac{te^{-r}}{r} \tag{10.5}$$

The first term is the present value of an untaxed unit increase in income starting a fraction, k, through the first period; the smaller is k, the larger the value of the pay increase. The second term is the perceived present value of the tax burden where the tax is imposed only after the end of the first period, and is lower the higher is r. Thus the higher the individual's marginal rate of time preference, the greater the tendency for the loss of future benefits to be discounted.

Major implications Fixed period awards have important policy implications. They enable the poor to raise their net income more easily, since benefit need not be lost at the time earnings rise. To that extent the tendency for families to be trapped in poverty is less acute than the traditional view suggests. Second, labour supply incentives may be improved. Temporary changes in earnings (e.g. overtime at Christmas) will not affect benefits; and even where increases are expected to persist, the tax rate relevant to labour supply decisions is that *perceived* by recipients, which, from equations (10.2) and (10.5), will depend on their time preference. This is almost certainly high, both because their income is low and because any increase in earnings may only be temporary. A poor worker is unlikely to reject an opportunity to increase his earnings because it might cost him benefit six months later.

There is little systematic evidence on rates of time preference, but inferences are possible. In Canada it normally takes about two months to process a claim for a tax refund. In order to get the money immediately, some people (before the practice was made illegal) would sell their title to a refund for between 30 and 70 per cent of its face value (Community Income Tax Service, 1976). The sale of a title to $100 in two months' time for $70 now implies a marginal rate of time preference of 600 per cent per year. From the second term in equation (10.5), $r = 6$ implies

$$t \, \frac{e^{-r}}{r} \, = \, 0.0004t$$

In other words, the perceived tax burden is almost zero. Even with less extreme cases the tax burden is reduced to under 40 per cent of its nominal value when $r = 100$ per cent, and to under 7 per cent when $r = 200$ per cent. If such rates of time preference are general, the tax effects of benefits withdrawn only some months after earnings have increased are likely to be heavily discounted, thereby considerably reducing the disincentive effect.

In addition to their beneficial impact on (a) family poverty and (b) labour supply, fixed period awards have two further advantages. If taxes are fully discounted, the withdrawal of benefit as income rises is analytically equivalent to a lump-sum tax collected at some time in the future, with all the welfare properties of lump-sum taxation. Second, fixed period awards ameliorate the dilemma faced by public policy between the desire to preserve incentives by keeping tax rates low, and the need to reduce costs by targeting benefits tightly on those in need (hence withdrawing benefits rapidly as income rises). Fixed period awards cushion the impact of high rates of withdrawal, while avoiding the high expenditure which would be involved in substantially reducing them.

3.3 Child Benefit

It has been argued that child benefit, in that it is not income tested, is poorly targeted. This section limits itself to discussion of this issue.

Targeting by income level As discussed in more detail in Chapter 11, vertical efficiency can be pursued in two ways.

1. Income testing targets benefit tightly on families with lower income, and thereby minimises direct benefit costs. Its disadvantages are the labour supply disincentive associated with high implicit tax rates, and high administrative costs.

2. Alternatively, benefit could be conditioned on one or more characteristics like being unemployed or having children. The greater the correlation between the characteristic and poverty, the more accurate is targeting.

Having children is highly correlated with poverty. Parents are typically in the younger segments of the population, and thus at a relatively low part of their lifetime earnings trajectory; and the arrival of children frequently reduces second-earner income. For both reasons, family income tends to be low precisely at the time when the demands on that income are high. For life-cycle reasons, families with children *systematically* have low income relative to needs. It is, of course, possible to point to specific high-income families with children; that merely makes the point that child benefit is not *perfectly* targeted. Pointing to exceptions is analogous to arguing that heavy smokers who live into their nineties disprove the ill-health effects of smoking.

This line of argument brings out the point that child benefit, in addition to any redistributive goals, has an efficiency function as a device which allows families to redistribute to themselves over their lifetime. A similar result could in theory be attained by borrowing; but capital market imperfections largely rule out that option in policy terms.

Targeting within the family Child benefit also assists targeting within the family. This has two aspects. First, if paid to the mother, the benefit helps to empower women. Second, and separately, limited systematic evidence and considerable casual empiricism suggest that paying child benefit to the mother improves the targeting of benefits on children.

Other aspects Because targeting is achieved without an income test, the labour supply disincentive of the benefit is considerably reduced.[4] The incentive, particularly for secondary earners, to work at least part-time is considerably enhanced.

The administration of an income test is costly, not least because information needs to be updated regularly. Child benefit is administratively cheap because it generally has a single, once-and-for-all information requirement – a birth certificate. Thereafter benefit can be paid automatically for 16 years; only if a child is in full-time education after age 16 is additional scrutiny needed. Administrative costs (including single-parent benefit) in 1990/1 were slightly over 2 per cent of benefit spending (UK, 1992e, Figure 28).

3.4 Empirical Issues and Evidence

The empirical literature on non-contributory benefits is surveyed by Atkinson (1987a) and Moffitt (1992). Two issues predominate: their effectiveness in relieving poverty; and their incentive effects.

THE EFFECTIVENESS OF NON-CONTRIBUTORY BENEFITS
IN RELIEVING POVERTY

The level of benefits The question here is whether benefits are sufficiently high to relieve poverty (assuming, initially, that people claim all the benefits to which they are entitled). For Britain, at least until 1980, the answer must be a qualified yes. Two points are noteworthy about the level of supplementary benefit/income support: it is set at 100 per cent of a notional

---

[4] There is a disincentive arising via the income effect but, unlike income testing, none via the substitution effect.

poverty line, rather than some fraction; and between 1948 and 1980 it retained its relativity to pre-tax average earnings, and hence rose relative to post-tax earnings (Barr, 1981). Partly for that reason, expenditure was high: in the early 1980s, about 8.4 per cent of GDP was transferred to the lowest income quintile (compared with about 10 per cent in Sweden and Germany, and 4.8 per cent in the USA) (Smeeding *et al.*, 1990, Table 2.3). As a result Beckerman (1979) found that cash benefits reduced the number of people below the supplementary benefit poverty line from 22.7 per cent of the population before all transfers to 3.3 per cent, and reduced the income gap (i.e. the aggregate shortfall of incomes below the poverty line) from £5.9 billion per year to £0.25 billion.[5]

Over the 1980s poverty, as measured by head count, increased. In 1979 there were 4 million poor families containing 6.1 million poor individuals; by 1985, there were 5.7 million families in poverty, embracing 9.4 million individuals (Barr and Coulter, 1990, Table 7.10; see also Coulter *et al.*, 1992). The measurement problems involved in such head count statistics are discussed by Johnson and Webb (1989).

Danziger *et al.* (1984) show that in 1983 cash benefits reduced the US poverty count (as defined by the official poverty line) from 24 per cent of the population pre-transfer to 15.2 per cent, and to between 10 and 13 per cent if transfers in kind are included. This is partly because there is no automatic relation between the official US poverty line (which is federal) and benefit levels (which are usually set by states). For further discussion of poverty in the USA, see Haveman (1987) and Sawhill (1988).

Living standards in utility terms depend not only on cash benefits, but also on the extent of stigma. Empirical studies are inconclusive mainly because stigma is not the only influence on take-up (another crucial variable being the extent to which claimants are aware of their potential entitlement). Serious statistical problems arise in attempting to separate two influences so different and so hard to measure (see Warlick, 1981; Moffitt, 1983; Duncan, 1984).

Targeting 1: horizontal efficiency First, do benefits go to those who need them (i.e. are they horizontally efficient)? This boils down mainly to take-up, of which there are two main measures: the *caseload* take-up rate refers to the proportion of eligible *claimants* who receive benefit; the *expenditure* measure relates to the fraction of total expenditure (assuming hypothetical full take-up) which is actually claimed. Take-up is far from easy to measure (see Atkinson, 1989, Ch. 11). Official estimates suggest that caseload take-up for supplementary benefit in the 1970s was typically between 70 and 75 per cent (for this and other estimates, see Barr and Coulter (1990, Table 7.6)). In the 1980s, take-up rose from 75 per cent in 1981 to 84 per cent in

[5] The concepts and problems involved in defining a poverty line and measuring the extent of poverty are discussed in Chapter 6:2.

1985 in caseload terms; take-up in expenditure terms was 91 per cent (UK, 1992e, para. 40).

Take-up was generally lower for the other main means-tested benefits. Caseload take-up for family income supplement (the predecessor of family credit) was typically around 50 per cent. Take-up of housing benefit in the mid-1980s is officially estimated at 78 per cent (caseload) and 90 per cent (expenditure). For further assessment, see Dorsett and Heady (1991).

In the USA, take-up of the main income-tested benefit, Aid to Families with Dependent Children, though low in the late 1960s (see the official study by Projector and Murray (1978)), increased considerably, largely because of positive action by administrators and rights workers. It is estimated that by 1977 take-up of the basic scheme was 94 per cent, and of the unemployed-parent scheme 72 per cent. For general discussion of the USA, see Sawhill (1988) and Levy (1988).

Drawing the threads together, cash benefits may fail to relieve poverty for three sets of reasons: (a) the absolute level of benefits may be too low; (b) coverage may be inadequate for certain groups, in the sense that they are poor but not eligible for benefit; and (c) take-up may be incomplete either (on the demand side) because of ignorance about entitlement, or stigma, or (on the supply side) out of maladministration and/or discrimination. In Britain (b) applies in the case of working families and some single-parent families, and (c) applies particularly to the elderly. In the USA problems arise under all three heads.

Targeting 2: vertical efficiency   The extent to which benefits are restricted to the poor has two aspects: to what extent does income testing restrict benefits to the poor; and how well-targeted are categorical benefits awarded on the basis of non-income criteria?

Looking first at income testing, there are two questions: how high are implicit tax rates; and how many people face them? The complexity of these issues was stressed in section 3.2; and further complications arise where tax rates are determined by the actual operation of the system, which may differ substantially from the scheme on paper.[6] According to government figures (based on work by Atkinson which investigated a large sample of individual families), about 600,000 tax units in 1980 faced marginal tax rates of over 50 per cent, of whom 120,000 faced marginal rates of 70 per cent and over (UK, 1983a, Table 15).

Reforms taking effect in April 1988 were intended to reduce the severity of the poverty trap. Under the old system, discussed in section 3.2, a person earning an extra pound could lose more than a pound in tax and benefit.

---

[6] Barr and Hall (1975) found that in 1967 in almost all major US cities the measurement of income by welfare caseworkers reduced the implicit tax rates embodied in Aid to Families with Dependent Children considerably below the 100 per cent rate specified in the regulations.

The 1988 reforms sought to avoid the problem by basing entitlement on income *net* of income tax, national insurance contributions and most cash benefits. The result was to make withdrawal rates in excess of 100 per cent considerably less likely. The overall withdrawal rate, however, remains high (see Dilnot and Webb, 1988). The reforms reduced the top rates of withdrawal, mainly by systematising arrangements. An almost inevitable result was that the reduction in the numbers of people facing marginal rates in excess of 100 per cent was accompanied by a sharp increase in the numbers facing marginal rates of 70 per cent or more. Both for this reason, and because of higher take-up, Barr and Coulter (1990, Table 7.15) estimate that after the reforms the numbers facing such rates had approximately doubled.

Where implicit tax rates, as imposed by the *de facto* operation of benefit systems, are high and faced by substantial numbers, the problem of the poverty trap with its inequities and disincentives becomes important. Where tax rates are low, the issue arises of potentially inaccurate targeting, in that the leakage of benefit may be excessive. Dilnot *et al.* (1984, Table 2.4) estimate that 100 per cent of supplementary benefit expenditure in 1981 went to those below the poverty line. Their conclusion is almost tautologous given that (a) they defined poverty in terms of the supplementary benefit level, and (b) supplementary benefit incorporates a 100 per cent withdrawal rate. For family income supplement and assistance with housing costs the corresponding figure was 37.5 per cent, i.e. 62.5 per cent of these benefits went to families with pre-transfer incomes *above* the supplementary benefit level, or were payments in excess of those necessary to bring incomes to that level. For cash benefits as a whole, 54 per cent of disbursements went to families whose post-transfer income did not exceed the poverty line.

It is not clear how these figures should be interpreted. Dilnot *et al.* take them to imply that the system is inefficient in that benefits 'leak out' to the non-poor. But to the extent that the harsher aspects of the poverty trap are thereby alleviated, the leakages may have benefits in incentive as well as in equity terms (it being remembered that recipients with incomes just above the supplementary benefit level can hardly be regarded as comfortably off).

A second aspect of vertical efficiency is the extent to which benefit can be targeted through non-income criteria. The *a priori* arguments why child benefit is likely to be well-targeted were set out in section 3.3. Table 10.2 shows the distribution of benefit expenditure for child benefit and the national insurance retirement pension in 1985. The bottom 10 per cent of households receive 21.6 per cent of total child benefit expenditure, receiving, on average, 5.5 times as much child benefit as a household in the top decile.

Table 10.2 *Distribution of benefit expenditure by income decile, UK, 1985*[a]

DECILE	PERCENTAGE OF BENEFIT GOING TO EACH DECILE		
	Child benefit	Retirement pension	Rent rebate
1	21.6 (21.6)[b]	35.4 (35.4)	38.4 (38.4)
2	7.4 (29.0)	26.5 (61.9)	29.6 (68.0)
3	7.6 (36.6)	9.5 (71.4)	19.5 (87.5)
4	8.7 (45.3)	7.4 (78.8)	6.9 (94.4)
5	12.6 (57.9)	5.3 (84.1)	2.4 (96.8)
6	12.5 (70.4)	4.2 (88.3)	1.5 (98.3)
7	11.0 (81.4)	4.1 (92.4)	1.0 (99.3)
8	8.9 (90.3)	2.8 (95.2)	0.3 (99.6)
9	5.6 (95.9)	3.0 (98.2)	0.4 (100)
10	3.9 (99.8)	1.7 (99.9)	0.0 (100)

Source: Atkinson (forthcoming, Table 1) and UK House of Commons Social Services Committee (1988b).

Notes: [a] Households are ranked into deciles of household gross income, excluding the benefit in question, and adjusted to reflect household composition. Thus the table should be read as follows: 21.6 per cent of expenditure on child benefit went to households in the bottom decile when ranked by income excluding child benefit.
[b] Figures in brackets are the cumulative distribution.

The effect in 1986 was to reduce the Gini coefficient by about 1.4 per cent (Barr and Coulter, 1990, Tables 7.10 and 7.11).

In terms of current income, the elderly, for life-cycle reasons, are also disproportionately represented at the lower end of the income distribution. Table 10.2 shows that the bottom income quintile received over 60 per cent of total pension spending. A typical household in the bottom decile received over 20 times as much pension expenditure as its counterpart in the top decile. Thus the retirement pension (which is not income tested) is tightly targeted on the least well-off. Figure 10.2 presents these data as a form of Lorenz curve (see Chapter 6:4.1). The diagonal line shows the position if pensions were distributed uniformly by income level; the difference between the actual distribution and the diagonal shows the extent to which pension expenditure is progressive. The effect of pensions in 1986 was to reduce the Gini coefficient by nearly 10 per cent (Barr and Coulter, 1990, Tables 7.11 and 7.12).

Finally, in assessing the effectiveness of income transfers in relieving poverty, we should remind ourselves of major and unavoidable methodological questions. First, there are the many problems in defining the poverty line, the unit of receipt, and the distribution of income within that unit (Chapter 6:2.1). Second is the value placed by recipients on the transfers: the value

Figure 10.2 *Cumulative distribution of expenditure on pensions by income decile, UK, 1985*

of cash benefits may be reduced by stigma, and that placed on in-kind transfers may be less than their market price (though see Chapter 4:4.2). Third, and possibly of greatest intractability, is the incidence of the transfers (Chapter 7:4.1). Calculations assume (because no other procedure is practicable) that a family's pre-transfer income is that which it would have been in the absence of any system of income support. This is, to say the least, a strong assumption. Similarly, it is assumed that benefits paid to those in work, including family credit and child benefit, have no effect on wage rates.

INCENTIVE EFFECTS

When turning to the incentive effects of cash transfers the waters are, if anything, even murkier. The incentive effects of unemployment benefit (Chapter 8:3.1) and pensions (Chapter 9:5.1) are closely linked with the present discussion, which is consequently brief. In the context of income-related benefits the main empirical questions concern their effects on labour supply and on family formation.

Labour supply Barr and Hall (1981) in a study of Aid to Families with Dependent Children in 1967, though not an explicit study of labour supply, found that recipients responded rationally to the budget constraint they faced, suggesting a negative relationship between benefit levels and labour supply. Levy (1979) showed that attempts to improve labour supply incentives in the US system may be successful for existing recipients; but labour supply overall may fall because benefits (being now more attractive) induce non-recipients to decrease their work effort and join the programme. This is precisely the reason (section 3.1) why lowering the tax rate implicit in income support is likely to be so costly.

Moffitt's (1992) survey of income-tested benefits concludes that, though the major US welfare benefits reduce labour supply, the effect is not strong enough to explain the long-term increase in the number of recipients. Recent policy developments (see Gramlich, 1989) seek improvements either through countervailing incentives or by policing individual behaviour. The categorical approach seeks to minimise distortions by paying more generous benefits to groups (e.g. pensioners) with less elastic labour supplies. The tax implicit in benefit withdrawal could be replaced by wage subsidies. Income support can be conditioned on work or job training, as in the Swedish active labour market policy (Flanagan, 1987). Child support from absent fathers can be pursued more vigorously.[7]

All such conclusions, however (and particularly numerical estimates of labour supply elasticities), should be read alongside the caveats in Chapter 8:3.1 about the empirical literature on unemployment benefits.

Effects on family formation Income support may affect family formation in various ways. Research has concentrated on the US welfare system, and the extent to which it gives families an incentive to split up. In particular, it has been argued that the sharp rise in the number of black female-headed households after 1960 was causally related to the increase in real benefits under Aid to Families with Dependent Children. Various studies, both time-series and cross-section, have investigated the question but, as with stigma, conclusions vary widely. Honig (1974) (see also Minarik and Goldfarb, 1976; Honig, 1976), using 1960 data, found a positive relationship

---

[7] In 1990 Australia introduced a system whereby child support is enforced through the income tax system.

between benefit levels and the proportion of female-headed families, with a stronger effect for non-white families. Barr and Hall (1981), using 1967 data, found that race exerted no independent effect on welfare dependency (though this does not rule out the possibility that black and white family formation were equally affected by increasing benefit levels). Yet other studies have failed to find any significant effects. The literature is surveyed by Atkinson (1987a).

3.5 Conclusion

Britain's income distribution, like that in almost all industrialised countries, is heavily skewed towards lower incomes. We want to support the poor (the level criterion), but the income distribution makes it inevitable that benefits must be withdrawn fairly rapidly if limited resources (the cost criterion) are to be targeted on the most needy. This focus can be achieved in various ways: benefit can be withdrawn as family income rises, either immediately (income support) or eventually (family credit); or it can be removed when an individual's status changes (e.g. the loss of unemployment benefit upon resumption of work, or loss of child benefit when a child reaches the age of 16). Whatever the method, a poverty trap in one form or another is largely inevitable, an observation which brings us naturally to Chapter 11.

Further Reading

The most comprehensive (and up-to-date) summaries of the institutions of non-contributory benefits are published annually by Tolley (1991) (which includes references to legislation). The background to the 1988 reforms is set out in UK (1985h).

For comment and criticism, see Meade (1978, Ch. 5), Atkinson (1989), UK (1983a) and Dilnot *et al.* (1984, Ch. 2). Dilnot and Webb (1988) assess the 1988 reforms. For a critique of the social fund, see Berthoud (1991), and Huby and Walker (1991). The construction and operation of housing benefit is assessed by Hills (1991, Ch. 10) and Glennerster (1992, Ch. 13).

The empirical literature on the incentive effects of income support schemes, and on their effectiveness in alleviating poverty, is vast. For estimates of poverty in the UK, see Beckerman (1979), Mack and Lansley (1985), and Atkinson (1989); and for a review of evidence between 1974 and 1985, Barr and Coulter (1990); on measurement problems, see Johnson and Webb (1989). For discussion of targeting, see Atkinson (forthcoming), Nichols and Zeckhauser (1982), Blackorby and Donaldson (1988) and Besley and Kanbur (1991).

For recent UK assessment of poverty and inequality, see Coulter *et al.* (1992). On the USA, see Danziger, Haveman and Plotnick (1984), Haveman (1987), Levy

(1988) and Sawhill (1988). Atkinson (1991) reviews evidence in various OECD countries. For international comparison, see Smeeding *et al.* (1990), and for a European perspective, Atkinson (1992). On redistributive effects see the Further Reading at the end of Chapter 7.

Chapter 11
Strategies for Reform

If a free society cannot help the many who are poor, it cannot save the few who are rich. [John F. Kennedy, 1961.]

1 Approaches to Income Support

The last three chapters discussed the cash side of the welfare state in some detail. This chapter considers more generally the pros and cons of different forms of income support. It is a discussion not of specific reform proposals, but of different *strategies*. The starting point is how most usefully to identify the poor. Two approaches stand out. Benefits can be conditioned on *income* (i.e. means-tested), the archetypal example being the sort of negative income tax discussed in section 2. Alternatively, as emerged in Chapter 10, they can be conditioned on the *characteristics* of recipients through categorical schemes which award benefits on the basis, for example, of being unemployed, sick or retired. This is the so-called 'Back to Beveridge' strategy, discussed in section 3. Section 4 considers mixed strategies. Section 5 summarises the major conclusions to emerge from Chapters 8 to 11.

The distinction between categorical and non-categorical schemes is important. The former stress the *causes* of poverty, and institute programmes for specific groups. Historically, it was thought that most people would be self-supporting through work, or through insurance against income loss due to unemployment, sickness or old age; and that the few who fell outside these groups could be categorised into the disabled, the blind, etc. Underlying this approach is the distinction between the 'deserving' poor (e.g. widows with young children) and the 'undeserving'. Such thinking lay behind the Poor Law, and permeated much of the 1930s New Deal legislation in the USA. The Beveridge Report, though liberal in its attitude, distinguished eight 'reasonable' causes of poverty (UK, 1942, pp. 124–5).

Non-categorical schemes, in contrast, regard recipients as a spectrum which includes the self-supporting, the very poor and a large number in between. Such schemes concentrate on *outcome* rather than cause, and classification is made only in terms of need. The approach is attractive because there are few gaps through which 'difficult' cases can fall, but it has the disadvantage of requiring a means test in one form or another.

A common thread throughout the chapter is that there are no easy solutions to poverty in countries with relatively large numbers of people with low incomes. This is not an argument against increased redistribution, but a warning that it will not be brought about without an awareness of the difficulties involved.

2 The Negative Income Tax Approach

2.1 The Idea

Negative income taxation is the archetype of cash support conditioned on an income test. This section discusses the way such schemes work, and considers briefly a British proposal which came close to implementation in the mid-1970s. Section 2.2 discusses large-scale negative income taxation, and section 2.3 a possible role for a small-scale scheme as part of a package of wider reform.

The principle is easily outlined in terms of the UK income tax system, shown in simplified form in Figure 11.1A by the line OBA: individual income is tax free up to £B; thereafter it is taxed at t per cent. Suppose that $B = £3000$ and $t = 35$ per cent. The simplest negative income tax is shown by the line G_0BA: if an individual's income is above £3000 he pays tax of 35 per cent of the excess over £3000; if it is below £3,000 he *receives* 35 per cent of the shortfall below £3000. Someone with an income of £3500 pays 35 per cent of £500, i.e. £175, while an individual with an income of £2500 receives £175. More generally, it is possible to have a different tax rate above and below the breakeven income (shown by the line G_1BA), and a higher breakeven for larger families.

Formally, the simplest negative income tax relates the individual's tax bill, T, (positive or negative) to his income, Y, as

$$T = t\,(Y - B) \tag{11.1}$$

where t is the tax rate applied above and below the breakeven income, B, as shown by the line G_0BA. It is often more useful to think of the system in a different way: an individual with zero income receives 35 per cent of the amount by which his income falls below £3000, i.e. £1050; from equation (11.1) it is entirely equivalent to give *everyone* a transfer of £1050, and to tax *all* other income at 35 per cent. Thus

$$T = tY - G \tag{11.2}$$

where $G = tB$ is a lump-sum transfer to the individual, who then pays tax

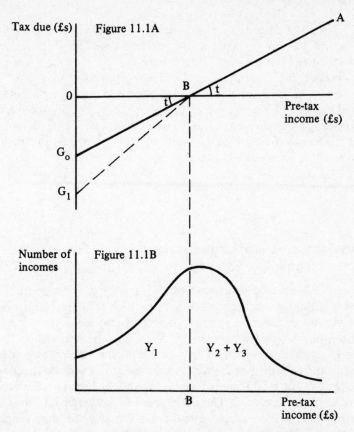

Figure 11.1 *The cost of negative income tax*

at a rate, t, on all his other income, Y. Similarly, an individual could be given a larger transfer, say G_1 in Figure 11.1A, and taxed at 50 per cent on the first £B of his income and 35 per cent thereafter. A scheme which gives everyone a lump sum and taxes all other income goes under the generic name of a *social dividend scheme*. Equations (11.1) and (11.2) show that social dividend schemes and negative income taxes are analytically identical. Such arrangements have been given various names: minimum income guarantee, reverse income tax, basic income guarantee, and guaranteed income schemes. Though their administration is very different, all are completely identified by two features: the size of the transfer, G, to an individual with no income; and the tax structure applied to any other income.

The tax credit scheme of the early 1970s (discussed in section 2.3) is an example of the social dividend approach.[1] It proposed weekly tax credits

[1] For the proposals, see UK (1972a); for assessments, UK (1973), Prest (1973), Barr and Roper (1974); and for a counter-view, Atkinson (1973).

(at 1972 prices) of £4 per single person, £6 per couple and £2 per child; all other income was to be taxed at 30 per cent (with higher rates for the highest incomes). For people with low earnings the tax credit was greater than their tax liability, thus raising take-home pay above gross pay. Certain groups were excluded, notably the self-employed and people below the poverty line, the latter because they almost certainly already received some sort of poverty relief, thereby (it was argued) complicating the administration of cash assistance if they received some of their income as tax-credit and the rest in other forms of income transfer.

2.2 An Assessment of Large-Scale Negative Income Tax Schemes

Negative income tax schemes have attracted widespread support (see the Further Reading): from libertarians because cash transfers are compatible with market allocation, and so can loosen what they see as the stranglehold of in-kind transfers under the welfare state; and from socialists because the scheme guarantees everyone at least a minimum income as a right of citizenship and without a means test. Additionally, it is claimed that negative income tax will boost take-up, reduce stigma and, by bringing all individuals under a single umbrella, enable government to be better-informed about the economic condition of the population. Possibly the most important claims are that negative income tax can solve two major problems – the poverty trap, and the failure of the welfare state to redistribute substantially more income.

Why then, despite such widespread support, has no country adopted a large-scale scheme? The short answer, for a nation with an income distribution like Britain's, is its cost. This implies a large increase in tax rates, which aggravates the poverty trap and/or creates labour supply disincentives.

ISSUES OF COST

A useful starting point is the distinction between a small-scale scheme, which offers a low guaranteed income like G_0 in Figure 11.1A, and a large-scale scheme giving a higher transfer like G_1. Under the first, the cost is not large, and no high tax rates are necessary; but the guaranteed income is low, so no substantial help is given to the poor, and the need for additional benefits remains. If negative income tax is the sole anti-poverty device, it is necessary to have a high guaranteed income like G_1. This raises problems of cost, as illustrated in Figure 11.1. The intercept, G_0 and slope, t, of negative income tax completely characterise the position of an individual or family. But the cost of the scheme and its redistributive strength depend *both* on the tax/benefit function *and* on the size distribution of income. The society shown in Figure 11.1B contains many poor people with income less than *B*, and relatively few rich people; consequently, the cost of the scheme shown in Figure 11.1A will be higher, because of the larger number of net beneficiaries relative to net contributors, than in a richer country (i.e. one in which the left-hand tail, Y_1, is smaller).

The logic of the cost issue Estimates for 1972 (Barr, 1975) suggest that a scheme which paid a universal transfer at the supplementary benefit/income support level would require close to a threefold increase in the average burden of income tax from 20 per cent of personal income to 50–60 per cent. Atkinson (1983a, p. 275) illustrates the point: if the guaranteed income for an average family is x per cent of average income, and if income tax currently raises y per cent of average income for purposes other than income support, then the average income tax rate must be $x + y$. With plausible values for x and y (Atkinson suggests 35 per cent and 15 per cent), the *average* rate of *income* tax (i.e. ignoring all indirect taxes, etc.) is at least 50 per cent.

Why are large-scale schemes so costly? The intuitive answer is that 'ordinary' income tax has to raise revenue to finance benefits *only* (or largely) for poor people, whereas negative income tax pays benefit to *everyone*. The resulting increase in taxation can be viewed in two ways: either because higher gross benefit payments require higher taxation; or because higher taxes are necessary to claw back benefits paid to rich people. The effect of universal benefits is to raise at least some marginal tax rates, even if the average tax rate (inclusive of benefits) is unchanged.

It is necessary, however, to dig deeper. Consider the society shown in Table 11.1 with five poor individuals (assumed to have no income) and ten rich people (whose income is £10,000 per year) as shown in lines 1 and 2. The tax base (i.e. pre-transfer personal income) is £100,000 (line 3), and the tax threshold £4000 under income tax and £0 under negative income tax (line 4). The poverty line, by assumption, is £4000 per year (line 5). Under 'ordinary' income tax (columns 1 and 2), £4000 is transferred to each of the five poor individuals in the form of 'welfare' benefits; rich individuals receive no transfer (line 6a). The total cost of the scheme is £20,000 (line 7), requiring a tax rate on income above the threshold of $33\frac{1}{3}$ per cent (lines 8 and 9); post-transfer incomes of poor and rich are £4000 and £8000, respectively (line 10). Under an otherwise identical negative income tax (columns 3 and 4), both poor *and* rich receive a transfer of £4000 (line 6b). The cost of the scheme is £60,000, requiring a tax rate on all income of 60 per cent (lines 7–9). Post-transfer incomes of rich and poor are identical to the income tax case: poor individuals have £4000; rich individuals each receive £4000 but have to pay £6000 in tax, leaving a net income of £8000. The introduction of a negative income tax with a uniform tax rate has had no effect on post-transfer incomes but, by tripling the cost of income support, has tripled the average tax rate (line 11) to ensure that rich individuals still pay £2000 net tax despite receiving an initial transfer of £4000.

However, Table 11.1 to some extent hides the fact that negative income tax may not increase taxation *per se*, so much as *replace implicit by explicit taxation*.[2] There are two cases. In the first, both the level of benefits and their coverage remain unchanged under negative income tax, as in Table 11.1. Identical recipients receive identical benefits; total net expenditure is unchanged; no increase in net revenue is necessary; and nobody's post-transfer income has changed. Negative income tax has produced an exact mimic of the previous system by a different administrative mechanism: nothing has been done to relieve poverty; and the poverty trap and labour supply disincentives are unchanged. The only difference is that in Table 11.1 someone whose income rises from £0 to £10,000 under income tax will (a) lose £4000 via implicit taxation, and (b) pay an additional £2000 in explicit income tax; under negative income tax he pays £6000 in explicit tax. The only effect of negative income tax in this case is to make *all* withdrawal of benefit part of *explicit* taxation. From one perspective this is more a difference of form than of substance; from another it forecloses the possibility of minimising incentive effects through devices like fixed period awards (Chapter 10:3.2), or the conditioning of benefits not on income but on, for example, health or employment status.

A second, and very different, case arises where net benefits and/or coverage are increased by negative income tax. This raises the net income of at least some poor people; but net expenditure rises, necessitating an increase in taxes over and above the replacement of implicit by explicit taxation.

The logic of what is happening is seen most easily in terms of two hypothetical states of the world, in which benefits are paid *only* to the poor (state A), or are paid to *everyone* (state B). Then:

1. *Total tax revenue*: gross expenditure, and hence on a revenue-neutral basis also gross tax revenues, must be higher in state B than state A.

2. *Average tax rate* (ATR): if tax revenues are greater in state B then ATR must be higher.

3. *Marginal tax rates* (MTR): if ATR is higher then MTR must be higher for at least some groups. There are two polar cases: *either* the increase in MTR is concentrated wholly on the poor, in which case (a) the poverty trap is institutionalised, and (b) there is a potential labour supply problem for the poor; *or* the increase in MTR is concentrated wholly on

---

[2] The concept of implicit taxation is discussed in Chapter 10:3.1.

Table 11.1 *Hypothetical effect of negative income tax on tax rates*[a]

	'ORDINARY' INCOME TAX AND BENEFITS		NEGATIVE INCOME TAX	
	Poor individual (1)	Rich individual (2)	Poor individual (3)	Rich individual (4)
ASSUMPTIONS				
(1) Number of individuals	5	10	5	10
(2) Pre-transfer income of each individual (per year)	0	£10,000	0	£10,000
(3) Tax base (=total pre-transfer personal income)	$10 \times £10{,}000 = £100{,}000$		$10 \times £10{,}000 = £100{,}000$	
(4) Tax threshold	£4000	£4000	£0	£0
(5) Poverty line (per year)	£4000	£4000	£4000	£4000
(6a) Cash transfer to each *poor* individual under income tax	£4000	0		
(6b) Guaranteed income to *all* individuals under negative income tax			£4000	£4000
IMPLICATIONS				
(7) Total cost of income support (line (1) × line (6))	$5 \times £4000 = £20{,}000$		$15 \times £4000 = £60{,}000$	
(8) Total taxable income (from lines (3) and (4))	$10 \times (£10{,}000 - £4000) = £60{,}000$		$10 \times £10{,}000 = £100{,}000$	
(9) Tax rate on taxable income (from lines (7) and (8))	$£20{,}000/£60{,}000 = 33\tfrac{1}{3}\%$		$£60{,}000/£100{,}000 = 60\%$	
(10) Post-transfer income	£4000	$£4000 + (1 - \tfrac{1}{3})£6000 = £8000$	£4000	$£4000 + (1 - 0.6)£10{,}000 = £8000$
(11) Average tax rate on personal income (from lines (7) and (3))	$£20{,}000/£100{,}000 = 20\%$		$£60{,}000/£100{,}000 = 60\%$	

Note: [a] Assumptions:
   (1) Taxation levied only to finance cash transfers.
   (2) No transactions costs.

the rich, in which case (a) the poverty trap is in principle 'solved', but (b) there is a potential labour supply problem for the rich.

Thus negative income tax inevitably raises explicit tax rates.

Formal analysis The cost of any scheme is the tax/benefit function in Figure 11.1A weighted by the income distribution in Figure 11.1B (non-technical readers can skip the equations). Thus:

$$C = AG - \int_0^\infty t(Y)D(Y)\mathrm{d}Y \tag{11.3}$$

where:

G = the guaranteed income per individual/family

A = the total number of individuals/families

Y = personal income

$t(Y)$ is the tax function (given in Figure 11.1A by the tax parameter, t), and

$D(Y)$ is the distribution of pre-tax income (given in Figure 11.1B).

Any issue of cost boils down to an empirical question about the elements of equation (11.3). For a given population, A, transfer, G, and tax function, $t(Y)$, the cost of the scheme and its redistributive strength depend on the size distribution of pre-tax personal income $D(Y)$, and in particular on the relative size of the left-hand tail of Figure 11.1B.

Within this framework it is possible (see Barr, 1975) to estimate the cost of different tax regimes – 'ordinary' income tax and two variants of negative income tax. Each of the systems comprises two elements – gross expenditure and gross revenue. For income tax, gross expenditure consists of total spending on cash benefits, S, and all remaining expenditure, R, out of income tax revenue. R, in other words, is the required surplus of income tax over expenditure on cash benefits. Under a large-scale negative income tax, S is omitted (since all existing cash benefits are, by assumption, abolished), and gross expenditure consists of R and the cost of the guaranteed income payments, AG in equation (11.3). On the revenue side, total personal income, Y, is split into three components: Y_1 is the income of 'poor' individuals/families with pre-transfer income below the tax threshold (i.e. the left-hand tail of Figure 11.1B); Y_2 is income below the tax threshold of families whose total income exceeds the tax threshold (equivalent to the personal allowances under income tax); and Y_3 is income above the tax threshold. Formally,

$$Y_1 = \int_0^B D(Y)\mathrm{d}Y$$

$$Y_2 + Y_3 = \int_B^\infty D(Y)\mathrm{d}Y \tag{11.4}$$

where B is the income tax threshold. Attention is focused on a very simple form of the tax function, $t(Y)$ in equation (11.3), with tax rates t_1 and t_2 applying, respectively, to income above and below the tax threshold.

Income tax is shown by the line OBA in Figure 11.2. Gross expenditure consists of cash benefits, S, plus the required surplus, R. On the revenue side, income below the tax threshold, $Y_1 + Y_2$, is not taxed (i.e. $t_1 = 0$); income above the threshold, Y_3, is taxed at the basic rate of income tax (including national insurance contributions), $\bar{t}$. Thus a simplified version of income tax is

$$C_1 = S + R - \bar{t}Y_3 \tag{11.5}$$

where, by definition, $C_1 = 0$.

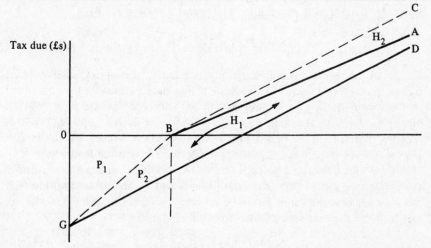

Figure 11.2 *The redistributive effects of negative income tax*

Dual-rate negative income tax consists on the expenditure side of the gross cost of the guaranteed income, AG (replacing existing cash benefits, S), and the required surplus, R. On the revenue side, taxes are levied at rates t_1 and t_2 on the relevant parts of the tax base, as shown by the line GBC in Figure 11.2. Dual-rate negative income tax is constructed so as to keep benefits in the hands of the poor by ensuring that all benefits are taxed away by the time the tax threshold, B, is reached. A benefit of £80 and a threshold of £100 implies that $t_1 = 80/100 = 0.8$, i.e. the restriction

$$t_1 = \frac{G}{B} \tag{11.6}$$

and the cost of the system is

$$C_2 = AG + R - \frac{G}{B}(Y_1 + Y_2) - t_2 Y_3 \tag{11.7}$$

Compared with income tax, the poor gain an amount related to the area P_1 in Figure 11.2.[3] Since all benefits are taxed away by the time the tax threshold is reached, the rich are invariant between the two systems if the tax rate on income above the threshold remains unchanged. But, as drawn, the dual-rate scheme imposes a higher rate than income tax above the tax threshold (i.e. BC has a steeper slope than BA), so the rich lose an amount related to the area H_2. Benefits remain in the hands of the poor.

Single-rate negative income tax is a special case where the same tax rate is levied on all income. Thus $t_1 = t_2$, and from equation (11.7)

$$C_3 = AG + R - t_2 Y \qquad (11.8)$$

where by definition (from Figure 11.1B and equation (11.4))

$$Y = \int_0^\infty D(Y)dY = Y_1 + Y_2 + Y_3 \qquad (11.9)$$

If the constraint of revenue neutrality is relaxed, this system is illustrated by the line GD in Figure 11.2. Income below the tax threshold is now taxed at the lower rate, t_2, so in comparison with income tax the poor gain an amount related to the area $P_1 + P_2$. As drawn, the rich gain H_1.[4] In this scheme, therefore, some benefit spills over to the rich, a result which remains true even if the single tax rate is chosen to ensure revenue neutrality.

A final and important point is the relation between the tax rate t under the single-rate scheme and the dual rates t_1 and t_2, on the assumption that the schemes cost the same. From equations (11.7), (11.8) and (11.9) the tax yields under the two schemes are equal if

$$tY = t_1(Y_1 + Y_2) + t_2 Y_3 \qquad (11.10)$$

Hence the relation between the single and dual rates is given by

$$t = \theta t_1 + (1 - \theta)t_2 \qquad (11.11)$$

where

$$\theta = \frac{Y_1 + Y_2}{Y} \qquad (11.12)$$

Two important implications follow from equation (11.11). First, t can be thought of as the marginal rate applied to all income; *or* as a weighted average of the dual rates; *or*, more generally, as the average of any set of marginal rates with the same tax yield. Second, if t_1 is higher than t_2 (which is likely if the poverty trap is a problem) then t is higher the larger is θ, i.e. the smaller is Y_3 as a proportion of total income.

Major implications   The foregoing apparatus demonstrates some earlier

---

[3] Understood as weighted by the appropriate section of the income distribution.
[4] Again weighted by the appropriate section of the income distribution.

results more precisely. Equation (11.6) shows that under the dual-rate scheme the tax rate, t, on low income rises *pari passu* with the level of benefits. Thus negative income tax recreates the poverty trap in another form. The first conclusion, therefore, is that *with the dual-rate scheme (which keeps all benefits in the hands of the poor) the more successfully poverty is alleviated, the more serious becomes the problem of the poverty trap.* The situation is no different from that under the present system of cash benefits.

The solution to the poverty trap is to withdraw benefits more slowly, in which case the breakeven income rises above the tax threshold. This is the case under the single-rate scheme, which lowers the marginal tax rate on the poor. But from equation (11.7) if the poor pay lower taxes on Y_1 then the rich pay lower taxes on Y_2. It follows, on an equi-cost basis, that more revenue will have to be collected from Y_3. Thus, for a given guaranteed income, *the poverty trap can be alleviated only by increased taxation of the rich.* This, as we shall see, can cause labour supply problems.

The last result is emphasised by equation (11.11), which shows that the average tax rate t (whether thought of as a single rate of tax applied to all income, or as the weighted average of a set of marginal rates) will be higher the smaller is Y_3 as a proportion of the tax base. This gives rise to a fundamental (but often overlooked) conclusion – that for a given level of benefit *it is the shape of the income distribution which 'creates' the poverty trap – changing the system of cash transfers will not solve the problem so long as benefits are conditioned on income.*

Negative income tax thus increases tax rates at some or all levels of income: it institutionalises the poverty trap and/or leads to higher tax rates on incomes above the poverty line. The only offsetting advantage is that the high tax rates on low income are at least systematic, in contrast with the often arbitrary pattern of the current system. In a country with Britain's income distribution the level of benefit and its cost can be reconciled only by the imposition of punitive taxation. This raises two consequential problems: the vertical efficiency[5] of negative income tax, as we shall see shortly, is not high despite the presence of high tax rates; and there is potentially a serious labour supply problem.

CONSEQUENTIAL ISSUES

Labour supply It is possible to draw on two sets of evidence. Econometric studies (e.g. Pencavel (1986), and various of the chapters in Ashenfelter and Layard (1986)) broadly confirm the conclusions of attitude surveys (Brown and Levin, 1974) that the labour supply of primary workers is wage inelastic. This might be taken to suggest that the introduction of a negative income tax would have no substantial effect on work effort, but several major caveats are necessary. First, labour supply estimates, being based on actual

[5] Vertical efficiency is defined in Chapter 10:2.

data, are derived for the most part from tax rates between 25 and 40 per cent; their conclusions are therefore valid only for tax rates within this range. The pitfalls of making predictions outside the range of data on which estimates are based are well-known. Second (see the relevant chapters in Ashenfelter and Layard (1986)), the supply elasticity of secondary workers (married women, teenagers, people past retiring age) can be substantial. Finally, there is the effect of perceptions on behaviour. The withdrawal of means-tested benefits as income rises can impose a 100 per cent implicit tax. Negative income taxation makes the tax explicit; and if taxation is thereby made more visible, labour supply disincentives might be strengthened.

A second source of evidence is a series of negative income tax experiments in the USA in the years after 1968. The main one, informally called the New Jersey Experiment, involved more than 1300 families, who received a guaranteed income between 50 and 125 per cent of the poverty line, and faced tax rates of between 30 and 70 per cent. The experiment spawned a vast literature (see the Further Reading). The initial consensus was that the data offered little evidence of substantial reductions in the labour supply of household heads. A number of doubts were subsequently raised: the conclusions applied for the most part only to primary workers; and the labour supply responses of participants may have been influenced by the limited duration of the experiment.

Redistributive effects   Negative income taxation has implications for both horizontal and vertical redistribution. A large-scale scheme paying benefits at the income support level can improve horizontal efficiency in two ways: it can increase take-up; and it can reduce stigma, because there is no longer a benefit system for the poor and a tax system for the non-poor, but one system in which everyone is treated similarly.

On vertical efficiency, negative income tax scores less well. At first glance it might appear that by benefiting the poor at the expense of the non-poor, it is strongly redistributive. This is not necessarily so. The cost of negative income tax, as we have seen, depends *inter alia* on the size distribution of income. So too does the redistributive strength of any particular scheme (i.e. the amount redistributed from those above to those below the breakeven income), simply because a 1 per cent increase in the average tax rate raises more revenue for redistribution to the poor the greater the proportion of taxpayers who are non-poor.

Barr (1975) shows that in a country with an income distribution like Britain's, negative income tax will not be a strong redistributor for two reasons. First, as benefits are increased, the average tax rate has to be raised to finance them. Second, there are many people with low incomes and relatively few with high incomes; the tax increase necessary to finance a high guaranteed income therefore falls substantially on those with low and average incomes, thus clawing back a substantial proportion of the benefit to the poor. In consequence the redistributive effects, though not trivial, are muted.

Conclusion 1 Given (a) the shape of the UK income distribution, (b) current benefit levels and (c) the fact that labour supply is potentially endogenous, two results follow. First, a universal negative income tax will be very costly; this will necessitate high tax rates which are likely to cause labour supply problems. Second, negative income taxation will not be a strong redistributor.

2.3 The Role of a Small-Scale Negative Income Tax

Given this conclusion, there are two ways of proceeding: one is the 'Back to Beveridge' approach discussed in the next section; the other is to retain the idea of a negative income tax, but to make it small-scale and combine it with other forms of income support.

Universal tax-credits A small-scale scheme will not, by definition, solve poverty, and is therefore relevant to poverty relief only if it makes other redistributive schemes more effective. The starting point is the tax-credit proposals described earlier. The scheme would have paid a weekly tax-credit, and taxed all other income at 30 per cent;[6] but it would have excluded the self-employed and, more importantly, the poor. The original proposals (UK, 1972a) as modified by Parliamentary discussion, were feasible and would have been implemented but for the General Election of February 1974. Furthermore, it would have cost only an extra £112 million (UK, 1973, Vol. II, p. 424) plus the cost of additional administration to make the scheme universal. Thus, a universal tax-credit scheme (i.e. a small-scale negative income tax) is financially feasible if the credits are chosen to supplement existing arrangements rather than to supplant them. For this purpose a tax-credit of roughly the value of the income tax personal allowance would suffice.

How useful would such a scheme be? We saw in Chapter 6:2.3 that one of the major difficulties in identifying and counting the poor lies in the fact that the Inland Revenue knows very little about them. The key feature of a universal tax-credit scheme is not that it would *per se* help the poor greatly (because the credit would be small), but that for the first time the great bulk of the population would be brought under the Inland Revenue umbrella. This would make it possible (Barr and Roper, 1974) to use computers to search out the poor (discussed shortly), thereby increasing the take-up of means-tested benefits. The strategy is to use a universal negative

---

[6] Except that those with higher incomes would have paid a higher marginal tax rate.

income tax not to *solve* poverty, but to enhance the effectiveness of benefits aimed specifically at the poor.

A scheme of this sort, as well as improving take-up, would alleviate the poverty trap in two ways. First, the tax-credits being universal, all other cash benefits become devices only for 'topping up' income, rather than mechanisms for total income support. This has the important advantage that the tax implicit in, for example, income support will apply over a shorter range of income. Suppose a family receives £50 in income support; under the present system (ignoring disregards) it faces a 100 per cent implicit tax on the first £50 of its net earnings. But if its weekly tax-credit were £30 it would receive only £20 in income support, and so face a 100 per cent tax rate on only the first £20 of net earnings. As a second improvement, fixed period awards (Chapter 10:3.2) would further reduce the poverty trap. A family in receipt of a £40 tax-credit, if awarded housing benefit of £20 per week for six months, would receive £60 per week *irrespective of changes in income*. Thus, by the back door, one is able to achieve the desirable result of paying a larger credit to families with low incomes. For a detailed proposal of a scheme of this type, see Parker (1989).

Administrative aspects It would be highly desirable, as a start, if existing means-tested benefits were rationalised. This should include standardising the definition of income used in assessing different benefits; standardising eligibility requirements (e.g. by extending the current system whereby families receiving income support or family credit are automatically entitled to various other benefits); merging some benefits; and, where possible, making use of fixed period awards.

Further work is also needed on computerisation of the tax and benefit systems, to enable a universal tax-credit scheme to be used as a search device to seek out the poor.[7] It is also possible to computerise benefit entitlement, speeding administration and making it easier to apply for benefit, thereby increasing both accuracy and take-up.

The resulting scheme would look broadly as follows. First, it would be open to anyone, at any time, to apply for benefit using an all-purpose application. In addition, because the tax-credits are universal, the tax authorities could combine their knowledge of (in theory) *everyone's* income with their computerised tax system to compile at the end of each tax year a list of all tax units with income below some specified amount. This list would be passed to the Department of Social Security. Everyone on the list would have a low income; but not everyone would be poor (e.g. a highly paid person who had started working in Britain only during the last month of the tax

---

[7] There would be other advantages. Computerisation makes possible self-assessment for income tax, which in turn makes it administratively feasible to dispense with the long basic rate band and replace it (if one so desires) by a structure of smoothly rising marginal tax rates. This is a somewhat technical administrative argument, but one with important policy implications – for details, see Barr *et al.* (1977).

year would (legitimately) have a low income for tax purposes, but would not be poor). The Department of Social Security would weed out the non-poor by sending each tax unit on the list an all-purpose benefit application form (completion of which would be *voluntary*). Completed returns would be processed, and benefit assessed, by computer.

If people could speedily ascertain their entitlement to *all* benefits with a single application, they would be more likely to apply; and if they did not apply, the 100 per cent survey of taxpayer incomes, even if conducted only annually, would take on average no more than six months (and at the outside slightly over a year) to 'catch' them. The result, almost certainly, is take-up rates above those achieved at present.

Conclusion 2 The proper role of a universal negative income tax is not as a major redistributor of income, but as a *search device* to discover low-income families. Take-up rates for means-tested benefits could thereby be substantially raised. In addition, the guaranteed income need be no higher than the value of current income tax personal allowances; hence the scheme does not raise benefit levels but only take-up rates; thus costs are not excessive, minimising problems with the poverty trap.

3 The 'Back to Beveridge' Approach

3.1 The Idea

Negative income taxation seeks to raise low incomes by paying benefits conditioned on income. The so-called 'Back to Beveridge' strategy makes benefits conditional on other characteristics, e.g. being unemployed, ill or retired, or having children. In its pure form, benefit is payable only on the basis of indicators like these; the issue of means testing does not arise.

The Meade proposals are an example of this approach (see also International Labour Office, 1984b). Meade (1978) argues that the existing system fails to prevent poverty because the main national insurance benefits and child benefit are below the poverty line defined by supplementary benefit/income support, thus violating a key Beveridge principle. His proposed reforms concentrate on rectifying this problem. They are: (a) raising all national insurance benefits to the income support level; (b) the payment of child benefit at the income support level; (c) the payment of additional benefits (to one-parent families, the disabled, etc.); and (d) the phasing out of many means-tested benefits. Income tax should be harmonised with the reformed system: in particular, (e) the income tax threshold should be raised to the income support level.

Proposals of this sort can alleviate the poverty trap in two important ways. First, the major benefits are at or above the poverty line, thus reducing the number of people receiving income support and facing its 100 per cent implicit tax. Second, these benefits are not affected by changes in income, but only by a change in the recipient's category, e.g. the loss of unemployment benefit upon resumption of work. This does not remove the poverty trap so much as sidestep it by concentrating the entire tax effect on the change in status.

The logic of the approach, in addition to alleviating the poverty trap, has important and much wider implications, which are worth exploring by way of a simple example. Assume:

1. Only redheads are poor.
2. All redheads are poor.
3. There is no hair-dyeing technology.

In these circumstances it would be possible completely to eliminate poverty, as defined by the poverty line, by paying a redhead benefit (this is known as *indicator targeting*). Additionally (and crucially), because benefits go *only* to the poor no substantial increase in tax rates is necessary.

These results follow for two reasons. First, in the terminology of Chapter 10:2, a redhead benefit is both horizontally and vertically efficient. Having red hair is a necessary condition for poverty (assumption 1); were this not the case a redhead benefit would leave gaps by failing to cover poor people who did not have red hair. It is also a sufficient condition (assumption 2); were this not the case, benefits would 'leak out' to redheads who were not poor. Thus having red hair is perfectly correlated with poverty. Second, having red hair is wholly exogenous to the individual (assumption 3). The ideal indicators on which to condition benefits are therefore *exogenous correlates* of poverty.

What would this strategy imply in practice? Empirically, the major correlates of poverty are unemployment; ill-health (sickness and disability); large families; single-parent families; old age; and high housing costs (empirical data on families with children and the elderly were discussed in Chapter 10:3.4). Benefits paid to people in these categories would embrace the great majority of the poor. How exogenous are these characteristics? The endogeneity of the level and duration of unemployment is highly controversial (Chapter 8:3.1). With ill-health, the problem is less acute because genuine ill-health is costly to the individual, and because policing is possible through certification procedures. The incidence of large families is exogenous with respect to benefits unless decisions to have children are influenced by the existence of child benefit and income support; and similarly, the occurrence of single-parent families is exogenous unless the decision by parents to separate is substantially influenced by the existence of cash benefits (see the discussion in Chapter 10:3.4 of the empirical literature on family formation). A crucial issue in this context is whether having children/separating is more strongly endogenous than labour supply.

Turning to old age, reaching retirement age is entirely beyond the individual's control. Individuals may choose voluntarily to defer retirement, but this works in the 'right' direction by increasing labour supply. Housing costs are far from exogenous under any system which, like housing benefit, bases assistance on *actual* costs. Matters could be improved if assistance were related to a regional index of *average* housing costs (see Chapter 14:5.2).

Some comments on indicator targeting are necessary. First, as we have seen, the strategy offers the possibility of sidestepping the poverty trap by concentrating the entire loss of benefit on a change of category (e.g. accepting a job, or regaining health). Exogeneity in this context is clearly crucial.

Second, some individuals with incomes below the poverty line will fall outside the characteristics just described (i.e. the characteristics are not completely horizontally efficient). For this group at least, a residual income-tested scheme would be necessary. There will also be people within the six categories (hence qualifying for benefit) whose pre-transfer income is above the poverty line (i.e. the categories are not completely vertically efficient). For this reason there is a case for making all benefits taxable in the same way as earned income.

Finally, it should be noted that the indicator approach can, at least in part, be organised through the institutions of social insurance (as currently for unemployment, ill-health and old age), but does not have to be (e.g. child benefit and child benefit increase). The issue of whether some forms of income support are organised through social insurance therefore remains open.

3.2 Combatting the Poverty Trap

An example of the indicator approach (UK, 1983a and b)[8] differs from most previous studies by basing its work not on an analysis of so-called 'typical' families but on a detailed study of a large sample of actual families. Such disaggregation makes it possible to show not only how the poverty trap arises, but also how many people it affects. This section draws out some of the more important strands of the argument.

Reforming national insurance contributions The starting point for reform according to the report is to iron out various anomalies by integrating income tax and national insurance contributions (UK, 1983a, paras 8.1, 8.2 and 8.10; UK, 1986a, Chs 6 and 7). The two taxes have different starting points and rate bands; and national insurance contributions, unlike income

[8] The document is referred to here for convenience as 'the report', though for Parliamentary reasons it does not have that status.

tax, are levied on a week-by-week basis, so that (see Table 7.3) someone earning £53.50 one week and £54.50 the next pays less than someone (with the same total income) earning £54 each week. The latter feature contrasts sharply with the operation of income tax.

To avoid these anomalies the report suggested that the two taxes be integrated. National insurance contributions were to have an *allowance* equal to the income tax personal allowance (thereby forgoing revenue), and the upper earnings limit was to be abolished (thereby gaining revenue).

Income tax thresholds   It is often argued that one way of mitigating the poverty trap is to raise the income tax threshold. The first major conclusion of the report was that this view is fallacious. The reason is simple: of 100 people taken out of tax by an increase in the threshold, 43 were pensioners (for whom incentive issues are largely irrelevant), nearly half were secondary workers, and only eight were earning household heads (Kay, 1984). As a result, an increase in the tax threshold left virtually unchanged the number of household heads facing marginal tax rates of over 50 per cent (UK, 1983a, para. 12.15).

Benefit levels   A more fruitful strategy, the report concluded, was to improve existing benefits. Thus the broad thrust of 'Package C' (UK, 1983a, paras 12.7 and 12.20) on the benefit side was (a) to increase sharply both child benefit and the increase for single parents, and (b) to increase retirement pensions. Because some gaps would remain, the coverage of supplementary benefit/income support was to be extended slightly; and to prevent too much 'leakage' to the non-poor, child benefit was to be taxed as earned income (as pensions are already).

The effect of these changes would be to increase the incomes of families with children and of the elderly, for the most part through benefits which are categorical rather than conditioned on income, thereby considerably reducing the number of people requiring means-tested benefits. As a result, the number of household heads facing marginal tax rates in excess of 50 per cent would be substantially reduced from 590,000 to 280,000, and the number with marginal tax rates in excess of 70 per cent from 110,000 to 50,000 (UK, 1983a, para. 12.20).

The approach embodied in the package thus reduces the poverty trap. In addition it is likely to have beneficial incentive effects, since the criteria on which benefits are awarded are largely exogenous to recipients (or, at least, are more exogenous than labour supply). To the extent that this is the case: (à) poverty is reduced (an equity gain); and (b) because costs are manageable, poverty trap tax rates can be reduced, thus improving labour supply incentives (an efficiency gain).

4 Mixed Strategies

Sections 2 and 3 discussed the two strategies for the most part in isolation. As a guide to practical policy, however, neither on its own is likely to succeed. Benefits conditioned on income generally run into problems of high tax rates; and pure categorical schemes face intractable problems of gaps in coverage, benefits 'leaking' to the non-poor, and problems with defining and administering borderline cases. Targeting, as Atkinson (forthcoming) points out, is a matter of some subtlety and has a number of different dimensions. The most likely path for reform is a judicious combination of the two approaches (for analysis of the interplay between income testing and categorical benefits, see Akerlof (1978), Stern (1982) and Kanbur and Keen (1989)). One example, as we saw in section 2.3, is a small-scale, universal negative income tax with additional benefits for the poor (Parker, 1989); the latter could be conditioned either on income, or on the characteristics of recipients.

The main purpose of this chapter has been to set out the logic of different strategies for reform, so no attempt is made here to go beyond a brief listing of some recent reform proposals (for a brief survey of early 1980s proposals, see Atkinson (1984)). Some tend more towards conditioning benefits on income. The Institute for Fiscal Studies proposals (Dilnot *et al.*, 1984) advocate a substantial integration of income taxation with benefits, whereby virtually all national insurance benefits and child benefit are replaced by a series of income-tested benefits with a high rate of withdrawal (in some instances over 80 per cent) at low incomes. The package, though clearing up some of what Dilnot *et al.* regarded as the worst difficulties of present arrangements, had its severe critics (Piachaud, 1984; O'Kelly, 1985), not least over its administrative feasibility.

The proposals of the Basic Income Research Group (Parker, 1989) are more obviously a negative income tax. The scheme has several variants, of which the most promising pays a guaranteed income which varies with family characteristics (e.g. extra payments are made for sickness, disability and old age). Some versions have the additional desirable characteristics that benefit is invariant to age (if below pensionable age), sex, marital status and employment status, thus minimising distortions in respect of labour market decisions and family formation. In many ways this scheme is a universal negative income tax whose intercept varies with the characteristics of recipients (and hence is very much a blend of the two approaches).

The most fully articulated 'Back to Beveridge' scheme is that discussed in section 3.2. The incomes of many of the poor would be raised by increasing child benefit and the national insurance pension. For recipients with pre-transfer incomes above the tax threshold these would be taxable under an integrated system of income tax and national insurance contributions.

A major overhaul of existing arrangements was suggested in a government consultative document (UK, 1985b) with several companion volumes (UK, 1985ċ, d, e), and a more circumspect set of proposals in a subsequent White Paper (UK, 1985h). The resulting changes to the state pension scheme were discussed in Chapter 9:5.1. Other changes, discussed in Chapter 10, included the transformation of supplementary benefit into income support, and of family income supplement into family credit. Some of the suggestions represent undoubted improvement, e.g. the partial move towards standardising the definition of income used in assessing benefits; and the choice of income definition under which marginal tax rates (though remaining high) are systematically kept below 100 per cent, thus removing the most glaring discontinuities in the structure of withdrawal rates. Other parts of the proposals, particularly the social fund, have been heavily criticised.

5 Conclusion: Cash Benefits

This section brings together the main conclusions of Part 2. The aims of cash benefits were set out in Chapter 1:2.2. Their achievement requires two sorts of mechanism. *Self-help* is necessary for people who are self-supporting on a lifetime basis but need a system which can reallocate income over time to iron out discontinuities. *Vertical redistribution* is necessary for those who are unable to support themselves over their lifetime as a whole.

The menu of methods of self-help includes private insurance and state activity, the latter in the form of social insurance, or through transfers out of current tax revenues. Vertical redistribution can be achieved by private charity, or through publicly organised transfers out of tax revenues (note that actuarial insurance cannot systematically redistribute from rich to poor). The respective merits of these methods can be summarised as follows.

Private versus social insurance The private market cannot always supply the efficient quantity and type of insurance against all causes of income loss.

1. Because non-insurance may cause an externality, there is an efficiency argument for making some forms of insurance compulsory (Chapter 8:2.1).

2. Private insurance in several important areas will be inefficient or non-existent: unemployment is an uninsurable risk, mainly because of moral hazard (Chapter 8:2.2); and so, in the context of pensions, is inflation (Chapter 9:3.1). This gives an efficiency justification for public provision of unemployment compensation and, at a minimum, provision on a PAYG basis of the indexation component of pension schemes. The efficiency arguments for public provision of sickness benefits and the smaller national insurance benefits are weaker.

Pension finance No definitive answer is possible.

1. Theoretical and empirical analysis of the effects of pension schemes on saving and labour supply have produced conflicting and inconclusive results (Chapter 9:5.1).

2. Moving national insurance pensions on to a funded basis will not by itself solve the future problem of pension finance (Chapter 9:5.1). The important changes are those which increase national output directly: through investment in new technology and improvements in the quality of labour (both of which increase productivity per worker); and through increased labour force participation, including a considerable reduction in unemployment, increased participation by women, and later retirement.

3. The choice between PAYG and funding depends mainly on views about income redistribution and financial flexibility (Chapter 9:3.2 and 9:5.3).

The insurance principle – is it possible, necessary or desirable? It is *possible* for the state to create institutions similar to private, actuarial insurance, e.g. the original Beveridge concept of flat-rate contributions based on average risk, giving entitlement to flat-rate benefits. For non-insurable risks (unemployment, inflation) these merely mimic private institutions but are not true insurance. It does not follow that actuarial institutions (i.e. with risk-related premiums) are *necessary*. If membership is compulsory it is possible, without the likelihood of substantial inefficiency, to charge premiums which are not based upon individual risk (Chapters 5:3.2 and 8:3.1).

It is an open question whether adherence to the insurance principle in a state scheme is desirable (Chapter 8:3.1). Social assistance has the advantage of flexibility, since entitlement to benefit does not depend on a contributions record; the corresponding disadvantages are that benefits conditioned on income may be stigmatising, and can cause a poverty trap (Chapter 10:3). Social insurance, while less flexible, may have advantages because it sidesteps the poverty trap (Chapter 11:3); because individuals might perceive contributions differently from taxes, with correspondingly different labour supply effects; and because recipients might feel less stigmatised by benefits conditioned on previous contributions rather than an income test.

Vertical redistribution In part because of the free-rider problem, redistribution through private charity is likely to be sub-optimal even from a libertarian perspective and *a fortiori* from a Rawlsian or socialist viewpoint (Chapter 4:4.1). Thus at least some publicly organised redistribution through the tax system can be justified under any theory of society, though with considerable disagreement about how much (Chapter 4:2.2 and 4:4.4). Any such redistribution will be constrained by the size distribution of income (Chapter 11:2.2).

National insurance in Britain Present arrangements (a) are social insurance not run on an actuarial basis (Chapter 8:3.1), and (b) (subject to qualifications) redistribute from rich to poor, from young to old, and from men to women (Chapter 8:3.2 and 9:5.2). Because the scheme is compulsory, (a) and (b) can be argued to cause no *major* inefficiency apart from a potential labour supply disincentive – an issue on which evidence to date is inconclusive (Chapter 8:3.1).

Non-contributory benefits in Britain

1. Income support is withdrawn rapidly as the income of recipients rises, thereby containing costs and targeting benefits on those with the lowest incomes. The price of these advantages is the poverty trap, which makes it difficult for families to increase their standard of living, and therefore creates a labour supply disincentive (Chapter 10:3.1).

2. Families not in receipt of income support may also face a poverty trap arising out of the withdrawal of other benefits for which entitlement is determined by an income test. Awarding benefit for a fixed period can mitigate the worst labour supply effects, but the complexity of the existing system makes firm conclusions difficult (Chapter 10:3.2).

Reform

1. Benefits conditioned on income (whether means-tested explicitly or in the form of a large-scale negative income tax) suffer from the necessity of high tax rates to finance them. This causes a poverty trap with major efficiency and equity costs.

2. For this reason large-scale negative income tax schemes cannot solve poverty on their own. Their cost is a consequence not of the negative income tax mechanism *per se* but of (a) the existing size distribution of income, (b) the poverty line chosen, and (c) the empirical fact that labour supply is not exogenous (Chapter 11:2.2).

3. Benefits conditioned on indicators other than income can circumvent some of these difficulties, particularly if the criteria are exogenous to the recipient and highly correlated with poverty. This 'Back to Beveridge' approach offers some hope of improvement (Chapter 11:3). The most hopeful route for reform is probably a careful blend of the two approaches (Chapter 11:4).

4. Reform is likely to be hampered by the political difficulties which can beset even small changes (Prest, 1983), and by the major difficulties of theory, measurement and methodology (Chapters 8:3.1, 9:5.1 and 10:3.4) which face empirical work.

What are the implications for policy of these largely technical arguments? The preferred libertarian methods of voluntary private insurance and voluntary charity rather fall by the wayside. Private insurance will frequently be inefficient, not primarily because people are unable to make rational decisions but because of technical problems on the supply side. Libertarians might therefore concede an element of compulsion in view of the externality caused by non-insurance (Chapter 8:2.1), and allow in addition a limited role for non-actuarial, tax-financed transfers to raise to subsistence those incomes which remain low despite private charity. This will be especially relevant to non-insurable risks. Libertarians criticise national insurance as exceeding the scope necessary to achieve this limited purpose, thereby curtailing the freedom of taxpayers to make their own decisions.

Socialists favour public organisation of cash transfers, financed by progressive taxation; benefits should be awarded on the basis of need, and should be above subsistence so as to reduce inequality. Whether insurable risks are dealt with out of tax revenues or by social insurance is an area of debate. However, many socialists abhor means testing, partly because of the poverty trap and partly as a legacy of the Poor Law. In the absence of a universal guaranteed income this brings us back to insurance, at which point there is some convergence between socialist and liberal views.

Further Reading

There is a huge literature on negative income taxation. For specific proposals, see UK (1972a) (a government proposal), Christopher *et al.* (1970) (tending to the libertarian); for a cogent liberal appeal, Meade (1972); and for a compendious proposal, Parker (1989). In the US context see Tobin *et al.* (1967), Green (1967), Tobin (1968) and Aaron (1973). On the costs of negative income tax see Barr (1975) and Atkinson (1989, Ch. 16).

One of the best accounts of the US negative income tax experiments, including details of the experimental design and an analysis of the labour supply responses, can be found in the contributions to Pechman and Timpane (1975). For a briefer review, see Haveman and Watts (1977); and for an account of the experiments in rural areas, Palmer and Pechman (1978).

On the case for 'Back to Beveridge', see Meade (1978, Ch. 13) and UK (1983a). On targeting issues more generally, see Atkinson (forthcoming), Nichols and Zeckhauser (1982), Blackorby and Donaldson (1988), and Besley and Kanbur (1991).

Reform proposals can be found in Dilnot *et al.* (1984) and Parker (1989). A scheme based more on the characteristics of recipients is UK (1983a, especially paras 12.7 and 12.20).

The 1988 reforms are based on UK (1985h). For early assessment of these, and earlier proposals in UK (1985b, c, d, e), see Davis *et al.* (1985a, b) (qualified support), Berthoud (1986) (qualified opposition), CPAG (1985) (unqualified opposition) and, for a Parliamentary view, UK (1985f). The outcomes are reviewed by Dilnot and Webb (1988).

Part 3
Benefits in Kind

Chapter 12
Health Care

Risk varies inversely with knowledge. [Irving Fisher, 1930.]

That any sane nation, having observed that you could provide for the supply of bread by giving bakers a pecuniary interest in baking for you, should go on to give a surgeon a pecuniary interest in cutting off your leg, is enough to make one despair of political humanity. [George Bernard Shaw, 1911.]

1 Introduction to Benefits in Kind

The questions Three intellectual threads run through this book: the social welfare maximisation problem, issues of social justice, and problems of definition and measurement. The discussion of cash benefits was concerned mainly with the first two; in the case of benefits in kind the third assumes special importance. Many of the arguments about health care and education turn crucially on the measurement of private and social costs and benefits, and also on the extent to which it is reasonable to assume perfect information.

In part because of these problems, the issues raised by benefits in kind are genuinely complex, and raise trickier problems of mixed public/private involvement than is the case with most cash benefits. It is therefore unfortunate that health care and education, more than most parts of the welfare state, are bedevilled by emotional polemics, most of which confuse aims and methods. The main purpose of these chapters is not to give the 'right' answer, but firmly to establish the right battleground.

Chapters 13–15 look at health care, education and housing respectively. Each chapter has a common outline. After a brief introduction (section 1), the aims of policy are discussed in section 2 and the theoretical arguments about state intervention in section 3. Policy analysis concentrates on assessment of the current British system (section 4) and possible reform strategies (section 5). The conclusions are set out in section 6. Many of the theoretical arguments, particularly as they apply to health care and education, are very similar. The theoretical sections of Chapters 12 and 13 are written to bring out the parallels rather than to be repetitive.

Given the size of the topics, the three chapters are inevitably eclectic. The main questions asked are: how efficient/just is a competitive market for health care/education/housing likely to be (the issue of 'privatisation'); to what extent would public production and allocation be more efficient/just; and would any intermediate system involving both public and private sectors perform better than either of the pure cases? There is limited discussion of the personal social services, but a number of other important issues receive little mention, including the detailed finances of health care and education (see Glennerster (1992), and the Further Reading).

Non-economic arguments   To clarify the approach, it is useful to remind ourselves of some arguments whose weakness was discussed earlier. Bad economic arguments about state intervention are generally of two sorts: either they fail to understand the nature and limitations of market allocation; or they confuse aims and methods. A common libertarian position is that health care is an 'ordinary' commodity which (like any other) should be distributed in accordance with income, tastes and relative prices; if we do not like the distribution of health care or education, we should change the distribution of income. It is argued below that this is a mistake of the first kind.

Arguments which confuse aims and methods were discussed in Chapter 4:7.2. The view that 'health care/education/housing are basic rights and therefore should be provided by the state' is illogical because the words 'and therefore' simply do not follow from the initial premise. If health care etc. are basic rights then so is food, which is provided well enough by the private sector. For the same reason, the argument that 'health care, etc. should be publicly provided because otherwise the poor could not afford them' does not stand up. Poverty may justify cash transfers but is not, without considerable qualification, a justification for public provision.

The same arguments can be viewed from the political perspectives discussed in Chapter 3. Many socialists believe that goods like health care, education and housing should be provided collectively. This view is tenable as a value judgement, but the consequent policies are unlikely to be successful unless they go with rather than against the grain of economic theory. It is argued here that health care can successfully be provided publicly, mostly without direct charge; but we shall see in Chapter 14 that the same cannot be said of housing. Libertarians argue that virtually all goods, including health care, education and housing, should be supplied privately because collective provision is both inefficient and a violation of individual liberty. This view, again, is workable in practice only if it accords with economic theory. Markets can fail entirely (unemployment insurance) or be inefficient (many forms of health care insurance) – devout hopes are not enough. Liberals reject both lines of argument because each makes the *method* of provision (market or state) a primary *aim*. It is argued in Chapter 4:7.2 that a better approach is to choose aims on the basis of personal values and ideology, and then to select on technical grounds whichever method best achieves them.

Institutions The institutions of the National Health Service (NHS) are described in section 4.1. During the early part of the chapter virtually no institutional knowledge is necessary. As a good approximation, the NHS is financed out of central government revenues, and health care (with minor exceptions) is provided publicly and without charge, both for treatment by a general practitioner (i.e. family doctor) and for hospital in- and out-patient treatment. Most hospital doctors and nurses in the NHS are paid a salary. Family doctors are paid in a complex way reflecting *inter alia* the numbers and ages of their patients. Throughout the NHS there is little fee-for-service. Alongside the NHS is a small private sector.

2 Aims

2.1 Concepts

Social welfare is maximised by the joint pursuit of economic efficiency[1] and social justice (or equity). This section outlines the meaning of these ideas as they apply to health care and then turns to the more difficult problem of measuring them. The fact that health care is important does not mean that it is not an economic commodity. Resources devoted to medical uses are not available for other purposes. There is a trade-off: if we spent nothing on health, some people would die unnecessarily of trivial complaints; if we spent the whole of national income on health care, there would be no food and we would all die of starvation. The optimal quantity clearly lies somewhere between – in principle where the value gained from the last unit of health care is equal to the marginal value which would be derived from the alternative use to which the resources involved could be put. This is the quantity X^* in Figure 4.1.

Efficiency in this sense must apply to two separate issues: the overall size of the health care system as a proportion of gross national product (this is the macro efficiency aim in Chapter 1:2.2); and the allocation of resources to different uses *within* health care (the micro efficiency aim), so as to produce the optimal quantity, quality and mix.

The concept of equity, as we have seen (Chapters 4:4 and 6:3.1), is more

---

[1] The concept of economic efficiency is defined in Chapter 4:2.1.

elusive.[2] Le Grand (1982, pp. 14–15) distinguishes four definitions of equity in consumption: equality of public expenditure; equality of use, i.e. individuals with the same need should consume the same quantity; equality of cost, i.e. *ceteris paribus* individuals should face the same 'price' for the service (including such factors as forgone earnings, time, etc.); and equality of outcome. Two definitions are of particular interest. Equality of utilisation implies that everyone in a given condition should receive the same quantity; the problem is that people differ in the extent to which they choose to consume health care or education. Equality of outcome implies an unequal allocation such that everyone enjoys an equal state of health or level of educational attainment. Whether or not such an aim is thought desirable, it is not fully feasible.

To avoid some of these difficulties equity will be defined as a form of *equality of opportunity*, as described in Chapter 6:3.1 (especially equation (6.18)). This does not mean that individuals can necessarily obtain as much health care as they want (since health care resources are scarce, it is probable that no system could satisfy everyone's wants). But it does mean that any individual should receive as much health care as anyone else in the same medical condition, regardless of any factors which are thought to be irrelevant, e.g. income. The same is true, *mutatis mutandis*, for education.

Once we have decided the efficient level of production of health care and its equitable distribution, the remaining question is who should pay for it, i.e. to what extent is it appropriate to finance health care progressively? This is the issue of vertical equity discussed in Chapter 4:4.1. It was argued in Chapter 4:7.2 that if, for example, health care is allocated efficiently by the market then equity aims are generally best achieved through cash transfers. But where health care is publicly produced and allocated for *efficiency* reasons, it may be appropriate to finance it out of progressive taxation; if so, it is possible, though not inevitable (section 4.3), that in-kind transfers will redistribute from rich to poor.

2.2 Measuring Costs and Benefits

The concept of efficiency is well-understood. But attempts to make it operational by measuring costs and benefits (Abel Smith, 1983; Aaron and Schwartz, 1984) must of necessity be somewhat rough-and-ready because of serious measurement problems, particularly in the quantification of benefits. The total cost of the NHS and its component parts is readily available (Table 12.1). The costs of different types of treatment are harder

---

[2] According to the White Paper on the founding of the National Health Service, 'the Government ... want to ensure that in the future every man and woman and child can rely on getting ... the best medical and other facilities available; that their getting them shall not depend on whether they can pay for them or on any other factor irrelevant to real need' (UK, 1944a). McLachlan and Maynard (1982, p. 521) correctly find these statements 'vague and Utopian'.

to establish, *inter alia* because of the familiar problem of apportioning overheads and the need to distinguish short- and long-run marginal costs, but these problems are not insurmountable.

On the benefit side there are three major problems: the nature of the maximand; the causal links between health care and improved health; and the valuation of improved health.

The nature of the maximand: health care is only an *input*; the output is improved health. Health, however, is determined not only by medical treatment, but also by such factors as diet, environment and lifestyle. Expenditure on health care can be estimated; but the output, health itself, cannot easily be measured (Culyer, 1983; Hunt *et al.*, 1980; Office of Health Economics, 1985).

Causality: to what extent is any reduction in suffering or output loss *caused* by medical care? A patient's complete recovery could be due entirely to the treatment he has received; or it could be due, wholly or in part, to his natural recuperative powers. The influence of intangible factors (e.g. the 'will to live') is crucial, but impossible to measure. Similarly, improvements in health outcomes (e.g. life expectancy) may be due to such factors as improved diet, reducing smoking, cleaner air, and the like. If such factors are ignored, we will tend to overestimate the benefits of health care.

The valuation of improved health: the difficulties are highlighted in the extensive literature on placing a monetary value on human life (see the Further Reading). Such attempts are sometimes regarded as distasteful or immoral. But all sorts of policies affect the risks faced by individuals, and hence on aggregate the number of deaths. Many accident victims would be saved if they could receive medical attention rapidly; nevertheless, we do not have casualty departments on every corner, nor ambulances constantly patrolling the streets. Thus we are not prepared to spend infinite sums of money to save one life. The question therefore arises of how much we should be prepared to spend to reduce the risk of death by 1 per cent or, more generally, to reduce the extent or duration of ill-health.

The measurement problems are obvious once we realise that the benefits of improved health are twofold. There are (or may be) *output benefits*, i.e. the increased output/income of the individual whose affliction is reduced or removed. This is hard enough to measure. In addition, there are intractable problems in measuring the *utility benefits* arising from any reduction in the physical and emotional suffering of the patient and his/her family.

Given these difficulties, cost–benefit studies of medical care (see Cullis and West, 1979, Ch. 8) are of necessity limited. They are useful as far as they go; but they do not go very far; nor is progress likely to be easy. Partly because of these problems, the more limited technique of cost effectiveness studies tackles a narrower issue by considering a specific medical condition, and examining the costs of alternative forms of treatment (Piachaud, 1972;

Williams, 1985). Here answers are possible largely because no attempt is made to measure benefits.

The conclusion to which this leads is simple but depressing. The efficiency aim is clear enough in principle for health care (and the same will turn out to be true for education), but measurement problems make definitive empirical answers unlikely, if not impossible. The definition of equity is more elusive but, as we shall see in section 4.3, empirical work has made some headway.

3 Methods

3.1 Theoretical Arguments for Intervention 1: Efficiency

This section looks at how the aims discussed in section 2 might be achieved, in particular *why* the state intervenes (sections 3.1 and 3.2) and *how* in theory it might intervene so as jointly to maximise efficiency and equity (section 3.3).

Private markets allocate efficiently only if the *standard assumptions* hold, i.e. perfect information, perfect competition and no market failures such as external effects (Chapter 4:3.2, and the Appendix to Chapter 4, paras 5–17). The underlying question is why health care is 'different' from equally vital commodities like food. Early literature was concerned with characteristics of the demand for medical care; later work concentrated more on the supply side, particularly on the behaviour of doctors individually, and on the medical profession as a corporate entity. A third, and completely different, set of arguments (section 3.2) centres on the notion of altruism, which, it has been argued, has particular relevance to health care.

INFORMATION PROBLEMS

Does medical care conform with the standard assumptions (Arrow, 1963; Culyer, 1971a)? First, are individuals perfectly informed about the nature of the product (in analytical terms, is their indifference map well-defined)? The answer, clearly, is no. Many people are unknowingly ill, particularly the elderly (Williamson *et al.*, 1964), and those with ailments like diabetes (Israel and Teeling-Smith, 1967; Florey, 1982) and hypertension (Hart, 1970), which can be largely without symptoms in their early stages. In addition, individuals are often ignorant about which types of treatment are available, and about the outcome of different treatments (which is often probabilistic). Furthermore, what little the patient knows is generally learned from a doctor (i.e. the supplier of health care services); and many types of treatment (e.g. setting a broken leg) are not repeated so that much of what a patient learns is of little future use.

There are other areas in which the consumer knows little and has to rely on the supplier for information (e.g. hi-fi, used cars). But in these cases it is usually possible to buy information (e.g. consumer magazines, or a report by the Automobile Association), and legislation offers increasing consumer protection.[3] With medical care:

1. Much (though not all) the information is technically complex, so that a person would not necessarily understand the information even if it were available.

2. The costs of mistaken choice are usually greater and less reversible than with most other commodities.

3. An individual generally does not have time to shop around if his condition is acute (contrast the situation with a car repair, which can be left until the car owner (a) has enough information, and (b) can afford the repair).

4. Consumers frequently lack the information to weigh one doctor's advice against another's.

5. Health and health care have strongly emotive connotations, e.g. ignorance may in part be a consequence of fear, superstition, etc.

To a considerable extent, therefore, consumers lack the information necessary for rational choice; and even if information were available, health care is inherently a technical subject, so that there is a limit to what consumers could understand without themselves becoming doctors. The problem is exacerbated by the existence of groups who would not be able to make use of information even if they had it, such as victims of road accidents.

To say that there is ignorance need not *ipso facto* be evidence of inefficiency. Information may be costly, and its acquisition therefore inefficient if the resulting gain is small. Some degree of ignorance may well be optimal, though almost certainly less than would prevail under a private health care market.

If consumers are to make rational choices, they need to have the necessary information, and also the power to enforce their decisions. Efficiency therefore requires equal power, in the sense that there should be no constraint on the ability of individuals to consume health care (or education) apart from differences in their money income, i.e. people may have different incomes, but there should be no discrimination. This assumption was presented in Chapter 4:3.2 as a precondition of perfect competition, but the issue is closely related to perfect information and so fits naturally into the discussion at this point. In the context of health care and education, power consists largely of knowledge about their uses and benefits; knowledge about one's rights in respect of the NHS and the educational system; and the ability and confidence to be articulate. It is somewhat implausible to

---

[3] It has been suggested that a consumer magazine about medicine might be called *Which Doctor?*

imagine that this is the state of affairs for all consumers, though in the final analysis the issue is empirical.

Because of imperfect information and unequal power, consumers will choose inefficiently, though there is room for debate about the extent of the problem (this is one of the key issues in any discussion of health care). It is also not clear whether the result will be under- or overconsumption. If the 'true' marginal private valuation in Figure 12.1 is shown by the curve *MPV*, consumer ignorance can result in demand curves *D1* (under-consumption) or *D2* (overconsumption). In addition, where knowledge and power are systematically related to socioeconomic status, there is also inequity (section 3.3).

Figure 12.1 *The effects of consumer ignorance on individual demand for health care/education*

What solutions exist? The provision of information on a scale sufficient for rational individual choice may be too costly, in which case decisions about treatment must be delegated to doctors. Minimal intervention takes the form of regulation, e.g. only individuals with approved qualifications are allowed to practise medicine. But where the information problem is serious the performance of the market may be so inefficient that more extensive state involvement, either through substantial regulation of private production, or through public production and allocation, might be a better solution. We return to this issue in section 4.2.

A separate issue is whether consumers are adequately informed about prices (formally, whether their budget constraint is well-defined). Here, again, it can be argued that most consumers are ignorant of what a particular form of treatment 'should' cost; and, because a great deal of medical care is not repeated, information often has no future use. Nor would it help if consumers were well-informed about prices. Rational choice requires sim-ultaneous knowledge *both* of prices *and* of the nature of the product (i.e. of both budget constraint and indifference map); knowledge of prices without adequate information about different types of treatment will not ensure efficiency.

The result is inefficiency of the type discussed above, and summarised in Figure 12.1. If the *only* problem were inadequate information about prices, the appropriate intervention would be regulation, either in the form of a published price list or through price controls. But where information about the nature of the product is imperfect, ignorance about prices adds further weight to the argument for more substantial state involvement.

INSURANCE PROBLEMS

The third information assumption – knowledge about the future – clearly fails with health care, as stressed by Arrow (1963). Patients do not know when, or how much, health care they will demand; they lack information about the probabilities of different outcomes for different types of treatment, and about the relative efficiency of different providers of health care; and they consume health care services infrequently, often at a time when their judgement and ability to acquire information are small. The problem of uncertainty is therefore serious.

In many instances the market solution is insurance. The real issue, therefore, is whether the private market can supply medical insurance efficiently. This, we saw in Chapter 5:3.1, requires five technical conditions to hold: the probability of needing treatment (see equation (5.12)) must be independent across individuals, and less than one; it must be known or estimable; and there must be no substantial problem of adverse selection or moral hazard (the last three conditions adding up to perfect information on the part of the insurance company). The extent to which these hold for health care is discussed *inter alia* by Arrow (1963) and Pauly (1974, 1986).

Looking at the first condition, the probabilities of different individuals requiring treatment are independent except during major epidemics. Second, the probability of requiring treatment of a particular type over a given period is less than one for ailments like appendicitis or a broken leg. But the condition fails for chronic medical problems (e.g. diabetes) arising before an insurance policy is taken out, and *a fortiori* for congenital problems.[4] In the absence of insurance starting before birth, the private market generally fails to cover these cases. The probabilities relevant to medical insurance are generally estimable, but problems arise of both adverse selection and moral hazard (Chapter 5:3.2).

Adverse selection occurs where an individual is able to conceal from the

[4] A related (but different) point is that treatment of long-term illness is generally expensive, so that competitive pressures act to reduce premiums at the expense of long-term coverage.

insurance company that he is a bad risk. In this situation equilibrium can be inefficient, unstable or non-existent. Akerlof (1970, pp. 492–3) asks why Americans over 65 cannot easily buy medical insurance, and concludes

that as the price [of insurance] rises the people who insure themselves will be those who are increasingly certain that they will need the insurance; for error in medical check-ups, doctors' sympathy with older patients, and so on make it much easier for the applicant to assess the risks involved than the insurance company.

Summers (1989), more broadly, argues that if employees know better than their employers whether they are likely to have high medical bills, the employers providing good medical benefits will disproportionately tend to have employees with health problems, thus discouraging the provision of fringe benefits.

There is discussion about the magnitude of the problem. Pauly (1986) attributes the lack of quantitative evidence to the difficulty of defining a strong test. There is, however, evidence about the instability of pooling equilibria (see Chapter 5:3.2) in the face of competitive pressures: Blue Cross/Blue Shield, the main US non-profit insurer, originally practised community rating (charging everyone in a locality the same premium), but was forced by competitive pressures from commercial insurers to adopt experience rating (related to the risk experience of individual subscribers).

Moral hazard can arise in two generic ways: patients may be able to influence either the probability of requiring medical treatment, or its cost. Taking the probability issue first, individuals with full insurance might take fewer health precautions; this is the problem (case 2 in Chapter 5:3.2) addressed by Pauly (1974, 1986). Second, both the decision to consult one's family doctor and pregnancy can be matters of *choice* which lead to the consumption of medical services. Elective medical care of this sort (case 3 in Chapter 5:3.2) is not well-covered by voluntary policies: some risks are uninsurable in private markets, at least for voluntary individual policies.

Moral hazard arises also where consumers can influence the cost of treatment. This is the *third-party payment* problem (case 4 in Chapter 5:3.2). It has two sources: the fact that the insurance company is largely divorced from the decisions of doctor and patient; and the fact that the doctor is paid a fee for service. Suppose medical insurance covers all costs. Health care is then 'free' to the patient; and the supplier is not constrained by the patient's ability to pay. Patient and doctor both face zero *private* costs, even though the *social* costs of health care are positive and frequently large, and both have an incentive to consume all health care which yields *any* private benefit. The result is overconsumption, i.e. Q_1, greater than the efficient outcome, Q^*, in Figure 12.2.

Figure 12.2 *A simple market for health care*

One additional problem requires discussion – that of transactions costs. We saw earlier (equation (5.17)) that insurance, even if efficient on the supply side, can be provided at a price which the individual is prepared to pay only if his degree of risk aversion is sufficient to cover the insurance company's administrative costs and normal profit. If transactions costs are too high, some risk-averse individuals will choose not to insure. This is not *per se* inefficient if high transactions costs are unavoidable. But it is inefficient if an alternative system could avoid them, e.g. private health care insurance in the USA has high accounting costs; these are avoided by the NHS, which rarely has to send patients a bill.

The theory thus predicts that conventional medical insurance will face two sets of problems: *gaps in coverage* arise for risks like chronic and congenital illness, the medical needs of the elderly, and primary health care; and *inefficiency* occurs in various forms, particularly overprescription of medical care as a result of third-party incentives. The first set of difficulties, plus the problem which arises if transactions costs are high, all lead to *underconsumption*. Third-party payments cause *overconsumption*.

Solutions There are two lines of attack on these problems: market solutions, and the adoption of different forms of intervention. Insurance companies have adopted various devices to contain costs in the face of the third-party payment problem. Pauly (1986) distinguishes two broad strategies influencing demand and supply, respectively. Insurers can limit coverage: premiums can rise disproportionately with the degree of cover sought; and there can be less-than-full cover through deductibles (where the insured person pays the first $X of any claim) and coinsurance (where the insured person pays x per cent of any claim). Such devices reduce the demand for treatment. None is a complete solution: deductibles, except for small claims, do nothing to face individuals with the *marginal* cost of treatment; and with a coinsurance rate of, say, 20 per cent, the patient's private marginal cost is only 20 per cent of marginal social cost. Alternatively, insurers can seek to influence the supply side by restricting treatment to certain providers, who then face competitive pressures to retain the insurance company's approved status.

However, there is no complete solution to moral hazard for two reasons: as discussed in Chapter 5:3.2, the root problem is the imperfect information of insurers about the behaviour of the insured; in addition, as discussed in section 2.2, 'health' is hard both to define and to measure, hampering contractual specification of individual loss as measured by the severity of illness.

Intervention can reduce inefficiency in a number of ways. Insurance could be compulsory to prevent the externalities caused by non-insurance (Chapter 8:2.1), with cover starting before birth to cope with the congenitally and chronically ill. As discussed in Chapter 5:3.2 a partial solution to adverse selection is to make membership (e.g. of an employer scheme) compulsory to prevent low risks opting out. Alternatively, regulation could prevent insurance companies from withholding cover from high-risk individuals, simultaneously regulating the conditions under which they could increase premiums. Compulsory membership of national/provincial systems of social insurance in various industrialised countries has a similar effect. Moral hazard would have to be left to dubiously effective devices like coinsurance, or to different types of insurance, like health maintenance organisations (discussed in section 5).

Most industrialised countries (the USA is an outlier in this respect) do not use private insurance as the primary method of financing health care. Two models predominate. Social insurance (as defined and discussed in Chapter 5:4.2) abandons the model of actuarial insurance because it does not fit health care very well. Alternatively, medical care can be financed via the tax system.

THE REMAINING ASSUMPTIONS

The assumption of equal power was discussed earlier. The next step is to consider the applicability of perfect competition, i.e. whether the markets for inputs like skilled manpower and drugs are competitive. In the case of doctors there are two issues: is the number of doctors restricted below its efficient level; and do doctors maximise profits, or have they other goals? The element of monopoly power resulting from barriers to entry imposed by medical associations is an old argument (see Friedman and Kuznets, 1945). Recent analysis focuses more on the behaviour of doctors. It is not argued that they act like the profit-maximising monopolist of elementary textbooks, but rather that they pursue several goals. It is suggested that a doctor's reputation depends more on the assessment of his/her fellow professionals than on direct evaluation by the consumer, and that the approval of colleagues is more easily achieved in the development of more advanced techniques (e.g. heart transplants). Thus, it is argued, there is a bias towards certain glamorous types of health care. Doctors' behaviour is then determined jointly by this type of motive and by their economic environment. As we have seen, doctors may not face the costs of their production decisions, but are reimbursed by insurance companies which tend not to question their activities. There is no budget constraint facing doctors individually; and on aggregate they are constrained only by the willingness of consumers or employers to pay insurance premiums.

These arguments, if true, point towards economic inefficiency in the form of oversupply of health care generally. In addition, the *composition* of that supply is distorted in favour of glamorous areas, and against low-prestige activities (e.g. general practice, occupational health). The consensus seems to be that the underprovision resulting from an undersupply of doctors is probably more than offset by the behaviour of individual doctors (of the *distribution* of that health care more will be said later). Perhaps the best that can be said of the market system is that two different forms of monopoly behaviour may to some extent cancel each other out.

What solutions exist for this non-competitive behaviour? At a minimum, regulation is required on standards (e.g. doctors must have approved qualifications). In addition, some regulation of prices and possibly also monitoring of doctors' activities might be appropriate. Another potential solution is the libertarian approach (see the Further Reading) of removing entry barriers to medical practice, thereby enhancing competitiveness on the supply side and largely removing the need for state intervention of the type just described. This solution may be more apparent than real. The advantages of competition are that it increases consumer choice and mini-mises costs. As we saw in Chapter 4:3.2, however, an increase in the range of choice is desirable only where consumers are sufficiently well-informed to choose between them, which is frequently not the case with health care; and if competitive forces push down prices consumers, for the same reason, will be unable to assess whether quality has declined, and if so whether they want the lower-quality product at the lower price. The counter-argument to the proponents of market systems for health care is that *the advantages of competition are contingent on perfect information.*

The conclusion is that supply-side deviations from competitive behaviour are likely to cause inefficiency; but removing restrictions to competition is unlikely *on its own* to improve economic welfare.

The remaining assumptions concern externalities and increasing returns to scale. The literature on health care distinguishes two sorts of externality: 'caring' externalities, such that my utility is reduced if you receive less health care than I think you should (these are a matter more of the *distribution* of health care than the efficiency of its production – see section 3.2); and technological externalities.[5] The latter arise mainly via communicable diseases (e.g. if I am vaccinated against polio I benefit, and also confer a benefit on you because you cannot now catch polio from me). In the context of today's medical technology these externalities, though real, are only a small fraction of the total value of health care. It is a standard proposition that technological external benefits, if uncorrected, cause underconsumption by creating a divergence between private and social benefits. The problem can be solved in a variety of ways, the most relevant here being regulation (e.g. making vaccination compulsory) or a Pigovian subsidy (see the Glossary). Externalities are not *per se* a justification for public production and allocation.

It is sometimes argued that health care is subject to increasing returns to scale (Chapter 4:3.2 and Figure 4.4). Were this the case, health care would be a natural monopoly which, if uncorrected, would lead to under-consumption. The theoretical solution is to regulate the industry (e.g. by setting a maximum price supporting the competitive output, and paying a lump-sum subsidy to make up the resultant losses), or to nationalise the industry. However, the range of output over which health care exhibits increasing returns to scale is small even with today's large-scale technology, so the problem is unlikely to arise except, possibly, in sparsely populated areas.

3.2 Theoretical Arguments for Intervention 2: Equity

Horizontal equity was discussed in Chapter 4:4.3 in terms of perfect information (which is necessary for rational decisions) and equal power (which is necessary to enforce those decisions). Both may be lacking for consumers of health care (and of education). Equity issues arise most acutely where these problems systematically affect the lower socioeconomic groups most strongly (a likely occurrence if information is costly to acquire). Thus lower-income individuals may have less information relevant to health care choices; in addition, they may be less able to make use of any information they acquire. In such cases intervention in the following forms may improve equity as well as efficiency.

Regulation would be concerned with the professional qualifications of doctors and nurses, with drugs, and with medical facilities in both public and private sectors.

Where imperfect information causes underconsumption, a **subsidy** might be applied either to prices (e.g. free medical prescriptions) or to incomes. In most circumstances price subsidies cost less than income subsidies

---

[5] On the definition and effects of externalities, and possible remedies, see Chapter 4:3.2, and/or the Appendix to Chapter 4, para. 15.

(Culyer, 1980, pp. 71–6; Lindsay, 1969). This is because if the price of health care is subsidised, consumption will increase via both income *and* substitution effects; with an income subsidy only the income effect operates, so a larger subsidy is generally needed to bring about a given increase in consumption.

Where problems of inadequate information and inequality of power are serious, efficiency and equity may jointly be maximised by public allocation and/or production. In broad terms this depends on two factors: whether the private or public sector is more efficient at producing health care; and whether monitoring of standards is more effective in one sector or the other. This issue is discussed in section 3.3.

Vertical equity concerns the extent to which health care does or should redistribute from rich to poor. We saw in Chapter 7:4 that (subject to various caveats) publicly provided health care is redistributive if (rich) individual R pays more tax contributions to its cost than (poor) P where each consumes the same quantity, and also if R consumes twice as much as P but pays more than twice as much in contributions. Why might this be thought desirable – why, in other words, might people care about the distribution of health care? A formal explanation is given by the voting model discussed in Chapter 4:4.2. Suppose R's utility rises both with his own consumption and with P's. In particular, suppose that R's utility rises with 'good' consumption by P (e.g. health care or education) but falls with P's 'bad' consumption, e.g. whisky. This is a consumption externality of the type described by equation (4.15). It might therefore be rational for R to make an in-kind transfer to P of health care costing, say, £300, but to offer a cash transfer of only £100 (since P might spend the latter on 'bad' consumption). Given these offers, P might prefer the in-kind transfer to the lower cash amount (see Figure 4.5). If the difference between the two offers is sufficiently large, both rich *and* poor might vote for compulsory in-kind transfers of health care.

It is worth delving more deeply into the nature of the consumption externality. 'Good' consumption by the poor can raise the utility of the rich for two entirely different reasons. The rich might vote for transfers to the poor of health care for reasons of efficiency/self-interest. They might believe that a healthy workforce fosters economic growth; or that increased health care for the poor raises their productivity and/or reduces the cost of caring for them; or that such transfers prevent social unrest. This is the 'national efficiency' argument (Chapter 2:2.1) which gives rise to the Marxist interpretation of the welfare state (Chapter 3:5.3). A completely different explanation is that some rich individuals care about the distribution of health care for reasons of *altruism* (Lindsay, 1969; Culyer, 1980, Ch. 3).

Thus, alongside efficiency arguments for public production and allocation, there may be powerful equity motives which make it politically easier to make transfers in kind. The rich may favour them for either selfish or altruistic reasons; and the poor may prefer them, either because the in-kind transfer is more generous than the cash offer for which they might realistically hope, and/or because they feel less stigmatised by receiving benefits in kind than in the form of means-tested cash transfers.

The voting model explains why *some* transfers of health care take place. But is the amount transferred *optimal*? This was discussed in Chapter 4:4.4. Libertarians support in-kind transfers (if at all) only as *voluntary* action by the rich, but not as a result of coercion by the poor via the ballot box (Chapter 4:4.1); they therefore argue that redistribution under the existing system is greater than optimal. Socialists support in-kind transfers for their own sake, because they increase equality, and argue that redistribution of health care is almost certainly sub-optimal.

The role of giving Previous discussion suggested two reasons for intervention to enhance equity: inadequacies of information or power may justify intervention to foster horizontal equity; and consumption externalities can explain in-kind transfers. The role of giving raises a third set of arguments. The analysis so far has treated health care as a commodity to which the standard economic arguments apply. But most societies, for generally accepted ethical reasons, decree that certain commodities, which in principle are readily marketable, should be excluded from the usual economic calculus. Thus, there is a free market for the purchase and sale of cattle but, in most countries, no similar market for babies, for wives or for slaves. Titmuss (1970) argues that for ethical and philosophical reasons there should similarly be no market for blood, which should be donated to recipients. This, he argues, is a morally superior method of distribution.

Two questions arise: how valid are Titmuss's views about blood; and to what extent do these arguments generalise to other commodities? Whether blood should be given rather than allocated by the market is ultimately one of social values, so that no answer is unambiguously right or wrong. But Titmuss's views are rightly respected on moral grounds, and also because certain characteristics of blood make its allocation as a gift both feasible and (arguably) also efficient. The reasons for the latter view are threefold: the opportunity cost of the act of giving blood (e.g. the time and discomfort) is small; and that of losing a pint of blood effectively zero; furthermore, blood donation can create an altruistic externality, inasmuch as donors often experience a utility gain, not from the act of giving but from the thought of the benefit the blood will confer on others. These considerations together suggest that the marginal social cost of blood is likely to be low, and may be zero. In this case giving might be both morally superior *and* efficient.

This makes blood a special case, so that it is dangerous indiscriminately to generalise the notion of giving into areas like health care and education (a mistake of which Titmuss himself was never guilty). The main reason is that the marginal social cost of, for example, health care is positive and often large. It is therefore an economic commodity. If a doctor spends more time with one patient, he/she will have less time to spend with others; and resources devoted to health care are at the expense of other uses (contrast the case of blood, the giving of which has virtually no opportunity cost to the donor, and which (*pace* Dracula) cannot be used for other than medical purposes).[6] Thus, voluntary giving of health care and education, even if regarded as morally superior, will generally run into major allocative problems which do not arise with blood (though see Sugden, 1984).

3.3 Types of Intervention

Sections 3.1 and 3.2 discussed *why* the state might intervene. The next question is *how* best it might do so. Since the aim is jointly to maximise efficiency and equity, they are discussed together. Three broad types of regime are considered: market production and allocation (with or without income transfers); public production and allocation; and intermediate strategies. The analysis of market production is closely linked to the issue of 'privatisation' discussed in Chapter 4:6, which should be read alongside this section (see especially Table 4.2, which is referred to extensively).

Medical technology used to be cheap, so that health care could be treated as a basic right like voting privileges; but costly advances are making this approach unsustainable.

The policy of meeting medical need, which once entailed little social waste, now threatens to cause considerable waste, largely through the provision of services that are medically needed (the benefit to the patient is positive), demanded (because marginal cost to the patient is zero or very low), and supplied (because providers are fully reimbursed or are indifferent between low- and high-benefit care), but that provide benefits worth less ... than social cost. [Aaron, 1981a, p. 25.]

Because of rising costs, the issue of macro efficiency (i.e. expenditure on health care as a proportion of national income) has become increasingly important in all industrial economies (section 4.1). It is therefore of more than usual importance to be dispassionate in considering methods of allocation.

Pure market provision Some writers (see the Further Reading) argue that health care is similar to food. On the demand side, consumers have preferences which they should be allowed to translate into their utility-maximising consumption pattern. Supply will adjust to these preferences

---

[6] Though resources used in *processing* and *storing* blood do have alternative uses and hence a positive opportunity cost.

more efficiently if it is competitive. Government intervention destroys the fit between demand and supply, and the destruction is greatest if intervention takes the form of public production. Writers of this ilk favour privatisation to the greatest extent possible, i.e. ideally line 1 in Table 4.2, or for low-income families line 2.

We saw in section 3.1 that health care comes nowhere near conformity with the standard assumptions, so that unrestricted market allocation is not a theoretically promising approach. But analysis of the pure market case is important to an understanding of the problems raised by health care. To focus the argument, discussion concentrates on two simple cases, initially assuming away non-competitive supply-side behaviour, and concentrating in particular on the problems of imperfect information on the demand side of the product market and the supply side of the insurance market.

Case 1: Assume initially that there is no insurance, so that consumption is constrained by price. In the presence of consumer ignorance (and to some extent also because of unequal power) the demand curve is not properly defined, but 'wobbly' as shown in Figure 12.1, so that the market-clearing quantity can be above or below the optimum. Uncorrected externalities lead to underconsumption, and non-competitive supply-side behaviour to under- or overconsumption, depending on what it is that doctors seek to maximise. The result is inefficiency in the total volume of resources (i.e. macro inefficiency), possibly substantial, though with no clear presumption of its direction, and also micro inefficiency (i.e. the allocation of resources to different types of health care). There is also considerable inequity; the distribution of health care is determined by inequalities in the income distribution; and these inequalities are heightened where knowledge and power are correlated with income (so that the poor are the least-informed), and also by the absence of insurance and perfect capital markets. The overall result is likely to be substantial *underconsumption* of health care.

Case 2: Assume that health insurance pays all medical bills in full. Consumption is no longer constrained by price, and is therefore determined mainly by the supplier; as a result, the indeterminacy of the patient's demand curve is less important. On the supply side, the doctor has no incentive to ration demand to the efficient quantity Q^* in Figure 12.2. Both patient and doctor can behave as though the cost of health care were zero, leading to consumption Q_1. From an efficiency viewpoint, this system leads unambiguously to *overconsumption*, since third-party payments give neither side of the market an incentive to moderate its consumption.[7] There is also inequity, inasmuch as some individuals are unable to buy insurance (the old, the chronically ill, etc.), and others cannot afford insurance premiums which overconsumption has raised to an inefficiently high level.

---

[7] There might be some pressures to economy, e.g. from employers who pay health care insurance premiums on behalf of their employees.

These arguments, it should be noted, do not necessarily apply on the input side. There is no reason why many material inputs should not be privately produced, e.g. food products (the NHS does not grow its own vegetables), drugs, beds, towels, X-ray machines and so on. Some inputs of services might also be privately produced, e.g. food or laundry, provided that the costs of quality control are not excessive.

Mixed public/private involvement To what extent might health care be based on mixed public/private involvement so as to avoid the worst problems of pure private provision? The desirability of such a package depends on two factors: would it be more efficient/equitable than any other method including the NHS; and might it be politically more acceptable than NHS-type arrangements (as might be the case, for instance, in the USA)? To be feasible it would have to be constructed out of various theoretical ingredients, relating to (a) production and (b) finance.

Production: the supply of medical treatment in a private market is crucially influenced by fee for service and third-party payments. The result, as we saw above, is that the market output, Q_1 in Figure 12.2, exceeds the efficient output, Q^*. Third-party payments create a divergence between private and social costs and benefits, and hence cause a particular kind of externality. These, we know, can be dealt with in a number of ways, of which two are of special relevance. First, output could be restricted to Q^* by *regulation*; this would involve policing doctors' decisions, either by administrative means or through the imposition of a budget constraint (e.g. line 3(b) in Table 4.2).

Alternatively, it is possible to *internalise the externality* by merging the activities of doctor and insurance company, thereby forcing doctors to face the social marginal cost of the treatment they prescribe. The outstanding example of this approach is the notion of a *health maintenance organisation* of the type now widespread in the USA (see the fuller discussion in section 5). The essence of a health maintenance organisation in this context is that *doctors* provide the insurance. As a result the externality is internalised and there is no longer an incentive to overprescribe. It might be possible by one of these methods to constrain private production to its efficient level.

Finance could be organised in one of two generic ways. One possibility is private finance plus residual state finance. 'Easy' cases (i.e. the insurable conditions of non-poor individuals) are financed by private insurance, subject to regulation in two ways: there would be minimum standards of coverage; and insurance would be compulsory because of the externality caused by non-insurance (see Chapter 8:2.1). Two difficulties arise: non-insurable risks, and the poor. The former, as we saw in section 3.1, include congenital and chronic health problems, the medical needs of the elderly, visits to general practitioners and pregnancy. The state could deal with these cases either by subsidising private insurance premiums through an explicit subsidy or via an untied cash transfer; or by paying the full cost of treatment through a residual public insurance scheme, or out of tax revenues. The poor could be assisted similarly. This approach raises a number of serious problems: there is the difficulty of defining borderlines, both as between the types of health care problem which qualify for state assistance, and over the income level below which the poor are subsidised; policing would be necessary to prevent oversupply; and the familiar poverty trap (Chapter 10:3) could arise for the poor.

A second possibility is state finance. Here the state pays medical bills through social insurance or out of tax revenues. An analytically equivalent arrangement is compulsory membership of regulated, private, non-profit insurance institutions acting, in effect, as agents of the state. The advantages of this arrangement are twofold: the scheme's compulsory nature makes it possible with no efficiency loss to gear premiums to ability to pay, rather than to risk (Chapter 5:4.1); and its universal coverage (with respect both to individuals and type of illness) avoids problems with borderlines. Such social insurance institutions, precisely because they are not strictly actuarial (i.e. because premiums are not risk-related on an individual basis), can avoid the gaps of private schemes (cf. Chapter 8:2.2 for the case of unemployment benefits).

These considerations suggest two coherent mixed strategies. Suppose that health care is *produced* by health maintenance organisations of some kind; that membership is compulsory for all individuals; and that insurance premiums are *financed* by individuals (in the case of the poor out of transfer incomes). This arrangement has the flavour of line 3(a) in Table 4.2. Alternatively, suppose health care is produced privately, but not by health maintenance organisations; payment is made by the state (directly, through social insurance, or through regulated medical insurance); and total output or expenditure is controlled by the state either directly or via a global budget constraint. This mechanism (broadly that of Canada) follows the general thrust of line 3(b) for health care *per se* and of line 6 for health care insurance. Policy aspects of such arrangements are discussed in section 4.

Public production, allocation and finance To justify this arrangement requires consideration of the different elements of line 8 in Table 4.2. Consumer sovereignty is appropriate where information is sufficient for rational choice, a process which may be assisted by regulation of quality. In the case of health care it can be argued that the patient's information is often so imperfect that the individual consumption decision is best made on his behalf by an expert (column 3).[8] The argument for publicly financed health

---

[8] There is a wealth of literature on the question of whether patient or doctor knows best. For further references and a review of the literature, see Illsley (1980, Chs 5 and 6).

care (column 4) rests on the problems just discussed of private insurance, viz. the imperfect information of insurance companies (which contributes to the third-party payment problem), and the fact that not all medical conditions are insurable. The third-party payment problem can also justify public production as a method of controlling the resulting large and inefficient increases in the output of health care (section 4.1). More formally, the imperfect information of consumers justifies control of *quality*, and that of insurance companies control of *quantity* (column 2). Both forms of policing might be more effective if production itself were public (column 1).

The argument for public production and allocation thus turns in a crucial though complex way on the issue of information. To justify this arrangement, however, it is necessary to show not only that the conditions for market efficiency fail, but also that public production and allocation are less inefficient than any alternative arrangement. The first point is relatively easy to establish, the second less so.

Because of information problems the NHS strategy can be regarded as feasible – an institution which arose historically largely for equity reasons works because it goes with the grain of *efficiency* considerations. The strategy has four cornerstones. Dealing with demand-side problems:

1. Treatment is decided by doctors, largely solving the difficulties caused by consumer ignorance.

2. Health care is financed (mostly) out of tax revenues, and is (mostly) free at the point of use.

These features avoid the problems of gaps in insurance cover by abandoning the insurance principle even as a fiction; and medical care is made available without stigma. On the supply side:

3. Doctors receive little or no fee for service, thus reducing third-party payment incentives to oversupply.

4. Health care is explicitly rationed, in part by administrative means, and partly by the existence of a budget constraint for the NHS as a whole. The idea, at least in principle, is to restrict consumption to the quantity Q^* in Figure 12.2.

Furthermore, once it is established that public production and allocation are justifiable on efficiency grounds, it is legitimate to finance health care so as to further distributional aims (Chapter 4:7.2). In theory, therefore, the strategy is feasible in both efficiency and equity terms. We turn now to assessment of the practice.

4 Assessment of the British System of Health Care

4.1 Institutions

This part of the chapter starts with an overview of the institutions of the National Health Service (NHS) and of private health care, and then attempts to assess the extent to which the NHS meets the aims of efficiency (section 4.2) and social justice (section 4.3).

Two points should be made immediately. First, expenditure on the NHS (around 6 per cent of national income) is low by international standards. However, expenditure has risen since the mid-1970s for several reasons. There was a 'bulge' in the birth rate in 1948 and another in the mid-1960s (Figure 9.1). The number of old people has increased, intensifying the demand on facilities (in 1989/90 health expenditure per person over 85 was sixteen times that on someone aged 16–44 (UK, 1992c, Figure 5)). Costly new techniques have led to increased expectations. The relative price effect has also acted to raise the cost of health care services by more than the average increase in prices.[9]

A second feature of the NHS, notwithstanding the problems discussed later, is its popularity. In the words of two American commentators,

the NHS promised high quality medical care to the acutely ill and increasingly delivered on that promise. It unquestionably spared patients the fear of financial ruin from medical bills. As a result, it became and remained one of the most popular institutions in Britain, second only to the Crown and a close second at that. [Aaron and Schwartz, 1984, p. 14.]

The major conclusions of a Parliamentary Report (UK House of Commons Social Services Committee, 1988a, p. lx) was that the 'strengths of the NHS should not be cast aside in a short term effort to remedy some of its weaknesses'.

THE OPERATION OF THE NATIONAL HEALTH SERVICE

The NHS in England[10] is the responsibility of the Secretary of State for Health, who is answerable to Parliament, and is responsible for the Department of Health. Under the Department are fourteen Regional Health Authorities, whose major function is twofold: to plan health care in the light of local needs, subject to a regional budget total set by central

---

[9] The relative price effect measures the extent to which the price of commodities like health care tends to rise faster than prices generally. There are two reasons: first, throughout the economy the price of labour tends to rise faster than the general price level (i.e. real earnings rise); and second, health care has a higher than average direct labour content, about three-quarters of NHS current spending being on directly employed staff. The same, broadly, is true of education. For details of the relative price effect, see UK (1972c, paras 68–71) and Rees and Thompson (1972).

[10] The Secretaries of State for Scotland, Wales and Northern Ireland are responsible *inter alia* for the NHS in those countries.

government; and to allocate resources to the second-tier bodies, the District Health Authorities, whose main task is to organise hospital and community health services in their areas. Primary health care (in particular family doctors) forms an entirely separate structure organised by Family Practitioner Committees appointed by the Secretary of State. A major reform of the NHS, set out in a White Paper in early 1989 (UK Department of Health, 1989a) was implemented over the early 1990s.

Discussion is organised round the four areas highlighted in Table 4.2: the production of health care; the individual consumption decision (i.e. how the system works from the viewpoint of the consumer); finance; and the aggregate production decision (i.e. budget setting).

Production of health care under the NHS has a tripartite structure of primary health care, hospitals, and community health care.

Primary health care: the main element is the system of general practitioners (i.e. family doctors). Every member of the community is registered with a general practitioner (GP), who deals with straightforward complaints and chronic conditions and, when necessary, refers patients to hospital and specialist services. In the latter case the GP acts both as a guide (to steer patients to the appropriate specialist) and as a filter (to prevent trivial complaints being taken to a specialist). GPs also have a role in preventive medicine, including immunisation, family planning, cervical screening, etc. The employment status of GPs is complex. Technically, they are self-employed professionals under contract to the local Family Practitioner Committee, though the central Medical Practitioners Committee has limited powers to prevent the establishment of new practices in well-provided areas.

The other major types of primary medical care are dentistry, pharmaceutical services and ophthalmic services, all of which fall under the aegis of the local Family Practitioner Committee. In England somewhat below 10,000 dentists work as independent contractors to their local Family Practitioner Committee, by whom they are paid a fee for service on an agreed scale, net of the consumer charges they levy (also on an agreed scale). Pharmacists dispense drugs, dressings, etc. as prescribed by doctors, for which they are paid (plus a profit margin, but net of the consumer charges discussed below) by the local Family Practitioner Committee.

Hospitals absorb about two-thirds of the resources of the NHS (Table 12.1). There are about 2800 NHS hospitals, covering the full range of medical care. The hospital sector in England directly employs 800,000 people, including 47,000 medical personnel, over 400,000 nurses and 84,000 professional technical staff such as radiographers (UK, 1992c, Table 30).

Hospital doctors are paid a salary rather than a fee for service, though, as discussed below, they are able to combine salaried work for the NHS with private practice. District hospitals are under the authority of the District General Manager. Self-managed hospital trusts, introduced by the

Table 12.1 *Health, UK, 1992/93 (est.) (£ million)*

	Current spending	Capital spending	Total
NATIONAL HEALTH SERVICE			
NHS hospitals, community health, etc.	20,552	1655[a]	
Family health services	6177		
Central health services	532	24	
Administration	290	31	
Total gross spending			29,262
Charges and capital revenues			−1410
Other			265
TOTAL PROGRAMME			28,117
EXPENDITURE IN SCOTLAND, WALES AND			
NORTHERN IRELAND			6749
TOTAL HEALTH			34,866

Sources: UK (1992c, Table 1); UK (1992f, Introductory Table); UK (1992g, Figure 1.03); UK (1992h, Table 1.1).
Note: [a] Includes expenditure on NHS Trusts.

1989 White Paper, are a new public provider. Such hospitals have greater freedom to manage their affairs than District hospitals, including the right to borrow (up to a limit) from both public and private sectors, and to set their own terms and conditions of employment (see Brazier *et al.*, 1990, Ch. 9).

The Community Health Service, the third branch of the NHS, has three functions: preventive health services, including health education, health visiting, screening and vaccination programmes, and maternity and child welfare clinics; liaison with the local authority, especially over matters of public health; and co-operation with personal social services departments, so that wherever possible health and social care can be dealt with together. A White Paper (UK Department of Health, 1989b), based on an earlier report (Griffiths, 1988) introduced a number of changes, some of which made it easier for purchasers of care on behalf of clients to buy from either the public or the private sector.

The individual consumption decision   As a first approximation, all health care under the NHS is free, except for the charges described below. The main source of health care for most people is their GP. Individuals are free to register with any NHS GP in their area who is prepared to add them to his/her list of patients. Anyone who wishes, for whatever reason, to change to another GP may do so. No charge is made for consultations or for home visits. The GP prescribes treatment or, in more complex/serious cases, refers the patient to an NHS hospital.

Where a GP prescribes drugs, the patient has in principle to pay the pharmacist a fixed charge per item, e.g. per bottle of tablets. The charge in

1993 was £3.75, having risen steeply since 1979,[11] though broad classes of people are exempt, e.g. children, expectant mothers, old people, certain chronically ill individuals, and people with low incomes (Tolley, 1991, Ch. 10). These groups include about 75 per cent of individuals, disproportionately those who make the greatest use of drugs. There is continued controversy over prescription charges, which are regarded by some as an anomaly in an otherwise largely free health service, and by others as a useful check on wasteful usage. As in many other countries, Britain's drug bill has increased sharply in recent years.

Individuals are also free to choose their dentist. In the past dental treatment was heavily subsidised, but by the early 1990s it was close to economic costs (though check-ups *per se* remain free, and broad classes of people are exempt from charges).

A patient is usually referred to hospital by his/her GP, but in emergencies this procedure is by-passed. All hospital treatment under the NHS is free, including test procedures, consultations with doctors, nursing, drugs and intensive care, whatever the type of complaint and however long the hospital stay. All the facilities of the NHS are available to anyone living in Britain, with the exception of temporary residents (i.e. those staying in the country for less than six months).

Finance The funding of the NHS is discussed in detail by Glennerster (1992, Ch. 10). Of the total cost of the NHS shown in Table 12.1, 80 per cent came from general (mainly central government) tax revenues, and 15 per cent from national insurance contributions. Thus some 95 per cent of the NHS was financed out of taxation, and only about 4 per cent from charges (UK, 1992c, Figure 1).

Hospitals in the past were, for the most part, financed from the District budget. The new structure introduced by the 1989 White Paper is somewhat more complex. A key objective of the reforms was to separate the finance of health care from its provision. District General Managers act as purchasing agents on behalf of their resident populations. The intention is that they should buy health care from the most efficient providers, public or private, inside or outside their District. Most hospital care will come from institutions within the District, but money will follow patients treated elsewhere.

Thus hospitals receive part of their funding from the District. They also receive income from GPs who act as budget holders for their patients. Under the 1990 Health Service and Community Care Act, implemented in April 1991, GPs working in practices with more than 9000 patients can elect to become budget holders, i.e to manage the budget for certain types of treatment for their patients, notably such things as X-rays, pathology tests, hernia repairs, varicose veins, and the like. Such doctors make their

[11] A charge of 5 pence was introduced in 1952; in early 1979 it was 20 pence.

own contracts with providers, and pay them from their own, larger, budget. For other medical care, the system of remuneration (discussed below) remains unchanged. The underlying idea is that larger numbers of smaller purchasing agents lead to a more competitive environment. The combined effect of increased powers for District General Managers and the ability of some GPs to make their own contracts with hospitals has considerably reduced the power of consultants (for an assessment, see Glennerster *et al.*, 1992).

Purchasing authorities (i.e. District General Managers and GP budget holders) make contracts (known as 'agreements') with providers. The agreements are not legally enforceable. Disputes are resolved by pendulum arbitration,[12] with appeal to the Secretary of State.

General practitioners' remuneration is complex (see Glennerster, 1992, Table 10.2). Somewhat to simplify, GPs receive three forms of payment. First, there are various allowances, mainly a basic practice allowance to cover running costs, plus other allowances, e.g. if the practice is an under-doctored area. Second, they receive a capitation payment of £X for each person on their register, where X is higher for older people. Third, there is a variety of other payments, *inter alia* for certain forms of preventive health care.

Two major changes were introduced in the early 1990s. As just discussed, large practices, from April 1991, could opt to become budget holders for certain types of treatment. Second, a new contract, imposed on GPs from April 1990, specified core services, established targets for the provision of those services, and offered extra payments for the achievement of certain targets, particularly for certain types of preventive care. The effect was to tip the balance between capitation and performance-related pay. A key point, and one to which we return, is that with few exceptions (notably payments to dentists, and for some types of preventive care to GPs), payment throughout the NHS takes the form more of a *salary* than a fee for service (for details, see Glennerster, 1992, Ch. 10).

The aggregate production decision, i.e. setting budget limits. The annual budget for the NHS as a whole is determined in the same way as the budget for national defence or any other government service, as the result of negotiation between the Treasury and spending departments, as modified by subsequent discussion in cabinet (Glennerster, 1992, Chs 4–6). The figure which emerges is a global budget for the NHS as a whole, which is divided between the relevant Secretaries of State. Within England and Wales, resources are allocated by the Secretary of State to each District according to a population-weighted formula. The procedure is therefore largely one of

[12] Under pendulum arbitration, the arbitrator does not seek a compromise solution, but must choose either party A's proposal in its entirety, or party B's. The system thus gives each party an incentive to seek the middle ground.

'top-down' allocation, substantially constrained by expenditure in previous years. GP budget holders, like Districts, will be cash-limited (i.e. they will have to operate within a fixed annual budget).

PRIVATE HEALTH CARE

Alongside the NHS is a system of private health care. Individuals can consult GPs privately (in which case they pay his/her fees and the full cost of any drugs), and/or obtain treatment in a private hospital or in a 'pay bed' in an NHS hospital, whether or not the original consultation with the GP was private. Though it has grown somewhat in recent years, the private sector remains small. In the late 1980s about 10 per cent of the population had some sort of private medical insurance, up from 4 per cent fifteen years earlier. Benefits paid are only a small fraction of NHS expenditure. Private medical care is used mainly by those wanting the convenience of a private room or (more contentiously) by those faced with a long wait for treatment under the NHS, and only for a narrow range of relatively uncomplicated treatment (see Propper and Maynard, 1990).

Most private health care is financed by voluntary insurance, which is cheap in Britain for four reasons (Aaron and Schwartz, 1984, p. 23): most patients use an NHS GP even if they see a specialist privately; the NHS provides a back-up in cases where patients present complications with which private hospitals are not equipped to deal; people with private insurance are usually young and employed (their health care insurance is often a fringe benefit of their job), and hence low risk; finally, health care is cheaper in Britain than, for example, the USA, not least because British doctors and nurses are paid less.

In the late 1980s, however, the expansion of private medical care slowed down: medical costs rose, and premiums could not easily be raised. Even the well-established private insurers faced a time of stringency, so that substantial growth of the sector is not likely, at least in the near future.

The relationship between private health care and the NHS is a source of substantial and continuing controversy. NHS hospitals have specialist consultants who are contracted to work for the NHS, but can choose whether to do so full-time or part-time. Most of them elect for the part-time option and practise in their consultative capacity both as part of the NHS and privately.[13] The existence of 'pay beds' within the NHS has aroused the greatest controversy. It is argued that people with money can jump the queue without necessarily paying the full economic cost of treatment, and many regard this as inequitable. Others argue that private patients bring extra income to some consultants, and that to ban private practice by NHS employees would result in large and costly pay demands,

[13] Consultants choosing the full-time option are allowed to earn up to 10 per cent of their income from private practice.

and possibly the loss of highly skilled specialists. The issue remains a political football. Speedy resolution is unlikely.

INTERNATIONAL COMPARISON

Before turning to an assessment of the NHS it is helpful to have some perspective on the organisation and problems of systems elsewhere (see also Hurst, 1991; Schieber *et al.*, 1991). In very broad terms all industrialised countries adopt one of the three models.

The quasi-actuarial approach is characterised by employer-based or individual purchase of private medical insurance, and by private ownership of medical factors of production. The closest approximation (and the only major example among OECD economies) is the USA.

Earnings-related social insurance contributions are characterised by compulsory coverage financed by earnings-related employee contributions and/or an employer payroll tax, possibly supplemented by tax funding. Such funding regimes are compatible with a larger (Canada) or smaller (Germany) role for the private sector.

'Universal' medical care is characterised by tax funding and public ownership and/or control of the factors of production (e.g. New Zealand, Sweden, the UK).

Problems Inspection of the international scene yields two major conclusions: the pervasiveness of regulation in *all* health care systems; and a dramatic escalation of health care costs in most countries in the later 1970s and early 1980s with, for the most part, a slowdown in the rate of expenditure growth since then (see Aaron, 1981a; Abel Smith, 1984, 1985; Barr, 1992, Table 3). Despite the variety of systems, there is considerable similarity in the difficulties they face. The most important arise out of the third-party payment problem (section 3.1).

Since fee for service paid by a third party is the most common way of paying doctors, it is not surprising, despite the variety of their institutions, that most countries experienced a dramatic escalation in health expenditures. The point is vital. According to the contributors to McLachlan and Maynard (1982):

The rising costs of medical care and, as a result, the problems of expenditures and cost containment ... is of major concern in the Federal Republic of Germany. [p. 235.]

... moves for a closer control to check the growth of expenditure [on health care in France] which is alarmingly high. [p. 267.]

In the US cost containment is the major driving force behind legislative and private sector health strategies. [p. 333.]

Nor is the problem confined to Western countries.

The cost of medical care in Japan has risen very rapidly ... The rate of increase has also grown steadily and so has, as a result, the percentage of the gross national product absorbed by medical care. [Chester and Ichien, 1983, p. 23; see also Noumi, 1983.]

The editors conclude that

however much health systems and policies may seem to differ from country to country all current policies have one major aim, cost containment which is an omnibus description of policies ... to contain not just *unit costs* but also *total* expenditure in both public and private sectors. [McLachlan and Maynard, 1982, p. 13, their emphasis.]

Of the countries covered by McLachlan and Maynard only two have not suffered a cost explosion: the UK, largely because of Parliamentary control of public expenditure;[14] and Canada, which imposes a global budget constraint at a provincial level on the expenditure of its publicly funded scheme.

The situation in the USA is a textbook example. The system until the mid-1960s (as a rough approximation) was one of private production financed by private health care insurance (for historical analysis, see Anderson (1968) and Russell (1980, pp. 171–8)). But problems arose, and as a response medicare (for the old) and medicaid (for the poor) were introduced in the mid-1960s. The modification they introduced was simple: the poor and old continued to receive private treatment; but their medical bills were now paid out of federal/state funds. The effect of these unlimited third-party payments was entirely predictable: public spending on health care rose from $6.6 billion in 1960 to $28 billion in 1970, to $105 billion in 1980, and to $207 billion in 1987 (for recent analysis, see Russell (1989) and Aaron (1991)). As a result, health care became the fourth largest item of federal expenditure after income support, defence and debt interest.

There are two possible arguments against the assertion that these cost escalations are caused by inadequately policed third-party payments. One is to argue that the USA has a greater taste for health care than, say, Britain (i.e. demand is higher in the USA); the other is that American citizens suffer more health problems than the British (i.e. need is greater in the USA). If the former, we would expect high-spending countries to enjoy better health; if the latter, that they suffer more illness. Neither phenomenon is the case (Culyer, 1976, Ch 10; Aaron and Schwartz, 1984, pp. 12–13). In 1992 the USA spent 12 per cent of GNP on health care; Britain spent 6.1 per cent. Yet, measured in terms of outcome measures like infant mortality and life expectancy, health in the USA is no better than in Britain.

Solutions   Two broad classes of solution – regulation, and the use of

---

[14] The ability of the NHS to act as a monopoly buyer is another contributory factor.

incentives – have been adopted to try to contain costs (see Barr (1992) for fuller discussion).

Regulation has been pervasive and, according to McLachlan and Maynard, is inescapable: 'insurance based systems are subject to regulations and controls similar (and sometimes greater) in effect to those that apply [in the UK]' (1982, p. 12). The logic is simple: expenditure = price x quantity. Successful cost containment must (a) control total spending directly, or (b) control price *and* quantity, or (c) use price control to reinforce an overall spending constraint. Control of medical fees (i.e. price control) with open-ended total budgets only partially contains costs because of the incentive for doctors to increase output to compensate for lost income. This is exactly what happened with medicare in the USA (Evans *et al.*, 1989). Canada, in contrast, managed to avoid the worst of the medicare cost explosion because it adopted both price control *and* a global budget ceiling. European countries, too, have developed systems which combine price and expenditure control (Abel Smith, 1984, 1985).

Whatever the system, successful methods of restricting supply to around its efficient level all include the imposition of budget limits either on public expenditure (Britain, Sweden) or on insurance disbursements (Canada). This is an important conclusion because the demand for health care will increase in the future not only with advances in medical technology but also because of the problem (Chapter 9:2 and 9:3.2) of ageing populations in almost all industrialised countries.

Incentives to economy take various forms. The third-party payment problem arises because health care providers are reimbursed retrospectively on what is, in effect, a cost-plus basis. The idea of *prospective payment* is becoming increasingly widespread. In one form, each hospital receives a fixed annual global budget which it can spend as it wishes. *Diagnosis related groups* (DRGs) are a refinement of the same idea: hospitals receive a fixed prospective price per patient depending mainly on the patient's DRG. Another form of prospective payment, *health maintenance organisations*, is discussed in section 5.

Other forms of incentive have also been tried, including cost sharing (where the patient pays part of the cost of treatment), privatisation, and (particularly in the USA) attempts to increase competition between providers. Though doubts have been expressed (Fuchs, 1988; Weisbrod, 1983) about uncritical adherence to competition, the European experience suggests that regulated competition may help to contain medical spending.

4.2 Assessment 1: Efficiency

As discussed in section 2.1, efficiency can be defined in principle but is hard to measure, mainly because of difficulties in measuring (a) the benefits of health care as opposed to other activities (the *macro* efficiency issue), and (b) the relative benefits in different areas of health care (*micro* efficiency). Quantitative work on both is scant (Cullis and West, 1979, Ch. 8; Aaron and Schwartz, 1984, Ch. 7), so discussion is to some extent a mixture of *a priori* argument with only a small leavening of empirical evidence.

Assessment of the efficiency, or otherwise, of the NHS is organised under four broad heads: advantages in principle; advantages in practice; criticisms with little validity; and criticisms which are valid. The NHS has at least four efficiency advantages in principle.

1. *Supply-side incentives* to economise on the use of resources arise, first, from the way remuneration is organised. Doctors are not generally paid a fee for service. Thus there is no financial incentive to oversupply, a point confirmed indirectly by evidence (UK, 1986b) of unnecessary treatment by dentists (who are paid a fee for service). There is no argument of principle against paying doctors a high salary – the crucial point in this context is that it is fixed. In the case of GPs these incentives may go too far, since the capitation payment system (section 4.1) gives GPs an incentive to increase the size of their lists, but to decrease the time spent with any one patient. To that extent there is an incentive for GPs either to *undersupply* or to pass patients to the hospital sector. This argument should not be overstated, however, since a patient who feels he/she is not receiving adequate attention from his/her GP can transfer to the list of another doctor, thereby reducing the original GP's income.[15]

A second form of constraint is the NHS budget (a macro efficiency point), coupled with the control exercised by the NHS over doctors' behaviour and the traditions of the medical profession in Britain. The overall result is that there is no financial incentive to supply excessive medical care, Q_1 in Figure 12.2, rather than the socially optimal quantity, Q^*. This is true both for health care as a whole and for different types of treatment, though with a question mark over the possibility of undersupply by GPs.

2. *The individual consumption decision.* The decision about treatment is generally made by doctors. This reduces the problem of imperfect information. In addition, the patient is more likely to trust a doctor's decision based on clinical judgement unclouded by financial motives.

3. *Finance* for the most part is out of general taxation, thereby avoiding problems in insurance markets, such as high probabilities of requiring treatment, adverse selection and moral hazard (Chapter 5:3 and section 3.1). To the extent that taxes are based on ability to pay there are also equity advantages, discussed below.

4. *Treatment* is mostly free at the point of use. This encourages early

[15] It can therefore be argued that the capitation element of GPs' pay under the NHS approximates to a voucher system.

diagnosis, reduces the externality problem, and also has equity advantages.

The system has advantages also in practical terms.

5. *Macro efficiency.* The NHS is cheap by international standards. It absorbs 6 per cent of national income; the US figure is approximately twice as large. Yet according to Aaron and Schwartz, '[these] large differences in per capita average medical expenditures between the two countries are not associated with large differences in life expectancy' (1984, p. 13). According to Klein (1984, p. 15), 'the NHS seems to be a remarkably successful instrument for making the rationing of scarce resources socially and politically acceptable'.

6. *Micro efficiency.* We shall see shortly that the NHS is not above criticism for the way it allocates resources to different areas of health care. But it also has advantages. Because of its unified structure and because payment is not generally based on fee for service,

the NHS has shown a greater ability than insurance-based systems to substitute medical time; to make use of the team approach and to provide a framework in which choices can be made between hospital and community care. Substitution can be seen in hospitals in the wide responsibility of the ward sister and outside the hospital in the roles of the district nurse and the health visitor. [Bosanquet, 1983, p. 154.]

Additionally, the unified structure of the NHS enables action to be taken on overall medical priorities (see points 10 and 11 below).

Two criticisms are made of the NHS (particularly in the USA) which do not hold water.

7. *The NHS is a monopoly.* The first argument is that consumers have no choice. This is not the case. They are free to choose (and change) their GP; to ask for a second opinion; or to opt for private medical care. A different argument is that the NHS devotes too many resources to bureaucracy. In fact, the NHS bureaucracy, like those in the health care systems of most countries, has increased. But it remains low by international standards. Administrative costs in the USA in the late 1980s were about 26 per cent of total current expenditure (Himmelstein and Woolhandler, 1986, 1991).[16] The NHS figure in 1987/8 was 2.9 per cent, in part because the NHS devotes virtually no resources to billing patients. A further counter-argument is that centralisation can have positive advantages by making it possible to set out priorities, and by enabling the NHS to negotiate low prices for drugs.

8. *Work effort.* Doctors, it is argued, work less hard if they are not paid a fee for service and/or the best and most innovative individuals will be lost

[16] If US administrative spending had been brought down to the average of countries which fund medical care through social insurance, the resulting savings in 1987 would have been around $50 billion.

to the profession (this is the issue of *dynamic* efficiency). There are two lines of attack on this position. It assumes uncritically that labour supply is motivated solely by financial gain, but loses plausibility if one allows for non-money wages and a tradition of service. Many professionals are paid salaries, e.g. academics, lawyers and accountants, yet it is not argued that they should be paid a fee for service. Though difficult to prove, it might be argued that Britain attracts to the medical profession individuals who gain substantial job satisfaction, while countries with private systems attract those with more strongly financial motives. If so, it does not follow that the latter group is either more able or harder working. A second counter-argument is that, even if work effort/innovation is substantially motivated by high pay, it might well suffice to base remuneration on high salaries rather than fee for service.

To rebut these arguments is not to say that no criticism is possible.

9. *Macro inefficiency.* Many commentators argue that too few resources in total are devoted to the NHS. Budget restrictions have aggravated waiting lists for non-urgent (and some urgent) treatment; and many hospital buildings are old. Pro-market writers argue that the NHS *causes* too few resources to be devoted to medical care; but international comparison suggests that private systems can lead to excessive production which regulation has only partly curtailed. There is widespread agreement (Kings Fund Institute, 1988; Owens and Glennerster, 1990) that the increase in the NHS budget over the 1980s was below that necessary to sustain standards in the face of an ageing population. If the NHS has too few resources, the appropriate solution is to relax the budget restrictions rather than substantially to alter the system.

Micro inefficiency arises in two important ways.

10. *Micro inefficiency in the spatial allocation of resources.* NHS resources are geographically misallocated, especially hospitals, whose location is largely a matter of historical accident. The Resource Allocation Working Party (RAWP) (UK Department of Health and Social Security, 1976) made specific proposals for geographical reallocation on the basis of such criteria as the size and demographic structure of the population in an area, health indicators such as local mortality and fertility, and gaps in existing provision. The overall effect of the recommendations was that resources should be shifted away from London and the south east of England. Subsequent policy reduced measured inequality (relative to a target index of 100 the best-provided region in 1977 was at 118 and the worst-off at 90; in 1987/8 the figures were 109 and 96). Under the 1989 reforms, the RAWP formula was replaced by more direct allocation of resources from the central Department of Health to Districts (see Carr-Hill, 1990). The issue of the extent to which London has a disproportionate share of resources is a

continuing controversy (see Mays and Bevan, 1987; UK Department of Health, 1992).

11. *Micro inefficiency in the allocation of resources to different types of health care.* Enthoven (1985) argued that the NHS was inefficient in several ways.

(a) Inadequate or inappropriate incentives: incentives to improve the efficiency of services were generally non-existent. In some instances incentives could be perverse: a consultant who treated more patients would get extra work but no extra resources; and since capital costs were generally paid by the central government, Districts and services generally did not have to face the opportunity cost of capital.

(b) Overcentralisation, particularly in the form of national pay agreements, led to staffing problems in high-wage parts of the country like London.

(c) Lack of accountability: no-one knew what anything cost or whether they were keeping within their budget.

(d) Inflexibility, e.g. the difficulty of closing an unwanted NHS hospital.

Greater efficiency requires two sorts of information: first, quantitative estimates of the costs and output benefits of different types of treatment (a technical question); and a set of weights to be applied to relevant non-medical criteria (e.g. whether the patient has dependants), which is almost entirely a social or political matter. Both sorts of information are relevant to the construction of systems which explicitly encourage efficient resource use. Thus a major efficiency criticism of the NHS (it is equally a criticism of other health care systems) is that it assembles and uses *too little information* (for further discussion, see Enthoven (1989) and Johnsson (1989)).

One approach to attempting to allocate resources more efficiently to different types of health care is the notion of a Quality Adjusted Life Year (QALY). A QALY starts from the premise that the outcome of medical care should be measured not only in terms of the quantity of extra life it produces, but also of its quality. Though the measurement of quality inevitably involves subjective judgement (e.g. of *how much* a restriction in mobility reduces the quality of life), the calculation of QALYs at least has the merit of incorporating subjective values explicitly and systematically. QALYs look at the extra years (adjusted for quality) resulting from treatment, and divide them by its cost. Some forms of treatment represent an inefficient use of resources, e.g. the treatment is unpleasant, it does not extend life by much, and the time remaining is full of pain and discomfort. Other types of treatment, in contrast, are underused. One example is a hip replacement: it is not expensive; and though it does not prolong life it considerably improves its quality. For further discussion, see Wagstaff (1991).

As well as improved management decisions, there is also a role for some competition on the supply side. A strategic proposal in this context is the use of internal markets within the NHS. The idea has two variants, one in which the *District* acts as budget holder (Enthoven, 1985), the other in which *GPs* act as budget holders (Maynard, 1986). The two approaches are discussed in section 5, below.

12. *Administrative inefficiency.* The argument that the NHS has a disproportionate number of bureaucrats does not stand up (point 7). There has, however, been a continuing problem over administrative co-ordination. After several official reports (UK, 1962, 1968, 1970, 1972b) there was some improvement, though administrative reform in 1974 was widely regarded as unsatisfactory (UK, 1979b; UK Department of Health and Social Security, 1979). After another round of reform in 1982 the appointment of professional managers was suggested (UK Department of Health and Social Security, 1983). There is also some evidence (UK National Audit Office, 1985) that nursing staff could be used more efficiently.

4.3 Assessment 2: Equity

As we saw in Chapter 4:2.2 and 4:4.3, equity cannot be defined unambiguously, but depends on political values; in addition (Chapter 6:3.1), the definition of equality is fraught with ambiguities. For present purposes horizontal equity is defined in terms of equality of opportunity in respect of health care, as set out in section 2.1. Thus individuals A and B with identical medical conditions should receive equal health care unless other relevant differences exist (e.g. one of them has young or old dependants); irrelevant considerations (e.g. that A is rich and B poor) should make no difference. How closely does the NHS approximate this ideal? Though there is room for disagreement, the equity advantages of the NHS can be listed as follows.

13. *The unimportance of income.* The quantity of health care an individual receives is largely (though as we shall see not wholly) unconstrained by his/her income. No one is denied health care because of poverty; and no one goes in fear of financial ruin as a result of expensive medical treatment. The latter is a particular problem in the USA where not only health care but also most health insurance is private.

14. *The distribution of health care and of health* is less unequal than in many other countries (but see point 17, below). As discussed earlier, however, the focus of interest for many purposes is not health care, but health. Attempts to measure the distribution of health have been controversial. Black's (1980) conclusion that disparities in health across UK socioeconomic groups had widened over the lifetime of the NHS were disputed by Le Grand (1987a). A different approach (Le Grand, 1987a; see also Illsley and Le Grand, 1987) attempts to measure inequality in health

outcomes by applying aggregate inequality measures such as the Gini coefficient (see Chapter 6:4) to individual data on age-at-death. Le Grand (1987a, Table 1) estimated mortality inequality and classified countries into three groups: the most equal group included the UK, the Netherlands and Sweden; the least equal group included the USA (measuring mortality inequality in terms of the Gini coefficient, the only country consistently less equal than the USA was Romania).

15. *The system accords with British notions of social justice* (McCreadie, 1976), and is highly popular politically (Halpern, 1985). A leaked report of a proposal in the late 1980s to introduce significant privatisation caused such a political backlash that the subsequent reform proposals (UK Department of Health, 1989a) preserved the basic principles of publicly funded and largely publicly produced health care.

Equity criticisms are twofold.

16. *Health care resources are distributed unequally by region*, though less so than hitherto, as discussed in point 10.

17. *Health care resources are distributed unequally across socioeconomic groups*. Three issues arise: the empirical facts; the explanation of those facts; and implications for policy. Le Grand (1982, Ch. 3) finds that inequalities of outcome persist; over a wide variety of indicators the higher socioeconomic groups enjoy better health and longer life than lower groups. His second conclusion, which confirms the findings of the Black Report (1980, Ch. 4), is that the NHS does not achieve equality of use. 'The evidence suggests that the top socioeconomic group receives 40 per cent more NHS expenditure per person reporting illness than the bottom one' (Le Grand, 1982, p. 46).

This result can be explained (see Figure 12.3) in terms of two sets of factors. The *benefits* of health care perceived by the lower socioeconomic groups (MPV_P) may be lower than those of the rich (MPV_R), e.g. if the poor have worse information; or the poor might rationally place a lower value on health (e.g. where someone's life is miserable, smoking might genuinely be one of his/her few pleasures); or the actual benefits to poorer people might be lower if doctors treat them with less care and compassion than middle-class patients. Probably of greater importance, the poor face higher *costs* of health care. Since treatment is free, the main cost is time. Travel time is generally higher for less advantaged people, who more often have to rely on public transport, and who may have further to travel. Once at the hospital or GP's consulting room, waiting time may be longer, e.g. because middle-class people with easier access to a telephone more often make an appointment. Finally, the cost of each hour's wait is generally higher for the poor, who more often lose pay if they spend a morning in a hospital out-patient clinic, a cost not faced by people on salaries. These

Figure 12.3 *Differences in the costs and benefits of health care/education by socioeconomic group*

factors taken together can explain why in practice Q_R in Figure 12.3 is 40 per cent higher than Q_P.

These results are not universally accepted. O'Donnell and Propper, using 1985 microdata, dispute the Le Grand result and also its methodology, concluding tentatively that the distribution of medical care under the NHS does not vary systematically with income. For continuing debate, see O'Donnell and Propper (1991), Propper and Upward (1992a, b), Wagstaff *et al.* (1991) and Le Grand (1991b).

What implications can be drawn from these results? To say that the NHS may not fully have achieved its objective of equal treatment for equal need does not mean that the NHS has not been an equalising force. First, the NHS cannot be regarded as a failure unless an alternative system of health care is more equalising. International comparison offers no strong evidence for such a proposition (Le Grand, 1989a).

The second reason why the NHS, despite unequal usage, can be an equalising force emerges when expenditure is discussed not in isolation but, more properly, in conjunction with the taxation which finances it (Chapter 7:4.2). The argument is important, and worth spelling out. Suppose that the pre-transfer incomes of poor and rich are 20 and 80; that all income is taxed away by the state to provide free goods and services; and that the rich receive twice as many goods and services as the (equally numerous) poor. As a result, the post-transfer incomes of poor and rich are $33\frac{1}{3}$ and $66\frac{2}{3}$, respectively. From the perspective of expenditure, the rich receive twice as much as the poor, suggesting that public allocation as an equalising force has failed. But when expenditure and taxation are considered together the picture is very different: the income of the poor has been raised both absolutely from 20 to $33\frac{1}{3}$, and relatively, from one-quarter of that enjoyed by the rich to one-half. On either count, the system taken as a whole is equalising.

18. *Redistributive effects of the NHS*. To what extent is the NHS thus financed progressively? In practice, measurement raises almost insuperable problems, *inter alia* because of the difficulty of measuring the incidence of taxes and benefits, but the *logic* is clear (Chapter 7:4.2, as qualified by Chapter 7:4.1). If (rich) individual R contributes on average, say, twice as much as (poor) P in whatever tax is used to pay for the NHS, but receives the same quantity of health care, then the NHS redistributes from rich to poor (i.e. is progressive). But if R contributes twice as much but consumes four times as much as P then the NHS is regressive.

If it is true (point 17) that, *ceteris paribus*, the 'rich' consume 40 per cent more health care per capita than the 'poor', then the NHS redistributes from rich to poor if on average the tax contribution towards the NHS of an individual in the highest socioeconomic group exceeds that of someone in the lowest by more than 40 per cent. The crucial words are 'tax contribution towards the NHS'. The NHS is progressive if we assume that it is financed by a progressive tax, or out of taxation generally (since the tax system overall is progressive). Even if it is financed out of proportional taxation the result is still likely to hold, since the income of individuals in the top socioeconomic group is on average more than 40 per cent higher than the average income of the poor. To argue that the NHS redistributes from rich to poor thus assumes that it is not financed specifically by regressive taxation, i.e. that the effect of abolishing the NHS would be a reduction in income tax, or in all taxes, but not lower tobacco taxation.

Additionally, even if the redistributive effect is weak, the NHS is still an equalising force if it reduces inequality more than any alternative system. The most plausible conclusion is not that the NHS has failed, but that it may not be as strong an equalising force as some of its supporters have hoped. This suggests that the aims of egalitarians are likely to be served better by keeping and improving the NHS than by replacing it.

5 Reform

Four sets of reform are considered: radical privatisation; the possible role of health maintenance organisations; a system of privately produced but publicly funded medical care; general possibilities for improving the NHS; and an assessment of the 1989 reform proposals.

Radical privatisation The failure of virtually all the standard assumptions[17] (section 3.1) suggests *a priori* that an unrestricted private market (i.e. lines 1 or 2 in Table 4.2) is likely to be highly inefficient for technical (i.e. non-ideological) reasons (section 3.1), and also inconsistent with many people's perceptions of social justice (section 3.2). This view, as we saw in section 4.1, is confirmed by empirical observation. Countries which have adopted careless *ad hoc* modifications to private health care systems have typically experienced sharp and unexpected cost increases. Nor does it follow that the private sector produces better quality health care than the NHS.[18]

An additional argument concerns the possible effects of any rapid expansion of private medical care in Britain. So long as private treatment is only a marginal activity it can serve as a useful device for enhancing consumer choice and alleviating excess demand. But if the private sector were to grow beyond a certain (unknown) size, it is possible that 'the most demanding consumers of health care [would] exit from the public sector so diminishing the political voice for more spending in the public sector' (Klein, 1984, pp. 23–4). This, it is argued, could lead to a two-tier system – high-quality private care for the better-off, and low-quality NHS treatment for the poor. Such an outcome would have two effects. It would shift medical resources from the poor to the rich; whether this is desirable depends on one's definition of social justice. In addition, if the private health care sector becomes large, it is likely to run into the cost containment problems faced by other countries (section 4.1), particularly the USA.

If radical privatisation is not the answer, what package of reform might be feasible? The main conclusion of the theoretical discussion in section 3 is that it is not possible to make health care efficient and equitable by *ad hoc* tinkering with private markets. What is needed is a *strategy*. Since virtually all health care is financed by third parties (i.e. insurance companies or the taxpayer) the marginal cost to the consumer is zero, and he will generally demand an inefficiently high quantity, Q_1 in Figure 12.2. The heart of the issue is therefore the rationing of treatment to Q^*. In principle this can be done in two ways: (a) by making doctors face the marginal social cost of health care; or (b) by imposing a budget constraint on total expenditure. The next two mixed public/private packages follow these two routes, the first being rather more private than the second. Each is presented only in outline to illustrate the approach; and other examples are, no doubt, possible.

Health maintenance organisations This is the case of private health care, private medical insurance and extensive regulation. The idea of a health

---

[17] I.e. the assumptions necessary for the market to allocate efficiently – see Chapter 4:3.2, or the Appendix to Chapter 4, paras 6–17.
[18] See, for instance, 'Private Health Treatment Not Necessarily Best, Survey Says', *The Times*, 7 June 1984, p. 4. The survey in question was by *Which?* magazine, a reputable consumer group.

maintenance organisation (HMO) is simple. Individuals pay a lump-sum annual contribution to a 'firm' of doctors (the HMO), which promises in return to provide the contributor and his/her family with a comprehensive range of medical services. The doctors provide primary care themselves, and buy in (and monitor) hospital care as necessary. The HMO's income, which consists of the contributions of its members, is used to pay for health care, including the salaries of the doctors. Any surplus (like that of any firm) can be distributed to the doctors as additional income, or to members in the form of lower contributions, or ploughed back into the HMO to improve its service.

An important theoretical advantage of HMOs is that the doctor provides both health care *and* medical insurance. The effect of an HMO is therefore analytically equivalent to merging the activities of doctor and insurance company. This internalises the externality caused by third-party payments (section 3.3). As a result, doctors as managers of the 'firm' have an incentive to economise, e.g. providing preventive care or early treatment to nip any incipient problem in the bud.

Evidence (Luft, 1981; Manning *et al.*, 1984) suggests that HMOs reduce medical costs by between 10 and 40 per cent in comparison with fee-for-service medicine, largely because of fewer hospital admissions, though some studies indicate that the reduction is a once-and-for-all effect. The precise form of HMO may also influence medical behaviour (Hillman *et al.*, 1989). Notwithstanding Enthoven's (1989) enthusiasm, it is well not to be too optimistic. First, HMOs may ameliorate one insurance problem – exploding costs; but they do nothing to deal with the other – uninsurable risks. Anecdotal evidence suggests that, as with any prepayment system, attempts are made in the USA to restrict membership to the best risks, an effect which is becoming stronger as the US population ages.[19] Second, HMOs do not *necessarily* provide the efficient quantity Q^* in Figure 12.2. Theory suggests that they will provide less than Q_1; but it does not follow that they will provide Q^*.

Any strategy based on HMOs would require non-trivial public involvement. *Production* of health care would be via HMOs. *Regulation* would be necessary in several forms: all HMOs would have to meet or exceed state-ordained minimum standards concerned with the range, duration and quality of service; HMOs would not be allowed to 'evict' high-risk members or individuals requiring expensive treatment; there would be a mandatory requirement on individuals to belong to an approved HMO (i.e. one which met minimum standards); and babies might have to be registered before birth. *Finance* by the state would have to include cash transfers to assist the poor. These could take the form of an untied income transfer; or the

---

[19] It is said that some HMOs have offices on the third floor of buildings with no elevator; if you are fit enough to get to the office, you are fit enough to join the HMO.

state could pay the subsidy directly to the HMO (cf. rent rebates for low-income tenants in UK local authority accommodation). In addition, the state might subsidise everyone's health care in recognition of the external benefits created by certain kinds of treatment. The system which emerges has the general flavour of lines 1 or 2 in Table 4.2 for health care, and of lines 3(a) or 4(a) for health insurance.

A package of this sort has several advantages. Everyone would receive health care of an approved standard (because membership of an approved HMO supported by cash transfers would be compulsory). Compulsory membership starting before birth would alleviate problems of pre-existing or congenital ill-health; it would also facilitate pooling the costs of GP visits and pregnancy, which raise potential problems of moral hazard. HMOs would have no incentive to oversupply. Finally, an element of consumer sovereignty is possible, in that each HMO can be thought of as a 'mini NHS'. Problems, however, remain. How is compulsory membership enforced? Might HMOs produce a sub-optimal output? There is also a problem with high-risk individuals who want to 'migrate' from one HMO to another because it offers a preferred package of health care; because they are moving to a different part of the country; or because their HMO goes out of business. Temporary or permanent immigrants raise similar problems. On the applicability or otherwise of HMOs to other countries, see Luft (1991).

Public finance of privately produced medical care This package of private production, public funding and extensive regulation embraces more public involvement than the previous one. *Production* of health care would be private, fee-for-service. There would be *regulation* of the quality of treatment and, crucially, also of its quantity. The latter, as discussed in section 4.1, could be achieved, as in Canada, through a combination of price control and global spending limits. *Finance* would be public, i.e. the state would pay all medical bills (private, non-profit institutions, acting in effect as agents of the state, could achieve the same result, e.g. Germany). Membership would be compulsory. Finance could be arranged in one of two ways. With compulsory insurance, premiums could be income-related with no efficiency loss (Chapter 5:4.1). Alternatively, the state could drop the idea of actuarial insurance because it does not fit health care very well, and finance the scheme from general taxation. The general thrust of these arrangements follows line 3(b) of Table 4.2 for health care, and line 6 for health insurance. This is broadly the Canadian system.

The advantages of this approach are twofold. The problems of private insurance are largely avoided; and the incentive to oversupply, resulting from fee for service and third-party payments, is moderated by constraining total expenditure. The strategy rests crucially on the effective imposition of a budget constraint. Such arrangements can undoubtedly be successful. A scheme of this sort has operated in Canada for many years; it works well and is widely popular (Evans *et al.*, 1989; Blendon and Taylor, 1989).

Possible improvements to the NHS We have seen that the NHS strategy (approximately line 8 in Table 4.2) has powerful advantages. But it also has problems, so that some reforms are desirable.

Efficiency issues: so far as macro efficiency is concerned, there is some evidence (though the issue is hard to quantify) that many problems (e.g. queues and old hospitals) are the result of underfunding. The solution is not to abandon the idea of the NHS, but to devote more resources to it. There are also problems of micro efficiency. This is inevitable, given the past lack of technical information on the costs and benefits of treatment, and of clearly stated priorities about different types of treatment and different classes of recipient. The solution is to gather more information of the type discussed in point 11. It is in this context that proposals for internal markets offer prospects of improvement. There are two models.

1. Districts as budget holders: Enthoven's (1985) proposal is that Districts should not be required to *provide* health care for their residents, but should be required to to *buy* care for their residents from whichever supplier could offer the most efficient and effective care. The role of Districts, in short, would be changed from that of *provider* to that of *purchasing agent*. The essence of the idea is to split the purchaser (i.e. the demand side of the market) from the provider (the supply side).

2. GPs as budget holders: Maynard (1986) argues that internal markets would best be mobilised by making GPs the purchasing agents on behalf of their patients. He argues, first, that Districts are too distant from the consumer. In addition, such a move would increase the power of GPs relative to consultants and hospitals, thus increasing pressure on hospitals to be efficient.

Both approaches have their problems. Contracts between purchasers (whether District or GP) and providers require accounting information which is costly to collect and is still poorly developed. The difficulty of quantifying outcome measures makes it hard to decide which supplier offers the most efficient and effective treatment. In many Districts and for many services competition is very limited. For further discussion, see Glennerster (1992, Ch. 10).

Equity issues arise in the NHS in two ways. Attempts have been made to equalise the geographical spread of resources by budgetary allocation and by financial incentives to doctors. These efforts should be continued and possibly intensified. The distribution of health care by social class could be made more equal by reducing the cost of treatment to the lower socioeconomic groups, e.g. by compensating outpatients for transport costs and forgone earnings (as is done already with jurors). This process would be assisted by more general equalising measures, e.g. further income redistribution, and better education, including information about the benefits of health care.

The distribution of medical care by social class is probably the most intractable of the problems discussed, and the measures suggested may appear to some readers to be rather pale. It may be that we simply have to accept that inequality in health care, like inequality generally, cannot easily be reduced beyond a certain point. This does not mean that we should not try – merely that we should not expect easy answers. At a minimum we should not forget that the distribution of health care under the NHS, unequal though it might be, is more equal than that in many (if not most) other countries. The balance between realism and complacency is never easy.

The 1989 reform proposals Since the reforms have not yet been fully implemented, it is possible only to comment on the proposals rather than the outcome (for more detailed discussion, see the references in the Further Reading). The idea behind the reforms is that the separation of provider and purchaser will lead to greater transparency. The intention is to make suppliers more accountable, and to use competitive forces to bring about greater efficiency.

The reforms can be commended in that, up to a point, they conform with the great weight of advice to the House of Commons inquiry (UK House of Commons Social Services Committee, 1988a; see also Barr *et al.*, 1989), namely to stick to tax funding, and to make efforts to introduce some competition on the supply side. Beyond that, however, there are three major sets of criticisms of the proposals.

The lines of financial control are unclear: the fact that there are two sets of budget holders, District General Managers and some GPs (i.e. both the Enthoven (1985) *and* the Maynard (1986) approaches), is likely to lead to co-ordination problems, particularly if the two groups have different priorities. In addition, GPs retain the right to refer patients to any supplier. District General Managers have little power to control GP referrals. For example, the District may have a contract for hernia repair with provider A, who is regarded as the most efficient. A GP, however, has the right to send a patient to provider B, with whom the District has no agreement. The District has to fund such treatment, making budget allocation uncertain.

Excessive optimism about the extent of and benefits from competition: the White Paper is optimistic about how much competition is feasible, and about its beneficial effects. Competition may be limited in at least three ways. Waiting lists in many areas suggest that there is at least some excess demand, reducing competitive pressures. Competition is likely to be limited outside the main metropolitan areas. Many relationships, even in the private sector, are not competitive in the short run; large enterprises often cultivate long-term relationships with suppliers on the grounds that it allows the purchaser greater regulatory power. As a separate point, the White Paper may overestimate the benefits of competition between health care providers. The literature offers no convincing evidence that hospital competition promotes efficiency (Culyer and Posnett, 1990).

The proposals contain no incentive to improve service to patients: at the heart of the proposals is a major and unavoidable tension. Either doctors face the costs of their decisions, or they do not. If they do not, they face no incentives to efficiency. But if doctors do face the costs of their decisions, downward cost pressures may affect quality, which imperfectly informed consumers may be unable to judge. Thus quality control and monitoring of medical outcomes becomes critical. The reform proposals, however, contain little evaluation of outcomes. Cost data under the old system were poor, but will rapidly improve. Management decisions are likely to be based increasingly on cost data rather than on data on medical outcomes. Thus there is a worry that doctors (like HMOs) will face incentives to try, by explicit refusal or by implicit methods, to weed out patients who fall into costly groups.

6 Conclusion: Health Care

No system of health care can be perfect – the real issue is to choose the least inefficient and inequitable form of organisation. Radical privatisation (as defined in Chapter 4:6) is no way of doing so. This conclusion rests not on personal values but on the *technical* nature of health care, and par- ticularly, though not exclusively, on information problems which are ignored in much of the pro-market literature.[20]

Health care conforms only minimally with the assumptions necessary for market efficiency. The imperfect information and unequal power of consumers, externalities, and technical difficulties with private medical insurance cause serious problems on the demand side of a hypothetical private market; non-competitive behaviour by doctors can cause problems with supply, and third-party payments cause inefficiency via both demand and supply (section 3.1). *A priori* there is an overwhelming presumption that an unrestricted private market will be highly inefficient, and also inconsistent with widely held notions of social justice. This view is confirmed by empirical observation (section 4.1). Countries with little public involve- ment in health care, or which adopted careless *ad hoc* modifications to private systems, typically experienced sharp, unplanned increases in expenditure. Efficiency requires, at a minimum, considerable regulation and state financial involvement (section 3.3).

---

[20] E.g. in the case of education see the classic piece by Friedman (1962, Ch. 6), and also Hayek (1960, Ch. 24).

Because of information problems the NHS strategy has major advantages – an institution motivated largely by equity can be successful because it goes with the grain of efficiency arguments. On the demand side, decisions about treatment are made by doctors, thus alleviating the effects of consumer ignorance; the problems of private insurance are resolved by abandoning the insurance principle even as a fiction; and treatment is largely free at the point of use, which reduces the externality problem and goes a long way towards eliminating the influence of the income distribution on consumption. On the supply side, doctors are not as a rule paid a fee for service, thus removing the financial incentive to oversupply. Health care is rationed partly by administrative means and partly by the NHS budget. Furthermore, if public production and allocation can be defended on efficiency grounds, it is legitimate to finance health care redistributively for reasons of social justice (Chapter 4:7.2). In theory, therefore, the strategy is feasible in both efficiency and equity terms.

The practice (section 4) is far from perfect. The NHS faces a shortage of resources; many hospital buildings are old; and there are waiting lists for non-urgent (and even some urgent) conditions. The distribution of health care by social class and by region is less equal than many people would wish; and there is room for improvement in the administration of the system. However, a good deal can be said on the plus side.

- The average quality of health care in Britain is good, in that health standards are not out of line with those in other countries.
- The NHS is cheaper than the health care system of any comparable country, and considerably cheaper than most.
- Doctors have no financial incentive to overprescribe and (partly because of this) patients generally trust their doctor.
- The variation in the quality and quantity of treatment by income level is smaller than in most other countries.
- Treatment is free whatever the extent and duration of illness; no-one is denied access because of low income; and no-one goes in fear of financial ruin.

The NHS thus has much to commend it; and many of its remaining problems could largely be resolved by giving it more resources and by gathering and using more and better information.

Its advantages notwithstanding, the NHS is not the only system of health care which makes sense, just as the governance of a country need not involve powers vested in a hereditary monarchy. But, like the Crown, the NHS is an institution which has served Britain well, is widely popular, and can be drastically changed only at considerable risk of throwing out the baby with the bath water. The study of health care in other countries shows that the adoption of a different system is likely to raise problems very similar to those of the NHS, and additional and more intense problems as well. 'Privatisation' (whatever its proponents mean by the term) will not solve old problems, and is likely to create new (and probably larger) ones. To imagine otherwise (to put it no more strongly) is naive dogmatism of the highest order. My preferred reform for Britain, therefore, is to keep the NHS; the principle should be retained, and the system improved within the existing strategy along the lines suggested in section 5.

However, the political economy and the structure of the medical profession in many other countries make it unlikely that they would readily adopt a system of public production. This is especially true of the USA with its tradition of private markets. For them the mixed public/private arrangements described in section 5 might be a more satisfactory solution. The Canadian model of publicly funded, privately produced health care has much to offer; and a system based on regulated health maintenance organisations buttressed by income transfers may offer an alternative. The crucial point is that any system of health care must constitute a genuine *strategy* – *ad hoc* tinkering is a guaranteed road to disaster.

Further Reading

For general discussion of the economics of health, see Stiglitz (1988, Ch. 11). On the nature of health care, including problems with insurance, see Arrow (1963) (the classic article) and Culyer (1989, 1993). Abel Smith (1983) discusses the measurement of efficiency in health care. On the human capital approach see Grossman (1972), and for a critique and extension, Dowie (1975). The literature on production and cost functions is set out in Cullis and West (1979, Chs 6 and 7). Problems with medical insurance are discussed by Pauly (1974, 1986) and Culyer (1993).

The literature on valuing life is summarised by Cullis and West (1979, Ch. 9). The human capital approach to valuing life is exemplified by Dawson (1967) and the 'willingness to pay' approach by Jones-Lee (1969) and, more formally, by Acton (1973). Marin and Psacharopoulos (1982) attempt to make the latter approach operational. For critiques, see Mishan (1971) and Broome (1978), and for an overview, Jones-Lee (1976). For other attempts to quantify the benefits of health care, see Wagstaff (1991).

The case for market provision of health care is set out by Lees (1961), Seldon (1981), Friedman and Friedman (1980, Ch. 4) and Minford (1984b); for a critique, see Bosanquet (1983, Chs 11 and 12). On the role of giving the classic work is Titmuss (1970).

For discussion of health care in an international context, see Barr (1992), Enthoven (1989), Johnsson (1989), Ham *et al.* (1990), Hurst (1991), and Schieber *et al.* (1991). On the USA specifically, see Russell (1989) and Aaron (1991).

On the institutions of the NHS see Glennerster (1992, Ch. 10); though slightly dated, Aaron and Schwartz (1984) give an excellent comparison of health care in Britain and the USA, including a brief institutional summary. On cost containment, see Abel Smith (1984, 1985). For assessment over the decade to the mid-1980s, see Le Grand *et al.* (1990).

The detailed financial institutions of health care are analysed by Glennerster (1992, Ch. 10). Le Grand (1982) discusses distributional aspects, and Le Grand and Robinson (1984) look at the possibility of privatising different parts of the welfare state.

A thoughtful (and sympathetic) discussion of reform within the NHS is by Enthoven (1985). The 1989 reforms are set out in UK Department of Health (1989a); for critiques, see Barr *et al.* (1989), Culyer *et al.* (1990), Day and Klein (1991), Enthoven (1991), Glennerster (1992, Ch.10), Green (1990) and Klein (1989).

Chapter 13
Education

Man is the most versatile of all forms of capital. [Irving Fisher, 1930.]

All that is spent during many years in opening the means of higher education to the masses would be well paid for if it called out one more Newton or Darwin, Shakespeare or Beethoven. [Alfred Marshall, 1842–1924.]

Introduction

The introductory discussion in Chapter 12:1 (which should be (re)read at this stage) applies equally to education. The role of the public sector in both finance and production is less clear-cut than with many types of cash benefits, particularly in the case of post-primary education. This chapter is concerned mainly with setting out the ground rules for policy analysis, rather than with asserting strong conclusions. The theoretical arguments are very similar to those for health care.

The rest of the chapter discusses the aims of the educational system (section 2), theoretical arguments about state intervention in pursuit of efficiency and equity (section 3), assessment of the British education system (section 4), the range of possible reforms (section 5), and major conclusions (section 6).

Institutions During the early part of the chapter little knowledge is needed of the institutions described in section 4.1. Education is compulsory to age 16. Primary (age 5 to 11) and secondary education (age 11 to 18) are provided publicly and without charge. There is also a small private sector. So-called further education is available beyond 16. For the most part these are all public-sector institutions funded by a mixture of central and local revenues. In contrast, university education is privately *produced* but largely (though to a decreasing extent) publicly *financed* out of central and local funds.[1]

---

[1] The distinction between public and private production and finance is set out in detail in Chapter 4:6.

2 Aims

2.1 Concepts

Social welfare is maximised through the pursuit of economic efficiency[2] and social justice (or equity). The importance of education in people's lives should not obscure its economic dimensions. Resources devoted to education cannot be used for other purposes. If we spent nothing on education, children would all be illiterate; if we spent the whole of national income on education, there would be no food or health care. The optimal quantity clearly lies somewhere between – in principle where the value gained from the last unit of education is equal to the marginal value which would be derived from the alternative use to which the resources involved could be put. This is the quantity X^* in Figure 4.1.

Efficiency in this sense must apply to the totality of resources devoted to education (the macro efficiency aim in Chapter 1:2.2), and also to the division of resources between different types and levels of education (the micro efficiency aim), so as to produce the optimal quantity, quality and mix.

The concept of equity is more elusive (see the discussion in Chapter 12:2.1). To sidestep some of these difficulties equity will be defined as a form of *equality of opportunity*, as described in Chapter 6:3.1 (especially equation (6.18)). This does not mean that individuals can necessarily obtain as much education as they want. However, it implies that if individuals A and B have similar tastes and ability, they should receive the same education, irrespective of factors which are thought to be irrelevant, e.g. income. This definition of equity has at least the merit that it apportions scarcity in a just way.

Once we have decided the efficient level of production of different types of education and their equitable distribution, the remaining question is how education should be financed. This is an issue of vertical equity discussed in Chapter 4:4.1. It was argued in Chapter 4:7.2 that if, for example, education is allocated efficiently by the market then equity aims are generally best achieved through income transfers. But where education is publicly produced and allocated for *efficiency* reasons, it may be appropriate to finance it out of progressive taxation; if so, it is possible, though not inevitable (section 4.3) that in-kind transfers will redistribute from rich to poor.

2.2 Measuring Costs and Benefits

Measuring the costs and benefits of education raises similar questions to those raised by health care (Chapter 12:2.2), but even greater problems. As with health care, the cost side presents no insurmountable problems. We

---

[2] The concept of economic efficiency is defined in Chapter 4:2.1.

know the direct costs of the state educational system and its components (Table 13.1). The problem of apportioning overheads is broadly the same as for health care. In addition, for individuals past school leaving age, it is necessary to include an estimate of forgone earnings as a measure of the output lost by their withdrawal from the labour market, taking into account the wage they would have received and the likelihood of their finding a job.

There are three major sets of problems in measuring benefits: (a) the concept of a 'good' education; (b) the valuation of education; and (c) the causal links between education and individual productivity.

The nature of the maximand raises a number of problems. First, what precisely do we mean by a good education? Families have widely different views about subject matter, the role of discipline, the place of religion and its type (see Coons and Sugarman, 1978). Second, the *process* of education is only part of the output, the rest consisting of such factors as increased individual productivity and future utility benefits such as job satisfaction and increased enjoyment of leisure.

The valuation of improved education: as the previous sentence suggests (see the more formal discussion below), education has at least three types of benefit: consumption benefits (i.e. enjoyment of the educational process itself), output benefits and utility benefits. Merely listing them makes clear the measurement problems.

Causality: as discussed later more fully, the 'screening hypothesis' questions the causal link between post-primary education and increased individual productivity. Put another way, the hypothesis calls into question the output benefits of education.

The human capital model attempts to explain the demand for education in terms of its production and utility benefits. It is argued, in the case of the former, that an individual who acquires more education becomes more skilful and productive. This approach sees education as a form of investment, analogous to improving machinery. From the individual viewpoint, such investment is profitable to the extent that it increases future income by more than its initial costs (including forgone earnings). Empirically there is a strong correlation between an individual's education and his lifetime earnings (see Psacharopoulos and Woodhall, 1985, Ch. 3). The overall pattern summarised by Blaug (1970, p. 27) is that 'within a few years after leaving school ... better educated people earn more than less educated people; their advantage continues to widen with age and ... the favourable differential persists until retirement'.

Utility benefits arise because the individual may derive utility from the educational process itself (i.e. education might have consumption benefits in the present as well as investment benefits in the future). The individual return to education also includes non-money rewards like job satisfaction and the enjoyment of leisure.

To clarify the *individual* return to education, it is helpful to set out formally the individual investment decision. The initial assumptions of the simplest human capital model are:

1. Education raises the individual's marginal product in the future and therefore his future money income.

2. This increase in money income is the *only* benefit from education, i.e. we rule out consumption benefits and future non-money returns.

If B_t is the benefit to the individual from an extra year's education, and r is his personal rate of time preference, the *gross present value*[3] (GPV) to the individual of an additional year of education is

$$GPV = \frac{B_1}{1+r} + \frac{B_2}{(1+r)^2} + \ldots + \frac{B_N}{(1+r)^N} \qquad (13.1)$$

The *net present value* (NPV) is

$$NPV = \sum_{t=0}^{N} \frac{B_t}{(1+r)^t} - C_0 \qquad (13.2)$$

where C_0 is the cost of an additional year of education (including forgone earnings). The individual will continue to acquire education so long as $GPV > C_0$, i.e. up to the point where $NPV = 0$. This is the level of education Q_0 in Figure 13.1, where the marginal private value (MPV) of education is the marginal gross present value from equation (13.1), and the marginal private cost (MPC) is the cost of education to the individual.

Relaxing the second assumption does not change the flavour of the results. Consumption benefits reduce C_0 in equation (13.2), and non-money returns increase B_t in equations (13.1) and (13.2). Either phenomenon increases the quantity of education an individual will choose to acquire.

The screening hypothesis It might seem, therefore, that by measuring the money income benefits (though not the utility benefits) to the individual we can establish a lower bound on the production benefits of education. This is valid if we are prepared to assume that education is *causally* related to increases in individual productivity. This is the strong first assumption made above. In contrast, the screening hypothesis argues that education is *associated* with increased productivity but does not *cause* it (the large literature on this and other aspects of the economics of education is surveyed by Blaug (1976, 1985) and Glennerster (1993)).

The screening hypothesis argues, first, that education beyond a basic level does not increase individual productivity and, second, that firms seek high-ability workers but are unable, prior to employing them, to distinguish them from those with low ability. The problem is analytically similar to adverse selection in insurance markets (Chapter 5:3.2), or more generally

---

[3] For further discussion of cost–benefit analysis, see Stiglitz (1988, Ch. 10), Brown and Jackson (1990, Ch. 8), Cullis and Jones (1992, Ch. 6), Musgrave and Musgrave (1989, Ch. 9) or Mishan (1982).

Figure 13.1 *A simple human capital model of the individual decision to invest in health care/education*

to 'lemons' (Akerlof, 1970), in the sense that one side of the market has more information than the other. Individuals therefore have an incentive to make themselves distinctive by some sort of signal (Spence, 1973; Arrow, 1973b; Varian, 1984, Ch. 8). According to the screening hypothesis, higher education fills exactly this function: it gives a signal to prospective employers, which it is in the *individuals'* (though not necessarily in society's) interests to acquire. Just as an individual's good health may be due more to a naturally strong constitution than to medical care so, according to this view, is productivity the result of natural ability rather than post-primary education.

There are various counter-arguments. Where education includes professional training (e.g. medicine), there is a direct contribution to productivity. The strong form of the hypothesis also assumes that there is only one type of job. In practice skills and job characteristics are heterogeneous, so that it is necessary to match workers and jobs, giving education an additional social return as a matching device. Whether there is *some* validity in the hypothesis is an empirical matter. The verdict is undecided and likely to remain so, since individual productivity is determined in part by unmeasurable influences like natural ability and family background.

The conclusion from the individual viewpoint is that it is possible to measure the money income benefits (but not the utility benefits) *associated* with different levels of education; but the *causal* relationship is less clear. The screening hypothesis leaves the *individual* decision to invest unaffected, and so leads to the same result as the human capital model. But, to the extent that it is true, screening has profound implications for the *socially* optimal level of investment in education, to which we turn next.

External benefits[4] Setting the screening hypothesis to one side for the moment, education may create benefits to society over and above those to the individual in a number of ways. There is at least one strong external benefit. Education, to the extent that it raises an individual's future earnings, increases his/her future tax payments; in the absence of any subsidy, an individual's investment in education confers a 'dividend' on future taxpayers.[5]

Does education create external benefits over and above this tax dividend? It is part of the conventional wisdom (Le Grand *et al.*, 1992, pp. 74–6) that it does. *Production benefits* arise if education not only makes someone more productive, but also contributes to the productivity of others (if people learn the same word processing package, they contribute to each others' productivity as well as to their own). Individuals may become more adaptable and better able to keep up with technological change. The economic spin-offs of higher education and a more mobile educated population are relevant in this context. It is not surprising that much 'high tech' industry is concentrated round clusters of universities, e.g. Cambridge (Massachusetts) and Cambridge (England). Measuring these benefits is difficult, not least because it is hard to separate the effects of education from other determinants of productivity, such as natural ability and the quantity and quality of capital equipment.

Education may also have broader benefits. First, there are *family benefits*. Schools viewed as a child-minding institution can create output benefits by enabling parents to work in the market sector (thereby raising their output and earnings) or in the household sector (thereby raising their output but not their earnings). Schools can also create utility benefits by enabling parents to enjoy more leisure. The value of these child-minding benefits could in principle be measured by what parents would be prepared to pay a child minder.[6] Education may also create *cultural benefits* external to the recipient in at least two ways. A common cultural experience (music, art, literature) may foster communication generally, both at the time and in the future. In addition, there may be neighbourhood effects; the mechanics of taking children to school, parent–teacher associations, etc. bring people into contact and may foster shared attitudes locally. Education in this

[4] See Chapter 4:3.2 and/or the Appendix to Chapter 4, para. 15.
[5] This line of argument can be used to justify a subsidy for any type of investment which raises future income. That is precisely what usually happens through the tax system in the case of business investment.
[6] While education clearly creates family benefits, it is arguable whether such benefits are external. In a world where parents make voluntary decisions about their children's education and pay the full market price for it, no issue of externalities arises. Where education is compulsory and provided free, the issue is less clear-cut.

context can be regarded as part of the socialisation process, as a device which fosters social cohesion.

These effects, however, can go both ways. Education encourages questioning attitudes and so, it might be argued, can create negative cultural benefits (Grosvenor Square, Paris and Berkeley in 1968). If education raises expectations unduly, the result could be individuals who are discontented with their job, with possible ill-effects on their productivity.

The previous paragraph is intended merely as a caution against blindly *assuming* that education has positive external benefits. If there are potential costs as well as benefits, the issue must be resolved empirically. Again, however, measurement problems make definitive answer impossible. Estimates of the private rate of return to education are suspect because, of necessity, they omit all non-money returns (job satisfaction, enjoyment of life generally). Estimates of the social rate of return are doubly suspect: they omit non-money returns and (since no other procedure is possible) they also ignore the screening problem.

The externality argument is strong in presumptive terms, but wholly satisfactory empirical verification is still lacking. Because of the 'tax dividend' point there is an unarguable external benefit, but it is not possible to show how much.

If education (a) increases individual productivity and (b) creates external production benefits, then the amount of education chosen by an individual in a market system, Q_0 in Figure 13.1, will generally be less than the optimal amount, Q^*, an issue discussed in more detail in section 3.1. However, if the claims of the screening hypothesis are valid then education leads to (but does not *cause*) an increase in individual income, but does not raise output. In this case individuals may acquire *more* education than is socially efficient.

Rate of return studies, despite these difficulties, have attempted to measure the benefits of education. The rate of return to education, r_0, is that rate of interest which equates the present value of the stream of future benefits in equation (13.2) to the initial cost of acquiring an additional unit of education. In other words, r_0 is the rate of interest which reduces the *net* present value of additional education to zero. It is vital to distinguish the private rate of return (which determines individual decisions) from the social rate (which is the relevant variable for efficient resource allocation).

Psacharopoulos (1973, 1980) and Psacharopoulos and Woodhall (1985, Chs 3 and 5) report private and social rates of return to different levels of education across countries. Two conclusions emerge: the rate of return is highest for primary education, and then declines; and the private rate of return exceeds the social rate at all levels of education (mainly because in all countries education subsidies reduce costs to the individual but not to society). These results must be heavily qualified. First, they are based on *money* returns. No account is (or can be) taken of the consumption value of education, nor of its non-money returns. Where these factors are present, empirical estimates *understate* both private and social benefits to an unknown extent. Second, such estimates can measure only the *association* between education and earnings. But to the extent that the screening hypothesis is true the causal link is weakened, in which case the measured social (though not the private) benefits of post-primary education will be *overstated* by an unknown amount. The estimation of rates of return, in short, is a heroic undertaking.

The relationship between education and economic growth, for these and other reasons, remains unclear. The rate of growth of output in any country depends on the increase in the quantity and quality of its capital stock; on the increase in quantity and quality of its labour force; and on a variety of non-economic factors. Education affects only one of these, the quality of the labour force. The problem is to separate the quantitative effect of this variable given the influence of all the others. Despite a great deal of work, little progress has been made (see Psacharopoulos (1984) and Psacharopoulos and Woodhall (1985, Ch. 2) for surveys). About the only firm conclusion to emerge is the unsurprising one that no country has experienced a substantial degree of economic development without first achieving a level of basic literacy in a substantial proportion of its population (various estimates agree that 40 per cent is about the minimum for 'take-off'). Beyond this, little has been established, Denison's (1962, 1967 and 1969) monumental work notwithstanding.

3 Methods

3.1 Theoretical Arguments for Intervention 1: Efficiency

The arguments about the conformity of education with the standard assumptions in many ways parallel those for health care (see the discussion in Chapter 12:3.1), so discussion is brief.

Perfect information Do consumers of education have perfect information about the nature of the product (i.e. are indifference maps well-defined); about prices (i.e. do they know their budget constraint); and about the future? Knowledge of the nature of the product is certainly not perfect. Children (the immediate consumers) are not well-informed. In a market system decisions are therefore left to parents, at least for early education. But parental preferences can cause inefficiency in two ways: they might themselves have imperfect information; or they might not consider the child's best interests but those of the family as a whole, themselves included. The issue is further complicated because the notion of 'the product' in education is even more elusive than with health care. As discussed in section

2.2, the definition of what constitutes a good education varies enormously between families.

Such complexities can make rational decision difficult. In addition, consumers of education are likely to differ in the extent of their confidence and articulateness (the issue of unequal power). The result of these factors is inefficiency, though both its extent and direction (see Figure 12.1) are open to debate. But it is likely that imperfect information leads to underconsumption, particularly by the lowest socioeconomic groups (see section 3.2).

Solutions can take several forms. In contrast with health care, the market itself might supply information, e.g. advisory centres, or a 'Good Schools Guide' which included relevant performance indicators. But it can be argued that where children or their families have imperfect information and/or where families cannot be relied on to act in their best interests, there is an efficiency argument for intervention, particularly in the form of regulation. This would embrace mandatory school attendance (discussed below), and the establishment of minimum standards and inspection to ensure conformity with those standards. Only if the information problem is regarded as major is there an argument on this account for public production and allocation.

A second issue is the extent to which consumers or their families are well-informed about prices. If education were privately produced, this information would be provided by the market. But, as with health care, it should be remembered that improved knowledge of prices increases efficiency only where consumers are well-informed also in other respects. If intervention on efficiency grounds were thought necessary, it would take the form of publishing a list of school fees, or regulating them.

The problem of information about the future is minor. Parents know that their children will need education at least until minimum school-leaving age. In a market system they would make financial provision for their children's education out of current income, out of savings or, if they were uncertain of their future income or lifespan, by taking out an endowment policy the proceeds of which could be used to pay school fees in the future. Uncertainty (as opposed to poverty) raises no substantial problems in this context.

Perfect competition The proposition that the advantages of a competitive market for health care are contingent on perfect information was discussed in Chapter 12:3.1 and is equally applicable here. But the information problem is arguably less severe for education, so this section is not concerned with the desirability of competition, but with its feasibility. Two issues arise: the supply of education; and the availability through the private market of finance for education.

There is no reason why schools in cities should not act competitively.

But a rural school may have a local monopoly and, if run to maximise profits, would underprovide. The standard solution is price regulation (Chapter 4:3.2). Education finance raises different issues. From an efficiency viewpoint we do not normally worry if an individual cannot afford more than x units of a good. If a student cannot afford smoked salmon and therefore buys none, there are no efficiency implications. But if an individual cannot afford an adequate diet and suffers malnutrition then, as well as equity costs, there are efficiency losses in the form of external costs to others. Similar losses arise if an individual cannot afford to buy the socially efficient amount of education, e.g. basic literacy and numeracy. With perfect capital markets, children could finance their own education by borrowing against their future earnings. But capital markets are not perfect; students seeking to borrow money can usually offer only human capital as collateral, whereas lending institutions require physical capital or financial wealth. In a pure market system this would result in underconsumption, giving an efficiency (as well as a possible equity) justification for intervention. This could take several forms: the state could act as guarantor for loans made by private institutions to children for educational purposes; it could provide loan finance itself; or it might choose to subsidise education.

Market failures Education is not a public good;[7] nor does it generally face increasing returns to scale. But we saw in section 2.2 that education can create three sorts of external benefit: the 'tax dividend' argument relates to future tax revenues; production benefits relate to productivity and economic growth; cultural benefits include social cohesion. The strength of these effects is hard to measure, but they cannot on that account be ignored. Intervention can involve regulation in the form of compulsory attendance at school until age sixteen to prevent underconsumption (see the analogous argument for compulsory membership of an unemployment insurance scheme in Chapter 8:2.1); and an appropriate Pigovian subsidy (see the Glossary) could in principle achieve a similar effect.

3.2 Theoretical Arguments for Intervention 2: Equity

Horizontal equity relates to perfect information (to assist rational choice) and equal power (to enforce that choice). Both may be lacking for consumers of education. A major equity issue arises where these problems are greater for individuals in lower socioeconomic groups (which is likely if information is costly to acquire). Thus parents with little education may have less information than better-educated parents in making decisions about their children; in addition, they may be less able to make use of any information

---

[7] See the definition of public goods in the Appendix to Chapter 4, paras 13 and 14.

they do acquire. In such cases intervention may improve equity as well as efficiency.

Regulation would be concerned with the professional qualifications of teachers, minimum physical facilities, school attendance and, possibly, curricula. Where imperfect information causes underconsumption, a subsidy might be applied either to prices or to incomes. Income subsidies usually take the form of cash transfers, but education vouchers (section 5) can be thought of as a form of tied transfer; so too can student educational grants.

Where problems of inadequate information and inequality of power are serious, efficiency and equity may both be increased by public allocation and/or production, depending on two factors: whether the private or public sector is more efficient at producing education; and whether regulation of standards is more effective in one sector or the other. The issue is discussed in section 3.3.

Vertical equity concerns the extent to which education does or should redistribute from rich to poor. As discussed in Chapter 7:4, publicly provided education, subject to caveats, is redistributive if (rich) individual R pays more tax contributions to its costs than (poor) P where each consumes the same quantity, and also if R consumes twice as much as P but pays more than twice as much in contributions. The voting model in Chapter 4:4.2 offers an explanation of why this might happen. If R's utility rises with P's 'good' consumption (education for P's children) but falls with P's 'bad' consumption, we have a consumption externality of the sort described by equation (4.15). In those circumstances, it might be rational for R to offer an in-kind transfer of education worth £300, but to make a cash offer of only £100 (since P might spend the latter on 'bad' consumption). If the difference between the two offers is large enough, P might prefer the in-kind offer to the lower cash amount (see Figure 4.5).

Analogous to the arguments about health care, the rich may have an interest in the education of the poor for two sets of reasons. They might support transfers of education for reasons of efficiency/self-interest: a well-educated workforce might foster economic growth, and/or might reduce social unrest. This is the 'national efficiency' argument (Chapter 2:2.1) which gave rise to the Marxist interpretation of the welfare state (Chapter 3:5.3). Alternatively, rich individuals might care about the distribution of education for altruistic/equity reasons.

Thus efficiency arguments for public production and allocation may be reinforced by equity motives which make it politically easier to make transfers in kind. The rich may favour them for selfish or altruistic reasons; and, if the offer is sufficiently generous, the poor might also prefer in-kind transfers.

The voting model offers an explanation of why *some* transfer of education takes place. But is the amount transferred *optimal*? As discussed in Chapter

4:4.4, libertarians support in-kind transfers only as *voluntary* action by the rich, but not as a result of government failure in the face of coercive electoral behaviour by the poor (Chapter 4:5). They therefore argue that redistribution under the current system is greater than optimal. Many socialists support in-kind transfers for their own sake (particularly in the case of education) because they increase equality, and argue that redistribution is almost certainly sub-optimal.

3.3 Types of Intervention

Sections 3.1 and 3.2 discussed *why* the state might intervene. The next issue is *how* best it might do so. The theoretical arguments raised by education largely parallel those for health care. The main differences are that the problem of information (though not of equal power) may be less acute; that problems with private insurance are not relevant; and that the issue of imperfect capital markets (and probably also of external effects) is probably of greater importance.

Pure market provision (i.e. lines 1 or 2 of Table 4.2). Critics of public provision (see the Further Reading) ideally wish to see education produced, allocated and financed privately. But recognising some of the difficulties described earlier, their policy proposals (section 5.1) are of private production, with mixed public/private finance and some regulation.

The argument against market production and allocation of pre-university education is the failure of many of the assumptions necessary for market efficiency. Regulation can be justified by imperfect information and unequal power, and the presence of externalities and local monopolies. Subsidies can be justified by externalities, and subsidies or the provision of loan guarantees (or of loans themselves) by capital market imperfections. The issue of public production rests largely on the extent of information problems. It should be clear that a pure market system is likely to be highly inefficient, and also inequitable to the extent that knowledge, power and access to capital markets are correlated with socioeconomic status. Unrestricted market provision of pre-university education is theoretically implausible and, in practice, does not exist in any country.

Mixed public/private involvement (e.g. line 4(a) in Table 4.2). The issue is whether it is possible to devise an efficient and equitable package whereby the state regulates education and subsidises it wholly or in part, but where production takes place in the private sector. This is the way universities operate in many countries, and proposals to extend these arrangements to schools (e.g. the so-called 'voucher' schemes) are discussed in section 5.1.

Several ingredients are necessary for this approach to be efficient and equitable. The state would have to regulate education in one or more of the following areas: mandatory school attendance to some minimum age; the range of curricula; minimum qualifications for teachers; certification of schools (i.e. would an individual need permission to start a school?); inspection to ensure an adequate quality of service; and fee levels (i.e. should schools be allowed to charge what they liked?). Though the principle of regulation is accepted, commentators disagree as to how far it should go.

Subsidies to education may be justifiable for both efficiency and equity reasons. In a libertarian world, individuals pay for the private benefits they receive from education, but are subsidised to the extent that external benefits are thereby conferred upon others.[8] This degree of subsidy might, however, be insufficient. Individuals from lower socioeconomic groups might face imperfect capital markets; in addition they (and their families) might systematically have poorer information about the benefits of education and/or be reluctant to incur large debts. Any resulting tendency to under-consumption suggests a larger subsidy than the externality argument implies, and maybe a 100 per cent subsidy, at least for school education. Additionally, if the subsidy is only partial, it may be necessary on both efficiency and equity grounds for the state to provide loan capital.

Private production is likely to be efficient only if its quality is adequately monitored. Libertarians dispute this view, arguing that dissatisfied parents could move their child to another school, and also that if a private school has a bad reputation it will go out of business. The weakness of this line of argument is twofold. First, parents may not have sufficient information to realise that their child is being badly educated or, if they do, may not have the confidence to do anything about it. Second, education is not a repeatable experiment. It is true that a restaurant which provides bad service will go out of business; its former clients will have suffered nothing worse than a bad meal, and can spend the rest of their lives going to better restaurants. But the application of this argument to education makes an unfounded leap in logic. Education is in large measure a once-and-for-all experience; a child who has had a year or two of bad education may never recover. In addition, a child may face high emotional costs (changing friends, etc.) in changing school. A more apt analogy is a restaurant which gives unknowing customers food so bad that it might cause permanent ill-health.

Finally, private consumption decisions are likely to be efficient and equitable only if families have sufficient information, and if they use it in the child's best interests. The issue of whether the state or the family is better qualified to make educational decisions in the name of an individual child is controversial to say the least. Some parents, maybe disproportionately in the higher socioeconomic groups, are capable of more

---

[8] Note that this approach is logically incompatible with the screening hypothesis (section 2.2).

informed decisions than the state; others make poorer decisions. If the quality of parental choice is systematically related to socioeconomic status and the effect is strong, then private allocation can be argued to be less equitable than state allocation, irrespective of the balance of argument about efficiency. It is not surprising that the advocates of parental choice almost invariably belong to the higher socioeconomic groups.

Public production, allocation and finance (i.e. line 8 in Table 4.2). The question is whether public funding, together with public production and (to a large extent) allocation is less inefficient and inequitable than the sort of arrangements just described. The allocation issue should be argued on the basis of perceptions about imperfect information and social cohesion, and that of public production on whether it is, or is not, likely to be more efficient than the private market. These issues, we have seen, turn crucially on the answers to two questions. First, do parents *on average* make better or worse decisions than the state about their children's education? Second, if the quality of parental choice varies systematically with socioeconomic status, how do we weigh the relative claims of middle-class children and their parents to be allowed private choice, against those of children in lower socioeconomic groups, whose interests might be served better by the state? The answer to the first question is empirical. The answer to the second depends on one's political stance. Libertarians argue that state allocation interferes with parental freedom and therefore reject it. To socialists the aim of equality is paramount; the claim of children from poorer families therefore takes priority, and state allocation is preferred. Liberals try to recognise the claims of both groups. This involves a system either of public allocation which takes account of stated parental preferences (this is the way the system set up under the 1944 Education Act was supposed to work), or of parental choice subject to careful scrutiny.

The *a priori* arguments about the public/private provision of education are more finely balanced than those about health care.[9] But it is fair to say that the failures of the assumptions necessary for market efficiency are sufficiently strong to make public production, allocation and finance of school education a tenable strategy. To the extent that this is the case on efficiency grounds, it is appropriate to finance education redistributively for reasons of social justice (Chapter 4:7.2).

Finally, since education is not a homogeneous whole, it is necessary to ask whether the same answers apply to all types of education. For instance, should there be one set of answers for compulsory education and another for education beyond the minimum school-leaving age; should some types of education be free and others not; are market solutions more applicable

[9] It is therefore curious that in practice the educational systems of different countries vary much *less* than their systems of health care. In particular it is surprising from an *economic* point of view that school education in the USA is publicly produced, allocated and financed (i.e. line 8 in Table 4.2).

to higher education than to school education; should higher education be financed in part by loans and, if so, on what terms should the loan be made or repaid? These and other questions are discussed in section 5.

4 Assessment of the British Educational System

4.1 Institutions

This section describes the operation of school education (public and private) and higher education under the four heads of Table 4.2, i.e. production, the individual consumption decision, finance, and the aggregate production decision. The efficiency and equity of the system are assessed in sections 4.2 and 4.3, respectively.

Public expenditure on education approximately doubled in real terms between 1960 and 1976, when it reached a peak of nearly 7 per cent of gross national product. The increase was partly the result of increased birth rates in the late 1940s and mid-1960s; partly because expectations about educational standards rose; and partly because of the relative price effect.[10] Thereafter, expenditure fell as a share of GDP, and from 1979/80 until the late 1980s fell in absolute terms (Glennerster and Low, 1990).

THE OPERATION OF SCHOOL EDUCATION

The ultimate responsibility for education in England and Wales[11] rests with the Secretary of State for Education, who is responsible for the Department for Education, and is accountable to Parliament. Under the Department are 104 Local Education Authorities (LEAs) which are the major employers of teachers and are the main providers of educational services. Since 1988, schools may opt out of LEA control and be under the direct jurisdiction of the Department for Education. In addition, a few schools are run by voluntary bodies, mostly religious, which provide the premises, but where most of the running costs are paid by the LEA. There is also a small private sector. Universities are not part of the legal framework established by the 1944 Education Act (Chapter 2:5.1), nor are they the responsibility of LEAs. They are therefore discussed separately.

Schools are inspected by a central body, Her Majesty's Inspectorate of Schools, which is entirely independent of the Secretary of State and the Department for Education to ensure that standards are policed without political influence. The inspectorate, which visits schools and publishes reports, is an important source of quality control by a central body of a

---

[10] See Chapter 12, footnote 9.

[11] The Secretaries of State for Scotland and Northern Ireland are responsible *inter alia* for education in those countries. The Scottish educational system differs in some important respects from the system described here.

locally provided service, a feature almost entirely lacking in the NHS.

The production of primary, secondary and further education All children
receive a compulsory primary education from age 5 to 11, usually at schools
provided by LEAs. Teachers are employed and paid on an agreed national
scale by the LEA. The total current cost of primary education in England
in 1992/3 (Table 13.1) was about £5.2 billion.

Secondary education is provided by LEAs, and to a limited extent by
opted-out schools, for children aged 11 to 19 years. It is free, and compulsory
up to 16 years. Most teachers are employed by the LEA and paid on an
agreed national scale. Total current public expenditure on secondary education in England in 1992/3 (Table 13.1) was £6.5 billion.

There have been a number of major controversies over secondary education: the introduction of comprehensive schools; raising the school-leaving
age; the reforms introduced by the Education Reform Act 1988; and the
issue of private education. The 1944 Education Act (Chapter 2:5.1) established three types of secondary school for children of different ability:
grammar schools (for the academically able), technical schools, and secondary modern schools (whose aim was to give a general education only
until the minimum leaving age). The choice of school for any particular
child was based on an examination at age 11 (the so-called 'eleven plus').
This structure was severely criticised. It was said to favour middle-class
children, to be unequal by geographical area, and to waste the talent of
many children from lower socioeconomic groups (on the last point, see the
Newsom Report (UK Central Advisory Council for Education, 1963)).

The debate over comprehensive schools was a political football for nearly
20 years. In 1965 LEAs were asked to submit plans for the reorganisation
of secondary education on comprehensive lines. By 1980 all had done so,
though in some cases only after considerable pressure. Many commentators
argued that the fierce controversy over the best way of organising schools,
despite its importance, obscured even more important educational objectives
like the content and quality of teaching, especially in rapidly changing and
increasingly technological times (for further discussion, see Glennerster and
Low (1990, p. 60 *et seq.*)).

The minimum leaving age was raised from 15 to 16 in 1972. The move
was not a total success, partly because many LEAs had been too much
taken up with the issue of comprehensive schools to devote sufficient
thought to the development of curricula suitable for an extra year of
schooling for non-academic adolescents. A second problem was the size of
many of the new schools, and the fact that the new system had not had
time to resolve its teething troubles. As a result, secondary education went
through a difficult time in the 1970s. Matters improved somewhat thereafter
as experience with the new system grew, and the number of children of
school age declined.

Table 13.1 *Education and science, UK, 1992/93 (est.) (£ million)*

CENTRAL GOVERNMENT OWN EXPENDITURE			
Schools	350		
Higher and further education	3195		
Science[a]	1054		
Other	264		
Total own expenditure		4863	
CENTRAL GOVERNMENT GRANTS			
TO LOCAL AUTHORITIES		3084	
TOTAL PROGRAMME		7947	
EXPENDITURE IN SCOTLAND, WALES			
AND NORTHERN IRELAND		1923	
TOTAL EDUCATION AND SCIENCE			9870
LOCAL AUTHORITY SPENDING[b]			
Schools			
Under-fives	815		
Primary	5168		
Secondary	6503		
Special schools	846		
Other	1259		
		14,591	
Higher and further education		2199	
Mandatory student awards		2059	
Administration and inspection		1146	
Other		582	
Total current spending		20,577	
Total capital spending		732	
Local authority spending in Scotland, Wales			
and Northern Ireland		3982	
TOTAL LOCAL AUTHORITY SPENDING			25,291
CENTRAL GOVERNMENT OWN SPENDING[c]			6786
TOTAL CENTRAL AND LOCAL SPENDING[d]			32,077

Sources: UK (1992d, Tables 1 and 2); UK (1992f, Introductory Table and Table 9.4); UK (1992g, Cm 1916, Figure 1.03 and Appendix 3); UK (1992h, Tables 1.1 and 12.2).

Notes: [a] Including postgraduate awards.

[b] Estimated by inflating the 1991–2 figures by 5 per cent.

[c] Includes expenditure in Scotland, Wales and Northern Ireland.

[d] Total public spending on education comprises central government spending and local authority spending. The latter derives from three main sources: transfers from the central Department of Education and Science (£3084 million in 1992–3 as the table shows); transfers from the central Department of the Environment (£30,800 million – see Table 7.1); and local authority own revenue (£14,200 million – see Table 7.1).

The Education Reform Act 1988 introduced far-reaching changes, though 'the length and depth of the consultation process was insultingly brief' (Glennerster *et al.*, 1991, p. 393). The Act included the introduction of a national curriculum (discussed below as part of the individual consumption decision), the possibility of schools opting out of LEA control (discussed under the finance of education), local management of schools (also discussed under the finance of education), and new procedures for establishing the size of schools (for description and assessment, see Glennerster (1992, Ch. 12); Glennerster *et al.*, (1991)).

The heated debate over the years concerning the place, if any, of private education is discussed below.

The third arm of the statutory system is further education, which covers the vocational, cultural, social and recreational needs of everyone over school-leaving age who is not in full-time secondary or higher (i.e. university) education. The system provides education relevant to people's working lives, and is often dovetailed with the practical training provided by industry (see Glennerster, 1992, Ch. 12). A second function is to provide for people's leisure. This involves a huge variety of courses, for many of which charges are levied. Since 1993, the funding of further education has been the responsibility of the central Further Education Funding Council.

This is not the place to discuss further education in detail, but one development in particular should be noted. A policy of rationalisation in the late 1950s culminated in a report (UK, 1966) which provided for polytechnics (which were then part of the LEA further education sector) to offer degree courses, leading to rapid expansion of degree courses by polytechnics, with standards supervised by a national body, the Council for National Academic Awards. Under the 1988 Education Reform Act, polytechnics became independent of LEA control, receiving their funding from central government through a new body, the Polytechnics and Colleges Funding Council. From 1992 the funding of universities and polytechnics was unified under the Higher Education Funding Council, and the technical distinction between university and polytechnic abolished. In the rest of the chapter, polytechnics are discussed alongside universities as part of a unified higher education sector.

Finally, LEAs have several additional functions. They are permitted (but not compelled) to provide nursery education for pre-school children; they are obliged to provide special education for physically and mentally handi-capped children; and they have a number of ancillary responsibilities including welfare activities like free school milk and school meals.

The individual consumption decision   We have seen that primary and secondary education is provided free, with compulsory attendance to 16 years. A child normally attends a local primary school, and then proceeds to a local comprehensive school. Exceptionally, if a child is particularly gifted and/or with adequate financial resources, he/she will go to a private school. Children who are less able or with lower expectations usually leave school at 16 with no, or few, qualifications. A bright child will take the

General Certificate of Secondary Education in six to eight subjects, both arts and sciences, at about the age of 16. The next step on the educational ladder is so-called Advanced Level ('A' level), taken at about the age of 18, often in a narrow range of two or three related subjects. Universities do not normally admit students unless they have two or three 'A' levels.

Issues of individual choice arise in at least three ways. First, there is the decision to continue education beyond the minimum leaving age. This is the individual investment decision discussed in section 2.2, to which we return later. Second is the extent to which parents can choose which school their child attends. The 1944 Education Act allowed parents considerable discretion, but often the exercise of this choice conflicted with attempts by the LEA to balance numbers and quality of intake across schools within their jurisdiction. Partly to assist parental choice, the 1988 Education Reform Act gives the Secretary of State for Education wide powers to determine the size of each school.

A third aspect of individual choice is the extent to which parents and their children have (or should have) any influence over the LEA and the teaching profession in the running of schools. After many years of debate (see UK, 1977), legislation in 1986 extended parental representation on schools' governing bodies. A major change under the 1988 Education Reform Act was the introduction of a national curriculum, which applies to all state schools. The Act specifies 'attainment targets', i.e. 'the knowledge, skill and understanding which pupils of different abilities and maturities' are expected to have reached by the ages of 7, 11, 14 and 16. The national curriculum specifies programmes of study to achieve these targets, and also establishes a system of assessment.

Finance   UK education spending is about the middle of the range by international standards (Glennerster, 1992, Table 12.2). Public spending is shared in roughly equal proportions by schools on the one hand and further and higher education on the other. The total cost of primary and secondary education in England in 1986/7 was £11.7 billion (Table 13.1). Since virtually no charges are levied, basic education is financed almost entirely by the state out of tax revenues. In the past (in contrast with the NHS), most expenditure took place at a local level. Since 1991, however, the bulk of the income of LEAs has derived directly from central government (Table 7.1).

Opting out: one of the major changes introduced by the Education Reform Act 1988 was the ability of schools to opt out of LEA control. The decision depends on a proposal to that effect by the school's governing body. A simple majority of a ballot of parents, together with the approval of the Secretary of State, can take the school into what is called 'grant maintained status'. The school is then run by an independent governing body, responsible to the Secretary of State, with representatives of parents, teachers and the locality. The school's property is transferred from the LEA to the governing body, which also becomes the employer of the teachers. By mid-1991, about 220 schools out of a total of about 29,000 had opted out. Such schools are the responsibility of the central Department for Education rather than of the LEA, and are centrally funded out of resources recovered from the LEA. Opted-out schools are thus funded directly by central government.

In addition to public funding, either from the LEA or central government, there are limited sources of non-governmental finance: to a small extent schools are able to raise funds through their own efforts to pay for 'extras'; and the voluntary sector contributes to the cost of some schools.

Local management of schools is another of the major changes introduced by the 1988 Education Reform Act. Under the Act, each LEA must establish a formula under which funds are allocated to individual schools (in effect, LEAs had always done this, but the Act requires the formulae to be approved by the Secretary of State). Once the budget is allocated, individual schools can manage their current resources as they wish (the same freedom does not apply to capital spending). Thus any pupil signing on at a state school triggers a payment by the LEA to the school, which it is free to allocate as it wishes. The scheme was introduced in most of the country in April 1990. For further detail of opting out and local management of schools, see Glennerster (1992, Ch. 12).

The aggregate production decision (i.e. setting budget limits). In the past most decisions about educational expenditure were a more or less complex mix of decisions at central and local levels. Since 1991, however, the bulk of education finance, and hence the aggregate production decision, has been a central government responsibility (Glennerster, 1992, Chs 4–6).

PRIVATE SCHOOLS

Alongside the state sector a small number of private schools (often confusingly called 'public' schools) provide day and residential education. In the mid-1980s, private schools catered for 6.4 per cent of all school children, absorbing about 14 per cent of current school expenditure. The existence of a private sector is controversial. Private schools over the years have come under heavy attack. It is argued that they cream off scarce resources of academically gifted children and teachers, and of finance, making it difficult for comprehensive schools to maintain high standards; and, through their hold on recruitment to key positions, that they perpetuate and accentuate economic and social divisions. The counter-arguments centre on their high quality, the beneficial effects of competition, and the freedom of parents to choose their favoured education.

The finance of private education is complex. The bulk of private schools' income comes from fees, though many have income from private endowments and from appeals to former pupils. They also benefit from tax expenditures. Their charitable status gives them tax advantages such as exemption from paying VAT on fees, and exemption from income tax and corporation tax. Private schools can also receive direct assistance. Under the 1902 Education Act so-called direct grant schools received financial assistance from central government if they took a specified number of children from the state sector. This scheme was abolished in 1976. Since 1981, under the assisted places scheme, central government has paid for a small number of gifted children from the state sector to be educated at a private school. By the late 1980s there were about 35,000 beneficiaries (for further discussion, see Glennerster and Low (1990) and Glennerster (1992, Ch. 12)).

HIGHER EDUCATION

Higher education comprises what used to be two sets of institutions: polytechnics (discussed earlier) and universities. Polytechnics, formerly under LEA control, became independent entities under the 1988 Education Reform Act. Universities have always been independent, self-governing bodies. The formal distinction between universities and polytechnics disappeared in 1992.

The individual consumption decision for British students is relatively straightforward. Universities offer places on the basis of academic qualifications, usually 'A' levels. Students do not have a right to a place; they are carefully selected, and the drop-out rate is low by international standards. The tuition fees of any UK undergraduate at a UK university are paid out of public funds, though the possibility of 'top-up' fees, which would not generally be publicly funded, was under discussion in the early 1990s.

British students in full-time higher education are also eligible for a maintenance grant. The system was introduced in 1962 after a government inquiry (UK, 1960) (the Anderson Report). The full grant varies according to where the student studies and whether or not he/she continues to live in the parental home. The grant is generally means-tested on parental income. Students from the best-off families receive no grant at all, though their fees are tax-funded. Where students receive less than the full grant, parents are expected to make a parental contribution to bring the student's income up to the full grant.

In its early days the system worked well, and the grant was sufficient for its purpose. Over the years, however, public spending constraints, in combination with increasing student numbers, put the system under increasing pressure. Partly to cope with these, a top-up loan scheme was introduced in 1990. The grant system is assessed later (see section 4.3, point 11) and the loan proposal discussed further in section 5.2. Higher education is thus subsidised for British students. Overseas students are not generally eligible for public funding. They have to pay tuition fees (which rose sharply in the early 1980s) and must finance their own living expenses.

Finance With hindsight, the 1960s were something of a golden age for British higher education (the same was true in the USA). The Anderson Report (UK, 1960) advocated a generous maintenance grant; and the Robbins Report (UK, 1963), whose importance to higher education has been compared with that of the 1944 Education Act to general education, recommended a sharp expansion in the number of students in higher education. As a result, higher education in the 1960s and early 1970s was generously funded out of tax revenues, with few questions asked. Universities received much of their funding from central government through the University Grants Committee (UGC), which divided government grants between universities, acted as a general link and a buffer between the Department of Education and the universities, and formulated a national policy for higher education. The Committee was an attempt to reconcile public funding with the independence of universities. The good times drew to a close in the mid-1970s. The UGC, alongside grants for universities, gave increasing 'guidance' as to how the money should be spent. In addition, taxpayer support declined in real terms.

The Education Reform Act 1988 strongly increased the extent of central planning of higher education. Universities are now funded by the Higher Education Funding Council (HEFC). Whereas the UGC had given *grants* (albeit with increasing strings attached), the HEFC awards *contracts*. Universities make 'bids' to teach N students at a price of $£X$, each. As a result, they receive public funds from three main sources: income from the HEFC; students' tuition fees, which are channelled through LEAs; and research funds, channelled largely through the Research Councils. Universities also increasingly earn money in the private sector: from the fees of privately funded UK students and of overseas students; from privately funded research activity; from a variety of commercial activities; and (in some cases) from their own endowments.

A further change, introduced in 1991 (UK Department of Education and Science, 1991), is the separation of the funding of teaching and research. Under the previous system, funding to higher education institutions covered academic salaries on the assumption that some 40 per cent of an academic's time was for research. Thus research was financed jointly with teaching. By funding teaching separately, higher education can be expanded at a cost per additional student place of around half the previous average cost. Research funding is to be concentrated on a small number of institutions with the best research records.

In 1992/3 direct public expenditure on universities in England was £4.3 billion, including £2.1 billion on mandatory student awards (Table

13.1), of which about £1.3 billion was on fees and £0.8 billion on maintenance grants.

The aggregate production decision has grown considerably more complicated. In the 1960s and early 1970s, somewhat to oversimplify, higher education institutions decided how many students they wished to admit, and the state made available sufficient funds to make this possible. There was a major expansion of the university sector in the aftermath of the Robbins Report; at the same time, as discussed earlier, there was an increase in degree opportunities at polytechnics. After 1975 these policies were to some extent reversed, or at any rate halted. By 1990 only about 15 per cent of the relevant age group started full-time degree courses. As well as restricting the *size* of the higher education sector, there was also growing government influence on its *composition*. What used to be virtually untied transfers to higher education have become increasingly like tied grants. Higher education is subject not only to the ordinary government budgetary process on aggregate expenditure, but also to an element of control over the disposition of public funds. For further detail, see Cave and Weale (1992).

In short, the production and finance of school education in the state sector are both public (approximating line 8 of Table 4.2). Private schools approximate to line 1, with elements of line 2. In the higher education sector, production is private and finance for British students largely public (line 2), but with increasing elements of line 4(b).

4.2 Assessment 1: Efficiency

The measurement problems discussed in section 2.2 make the assessment of efficiency problematic both for macro and micro efficiency (see the Glossary). Much of the argument is therefore of necessity *a priori*. Efficiency advantages and disadvantages are much more finely balanced than in the case of health care – one person's 'sign of a civilised society' is another's 'violation of individual freedom'. Discussion of efficiency therefore concentrates on seven areas, with no attempt at division into advantages and disadvantages.

   1. *The individual consumption decision* is substantially influenced by the state and the teaching profession both centrally and locally. Children must attend school until they are 16; the LEA (see the Glossary) can influence (or in some cases control) the choice of school; and state schools are bound by the national curriculum. These constraints mitigate to some extent the problem of imperfect information, but at the expense of consumer sovereignty. As discussed earlier (section 3.3), there is heated debate about

whether the LEA or the parent is better able to make decisions in the child's interests (see Green, 1991).

2. *Primary and secondary education is free*, or nearly so, and higher education is subsidised. Such subsidies avoid the externality problem and have equity advantages; but according to the screening hypothesis (section 2.2) they are inefficient, at least for university education.[12]

3. *Macro efficiency: schools.* There is little hard evidence about whether or not too few resources are devoted to education, save that it absorbs about the same proportion of national income as in most other industrial countries. A study of British secondary education by Blaug and Woodhall (1968) was severely qualified, as the authors make clear, by the measurement problems discussed in section 2.2. First, there is no single definition of the purpose of education, and so it is not possible to measure output unambiguously. Second, though the quantity of inputs (teachers' and pupils' time, buildings, equipment) can be measured, their quality is largely unmeasurable. Finally, it is not possible to relate the output to inputs. This is, first, because neither can be measured properly. Thus there is a tendency to measure output by the quantity of input, i.e. to assume that education is better simply because it costs more. It is thought, for example, that pupils do better if they are taught in smaller groups, although empirical evidence lends little support to this proposition. But even if output and inputs could be measured, there remains a second problem – that of establishing a causal relationship between the two. This brings us back to the screening hypothesis (section 2.2). Is an individual productive because he/she is naturally able, or because he/she has been well educated – and if both, what are the proportional contributions?

An early study of high school students in large American cities (Burkhead *et al.*, 1967) found that variations in test scores depended almost entirely on factors unrelated to the school system, e.g. family income and the character of the neighbourhood. A study of fundamental importance by Jencks (1972) reached two even stronger conclusions: that differences in educational inputs offered no explanation of differences in educational attainment; and that differences in educational attainment made no independent contribution to explaining disparities in income. These results, taken together, suggest that attempts to equalise the distribution of educational inputs may do little to reduce inequality. Not surprisingly, these conclusions were controversial, and led to further research (for a British study see Rutter *et al.*, 1979), but the issue remains unsettled. Are the Jencks conclusions a statistical artefact arising out of measurement errors, or are factors other than education the dominant determinants of pupil achievement? The issue is crucial to reasoned decisions about the volume

[12] And maybe also inequitable – see points 11 and 12, below.

of resources to be devoted to school education. For a survey of the evidence, see Hanushek (1986).

4. *Macro efficiency: higher education.* It is argued (Barr, 1989a, Ch. 1) that the British higher education sector is too small. In 1960/1 about 7 per cent of the relevant age group embarked on degree courses; 30 years later the figure was barely 15 per cent, far short of the comparable figure in most other industrial countries (see UK Department of Education and Science, 1988). Farmer and Barrell (1982) argue that this is inefficient (and also inequitable – see section 4.3, point 11). For instance, the earnings differential between graduates and non-graduates, though reduced by the post-Robbins expansion, is large by international standards. Such differentials, it is argued, are the result of entry restrictions to university education, with effects on graduate earnings comparable to the result of efforts over the years in the USA to restrict entry to the medical profession. This evidence, though no more than indicative, lends at least qualified support to the view that the British higher education sector is too small.

5. *Micro efficiency: schools.* Because of the measurement problems discussed in point 3, little can be said about the efficiency with which resources are divided between different areas of education. A variety of government reports on different parts of the system were mentioned in section 4.1. They ranged over primary, secondary, further and higher education; without exception all gave plausible and laudable reasons why more resources should be devoted to 'their bit' of the system. Measurement problems make it impossible on a quantitative basis to choose between them; and resource constraints and political realities make it impossible to implement all their recommendations. Criticism by the schools' inspectorate, however, carries weight because of its source. It was reported (UK Department of Education and Science, 1986) that many schools suffered shortages of equipment and neglected buildings, and that in some instances management was ineffective. This might be attributed in part to expenditure cuts (an issue of macro efficiency) – but micro inefficiency was also involved even if it could not fully be measured. One response to these problems, local management of schools, is too recent to be assessed, though early reports suggest that the reform is not without its problems.

6. *Micro efficiency: higher education.* A separate issue is the extent to which the higher education sector is subject to excessive central planning. The argument against present arrangements is that the division of public funds between different higher education institutions is centrally decided. Such a process is inevitably bureaucratic. The UGC came under increasing criticism: its decisions were attacked, and so was the way it made those decisions, with suspicions (rightly or wrongly) of arbitrariness and bias, i.e. both the outcome *and* the process were questioned. In addition, there was an increasingly burdensome paper chase. The UGC issued at least 40 circulars to universities each year, many of them asking questions which

required data to be collected. Such data collection was expensive, the more so since much of it was collected *only* because of UGC requests (for a fuller critique of the UGC mechanism, see Barnes and Barr (1988, Ch. 3)). Early experience with the Funding Councils suggests little improvement. Such an administrative burden might be inevitable if all other solutions were less efficient. As discussed in section 5.2, however, that is almost certainly not the case.

7. *Administrative efficiency.* There is some evidence (Lord, 1983) that the organisation and administration of the educational system could be improved. The switch to comprehensive schools is argued to have been less co-ordinated than it might have been. It is also argued that there was too little advance planning before the school leaving age was raised. At a more technical level, Knight (1983) argued that localities gather too little detailed cost data, and do not make the best use of the data they have.

4.3 Assessment 2: Equity

As discussed in Chapter 4:2.2 and 4:4.3, equity is hard to define, and depends in part on political perspective. Following section 2.1, horizontal equity is taken to imply that children A and B should have an equal *opportunity* (as defined in Chapter 6:3.1) to acquire an education of equal quality and duration, irrespective of whether, for example, A comes from a middle-class family and B from a low socioeconomic group. Equality of opportunity, as discussed in Chapter 6:3, does not necessarily imply equality of outcome for at least three reasons: A may be luckier than B; A and B may have different tastes where (and the proviso is crucial) both have perfect information; and A may be more 'able' than B, where such differences are not related to educational and other circumstances earlier in their lives.

8. *The role of income.* The intention of the 1944 Education Act and subsequent policies, including the implementation of the Robbins Report, was that access to education at all levels should not be constrained by family income. This aim has not been fully achieved for either schools or higher education. Though no fees are charged, school attendance still involves parental expenditure, e.g. on uniforms or sports gear (Bull, 1980); and many children leave school at 16 not because they want to or because they do not have the ability to proceed further, but because their family needs their earnings. It has been estimated (Piachaud, 1975) that the *absolute* costs of education for a child between 15 and 17 are higher for low-income parents. School education after age 16 (for which maintenance grants are very limited), like health care under the NHS, is not 'free', but imposes a cost in forgone earnings which bears disproportionately on the lower socioeconomic groups. This disproportion has major implications (discussed below) for university attendance.

9. *The distribution of school education by quality is unequal by social class.* Middle-class parents are better able to exercise choice within the state sector, and some increase their choice further by sending their children to private schools. At this point the conflict between equity and individual freedom is at its sharpest.

Some improvement has been sought. There have been attempts to direct additional resources towards primary schools in areas with a disproportionate number of disadvantaged children; and the mechanism by which funds are channelled from central government via LEAs to individual schools could assist such a process (Glennerster, 1992, Ch. 12). The move to comprehensive secondary schools was motivated mainly by a desire to increase horizontal equity. Whether these policies are desirable, and whether they go far enough, depends on the importance attached to the aim of equality and on how one weights the relative claims on scarce resources of children from more and less fortunate backgrounds.

10. *The distribution of school education by quantity is unequal by social class.* There are persistent inequalities both in educational expenditures (i.e. inputs) and in outcomes. As measured by public expenditure, a child from socioeconomic group 1 consumes on average about $1\frac{3}{4}$ times as much post-compulsory secondary education as a child from the lowest socioeconomic group (Le Grand, 1982, Table 4.1). This figure, as Le Grand points out, understates the true difference in consumption of educational inputs because children (mainly from socioeconomic group 1) attending private schools are not included. On the output side, the picture is similar. The children of better-off families disproportionately stay longer at school and obtain more and better qualifications than their less fortunate confrères.[13] For a recent study of the causes of these results, see Bennett *et al.* (1992).

11. *The distribution of higher education is unequal by social class.* Reasons cited include poorer information about the value of education, lower-quality schools, and the cost in terms of forgone earnings of post-compulsory education, all of which help to explain why children in lower socioeconomic groups leave school earlier. The nature of the 'A' level system and the workings of the grant system itself (discussed shortly) are also said to reduce working-class attendance (for further discussion of causation, see Barr and Low (1988) and Glennerster and Low (1990, p. 65 *et seq.*)). The results are clear. Farmer and Barrell (1982, p. 20) report that of the $12\frac{1}{2}$ per cent of the relevant age group attending university in 1979, only 22 per cent came from a working-class background (see also Universities Central Council on Admissions, 1985); in the USA in 1972, 36 per cent of the age group attended college, of whom 42 per cent came from less advantaged backgrounds.[14]

---

[13] This *could* be entirely the result of differences in tastes – a point to which we return shortly.

[14] It has been argued that the fact that the UK figure of 22 per cent remained largely unchanged by the Robbins expansion represents a considerable *success* in equity terms, in that one would expect a large and rapid expansion of the university system, *ceteris paribus*, to *reduce* working-class attendance as a proportion of the total.

The role of the system of tax-funded maintenance grants in this context should not be overlooked. The intention was to pay students from poorer backgrounds a grant to cover living costs, thereby, it was hoped, removing impediments to access to higher education. The system, in reality, has three major problems.

(a) Student poverty: the real value of the grant fell under all governments, so that its purchasing power in 1989 was 25 per cent below its 1962 level. The full grant became too low to support a typical student; and many students did not receive even that limited amount because the parental contributions system worked badly. About half the students entitled to a parental contribution received less than the assessed amount, and the shortfall was substantial; students whose parents gave less than supposed, received only £53 of every £100 of assessed parental contribution (Barr and Low, 1988, pp. 31–4). As a result, one student in 13 in the early 1980s remained below the poverty line, even when income from all sources was included (ibid., Table 6).

(b) Parental wealth: though many students are poor, their parents, typically, are not. Le Grand (1982, Table 4.1) found that public expenditure on university education for the average student from socioeconomic group 1 was $5\frac{1}{2}$ times that for a child from the lowest socioeconomic group. As with school education this figure understates the true difference. His data relate to public expenditure, which is *lower* for the child of a wealthy family because he/she receives a lower maintenance grant. It follows that on average a child from a wealthy family is *more* than $5\frac{1}{2}$ times as likely to go to university. Barr and Low (1988) report that, compared with the population at large, students are twice as likely to come from high-income families (the top 40 per cent), and over three times as likely to come from the highest incomes (the top $12\frac{1}{2}$ per cent).

(c) The cost of the system: when account is taken of tax-funded tuition fees and the maintenance grant, the UK taxpayer makes one of the largest contributions to students of any country (UK Department of Education and Science, 1988, Chart 6). The grant system is thus expensive. This, it is argued, has kept the higher education sector in Britain small, since the taxpayer cost of expanding the system is high. The grant system, far from increasing opportunity, can be regarded as an *impediment* to expansion. Since the higher socioeconomic groups tend to do better in any race for scarce resources (see Le Grand, 1987b), it should not be surprising that the class gradient in higher education attendance is steep.

How should these findings be interpreted? Several issues arise. First, the difference *could* in principle be caused entirely by exogenous differences in tastes and abilities, in which case no issue of inequality arises.[15] A person would be brave (or foolish) to argue that this is the whole explanation. But to the extent that it is part of the story, a simple observation of outcomes tends to overstate inequality. Second, if this inequality is genuine, should we be concerned about it? Is education the engine of economic prosperity or the plaything of the rich? If the former, it is appropriate to be concerned about its distribution on efficiency as well as equity grounds. If the latter (i.e. if the screening hypothesis holds), post-compulsory education may have no *social* benefits, thereby diminishing the importance of the efficiency question. But since education confers *private* benefits, its distribution, if inequitable, remains a proper concern. Third, it is necessary to remind ourselves that a different system of education would not *necessarily* be more egalitarian. As with the NHS, it is not enough to argue that the present system is imperfect; it is also necessary to suggest an alternative which will do better. If none can be found, egalitarian goals must be pursued by other means.

These caveats notwithstanding, it is hard to resist the conclusion that the distribution of education is influenced by inequalities in society. Individuals from less fortunate backgrounds have less information about the value of education, and less of the *savoir faire* necessary to make the best use of 'the system'. They have lower incomes, and are therefore less able to afford the earnings forgone by continuing education. Nor should it be forgotten that education is an investment which, like all investments, takes time to pay off; but the pursuit of long-run goals requires *hope*; and hope, too, is distributed unequally by social class. The expectations of children are formed largely on the experience of their parents, whose lives may give little encouragement to long-run optimism. For all these reasons, children from low-income families tend to receive education of a lower quality, and to avail themselves of a smaller quantity. There is inequality in education, and the inequality is much greater than in health care.

12. *Redistributive effects of the educational system.* We have seen (Chapter 7:4.2 as qualified by Chapter 7:4.1) that education is financed progressively even if (rich) individual R consumes (say) twice as much education as (poor) individual P, so long as R (or his/her parents) pays more than twice as much as B in the taxes which pay for education. For the system as a whole, educational expenditure on a child of a family in socioeconomic group 1 (henceforth for short a 'rich' child) is about 50 per cent higher than for a 'poor' child, i.e. one in the lowest socioeconomic group (Le Grand, 1982, Table 4.1). Thus the system is financed progressively if on average the tax contribution towards education of an individual in the highest socio-

---

[15] See Murphy (1981) for discussion from a sociological perspective. He sums up the issue neatly: 'though no necessary relationship exists between class *disparity* in education and class *inequality* in education, educational commentators have conventionally taken the existence of one to indicate the existence of the other' (p. 182, my emphasis).

economic group exceeds that of someone in the lowest by more than 50 per cent. As with the NHS (see the discussion in Chapter 12:4.3) this is likely if we are prepared to assume that education is financed out of taxation generally – i.e. that if all public expenditure on education were withdrawn, there would be, for example, a reduction in income tax, or an equi-proportionate reduction in all taxes, rather than a reduction of a regressive tax.

In contrast with the NHS, however, matters cannot be left there. The picture for different parts of the educational system must be discussed; and so must its intergenerational impact. The ratio of public expenditure on 'rich' children to 'poor' for education as a whole is about 1.5. For secondary education after age 16, for further education and for university education, the ratios are approximately 1.75, 3.5 and 5.5, respectively (Le Grand, 1982, Table 4.1). It is possible, subject to the caveats in the previous paragraph, to argue that post-compulsory secondary education might still be pro-gressive; but the finance of further education is at best proportional, and that of universities almost certainly regressive. A similar conclusion was reached, for similar reasons, by Hansen and Weisbrod (1969 and 1978) (see also Pechman, 1970) for the heavily subsidised system of public higher education in California.

The regressivity of university finance is compounded by noting that education, more than health care, has intergenerational aspects. One of the main conclusions of Atkinson *et al.* (1983) is that nearly half of their sample of poor people came from poor parents. In part, this is because children of poor parents tend to have lower-quality education, and less of it. Thus the taxes of poor families contribute to consumption by the rich of a university education which helps to keep them rich.

5 Reform

Section 5.1 looks at four sets of reforms for schools: radical privatisation; voucher schemes; possible improvements within the existing system; and early assessment of the 1988 Education Reform Act. Section 5.2 discusses voucher proposals and student loans for higher education.

5.1 School Education

Radical privatisation Section 3.1 discusses the failure of many of the standard assumptions.[16] *A priori* we would therefore expect an unrestricted private market for school education (i.e. line 1 or 2 in Table 4.2) to be

---

[16] I.e. the assumptions necessary for the market to allocate efficiently – see Chapter 4:3.2, or the Appendix to Chapter 4, paras 6–17.

inefficient for technical reasons (section 3.1), and also inconsistent with widely held views of social justice (section 3.2). Complete privatisation offers no solution, and so it is not surprising that no advanced country has a system of school education which remotely approximates a pure private market. It is more useful to ask whether any mixed public/private package offers hope of improvement, considering separately the school and university systems.

Voucher schemes for school education   The idea is that parents receive an education voucher for each of their children, i.e. a form of tied grant which can be 'spent' by parents at a school of their choice. There are many variants (see the Further Reading), but Bosanquet (1983, Ch. 12) distinguishes two archetypal schemes.[17] The Friedman (1962) proposal (see also Maynard, 1975) has three defining characteristics. First, the value of the voucher is the average cost of a place in a state school, or a proportion of that cost. Second, 'topping up' is allowed (i.e. if the voucher failed fully to cover fees, parents could top it up out of their own pockets). Third, parents and schools are unconstrained: parents can spend the voucher at any school, public or private, and schools have complete freedom in their choice of pupils and organisation of waiting lists.

Jencks' (1970) scheme is very different. The basic voucher covers the full average cost of state education. Topping up is not allowed, but low-income parents receive a compensatory increment to the basic voucher, thereby diverting resources to schools with disproportionate numbers of children from poor backgrounds. Schools where demand exceeds supply are constrained in that they must allocate at least half of the available places at random. The Jencks' scheme, consequently, has more of an equalising effect on expenditure. Both Friedman and Jencks are concerned with consumer sovereignty and efficiency, but Jencks' scheme places more emphasis on distributional goals.

The essence of the voucher idea is that education is at least in part produced in the private sector, with intervention to increase efficiency and equity by subsidy (i.e. the voucher) and regulation (e.g. compulsory school attendance, minimum standards and, in some schemes, restrictions on topping up and the allocation of places). The Friedman scheme is therefore a mixture of lines 1 and 2 of Table 4.2 (because parents can choose their child's school, and are free to top up the voucher) and line 4(a) (since education up to a certain age is compulsory). The Jencks scheme is a combination of line 2 and line 4(b), the latter because the 'no topping-up' rule imposes a constraint on total output.

Voucher schemes, it is argued, increase efficiency, enhance consumer sovereignty, and reduce the risk of political indoctrination. Parents choose

---

[17] See Blaug (1984, pp. 161–5) for a more detailed breakdown of different voucher options.

their child's school; education is privately produced and competitive, so that schools are responsive to parental demand; and voucher schemes avoid the present (arguable) inequity whereby parents who send their children to private schools receive no tax relief in respect of costs from which they thereby relieve the state system.

To opponents of voucher schemes, their efficiency advantages are debatable and their equity effects almost certainly deleterious. The efficiency issue, as we saw in section 3.1, hinges on whether parents are sufficiently well-informed to police the standards of their child's school and, if not, whether a publicly organised inspectorate will be more effective with public or private production. In equity terms, it is argued that voucher schemes will increase inequalities in the distribution of education (both quantity and quality) by social class (though less so in the case of a Jencks type of scheme than under the Friedman proposals). Vouchers might well have advantages for middle-class families, but only at the expense of less well-informed choices by lower socioeconomic groups. The equity issue therefore turns on the relative weight given to the claims of the two groups. Finally, voucher schemes are criticised because privately produced education is likely to reduce social cohesion.

Empirical evidence is scant. There has been one small, short-lived and inconclusive experiment with vouchers in the USA (see Bosanquet, 1983, pp. 167–70; Blaug, 1984), and one feasibility study in Britain (Kent County Council, 1978). According to Bosanquet, 'voucher schemes have not shown a robust Hayekian will to evolve. They have not been a socially selected institution which has grown' (1983, p. 170).

Possible improvements within the existing system The strategy of public production, regulation and finance (line 8 in Table 4.2), at least for school education, is common to all industrialised countries. The evidence on the efficiency of the British system is scant (section 4.2), so discussion of reform is concerned mainly with equity. The first issue is that imperfect information arises differentially by social class. Partly as a result, the *quality* of school education varies with socioeconomic status. Attempts to increase the information available to working-class parents are unlikely to have much impact. A more plausible approach, where disadvantage is geographically concentrated, is to strengthen efforts to increase the resources available to primary and secondary schools with disproportionate numbers of disadvantaged children. There is also discussion of the use of quasi-markets which fall short of vouchers (see Glennerster (1991) for a survey of the arguments).

The information problem is also one of the causes of the unequal distribution of the *quantity* of education (see Bennett *et al.*, 1992). In addition to better information, children from poor families might be induced to consume more education by a grant, probably income-related, for those who continue with education/training after the minimum school leaving age.

The 1988 Education Reform Act Since the reforms are in their early stages, it is possible only to comment on the proposals rather than the outcome (for further discussion, see the references in the Further Reading, especially Glennerster *et al.* (1991) and Glennerster (1991)). Four changes, in particular, require discussion: the national curriculum, local management of schools, opting out, and the role of competition.

The *national curriculum* can be viewed in at least three ways. According to the first view, it exemplifies a centralising tendency and interferes with the individual/family consumption decision. As discussed earlier, there is little agreement about what constitutes a 'good' education, so that the family is best at making choices about a child's education. Schools wishing to experiment, which was possible under the old system subject to *local* agreement, now require *central* agreement from the Secretary of State. The only parents with real freedom are those who can afford private education (private schools are not bound by the national curriculum). The national curriculum, according to this view, reduces efficiency, equity and individual freedom.

A second view is that the national curriculum increases equality of opportunity by spreading best practice. The assessment targets are outcome measures against which school performance can be measured. Where a school does badly, positive discrimination could be used to raise the standards of the lowest achievers.

A third view, which draws on the experience of other countries, is that the national curriculum politicises education achievement, since politicians will not like to see large numbers of pupils failing the tests. 'If politicians can influence the unemployment figures, why not assessment standards?' (Glennerster *et al.*, 1991, p. 396).

Local management of schools: as discussed earlier (section 4.2, point 6) in the context of higher education, the argument for decentralised management is that it improves efficiency. Local managers have better information than managers at the LEA or the Department for Education. In addition, if management is central, information flows become distorted by local managers in an attempt to maximise their freedom. Empirical evidence from the USA (Chubb and Moe, 1990) supports the view that decentralised schooling systems produce better results, measured in terms of educational outcomes. There are therefore grounds for hoping that local management of schools will improve efficiency.

Opting out, according to one view, is a device to improve the freedom of schools. The argument is that parents and governors, through their ability to opt out, have countervailing power in the face of inefficient LEA governance. However, opted-out schools are controlled by central government in broadly the same way as would occur under the LEA, so that it is not clear how much additional freedom would actually result.

A second view is that opting out is a Trojan Horse to bring in vouchers. Schools receive a per capita grant; and parents, in theory at least, have the right to choose their child's school. As Glennerster *et al.* (1991, p. 396) point out, this is a short step from genuinely independent schools financed by vouchers. The route to such reform would be twofold: to encourage large numbers of schools to opt out; and then to allow genuine independence.

The counter-argument (view 3) is that opting out is a device to centralise control of schools. The policy, it can be argued, was designed to break LEA control of schools. A bureaucratic theory of government (Chapter 4:5) predicts that once the Department for Education has acquired control of schools it will be reluctant to let it go; and the argument is reinforced by the reluctance of the Treasury to hand large sums of taxpayer money to independent private institutions. According to Glennerster *et al.* (1991, p. 397), 'the potential powers handed to a centralist government are disturbing'.

The role of competition: one of the main thrusts of government policy in the late 1980s, in health care as well as education, was to separate the production of services from their finance (i.e. to separate demand from supply), in pursuit of the efficiency advantages of competition. With education, as with health care, optimism should not be uncritical. Problems include imperfect consumer information on the demand side, and local monopoly on the supply side. In addition, Chapter 12 discussed at length the problems which arise when private medical insurers attempt to screen out all but the best risks. Glennerster (1991) points out that a similar problem arises with education. He observes that the socioeconomic background of pupils remains empirically the best predictor of pupil performance. In a competitive environment, schools will therefore compete to enrol children from higher socioeconomic backgrounds in order to maximise their performance measured in terms of educational outcome (a key indicator in attracting new parents). Just as medical insurers seek potentially healthy clients, schools seek potentially high-achieving pupils. Such competition causes inefficiency; and by restricting the choices of children from poorer backgrounds, it is also inequitable.

5.2 Higher Education

VOUCHERS FOR HIGHER EDUCATION

The problem As discussed in section 4.2, point 6, central planning does not foster efficiency in higher education. One approach to decentralised funding is the voucher mechanism. As applied to higher education, the government would largely stop giving money to *institutions* (i.e. universities) and would instead give it to *students*. Universities in the early 1990s received about £3000 per year for teaching each non-science student; the government could instead give each student a fee bursary worth £3000, and universities would then compete for students. Two overarching questions arise: how capable are students of making informed choices; and how appropriate is competition to higher education? The following is only a brief summary of the arguments (for fuller discussion, see Barnes and Barr (1988, Chs 1, 5 and 6); on the demand for higher education generally, see Pissarides (1982)).

Students as consumers   Are students sufficiently well-informed to be able to make rational choices? There are several reasons why the answer for students in higher education might be different than for parents of school children. First, information is available, and more can be made available (note that the number of universities is much smaller than the number of schools). Second, the information, for the most part, is sufficiently simple for the student to be able to understand and evaluate it. Third, the student has time to acquire the information he/she needs, and time to seek advice. It should be noted, fourth, that students make choices already. Though the matter is controversial, it can be argued that the assumption of well-informed (or potentially well-informed) consumers holds for higher education much more than for school education.

In addition to making choices to maximise their individual welfare, are students more capable than central planners of making choices which conform with the needs of the economy? The little available evidence suggests that they are. Research connected with the Robbins Report (UK, 1963) showed the difficulty of trying to project medium-term manpower needs. To illustrate the point anecdotally, in Canada in the early 1990s the graduates in greatest demand were those with degrees in philosophy, since one of the leading edges in information technology was 'fuzzy logic'. Philosophy departments in Britain at the time were under serious threat from the central planners.

Consumer sovereignty can therefore be regarded as a more useful instrument for higher education than for schools.

The role of regulation   Universities are not the conventional firms of economic theory: they do not make a homogeneous product; they do not seek to maximise profit; and the 'product' is not well-defined. To argue against unconstrained competition, however, does not imply that the only answer is central planning. A more appropriate policy is regulation. First, should some subjects be protected? Subjects like accounting, law and economics can look after themselves. On the other hand, classics or music, if protection were thought necessary, could be protected by issuing vouchers tied to the study of those subjects. Institutions could be protected similarly. Thus for reasons of regional balance there could be vouchers tied to, say, the Scottish universities.

Second, would competition degrade the quality of higher education? One way of guarding against any such tendency would be to monitor quality and publish the results. There is a clear regulatory role for a government or para-governmental body to ensure the prompt publication of accurate performance data. Once published, such data would enable potential students to vote with their feet (see Cave *et al.*, 1992).

Intervention is possible also in pursuit of distributional goals. It would be possible (and, I would argue, highly desirable) to offer larger vouchers to students from poorer backgrounds (for the use of vouchers, more generally, as a redistributive device, see Le Grand (1989b)).

The vouchers mechanism allows intervention to foster both educational and distributional objectives. The degree of competition is a policy variable; different answers are possible for different subjects; and the system can be as strongly redistributive as desired. In the case of higher education, there is a strong case for replacing a planning mechanism by one where funding remains largely (though not wholly) public, with production organised through consumer sovereignty and regulated competition.

STUDENT LOANS[18]

Problems Higher education has three sets of problems. The system is too centrally planned (section 4.2, point 6); as just discussed, reform possibilities include a move towards a regulated market mechanism. The system is also too small (section 4.2, point 4), and with a heavy class bias (section 4.3, point 11). Reform is therefore needed to bring about expansion and improved access. The grant system is not the answer. Substantial expansion of higher education via that route would be expensive in public expenditure terms, ruling it out under a Conservative government; and its expense and regressivity would rule it out under a Labour government, given other public spending priorities such as nursery schools, education for the 16–19 age group, and the NHS.

This section discusses how student loans might help, discussing in turn the arguments against mortgage-type loans; the UK government scheme introduced in 1990; and an alternative set of proposals which, it is argued, contribute more to expansion and improved access.

Mortgage loans are organised like a mortgage or bank overdraft, i.e. repayments are related to the size of the loan, the interest rate and the repayment period, but not to the income of the individual borrower. Income-contingent repayments, in contrast, take the form of a fraction of the individual borrower's subsequent income. They can take two generic forms.

---

[18] The arguments in this section are set out in more detail in Barr (1989a, 1991).

- With *income-contingent loans* repayment ceases once the loan plus interest has been repaid; thus no-one repays more than he/she has borrowed.
- With a *graduate tax*, repayments continue for life, or until retirement. High-earning graduates may therefore repay more than they have borrowed.

Because of major capital market imperfections facing potential student borrowers, mortgage loans create problems on both sides of the market. On the demand side, they are risky from the student's viewpoint and so are likely to deter applicants, particularly from disadvantaged backgrounds. This is inefficient because it wastes talent, and inequitable because it reduces intergenerational mobility.

It is sometimes argued (UK Department of Education and Science, 1988, Chart J) that people from lower socioeconomic groups will borrow to buy a house, so why not to buy a degree? Apart from the tax advantages, when someone buys a house (a) he knows what he is buying (since he has lived in a house all his life), (b) the house is unlikely to fall down, and (c) at least until the early 1990s, the value of the house is likely to go up. When people borrow for a degree (a) they are imperfectly informed about the nature of the product (particularly if they come from a family with no graduates), (b) there is a high risk (or at least a high perceived risk) of failing the degree outright, and (c) not all degrees carry a high rate of return. More generally, though the *average* private return to a degree is positive (UK Department of Education and Science, 1988, Annex D), there is a considerable variance around it. For all three reasons, borrowing to buy a degree is considerably more risky than borrowing to buy a house, and the risks are likely to be greater for people from poorer backgrounds and for women.

On the supply side, long-term loans are risky also to the lender. There is no collateral (contrast the case of lending for house purchase). Since slavery is illegal, the private sector will make long-term unsecured loans only with a government guarantee, which would be costly. A second form of risk to the lender is asymmetric information, in that students are better-informed than lenders whether they aspire to careers in financial markets or the arts.

Because the guarantee is expensive, total lending will be strictly policed, creating the sorts of supply-side constraint discussed in section 4.3, point 11. There are also high administrative costs, particularly for more risky students. Lending institutions have to keep detailed records of each borrower. The cost of chasing repayments is also substantial, the more so because the loan is unsecured.

Friedman (1962) was very clear about these capital market imperfections, in particular the riskiness of student loans (e.g. the absence of any security). He pointed out that

[t]he device adopted to meet the corresponding problem for other risky invest-

ments is equity investment plus limited liability on the part of shareholders. The counter-part for education would be to 'buy' a share in an individual's earning prospects; to advance him the funds needed to finance his training on condition that he agree to pay the lender a specified fraction of his future earnings. [1962, p. 103.]

On that basis he advocated loans from government, in return for which

[t]he individual ... would agree to pay to the government in each future year a specified percentage of his earnings in excess of a specified sum for each £1000 that he received ... The payment could easily be combined with payment of income tax and so involve a minimum of additional administrative expense. [p. 105.]

Thus Friedman, starting from the benefit principle (i.e. he who benefits should pay), ends up advocating a graduate tax (in the sense described above). A different approach starts from a predisposition towards free, tax-financed education, abandoning that model only because of its regressiveness when applied to higher education. Glennerster *et al.* (1968, p. 26) point out that

in the United Kingdom, higher education is now financed as a social service. Nearly all the costs are borne out of general taxation ... But it differs radically from other social services. It is reserved for a small and highly selected group ... It is exceptionally expensive ... [And] education confers benefits which reveal themselves in the form of higher earnings. A graduate tax would enable the community to recover the value of the resources devoted to higher education from those who have themselves derived such substantial benefit from it.

The conclusion is that the benefit principle and the ability-to-pay approach, despite their very different starting points, lead to identical policy prescriptions – income-contingent repayments.

The government loan scheme Loan schemes are common in other countries (Barr, 1989a, Ch. 3, 1991; Johnstone, 1986); indeed, Britain was an outlier in having no such scheme. The UK scheme (UK Department of Education and Science, 1988) was introduced in 1990 with the objective of reducing the taxpayer cost per student. Under the proposals, students take out a loan to supplement the maintenance grant; the grant is frozen until student support comprises 50 per cent grant and parental contribution, and 50 per cent loan. The loan bears a zero real interest rate, and is repaid in (usually) ten instalments (i.e. mortgage-type repayments), suspended for those earning below 85 per cent of the national average. Students borrow Treasury money, but in the original proposal both the issuing of the loan and the collection of repayments were to be administered by the banks.

The scheme has strategic flaws. First, for the reasons just discussed, mortgage-type loans are likely to harm access. Second, the original proposal was that students borrow Treasury money, with repayment collected by the banks. Both legs were misspecified. First, a loan scheme in which students borrow Treasury money yields no public-sector savings in the short or medium term, when students are borrowing in large numbers, but few are yet making repayments. Second, the administrative costs of a completely new repayment system run by the banks are high, eroding most of the long-term savings. The Government admitted (*Hansard*, Written Answers, 24 July 1989, col. 441) that the scheme produced no cumulative net saving for at least 25 years. Even that figure was an underestimate, in that it omitted any interest charge on the cumulative deficit over those years. Thus the scheme yielded no savings for a long time, and hence freed no resources for expansion; at the same time it risked harming access. Even in its own terms the scheme failed to achieve any desirable objective.

Nor was the scheme liked by the banks, which were not prepared to assume the administrative costs associated with a completely new repayment mechanism, and which were concerned about relations with their prospective best customers. For both reasons the banks contemplated participation only if repayments were collected by an arm's length institution, the Student Loans Company, owned jointly by the banks, whose costs would be met by government. The result was a strange beast: a private-sector, publicly funded quango.[19] In December 1989, however, after a year of discussion with government, the banks withdrew, and the government decided to run the Student Loans Company itself. The scheme came into effect in 1990.

The national insurance loan scheme An alternative proposal (Barnes and Barr, 1988; Barr, 1989a, b) was designed with the explicit objectives of expansion and improved access. Its key characteristics are:

- The loan would supplement, but not wholly replace, the maintenance grant.
- The loan would bear a real interest rate of 3 per cent.
- Repayment would take the form of an addition to the individual's national insurance contribution (NIC); an indexed loan equal to half the maintenance grant could be repaid by a graduate with average earnings over 25 years by a 1 per cent addition to the NIC.
- The additional repayment would be 'switched off' once the individual had repaid the loan plus interest. The scheme thus offers a genuine loan in which no-one would repay more than he/she had borrowed.
- Because repayments (a) bear a realistic real interest rate, and (b) are secure, it is possible for the money students borrow (subject to a partial Treasury guarantee) to come from the private sector.

The scheme has various advantages.

- *Expansion and access* are enhanced. Income-contingent repayments do

[19] Quasi autonomous non-governmental organisation.

not discourage applicants; and low earners, women working in the home, and unemployed individuals are automatically protected.

- *Administration* is simple and cheap because it 'piggy backs' on to an existing system, and uses a well-established tax base.
- *Security of repayment*: defaults are minimal. NICs are hard to evade; and, because they give title to future benefits, there is little *incentive* to evade. Security also facilitates repayment over an extended period, thus allowing a low repayment rate. Since the asset is long-lived, this arrangement is efficient. Secure repayment also facilitates private-sector funding.
- *Private-sector funds*: the possibility of funding loans largely from the private sector opens up the possibility of *immediate* public expenditure savings, thus freeing resources for expansion and proactive measures to improve access.
- *Micro efficiency is enhanced*: the scheme gets round the worst of the capital market imperfections, and hence allows individuals to borrow against their future earnings. In addition, individuals pay at least something in recognition of the private benefits of higher education, but are subsidised to the extent of the external benefit conferred on others.
- *Reduced dependence on parental contributions*: if part of student support came from a loan, more or less compulsory reliance on parental contributions would decline. If a sufficiently large loan facility were available, it would be possible for students, if they wished, to be entirely independent of their parents.

6 Conclusion: Education

Many of the assumptions necessary for market efficiency fail, the main problems being imperfect information, imperfect capital markets and external effects. From an equity viewpoint, the most important problem is that knowledge about the operation and value of education is likely to be correlated with socioeconomic status. Substantial public involvement is therefore essential (section 3.3), although, because the information problem is less acute than with health care, the theoretical arguments about public production (as opposed to regulation and finance) are rather more finely balanced. It is therefore not surprising that no advanced country has a system of school education which even remotely approximates a pure private market. State school systems universally are publicly regulated and financed; they are also all publicly produced. To the extent that this strategy is valid on efficiency grounds, it is legitimate for education to be financed in accordance with distributional goals (Chapter 4:7.2).

The practice of education in Britain is far from unblemished. The conclusion on the efficiency of the system is that we simply do not know (section 4.2); and because measurement problems are so intractable (section 2.2) it is unlikely that it will ever be possible to collect the information necessary to produce definitive answers. From an equity viewpoint, the educational system is less egalitarian than the NHS. There is strong (many would say irrefutable) evidence that the rich receive higher-quality school education and make considerably more intensive use of the system, particularly of higher education. The latter difference cannot be explained entirely by differences in tastes and ability. Additionally, though it can be argued that about four-fifths of educational expenditure is financed progressively or proportionately, the finance of the university sector is almost certainly regressive. For this sector at least, the hopes of the founders of the welfare state have not been met.

The performance of the educational system is thus more mixed than that of the NHS. But its critics have to show not that it is less than wholly efficient or equitable (which is not in dispute), but that a more market-oriented solution would do better. So far as school education is concerned, opponents of the broad thrust of existing arrangements have (to put it no more strongly) yet to prove their case. The advocates of a mixed public/private system of school education offer only limited evidence in support of their views. The efficiency effects of vouchers for schools are unclear *a priori* and not proven empirically. In equity terms they are likely to increase inequalities in the distribution of education, and in particular to benefit the middle class at the expense of lower socioeconomic groups (section 4.3).

A well-designed loan scheme (section 5.2) would enable higher education to expand, bringing it more into line with the size of systems abroad. Such a scheme can contribute to expansion (improving macro efficiency) and open up capital markets facing students (a micro efficiency gain). Loans can also improve equity, both because expansion improves the chances of working-class attendance and by reducing the regressivity of higher education finance. Loans, however, are not a complete answer to the problems of UK higher education. The regressivity of university finance has two roots: the extent of tax finance; and the fact that few children from a working-class background go to university. Loan schemes tackle the problem by altering the system of finance, which deals with the first root but does less to eradicate the second. Increasing university attendance by working-class children requires not only expansion of higher education, but also, and importantly, improvements in the equity of the school system.

The essential first step towards equality of opportunity is thus to reduce inequalities in the quantity and quality of school education by social class in the ways described in section 5.1. But there might be limits to the extent to which this can be achieved solely within the confines of the educational system. To the extent that inequalities in education are the result of broader inequalities, progress in the former will depend in part on improvements in the latter. International comparison suggests that the British record in education, in contrast with health care, leaves considerable room for improvement.

Further Reading

The case for market provision of education is set out by Lees (1961), Seldon (1981), Friedman and Friedman (1980, Ch. 6), and Minford (1984b); for a critique, see Bosanquet (1983, Chs 11 and 12).

The best general book on the economics of education is Blaug (1970). For general discussion, see Stiglitz (1988, Ch. 15), and for an up-to-date survey, Glennerster (1993). On the vast literature on the theory of human capital and its application, see Blaug (1970, Ch.1) for an excellent introduction; the classic work is Becker (1975). The screening literature is surveyed by Blaug (1976, 1985) and Varian (1984, Ch. 8). For a survey of economic aspects of education, see Psacharopoulos and Woodhall (1985). See also the Further Reading on the theoretical literature on information problems at the end of Chapter 5.

Institutional and other aspects of the educational system are discussed by Glennerster (1992, Ch. 12). For the relationship (or lack of it) between educational inputs, educational attainment and the distribution of income, see Jencks (1972), Averch *et al.* (1972) and Hanushek (1986) in a US context, and Bennett *et al.* (1992) for a British study. Contrasting views of the British educational system and various voucher schemes are contained in Friedman (1962, Ch. 6), Jencks (1970), Maynard (1975), Friedman and Friedman (1980, Ch. 6) and Bosanquet (1983, Ch. 12); for a summary of the voucher issue and an assessment of practical experience, see Blaug (1984). For an assessment of the decade to the mid-1980s, see Glennerster and Low (1990).

The detailed financial institutions of education are analysed by Glennerster (1992, Ch. 12). Le Grand (1982) discusses distributional aspects, and Le Grand and Robinson (1984) look at the possibility of privatising different parts of the welfare state. On additional discussion of the class bias in educational attendance and attainment, see Le Grand (1987b).

The 1988 Education Reform Act is discussed by Glennerster (1991, 1993) and Glennerster *et al.* (1991). On the background to the late 1980s debate on British higher education, see Barnes and Barr (1988, Ch. 2) and Barr (1989a, Ch. 1). On international comparisons of loan schemes, see Woodhall (1983), Johnstone (1986) and Barr (1989a, Ch. 3). The government's loan scheme is set out in UK Department of Education and Science (1988). For critiques and an alternative, see Barr (1989a, b, 1991, 1993).

Chapter 14
Housing

An Englishman's home is his tax haven. [*The Economist*, 1979.]

1 Introduction

This chapter argues that housing is the least successful part of the welfare state, largely because (with the wisdom of hindsight) it is apparent that policy-makers blurred the distinction between aims and methods. In part by historical accident the post-war Labour government chose a method of achieving its health care objectives which broadly accords with the predictions of economic theory. It is therefore not surprising that health care in Britain, by and large, has worked well. Housing policy, in contrast, has gone wrong not because its aims have been inappropriate, but because historically methods were chosen which have been unable to achieve them. The resulting problems are entirely predictable. The present system misallocates housing. Poor people can be homeless or overcrowded. At the same time, owner-occupiers and people fortunate enough to occupy local authority housing face incentives to consume inefficiently large quantities, so that the system simultaneously creates overoccupation and underoccupation, and at the same time subsidises the rich. Starting *tabula rasa*, no-one would knowingly devise such a system.

The main questions are concerned with the efficiency and equity of different ways of organising the housing market. A number of important matters are not discussed, particularly inner city problems, the planning of land use (other than consideration in a general way of the importance of regulation), and private rental outside the scope of the 1977 Rent Act (on all of which see the Further Reading). The aims of housing policy are discussed in section 2. Section 3 discusses in principle whether housing as a commodity accords with the standard assumptions[1] and, where it does

[1] I.e. the assumptions necessary for the market to allocate efficiently – see Chapter 4:3.2, and/or the Appendix to Chapter 4, paras 6–17.

not, what type of intervention might be appropriate. The conclusion is that economic theory offers no strong arguments for public production of housing, and powerful arguments against general subsidies of house *prices* as opposed to subsidies of individual/family *incomes*. Section 4 assesses the practice, looking in particular at the inequities and inefficiencies resulting from past and present policies. This sets the scene for discussion in section 5 of possibilities for reform.

2 Aims

A Conservative White Paper (UK Department of the Environment, 1971) listed three objectives of housing policy.
 1. A decent home for every family at a price within their means.
 2. A fairer choice between owning a home and renting one.
 3. Fairness between one citizen and another in giving and receiving help towards housing costs.
 A subsequent Green Paper under a Labour government (UK Department of the Environment, 1977a, para. 2.16) added six further aims.
 4. ... A better balance between investment in new houses and the improvement and repair of older houses ...
 5. Housing costs should be a reasonably stable element in family finances.
 6. [Increased] scope for mobility in housing ...
 7. A reasonable degree of priority in access ... for people in housing need who in the past have found themselves at the end of the queue ...
 8. [The necessity to] safeguard the independence of tenants ...
 9. [The necessity to] ensure that the housing needs of groups such as frail elderly people, the disabled and the handicapped are met.[2]
 Various of these goals reappear, more recently, in UK Department of the Environment (1987a). It is helpful for subsequent discussion if some order is imposed on these objectives. Efficiency in the context of housing arises in three ways: the size and quality of the housing stock, tenure neutrality and mobility.

The size and quality of the housing stock must be efficient. Housing faces the same trade-off as, for example, health care: clearly it is inefficient to spend nothing on housing; equally, if the whole of national income were devoted to accommodation, there would be no resources for the production of food and health care. The optimal quantity lies somewhere in between – in principle where the value placed on the marginal unit of housing equals the marginal social cost of the resources used. This is the quantity Q^* in

[2] For further discussion of the goals of housing policy, see Hills (1991, Ch. 2) and, in a US context, Aaron (1981b, pp. 70–6) and Levine (1978).

Figure 14.1 (see Chapter 4:2.1, and the Appendix to Chapter 4, paras 2–4). Part of this aim is captured by objective 4, above.

Figure 14.1 *Efficiency in the housing market*

Tenure neutrality (captured by objective 2) exists when competitive markets leave individuals (on average and in the long run) financially indifferent between buying accommodation and renting it, with no artificial distortions (e.g. via the tax system) of their relative costs. An approximate example of tenure neutrality is the case of television purchase and rental in the UK. The concept, which has both efficiency and equity implications, is important and requires careful explanation (non-technical readers can skip the equations).

Formal analysis: consider the flow of housing services[3] (net of maintenance costs) $R_1, R_2, \ldots, R_N$ for a rational individual with a constant rate of time preference, r. The present value of the benefit stream is

$$PVB = \sum_{t=1}^{N} \frac{R_t}{(1+r)^t} \qquad (14.1)$$

To simplify, let $R_t = R$ for all t. Then in perpetuity[4]

---

[3] I.e the value placed by occupants on housing of a given quality/type, as measured by the annual rent they would be willing to pay. The concept of the flow of services from physical wealth is discussed in Chapter 6:1.1.

[4] The easiest way to prove equation (14.2) is to express the flow of benefits in continuous terms. Then

$$PVB = \int_0^\infty Re^{-rt}dt = -\frac{R}{r}\left[e^{-rt}\right]_0^\infty = \frac{R}{r}$$

For exposition of the present value formula, see Brown and Jackson (1990, Ch. 8), Cullis and Jones (1992, Ch. 6), Stiglitz (1988, Ch. 10), Musgrave and Musgrave (1989, Ch. 9) or Mishan (1982).

$$PVB = \frac{R}{r} \qquad (14.2)$$

and the individual will buy the house only if $R/r > P$ where P is the purchase price. On the cost side, consider the individual decision whether to buy the house outright, or to borrow P at the market rate of interest, i. Suppose, for simplicity, that for the duration of the mortgage he repays interest only (i.e. his repayments are iP per period); at the end he repays the principal. The present value of the stream of costs is

$$PVC = \sum_{t=1}^{N} \frac{iP}{(1 + r)^t} + \frac{P}{(1 + r)^{N + 1}} \qquad (14.3)$$

Assume that N is large (so that the second term on the right-hand side of equation (14.3) drops out); and that i and P are constant. Then

$$PVC = \frac{iP}{r} \qquad (14.4)$$

Equations (14.2) and (14.4) have been derived via assumptions which are purely analytical. At this stage two important *behavioural* assumptions are introduced. Assume, first, that the market for housing is competitive for both purchase (so that $PVB = P$ in equation (14.2)) and rental, so that R (the flow of housing services per period) equals the competitive market rent R_c at the margin. Hence equation (14.2) becomes

$$PVB = \frac{R_c}{r} = P \qquad (14.5)$$

The second assumption is that capital markets are perfect; thus $i = r$. Two important results follow. First, from equation (14.5)

$$\frac{R_c}{i} = P \rightarrow R_c = iP \qquad (14.6)$$

i.e. *there is an economic relationship between the market rent, R_c and the purchase price, P,* i.e. between the flow and the stock prices. Thus there is no artificial incentive to rent or buy. Second, from equation (14.4)

$$PVC = P \qquad (14.7)$$

Equation (14.7) shows that the cost of borrowing and the purchase price are equal; *a rational individual is indifferent between taking out a mortgage or making an outright purchase* – there is no artificial incentive to borrow.

Implications: equations (14.6) and (14.7) show that tenure neutrality requires two conditions: a competitive market for purchase and rental; *and* a perfect capital market, in the sense that mortgage finance should be available competitively and on a non-discriminatory basis. In practice, matters are complicated, *inter alia* by uncertainties about future rates of inflation, which may cause unforeseen variations in real interest rates and house prices. These factors make the relationship between purchase price, rent and borrowing costs more complex than equations (14.6) and (14.7) suggest. But the meaning of the condition remains unchanged – even in a world of uncertainty, tenure neutrality implies an undistorted economic relationship between purchase price and annual rent, and requires perfect capital markets.

Mobility (objective 6) arises out of the fixed location of housing. The issue does not occur with, for example, food. If an individual moves to another part of the country, he simply buys his food in a different shop. But he cannot take housing with him, nor buy it off a supermarket shelf. It is therefore important that the housing market is sufficiently flexible to prevent persistent excess demand – a desirable aim for many reasons, and in the context of mobility because excess demand could hinder or prevent an individual who lives in area A from taking a job in area B.

Turning to distributional issues, the definition of horizontal equity, as we have seen (Chapters 4:4.3 and 6:3.1), is elusive. For housing it can refer to a minimum standard, or to equality of cost, equality of subsidy or equality of final outcome. All are different, and all lead to different results. For present purposes, as with health care and education, horizontal equity is defined in terms of equality of opportunity and minimum standards.

Equality of opportunity, as defined in Chapter 6:3.1, refers to access to housing of at least some minimum standard, analogous to the implicit but widely accepted aim for food, that everyone should have a healthy diet such that no-one starves. Equality of opportunity applies in two ways: access to adequate housing generally (this is the 'decent home for every family' in objective 1, and also includes objectives 7 and 9); and access to different tenures, i.e. tenure neutrality expressed in objective 2. If the price of different tenures or access to capital markets favours the better-off, then issues of equity as well as efficiency arise.

Minimum standards (objectives 1 and to some extent 8) can be justified on efficiency grounds by imperfect information and by certain types of externality, and on equity grounds if information and power are systematically correlated with income (Chapter 4:3.2 and 4:4.3). They might also be necessary to protect children. There is considerable disagreement as to where the minimum standard should be set (see section 5.2).

Vertical equity   Once the efficient quantity/quality of housing and its equitable distribution have been decided, the remaining question is how housing should be financed. This concerns vertical equity (see the Glossary), expressed in objectives 3 and 5, and also in the second part of objective 1 ('at a price within their means'). The quotation is important. Vertical equity can be pursued *either* by reducing 'price' (e.g. health care) *or* by increasing 'means' (e.g. food). It was argued in Chapter 4:7.2 that in general the former is appropriate to achieve vertical equity only where there exist *efficiency* grounds for subsidy or for public production and allocation; in their absence, the latter policy (i.e. cash transfers) will generally contribute more to efficiency and social justice.[5] The extent of vertical redistribution will depend largely on one's political perspective (Chapter 4:2.2).

3 Methods

3.1 The Simple Theory of the Housing Market

One of the key characteristics of housing is its durability. A family of four may over its lifetime spend £200,000 on, say, food. But consumption, expenditure and (crucially) production take place on a day-by-day basis, so supply can respond fairly rapidly to changes in demand. It is possible to make a loaf which lasts for two days; but it is not possible to build a two-day house, e.g. out of cardboard.[6] Though the consumption of housing *services* occurs on a daily basis, the *stock* (i.e. the building itself) can last a lifetime. New building is therefore only a small proportion of the existing housing stock, and so total supply can increase only slowly (in Britain at an annual average of less than 2 per cent (Hills, 1991, Table 1.2)). Thus short-run supply is highly inelastic, even though it may be elastic in the long run. The best representation of the housing market is therefore by a disequilibrium stock-adjustment model.

The left-hand diagram in Figure 14.2 shows the market for the stock of housing; the right-hand diagram, the *flow* of new housing (i.e. net additions to the housing stock). No distinction is made between accommodation for rent and for owner occupation. The curve D_1 shows the demand for housing at different prices, given the prices of other goods, the level of income and its dispersion, and the size and demographic structure of the population. The curve SRS_1 is the highly inelastic *short-run* stock supply of housing. The curve S in the right-hand diagram shows the supply schedule for new housing as a function of its price, based on two simplifications. First, building activity empirically depends less on current prices than on

---

[5] Note the theoretical caveat in Chapter 4:7.2 that the optimal taxation approach can give a different result. The taxation necessary to finance income transfers may cause a substantial labour supply disincentive. If so, it may be possible to improve both efficiency and equity by subsidising the *prices* of goods consumed by the poor if (a) such goods are consumed only (or mainly) by the poor, and (b) the consumption of such goods is not strongly complementary to leisure. Since neither condition applies to housing, the argument, even as a theoretical proposition, is not of immediate relevance.

[6] Such dwellings do exist in some developing economies. But they are largely ruled out in industrial economies by prevailing attitudes, by legally binding minimum standards, and often also by the climate.

expectations about future prices (Robinson, 1979, Ch. 5); second, current completions depend on past decisions. The model at its simplest assumes that completions this period are a function of the stock price last period (Robinson, 1979; Muth, 1960; Whitehead, 1974). The net addition to the stock of housing in any period is total completions minus losses through depreciation and demolition.

Figure 14.2 *A simple stock-adjustment model of the housing market*

Consider a point of initial equilibrium in Figure 14.2. With demand shown by D_1 and stock supply by SRS_1 the total housing stock is Q^*. The price p^* serves two functions: it clears the market for the stock of housing; and it induces new building (q^* in the right-hand diagram) just sufficient to offset losses through depreciation. Thus the net stock of housing is exactly maintained, and the market remains in equilibrium. Now suppose that there is an increase in demand, shown by an outward shift in the demand curve to D_2. The stock price rises to P_1, so additions to the stock one period later rise to q_1 in the right-hand diagram. Since this exceeds the rate of depreciation q^* the net stock of housing increases, as shown by the new short-run stock supply curve SRS_2. The new stock price is P_2, lower than p_1 but still higher than the equilibrium price p^*. Net additions to stock therefore continue until the price returns to p^*. With demand shown by D_2 this occurs with a housing stock of Q^{**}. *Long-run* supply can therefore be represented by the curve LRS.

In practice, the market for a number of reasons is unlikely to converge smoothly to a new equilibrium. It is more realistic to think of the housing market as in continual disequilibrium as the result of random shocks, but generally tending towards equilibrium. Nevertheless, the stock-adjustment model, even in its simplest form, is useful because it illustrates the behaviour of a market where supply is inelastic in the short run but elastic over a longer period (for a survey, see Smith *et al.* (1988)).

3.2 Theoretical Arguments for Intervention 1: Efficiency

The rest of section 3 discusses the theoretical arguments for public involvement in housing. We know (Chapter 4:3.2) that the market allocates
resources efficiently only if the standard assumptions hold, i.e. perfect
information, perfect competition and no market failures such as external
effects, public goods or increasing returns to scale. The argument in this
section considers the nature of housing as a commodity, and in particular
the extent to which these assumptions hold; section 3.3 looks at equity
arguments.

Perfect information Are individuals well-informed about the nature of the
product, i.e. are their indifference maps well-defined? If an individual
inspects a house, does he thereby acquire full information about its qualities?
For many characteristics, e.g. size and location, the answer is yes; but most
house buyers have highly imperfect information on technical matters like
rising damp. This does not necessarily imply state intervention, because
market institutions (e.g. surveyors) have developed to supply information.
Furthermore, housing, from the viewpoint of the consumer, is not as
highly complex a commodity as health care,[7] so that consumers generally
understand the information they acquire. To that extent, market institutions
deal more effectively with information problems with housing than with
health care.

A second question is whether consumers are adequately informed about
prices (formally, whether their budget constraint is well-defined). This,
typically, is the case for homogeneous commodities which are bought
repeatedly (e.g. food), so that information is regularly updated. Where a
good is bought infrequently but is homogeneous (e.g. train fares) out-of-
date information can speedily be rectified. Housing, in contrast, is both an
irregular purchase (taken to include renting) and highly heterogeneous, so
that buyers will not have perfect knowledge. Again, however, the market
has developed institutions such as estate agents to improve consumer
information; or the buyer can commission a professional valuation from an
independent expert.

The third information assumption concerns knowledge about the future.
One problem is uncertainty about whether one's house will be destroyed,
e.g. by fire. The market solution is to supply house structure insurance,
which is efficient because it conforms with the technical conditions necessary
for private insurance (Chapter 5:3). Other forms of uncertainty, e.g. a
decline in property values, either generally or in one's locality, are not
directly insurable; but by renting rather than buying, the worst of such risks
can often be transferred to the landlord.

Though none of the information assumptions hold fully, the problems

[7] See Chapter 12:3.1, for the complexities of health care as a commodity.

which arise are those which the market itself is often able to solve. The role of the state in this context is to regulate minimum standards for the surveying and valuation professions, and for house insurance policies.

Perfect competition Because housing is durable its short-run supply elasticity is low. As a result, an increase in demand (e.g. from D_1 to D_2 in Figure 14.2) can cause a short-run, sharp increase in price from p^* to p_1, though in the long run, as new houses are built, the price will tend to return to p^*. The fact that house prices and rents can change substantially in the short run may cause equity problems (discussed below), but is neither uncompetitive nor inefficient (cf. the sharp rise in coffee prices after a bad harvest). Inelastic supply is not *per se* a violation of perfect competition. It is sometimes argued that supply is less than fully competitive in other respects, because housing is heterogeneous, and because the construction industry is not fully competitive (Bowley, 1966). Nevertheless, the supply of housing displays no *major* violations of the competitive assumption.

Competition can, however, fail in two ways: the assumption of equal power; and the issue of perfect capital markets. The equal power assumption can be violated with rented accommodation because, in brief, a 'house' over time becomes a 'home', thus giving the landlord an element of monopoly power. Consider an individual who moves to a new area. At least in principle, he faces a competitive market, so that he pays a rent (say £100 per week) equal to his marginal valuation of the property. But once he has moved in, the house, for at least three reasons, becomes over time that mystical thing, a home. This is first because of the pictures and other personal effects he puts up (which features could all be transferred if he moved). Second, he (or his landlord) might redecorate or improve the house; this is investment in physical capital, which raises the value of the property. Third (and crucially), he learns about the area (the best school, the best bakery), and makes friends. These last are investments in human capital. They do not raise the value of the property; nor are they transferrable if he moves elsewhere.

These factors, and especially the third, raise the marginal value (MV) of the house to the individual, i.e. MV (home) $> MV$ (house). Ignoring inflation, the individual would be prepared to pay a higher rent (say £125) to stay there, both to protect his investment in human capital, and to avoid the substantial transactions costs (search time, removal expenses, etc.) of moving elsewhere.[8] At a rent of £100 he is intra-marginal, and this gives the landlord monopoly power,[9] though its strength is an empirical

[8] On the general topic of mobility in the context of housing transactions costs, see Venti and Wise (1984).
[9] A similar phenomenon can occur with owner-occupiers. An individual buys a house as a marginal decision. Over time it becomes a home, and its marginal value to the individual rises, and can often exceed the market price of the house (proof: try knocking on people's doors and asking if they would agree to sell their house at its market price plus moving costs, etc.). It is therefore iniquitous that governments can compulsorily purchase houses at their market price. Such an action steals from the individual the difference

question.[10] If the problem is thought to be serious, the simplest solution is regulation, not via rent control but through a tribunal with the power to reduce rents if a landlord exploits his monopoly by raising the rent to £125, when new tenancies for similar property are fetching only £110.

In the case of owner-occupiers the assumption of perfect competition applies not only to the housing market *per se* but also to capital markets. As we have seen (equations (14.6) and (14.7)), both conditions are essential for tenure neutrality. But capital markets in practice may be (and often are) far from perfect, e.g. if lending institutions refuse loans to all but the safest cases. Intervention could take the form of public provision of loan finance, or of loan guarantees, i.e. the state would indemnify lending institutions against losses incurred if an individual defaulted on repayments. Such intervention could have equity as well as efficiency advantages.

The remaining assumptions   Externalities[11] arise in several ways. Houses which are structurally unsafe or fire hazards threaten their occupants and neighbours, the fire hazard point being recognised in local by-laws as long ago as the Middle Ages. Similarly, a house with improper sanitation creates public health hazards (UK, 1842, discussed in Chapter 2:1.2). One solution is to subsidise the maintenance of building standards. But the aim in this case is not so much to encourage building quality as to ensure that it does not fall below a minimum level. This might be achieved more directly through regulation of minimum standards of individual dwellings.

A related but different phenomenon is that housing can create a spatial externality. This arises in one form if I build a factory in my back garden, which imposes costs on my neighbours as an eyesore and a general reduction in the amenities they enjoy. There is a conflict between my freedom to do what I like on my land, and the freedom of others to be unaffected by my activities. This problem can sometimes be resolved by the market, if property rights are unambiguously assigned and enforceable (Coase, 1960). Another solution is a Pigovian 'eyesore tax' (see the Glossary), though this faces serious measurement problems. The most direct intervention is regulation of land use in the form of zoning and planning controls, though with room for disagreement as to their extent, e.g. should I be allowed to paint my house psychedelic orange?

A different type of spatial externality arises out of slums. A slum landlord (particularly if subject to rent control) faces incentives to reduce expenditure

between MV (home) and MV (house) – it is a theft of the value of comfort, habit and of the human capital the individual has built up in the locality. Setting measurement problems to one side, the equitable compensation for compulsory purchase should in principle be that sum for which the individual would agree to move voluntarily. This would include not only the value of the garage which he has added (i.e. physical capital), but also his accumulation of human capital.

[10] There may be an element of monopoly power in the opposite direction, since landlords also face costs if a tenancy changes hands.

[11] See Chapter 4:3.2 and the Appendix to Chapter 4, para. 15.

on his property (see section 4.2), which then deteriorates, thereby reducing the value of surrounding property. Slum neighbourhood characteristics generally dominate attempts at improvement by any *individual* landlord because he cannot find tenants prepared to pay a rent high enough to cover the costs of improvement. Once the slum process has started, it tends to continue, creating *inter alia* a public health problem. Two solutions are possible. If the houses are worth saving, subsidies (e.g. improvement grants) can lead to 'gentrification' and are therefore justifiable in efficiency terms. If the houses are not worth saving, because they are old or their density exceeds minimum standards, regulation in the form of planning controls may be appropriate (see Gauldie's (1974, pp. 279–80) description of how Birmingham in the nineteenth century purchased both houses and factories in areas it wished to improve).

A further problem, with the same analytical characteristics as externalities, arises if the private discount rate exceeds the social discount rate. In such cases, private markets tend to underinvest in terms of both quantity and quality. This gives rise to one of the few efficiency arguments for financial assistance with housing costs in the form of a general *price* subsidy.

The issue of public goods[12] arises over the provision of parks and open space. Though it is possible in principle to practise exclusion (i.e. to charge for admission to parks), the marginal cost of an extra user is zero if the park is not full. Thus the efficient price is zero, in which case private developers have no incentive to provide the efficient quantity of public open space, and may have no incentive to provide any at all. The most direct solution, again, is regulation in the form of planning controls, e.g. that at least x per cent of any development should be public open space.

Amenities such as sewers, drains, water and the distribution (though not the production) of domestic gas and electricity, face increasing returns to scale. If, for example, electricity is supplied to a particular area, it is obviously cheaper to run a main cable down a whole street with a branch to each house than to supply each house separately. The solution is regulation – in this case that all property developments should include provision of these services.

Before proceeding, it is worth spelling out a number of complexities implicit in earlier discussion. First, housing is a heterogeneous commodity, so that there is not a single market, but a series of interrelated ones. Second, the longevity of housing, and its consequent nature as a capital asset, mean that the operation of the housing market is related to the availability of finance, and hence to financial markets. Third is the problem of indivisibilities, both in terms of the 'lumpiness' of much housing expenditure and in changing the quality of a given dwelling. Fourth, changing one's

---

[12] See Chapter 4:3.2 and in the Appendix to Chapter 4, paras 13 and 14.

house can involve substantial transactions costs in both financial and utility terms. None of these features necessarily prevents housing markets from operating efficiently, but they may well prevent them from operating quickly (as shown in the stock-adjustment model in section 3.1) and/or may necessitate regulation. Policy design needs to take account of these factors. For further discussion of the nature of housing, see MacLennan and Gibb (1993).

The conclusion is that efficiency is likely to be enhanced by regulation in a variety of forms; by limited subsidies for specific reasons; and by public provision of loan finance or loan guarantees. It should be noted that none of the efficiency arguments points towards either public production of housing or state allocation to the individual.

3.3 Theoretical Arguments for Intervention 2: Equity

Horizontal equity raises two issues: access to housing; and access to capital markets. The latter can be dealt with briefly. Capital market imperfections may bear disproportionately on the lower socioeconomic groups. The problem is less that the poor are charged a higher interest rate (which would be justifiable on efficiency grounds to the extent that they were worse risks), than that those with lower and/or fluctuating incomes may not be able to borrow at *any* interest rate. Public intervention in the form of loans or loan guarantees may therefore be desirable to enhance tenure neutrality for equity as well as efficiency reasons.

Turning to access to housing *per se*, the crucial assumptions for horizontal equity (Chapter 4:4.3) are perfect information (to enable consumers to make rational decisions) and equal power (to enable them to enforce those decisions). If these assumptions hold, there is little reason for the state to intervene. The question we need to ask, therefore, is why the state might wish to encourage or force people to consume more or better housing than they would voluntarily choose. Several reasons have been suggested. Individuals, it is argued, may not accurately perceive the benefits of housing (i.e. an aspect of imperfect information), and may therefore consume less than is efficient. If this problem disproportionately afflicts the lower socioeconomic groups, we have equity as well as efficiency grounds for intervention. Whether this is in fact the case is an empirical question, and a crucial one. But it can be argued that imperfect information is not a *major* problem with housing – poor people live in sub-standard accommodation less because they misperceive the benefits of housing than because they cannot afford anything better. A second argument is that individuals may accurately perceive the value of housing to themselves, but fail to take account of the effects of their decisions on others, e.g. the public health argument. This problem is real and, where it affects the poor disproportionately, again gives equity as well as efficiency grounds for intervention.

In either case, what intervention is appropriate? One form involves regulation of building standards and of land use generally. Alternatively, the state could seek to encourage consumption through subsidies applied either to prices or to incomes. The problems of price subsidies for housing (discussed in section 4) suggest that regulation will usually be more satisfactory.

Vertical equity involves intervention either via income redistribution, allowing individuals to make their own consumption decisions, or through direct transfers of housing. Consumption externalities (Chapter 4:4.2) offer one explanation of in-kind transfers: the utility of a representative rich individual, R, rises with his own consumption, rises with the 'good' consumption (e.g. housing) of a representative poor man, P, but falls with P's 'bad' consumption. In this situation, R might agree to an in-kind transfer to P of housing worth, say, £1000, but offer a cash transfer (which might be spent on 'bad' consumption) of only £200, in which case both rich and poor might prefer the in-kind transfer (see Figure 4.5).

The rich might also favour this approach for other reasons, including their own self-interest. They might believe that good housing improves the health and productivity of the workforce or that good housing prevents social unrest (Chapter 3:5.3). Another argument (discussed by Culyer, 1971b) is that housing is such an important part of community welfare that individuals should be compelled to consume at least some minimum quantity. This is the 'merit good' argument (Chapter 4:4.2) in its pure form. The poor may prefer direct transfers of housing either because of the generosity of the in-kind transfer in comparison with the cash offer they would otherwise receive, or because they feel less stigmatised by receiving benefits in kind than in the form of means-tested cash transfers. For all these reasons it may be politically easier to transfer housing in kind.

3.4 Types of Intervention

The preceding two sections considered *why* the state intervenes. This section discusses in principle *how* best it might do so (i.e. the question of method).

Pure market provision according to the theoretical analysis, is likely to be inefficient and inequitable. Many of the assumptions necessary for efficiency can fail: landlords have potential monopoly power; capital markets may be imperfect; and housing creates a wide range of external effects. If these problems disproportionately affect the lower socioeconomic groups, there is also a problem of horizontal equity; and in the absence of redistributive policies, inequalities in the distribution of income would lead to wider inequalities in the distribution of housing than most people would like. Proponents of a free market for housing (Friedman and Stigler, 1972; Friedman, 1962, pp. 178–80; Hayek, 1960, Ch. 22) point to the undoubted problems with housing in Britain. They are correct in attributing some of them to inappropriate intervention. But advocacy of unrestricted markets is implausible; a better solution is not to adopt a 'hands-off' policy, but to choose more effective policy instruments.

Mixed public/private provision involves the design of a theoretical package of regulation and subsidy such that private production and allocation is efficient and equitable. Such a scheme (whose policy aspects are discussed in section 5) would involve the following ingredients.

Regulation on the supply side would include minimum standards, *inter alia* because of the public health externality; planning of land use (because of spatial and other externalities); regulation of professional standards for surveyors and valuers (thus improving information about the quality of housing); and regulation of landlords, as a counter-weight to any monopoly power they acquire in the long run.

Finance: there is a strong case for public provision of loan finance or loan guarantees if capital markets are imperfect, not least to encourage tenure neutrality. In addition, price subsidies may be appropriate in strictly limited cases: in the presence of slum-type externalities; where there is a divergence between private and social discount rates; and possibly on equity grounds if short-run supply inelasticity causes financial hardship (though the latter subsidy should be of limited duration).

The arguments of principle suggest that state intervention along these lines could achieve efficiency and horizontal equity. Three major theoretical conclusions emerge. First, information problems are not overriding. Individuals (with professional assistance if necessary) generally have sufficient information about the quality and price of housing to make rational decisions. In the case of housing, much more than with health care (Chapter 12:3.1), one can argue that consumer sovereignty is useful (not morally better or worse, *useful*). Second, there is an efficiency justification for *general* price subsidies only if the private discount rate is thought to be inefficiently high. Together with the first point, this suggests powerful advantages if prices are kept at their efficient level, p^* in Figure 14.1, and vertical equity aims are pursued through cash transfers (Chapter 4:7.2).[13] Third, the theory offers no efficiency justification for public production of housing (as opposed to regulation of private supply). This is *not* an argument against public production. But, taken together with the previous two points, it suggests that the aims set out in section 2 are more likely to be achieved if housing is allocated via efficient prices, supported by income transfers. If untied cash transfers are politically unacceptable, or if the untied transfer necessary

[13] Though see footnote 5 above.

to raise the consumption of housing to the desired level is too expensive, cash transfers could be tied to expenditure on housing. The kernel of the argument is its suggestion that *Britain's housing difficulties are not a market allocation problem but an income distribution problem*. In other words, as argued in sections 4 and 5, the technical nature of housing makes it more like food than like health care.[14]

Public production and allocation to the individual at a zero or subsidised price (i.e. less than p^* in Figure 14.1) are theoretically defensible for health care (Chapter 12:3.3). Precisely the same theoretical considerations suggest that this approach is unlikely to work well with housing. First, there are problems with allocating accommodation to individuals by administrative decision. When faced with efficient prices, consumers are likely to make better decisions than housing administrators for two sets of reasons: because they have better information about their own tastes and requirements; and because tastes about housing vary widely across individuals. Both aspects contrast sharply with health care (Chapter 12:3.1).

A second problem arises if prices are inefficiently low. Unless the demand for housing is completely price inelastic, any subsidy of rents/prices greater than justified for efficiency reasons (e.g. P_1 instead of P^* in Figure 14.1) will raise demand to Q_1. One or both of two consequences follow: if supply increases to Q_1 the result is a housing stock larger than the efficient quantity/quality Q^*; and if it remains at Q^* the result is excess demand, e.g. waiting lists, immobility and/or homelessness as discussed in section 4.

The theoretical arguments therefore suggest that a strategy of public allocation of housing by administrative decision at a subsidised price will be inefficient and inequitable. There is a fundamental conflict between this approach and the mixed public/private strategy discussed previously, in which housing is allocated by individual consumption decisions constrained by efficient prices, and supported by income transfers. This conflict emerges repeatedly, both in assessing the British system in practice, and in considering options for reform.

4 Assessment of British Housing Institutions

4.1 Institutions

Public intervention in housing is far-reaching and diverse. It involves regulation, subsidy, and public production and allocation, though with considerable variation between the three main types of tenure – owner

[14] The debate is an old one, going back at least as far as the Land Enquiry Committee (UK, 1914), whose long-term solution, according to Swenarton (1981, p. 41), 'was to ensure that everyone could afford an economic rent through minimum wage legislation; in the short-term, the housing shortage could be alleviated by state provision of houses, so long as they were built and let at a strictly economic rent'.

occupation, the local authority rental sector and private rented accommodation. Because of the complexity of these institutions it is impossible to give a comprehensive picture (see the Further Reading). This section seeks to sketch out the main institutional features. Section 4.2 assesses the extent to which different parts of the housing market meet the aims discussed in section 2; the housing market as a whole is discussed in section 4.3. Throughout, the term 'house' is used to include flats, apartments, etc.

HOUSING AS A WHOLE

The historical background is probably more relevant to the current situation in housing than in any other part of the welfare state. Government involvement at a national level began in the second half of the nineteenth century (Chapter 2:1.2) mainly out of concern with public health. Legislation established two powers: to set minimum standards for new houses, and to demolish unsafe or unhealthy dwellings. These simultaneously increased the cost of housing and reduced its supply. As a result, many families could not pay the market rent of minimum standard accommodation.[15] The main response in the nineteenth century was private philanthropy.

By the early twentieth century this approach was increasingly regarded as unsatisfactory. Two solutions were discussed: provision by local authorities of housing for the poor at subsidised rents; and income subsidies for the poor. The latter policy commanded little support at the time, partly for ideological reasons and partly for lack of a suitable administrative structure to distribute income transfers. The Housing and Town Planning Act 1919 (the Addison Act) imposed on local authorities the duty of remedying housing deficiencies in their area (Chapter 2:3.1). Wartime exigencies had already led to the imposition of rent controls in 1915. The rejection of income subsidies at a time of acute housing shortage thus led over a four-year period to the adoption of two sets of policies: rent (i.e. price) subsidies in the form of rent control, and public provision of housing. These policies continued in various forms during the inter- and post-war periods, and remain largely in force today.

Central and local government responsibilities Central government policy is formulated by the Department of Environment. Housing itself is provided by local authorities, housing associations and private landlords (for rent) and by private builders (for purchase). Local authorities have a general responsibility for meeting housing need in their area, including the clearance of individual unfit dwellings, the exercise of planning controls to enforce minimum standards, and the building, managing and letting of housing.

[15] See the evidence presented to the Royal Commission on the Housing of the Working Class (UK, 1885). This was, and still is, the last Royal Commission on housing in Britain, though see National Federation of Housing Associations (1985) (and its follow-up, Inquiry into British Housing (1991)) for a non-governmental attempt, chaired by HRH The Duke of Edinburgh, to fill the gap.

Planning of the quantity, quality and location of housing is conducted by local authorities in consultation with central government. Under the Town and Country Planning Act 1968 each local authority submits to central government a general plan for land use, after public enquiry. Once the overall plan has been approved, its detailed implementation is the responsibility of the local authority. Any proposal to construct a new development or modify an existing one must be approved by the local authority. Unsuccessful applicants can appeal to the Minister, who has the power to reverse local decisions.

Public expenditure on housing is shown in Table 14.1. Current expenditure in England in 1992/3 was £4 billion, mostly in the form of subsidies to local authority housing; capital spending (net of sales and repayment of loans) was £3.7 billion. The UK total of £9 billion is a rather narrow definition of public expenditure on housing. It omits income transfers such as housing benefit (Table 7.5), and also implicit spending in the form of various tax concessions to owner-occupiers (i.e. tax expenditures, discussed in Chapter 7:1.1).[16] Table 14.2 gives a more complete picture. Total spending on local authority and related housing, including price and income subsidies, was £8.5 billion. The main tax expenditures on owner occupation are mortgage interest relief[17] and relief from capital gains tax, amounting together to some £8.1 billion. Subsidies to the private rented sector consisted of £2.5 billion for income subsidies, plus an unknown revenue loss due to rent control. Table 14.2 shows public expenditure on housing in 1992/3 of around £20 billion, mostly in the form of subsidies, and much of it subsidising prices rather than incomes (for further discussion of housing expenditure, see Hills (1991, Ch. 3)). Given this vast expenditure, what has been achieved?

The quantity and quality of housing There is a consensus that during the 1970s there was no *general* housing shortage (UK Department of the Environment, 1977a, para. 3.05). By the mid-1980s, however, pressure on accommodation was growing especially (though not only) in the London area (UK Department of the Environment, 1985a, Table 3). The average quality of housing in the mid-1970s was high by international standards (UK Department of the Environment, 1977a, para. 3.01; Lansley, 1979, p. 133), though with wide variation. Over one-quarter of the housing stock was old (i.e. pre-1914). There was rapid improvement over the 1960s and early 1970s; but from the late 1970s the condition of the housing stock declined sharply. The number of properties in serious disrepair increased, and slum clearance fell substantially despite persisting problems of unfitness

---

[16] It also omits the transfer to tenants resulting from rent control, which exemplifies a more general phenomenon – regulation as a form of implicit taxation/expenditure; for an analysis, see Prest (1985).
[17] We discuss later whether the true tax expenditure should not be the revenue forgone because the imputed income of owner-occupiers is not taxed.

Table 14.1 *Public expenditure on housing, UK, 1992/93 (est.) (£ million)*

CURRENT EXPENDITURE			
Central government subsidies to local authorities			
Housing element	1009		
Rent rebate element	2747		
		3756	
Central government subsidies to Housing			
Corporation and Housing Associations		158	
Other		123	
Total current expenditure			4036
CAPITAL EXPENDITURE			
Local authority[a]			
Credit approvals	1493		
Capital grants	440		
		1933	
Housing corporation			
Capital programme	1731		
Other	−25		
		1707	
Other		40	
Total capital expenditure			3680
TOTAL PROGRAMME			7716
EXPENDITURE IN SCOTLAND, WALES AND			
NORTHERN IRELAND			1259
TOTAL NET DIRECT EXPENDITURE ON HOUSING			8975

Sources: UK (1992b, Figure 82); UK (1992f, Introductory Table and Table 9.4); UK (1992g, Figure 1.03 and Appendix 3); UK (1992h, Table 1.1).
Note: [a] The figure excludes local authorities' self-financed expenditure.

(National Federation of Housing Associations, 1985, Ch. 2). As a partial response, the system of improvement grants was revised in the late 1980s.

Tenure patterns have shifted dramatically over the post-war period from private rented accommodation to owner occupation and the local authority sector. In 1988, 65 per cent of houses were owner-occupied (30 per cent in 1950), 25 per cent rented from local authorities or new towns (18 per cent), and 7 per cent from private landlords (52 per cent) (Hills and Mullings, 1990, Table 5.14).

Because the tenures are organised so differently, they are discussed separately, using the same four heads as health care and education (see also Table 4.2), i.e. production, the aggregate production decision, the individual consumption decision, and finance.

Table 14.2 *Public expenditure (more broadly defined) on housing, UK, 1992/93 (est.)* *(£ million)*

LOCAL AUTHORITY HOUSING[a,d]			
General current subsidies	1009		
Rent rebates	3652		
Capital expenditure (net)	1933		
		6594	
HOUSING CORPORATION AND HOUSING ASSOCIATIONS[a,d]			
General current subsidies	158		
Capital expenditure	1747		
		1905	
TOTAL LOCAL AUTHORITY AND HOUSING ASSOCIATION			8499
OWNER OCCUPATION[b,e]			
Mortgage interest relief for owner-occupiers		6100	
Capital gains tax relief on main residence		2000	
Total owner occupation			8100
PRIVATE RENTED HOUSING			
Rent allowances[c,d]		2522	
Rent control		unknown	
Total private rented housing			2522[f]
EXPENDITURE IN SCOTLAND, WALES AND NORTHERN IRELAND			1259
TOTAL PUBLIC EXPENDITURE ON HOUSING			20,380[f]

Sources: [a] UK (1992b, Figure 82).
                [b] UK (1992a, Table 4B.1).
                [c] UK (1992e, Tables 1 and 3).
Notes: [d] Excludes expenditure in Scotland, Wales and Northern Ireland.
                [e] Figure relates to 1991/2.
                [f] Figure only a lower bound.

THE OWNER-OCCUPIED SECTOR

Production of owner-occupied housing is by private individuals or property developers, subject to planning controls, and to considerable regulation of minimum standards of design and materials. The aggregate production decision is private, though again tempered by the need to obtain planning permission and by more general land policies.

The individual consumption decision is private in the sense that individuals can choose which house they want to buy. But decisions are generally constrained by the availability of mortgage finance which, as we shall see, is a greater problem for some people than others.

Finance for house purchase is generally private, though with heavy subsidies, mainly in the form of tax relief. The most common source of loan finance for owner-occupiers in Britain are the building societies (see Cullingworth, 1979, Ch. 1). They are non-profit institutions enjoying limited tax advantages, which make long-term (20–25-year) loans to individuals for house purchase or home improvement. Over the 1980s banks entered the mortgage market.

Owner-occupiers receive substantial tax relief. Interest repayments on the first £30,000 of a mortgage are deductible at the basic rate of income tax (25 per cent in the early 1990s); equivalent assistance is given also to individuals below the tax threshold.[18] Such tax relief applies to an individual's 'principal private residence' (i.e. not to second homes). A second major tax advantage is that no capital gains tax is charged on the increase in the real value of an individual's principal private residence (for discussion of the taxation of housing, see Hills (1991, Chs 11 and 12)).

These reliefs require explanation. Businesses pay tax on their net profits. Analogously, a landlord pays tax on his *net* rent receipts, i.e. the excess of his gross rent receipts over total costs, including maintenance and repair costs and any interest costs on borrowed money. Historically, if the landlord let the house to himself (i.e. was an owner-occupier), he would pay tax on a similar sum. He would have imputed to him the gross rent he would receive if he let the house to a third party; from this he could deduct maintenance costs and mortgage interest payments. So long as an owner-occupier paid tax on this imputed income (so-called 'Schedule A' receipts), it was entirely proper for mortgage interest to be deductible. But over time the income imputed to individuals was eroded, partly by inflation, partly because rent control made it difficult to estimate market rents, and partly because the tax was politically unpopular. It was abolished in 1962. It is thus open to debate whether the transfer to owner-occupiers is the deductibility of mortgage interest or the non-taxation of imputed housing income. However the tax advantages are measured, owner-occupied housing is favourably treated relative to most other investments and to other consumption goods, with important implications for tenure neutrality (see section 4.3, point 23).

These tax advantages all have the effect of offering owner-occupiers a price subsidy. In addition, poor homeowners are eligible for a limited range of income subsidies under housing benefit (Chapter 10:1).

LOCAL AUTHORITY HOUSING

Production Local authority housing is publicly designed and planned, though its construction may be contracted out to private builders. Main-

---

[18] This is administratively simple, since an individual whose tax rate is 25 per cent and who pays £100 gross mortgage interest sends £75 to the building society, which receives the remaining £25 from the tax authorities. For details of the UK system of income tax, see Kay and King (1990, Ch. 2).

tenance is usually carried out by local authority employees, though in recent years there has been some contracting out. The aggregate production decision rests in principle with local authorities, but has latterly been severely constrained. Net capital spending fell from about £8 billion in the mid-1970s to £1 billion by 1990 (both figures in 1989 prices) (for further discussion, see Hills (1991) and Forrest and Murie (1990)). In addition, under the Housing Act 1980, tenants were given the right to buy the local authority property in which they lived at a discount whose size depended on the time the tenant had lived there. Over the 1980s about 1.5 million local authority dwellings were sold this way, and the number of such dwellings fell from about a third to about a quarter of all dwellings (for discussion and analysis of the sale of local authority housing, see Forrest and Murie (1990)).

The individual consumption decision   Local authorities have a statutory duty to meet housing need. Families signal their demand by asking to be put on an authority's waiting list. In practice, however, few people are able to acquire a local authority tenancy unless they are homeless. In large measure, therefore, the individual consumption decision is beyond both the individual and the local authority.

The finance of local authority housing is a morass which will be touched on only briefly (for fuller discussion, see Hills (1991, Ch. 7) and Glennerster (1992, Ch. 13)). Each local authority has a *Housing Revenue Account*, which shows all expenditure and revenue on a cash flow basis, including interest payments on past loans, and subsidies from central and local government. In the past, there was a requirement that the account should balance on a current basis, with important implications: by 'pooling' its rent income a local authority could spread the high costs of new building across the whole of its housing stock; similarly, the interest charges to the Housing Revenue Account were the average 'pooled' interest rates paid by the local authority on its historical borrowing. Rents in a given local authority therefore depended on two factors: the average age of the housing stock (which determined the historic cost of building, and hence interest charges); and the extent of subsidy from central and local government.

A reformed system of local authority housing subsidies came into effect in April 1990, as a result of the 1989 Local Government and Housing Act. Two changes were of particular importance. First, each local authority's Housing Revenue Account was 'ring fenced', so that local authorities could no longer subsidise the Account from other sources. Second, the calculation of central government grant was changed in such a way as to reduce the advantage of local authorities with an older housing stock. The overall result of the changes was twofold: subsidies to different local authorities became somewhat more systematic; and the extent of subsidy declined from around 44 per cent in the later 1970s to around 15 per cent in the later

1980s (see Hills and Mullings, 1990, Figure 5.3; Hills, 1991, Table 3.3).

Local authority (and private) tenants are eligible also for housing benefit (Chapter 10:1). The basic idea, in the words of an earlier debate, is 'to subsidise people rather than houses'; poor tenants in local authority and private rented accommodation receive assistance in paying their rent. Such assistance is higher the lower the family's income, the higher its housing costs, and the larger the family size. Though sound in principle, the scheme has been criticised (see Hills, 1991, Ch. 10). One of the overall effects of the 1980s was to tip the balance from *general* subsidies to local authority housing towards subsidies to individuals. Section 5 argues in favour of such a substitution of income subsidies for price subsidies.

Housing associations can be thought of as decentralised, quasi-public housing at below-market rents. Governments from the 1960s onwards sought to diversify sources of housing for poorer tenants. In 1974 a housing association grant was established to offer capital grants to housing associations at the start of a new scheme. The size of this Housing Association Grant (HAG) was set to reduce loan repayments sufficiently to enable poorer tenants to pay the rent.

The problem with the system was that all calculations were based on the nominal values prevailing at the time the HAG was made so that, as prices rose over time, the real burden of rent fell below rents for comparable dwellings in other sectors. The Housing Act 1988 sought to rectify the problem by changing the basis on which the grant was calculated. For further details of the intricacies of housing association finance and criticisms of current arrangements, see Hills (1991, Ch. 8) and Glennerster (1992, Ch. 13).

THE PRIVATE RENTED SECTOR

Production of new housing for private rental is in principle decided by property developers, subject to planning controls and regulation of minimum standards, though in practice there has not been much new building for private rental in the UK in recent years.[19] Total supply is determined privately, including decisions about building new rental property, and also whether new or existing stock is used for private rental or sold for owner occupation.

The individual consumption decision is private in the sense that individuals can choose whether to seek a private tenancy. But choices are severely constrained by the availability of such accommodation, for which, as we shall see, there is considerable excess demand in some areas.

---

[19] There has been a small amount of new building as a result of tax concessions through the Business Expansion Scheme (see Crook *et al.*, 1991).

The finance of private rented accommodation is private, subject to two major qualifications: poor tenants are eligible for housing benefit as described above; and some private tenancies are subject to considerable regulation, particularly in connection with security of tenure and (for tenancies starting before 1988) rent control. Rent control was first introduced in 1915.[20] Its history and institutions are complex (see Chapter 2:3.1, and the Further Reading). Two points are crucial for our purposes and have major implications: rent control is a form of implicit price subsidy; and it is not financed by government (i.e. the taxpayer) but is a transfer from landlord to tenant.

CONCLUSION

A key conclusion is the pervasiveness of subsidies to housing. The first point is their *scale*. From Table 14.2, public expenditure (including tax expenditures) on housing in 1992/3 was about £20 billion (expenditure on the National Health Service in England was £35 billion (Table 12.1). Second, much of this expenditure was on *price* subsidies. Owner-occupiers receive substantial tax reliefs which serve, *ceteris paribus*, to reduce the cost of buying a house.[21] Though the relative importance of income subsidies in the local authority sector has increased, local authority rents are still generally reduced by subsidies. Rents in parts of the private sector are reduced by rent control. The analysis of section 3.2 suggests that there is efficiency justification neither for such heavy price subsidies, nor for their application to such a large proportion of the housing stock.

Until the early 1980s there was no general housing shortage, and Britain had a higher average standard of housing than many richer countries. Yet many families live in poor housing, and homelessness is a growing problem. This suggests that the housing stock is misallocated, causing both inefficiency and inequity. The next two sections seek to explain how this has come about.

4.2 Problems in Individual Parts of the Housing Market

The owner-occupied sector This section is concerned not with the detailed workings of different parts of the UK housing market, but with the overall pattern. The conclusion is that the substantial problems of the system conform strikingly with the predictions of economic theory. The owner-occupied sector has major efficiency problems.

1. *Underoccupation.* Price subsidies to owner-occupiers, mainly in the form of tax reliefs, lead to overconsumption and underoccupation. The

---

[20] For a one-page summary of the history of rent control since 1915, see Robinson (1979, Table 6.1).

[21] These tax advantages are likely at least partially to be capitalised in house prices, thereby reducing the subsidy element – see section 4.2, point 5.

theory is simple. If house prices are p_1 rather than p^* in Figure 14.1, demand will be Q_1, greater than the efficient quantity/quality, Q^*, unless price elasticity is zero. As an empirical matter, though not without their econometric difficulties, estimates agree that the elasticity of housing demand is greater than zero with respect to both prices and incomes, with a rough consensus round a price elasticity of 0.5 (Byatt *et al.*, 1973; MacLennan, 1982, Ch. 2; King, 1980); if the price of housing halves, demand will increase on average by 50 per cent. Furthermore, since the subsidy is paid out of tax revenues (rather than by private builders), supply will increase to Q_1. In practical terms the main effect is overconsumption. People tend to live in larger/higher-quality housing than they would if prices were set at p^*. This is partly because at a subsidised price they choose to consume more housing services (a consumption motive). There is also an asset motive, to the extent that housing is treated more favourably than other forms of private asset accumulation. The result is underoccupation (UK Department of the Environment, 1977b, Ch. 2, especially paras 32–3).

2. *Tax reliefs artificially raise the return to housing* above that on many other forms of saving available to private individuals. As a result, a disproportionate share of limited savings is attracted to housing finance, though this effect has been reduced by increasing tax concessions over the later 1980s for other forms of private saving.

There are also serious equity criticisms.

3. *Access to mortgage finance is unequal.* Lending policies of building societies and banks generally exclude individuals with low or irregular earnings and those without sufficient savings to pay the initial deposit on a house. This disproportionately affects the lower socioeconomic groups, thereby causing inefficiency, and also inequity which is only partially mitigated because many local authority tenants, since the passage of the 1980 Housing Act, are able to buy the property they formerly rented. The result is a housing market which is largely segmented, with poorer families restricted for the most part to rented accommodation.

4. *The tax reliefs to owner occupation are largely regressive.* Individuals with higher incomes generally have larger mortgages. In the past they also received tax relief at a higher rate. The result is shown in column (2) of Table 14.3. Families with high incomes in 1974/5 received on average six times as much mortgage interest relief as poor families. Le Grand (1982, Table 5.1), using the non-taxation of imputed income as a measure of the tax concession, reached a similar conclusion.[22] Official figures (*Hansard*, 3 February 1984) confirm the pattern: mortgage interest relief in 1983/4 was nearly twelve times as high, on average, for mortgage holders with incomes

---

[22] The distribution of the tax concession differs substantially, depending on whether it is measured as mortgage interest relief, or as the non-taxation of imputed income – see point 23.

over £20,000 per year as for those with income under £5,000. In 1989/90, tax advantages continued to be higher for the best-off (Hills, 1991, Ch. 14). The effect persists, though somewhat reduced from 1991, when mortage relief was restricted to the basic rate of income tax. Capital gains tax relief is also regressive, since individuals with higher incomes tend to own larger houses and so make larger capital gains. *Prima facie* both forms of tax relief go mainly to the better-off.

A partial counter-argument is that subsidies lead to a 'filtering' process, whereby families who (partly because of tax reliefs) move into more expensive housing release cheaper accommodation to households with lower incomes. Empirical evidence, though limited, lends little support to the hypothesis (Robinson, 1979, pp. 30–1).

Table 14.3 *Mortgage interest tax relief and subsidies for local authority housing by level of pre-tax income, 1974/75*

Income of head of household and wife (£s per year) (1)	Average mortgage interest tax relief per owner-occupier (£s per year) (2)	Average subsidy per local authority tenant (£s per year) (3)
Under £1000	59	168
£1000–1499	73	168
£1500–1999	91	159
£2000–2499	104	160
£2500–2999	101	137
£3000–3499	129	147
£3500–3999	129	154
£4000–4999	148	164
£5000–5999	179 }	154
£6000 and over	369 }	

Source: *Housing Policy, Technical Volume 1*, Table IV. 34 and IV. 36 (HMSO, 1977).

5. *Tax capitalisation.* A second counter-argument to the regressivity of tax reliefs is that they are capitalised. As a result, house prices are higher than they would otherwise be, thereby depriving owner-occupiers of the benefit of the tax concessions. The argument is best illustrated by example. Suppose that mortgage repayments consist only of interest, and that an individual wants to buy the largest house he can afford with mortgage repayments of £400 per month. In a world with no tax reliefs, suppose he can buy a house costing £100,000. If tax relief at 50 per cent is introduced, he can now afford monthly repayments of £800 (because the government pays half), and so can buy a house costing £200,000. But if the supply of housing is totally inelastic, his extra purchasing power (together with that of other similarly placed individuals) will double house prices, leaving him

in exactly the same position as before. In this case, the introduction of tax relief does not benefit new house buyers, but only existing homeowners, who make large capital gains.

In practice, however, the long-run supply of housing is not completely inelastic, so house prices in the previous example would not rise by 100 per cent. Thus tax reliefs do benefit owner-occupiers, though probably by less than the tax expenditure figures suggest.[23] The regressivity argument therefore stands. A different argument follows from the observation that the real burden of income tax rose fairly steadily from 1948 until the mid-1980s. This suggests that an *increasing* amount of tax relief has been capitalised, an argument strengthened by the gradual erosion and eventual abolition of the taxation of imputed income. As a result, the tax system can be argued to have exerted not a once-and-for-all effect on house prices, but a fairly steady upward pressure. The effect has been to confer capital gains on earlier house buyers at the expense of more recent purchasers.

The conclusion on vertical equity is that various tax reliefs worth some £8.1 billion in 1992/3 have benefited mainly the better-off, though probably by less than the figures in Table 14.2 suggest; and to the extent that capital gains have accrued disproportionately to earlier buyers, redistribution has also been arbitrary (see Whitehead, 1980, pp. 95–8; Le Grand, 1982, pp. 90–5).

Local authority housing In efficiency terms there is little theoretical justification for price subsidies (section 3.2). Yet local authority rents in the early 1970s covered on average only 40 per cent of the historic cost of housing, rising to 85 per cent by 1990 (UK, 1992b, Figure 93). In most areas, therefore, local authority rents are below their efficient level, though it is hard to say by how much. At least four consequential efficiency problems arise.

6. *Subsidised rents lead to overconsumption/underoccupation.* If rents are shown by $p_1 < p^*$ in Figure 14.1, people will wish to consume quantity/quality $Q_1 > Q^*$. Local authority tenants will demand a larger/higher-quality house than they would if they had to pay an efficient rent, p^*, which reflects the marginal social cost of housing. The crucial point for efficiency (given that demand, empirically, is price elastic) is that the *marginal* cost of rented accommodation should be p^*. Since administrative allocation is not, in practice, fully efficient (see point 10 below), subsidised rents create an incentive to overconsumption/underoccupation.

7. *Excess demand.* As another aspect of the same problem, subsidised rents lead to excess demand for local authority housing, thereby contributing

[23] If supply is not totally elastic, landowners and property developers will also benefit from the tax concessions.

to overcrowding (usually in the other sectors) and to homelessness.[24] If rents in Figure 14.1 are shown by p_1 people will demand Q_1. If local authorities increased the supply of housing to Q_1 demand would be satisfied, but only at the expense of overinvestment in housing (since $Q_1 > Q^*$). In practice this has not happened. As a result, there is excess demand for local authority housing, as manifested by waiting lists in most areas; many people want local authority housing (or want larger or higher-quality housing) but are unable to obtain it. Frequently they are unable to move into the owner-occupied sector, because they cannot afford to do so, and/or because of inequalities in access to mortgage finance (point 3 above); nor can they find suitable private rented accommodation, because rent control leads to excess demand in that sector (point 15 below). Two results follow. Families who already have local authority housing but want more spacious accommodation (e.g. because their family has grown) suffer overcrowding; and families still on the waiting list suffer from low-quality (often private rented) accommodation and/or from overcrowding (e.g. if they are living with family or friends), or from homelessness (Donnison and Ungerson, 1982, Ch. 16; UK Department of the Environment, 1985a, Table 3).

Points 6 and 7 taken together show that (unless there is *overinvestment* in housing, i.e. Q_1 in Figure 14.1), inefficiently low rents can *simultaneously* cause underoccupation, overcrowding and homelessness. The proponents of price subsidies had unimpeachable aims; but the method they chose is questionable, to say the very least.

8. *Labour immobility* is a further consequence of excess demand, in that existing tenants may be unable to take up work in a different locality because they would have to go on the waiting list in the new area. Immobility is reinforced, for the reasons given in point 7, by the inability of many local authority tenants to find accommodation in other sectors of the housing market. As cases in point, Lomas (1974) and Shankland *et al.* (1977) describe how unemployed people in local authority housing in inner London are unable for this reason to move to areas with better job prospects. A more general study by Hughes and McCormick (1981) concludes that, *ceteris paribus*, local authority tenants have lower migration rates (except for moves within a locality) than owner-occupiers.

9. *Hard-to-let* property results largely from charging rents on the basis of 'pooled' historic costs (section 4.1). Its existence is telling evidence that not only absolute rents, but also rent *differentials* for different properties are inefficiently small. Efficiency requires that if house P ('penthouse') is four times as attractive as house T ('terrace') in terms of quantity and quality, then its rent should be about four times as high. Because of rent pooling this is not the case in many localities. Furthermore, a family on

---

[24] A rough association has been remarked between administrative allocation schemes and homelessness (UK, Holland, Germany), and between market allocation and overcrowding.

the waiting list knows that if it accepts house T, it is unlikely subsequently to be able to transfer to P. For this reason, and because the rent of T is not sufficiently lower than the rent of P (which is itself inefficiently low), the family is likely to refuse T in the hope of later being offered P. Consequently, T is hard to let. This occurs only because both rents on average, and in particular rent relativities, are inefficiently low. The problem is much smaller in the owner-occupied sector, because *relative* prices are determined by the market, even if absolute house prices are subsidised – long-run problems of hard-to-sell are therefore minimal.

Local authority housing can also cause inequity.

10. *Access to local authority housing in a given area can be arbitrary.* The first source of the problem is the imperfect knowledge of housing administrators, who cannot have complete information about the circumstances of individuals on the waiting list (on the inefficiencies and inequities of administrative allocation, see Power (1984) and UK Audit Commission (1986)). Inequity arises, second, if housing allocation is influenced by extraneous considerations like racial prejudice (see Commission for Racial Equality, 1983); and some survey evidence suggests that the least desirable local authority housing tends to be occupied by the most disadvantaged people (Harrison, 1985). A third source of mismatch between 'need' and housing allocation arises over time. A needy family in the past may quite properly have been given local authority housing; but if the family's income rose substantially over the years, it was possible neither to evict it nor to raise its rent to an efficient level.[25] The effect is strengthened by the fact that in certain circumstances local authority tenancies can be transferred within a family from one generation to the next (i.e. tenancies can be inherited), but weakened by the shifting balance over the 1980s away from rent subsidies towards income-tested housing benefit.

Local authority housing can thus fail to be allocated to those in greatest need for at least these three reasons. The result is arbitrariness, and hence horizontal inequity. Because of excess demand, the system benefits those who obtain local authority housing at the expense of those on the waiting list, with no guarantee that the former group is necessarily the more needy.

11. *Regional inequality in access to local authority housing* arises because waiting lists vary by region. Some authorities, for historical reasons, have a large housing stock, but demand may be relatively low, e.g. because of out-migration. Elsewhere the situation is reversed. Thus it is easier to obtain local authority housing in some parts of the country than in others.[26]

[25] For a particularly lurid example of the problem which used to exist, see 'Council House Tenant's Rolls-Royce', *The Times*, 10 February 1983.
[26] It should be noted that waiting lists, to the extent that they are longest in areas with the highest economic activity, are not arbitrary, but systematic. If so, waiting lists are inefficient, but not as inequitable as point 11 suggests.

12. *Redistribution via price subsidy* is arbitrary in at least three ways. Consider two areas A and B. A's housing stock for historical reasons is older than B's but of equal quality. The determination of rents on the basis of historic cost implies that rents in A will be lower than in B, even if tenants in the two areas have the same average income. Redistribution is thus arbitrary by region. Second, within a given area, the fact that housing costs are pooled can imply, depending on the precise method of rent setting, that tenants in newer (and hence higher-cost) housing are subsidised by those in older accommodation. The result of these two effects is that redistribution by income level can easily be arbitrary. Column (3) of Table 14.3 shows that average subsidies were virtually invariant to the income of tenants. The reduction in subsidy over the 1980s reduced this form of arbitrariness somewhat: in the late 1980s, low-income tenants benefited most (because of the importance of housing benefit); above the lowest incomes, the distribution of subsidy varied little with income (Hills, 1991, Figures 14.1 and 14.3). Finally, because there is excess demand, families with local authority tenancies benefit at the expense of those on the waiting list. The overall result has been described as redistribution by luck.

13. *Redistribution via income subsidies* is progressive. Housing benefit is paid to low-income families, and is withdrawn as family income rises. The scheme, however, is not without its problems (see Hills, 1991, Ch. 10). Table 10.2 shows that almost all spending on rent rebates goes to families in the bottom half of the income distribution.

The conclusion on vertical equity is that the redistributive effects of rent rebates and allowances (£6.1 billion in 1992/3 – Table 14.2) is progressive, but that other expenditure on local authority housing was largely arbitrary.

The private rented sector Many problems in this sector can be attributed to rent control (a form of implicit price subsidy), and to the fact that many individuals in regulated tenancies enjoy considerable security of tenure.

14. *Rent controls lead to overconsumption/underoccupation.* The argument is similar to that in point 6. Rent control reduces rents to $p_1 < p^*$ in Figure 14.1. Since demand is price elastic, people wish to consume more and/or higher-quality accommodation, Q_1, than they would at the efficient rent, p^*. The result, for tenants who are able to find regulated private rented accommodation, is overconsumption/underoccupation. At a minimum it is likely to reduce the downward adjustment which would normally be expected in the later stages of a family's life cycle.

15. *Excess demand* is a related consequence, which aggravates over-crowding and homelessness. The argument is similar to that in point 7. Assume for the moment (the assumption is relaxed in point 16) that the supply of rented accommodation is Q^*. If rents in Figure 14.1 are shown by p_1, people will demand $Q_1 > Q^*$. The result is excess demand. Many families want private rented accommodation (or want larger/higher-quality

accommodation) but are not able to find any. Frequently they are not able to move into the owner-occupied sector because of unequal access to mortgage finance etc. (point 3), nor into local authority housing because of the existence of waiting lists (point 7). Thus individuals who already have private rented accommodation, but want more space as their family grows, experience overcrowding; and families without accommodation may suffer homelessness.

The previous two points are accentuated by the fact that the price subsidy implicit in rent control is paid not from public funds, but by the landlord. This can have two effects.

16. *Reduction in quantity supplied.* The standard argument is that if controls reduce rents from p^* to p_1 in Figure 14.1, landlords will respond by reducing the supply of private rented accommodation from its optimum level, Q^* to Q_2, thereby accentuating excess demand. This argument is naive even in theory. A more realistic picture is given by the stock-adjustment model in section 3.1 (see Figure 14.2). Suppose that the market rent in long-run equilibrium is p^*. If demand increases from D_1 to D_2, the short-run equilibrium rent rises to p_1. In the absence of rent control, new houses are built at a more rapid rate, q_1 in the right-hand part of the diagram, a process which continues until the total stock has increased to Q^{**} restoring equilibrium rents to p^*. If rents, instead, are held at p_2, new construction will be slower (q_2 in the right-hand diagram), but in the long run the housing market still returns to equilibrium, restoring rents to p^*. The theoretical conclusion, therefore, is that rent controls do not reduce long-run supply so long as controlled rents exceed the long-run (though not necessarily the short-run) equilibrium. Only if rents are held below their long-run equilibrium, p^*, does the conclusion of the naive model hold.

Empirical investigation is complex and hampered by data problems. But there is consensus that for most (though not all) of the period since 1915 rents have been held below their long-run equilibrium; and that this has acted to reduce the supply of private rented accommodation, but is not the sole explanation of the dramatic decline in the private rented sector (Robinson, 1979, pp. 76–9 and 84–9).

17. *Reduction in quality supplied.* The fact that rent control is a subsidy from landlord to tenant is argued also to have reduced the *quality* of private rented accommodation below its optimum. The theoretical argument is shown in Figure 14.3.[27] A given house yields a flow of services, of which some are fixed (e.g. its size) and some variable (its state of decoration and repair); taken together these services determine quality. The price of each unit of service, v, is measured on the vertical axis, and their quantity, R, on the horizontal axis. When the rental market is in long-run equilibrium

[27] This approach is taken from Culyer (1980, Ch. 10).

the market rent, p^*, is shown in Figure 14.3 by the rectangle Ov^*aR^*, i.e. $p^* = v^*R^*$ shown at point a. If rents are restricted to $p_1 < p^*$, the landlord's receipts are reduced to the rectangle Ov_1bR^*, and the implied price per unit of service to v_1 as shown at point b.

Figure 14.3 *The effect of rent control on the quality of housing*

A possible response by landlords, while observing the restriction of their receipts to p_1, is to reduce costs and hence to increase their profits by reducing the quality of the house, cutting expenditure on repairs and maintenance. The line bcd is a rectangular hyperbola; it therefore shows all combinations of v and R which yield the same revenue (i.e. rent) as the rectangle Ov_1bR^*. Suppose the landlord reduces quality to R_2. His receipts are shown by the rectangle $Ov^*cR_2 = Ov_1bR^*$. However, at this implied price per unit of service, v^*, there will be excess demand (at price v^*, demand will be R^*, supply R_2). The market-clearing quantity is R_3, with an implied price per unit of service v_2. The landlord can obtain his required return at any price at or above v^*, hence at any quality at or below R_2. If legislation on minimum standards prevents him from lowering quality to R_3 (but allows him to lower it below R_2), he will still obtain his required return, but there will be excess demand for rented accommodation.

The theoretical conclusion is that rent control creates incentives to reduce the quality of housing, but the reduction in quality may not prevent excess demand. Empirically, the average quality of housing in the private rented sector is dramatically lower than in the other tenures, the prevalence of dwellings which are unfit, lacking in amenities or in serious disrepair being markedly higher than for other tenures (Hills and Mullings, 1990, Table 5.19). Though causality is hard to establish, there is a strong implication that rent control has been a contributory, though not necessarily the only, factor.

18. *Labour immobility* is a consequence of rent control to the extent that it creates excess demand. A tenant who leaves a controlled property may find no accommodation at a similar rent, and is therefore less likely to move. This reinforces the immobility caused by local authority waiting lists (point 8 above), though its quantitative magnitude is smaller, partly because the sector is smaller, and partly because relatively few people in the controlled private rented sector are members of the labour force.

Equity effects can be listed more briefly.

19. *Access to regulated tenancies is arbitrary*, with some tendency in addition to exclude those in greatest need. Rent control and security of tenure, by creating excess demand, benefit tenants already in controlled accommodation at the expense of those unable to obtain a regulated tenancy. To some extent it is the most needy who find it hardest to obtain such accommodation. Because of security of tenure, landlords choose tenants so as to minimise risk, which tends to exclude those who impose the greatest costs. These, disproportionately, are people in greatest housing need, e.g. large families with low incomes, and individuals with personal handicaps.

20. *Minimum standards are enforced least* in private rented accommodation, whose average standard (point 17) is lower than in the other sectors. This quality differential disproportionately affects the lowest socio-economic group (point 25).

21. *The redistributive effects of rent control may be arbitrary*. Not all landlords are rich and not all tenants poor. The transfer from landlord to tenant can therefore be distributionally arbitrary in individual cases, even though on average it is probably progressive because most tenants in the regulated rental sector are poor.

22. *Redistribution via income subsidies*, as with local authority housing, is progressive (see Table 10.2).

4.3 Housing as a Whole: Tenure Neutrality and the Distribution of Housing

This section discusses three aspects of the housing market as a whole: the relative subsidy to the different tenures, equality of access to different tenures (which are two aspects of tenure neutrality) and the distribution of housing.

23. *The relative subsidy to different tenures is unequal.* The subsidy to owner occupation is discussed by Robinson (1979, pp. 129–30) drawing on Rosenthal (1975). A renter and a homeowner have pre-tax money incomes Y_R and Y_O, respectively, and live in identical houses with the same market value, P. The owner-occupier receives an imputed income from his house of iE, where i is the (uniform) rate of return on capital and E his equity holding in his house. The two are assumed to have equal total (money plus imputed) incomes. Thus:

$$Y_R = Y_O + iE \tag{14.8}$$

The renter (ignoring maintenance costs, etc.) is assumed to pay a competitive market rent, iP. If we now introduce tax at a constant rate t on money income, but not on imputed income or mortgage interest payments, the disposable income (i.e. net of tax and housing costs) of the renter is

$$YD_R = (1 - t)Y_R - iP \tag{14.9}$$

For the owner-occupier, income after tax and housing costs is

$$YD_O = (1 - t)Y_O - i(P - E) + ti(P - E) \tag{14.10}$$

where $(P - E)$ is the size of the mortgage, $i(P - E)$ the mortgage interest payment and $ti(P - E)$ the mortgage tax relief. Comparing the disposable incomes of the two individuals by subtracting equation (14.9) from (14.10) gives

$$YD_O - YD_R = (1 - t)(Y_O - Y_R) + (1 - t)iE + tiP \tag{14.11}$$

We know from equation (14.8) that $Y_O - Y_R = -iE$; hence substituting into equation (14.11) the first two right-hand terms cancel and

$$YD_O - YD_R = tiP \tag{14.12}$$

The advantage to the owner-occupier, *ceteris paribus*, is tiP, the tax relief on the imputed income from his house.

The difference between the tax relief on imputed income and that on mortgage interest payments is much more than a technicality in two important respects. First, the relief on imputed income, iP, is related to the current market value of the house and will therefore rise as P appreciates, whereas mortgage interest payments, $i(P_O - E)$, and hence the associated tax relief, are related to the initial purchase price, P_O, and so remain constant or decline over time. Thus, for any particular house, the tax base would be increased more by restoring the taxation of imputed housing income than by abolishing mortgage interest relief, since $iP > i(P_0 - E)$ and the difference increases over time.[28] A second major difference is that taxation of imputed income applies not just to individuals with a mortgage (who could offset their interest payments against their imputed income), but to all owner-occupiers, including the 50 per cent (largely the elderly) without a mortgage.

It is open to debate whether the tax relief on imputed income, tiP, or on mortgage interest, $ti(P_0 - E)$, is the better measure of the transfer to homeowners. As so often, the answer depends on what is being compared with what. The tax relief on imputed income shows the advantage of owner occupation relative to renting; and the tax relief on mortgage interest is a measure of the advantage relative to investment in other consumer durables like cars, interest payments for which receive no tax concessions.

To these reliefs, however measured, is added the transfer to owner-occupiers due to the exemption from capital gains tax. The value of this relief has declined since 1984, when extensions to the indexation of capital gains reduced the impact of the tax on non-housing assets. It is possible at least approximately to measure the *actual* value of this relief; but it is much harder to measure the concession relative to 'true' capital gains, given the well-known difficulties of choosing an appropriate base for the tax. A complete measure of the tax benefit to owner-occupiers would have to resolve the ambiguities of all the various tax reliefs, as well as considering the extent to which they are capitalised in house prices (point 5).

Transfers to local authority tenants can be discussed more briefly. The subsidy can be measured by comparing the actual rent (net of housing benefit) with *either* the historic cost of housing *or* the notional competitive market rent. The latter is the more appropriate in economic terms (Rosenthal, 1977; Robinson, 1979, pp. 132–3; Piggott, 1984) though much harder to measure. The former is more relevant to public expenditure, and is therefore the figure used in official publications. In the early 1990s, according to official figures, local authority rents were about 85 per cent of broadly comparable private rents (UK, 1992b, Figure 93).

The transfer due to rent control is the difference between the controlled rent (again net of housing benefit) and the market rent, though with ambiguity as to whether the comparison should be with the short-run equilibrium rent (p_1 in Figure 14.2) or the theoretical long-run equilibrium, p^*.

Though conceptually it is all but impossible to disentangle an unambiguous

---

[28] The widening difference is offset only in part by the tendency for P_0 to increase as individuals move to a larger house.

definition of equality of subsidy, empirical evidence suggests that owner occupation is favoured more than the other tenures (Whitehead, 1983, para. 5), and that the differential has widened in recent years (Glennerster, 1992, Ch. 13). Owner-occupiers have built up substantial wealth over the post-war period, in part through their own contributions. But they have also received two forms of transfer: from taxpayers generally (because of the non-taxation of mortgage interest and capital gains), and from savers. The latter transfer results from the redistributive effects of unanticipated inflation, which led to periods of negative real interest rates; and mortgage repayments for many individuals fell as a proportion of their income. Over the same period, tenants had to pay rising rents and built up no housing wealth.

24. *Access to different tenures is unequal.* This is a second aspect of tenure neutrality. Access to owner occupation is restricted by capital market imperfections, to the detriment of the worst-off (point 3). The allocation of local authority housing is marred by the way tenants are selected from the waiting list, and also because needy tenants may over time become less needy (point 10); and regional inequalities cause further problems (point 11). Excess demand for private rented accommodation and risk-averting behaviour by landlords together create arbitrariness in access to regulated tenancies, with particular difficulties for those in greatest housing need (point 19).

Tenure neutrality is thus achieved in terms of neither equality of subsidy nor equality of opportunity. In both respects, the system tends to work to the advantage of the better-off, with an added element of arbitrariness. This conclusion is borne out by empirical evidence (UK Department of the Environment, 1977c, Ch. 5). We have already seen that the crude distribution of subsidies is unequal. Table 14.3 shows (column (2)) that mortgage tax relief disproportionately benefits the better-off, though these data are qualified in that tax advantages may partly be capitalised in house prices (point 5). At the same time (column (3)), the distribution of subsidies to local authority tenants, at least until the early 1980s, was largely invariant to income. Le Grand (1982, Table 5.1) reaches similar conclusions.

The evidence on the relation between tenure and socieconomic status is also persuasive (though not conclusive). Table 14.4 shows that 82 per cent of households in the highest socioeconomic group are owner-occupiers, while only 8 per cent are local authority tenants and 6 per cent private tenants. Column (1) shows that the higher socioeconomic groups are disproportionately owner-occupiers while local authority tenants (column (2)) are concentrated among the less well-off. As a descriptive matter the housing market is not completely segmented (29 per cent of semi- and unskilled manual workers are owner-occupiers), but differences in household tenure by socioeconomic group are systematic and strong. In behavioural terms, these disparities can be explained by differences in tastes (in which case no issue of inequality arises), or by differences in constraints, or by a combination of the two. The difficulty of separating these effects qualifies the stark appearance of the data. The conclusion (Whitehead, 1980, p. 112) is that

fiscal neutrality and 'appropriate' incentives are not obtained: between consumers, between different types of investment, within housing, between housing and other assets, or between consumption, saving and investment. Horizontal inequalities between tenures are particularly common and, especially for people living in the private rental sector, assistance helps to exacerbate the strong vertical inequities of the system.

25. *The distribution of housing*. The lower socioeconomic groups are twice as likely as better-off households to live at a density of more than one

Table 14.4 *Household tenure by socioeconomic group, Great Britain, 1978*

SOCIOECONOMIC GROUP	TYPE OF TENURE (%)			
	Owner-occupied (1)	Rented from local authority (2)	Private rented (3)	Other (4)
Professionals, employers and managers	82	8	6	5
Intermediate and junior non-manual	59	25	12	5
Skilled manual	49	40	9	3
Semi-skilled and skilled manual	29	56	11	3

Source: Le Grand (1982, Table 5.2).
Note: Percentages may not add up because of rounding.

person per room (Le Grand, 1982, Table 5.4). Four per cent of households in 1977 had less than the 'standard' number of rooms given their size; the incidence of this type of overcrowding was six times as high for the lowest socioeconomic groups as for households in the top socioeconomic group (Reid, 1981, Table 5.30). Overcrowding also varies substantially by tenure. Only 0.5 per cent of owner-occupiers in 1971 lived at a density of more than 1.5 people per room; for local authority tenants the proportion was 1.8 per cent, and for private tenants in furnished accommodation over 8 per cent (UK Department of the Environment, 1977b, Table II.14). Hills and Mullings (1990, pp. 181–2) found that housing improvements over the 1980s had not benefited the lowest income quintile, whose relative position therefore worsened. The extreme case of shortage of space is homelessness. To an even greater extent than overcrowding, this disproportionately afflicts the lowest socioeconomic groups.

Similar variations occur in the quality of housing. In 1977, families in the top socioeconomic group were more than twice as likely as the bottom group to have central heating, and nearly twice as likely to live in a detached or semi-detached house (Le Grand, 1982, Table 5.4). The distribution of housing by annual income shows even more marked inequalities (Townsend, 1979, Ch. 13; Le Grand, 1982, Ch. 5); and inequalities in tenure, density and amenities tend to persist across generations (Jenkins and Maynard, 1983).

The overwhelming conclusion is that, though subsidies may have led to some equalisation, sizeable inequalities remain. Whether they are *too* large depends partly on whether the housing standards of the lower socioeconomic groups are *inefficiently* low, and partly on the weight attached to equality.

5 Reform

5.1 The Debate Over Reform

In view of the arguments in section 4 it is not surprising that proponents of the status quo are few. The argument that mortgage interest tax relief is not a subsidy does not bear close examination. As we have seen (Chapter 7:1.1), tax expenditures should properly be included in public spending.[29] Possibly the only plausible argument for the status quo is that radical change may be impossible for political reasons because the interests of so many individuals would be affected. A fundamental reform of housing finance has been on the political agenda for a long time (UK Department of the Environment, 1971, 1977a), but change has been limited.

An early proposal for reform by Nevitt (1966)[30] advocated tenure-neutral taxation together with a unified system of subsidies for all tenures, under which poor families receive assistance scaled to their housing need, and better-off families receive no subsidy at all. The scheme suggested in section 5.2 is in many ways similar.

Donnison and Ungerson (1982) suggest a scheme which pays the full cost of housing for low-income families, the benefit to be withdrawn as family income rises. The problem with this proposal is its expense. If it were financed through the abolition of mortgage interest relief, the package would resemble the scheme in the previous paragraph. Lansley (1982) advocates a universal, flat-rate (i.e. non-means-tested) housing allowance based on family size and an index of regional housing costs, where the allowance covers the full cost of minimum standard accommodation. Conceptually, this scheme is a form of negative income tax, and so raises the problems discussed in Chapter 11. Its universal nature makes it

[29] Since 1983 mortgage interest in the UK has been paid net of tax (see footnote 18, above). Thus tax relief for owner-occupiers is paid by the Inland Revenue to the building societies, etc. For local authority tenants, housing benefit is paid by the Department of Social Security to local authorities. The latter payments appear in the public expenditure figures, the former do not. See Barr (1986) for criticism.

[30] Subsequently echoed in part by the Housing Finance Act 1972, and more recently by the National Federation of Housing Associations (1985) and Inquiry into British Housing (1991).

immensely costly, and therefore requires a sharp increase in tax rates (on these and other proposals, see Glennerster (1992, Ch. 13) and Hills (1991, Ch. 16)).

The USA has also seen its fair share of reform proposals, concerned particularly with improving the housing conditions of the poor. Most schemes focus on income subsidies rather than public production of housing at subsidised rents. In 1973 the US Department of Housing and Urban Development funded a series of experiments in twelve cities to test the feasibility of housing allowances. For a variety of reasons the experiment met with mixed success (see Bradbury and Downs (1987), especially the chapter by Aaron).

5.2 Designing a System for a Brand New Country

This section discusses how housing finance in Britain might be reformed, assuming that we start *ab initio* to design a system for a hypothetical brand new country. Section 5.3 considers how such a system might be implemented in practice. The two aspects of reform are discussed more fully by Hills (1991, Chs 16 and 17).

Regulation is essential. First, there would be minimum standards for individual dwellings, partly because of the public health externality and also (though more arguably) on the grounds of horizontal equity. Minimum standards to protect the poor 'for their own good' (i.e. the merit good argument discussed in Chapter 4:4.2) should not be accepted uncritically. If they are set at a level higher than is justified on *efficiency* grounds, the cost of minimum standard housing will (a) be inefficiently high for those who would rationally choose housing of lesser (but still efficient) quality, and (b) be beyond the reach of those with lower incomes. Given its longevity, there are enough unavoidable problems over the affordability of housing without aggravating them unnecessarily (though with the best of motives) by setting standards which can worsen the housing problem to the detriment particularly of the poor. It can be argued that the only *equity* justification for minimum standards is the protection of children and possibly also the elderly.

Zoning and planning controls over land use would be concerned with housing density (because of the public health externality); the separation of residential housing from factories (because of the spatial externality); and the provision of amenities such as public open space (which has public good attributes) and water, gas, electricity and sewerage (for reasons of public health, and because their distribution displays increasing returns to scale). Third, there would be some regulation of private landlords to prevent exploitation of monopoly power over tenants (see section 3.2), and to protect tenants against arbitrary eviction. This type of regulation is necessary for the fulfilment of the 'equal power' assumption (Chapter 4:3.2), thereby increasing both efficiency and horizontal equity. Finally, it may be necessary to regulate the professional standards of surveyors and valuers to ensure adequate consumer information about the quality and price of housing (cf. hygiene laws for food).

Production of housing would be subject to the relevant regulation; it could take place in either or both public and private sectors. In terms of economic efficiency the issues of public/private production of the housing stock and its ownership are much less important than its *price*.

Finance Three issues are important: the supply of mortgage finance; the price of housing; and vertical equity. *The supply of loan finance* could remain in the private sector, but with the addition of publicly provided loans or loan guarantees for individuals who have difficulty in obtaining an adequate mortgage in the private sector; and all mortgages would be fully indexed to the real value of the initial loan. These interventions would make access to capital markets more equitable, and would aid tenure neutrality; the supply of mortgages would not be artificially restricted; and there would be no arbitrary transfer from savers to mortgage holders.

House prices (both purchase price and rent) would be market prices with only three possible exceptions. There would be price subsidies in respect of a limited number of externalities, e.g. to prevent the spread of slums and/or to encourage 'gentrification' (see UK Department of the Environment, 1985b). Subsidies of this type are likely to be small in amount, and would apply only to a limited proportion of the total housing stock. The only argument for a *general* price subsidy is if it is believed that the private discount rate systematically exceeds the social discount rate. These two forms of subsidy perform an efficiency function.

The third exception is that it may be necessary for equity reasons to subsidise rents to prevent hardship if housing demand in an area rises, thereby (because short-run supply is inelastic) causing rents to rise sharply. These subsidies could be implemented in various ways: as additional income transfers to poor tenants in high-rent areas; or as a price subsidy paid by the *state* to prevent the contraction of private supply (measured in quantity and quality) resulting from rent control. Rent control is probably the least attractive method, and should be adopted, if at all, only as a temporary expedient;[31] and it is essential that controlled rents equal or exceed the long-run equilibrium, p^* in Figure 14.2, though they should obviously be below the (temporarily high) short-run market-clearing rent. This last solution has the disadvantages that it is likely to slow adjustment to the

---

[31] Though this was the intention in 1915. Income tax was also originally intended to be temporary.

higher level of demand (point 16), and also has arbitrary distributional effects (point 21).

The adoption of market prices implies the removal of all price subsidies except in the cases just discussed. For owner occupation this should ideally take the form of taxing imputed housing income. If this is not possible for administrative or political reasons, there should be no mortgage interest tax relief. In either case it would be necessary to apply capital gains tax, indexed in some sensible way, to owner-occupied houses. There would be no subsidies from central and local revenues to local authority housing, and local authorities would pay market interest rates on borrowed funds. In the private sector there would be no rent control except, possibly, in the circumstances just discussed, in which case it should be strictly limited as to time and place. House prices and rents, in short, would be *market* prices, subject to long-run modification only for very specific reasons.

Income transfers would be the main vehicle for pursuing vertical equity. There would be one system applying to all tenures. Consider first the transfer to a householder with no income. He/she would receive £X per week, related to family size. In strict efficiency terms the subsidy would not vary regionally, so as to leave migration decisions undistorted. But housing costs vary so substantially in different areas that this policy conflicts with equity considerations. It can therefore be argued that the income subsidy should be higher in areas with higher *average* housing costs (ideally the transfer should not be directly related to a family's *actual* housing costs because this would interfere with marginal decisions). The transfer could be untied (i.e paid in cash), or tied to expenditure on housing if this were necessary for political or other reasons (e.g. to protect children). The transfer would be reduced as family income increased, and above a certain income would cease entirely.

A veil is deliberately being drawn over the size of the basic transfer and its relation to family income, both of which require detailed study. But the scheme is undoubtedly feasible in purely *financial* terms. Public expenditure (broadly defined) on housing in 1992/3 was around £20 billion (Table 14.2), much of it benefiting the better-off. The scheme just described would use this sum to pay an income-related (i.e. unambiguously progressive) transfer. It follows as a proposition in pure logic that on a revenue-neutral basis the poor on average must benefit at the expense of the non-poor.[32] Herein lies the problem of the scheme, which is not its financial but its political feasibility.

The individual consumption decision Individuals would make a utility-maximising decision constrained by their income (including the housing

[32] The point in the income distribution at which people would receive less assistance than currently would depend on the precise details of the transfer.

transfer) and subject in all tenures to the (generally) market price/rent of housing.

These proposals are likely to sound abhorrent to those who regard the market as inequitable. Such readers are asked to bear with the argument, and invited to remember the aims of housing policy outlined in section 2; to acknowledge (at least in part) the magnitude of the failure of the existing system to achieve them (section 4); and to consider the advantages of the scheme outlined above, advantages in terms of efficiency and, possibly even more, in terms of horizontal and vertical equity.

In efficiency terms, market prices, modified if at all only for the three reasons discussed, avert incentives to underoccupy, thereby avoiding many of the forces contributing to overcrowding and homelessness. Owner-occupiers have no incentive to buy a large house as an artificially inflated asset; and the existence of market (or modified market) rents prevents systematic excess demand in both rental sectors, thus avoiding the worst of the problems discussed in section 4.2. Waiting lists would no longer be a permanent part of the landscape, though it would be desirable for local authorities to have some housing under their control for emergency cases, and also because housing markets take time to adjust. Additionally, market pricing together with indexed mortgages result, at least approximately, in tenure neutrality.

The system also contributes substantially to horizontal equity. Access to mortgage finance would be more equal; arbitrariness in the allocation of rented accommodation in both public and private sectors would be reduced; and regional inequalities in access to local authority housing would be less important because there would be approximate neutrality between local authority housing and the other tenures. Access to housing would be determined not by administrative decision but by individual choice (see English, 1982); and the distribution of housing by income level could be adjusted via the size of the housing transfer and its relation to family income.[33]

In terms of vertical equity the housing transfer is unambiguously progressive (see Table 10.2). In comparison with the present system, transfers would go to those in greatest need, with no subsidy at all for the well-off. As a result, access to housing for the poor would be increased; for the rich it would be reduced. Additionally, the indexation of loans for house purchase eliminates the arbitrary transfer from savers to mortgage holders.

In terms of cost, the system would either be cheaper because individuals who were not poor would no longer receive subsidies; or if it were not

---

[33] Another result is that council house sales would be less controversial. On the supply side, state intervention in mortgage markets would make owner occupation more generally available; on the demand side, tenure neutrality would remove the financial advantages of owner occupation relative to renting.

cheaper, but revenue-neutral, would be more cost-effective because benefits would be focused more systematically.

5.3 How to Get from Here to There

The final part of the argument is to consider the major difficulties involved in changing the present UK system to a very different set of arrangements. The design of any such change would require an immense amount of work, and what follows is the barest of outlines (for a more detailed set of rather similar proposals see National Federation of Housing Associations (1985) and Inquiry into British Housing (1991)). The sorts of change envisaged would obviously set in train a series of long-run adjustments in all sectors of the housing market, implying that any new system should be phased in gradually.

Adjustment problems are likely to be particularly acute in the owner-occupied sector. The instant removal of all tax reliefs for owner-occupiers would at least partly be capitalised (Whitehead, 1983, paras 16–18). House prices would fall sharply, imposing heavy capital losses, with the result in some cases that house values would be lower than existing mortgages (i.e. an individual could find himself with a £100,000 mortgage on a house now worth only £90,000). It would therefore probably be necessary to phase out mortgage interest relief gradually, by reducing the amount of mortgage qualifying for tax relief (currently £30,000) by, say, £500 per year, thereby removing the tax concession over a 20-year period;[34] or the rate at which tax relief is granted could gradually be reduced. As a step in the right direction, mortgage interest relief, since 1991, is given only at the basic rate of income tax. Alternatively, mortgage interest relief could be retained, and the taxation of imputed housing income gradually reintroduced. The main difficulties with this approach are its administrative complexity and the likelihood, for political reasons, that the assessment of imputed income would never reach the full market value of the flow of housing services, not least because such taxation would bear more heavily on the elderly than present arrangements. It might therefore be more realistic to phase out mortgage interest relief. The removal of capital gains tax relief could be phased in more easily, by bringing into tax only the real gains arising after some date subsequent to legislation (i.e. only gains arising *after* the market had at least partly adjusted to the new system).

The withdrawal of price subsidies for local authority housing would present no insuperable problems if accompanied by a suitable phasing in of the income-related housing transfer. For reasons of horizontal equity the time-scale might be the same as for the tax changes for owner-occupiers.

---

[34] The proposals of the National Federation of Housing Associations (1985, p. 19) suggest that tax relief should be phased out over 10–12 years.

Similarly, the gradual removal of rent control over the same period would be accompanied by the phased introduction of the housing transfer. In both cases, the only losers would be tenants with incomes too high to qualify for the income subsidy.

Several problems are harder to solve. First, an income-related housing transfer could aggravate the poverty trap, inasmuch as the transfer would be reduced as family income rose. To the extent that a solution exists it would depend on more general reform of income support along the lines discussed in Chapter 11. Second, the precise details of the transfer would need to take account of difficulties with take-up, links with other forms of income support, and similar such problems as arose with housing benefit (Chapter 10:1).

6 Conclusion: Housing

Housing fails in various ways to conform with the conditions necessary for an unrestricted private market to be efficient. The specific failures justify substantial regulation, price subsidies for strictly limited reasons, and public provision of loan finance or loan guarantees. The theoretical discussion in sections 3.2 and 3.3 suggests that state intervention along these lines would improve efficiency and horizontal equity.

Three conclusions follow (section 3.4). First, in sharp contrast with health care, the information problems which arise are of a type which the market itself is able to solve; individuals (with professional advice if necessary) are generally able to make rational choices. Second, the efficiency justification for *general* price subsidies is highly qualified. This point, together with the first, implies that there are powerful advantages to keeping prices at the level dictated by efficiency, and seeking to achieve distributional objectives through cash transfers. Third, no efficiency justification emerges for public production of housing (as opposed to regulation of private supply). This is not an argument *against* public production. But the three points taken together suggest that the aims of housing policy (section 2) are more likely to be achieved if housing is allocated through individual consumption decisions, subject to regulation on minimum standards and efficient prices, and supported by income transfers.

British housing institutions (section 4.1), characterised by substantial and pervasive subsidies, are strongly at variance with this model. Public expenditure, as set out in Table 14.2, is large (nearly 60 per cent of spending on the National Health Service), and involves substantial *price* subsidies. Owner-occupiers receive considerable tax relief; local authority rents are subsidised in a number of ways; and private-sector rents are often reduced by rent control.

Many of these institutions date from decisions made during and just after the First World War (Chapter 2:3.1). For the reasons discussed in section 3 there is no efficiency justification for such large subsidies, nor for their application to such a large proportion of the housing stock. The result (section 4.2) is that price subsidies in each sector of the housing market create excess demand, which reinforces excess demand in the other sectors. In consequence, there is evidence simultaneously of underoccupation, over-crowding and homelessness; the quantity and quality of the regulated private rental stock has deteriorated; labour mobility is hindered; and the system is decidedly not tenure-neutral. The system also performs badly in terms of horizontal equity. Access to mortgage finance favours the higher socio-economic groups; and access to rental accommodation in both public and private sectors has a strong arbitrary element. The redistributive effects of housing finance can also be perverse. The tax advantages to owner-occupiers are regressive. The distributional impact of price subsidies to local authority tenants and (in a very different way) to households living in regulated private rented accommodation are largely arbitrary. Income subsidies to households in rented accommodation are progressive, but take-up and administration are still patchy.

These problems are an entirely predictable consequence of price subsidies introduced mainly to increase equity.[35] The conclusion is clear. The use of price subsidies *only* for equity reasons is a confusion of aims and methods which is almost bound to cause inefficiency and inequity (Chapter 4:7.2). In the absence of an efficiency justification, price subsidies are likely to cause excess demand and/or overconsumption unless demand can be rationed efficiently by administrative means. This is possible with health care but works less well with housing. In the latter case, equity (as well as efficiency) aims are more likely to be achieved by income subsidies. No policy-maker starting from scratch with the vast sum currently spent on housing would choose to spend it in the manner described in section 4.1.

The strategy for reform in section 5.2 draws on the theoretical discussion of section 3, supported by the analysis of section 4, which shows how the shortcomings just described are readily explicable in terms of the theory. The state would retain wide regulatory powers over individual dwellings and over land use generally; and there would be regulation to prevent private landlords from abusing their power. The production of housing, subject to regulation, could be private, public or both. Housing finance would be reformed in three ways. First, the state would take action to improve access to capital markets. Second, with only limited exceptions, house prices and rents would over time be brought into line with market-

[35] Many other countries avoid at least some of these problems. It is noteworthy that a major American study of priorities for the 1980s in both foreign and domestic policy (Pechman, 1980) had a chapter on health care, another on education, another on the environment (pollution, safety, etc.). But in a volume of 500 pages there was scarcely a mention of housing (or of food).

clearing prices by the phased withdrawal of tax reliefs for owner-occupiers, price subsidies to local authority tenants and the implied price subsidy of rent control. Third, the revenue thereby released would be used to pay income-related transfers.

The result would come much closer than existing arrangements to tenure neutrality, and would greatly reduce underoccupation, overcrowding, immobility and homelessness. Vertical equity would be improved because subsidies would be systematically related to income, rather than arbitrary; and those with above-average incomes would no longer be subsidised at all.

These arrangements approximate more closely to the case of food than to the National Health Service. The implied suggestion is that difficulties with housing are more an income distribution problem than a market allocation problem. The strategy is chosen *not* for ideological reasons, but because it is more likely to achieve the aims set out in section 2. The National Health Service strategy of free provision via administrative decision works well for health care, for the reasons given in Chapter 12; it does not work well for housing. Individuals have diverse tastes about housing, and can generally make better decisions than housing administrators because they have better information than officials (contrast the case of health care). The nature of housing as a commodity thus approximates more closely to food than to health care. This *technical* observation is the basis of the reforms proposed in sections 5.2 and 5.3. Their major difficulty is less an economic one than their requirement of a long-run policy based on widespread support. In political terms this may not be forthcoming, partly for ideological reasons and partly because the reforms produce losers as well as gainers. Despite the political problem, however, it is clear that Britain needs a *strategy* for the reform of housing finance, not just *ad hoc* tinkering.

It is important, in conclusion, to be clear what I am *not* saying. I am not arguing for the abolition of subsidies to local authority housing, nor simply for the abolition of rent control, nor even for the abolition of all housing subsidies. What is being suggested, quite simply, is that over time *price* subsidies should be replaced by *income* subsidies in all sectors of the housing market.

Further Reading

On the historical background see UK Department of the Environment (1977b, Ch. 1), Robinson (1979, Ch. 6), Gauldie (1974) and Swenarton (1981). On the quantity and quality of the housing stock see National Federation of Housing Associations (1985, Ch. 2). Details of housing benefit and its reform are contained in UK (1985e, 1985h, Ch. 3) (see also the Further Reading to Chapter 10). Recent housing policy is contained in UK Department of the Environment (1987a, b, c). For analytical discussion of financial aspects, see Glennerster (1992, Ch. 12) and Hills (1991). The planning process and its effects are discussed by Hall (1982), and inner city problems by Hall (1981), Donnison and Soto (1980) and Bassett and Short (1980).

The best discussions of housing economics, both theoretical and with a review of empirical evidence, are by Robinson (1979), MacLennan (1982), Hills (1991) and Muth and Goodman (1989). For a survey, see Smith *et al.* (1988).

For assessment of British housing policy, see Hills (1991), Forrest and Murie (1990) and MacLennan and Gibb (1993).

The most complete early proposal for reform is by Nevitt (1966); a recent inquiry chaired by HRH The Duke of Edinburgh (National Federation of Housing Associations, 1985) and a second inquiry (Inquiry into British Housing, 1991) reached similar conclusions; see also Hills (1991, Chs 16 and 17).

Part 4
Epilogue

Chapter 15
Conclusion

A democratic capitalist society will keep searching for better ways of drawing the boundary lines between the domain of rights and the domain of dollars. And it can make progress. To be sure, it will never solve the problem, for the conflict between equality and economic efficiency is inescapable. In that sense, capitalism and democracy are really a most improbable mixture. Maybe that is why they need each other – to put some rationality into equality and some humanity into efficiency. [Arthur M. Okun, 1975.]

1 Arguments for a Welfare State

1.1 Theory

The British welfare state is the outcome of diverse forces over nearly four centuries of developing social policy. Two aspects, in particular, stand out from the historical discussion in Chapter 2: debates about ideology (which are taken up in Chapter 3), and the welfare state's functional purposes, notably economic efficiency (Chapters 4 and 5). Ideological aims vary widely. To libertarians (Chapter 3:2) the primary goal is individual freedom, which is best achieved by unrestricted private markets. Empirical libertarians like Hayek and Friedman therefore espouse minimal intervention and oppose all but the most austere welfare systems, whose purpose is limited to poverty relief. Marxists (Chapter 3:4.2) regard the market system by its very nature as incompatible with their primary aim of meeting need. They therefore reject it, and give the state a primary role in production and allocation. Marxists have mixed feelings about the welfare state (Chapter 3:5.3). In part it accords with their aim of meeting need and is therefore to be applauded; yet it serves also to support a capitalist system which they regard as inherently unjust.

Liberals take a more eclectic view. The utilitarian aim (Chapter 3:3.1) is the maximisation of total welfare, leaving open the question of whether it is to be achieved by private markets, by public production and allocation, or by a mix of the two. Rawls (Chapter 3:3.2) argues that goods, liberty and opportunity should be distributed equally unless any other arrangement is to the advantage of the least well-off. Again, the issue of how this is best achieved is left open. For the purposes of this book the single feature which above all distinguishes liberal theories is the treatment of private property as an issue which is contingent, not dogmatic, i.e. the treatment of private property is not an end in itself but a means towards the achievement of stated aims (see Okun, 1975).

Society has functional as well as ideological goals, notably the achievement of economic efficiency, as defined in Chapter 4:2.1. Where there is a trade-off between efficiency and social justice their relative weights will vary between libertarians, liberals and Marxists. But an increase in efficiency which does not impair social justice is an unambiguous gain under *any* of these theories of society (Chapter 4:2.2).

Efficiency can be achieved as the outcome of a market-clearing process, notably in a competitive environment with no market failures and, importantly, with no significant information failures (Chapter 4:3.2). Similar conditions are necessary if insurance is to be efficient: at least some individuals must be risk-averse (Chapter 5:2.1), and there must be no technical problems with privately supplied insurance (Chapter 5:3). These conditions, referred to collectively as the *standard assumptions*, must all hold if the market is to be relied on to allocate efficiently.

The distinction between *aims* and *methods* is crucial. The ideological and functional aims of policy can be encapsulated in large measure in the twin goals of economic efficiency and social justice. Once the aims have been chosen, the next step is to select methods to achieve them, including (Chapter 4:3.1) no state intervention at all; intervention in the form of cash transfers; or interference with the market mechanism through regulation, through financial involvement and/or through public production. The approach can be summarised in two statements: (a) the proper place of ideology is in the choice of aims, particularly the definition of social justice and its trade-off with economic efficiency; (b) once these aims have been agreed, the choice of method should be treated as a *technical* issue.

Whether a good is better produced publicly or privately should be decided on the basis of which method more closely achieves specified aims; and a major purpose has been to give a rationale in any situation for choosing the method(s) most likely to do so. This was given in the form of two propositions (Chapter 4:7.2).

1. If the standard assumptions hold, market allocation will be efficient; in this case social justice should generally be pursued via income transfers (e.g. so that poor people can buy food at market prices).

2. Suppose the standard assumptions fail in a way that justifies public production and allocation on *efficiency* grounds; social justice may then

appropriately be pursued through direct transfers in kind (e.g. free medical care under the National Health Service).

Whether a particular commodity should be publicly or privately produced is thus contingent on its technical characteristics, i.e. a liberal approach in the sense described above (for libertarian and Marxist counter-arguments, see Chapter 4:7.3). The welfare state should not be judged in dogmatic terms, but should be supported only if it contributes more than alternative arrangements to the achievement of agreed policy objectives.

1.2 Policy

Chapter 1 started with two questions: what theoretical arguments justify the existence of the various parts of the welfare state; and given these arguments of principle, how well do the British and other systems perform? The answers are summarised in Chapter 4:7 for the underlying theory, Chapter 11:5 for cash benefits, and the concluding sections of Chapters 12, 13 and 14 for health care, education and housing, respectively, so only the most important conclusions are set out here.

The aims of cash benefits (Chapter 1:2.2) include the relief of poverty (about which there is general agreement) and, more controversially, the protection of accustomed living standards and the reduction of inequality. Their achievement requires mechanisms to foster self-help and vertical redistribution.

Self-help is necessary for an individual/family who is self-supporting over his/her lifetime, but who needs a system of income smoothing to facilitate redistribution from himself at one time (e.g. when working) to himself at another (e.g. when unemployed or retired). The answer in principle is voluntary private insurance. This, however, is not a tenable strategy (Chapters 8 and 9). On the demand side, non-insurance imposes external costs on various groups including taxpayers, giving an efficiency reason for making insurance compulsory (Chapter 8:2.1). On the supply side, the private market is unable for technical reasons to provide the efficient quantity and type of insurance against all causes of income loss; in particular, unemployment and inflation are not insurable risks.

Several important results follow. There are strong efficiency grounds for public provision of unemployment compensation (Chapter 8:2.2) and at least the indexation component of retirement pensions (Chapter 9:3.1). For these benefits at least, public involvement, whatever the form it takes, will not (because it cannot) be actuarially related to individual risks; and the same can be said of any institutions in these areas. For the major risks covered by the state scheme, adherence to strict actuarial principles is neither possible (except as a mimic of private institutions) nor necessary, and only arguably desirable. Various reforms of the insurance system are possible, but a substantial return to voluntary private insurance and pure, private, funded pensions is not one of them (Chapters 8:3.1 and 9:5.1). Social policy requires that individuals are protected against income loss; but strict adherence to market supply enables them to acquire protection only where risks are insurable. This puts the cart before the horse by making *social* policy subservient to *technical* considerations.

Vertical redistribution is relevant to those who cannot support themselves over their lifetime. In principle it can be organised through private charity or by the state. Partly because of the free-rider problem, redistribution through private charity is likely to be sub-optimal even by libertarian standards, and even further below the Rawlsian or socialist optimum (Chapter 4:4.1). Redistribution through the tax system may therefore be justified in both efficiency and equity terms (Chapter 10:2) under any theory of society, though with considerable disagreement as to how much redistribution is desirable (Chapter 4:4.4) or feasible (Chapter 11). The overall success of cash benefits in practice is also controversial (Chapters 8:3, 9:5 and 10:3). The UK has a wide-ranging system of insurance benefits whose effect, albeit imperfectly, is redistributive from rich to poor; these are buttressed by assistance benefits organised on a national basis, for which *everyone* is potentially eligible. Many other countries have less comprehensive systems (Chapter 2:6). Nevertheless, poverty remains (Chapter 10:3.4). Nor is this simply because the poverty line has been moved up over the years; for many there is not just *relative* poverty, but a life of harsh discomfort which persists to the present.

Reform can follow one of two strategies. Benefits can be conditioned on income by an explicit means test or through a negative income tax (Chapter 11:2), though this approach can easily aggravate the poverty trap (see the Glossary), with important efficiency and equity costs. Alternatively, it may be possible to side-step the worst of the poverty trap by adopting the 'Back to Beveridge' approach (Chapter 11:3), under which benefits are conditioned on carefully chosen characteristics of recipients, such as being unemployed or retired, or having children. A judicious combination of the two approaches (Chapter 11.4) might be to raise the main national insurance benefits to the income support level, to increase child benefit, and to make all these benefits taxable.

Benefits in kind The theoretical discussion of public involvement in health care and education is set out in the early parts of Chapters 12 and 13, respectively. The issues are complex, not least because of intractable measurement problems (Chapters 12:2.2 and 13:2.2). There are strong *a priori* arguments suggesting that unrestricted private markets for health care and education (Chapters 12:3 and 13:3) will be inefficient, and also inequitable to the extent that information, power and access to capital markets are correlated with socioeconomic status. The precise form of public involvement has two aspects. The *allocation* issue rests crucially on whether individuals or 'experts' (doctors, teachers, etc.) are better informed and/or better able to act in the interests of consumers. The question of *production* depends largely on whether quality/quantity can be monitored more effectively with production in the public or private sector. The theoretical arguments for public production and allocation of health care and education (Chapters 12:3.3 and 13:3.3), though not irrefutable, are strong, largely because of information problems, particularly in the case of health care.

The National Health Service is not above criticism, but it has powerful advantages (Chapter 12:4). By international standards the system is cheap and, for the most part, provides high-quality care. Theoretical argument and international comparison both suggest that radical 'privatisation' (whatever its advocates mean by the term) will not solve old problems, and is likely to create new and larger ones. The evidence for Britain, overwhelmingly, is that the National Health Service should be retained, and improvement sought within the existing strategy by increasing its resources, gathering and using more and better information, and the introduction of a measure of competition on the supply side. This is not to say that public production is the only possible model. Other countries with different political traditions and different medical structures have adopted other sensible *strategies* of mixed public/private provision, e.g. private production and public funding subject to a budget constraint, as in Canada (Chapter 12:5).

The educational system fares less well (Chapter 13:4). The evidence suggests that middle-class children on average receive a disproportionate share of educational resources in terms of both quantity and quality; and that these differentials cannot be attributed solely to differences in tastes. In addition, the finance of university education restricts the size of the sector, and is regressive. It is open to question to what extent these features are *necessarily* an indictment of the present system. Opponents have to show not that the state sector is imperfect (which is not in dispute), but that a more market-oriented system would do better. Vouchers for school education (Chapter 13:5.1) offer no such prospect. Their efficiency effects are unclear *a priori* and unproven empirically; in equity terms they are likely to benefit middle-class children more than other groups. Loans for university education have also been suggested. It is argued (Chapter 13:5.2) that a well-designed system would improve efficiency by allowing higher education to expand, and this would also be an equalising measure, both because rich students would to that extent no longer be financed by lower-income taxpayers, and because expansion would improve access for students from poorer backgrounds.

Housing is the one major area where the welfare state has performed badly, not through choosing controversial aims (Chapter 14:2), but by adopting methods which are unlikely to achieve them. The theoretical arguments (Chapter 14:3) support a substantial efficiency role for the state through widespread regulation, limited price subsidies for very specific reasons, and intervention in the market for loans. There is little necessity for public production of housing, and no justification for state allocation to the individual. Equity objectives are thus likely to be met most effectively by market or near-market prices and regulation, supported by income transfers.

The historical strategy, however, has been based on price subsidies (Chapter 14:4.1), with substantial public production allocated by administrative means. The system has not worked well. It is explained (Chapter 14:4.2) how price subsidies in each sector of the housing market have led to excess demand and misallocation, with problems simultaneously of underoccupation, overcrowding, immobility and homelessness; the quantity and quality of the private rental housing stock has declined; and the system is nowhere near tenure-neutral (see the Glossary). The distributional effects of the subsidies are also largely perverse (Chapter 14:4.3): owner-occupiers (mainly in the higher socioeconomic groups) benefit disproportionately; and the redistributive impact of rent control and remaining rent subsidies is arbitrary. The reforms set out in Chapter 14:5 therefore adopt a strategy in which *price* subsidies (i.e. mortgage interest relief, subsidised local authority rents and rent control) are gradually replaced by *income* subsidies. Housing would be allocated by individual choice in the face of efficient (i.e. for the most part market) prices, supported by income transfers.

One of the most important points I have tried to convey in this book is that the approach to housing (and to the other areas) is advocated *not* for ideological reasons but because it would have substantial advantages in terms of efficiency and, possibly even more, of social justice. Housing and health care are equally important from the viewpoint of *social* policy; but there are substantial differences in their *technical* natures. As a result, they require different solutions.

1.3 Why Have a Welfare State?

The welfare state has two purposes: one is redistributive, or compensatory, to enhance social justice, the other functional, e.g. to deal with varying forms of market failure, thereby increasing economic efficiency. Virtually all parts of the welfare state display both aspects. Education from a functional perspective is a form of investment in the next generation of workers and citizens, but provided 'free' it acts also to help the poor; and analogous arguments apply to health care. Publicly provided income transfers, similarly, have an efficiency role where the private market is unable to supply insurance (e.g. against unemployment) even to individuals able to support themselves on a lifetime basis.

Several important conclusions emerge. First, to the extent that the welfare state has a substantial functional aspect, opposition by writers like Hayek and Friedman is misplaced. The single theoretical issue which, more than any other, divides their arguments from those in this book is their failure to acknowledge the major implications of information problems, which affect consumers of increasingly complex products, and also arise in important ways in insurance markets. Information problems of this sort greatly strengthen the efficiency case for the welfare state. The debate with libertarians (Chapter 4:7.3), surprisingly, turns out to be at least as much technical as ideological. As a result, it is less public involvement *per se* which should be a matter for controversy, than its precise form and the choice of its distributional objectives.

This theoretical conclusion is supported by recent history. A British study concluded that

the welfare state, and indeed welfare itself, is very robust. Over the thirteen years from 1974 to 1987, welfare policy successfully weathered an economic hurricane in the mid-1970s and an ideological blizzard in the 1980s. The resources going to public welfare were maintained; [and] welfare indicators continued to show a steady improvement. [Le Grand, 1990, p. 350.]

In the USA,

the Reagan era ended with the welfare state substantially intact, though somewhat frayed around the edges. It is now tilted more toward its middle-class beneficiaries than it was a decade ago, but the broad contours remain essentially as they have evolved since the 1930s, when the welfare state began. [Peterson, 1991, p. 133.]

Once the welfare state's efficiency role is understood, it is no longer surprising that neither in Britain nor in the USA, despite determined efforts during the 1980s, was government able to roll back the frontiers of the state in these areas. The same has been true in all industrialised countries (see Barr, 1992, Table 1). The argument is not diminished by the fact that it can explain only part of the variation across countries. The major efficiency role of social institutions makes them relevant to the population at large, not just to the poor. The welfare state is much more than a safety net; it is justified not simply by any redistributive aims one may (or may not) have, but because it does things which private markets for technical reasons either would not do at all, or would do inefficiently. We need a welfare state of some sort for efficiency reasons, and would continue to do so even if all distributional problems had been solved.

2 Broader Perspectives

2.1 Other Reforms

This last section sets the subject matter of the book into its broader perspective. Imagine a situation in which all the reforms discussed earlier had been implemented; that the public/private mix was optimal in all parts of the welfare state; that the resources absorbed were optimal for the welfare state as a whole and for its constituent parts; and that market allocation and actuarially fair insurance were applied where they contributed to efficiency and social justice, and were rejected where they did not. Would the agenda for reform then be complete? The answer, obviously, is no. The welfare state may make unemployment more bearable, but it does little to reduce the number of people out of work; nor does it improve working conditions for those in employment; and many people, e.g. the disabled, ethnic minorities and women, are underprivileged for reasons not directly connected with poverty. There is room for debate about the nature of these problems and about appropriate ameliorative action, but little disagreement that each is a legitimate concern of public policy (for detailed discussion, see Glennerster, (1983)).

I shall not dwell on these problems, not because they are unimportant but because (with the exception of unemployment) economics has little to say about them. I want instead to turn to an issue which runs implicitly through the whole book. The welfare state, despite its faults, is an equalising force; but various writers argue that it is not sufficiently equalising and/or that on its own it cannot be. This raises the question of how to increase equality without creating incentive problems – the issue, in short, of the extent to which greater equality is compatible with a capitalist system. I make no attempt at any strategic answer to such a vast question. But I should like to suggest that, by exercising some imagination, the mixed economy can be made more flexible than many people (both libertarian and Marxist) believe.

It is conventionally argued that the advantage of capitalism is its dynamism, i.e. its tendency to encourage innovation and economic growth; its disadvantage is the inequality it creates. To Marxists the price of inequality is too high, so they reject capitalism; to libertarians the price of reducing inequality is too high, so they reject the aim of equality. Both solutions can be regarded as extreme. To avoid the disadvantages of capitalism by abandoning the market system entirely is to throw the baby out with the bath water, as the collapse of centrally planned regimes in central and eastern Europe and the former Soviet Union has shown. A better solution is to accept *some* price in inequality for the benefits of innovation and output growth, but to seek to minimise it.

To illustrate the argument I want to suggest that inequality could be reduced by two measures: the imposition of heavier (but carefully designed) taxation on the transmission of wealth; and profit sharing. The standard argument against death duties and inheritance taxes is that they create disincentives, i.e. the price of greater equality in terms of lost output is high. This need not be inevitable. Consider two individuals: C (Chip) inherits nothing, but over his lifetime builds a computer business worth £100 million; D (Duke) inherits £100 million and earns nothing. C's enterprise has made him rich and has also benefited others. One way of retaining these benefits, while simultaneously reducing both the disincentive problem and the tendency of inherited wealth to perpetuate inequality, is to tax C's bequest less heavily than D's. Specifically, suppose that an individual is allowed to bequeath £X to his heirs, where X is a measure of his lifetime production as represented, for instance, by his lifetime earnings.[1] C could leave his fortune to his son or daughter on generous terms, while the greater proportion of D's wealth would be taxed away. C's son could leave a large fortune to *his* children only if he himself were productive. The resulting system would not tax the *creation* of wealth; and the taxation of its transmission, far from creating disincentives, would actively encourage economic growth by giving legatees a tax incentive to maximise their lifetime output.

A possible objection is that C's fortune is built on the backs of his workers who do not die rich. This might well be true – but again the solution may not be to throw out the benefits of capitalism to avoid its cost, but to share the benefits more equally. One way of doing so is to pay workers in part with shares in the firm where they work. They could, if they wished, sell these shares for cash; or they could build up an asset-holding, and share in C's fortune. In the latter case, workers would increasingly have the same incentives as owner-managers; in addition, as shareholders they would have some power in running the firm. The resulting system avoids conflict between labour and capital by creating worker-capitalists and manager-capitalists with shared interests;[2] and other ways of reducing the tension between distributional goals and dynamic efficiency are, doubtless, possible.

2.2 The Political Economy of the Future

This book has concentrated on problems with the welfare state *qua* welfare state. But difficulties can arise also from much broader causes. These include a changed ideological climate on both sides of the Atlantic and changes in external economic conditions, particularly the decline in growth rates, and

---

[1] Note that this would give a wealthy individual a powerful countervailing incentive not to cheat on his income tax (at least as regards earned income).
[2] See, for instance, 'John Lewis to Pay Worker-Partners Record £25 million Bonus', *The Times*, 9 March 1984; on analytical aspects, see Meade (1984) and Weitzman (1984).

sharp increases in unemployment in many countries since the mid-1970s. These problems give rise to two central controversies which transcend the boundaries of the book.

Is a welfare state compatible with high unemployment?   We have seen (Chapters 5:3.2 and 8:2.2) that unemployment, for technical reasons, is an uninsurable risk. For this reason the Beveridge strategy had *two* legs – social insurance and high employment (which Beveridge rightly regarded as a precondition for the success of the insurance arrangements). There is general agreement that high levels of employment and rising living standards have been at least as much an equalising force as redistribution over the past 45 years. The post-war consensus was that welfare spending made a twofold contribution, through its redistributive impact, and through its multiplier effect on employment. Adherents of this view (broadly the Labour and Liberal Democratic parties in Britain, and Liberal Democrats in the USA) argue that current difficulties represent a failure not of the welfare state but of macroeconomic policy. The counter-view, espoused by so-called 'supply-siders', including the Conservative and Republican administrations of the 1980s, is that the causal chain goes the other way – that it is high public (and particularly social) spending which is a *cause* of high unemployment, rather than its cure (see Murray (1984) and, for counter-views, Levy (1988) and Marmor *et al.* (1990)). The debate is a continuing one.

The relation between the welfare state and economic growth is also complex. Total spending on the welfare state in Britain rose sevenfold in real terms between 1948 and the early 1990s, from 10 per cent of gross domestic product to about 23.6 per cent (Table 7.2), and the experience of other countries, including the USA, Canada and Japan, has been similar. That social spending and consequently also taxation have increased is fact. What is controversial are the two effects of (a) higher benefits on work effort and (b) higher taxation on economic growth. The answers to these questions, as we saw in Chapters 8:3.1 and 9:5.1, rest ultimately on empirical magnitudes which we do not, and may never fully know. The effect of the welfare state on capital accumulation and output growth, despite much research and strident polemics, remains largely *terra incognita*.

The opposite question – the effect of economic growth on welfare spending – is at least as much political as economic. There is a flourishing debate about whether Britain or other countries can afford a welfare state. The easy complacency of earlier years about the continued growth of social spending has been replaced by discussion of whether or not there is a 'crisis in welfare'. The argument in this book is that the discussion should not be about *whether* there should be a welfare state, but about its precise form and its distributional objectives. Glennerster reaches a similar conclusion. He points out two crucial facts. First, the level of taxation and social spending, though high in all industrialised economies, varies widely and is not correlated in any obvious way with economic performance. These facts contradict the simple view that the present scale of the welfare state or something rather larger or smaller is incompatible with a substantial capitalist sector. Second, '[f]orty five years ago, in a ravaged economy, when real incomes were less than half what they are today, people voted for what came to be called a welfare state, and paid the price, and voted to continue affording it' (Glennerster, 1992, p. 284).

This brings out a final point – that the future of the welfare state depends not only on economic feasibility, but also very much on what people, through the political process, decide that they want.

None of the ideas in this book has been intended as a detailed blueprint, but more as an illustration of an approach which has been, throughout, to entertain moderately egalitarian aims while avoiding dogmatism about methods. The result shows how, with care, it is possible to create institutions both within the welfare state and more broadly which contribute to a society characterised simultaneously by economic efficiency and social justice.

Further Reading

For a classic defence of the mixed economy, see Okun (1975). The 'crisis in welfare' is discussed by libertarians (Harris and Seldon, 1979; Seldon, 1981) and Marxists (Gough, 1979; Ginsburg, 1979). For more general discussion, see Mishra (1984), Glennerster (1983, 1992, Ch. 15) and Heald (1983); and for two opposing views about the effects of the welfare state, Murray (1984) and Marmor *et al.* (1990).

Glossary

Absolute Poverty: poverty line defined in terms of a subsistence standard of living; as opposed to **Relative Poverty.**

Actuarial: an actuarial contribution is based on two factors: (a) the size of the benefit to be paid if the insured event (e.g. becoming ill) occurs; and (b) the probability of the event occurring. The probability needs to take into account mortality, morbidity, inflation and all other relevant factors. This is the way in which private insurance works.

Adverse Selection: situation in which an individual who is a poor risk can conceal the fact from the insurance company.

AFDC: Aid to Families with Dependent Children.

Aid to Families with Dependent Children: the main US **Income-Tested Benefit** for families with no (or virtually no) other income.

Allocative Efficiency: see **Economic Efficiency.**

Annuity: the payment of an income of £X per year for life; often given to an individual in exchange for a single, lump-sum payment at the time he/she retires. See Chapter 5:2.3.

Building Society: UK financial institution which lends money to individuals for the purpose of buying a house. The US equivalent, broadly, is a savings and loan association.

Cardinal Utility: if utility is *cardinally* measurable, we can make statements like 'A gets twice as much utility from his first ice cream as from his second' or 'B gets the same utility as A from an ice cream.' When utility is measurable only *ordinally* we can say only that A gets *more* utility from his first ice cream than from his second, but not how much more; and it is not possible to make interpersonal comparisons between A's and B's utility. See also **Utility.**

Cash Benefits: income support for individuals in the form of cash, in contrast with benefits in kind like free health care. Cash benefits generally include **Social Insurance** and **Social Assistance.**

Child Benefit: UK system of weekly, tax-free cash payment of £X for each child in the family, generally payable to the mother.

Child Benefit Increase: UK system of paying an addition to **Child Benefit** to a parent with single-handed responsibility for one or more children.

Collectivist: view which gives priority to the achievement of equality or meeting need. Can take various forms including **Fabian Socialist** or **Marxist.**

Comprehensive School: UK secondary school for pupils of all abilities, generally covering the age range 11–18.

Contributory Benefit: benefit payable only to individuals who (a) have a **National Insurance** contribution record, and (b) are unemployed, retired or suffering from ill-health, etc. See also **Social Insurance** and **Non-Contributory Benefit.**

Cross-Section: series of observations on different entities during a single period of time, e.g. the Family Expenditure Survey gathers data on the expenditure patterns of a large number of families in a given week; as opposed to **Time-Series.**

Disregard: amount of earnings or other income which is disregarded (i.e. ignored) in calculating the benefit to which an individual or family is entitled.

Earnings-Related Benefits, in contrast with **Flat-Rate Benefits,** are paid as a percentage of previous earnings; thus, individuals with higher previous earnings receive higher benefits.

Economic Efficiency: the allocation of scarce resources in such a way that no reallocation can make any individual better-off without making at least one other individual worse-off. Also referred to as efficiency, allocative efficiency, Pareto efficiency or Pareto optimality.

Efficiency: see **Economic Efficiency.**

Equity: a goal relating to the way in which resources should be distributed or shared between individuals, hence synonymous with **Social Justice;** see also **Horizontal Equity** and **Vertical Equity.** Equity *may* imply equality, but does not have to – see also **Libertarian, Liberal, Collectivist.**

Estate Agent: institution to assist with the purchase and sale of property; in the US a realtor.

Fabian Socialist: view that **Collectivist** goals can be achieved within a mixed economy. See also **Libertarian, Liberal, Marxist.**

Family Credit: UK system of supplementing the incomes of low-income working families, introduced in 1988 to replace Family Income Supplement.

Family Income Supplement: see **Family Credit.**

FIS: Family Income Supplement.

Flat-Rate Benefits, in contrast with **Earnings-Related Benefits,** are paid at a fixed monthly rate (though they may be higher for larger families) and are not related to previous income. Thus, for a given family type, all recipients receive the same benefits.

Funded pensions are paid from an accumulated fund built up over a period of years out of contributions of its members. Contrasts with **Pay-As-You-Go** schemes.

General Practitioner: family doctor.

Gini Coefficient: a measure of the overall inequality in society; it takes on values between zero (when income is distributed equally) and one (when one individual has all the income).

GP: General Practitioner.

Green Paper: consultative document issued by UK central government, inviting discussion and comment; as distinct from a **White Paper.**

Health Maintenance Organisation: a 'firm' of doctors, which charges individuals/families an annual premium, in return for which it provides the individual/family with a comprehensive range of medical services. See Chapter 12:5.

Higher Education Funding Council (HEFC): a body which finances universities and colleges on the basis of contracts; replaces the former **Polytechnics and Colleges Funding Council** and **Universities Funding Council.**

HMO: Health Maintenance Organisation.

HMSO: Her Majesty's Stationery Office.

Horizontal Equity: distribution in accordance with equal treatment of equals, e.g. the relative tax treatment of families of different sizes at a given level of income. See also **Equity** and **Vertical Equity.**

Housing Benefit: UK system of assistance with rent and local taxation for low-income householders.

Housing Revenue Account: shows housing revenue and expenditure in each local authority on a cash flow basis, including interest payments on past loans, rental income, and central and local subsidies.

HRA: Housing Revenue Account.

Implicit Tax Rate: a tax which arises when a family in receipt of an **Income-Tested Benefit** earns extra income, and as a consequence loses benefit. If benefit is lost pound for pound with earnings, the implicit tax rate is 100 per cent. See Chapter 10:3.

Income-Related Benefit: see **Income-Tested Benefit.**

Income Support: UK system of **Means-Tested, Non-Contributory** benefits, for which individuals/families are eligible if their income from all other sources is less than the poverty standard. Replaced **Supplementary Benefit** in 1988.

Income-Tested Benefit: benefit awarded to individuals/families with low incomes, and withdrawn as income rises; as distinct from benefits awarded on the basis of other criteria, e.g. having a contributions record. Also referred to as income-related benefit. See also **Contributory Benefit** and **Means-Tested Benefit.**

Laissez-Faire: the term is used in this book in its most frequent sense as 'a belief in the efficacy of a free market economy' (Taylor, 1972, p. 11.). See also **Libertarian.**

LEA: see **Local Education Authority.**

Less Eligibility: condition that the standard of living of those in receipt of **Poor Law** benefits should be lower than that of the poorest worker.

Liberal: view of property rights and income distribution as contingent matters rather than as items of dogma. Note the confusing ambiguity in the use of the word. In the nineteenth century it was used as a label for Classical liberal thinkers like Bentham and Nassau Senior; and today a writer like Friedman, in calling himself a liberal, is using the term in the same way. Throughout the book such writers are referred to as **Libertarians.**

Libertarian: view which gives priority to individual liberty, usually associated with a belief in the free market and **Laissez-Faire.** See also **Liberal** and **Collectivist.**

Local Education Authority: the body which organises most forms of education at a local level, including building schools and employing teachers.

Local Rates: former UK system of local taxation, based on the annual rental value of property.

Macro Efficiency: concerns the proportion of national resources devoted to a particular activity such as health care or education; as opposed to **Micro Efficiency.**

Market Failure: impediment to the efficient working of the market, in particular externalities, public goods or increasing returns to scale (see Appendix to Chapter 4, paras 12–16).

Marxist: view that **Collectivist** goals are incompatible with capitalism, and can be achieved only under state ownership of major productive resources. See also **Libertarian, Liberal** and **Fabian Socialist.**

Means Test: see **Means-Tested Benefits.**

Means-Tested Benefits are paid only to individuals whose income and/or wealth from all other sources are below a given amount. The term thus embraces both income testing and wealth testing.

Micro Efficiency: concerns the division of total medical resources between the different parts of the health care system, or that of educational resources between different areas of education, etc.; as opposed to **Macro Efficiency.**

Moral Hazard: situation in which an insured person can affect the insurance company's liability without its knowledge.

National Health Service: UK system under which medical care is (a) provided by the state, (b) financed mainly out of general tax revenues and (c) supplied to patients without charge, apart from a contribution towards the cost of drugs (from which the young, the old and the poor are exempt).

National Insurance: UK system of **Social Insurance** in respect, for example, of unemployment, ill-health and retirement. See also **Contributory Benefit.**

Negative Income Tax: a system in which income support and income taxation are integrated by using the tax system both to pay benefits to those with low incomes and to levy taxes on those with higher incomes.

NHS: the UK **National Health Service.**

NIT: Negative Income Tax.

Non-Contributory Benefit: benefit awarded without the need for a contributions record, and financed out of general tax revenues (in contrast with a **Contributory**

Benefit). May be **Income-Tested,** or awarded on the basis of non-income criteria, e.g. **Child Benefit.**

Ordinal Utility: see **Cardinal Utility.**

Original Position: hypothetical situation (used by the philosopher John Rawls) in which rational negotiators behind the **Veil of Ignorance** negotiate a just constitution for a country in which they will all have to live.

Outdoor Relief: benefits paid under the **Poor Law** to individuals, principally the elderly, who were not required to live in the **Workhouse.**

Pareto Efficiency: see **Economic Efficiency.**

Pareto Optimality: see **Economic Efficiency.**

Pay-As-You-Go: pensions paid (usually by the state) out of current tax revenues, rather than out of an accumulated fund; contrasts with **Funded** schemes.

PAYG: Pay-As-You-Go.

Pigovian Subsidy/Tax: where an activity creates an external benefit, an unrestricted private market will supply an inefficiently small quantity. One way of restoring supply to its efficient level is to to pay a so-called Pigovian subsidy. Analogously, a Pigovian tax discourages excessive supply in the presence of an external cost. See Chapter 4:3.2 and/or the Appendix to Chapter 4, para. 15.

Polytechnics and Colleges Funding Council (PCFC): a body which financed polytechnics and colleges in Britain on the basis of contracts from 1990 to 1993, after which it was replaced by the **Higher Education Funding Council.**

Poor Law: UK system for the relief of destitution, from late sixteenth century; it was phased out over the first half of the twentieth century.

Poverty Trap: situation in which individuals/families earning an extra £1 lose £1 or more in **Income-Tested Benefits**, and hence make themselves absolutely worse-off. See also **Implicit Tax Rate.**

Progressive Taxation: tax system in which tax paid as a proportion of income is higher for individuals with higher incomes. See also **Proportional Taxation** and **Regressive Taxation.**

Proportional Taxation: tax system in which tax paid is the same proportion of income at all income levels. See also **Progressive Taxation** and **Regressive Taxation.**

Rates: see **Local Rates.**

Regressive Taxation: tax system in which tax paid as a proportion of income is lower for individuals with higher incomes. See also **Progressive Taxation** and **Proportional Taxation.**

Relative Poverty: poverty line defined relative to the average standard of living, e.g. as a proportion of average income. As opposed to **Absolute Poverty.**

Replacement Ratio: ratio of income when unemployed, to income (post-tax and transfers) when in work.

Revenue-Neutral: a policy change is revenue-neutral if any resulting increase in expenditure is accompanied by a matching increase in taxation.

SB: Supplementary Benefit.

Serps: UK state earnings-related pension scheme.

Social Assistance: state benefits paid out of general tax revenues without contribution condition, but usually subject to a **Means Test.** See also **Income-Tested Benefit.**

Social Dividend Scheme: form of **Negative Income Tax.**

Social Insurance: form of organisation, originally modelled on private insurance, under which individuals receive state benefits in respect of, for example, unemployment or retirement, often without any test of means or need, on the basis of previous (usually compulsory) contributions. See also **Contributory Benefit** and **National Insurance.**

Social Justice: a goal relating to the way in which resources should be distributed or shared between individuals. See also **Equity, Horizontal Equity** and **Vertical Equity.** For different definitions of social justice, see **Libertarian, Liberal, Collectivist.**

Social Security: all publicly provided cash benefits. Note that this standard British usage differs from the narrower American definition of social security as retirement benefits, and the broader EC definition which includes health services. Throughout the book the term is used with its British meaning.

Standard Assumptions: the assumptions under which the market will, in theory, allocate resources efficiently, viz, perfect information, perfect competition and no **Market Failures** (see Chapter 4:3.2 or the Appendix to Chapter 4, paras 5–17).

Stigma: loss of **Utility** because income is received in the form of (usually) **Income-Tested Benefits,** rather than from some more congenial source (e.g. earnings or insurance benefits).

Supplementary Benefit: former UK system of **Means-Tested, Non-Contributory Benefits,** for which individuals/families were eligible if their income from all other sources was less than the poverty standard. Replaced the earlier system of National Assistance in 1966. Replaced in 1988 by **Income Support.**

Take-Up: the number of people receiving a particular benefit as a proportion of those potentially eligible.

Tax Expenditures: public expenditure implicit in the granting of tax relief to certain activities, e.g. approved private pension contributions or mortgage interest payments, as opposed to explicit expenditure. See Chapter 7:1.1.

Tenure Neutrality: an aim of housing policy, whereby individuals (on average and in the long run) are financially indifferent between buying accommodation and renting it. See Chapter 14:2.

Third-Party Payment Problem: situation in which the insurance company pays the whole of an individual's medical bill, for example; as a result neither patient nor doctor has an incentive to economise. Technically, a form of **Moral Hazard.**

Time-Series: series of observations on a single entity (or aggregate) over several periods, e.g. data on the level of unemployment benefits, the number of people out of work, etc. in a country each year from 1960 to 1980. As opposed to **Cross-Section**.

Unemployment Trap: situation in which an individual/family is better-off (or little worse-off) when unemployed than when in work. This situation arises particularly for those with low earnings and/or with large families.

Unfunded: see **Pay-As-You-Go**.

Universities Funding Council (UFC): a body which financed universities in Britain on the basis of contracts from 1990 to 1993, after which it was replaced by the **Higher Education Funding Council.**

Uprating: increase in the value of almost all cash benefits, usually at annual intervals, and usually in line with changes in the price level.

Utility: individual well-being or satisfaction. See also **Cardinal Utility.**

Veil of Ignorance: hypothetical situation in which rational individuals in the **Original Position** have to negotiate a just constitution for a country in which they will all have to live, but *without knowing who they will be* (i.e. whether they will be born as one of the most or least fortunate).

Vertical Equity: the extent of redistribution of income, consumption or wealth from rich to poor. See also **Equity** and **Horizontal Equity.**

Welfare: US usage for **Income-Tested Benefits**. See also **Social Assistance.**

White Paper: firm statement of government intent; as distinct from a **Green Paper.**

Workhouse: institution giving work and rudimentary accommodation to the destitute, under the **Poor Law.**

Workhouse Test: condition that recipients of benefits under the **Poor Law** must live in the **Workhouse.**

References

AARON, HENRY J. (1973), *Why is Welfare so Hard to Reform?*, Washington, DC: The Brookings Institution.

AARON, HENRY J. (1981a), 'Economic Aspects of the Role of Government in Health Care', in van der Gaag, J. and Perlman, M. (eds), *Health, Economics, and Health Economics*, Amsterdam: North Holland.

AARON, HENRY J. (1981b), 'Policy Implications: A Progress Report' in Bradbury, K. L., and Downs, A. (1981).

AARON, HENRY J. (1982), *Economic Effects of Social Security*, Washington, DC: The Brookings Institution.

AARON, HENRY J. (1984), 'Social Welfare in Australia', in Caves, Richard E., and Krause, Lawrence B. (eds), *The Australian Economy: A View from the North*, Washington, DC: The Brookings Institution.

AARON, HENRY J. (1991), *Serious and Unstable Condition: Financing America's Health Care*, Washington, DC: The Brookings Institution.

AARON, HENRY J., and BURTLESS, GARY (eds) (1984), *Retirement and Economic Behavior*, Washington, DC: The Brookings Institution.

AARON, HENRY J., and PECHMAN, JOSEPH A. (1981), *How Taxes Affect Economic Behavior*, Washington, DC: The Brookings Institution.

AARON, HENRY J., and SCHWARTZ, WILLIAM B. (1984), *The Painful Prescription: Rationing Hospital Care*, Washington, DC: The Brookings Institution.

AARON, HENRY J., BOSWORTH, BARRY P., and BURTLESS, GARY T. (1989), *Can America Afford to Grow Old?*, Washington, DC: The Brookings Institution.

ABEL SMITH, BRIAN (1964), *The Hospitals, 1800–1948*, London: Heinemann.

ABEL SMITH, BRIAN (1976), *Value for Money in Health Services*, London: Heinemann.

ABEL SMITH, BRIAN (1983), 'Economic Efficiency in Health Care Delivery', *International Social Security Review*, Vol. 36, No. 2, pp. 165–79.

ABEL SMITH, BRIAN (1984), *Cost Containment in Health Care*, Occasional Papers in Social Administration No. 73, London: Bedford Square Press.

ABEL SMITH, BRIAN (1985), 'Who is the Odd Man Out?: The Experience of Western Europe in Containing the Costs of Health Care', *Health and Society*, Vol. 63, No. 1, pp. 1–17.

ABEL SMITH, BRIAN, and TOWNSEND, PETER (1965), *The Poor and the Poorest*, London: Bell and Sons.

ACTON, J. P. (1973), *Evaluating Public Programmes to Save Lives: The Case of Heart Attacks*, Santa Monica: Rand Corporation.

AKERLOF, GEORGE A. (1970), 'The Market for "Lemons": Qualitative Uncertainty and the Market Mechanism', *Quarterly Journal of Economics*, Vol. 84, pp. 488–500, August.

AKERLOF, GEORGE A. (1978), 'The Economics of "Tagging" as Applied to the Optimal Income Tax, Welfare Programs and Manpower Planning', *American Economic Review*, Vol. 68, pp. 8–19.

ALTMEYER, A. J. (1966), *The Formative Years of Social Security*, Madison: University of Wisconsin Press.

ANDERSON, O. W. (1968), *The Uneasy Equilibrium: Private and Public Financing of Health Services in the United States 1875–1965*, New Haven: College and University Press.

APPS, PATRICIA F. (1981), *A Theory of Inequality and Taxation*, Cambridge: Cambridge University Press.

ARROW, KENNETH F. (1963), 'Uncertainty and the Welfare Economics of Medical Care', *American Economic Review*, Vol. 53, pp. 941–73, reprinted in Cooper and Culyer (1973) and Diamond and Rothschild (1978).

ARROW, KENNETH J. (1971), 'Models of Job Discrimination', in Pascal, A. H. (ed.), *Racial Discrimination in Economic Life*, Lexington Press, reprinted in Atkinson (1980).

ARROW, KENNETH J. (1973a), 'Some Ordinalist-Utilitarian Notes on Rawls's *Theory of Justice*', *Journal of Philosophy*, Vol. 70, May, pp. 245–63.

ARROW, KENNETH J. (1973b), 'Higher Education as a Filter', *Journal of Public Economics*, Vol. 2, pp. 193–216.

ASHENFELTER, ORLEY, and LAYARD, RICHARD (eds) (1986), *Handbook of Labor Economics*, Vol. 2, Amsterdam: North Holland.

ATKINSON, ANTHONY B. (1970), 'On the Measurement of Inequality', *Journal of Economic Theory*, Vol. 2, pp. 244–63, reprinted in Atkinson (1980, pp. 23–43) (including a non-mathematical summary).

ATKINSON, ANTHONY B. (1973), *The Tax Credit Scheme and the Redistribution of Income*, London: Institute for Fiscal Studies.

ATKINSON, ANTHONY B. (1974), *Unequal Shares*, London: Penguin.

ATKINSON, ANTHONY B. (ed.) (1980), *Wealth, Income and Inequality*, 2nd edn, Oxford: Oxford University Press.

ATKINSON, ANTHONY B. (1983a), *The Economics of Inequality*, 2nd edn, Oxford: Oxford University Press.

ATKINSON, ANTHONY B. (1983b), *Social Justice and Public Policy*, Brighton, Sussex: Harvester Press.

ATKINSON, ANTHONY B. (1984), 'A Guide to the Reform of Social Security', *New Society*, 13 December, pp. 426–8.

ATKINSON, ANTHONY B. (1987a), 'Income Maintenance and Social Insurance', in Auerbach, Alan J., and Feldstein, Martin S. (eds), *Handbook of Public Economics*, Vol. 2, Amsterdam: North Holland.

ATKINSON, A. B. (1987b), 'On the Measurement of Poverty', *Econometrica*, Vol. 55, pp. 749–64.

ATKINSON, ANTHONY B. (1989), *Poverty and Social Security*, Brighton, Sussex: Harvester Press.

ATKINSON, A. B. (1991), 'Poverty, Economic Performance and Income Transfer Policy in OECD Countries', *World Bank Economic Review*, Vol. 5, No. 1, January, pp. 3–21.

ATKINSON, A. B. (1992), 'Towards a European Social Safety Net?', *Fiscal Studies*, Vol. 13, No. 3, August, pp. 41–53.

ATKINSON, A. B. (forthcoming), 'On Targeting Social Security', *World Bank Conference on Public Expenditures and the Poor*, 1992.

ATKINSON, ANTHONY B., and FLEMMING, JOHN S. (1978), 'Unemployment, Social Security and Incentives', *Midland Bank Review*, pp. 6–16.

ATKINSON, ANTHONY B., and HARRISON, A. J. (1978), *The Distribution of Personal Wealth in Britain*, Cambridge: Cambridge University Press.

ATKINSON, ANTHONY B., and MICKLEWRIGHT, JOHN (1991), 'Unemployment Compensation and Labour Market Transitions: A Critical Review', *Journal of Economic Literature*, Vol. 29, No. 4, December, pp. 1679–727.

ATKINSON, ANTHONY B., and STIGLITZ, JOSEPH E. (1980), *Lectures on Public Economics*, London and New York: McGraw-Hill.

ATKINSON, ANTHONY B., KING, MERVYN A., and STERN, NICHOLAS H. (1989), 'The Poverty Trap in Britain', in Atkinson (1989).

ATKINSON, ANTHONY B., MAYNARD, ALAN K., and TRINDER, CHRIS (1983), *Parents and Children*, London: Heinemann.

AUERBACH, ALAN J., and KOTLIKOFF, LAURENCE J. (1990), 'Demographics, Fiscal Policy and US Saving in the 1980s and Beyond', in Summers, Lawrence H. (ed.), *Tax Policy and the Economy*, Vol. 4, Cambridge, Mass: MIT Press.

AUERBACH, ALAN J., *et al.* (1989), 'The Economic Dynamics of Ageing Populations: The Case of Four OECD Economies', *OECD Economic Studies*, Spring, pp. 97–130.

AVERCH, H. A., *et al.* (1972), *How Effective is Schooling? A Critical Review and Synthesis of Research Findings*, Santa Monica, Calif.: The Rand Corporation.

BARNES, JOHN, and BARR, NICHOLAS (1988), *Strategies for Higher Education: The Alternative White Paper*, Aberdeen University Press for the David Hume Institute, Edinburgh, and the Suntory-Toyota International Centre for Economics and Related Disciplines, London School of Economics.

BARR, NICHOLAS A. (1975), 'Negative Income Taxation and the Redistribution of Income', *Oxford Bulletin of Economics and Statistics*, Vol. 37, No. 1, February, as amended in Vol. 38, No. 2, May 1976.

BARR, NICHOLAS A. (1979), 'Myths My Grandpa Taught Me', *Three Banks Review*, No. 124, December.

BARR, NICHOLAS A. (1980), 'The Taxation of Married Women's Incomes', *British Tax Review*, Nos 5 and 6.

BARR, NICHOLAS A. (1981), 'Empirical Definitions of the Poverty Line', *Policy and Politics*, Vol. 9, No. 1.

BARR, NICHOLAS A. (1985), 'Economic Welfare and Social Justice', *Journal of Social Policy*, Vol. 14, No. 2, April, pp. 175–87.

BARR, NICHOLAS A. (1986), 'Revenue, Expenditure and the Government Accounts', *British Tax Review*, No. 6, pp. 340–6.

BARR, NICHOLAS (1989a), *Student Loans: The Next Steps*, Aberdeen University Press for the David Hume Institute, Edinburgh, and the Suntory-Toyota International Centre for Economics and Related Disciplines, London School of Economics.

BARR, NICHOLAS (1989b), 'The White Paper on Student Loans', *Journal of Social Policy*, Vol. 18, No. 3, July.

BARR, NICHOLAS (1991), 'Income-Contingent Student Loans: An Idea Whose Time has Come', in Shaw, G. K. (ed.), *Economics, Culture and Education: Essays in Honour of Mark Blaug*, Cheltenham: Edward Elgar.

BARR, NICHOLAS (1992), 'Economic Theory and the Welfare State: A Survey and Interpretation', *Journal of Economic Literature*, Vol. 30, No. 2, pp. 741–803.

BARR, NICHOLAS (1993), 'Alternative Funding Resources for Higher Education', *Economic Journal*, Vol. 103, No. 418, May.

BARR, NICHOLAS, and COULTER, FIONA (1990), 'Social Security: Solution or Problem?', in Hills (1990).

BARR, NICHOLAS A., and HALL, ROBERT E. (1975), 'The Taxation of Earnings Under Public Assistance', *Economica*, Vol. 42, No. 168, November, pp. 373–84.

BARR, NICHOLAS A., and HALL, ROBERT E. (1981), 'The Probability of Dependence on Public Assistance', *Economica*, Vol. 48, No. 190, May, pp. 109–23.

BARR, NICHOLAS, and LOW, WILLIAM (1988), *Student Grants and Student Poverty*, Welfare State Programme, Discussion Paper No. WSP/28, London: London School of Economics.

BARR, NICHOLAS A., and ROPER, JOHN F. H. (1974), 'Tax-Credits: An Optimistic Appraisal', *Three Banks Review*, No. 101, March.

BARR, NICHOLAS, and WHYNES, DAVID (eds) (1993), *Issues in the Economics of the Welfare State*, London: Macmillan.

BARR, NICHOLAS, GLENNERSTER, HOWARD, and LE GRAND, JULIAN (1989), 'Working for Patients? The Right Approach?', in *Resourcing the National Health Service: The Government's White Paper; Working for Patients*, House of Commons Social Services Committee, Session 1988–89, HC 214–I, London: HMSO, reprinted in *Social Policy and Administration*, Vol. 23, No. 2, August.

BARR, NICHOLAS A., JAMES, SIMON R., and PREST, ALAN R. (1977), *Self-Assessment for Income Tax*, London: Heinemann.

BARRO, ROBERT J. (1974), 'Are Government Bonds Net Wealth?', *Journal of Political Economy*, Vol. 84, pp. 1095–117.

BARRO, ROBERT J. (1978), *The Impact of Social Security on Private Saving: Evidence from the US Time Series*, Washington, DC: The American Enterprise Institute.

BARRY, BRIAN (1973), *The Liberal Theory of Social Justice*, Oxford: Clarendon Press.

BASSETT, K., and SHORT, J. (1980), *Housing and Residential Structure: Alternative Approaches*, London: Routledge and Kegan Paul.

BAUMOL, WILLIAM J., and BLINDER, ALAN S. (1991), *Economics: Principles and Policy*, 5th edn, London and New York: Harcourt Brace Jovanovich.

BAUMOL, WILLIAM J., and OATES, WALLACE E. (1979), *The Theory of Environmental Policy*, Englewood Cliffs, New Jersey: Prentice Hall.

BECKER, GARY (1975), *Human Capital*, 2nd edn, Cambridge, Mass.: National Bureau of Economic Research.

BECKER, GARY (1983), 'A Theory of Competition among Pressure Groups for Political Influence', *Quarterly Journal of Economics*, Vol. 98, August, pp. 371–400.

BECKER, GARY (1985), 'Public Policies, Pressure Groups, and Dead Weight Costs', *Journal of Public Economics*, Vol. 28, December, pp. 329–47.

BECKERMAN, WILFRED (1979), 'The Impact of Income Maintenance Payments on Poverty: 1975', *Economic Journal*, Vol. 89, pp. 261–79.

BEENSTOCK, MICHAEL, and BRASSE, VALERIE (1986), *Insurance for Unemployment*, London: Allen and Unwin.

BEESLEY, MICHAEL, and LITTLECHILD, STEPHEN (1983), 'Privatisation: Principles, Problems and Priorities', *Lloyds Bank Review*, July.

BENNETT, ROBERT, GLENNERSTER, HOWARD, and NEVISON, DOUGLAS (1992), 'Investing in Skill: To Stay On or Not To Stay On', *Oxford Review of Economic Policy*, Vol. 8, No. 2, pp. 130–45.

BENTHAM, JEREMY (1789), *An Introduction to the Principles of Morals and Legislation*, London: Payne.

BERTHOUD, RICHARD (1984), *The Reform of Supplementary Benefit – Summary of Findings*, London: Policy Studies Institute.

BERTHOUD, RICHARD (1986), *Selective Social Security*, London: Policy Studies Institute.

BERTHOUD, RICHARD (1991), 'The Social Fund – Is It Working?', *Policy Studies*, Vol. 12, No. 1, Spring.

BESLEY, TIMOTHY, and KANBUR, RAVI (1991), 'The Principles of Targeting', in Balasubramanyam, V. N., and Lall, Sanjaya (eds), *Current Issues in Development Economics*, London: Macmillan.

BEVERIDGE, WILLIAM (1944), *Full Employment in a Free Society*, London: Allen and Unwin.

BJORKLUND, ANDERS, and HOLMLUND, BERTIL (1989), 'Effects of Extended Unemployment Compensation in Sweden', in Gustafsson, Bjorn A., and Klevmarken, N. Anders (eds), *The Political Economy of Social Security*, Amsterdam: North Holland.

BLACK, DOUGLAS (1980), *Inequalities in Health* (the Black Report), Report of a Research Working Group chaired by Sir Douglas Black (Department of Health and Social Security, London), published in Townsend and Davidson (1982).

BLACKORBY, CHARLES, and DONALDSON, DAVID (1988), 'Cash Versus Kind, Self-Selection, and Efficient Transfers', *American Economic Review*, Vol. 78, pp. 691–700.

BLAUG, MARK (1970), *An Introduction to the Economics of Education*, London: Penguin.

BLAUG, MARK (1976), 'The Empirical Status of Human Capital Theory: A Slightly Jaundiced Survey', *Journal of Economic Literature*, September, pp. 827–56, reprinted in Blaug (1987).

BLAUG, MARK (1984), 'Education Vouchers – It All Depends on What You Mean', in Le Grand and Robinson (1984).

BLAUG, MARK (1985), 'Where Are We Now in the Economics of Education?', *Economics of Education Review*, Vol. 4, No. 1, pp. 17–28, reprinted in Blaug (1987).

BLAUG, MARK (1987) *The Economics of Education and the Education of an Economist*, Aldershot: Edward Elgar.

BLAUG, MARK, and WOODHALL, MAUREEN (1968), 'Productivity Trends in British Secondary Education, 1950–63', *Sociology of Education*, Winter.

BLENDON, ROBERT J., and TAYLOR, HUMPHREY (1989), 'Views on Health Care: Public Opinion in Three Nations', *Health Affairs*, Vol. 8, No. 1, pp. 149–57.

BODIE, ZVI (1989), 'Inflation Insurance', Working Paper No. 3009, Cambridge, Mass.: National Bureau of Economic Research.

BODIE, ZVI (1990), 'Pensions as Retirement Income Insurance', *Journal of Economic Literature*, Vol. 28, March, pp. 28–49.

BOOTH, CHARLES (1902), *Life and Labour of the People of London*, 17 vols (London).

BOS, DIETER (1984), 'Income Taxation, Public Sector Pricing and Redistribution', *Scandinavian Journal of Economics*, Vol. 84, pp. 166–83.

BOSANQUET, NICHOLAS (1983), *After the New Right*, London: Heinemann.

BOSKIN, MICHAEL J. (1977), 'Social Security and Retirement Decisions', *Economic Inquiry*, Vol. 15, pp. 1–25.

BOSKIN, MICHAEL J., and HURD, MICHAEL D. (1978), 'The Effect of Social Security on Early Retirement', *Journal of Public Economics*, Vol. 10, pp. 361–77.

BOWLES, S. (1973), 'Understanding Unequal Economic Opportunity', *American Economic Review*, Vol. 63, pp. 346–56, reprinted in Atkinson (1980).

BOWLEY, MARION (1937), *Nassau Senior and Classical Economics*, London: Allen and Unwin.

BOWLEY, MARION (1966), *The British Building Industry*, Cambridge: Cambridge University Press.

BRADBURY, K. L., and DOWNS, A. (eds) (1981), *Do Housing Allowances Work?*, Washington, DC: The Brookings Institution.

BRADSHAW, JONATHAN, DITCH, JOHN, and WHITEFORD, PETER (forthcoming), *Comparative Study of Child Support in the EC*, York University.

BRAZIER, JOHN, HUTTON, JOHN, and JEAVONS, RICHARD (1990), 'Evaluating the Reform of the NHS', in Culyer *et al.* (1990).

BRIGGS, ASA (1961a), 'The Welfare State in Historical Perspective', *Archives euro-péennes de Sociologie*, Vol. 2, No. 2, pp. 221–59.

BRIGGS, ASA (1961b), *Social Thought and Social Action: A Study of the Work of Seebohm Rowntree, 1917–1954*, London: Longman.

BRITTAIN, J. A. (1977), *The Inheritance of Economic Status*, Washington, DC: The Brookings Institution.

BRITTAIN, J. A. (1978), *Inheritance and the Inequality of Material Wealth*, Washington, DC: The Brookings Institution.

BRITTAN, SAMUEL (1986), 'Privatisation: A Comment on Kay and Thompson', *Economic Journal*, Vol. 96, No. 381, pp. 33–8.

BROOME, JOHN (1978), 'Trying to Value a Human Life', *Journal of Public Economics*, Vol. 9, No. 1, and discussion in the same journal, Vol. 12, No. 2, 1979.

BROWN, CHARLES V. (1983), *Taxation and the Incentive to Work*, 2nd edn, Oxford: Oxford University Press.

BROWN, CHARLES V., and JACKSON, PETER M. (1990), *Public Sector Economics*, 4th edn, Oxford: Basil Blackwell.

BROWN, CHARLES V., and LEVIN, E. (1974), 'The Effects of Income Taxation on Overtime: The Results of a National Survey', *Economic Journal*, Vol. 84, No. 336, December, pp. 833–48.

BRUCE, MAURICE (1972), *The Coming of the Welfare State*, 4th edn, London: Batsford.

BUCHANAN, JAMES M., and TULLOCK, GORDON (1962), *The Calculus of Consent*, Ann Arbor: University of Michigan Press.

BUHMANN, BRIGITTE, RAINWATER, LEE, SCHMAUS, GUENTHER, and SMEEDING, TIMOTHY (1988), 'Equivalence Scales, Well-Being, Inequality, and Poverty: Sensitivity Estimates across Ten Countries, Using the Luxembourg Income Study (LIS) Database', *Review of Income and Wealth*, Vol. 34, No. 2, pp. 115–42.

BULL, D. (1980), *What Price Education?*, Poverty Pamphlet 48, London: Child Poverty Action Group.

BURKHEAD, J., FOX, T. G., and HOLLAND, J. W. (1967), *Input and Output in Large City High Schools*, New York: Syracuse University Press.

BURTLESS, GARY, and MOFFITT, ROBERT A. (1984), 'The Effect of Social Security Benefits on the Labor Supply of the Aged', in Aaron and Burtless (1984).

BYATT, I. C. R., HOLMANS, A. E., LAIDLER, D. E. W., and NICHOLSON, R. J. (1973), 'Income and the Demand for Housing', in Parkin, Michael (ed.), *Essays in Modern Economics*, London: Longman.

CARR-HILL, ROY (1990), 'RAWP Is Dead: Long Live RAWP', in Culyer *et al.* (1990).

CAVE, MARTIN, and WEALE, MARTIN (1992), 'The Assessment: Higher Education: The State of Play', *Oxford Review of Economic Policy*, Vol. 8, No. 2, pp. 1–18.

CAVE, MARTIN, DODSWORTH, RUTH, and THOMPSON, DAVID (1992), 'Regulatory Reform in Higher Education in the UK: Incentives for Efficiency and Product Quality', *Oxford Review of Economic Policy*, Vol. 8, No. 2, pp. 79–102.

CAVES, D. W., and CHRISTENSEN, L. R. (1980), 'The Relative Efficiency of Public and Private Firms in a Competitive Environment: The Case of Canadian Railroads', *Journal of Political Economy*, Vol. 88, No. 5, October, pp. 958–76.

CHESTER, T. E., and ICHIEN, M. (1983), 'Health Care in Japan – Its Development, Structure and Problems', *Three Banks Review*, No. 137, March, pp. 17–26.

CHRISTOPHER, A., *et al.* (1970), *Policy for Poverty*, Research Monograph 20, London: Institute of Economic Affairs.

CHUBB, J. E., and MOE, T. M. (1990), *Politics, Markets and America's Schools*, Washington, DC: The Brookings Institution.

COASE, RONALD H. (1960), 'The Problem of Social Cost', *Journal of Law and Economics*, October.

COLLARD, DAVID (1983), 'Economics of Philanthropy: A Comment', *Economic Journal*, Vol. 93, No. 371, September, pp. 637–8.

COMMISSION FOR RACIAL EQUALITY (1983), *Housing in the London Borough of Hackney: Report of a Formal Investigation*, London: Commission for Racial Equality.

COMMUNITY INCOME TAX SERVICE (1976), *Annual Report*, Winnipeg, Manitoba.

COOKE, K., and BALDWIN, S., (1984), 'How Much is Enough?', *New Society*, Vol. 70, No. 1138, 11 October, pp. 67–8.

COONS, J., and SUGARMAN, S., (1978), *Education by Choice: The Case for Family Control*, Berkeley: University of California Press.

COOPER, MICHAEL H., and CULYER, ANTHONY J. (eds) (1973), *Health Economics*, London: Penguin.

COULTER, FIONA, COWELL, FRANK, and JENKINS, STEVEN (1992), 'Equivalence Scale Relativities and the Extent of Inequality and Poverty', *Economic Journal*, Vol. 102, No. 414, September, pp. 1067–82.

COWELL, FRANK A. (1977), *Measuring Inequality*, Oxford: Philip Allan.

CPAG (1984), *Double Discrimination: Racism in Social Security*, London: Child Poverty Action Group.

CPAG (1985), *Burying Beveridge, A Detailed Response to the Green Paper: Reform of Social Security*, London: Child Poverty Action Group.

CREEDY, JOHN (1982), *State Pensions in Britain*, Cambridge: Cambridge University Press.

CREEDY, JOHN, and DISNEY, RICHARD (1985), *Social Insurance in Transition*, Oxford: Oxford University Press.

CROOK, TONY, KEMP, PETER, ANDERSON, ISOBEL, and BOWMAN, STUART (1991), *The Business Expansion Scheme and Rented Housing*, York: Joseph Rowntree Foundation.

CROSLAND, ANTHONY (1956), *The Future of Socialism*, London: Cape.

CULLINGWORTH, J. B. (1979), *Essays on Housing Policy: the British Scene*, London: George Allen and Unwin.

CULLIS, JOHN, and JONES, PHILIP (1992), *Public Finance and Public Choice: Analytical Perspectives*, London: McGraw-Hill.

CULLIS, JOHN, and WEST, PETER (1979), *The Economics of Health*, Oxford: Martin Robertson.

CULLIS, J. G., JONES, P. R., and MORRISSEY, O. (1991), 'Public Choice Perspectives on the Poll Tax', *Economic Journal*, Vol. 101, No. 406, May, pp. 600–14.

CULYER, ANTHONY J. (1971a), 'The Nature of the Commodity "Health Care" and Its Efficient Allocation', *Oxford Economic Papers*, Vol. 23, pp. 189–211, reprinted in Cooper and Culyer (1973).

CULYER, ANTHONY J. (1971b), 'Merit Goods and the Welfare Economics of Coercion', *Public Finance*, No. 4.

CULYER, ANTHONY J. (1976), *Need and the National Health Service*, Oxford: Martin Robertson.

CULYER, ANTHONY J. (1980), *The Political Economy of Social Policy*, Oxford: Martin Robertson.

CULYER, ANTHONY J. (ed.) (1983), *Health Indicators*, Oxford: Martin Robertson.

CULYER, ANTHONY J. (1989), 'The Normative Economics of Health Care Finance and Provision', *Oxford Review of Economic Policy*, Vol. 5, pp. 34–58.

CULYER, ANTHONY J. (1993), 'Health Care Insurance and Provision', in Barr and Whynes (1993).

CULYER, ANTHONY J., and POSNETT, JOHN P. (1990), 'Hospital Behaviour and Competition', in Culyer *et al.* (1990).

CULYER, ANTHONY J., and MAYNARD, ALAN K., and POSNETT, JOHN P. (eds) (1990), *Competition in Health Care: Reforming the NHS*, London: Macmillan.

DALTON, H. (1920), 'The Measurement of the Inequality of Incomes', *Economic Journal*, Vol. 30, pp. 348–61.

DANIELS, N. (ed.) (1975), *Reading Rawls*, Oxford: Basil Blackwell.

DANZIGER, SHELDON, HAVEMAN, ROBERT, and PLOTNICK, ROBERT (1981), 'How Income Transfer Programs Affect Work, Savings and the Income Distribution: A Critical Review', *Journal of Economic Literature*, Vol. 19.

DANZIGER, SHELDON, HAVEMAN, ROBERT, and PLOTNICK, ROBERT (1984), *Anti-poverty Policy: Effects on the Poor and Nonpoor*, discussion paper, Madison: University of Wisconsin.

DANZIGER, SHELDON, VAN DER GAAG, JACQUES, SMOLENSKY, EUGENE, and TAUSSIG, MICHAEL (1984), 'Implications of the Relative Economic Status of the Elderly for Transfer Policy', in Aaron and Burtless (1984).

DAVIS, EVAN, *et al.* (1985a), *1985 Benefit Reviews: The Effect of the Proposals*, Report Series No. 17, London: Institute for Fiscal Studies.

DAVIS, EVAN, *et al.* (1985b), 'The Social Security Green Paper', *Fiscal Studies*, Vol. 6, No. 3, August, pp. 1–8.

DAVIS, O. E., and WHINSTON, A. (1965), 'Welfare Economics and the Theory of Second Best', *Review of Economic Studies*, Vol. XXXII, No. 89, January, pp. 1–14.

DAWSON, R. F. F. (1967), *Cost of Road Accidents in Great Britain*, London: Ministry of Transport, Road Research Laboratory, reprinted in Cooper and Culyer (1973).

DAY, PATRICIA, and KLEIN, RUDOLF (1991), 'Britain's Health Care Experiment', *Health Affairs*, Vol. 10, No. 3, pp. 39–59.

DEATON, ANGUS S., and MUELLBAUER, JOHN (1980), *Economics and Consumer Behaviour*, Cambridge: Cambridge University Press.

DENISON, EDWARD F. (1962), *The Sources of Economic Growth in the United States and the Alternatives Before Us*, New York: Committee for Economic Development.

DENISON, EDWARD F. (1967), *Why Growth Rates Differ. Postwar Experience in Nine Western Countries*, Washington, DC: The Brookings Institution.

DENISON, EDWARD F. (1969), 'The Contribution of Education to the Quality of Labor: Comment', *American Economic Review*, December.

DERTHICK, MARTHA (1979), *Policymaking for Social Security*, Washington, DC: The Brookings Institution.

DESAI, MEGHNAD (1979), *Marxian Economics*, Oxford: Basil Blackwell.

DIAMOND, PETER A., and HAUSMAN, JERRY A. (1984), 'The Retirement and Unemployment Behavior of Older Men', in Aaron and Burtless (1984).

DIAMOND, PETER A., and ROTHSCHILD, MICHAEL (eds) (1978), *Uncertainty in Economics: Readings and Exercises*, New York: Academic Press.

DILNOT, ANDREW, and DISNEY, RICHARD (1989), 'Pensions Schemes after the 1989 Budget', *Fiscal Studies*, Vol. 10, No. 3, August, pp. 34–49.

DILNOT, ANDREW, and STARK, GRAHAM (1986), 'The Poverty Trap, Tax Cuts, and the Reform of Social Security', *Fiscal Studies*, Vol. 7, No. 1, February, pp. 1–10.

DILNOT, ANDREW, and WEBB, STEVEN (1988), 'The 1988 Social Security Reforms', *Fiscal Studies*, Vol. 9, No. 3, August, pp. 26–53.

DILNOT, ANDREW, KAY, JOHN, and MORRIS, NICK (1984), *The Reform of Social Security*, Oxford: Clarendon Press, for the Institute for Fiscal Studies, London.

DISNEY, RICHARD, and WHITEHOUSE, EDWARD (1991), 'How Should Pensions in the UK Be Indexed?', *Fiscal Studies*, Vol. 12, No. 3, August, pp. 47–61.

DONNISON, DAVID (1972), 'Ideologies and Policies', *Journal of Social Policy*, Vol. 1, Pt 2, April, pp. 97–117.

DONNISON, DAVID, and UNGERSON, CLARE (1982), *Housing Policy*, London: Penguin.

DONNISON, D. with SOTO, P. (1980), *The Good City: A Study of Urban Development and Policy in Britain*, London: Heinemann.

DORSETT, RICHARD, and HEADY, CHRISTOPHER (1991), 'The Take-Up of Means-Tested Benefits by Working Families with Children', *Fiscal Studies*, Vol. 12, No. 4, November, pp. 22–32.

DOUGLAS, P. H. (1925), *Wages and the Family*, Chicago: University of Chicago Press.

DOUGLAS, P. H. (1939), *Social Security in the United States: An Analysis of the Federal Social Security Act*, New York: McGraw-Hill.

DOWIE, J. (1975), 'The Portfolio Approach to Health Behaviour', *Social Science and Medicine*, Vol. 9, No. 11/12, November/December, pp. 619–31.

DOWNS, ANTHONY (1957), *An Economic Theory of Democracy*, New York: Harper and Row.

DUNCAN, G. J. (ed.) (1984), *Years of Poverty, Years of Plenty*, Michigan: Institute for Social Research.

DUNLEAVY, PATRICK (1985), 'Bureaucrats, Budgets and the Growth of the State: Reconstructing an Instrumental Model', *British Journal of Political Science*, Vol. 15, pp. 299–328.

ENGLISH J., (1982), 'Must Council Housing Become Welfare Housing?', *Housing Review*, November–December, pp. 212–13.

ENTHOVEN, ALAIN C. (1985), *Reflections on the Management of the National Health Service: An American Looks at Incentives to Efficiency in Health Services Management in the UK*, London: Nuffield Provincial Hospitals Trust (a summary is contained in *The Economist*, 22 June 1985, pp. 19–20).

ENTHOVEN, ALAIN (1989), 'What Can Europeans Learn from Americans?', in US HCFA (1989).

ENTHOVEN, ALAIN (1991), 'Internal Market Reform of the British National Health Service', *Health Affairs*, Vol. 10, No. 3, pp. 60–70.

ERMISCH, JOHN F. (1980), *Paying the Piper: Demographic Changes and Pension Contributions*, London: Policy Studies Institute.

ERMISCH, JOHN F. (1983), *The Political Economy of Demographic Change*, London: Policy Studies Institute, and Gower.

ESPING-ANDERSON, G. (1990), *The Three Worlds of Welfare Capitalism*, Cambridge: Polity Press.

EVANS, ROBERT G., LOMAS, JONATHAN, BARER, MORRIS L., *et al.* (1989), 'Controlling Health Expenditures: The Canadian Reality', *New England Journal of Medicine*, Vol. 320, No. 9, pp. 571–77.

FALKINGHAM, JANE (1989), 'Dependency and Ageing in Britain: A Re-Examination of the Evidence', *Journal of Social Policy*, Vol. 18, No. 2, pp. 211–33.

FARMER, M., and BARRELL, R. (1982), 'Why Student Loans Are Fairer Than Grants', *Public Money*, Vol. 2, No. 1, June, pp. 19–24.

FEINSTEIN, C. H. (1972), *Statistical Tables of National Income, Expenditure and Output of the UK, 1855–1965*, Cambridge: Cambridge University Press.

FELDSTEIN, MARTIN S. (1974), 'Social Security, Induced Retirement and Aggregate Capital Accumulation', *Journal of Political Economy*, Vol. 82, pp. 905–26.

FELDSTEIN, MARTIN S. (1979), 'Social Security Hobbles Our Capital Formation', *Harvard Business Review*, July–August.

FIEGEHEN, GUY, and LANSLEY, STEWART (1976), 'The Measurement of Poverty', *Journal of the Royal Statistical Society*, Vol. 139, pp. 508–18.

FIEGEHEN, G. C., LANSLEY, P. S., and SMITH, A. D. (1977), *Poverty and Progress in Britain, 1953–73,* Cambridge: Cambridge University Press.

FINE, BEN (1975), *Marx's Capital*, London: Macmillan.

FINER, S. E. (1952), *The Life and Times of Sir Edwin Chadwick*, London: Methuen.

FISHER, IRVING (1930), *The Theory of Interest*, New York: Macmillan.

FLANAGAN, ROBERT J. (1987), 'Efficiency and Equality in Swedish Labor Markets', in Bosworth, Barry P., and Rivlin, Alice M. (eds) *The Swedish Economy*, Washington, DC: The Brookings Institution.

FLOREY, C. DU V. (1982), 'Diabetis Mellitus', in Miller, D. L., and Farmer, R.D.T. (eds), *Epidemiology of Diseases*, Oxford: Blackwell Scientific.

FORREST, R., and MURIE, A. (1990), *Selling the Welfare State: The Privatisation of Public Housing*, London: Routledge.

FOSTER, JAMES E. (1984), 'On Economic Poverty: A Survey of Aggregate Measures', *Advances in Econometrics*, Vol. 3, pp. 215–51.

FRASER, DEREK (1984), *The Evolution of the British Welfare State*, 2nd edn, London: Macmillan.

FREEDEN, M. (1978), *The New Liberalism: An Ideology of Social Reform*, Oxford: Oxford University Press.

FRIEDMAN, MILTON (1962), *Capitalism and Freedom*, Chicago: University of Chicago Press.

FRIEDMAN, MILTON, and FRIEDMAN, ROSE (1980), *Free to Choose*, London: Penguin.

FRIEDMAN, MILTON, and KUZNETS, SIMON (1945), *Income from Independent Professional Practice*, New York: National Bureau of Economic Research.

FRIEDMAN, MILTON, and STIGLER, GEORGE (1972), 'Roofs or Ceilings? The Current Housing Problem', in Hayek, Friedrich, *et al.*, *Verdict on Rent Control*, London: Institute of Economic Affairs.

FUCHS, VICTOR R. (1988), 'The "Competition Revolution" in Health Care', *Health Affairs*, Vol. 7, No. 3, pp. 5–24.

GAULDIE, E. (1974), *Cruel Habitations: A History of Working-Class Housing, 1780–1918*, London: George Allen and Unwin.

GEORGE, VICTOR, and WILDING, PAUL (1976), *Ideology and Social Welfare*, London: Routledge and Kegan Paul.

GILBERT, BENTLEY B. (1973), *The Evolution of National Insurance in Great Britain*, London: Michael Joseph.

GINSBURG, N. (1979), *Class, Capital and Social Policy*, London: Macmillan.

GINTIS, H., and BOWLES, S. (1982), 'The Welfare State and Long-Term Economic Growth: Marxian, Neoclassical and Keynesian Approaches', *American Economic Review*, Papers and Proceedings, Vol. 72, No. 1, pp. 341–5.

GLENNERSTER, HOWARD (ed.) (1983), *The Future of the Welfare State: Remaking Social Policy*, London: Heinemann.

GLENNERSTER, HOWARD (1990), 'Social Policy since the Second World War', in Hills (1990).

GLENNERSTER, HOWARD (1991), 'Quasi-markets for Education?', *Economic Journal*, Vol. 101, No. 408, September, pp. 1268–76.

GLENNERSTER, HOWARD (1992), *Paying for Welfare: The 1990s*, London: Harvester Wheatsheaf.

GLENNERSTER, HOWARD (1993), 'The Economics of Education: Changing Fortunes', in Barr and Whynes (1993).

GLENNERSTER, HOWARD, and LOW, WILLIAM (1990), 'Education and the Welfare State: Does It All Add Up?', in Hills (1990).

GLENNERSTER, HOWARD, MERRETT, STEPHEN, and WILSON, GAIL (1968), 'A Graduate Tax', *Higher Education Review*, Vol. 1, No. 1.

GLENNERSTER, HOWARD, OWENS, PATRICIA, and MATSAGANIS, MANOS (1992), *A Foothold for Fundholding*, London: Kings Fund Institute.

GLENNERSTER, HOWARD, POWER, ANNE, and TRAVERS, TONY (1991), 'A New Era for Social Policy: A New Enlightenment or a New Leviathan?', *Journal of Social Policy*, Vol. 20, No. 3, July, pp. 389–414.

GOLDFARB, R. S. (1970), 'Pareto Optimal Distribution: A Comment', *American Economic Review*, Vol. LX, No. 5, December.

GOODIN, ROBERT, and LE GRAND, JULIAN (1987), *Not Only the Poor: The Middle Classes and the Welfare State*, London: Allen and Unwin.

GORDON, DAVID M. (1969), 'Income and Welfare in New York City', *Public Interest*, Winter.

GORDON, MARGARET (1988), *Social Security Policies in Industrial Countries: A Comparative Analysis*, Cambridge: Cambridge University Press.

GORDON, ROBERT J., and BLINDER, ALAN S. (1980), 'Market Wages, Reservation Wages and Retirement Decisions', *Journal of Public Economics*, Vol. 14, pp. 277–308.

GOROVITZ, S. (1975), 'John Rawls: A Theory of Justice', in Crespigny, A. de, and Minogue, K. R. (eds), *Contemporary Political Philosophers*, London: Methuen.

GOUGH, I. (1979), *The Political Economy of the Welfare State*, London: Macmillan.

GRAMLICH, EDWARD M. (1989), 'Economists' View of the Welfare System', *American Economic Review*, Vol. 79, No. 2, May, pp. 191–6.

GREEN, CHRISTOPHER (1967), *Negative Taxes and the Poverty Problem*, Washington, DC: The Brookings Institution.

GREEN, DAVID (ed.) (1990), *The NHS Reforms: Whatever Happened to Consumer Choice?*, Health Series No. 11, London: Institute for Economic Affairs.

GREEN, DAVID (ed.) (1991), *Empowering the Parents: How to Break the Schools Monopoly*, London: Institute of Economic Affairs.

GRIFFITHS, ROY (1988), *Community Care: An Agenda for Action*, London: HMSO.

GRONBJERG, K., STREET, D., and SUTTLES, G. D. (1978), *Poverty and Social Change*, Chicago: University of Chicago Press.

GROSSMAN, M. (1972), *The Demand for Health: A Theoretical and Empirical Investigation*, Occasional Paper 119, Cambridge, Mass.: National Bureau of Economic Research.

GRUBEL, H. G., and MAKI, D. R. (1976), 'The Effects of Unemployment Benefits on US Unemployment Rates', *Weltwirtschaftliches Archiv*, Vol. 112, pp. 274–97.

HALL, PETER (1981), *The Inner City in Context*, Final Report to the Social Science

Research Council Inner Cities Working Party, London: Heinemann.

HALL, PETER (1982), *Urban and Regional Planning*, London: Penguin.

HALPERN, JANICE, and HAUSMAN, JERRY A. (1986), 'Choice Under Uncertainty: A Model of Applications for the Social Security Disability Insurance Program', *Journal of Public Economics*, Vol. 14, No. 2, pp. 161–94.

HALPERN, S. (1985), 'What the Public Thinks of the NHS', *Health and Social Service Journal*, 6 June, pp. 702–4.

HAM, CHRIS, ROBINSON, RAY, and BENZEVAL, MICHAELA (1990), *Health Check: Health Care Reforms in an International Context*, London: Kings Fund Institute.

HAMERMESH, DANIEL S. (1984), 'Life-Cycle Effects on Consumption and Retirement', *Journal of Labor Economics*, Vol. 2, pp. 353–70.

HANNAH, LESLIE (1986), *Inventing Private Pensions*, Cambridge: Cambridge University Press.

HANSEN, W. LEE, and WEISBROD, BURTON A. (1969), 'The Distribution of Costs and Direct Benefits of Public Higher Education: the Case of California', *Journal of Human Resources*, Vol. IV, No. 2, Spring, pp. 176–91.

HANSEN, W. LEE, and WEISBROD, BURTON A. (1978), 'The Distribution of Subsidies to Students in California Public Higher Education: Reply', *Journal of Human Resources*, Vol. XIII, No. 1, Winter, pp. 137–9.

HANUSHEK, ERIC A. (1986), 'The Economics of Schooling: Production and Efficiency in Public Schools', *Journal of Economic Literature*, Vol. 23, No. 3, pp. 1141–77.

HARBERGER, A. C. (1962), 'The Incidence of the Corporation Income Tax', *Journal of Political Economy*, June.

HARRIS, JOSE F. (1972), *Unemployment and Politics, 1886–1914*, Oxford: Oxford University Press.

HARRIS, JOSE F. (1977), *William Beveridge: A Biography*, Oxford: Oxford University Press.

HARRIS, RALPH, and SELDON, ARTHUR (1979), *Over-Ruled on Welfare*, Hobart Paperback No. 13, London: Institute of Economic Affairs.

HARRISON, A. J. (1979), *The Distribution of Wealth in Ten Countries*, Background Paper No. 7, Royal Commission on the Distribution of Income and Wealth, London: HMSO.

HARRISON, J. (1978), *Marxist Economics for Socialists*, London: Pluto.

HARRISON, P. (1985), *Inside the Inner City*, revised edn, London: Penguin.

HART, J. T. (1970), 'Semicontinuous Screening of a Whole Community for Hypertension', *Lancet*, 1 August.

HAVEMAN, ROBERT H. (1987), *Poverty Policy and Poverty Research: The Great Society and the Social Sciences*, Madison: University of Wisconsin Press.

HAVEMAN, ROBERT H., and WATTS, HAROLD W. (1977), 'Social Experimentation as Policy Research; A Review of Negative Income Tax Experiments', in Halberstadt, V., and Culyer, J. (eds), *Public Economics and Human Resources*, Paris: Cujas.

HAVEMAN, ROBERT H., and WOLFE, BARBARA L. (1984), 'Disability Transfers and

Early Retirement: A Causal Relationship?', *Journal of Public Economics*, Vol. 24, pp. 47–66.

HAVEMAN, ROBERT H., WOLFE, BARBARA L., and WARLICK, JENNIFER L. (1984), 'Disability Transfers, Early Retirement and Retrenchment', in Aaron and Burtless (1984).

HAY, J. R. (1975), *The Origins of the Liberal Welfare Reforms 1906–1914*, London: Macmillan.

HAYEK, FRIEDRICH A. (1944), *The Road to Serfdom*, London and Chicago: Routledge and Chicago University Press.

HAYEK, FRIEDRICH A. (1945), 'The Use of Knowledge in Society', *American Economic Review*, Vol. 35, pp. 519–30.

HAYEK, FRIEDRICH A. (1960), *The Constitution of Liberty*, London and Chicago: Routledge and Kegan Paul, and Chicago University Press.

HAYEK, FRIEDRICH A. (1976), *Law, Legislation and Liberty*, Vol. 2, 'The Mirage of Social Justice', London: Routledge and Kegan Paul.

HEALD, DAVID (1983), *Public Expenditure: Its Defence and Reform*, Oxford: Martin Robertson.

HELLWIG, MARTIN (1987), 'Some Recent Developments in the Theory of Competition in Markets with Adverse Selection', *European Economic Review*, Vol. 31, pp. 319–25.

HEMMING, RICHARD (1984), *Poverty and Incentives*, Oxford: Oxford University Press.

HEMMING, RICHARD, and KAY, JOHN (1982a), 'Great Britain', in Rosa (1982).

HEMMING, RICHARD, and KAY, JOHN (1982b), 'The Costs of the State Earnings-Related Pension Scheme', *Economic Journal*, Vol. 92, No. 366, June, pp. 300–19.

HICKS, JOHN R. (1946), *Value and Capital*, 2nd edn, Oxford: Clarendon Press.

HIGGINS, JOAN (1981), *States of Welfare: Comparative Analysis in Social Policy*, Oxford: Basil Blackwell and Martin Robertson.

HILLMAN, ALAN L., PAULY, MARK V., and KERSTEIN, JOSEPH J. (1989), 'How Do Financial Incentives Affect Physicians' Clinical Decisions and the Financial Performance of Health Maintenance Organizations?', *New England Journal of Medicine*, Vol. 321, No. 2, pp. 86–92.

HILLS, JOHN (ed.) (1990), *The State of Welfare: The Welfare State in Britain since 1974*, Oxford: Oxford University Press.

HILLS, JOHN (1991), *Unravelling Housing Finance*, Oxford: Oxford University Press.

HILLS, JOHN, and MULLINGS, BEVERLY (1990), 'Housing: A Decent Home for All at a Price within their Means?', in Hills (1990).

HIMMELFARB, GERTRUDE (1984), *The Idea of Poverty: England in the Early Industrial Age*, London: Faber.

HIMMELSTEIN, DAVID U., and WOOLHANDLER, STEFFIE (1986), 'Cost without Benefit: Administrative Waste in US Health Care', *New England Journal of Medicine*, Vol. 314, No. 7, pp. 441–5.

HIMMELSTEIN, DAVID U., and WOOLHANDLER, STEFFIE (1991), 'The Deteriorating Administrative Efficiency of the US Health Care System', *New England Journal of Medicine*, Vol. 324, No. 18, pp. 1253–7.

HIRSHLEIFER, J. (1980), *Price Theory and Applications*, 2nd edn, London: Prentice Hall.

HOBSBAWM, E. J. (1964), *Labouring Men*, London: Weidenfeld and Nicolson.

HOBSON, J. A. (1908), *The Problem of the Unemployed*, 4th edn (London).

HOBSON, J. A. (1909), *The Crisis of Liberalism: New Issues of Democracy*, London: King and Son.

HOCHMAN, HAROLD, and RODGERS, JAMES (1969), 'Pareto Optimal Distribution', *American Economic Review*, Vol. LIX, No. 4.

HOCHMAN, HAROLD, and RODGERS, JAMES (1970), 'Reply', *American Economic Review*, Vol. LX, No. 5, December.

HOLZMANN, ROBERT (1988), 'Ageing and Social Security Costs', *European Journal of Population*, Vol. 3, pp. 411–37.

HONIG, MARJORIE (1974), 'AFDC Income, Recipient Rates, and Family Dissolution', *Journal of Human Resources*, Vol. 9, pp. 303–22.

HONIG, MARJORIE (1976), 'AFDC Income, Recipient Rates, and Family Dissolution: A Reply', *Journal of Human Resources*, Vol. 11, pp. 250–9.

HUBY, M., and WALKER, R. (1991), 'The Social Fund and Territorial Justice', *Policy and Politics*.

HUGHES, G., and MCCORMICK, B. (1981), 'Do Council Housing Policies Reduce Migration Between Regions?', *Economic Journal*, Vol. 91, No. 364, December, pp. 919–37.

HUME, DAVID (1770), 'Enquiry Concerning the Principles of Morals', in *Essays and Treatises on Several Subjects*, London: Cadell.

HUNT, EDWARD H. (1981), *British Labour History, 1815–1914*, London: Weidenfeld and Nicolson.

HUNT, S. M., *et al.* (1980), 'A Quantitative Approach to Perceived Health Status: A Validation Study', *Journal of Epidemiology and Community Health*, Vol. 34.

HURD, MICHAEL (1990), 'Research on the Elderly: Economic Status, Retirement and Consumption and Saving', *Jo. of Economic Literature*, Vol. 28, pp. 565–637.

HURLEY, S. I. (1985), 'The Unit of Taxation Under an Ideal Progressive Income Tax', *Oxford Journal of Legal Studies*, Vol. 4, No. 2, pp. 157–97.

HURST, JEREMY W. (1991), 'Reforming Health Care in Seven European Nations', *Health Affairs*, Vol. 10, No. 3, pp. 7–21.

ILLSLEY, RAYMOND (1980), *Professional or Public Health*, London: Nuffield Provincial Hospitals Trust.

ILLSLEY, RAYMOND, and LE GRAND, JULIAN (1987), *The Measurement of Health Inequality*, Welfare State Programme, Discussion Paper No. WSP/12, London: London School of Economics.

INMAN, ROBERT P. (1987), 'Markets, Governments and the "New" Political Economy', in Auerbach, Alan J., and Feldstein, Martin S. (eds), *Handbook in Public Economics*, Vol. II, Amsterdam: North Holland.

INQUIRY INTO BRITISH HOUSING (1991), *Second Report*, York: Joseph Rowntree Foundation.

INTERNATIONAL LABOUR OFFICE (1984a), *Introduction to Social Security*, Geneva: International Labour Office.

INTERNATIONAL LABOUR OFFICE (1984b), *Into the Twenty-first Century: The Development of Social Security*, Geneva: International Labour Office.

ISRAEL, STEVEN, and TEELING-SMITH, GEORGE (1967), 'The Submerged Iceberg of Sickness in Society', *Social and Economic Administration*, Vol. 1, pp. 43–56.

JENCKS, CHRISTOPHER (1970), *Education Vouchers: A Report on the Financing of Elementary Education by Grants to Parents*, Cambridge, Mass.: Cambridge Center for the Study of Public Policy.

JENCKS, CHRISTOPHER (1972), *Inequality: A Reassessment of the Effect of Family and Schooling in America*, New York and London: Basic Books and Allen Lane.

JENKINS, STEPHEN P., and MAYNARD, ALAN K. (1983), 'Intergenerational Continuities in Housing', *Urban Studies*, Vol. 20, No. 374, pp. 431–8.

JOHNSON, GEORGE, and LAYARD, RICHARD (1986), 'The Natural Rate of Unemployment: Explanation and Policy', in Ashenfelter and Layard (1986).

JOHNSON, PAUL, and FALKINGHAM, JANE (1992), *Ageing and Economic Welfare*, London: Sage.

JOHNSON, PAUL, and FALKINGHAM, JANE (forthcoming), 'Is There a Future for the Beveridge Pension Scheme?', in Baldwin, Sally, and Falkingham, Jane (eds), *Social Security and Social Change: New Challenges to Beveridge*, London: Harvester Wheatsheaf.

JOHNSON, PAUL, and WEBB, STEVEN (1989), 'Counting People with Low Incomes: The Impact of Recent Changes in Official Statistics', *Fiscal Studies*, Vol. 10, No. 4, December, pp. 66–82.

JOHNSSON, BENGT (1989), 'What Americans Can Learn from Europeans', in US HCFA (1989).

JOHNSTONE, D. BRUCE (1986), *Sharing the Costs of Higher Education*, New York: College Entrance Examination Board.

JONES, ANDREW M., and POSNETT, JOHN W. (1993), 'The Economics of Charity', in Barr and Whynes (1993).

JONES-LEE, M. (1969), 'Valuation of Production in Probability of Death by Road Accident', *Journal of Transport Economics and Policy*, Vol. 3, pp. 37–47, reprinted in Cooper and Culyer (1973).

JONES-LEE, M. (1976), *The Value of Life: An Economic Assessment*, Oxford: Martin Robertson.

KAIM-CAUDLE, P. (1973), *Comparative Social Policy and Social Security: A Ten-Country Study*, Oxford: Martin Robertson.

KALDOR, NICHOLAS (1955), *An Expenditure Tax*, London: Allen and Unwin.

KAMERMAN, SHEILA B., and KAHN, ALFRED J. (1991), *Government Expenditures for Children and their Families in Advanced Industrialized Countries*, UNICEF, Economic Policy Series No. 20.

KANBUR, RAVI, and KEEN, MICHAEL (1989), 'Poverty, Incentives, and Linear Income Taxation', in Dilnot, Andrew, and Walker, Ian (eds), *The Economics of Social Security*, Oxford: Oxford University Press.

KATZNELSON, I. (1978), 'Considerations on Social Democracy in the United States', *Comparative Politics*, October.

KAY, JOHN A. (1984), 'The Effects of Increasing Tax Thresholds on the Poverty and Unemployment Traps', *Fiscal Studies*, Vol. 5, No. 1, February, pp. 32–4.

KAY, JOHN, and KING, MERVYN A. (1990), *The British Tax System*, 5th edn, Oxford: Oxford University Press.

KAY, J. A., and THOMPSON, D. J. (1986), 'Privatisation: A Policy in Search of a Rationale', *Economic Journal*, Vol. 96, No. 381, March, pp. 18–32.

KAY, JOHN, MAYER, COLIN, and THOMPSON, DAVID (eds) (1986), *Privatisation and Regulation: The UK Experience*, Oxford: Clarendon Press.

KENT COUNTY COUNCIL (1978), *Education Vouchers in Kent*, Maidstone: Kent County Council.

KING, MERVYN A. (1980), 'An Econometric Model of Tenure Choice and Demand for Housing as a Joint Decision', *Journal of Public Economics*, Vol. 14, No. 2, October, pp. 137–59.

KING, MERVYN A. (1983), 'An Index of Inequality: with Applications to Horizontal Equity and Social Mobility', *Econometrica*, Vol. 51, pp. 99–115.

KINGS FUND INSTITUTE (1988), *Health Finance: Assessing the Options*, London: Kings Fund Institute.

KLEIN, RUDOLF (1984), 'Privatisation and the Welfare State', *Lloyds Bank Review*, No. 151, January, pp. 12–29.

KLEIN, RUDOLF (1989), *The Politics of the NHS*, 2nd edn, London: Longman.

KNIGHT, B. (1983), 'Accounting for Educational Priorities', *Public Money*, Vol. 3, No. 3, December, pp. 37–40.

KOTLIKOFF, LAURENCE J. (1989a), *What Determines Savings?*, Cambridge, Mass.: MIT Press.

KOTLIKOFF, LAURENCE J. (1989b), 'On the Contribution of Economics to the Evaluation and Formation of Social Insurance Policy', *American Economic Review*, Vol. 79, No. 2, May, pp. 184–90.

KREPS, DAVID M. (1990), *A Course in Microeconomic Theory*, New Jersey and London: Princeton University Press and Harvester Wheatsheaf.

LAFFONT, JEAN-JACQUES (1989), *The Economics of Uncertainty and Information*, London and Cambridge, Mass.: MIT Press.

LAIDLER, DAVID, and ESTRIN, SAUL (1989), *Introduction to Microeconomics*, 3rd edn, London and New York: Philip Allan.

LAMPMAN, ROBERT J. (1984), *Social Welfare Spending: Accounting for Changes from 1950 to 1978*, New York: Academic Press.

LANSLEY, STEWART (1979), *Housing and Public Policy*, London: Croom Helm.

LANSLEY, STEWART (1982), *Housing Policy: New Policies for Labour*, London: Labour Housing Group.

LASKI, HAROLD (1967), *A Grammar of Politics*, 5th edn, London: Allen and Unwin.

LAYARD, RICHARD, and WALTERS, ALAN (1978), *Microeconomic Theory*, London: McGraw-Hill.

LAYARD, RICHARD, NICKELL, STEPHEN, and JACKMAN, RICHARD (1991), *Unemployment*, Oxford: Oxford University Press.

LAZEAR, EDWARD (1986a), 'Retirement from the Labor Force', in Ashenfelter, Orley, and Layard, Richard (eds), *Handbook of Labor Economics*, Amsterdam: North Holland.

LAZEAR, EDWARD P. (1986b), 'Incentive Effects of Pensions', in Wise, David A. (ed.), *Pensions, Labor and Individual Behavior*, Chicago: University of Chicago Press.

LAZEAR, E. P., and MICHAEL, R. T. (1980), 'Family Size and the Distribution of Real Per Capita Income', *American Economic Review*, Vol. 70, pp. 91–107.

LE GRAND, JULIAN (1982), *The Strategy of Equality*, London: George Allen and Unwin.

LE GRAND, JULIAN (1984), 'Equity as an Economic Objective', *Journal of Applied Philosophy*, Vol. 1, No. 1, pp. 39–51.

LE GRAND, JULIAN (1987a), 'Inequalities in Health: Some International Comparisons', *European Economic Review*, Vol. 31, pp. 182–91.

LE GRAND, JULIAN (1987b), 'The Middle-Class Use of the British Social Services', in Goodin and Le Grand (1987).

LE GRAND, JULIAN (1987c), 'Measuring the Distributional Impact of the Welfare State: Methodological Issues', in Goodin and Le Grand (1987).

LE GRAND, JULIAN (1989a), 'An International Comparison of Distribution of Age-at-Death', in Fox, J. (ed.), *Health Inequalities in European Countries*, London: Gower.

LE GRAND, JULIAN (1989b), 'Markets, Welfare and Equality', in Le Grand and Estrin (1989).

LE GRAND, JULIAN (1990), 'The State of Welfare', in Hills (1990).

LE GRAND, JULIAN (1991a), *Equity and Choice: An Essay in Applied Philosophy*, London and New York: HarperCollins.

LE GRAND, JULIAN (1991b), 'The Distribution of Health Care Revisited: A Commentary on Wagstaff, van Doorslaer and Paci, and O'Donnell and Propper', *Journal of Health Economics*, Vol. 10, pp. 239–45.

LE GRAND, JULIAN, and ESTRIN, SAUL (eds) (1989), *Market Socialism*, Oxford: Clarendon Press.

LE GRAND, JULIAN, and ROBINSON, RAY (1984), *Privatisation and the Welfare State*, London: George Allen and Unwin.

LE GRAND, JULIAN, PROPPER, CAROL, and ROBINSON, RAY (1992), *The Economics of Social Problems*, 3rd edn, London: Macmillan.

LE GRAND, JULIAN, WINTER, DAVID, and WOOLLEY, FRANCIS (1990), 'The National Health Service: Safe in Whose Hands?', in Hills (1990).

LEES, DENNIS S. (1961), *Health Through Choice*, London: Institute of Economic Affairs.

LEIMER, DEAN R., and LESNOY, SELIG D. (1982), 'Social Security and Private Saving: New Time-Series Evidence', *Journal of Political Economy*, Vol. 90, pp. 606–42.

LETWIN, WILLIAM (ed.) (1983), *Against Equality*, London: Macmillan.

LEVINE, M. D. (1978), *Federal Housing Policy: Current Programs and Recurring Issues*, Congressional Budget Office, Background Paper, Washington, DC: Government Printing Office.

LEVY, FRANK (1979), 'The Labor Supply of Female Household Heads, or AFDC Work Incentives Don't Work Too Well', *Journal of Human Resources*, Vol. XIV, No. 1, Winter, pp. 76–97.

LEVY, FRANK (1988), *Dollars and Dreams: The Changing American Income Distribution*, New York: Norton.

LINDERT, P. H., and WILLIAMSON, J. G. (1982), 'Revising England's Social Tables 1688–1812', *Explorations in Economic History*, Vol. 19, pp. 385–408.

LINDERT, P. H., and WILLIAMSON, J. G. (1983), 'Reinterpreting Britain's Social Tables, 1688–1913', *Explorations in Economic History*, Vol. 20, pp. 94–109.

LINDSAY, C. M. (1969), 'Medical Care and the Economics of Sharing', *Economica*, Vol. XXXVI, pp. 351–62, reprinted in Cooper and Culyer (1973).

LIPSEY, RICHARD G., and LANCASTER, KELVIN (1956), 'The General Theory of Second-Best', *Review of Economic Studies*, Vol. XXIV, No. 63, January, pp. 11–32.

LISTER, RUTH (1983), *Poverty*, No. 54, April.

LOMAS, G. (1974), *The Inner City*, London: London Voluntary Service Council.

LORD, RODNEY (1983), 'Value for Money in the Education Service', *Public Money*, Vol. 3, No. 2, September, pp. 15–22.

LORENZ, M. C. (1905), 'Methods of Measuring the Concentration of Wealth', *Publications of the American Statistical Association*, Vol. 9, pp. 209–16.

LUCAS, ROBERT E. (1987), *Models of Business Cycles*, Oxford: Basil Blackwell.

LUFT, HAROLD S. (1981), *Health Maintenance Organizations: Dimensions of Performance*, New York: Wiley.

LUFT, HAROLD S. (1991), 'Translating US HMO Experience to Other Health Systems', *Health Affairs*, Vol. 10, No. 3, pp. 172–86.

LUKES, STEVEN (1972), 'An Archimedean Point', *Observer Review*, 4 June.

LYDALL, HAROLD F. (1979), 'Some Problems in Making International Comparisons of Inequality', in Moroney, J. R. (ed.), *Income Inequality: Trends and International Comparisons*, Lexington, Mass.: Lexington Books.

LYNES, ANTHONY (1986), *Paying for Pensions: The French Experience*, London: London School of Economics.

MACK, JOANNA, and LANSLEY, STEWART (1985), *Poor Britain*, London: Allen and Unwin.

MACLENNAN, DUNCAN (1982), *Housing Economics: An Applied Approach*, London: Longman.

MACLENNAN, DUNCAN, and GIBB, KENNETH (1993), 'Political Economy, Applied Welfare Economics and Housing in the UK', in Barr and Whynes (1993).

MAKI, D. R., and SPINDLER, Z. A. (1975), 'The Effect of Unemployment Compensation on the Rate of Unemployment in Great Britain', *Oxford Economic Papers*, Vol. 27, pp. 440–54.

MANDEL, E. (1976), 'Introduction' to Karl Marx, *Capital*, vol. 1, London: Penguin.

MANNING, WILLARD, *et al.* (1984), 'A Controlled Trial of the Effect of a Prepaid Group Practice on Use of Services', *New England Journal of Medicine*, No. 301, 7 June, pp. 1505–10.

MARIN, ALAN (1983), 'Your Money or Your Life?', *Three Banks Review*, No. 38, June, pp. 20–37.

MARIN, ALAN, and PSACHAROPOULOS, GEORGE (1982), 'The Reward for Risk in the Labour Market', *Journal of Political Economy*, Vol. 90, No. 4, July/August.

MARMOR, THEODORE, MASHAW, JERRY, and HARVEY, PHILIP (1990), *America's Misunderstood Welfare State: Persistent Myths, Enduring Realities*, London and New York, HarperCollins and Basic Books.

MARSH, D. (1980), *The Welfare State*, 2nd edn, London: Longman.

MARSHALL, THOMAS H. (1975), *Social Policy in the Twentieth Century*, 4th edn, London: Hutchinson.

MARX, KARL (1976), *Capital*, Vol. 1, London: Penguin.

MARX, KARL (1978), *Capital*, Vol. 2, London: Penguin.

MARX, KARL (1981), *Capital*, Vol. 3, London: Penguin.

MAYNARD, ALAN K. (1975), *Experiment with Choice in Education*, London: Institute of Economic Affairs.

MAYNARD, ALAN K. (1982), 'The Private Health Care Sector in Great Britain', in McLachlan and Maynard (1982).

MAYNARD, ALAN K. (1986), 'Performance Incentives in General Practice', in *Health Education and General Practice*, London: Office of Health Economics.

MAYS, NICHOLAS, and BEVAN, GWYN (1987), *Resource Allocation in the National Health Service*, Occasional Papers on Social Administration No. 81, London: Bedford Square Press.

MCCLEMENTS, LESLIE D. (1977), 'Equivalence Scales for Children', *Journal of Public Economics*, Vol. 8.

MCCLEMENTS, LESLIE D. (1978), *The Economics of Social Security*, London: Heinemann.

MCCREADIE, C. (1976), 'Rawlsian Justice and the Financing of the National Health Service', *Journal of Social Policy*, Vol. 5, Pt 2, April.

MCDANIEL, P. R., and SURREY, S. S. (1984), *International Aspects of Tax Expenditures: A Comparative Study*, Deventer: Kluwer.

MCDONAGH, O. (1960), 'The Nineteenth Century Revolution in Government: A Reappraisal Reappraised', *Historical Journal*, II.

MCLACHLAN, GORDON, and MAYNARD, ALAN K. (eds) (1982), *The Public/Private Mix for Health*, London: The Nuffield Provincial Hospitals Trust.

MEADE, JAMES E. (1952), 'External Economies and Diseconomies in a Competitive Situation', *Economic Journal*, Vol. 62, pp. 54–67.

MEADE, JAMES E. (1972), 'Poverty in the Welfare State', *Oxford Economic Papers*, Vol. 24.

MEADE, JAMES E. (1974), *The Inheritance of Inequalities*, Bristol Academy/Oxford University Press, reprinted in Atkinson (1980).

MEADE, JAMES E. (1978), *The Structure and Reform of Direct Taxation*, London: Institute for Fiscal Studies and George Allen and Unwin.

MEADE, JAMES E. (1984), 'Full Employment, New Technologies and the Distribution of Income', *Journal of Social Policy*, Vol. 13, No. 2, April, pp. 129–46.

MENSCHER, S. (1967), *Poor Law to Poverty Program*, Pittsburgh: University of Pittsburgh Press.

MERRETT, STEPHEN (1979), *State Housing in Britain*, London: Routledge and Kegan Paul.

MESA-LAGO, CARMELO (1990), *Economic and Financial Aspects of Social Security in Latin America and the Caribbean: Tendencies, Problems and Alternatives for the Year 2000*, World Bank, Latin American and the Caribbean Region, Technical Department, Human Resources Division, Report No. IDP–095.

MEYER, P. A., and SHIPLEY, J. J. (1970), 'Pareto Optimal Distribution: A Comment', *American Economic Review*, Vol. LX, No. 5, December.

MILIBAND, RALPH (1969), *The State in a Capitalist Society*, London: Weidenfeld and Nicolson.

MILL, JOHN STUART (1863), *Utilitarianism*, London: Parker, Son and Bourn.

MILLER, DAVID (1976), *Social Justice*, Oxford: Clarendon Press.

MINARIK, J. J., and GOLDFARB, R. S. (1976), 'AFDC Income, Recipient Rates, and Family Dissolution: A Comment', *Journal of Human Resources*, Vol. 11, pp. 243–50.

MINFORD, PATRICK (1984a), 'Response to Nickell', *Economic Journal*, Vol. 94, No. 376, December.

MINFORD, PATRICK (1984b), 'State Expenditure: A Study in Waste', supplement to *Economic Affairs*, London: Institute of Economic Affairs.

MINFORD, P., with ASHTON, P., PEEL, M., DAVIES, D., and SPRAGUE, A. (1985), *Unemployment: Cause and Cure*, 2nd edn, Oxford: Basil Blackwell.

MISHAN, EDWARD J. (1971), 'Evaluation of Life and Limb, A Theoretical Approach', *Journal of Political Economy*, Vol. 79, No. 4, July/August, pp. 687–705.

MISHAN, EDWARD J. (1982), *Cost–Benefit Analysis: An Informal Introduction*, 3rd edn, London: George Allen and Unwin.

MISHRA, RAMESH (1981), *Society and Social Policy*, London: Macmillan.

MISHRA, RAMESH (1984), *The Welfare State in Crisis*, Brighton, Sussex: Harvester Press.

MITCHELL, OLIVIA S., and FIELDS, GARY S. (1981), 'The Effects of Pensions and Earnings on Retirement: A Review Essay', Working Paper 772, Cambridge, Mass.: National Bureau of Economic Research.

MOFFITT, ROBERT A. (1983), 'An Economic Model of Welfare Stigma', *American Economic Review*, Vol. 73, pp. 1023–35.

MOFFITT, ROBERT A. (1992), 'Incentive Effects of the US Welfare System: A Review', *Journal of Economic Literature*, Vol. 30, No. 1, March, pp. 1–61.

MORGAN, E. VICTOR (1984), *Choice in Pensions: The Political Economy of Saving for Retirement*, London: Institute of Economic Affairs.

MORTENSEN, DALE T. (1986), 'Job Search and Labor Market Analysis', in Ashenfelter and Layard (1986).

MUELLBAUER, JOHN (1977), 'Testing the Barten Model of Household Composition Effects and the Cost of Children', *Economic Journal*, Vol. 87.

MUELLBAUER, JOHN (1979), 'McClements on Equivalence Scales for Children', *Journal of Public Economics*, Vol. 12.

MUELLBAUER, JOHN (1980), 'The Estimation of the Prais-Houthakker Model of Equivalence Scales', *Econometrica*, Vol. 48.

MUELLER, DENNIS C. (1989), *Public Choice II*, Cambridge: Cambridge University Press.

MUNNELL, ALICIA H. (1982), *The Economics of Private Pensions*, Washington, DC: The Brookings Institution.

MURPHY, J. (1981), 'Class Inequality in Education: Two Justifications, One Evaluation but No Hard Evidence', *British Journal of Sociology*, Vol. 32, No. 2, June, pp. 182–201.

MURRAY, CHARLES (1984), *Losing Ground: American Social Policy, 1950–1980*, New York: Basic Books.

MUSGRAVE, RICHARD A., (1970), 'Pareto Optimal Distribution: A Comment', *American Economic Review*, Vol. LX, No. 5, December.

MUSGRAVE, RICHARD A., and MUSGRAVE, PEGGY B. (1989), *Public Finance in Theory and Practice*, 5th edn, London and New York: McGraw-Hill.

MUTH, R. F. (1960), 'The Demand for Non-Farm Housing', in Harberger, A. C. (ed.), *The Demand for Durable Goods*, Chicago: University of Chicago Press.

MUTH, RICHARD F., and GOODMAN, ALLEN C. (1989), *The Economics of Housing Markets*, London and New York: Chur.

MYERS, R. J. (1965), *Social Insurance and Allied Government Programs*, New York: Irwin.

NATIONAL FEDERATION OF HOUSING ASSOCIATIONS (1985), *Inquiry into British Housing: Report*, London: National Federation of Housing Associations.

NATIONAL SUPERANNUATION COMMITTEE OF INQUIRY (1976), *A National Super-*

annuation Scheme for Australia, Canberra: Australian Government Publishing Service.

NATIONAL SUPERANNUATION COMMITTEE OF INQUIRY (1977), *Occupational Superannuation in Australia*, Canberra: Australian Government Publishing Service.

NEVITT, ADELLA A. (1966), *Housing, Taxation and Subsidies*, London: Nelson.

NEWFIELD, JACK (1978), *Robert F. Kennedy: A Memoir*, New York: Berkley Publishing Corporation.

NICHOLS, ALBERT L., and ZECKHAUSER, RICHARD J. (1982), 'Targeting Transfers through Restrictions on Recipients', *American Economic Review* (Papers and Proceedings), Vol. 72, pp. 372–7.

NICHOLSON, JOHN L. (1974), 'The Distribution and Redistribution of Income in the United Kingdom', in Wedderburn, Dorothy (ed.), *Poverty, Inequality and Class Structure*, Cambridge: Cambridge University Press.

NICHOLSON, JOHN L. (1976), 'Appraisal of Different Methods of Estimating Equivalence Scales and Their Results', *Review of Income and Wealth*, Series 22, No. 1, March.

NICKELL, STEPHEN J. (1984), 'A Review of *Unemployment: Cause and Cure*, by Patrick Minford with David Davies, Michael Peel and Alison Sprague', *Economic Journal*, Vol. 94, No. 376, December.

NISBET, R. (1974), 'The Pursuit of Equality', *The Public Interest*, Vol. 35, Spring, pp. 103–20, reprinted in Letwin (1983).

NISKANEN, WILLIAM A. (1971), *Bureaucracy and Representative Government*, Chicago: Aldine Atherton.

NOUMI, K. (1983), 'Financing of Social Security Medical Care Schemes and the Containment of Costs: The Japanese Experience', *International Social Security Review*, Vol. 36, No. 2, pp. 180–90.

NOZICK, ROBERT (1974), *Anarchy, State and Utopia*, Oxford: Basil Blackwell.

O'DONNELL, OWEN, and PROPPER, CAROL (1991), 'Equity and the Distribution of UK National Health Service Resources', *Journal of Health Economics*, Vol. 10, pp. 1–21.

O'HIGGINS, MICHAEL (1980), 'The Redistributive Effect of Public Expenditure and Taxation', in Sandford *et al.* (1980).

O'HIGGINS, MICHAEL, *et al.* (1990), 'Income Distribution and Redistribution: A Microdata Analysis for Seven Countries', in Smeeding *et al.* (1990).

O'KELLY, RORY (1985), 'The Future of Social Security', Submission by the Fabian Society to the Labour Party's National Executive Committee, London: The Fabian Society.

OECD (1988), *Ageing Populations: The Social Policy Implications*, Paris: OECD.

OECD (1990), *Health Care Systems in Transition: The Search for Efficiency*, Paris: OECD (also published as US HCFA (1989)).

OFFICE OF HEALTH ECONOMICS (1985), *Measurement of Health*, London: Office of Health Economics.

OKUN, ARTHUR M. (1975), *Equality and Efficiency: The Big Tradeoff*, Washington, DC: The Brookings Institution.

OLIVER, M. (1989), *The Politics of Disablement*, London: Free Association Books.

ORSHANSKY, MOLLY (1965), 'Counting the Poor: Another Look at the Poverty Problem', *Social Security Bulletin*, Vol. 28, pp. 3–29.

OWENS, PATRICIA, and GLENNERSTER, HOWARD (1990), *Nursing in Conflict*, London: Macmillan.

PALMER, J. L., and PECHMAN, J. A. (eds) (1978), *Welfare in Rural Areas: The North Carolina–Iowa Income Maintenance Experiment*, Washington, DC: The Brookings Institution.

PARKER, HERMIONE (1989), *Instead of the Dole: An Enquiry into Integration of the Tax and Benefit System*, London: Routledge.

PARSONS, D. O. (1980), 'The Decline in Male Labor Force Participation', *Journal of Political Economy*, Vol. 88, pp. 117–24.

PAULY, MARK V. (1974), 'Overinsurance and Public Provision of Insurance: The Roles of Moral Hazard and Adverse Selection', *Quarterly Journal of Economics*, Vol. 88, pp. 44–62.

PAULY, MARK V. (1986), 'Taxation, Health Insurance and Market Failure in the Medical Economy', *Journal of Economic Literature*, Vol. 24, June, pp. 629–75.

PEACOCK, ALAN T. (1984), 'Privatisation in Perspective', *Three Banks Review*, No. 144, December, pp. 3–25.

PEACOCK, ALAN T., and SHANNON, ROBIN (1968), 'The Welfare State and the Redistribution of Income', *Westminster Bank Review*, August, pp. 30–46.

PEACOCK, ALAN T., and WISEMAN, JACK (1967), *The Growth of Public Expenditure in the United Kingdom*, revised edn, London: George Allen and Unwin.

PECHMAN, JOSEPH A. (1970), 'The Distributional Effects of Public Higher Education in California', *Journal of Human Resources*, Vol. 5, pp. 310–70.

PECHMAN, JOSEPH A. (ed.) (1980), *Setting National Priorities: Agenda for the 1980s*, Washington, DC: The Brookings Institution.

PECHMAN, JOSEPH A. (ed.) (1983), *Setting National Priorities: The 1984 Budget*, Washington, DC: The Brookings Institution.

PECHMAN, JOSEPH A. (1985), *Who Paid the Taxes, 1966–85*, Washington, DC: The Brookings Institution.

PECHMAN, JOSEPH A., and TIMPANE, P. MICHAEL (eds) (1975), *Work Incentives and Income Guarantees: The New Jersey Negative Income Tax Experiment*, Washington, DC: The Brookings Institution.

PECHMAN, JOSEPH A., AARON, HENRY J., and TAUSSIG, MICHAEL K. (1968), *Social Security: Perspectives for Reform*, Washington, DC: The Brookings Institution.

PELLING, HENRY (1979), *Popular Politics and Society in Late Victorian Britain*, 2nd edn, London: Macmillan.

PELZMANN, SAMUEL (1976), 'Towards a More General Theory of Regulation', *Journal of Law and Economics*, Vol. 19, August, pp. 211–40.

PEN, JAN (1971), 'A Parade of Dwarfs (and a Few Giants)', extract from *Income Distribution*, London: Penguin, reprinted in Atkinson (1980).

PENCAVEL, JOHN (1986), 'Labor Supply of Men: A Survey', in Ashenfelter and Layard (1986).

PETERSON, WALLACE C. (1991), *Transfer Spending, Taxes and the American Welfare State*, Boston, Mass.: Kluwer.

PIACHAUD, DAVID (1972), 'The Economics of Treating Varicose Veins', *International Journal of Epidemiology*, Vol. 1, Autumn.

PIACHAUD, DAVID (1975), 'The Economics of Educational Opportunity', *Higher Education*, Vol. 4, No. 2.

PIACHAUD, DAVID (1981), 'Peter Townsend and the Holy Grail', *New Society*, 10 September, pp. 419–21.

PIACHAUD, DAVID (1984), 'The Means Test State', *New Socialist*, October, pp. 53–4.

PIACHAUD, DAVID (1987), 'Problems in the Definition and Measurement of Poverty', *Journal of Social Policy*, Vol. 16, No. 2.

PIACHAUD, DAVID (1993), 'The Definition and Measurement of Poverty and Inequality', in Barr and Whynes (1993).

PIGGOTT, JOHN (1984), 'The Value of Tenant Benefits from UK Council House Subsidies', *Economic Journal*, Vol. 94, No. 374, June, pp. 384–9.

PIGGOTT, JOHN, and WHALLEY, JOHN (1985), *UK Tax Policy and Applied General Equilibrium Analysis*, Cambridge: Cambridge University Press.

PIGGOTT, JOHN, and WHALLEY, JOHN (eds) (1986), *New Developments in Applied General Equilibrium Analysis*, Cambridge: Cambridge University Press.

PINKER, ROBERT (1979), *The Idea of Welfare*, London: Heinemann.

PISSARIDES, CHRISTOPHER (1982), 'From School to University: The Demand for Post-Compulsory Education in Britain', *Economic Journal*, Vol. 92, September, pp. 654–67.

POSNER, RICHARD A. (1975), 'The Social Costs of Monopoly and Regulation', *Journal of Political Economy*, Vol. 83, August, pp. 807–27.

POWER, ANNE (1984), *Local Housing Management, A Priority Estates Project Survey*, London: Department of the Environment.

PREST, ALAN R. (1968), 'The Budget and Interpersonal Redistribution', *Public Finance*, Vol. 23, pp. 80–98.

PREST, ALAN R. (1973), 'Proposals for a Tax-Credit System', *British Tax Review*, No. 1.

PREST, ALAN R. (1983), 'The Social Security Reform Minefield', *British Tax Review*, No. 1, pp. 44–53.

PREST, ALAN R. (1985), 'Implicit Taxes: Are We Taxed More than We Think?', *Royal Bank of Scotland Review*, No. 147, September, pp. 10–26.

PREST, ALAN R., and BARR, NICHOLAS A. (1985), *Public Finance in Theory and Practice*, 7th edn, London: Weidenfeld and Nicolson.

PROJECTOR, DOROTHY S., and MURRAY, ELLEN G. (1978), *Eligibility for Welfare and Participation Rates, 1970*, Studies in Income Distribution No. 7, Washington, DC: US Department of Health, Education and Welfare.

PROPPER, CAROL, and MAYNARD, ALAN (1990), 'Whither the Private Health Care Sector?', in Culyer *et al.* (1990).

PROPPER, CAROL, and UPWARD, RICHARD (1992a), 'Need, Equity and the NHS: The Distribution of Health Care Expenditure 1974–87', *Fiscal Studies*, Vol. 13, No. 7, May, pp. 1–21.

PROPPER, CAROL, and UPWARD, RICHARD (1992b), 'Equity in the Finance and Delivery of Health Care in Britain', in van Doorslaer, Eddy, Wagstaff, Adam, and Rutten, F. (eds), *Equity in the Finance and Delivery of Health Care: An International Perspective*, Oxford: Oxford University Press.

PRYKE, R. (1982), 'The Comparative Performance of Public and Private Enterprise', *Fiscal Studies*, Vol. 3, No. 2, July.

PSACHAROPOULOS, GEORGE (1973), *Returns to Education: An International Comparison*, Amsterdam: Elsevier.

PSACHAROPOULOS, GEORGE (1980), *Education and Income*, World Bank Staff Working Paper No. 402, Washington, DC: The World Bank.

PSACHAROPOULOS, GEORGE (1984), 'The Contribution of Education to Economic Growth: International Comparisons', in Kendrick, J (ed.), *International Productivity Comparisons and the Causes of the Slowdown*, Cambridge, Mass.: Ballinger.

PSACHAROPOULOS, GEORGE, and WOODHALL, MAUREEN (1985), *Education for Development: An Analysis of Investment Choices*, Oxford: Oxford University Press.

RADFORD, R. A. (1945), 'The Economic Organisation of a POW Camp', *Economica*, NS Vol. XII, No. 48, November, pp. 189–201.

RAVALLION, MARTIN (1991), 'Reaching the Rural Poor through Public Employment: Arguments, Evidence and Lessons from South Asia', *World Bank Research Observer*, Vol. 6, No. 2, July, pp. 153–75.

RAWLS, JOHN (1972), *A Theory of Justice*, Oxford: Oxford University Press.

REES, P. M., and THOMPSON, F. P. (1972), 'The Relative Price Effect in Public Expenditure: Its Nature and Method of Calculation', *Statistical News*, No. 18, August, London: HMSO.

REID, I. (1981), *Social Class Differences in Britain*, London: Grant McIntyre.

RICARDO, DAVID (1817), *On the Principles of Political Economy and Taxation*, London: Murray.

RIMLINGER, G. (1971), *Welfare Policy and Industrialisation in Europe, America and Russia*, New York: Wiley.

ROBBINS, LIONEL C. (1977), *Political Economy Past and Present: A Review of Leading Theories of Economic Policy*, London: Macmillan.

ROBBINS, LIONEL C. (1978), *The Theory of Economic Policy in English Classical Political Economy*, 2nd edn, London: Macmillan.

ROBINSON, JOAN, and EATWELL, JOHN (1973), *An Introduction to Modern Economics*, London: McGraw-Hill.

ROBINSON, RAY (1979), *Housing Economics and Public Policy*, London: Macmillan.

ROBSON, WILLIAM A. (1976), *Welfare State and Welfare Society*, London: George Allen and Unwin.

ROSA, JEAN-JACQUES (ed.) (1982), *The World Crisis in Social Security*, Paris and San Francisco: Fondation Nationale d'Economie Politique and Institute for Contemporary Studies.

ROSE, M. E. (1972), *The Relief of Poverty 1834–1914*, London: Macmillan.

ROSEN, S. (1982), 'United States', in Rosa (1982).

ROSENTHAL, L. (1975), 'The Nature of Council House Subsidies', PhD thesis, University of Essex.

ROSENTHAL, L. (1977), 'The Regional and Income Distribution of Council House Subsidy in the United Kingdom', *The Manchester School*, Vol. 45, pp. 127–40.

ROTHSCHILD, MICHAEL, and STIGLITZ, JOSEPH E. (1976), 'Equilibrium in Competitive Insurance Markets: An Essay on the Economics of Imperfect Information', *Quarterly Journal of Economics*, Vol. 90, pp. 629–49.

ROWLEY, CHARLES K., and PEACOCK, ALAN T. (1975), *Welfare Economics: A Liberal Restatement*, Oxford: Martin Robertson.

ROWNTREE, B. SEEBOHM (1901), *Poverty: A Study of Town Life*, London: Longman.

ROWNTREE, B. SEEBOHM (1941), *Poverty and Progress: A Second Social Survey of York*, London: Longman.

ROWNTREE, B. SEEBOHM, and LAVERS, G. R. (1951), *Poverty and the Welfare State*, London: Longman.

RUNCIMAN, W. G. (1972), *Relative Deprivation and Social Justice*, London: Penguin.

RUSSELL, LOUISE B. (1980), 'Medical Care', in Pechman (1980).

RUSSELL, LOUISE B. (1989), *Medicare's New Hospital Payment System: Is It Working?*, Washington, DC: The Brookings Institution.

RUTTER, M., MAUGHAN, B., MORTIMORE, P., and OUSTON, J. (1979), *Fifteen Thousand Hours: Secondary Schools and Their Effects on Children*, London: Open Books.

SAINSBURY, SALLY (1986), *Deaf Worlds*, London: Hutchinson.

SAINSBURY, SALLY (1989), *Regulating Residential Care*, London: Gower.

SALOP, JOANNE, and SALOP, STEVEN (1976), 'Self-Selection and Turnover in the Labor Market', *Quarterly Journal of Economics*, Vol. 90, No. 4, November, pp. 619–27.

SAMUELSON, PAUL A. (1954), 'The Pure Theory of Public Expenditures', *Review of Economics and Statistics*, Vol. XXXVI, November.

SAMUELSON, PAUL A. (1958), 'An Exact Consumption-Loan Model of Interest with or without the Social Contrivance of Money', *Journal of Political Economy*, Vol. LXVI, No. 6, December, pp. 467–82.

SANDFORD, CEDRIC, POND, CHRISTOPHER, and WALKER, ROBERT (eds) (1980), *Taxation and Social Policy*, London: Heinemann.

SAWHILL, ISABEL V. (1988), 'Poverty in the US: Why Is It So Persistent?', *Journal of Economic Literature*, Vol. 26, pp. 1073–119.

SCHIEBER, GEORGE J., POULLIER, JEAN-PIERRE, and GREENWALD, LESLIE M. (1991), 'Health Care Systems in Twenty-Four Countries', *Health Affairs*, Vol. 10, No. 3, pp. 22–38.

SCHOTTLAND, C. I. (1963), *The Social Security Program in the United States*, New York: Appleton-Century-Crofts.

SELDON, ARTHUR (1981), *Wither the Welfare State*, London: Institute of Economic Affairs.

SEN, AMARTYA K. (1970), 'The Impossibility of a Paretian Liberal', *Journal of Political Economy*, Vol. 78, No. 1, January/February, pp. 152–7.

SEN, AMARTYA K. (1973), *On Economic Inequality*, Oxford: Oxford University Press.

SEN, AMARTYA K. (1979), 'Personal Utilities and Public Judgements: Or What's Wrong with Welfare Economics?', *Economic Journal*, Vol. 89, No. 355, September, pp. 537–58.

SEN, AMARTYA K. (1983), 'Poor, Relatively Speaking', *Oxford Economic Papers*, Vol. 35, pp. 153–69.

SEN, AMARTYA K. (1992), *Inequality Reexamined*, Oxford: Clarendon Press.

SHANKLAND, G., WILLMOTT, P., and JORDAN, D. (1977), *Inner London: Policies for Dispersal and Balance*, Department of the Environment, London: HMSO.

SHAVELL, STEVEN (1979), 'On Moral Hazard and Insurance', *Quarterly Journal of Economics*, Vol. 93, pp. 541–62.

SHORROCKS, A. F. (1983), 'Ranking Income Distributions', *Economica*, Vol. 50, No. 197, February, pp. 3–17.

SIMONS, HERBERT (1938), *Personal Income Taxation*, Chicago: University of Chicago Press.

SMEEDING, TIMOTHY, et al., (1990), 'Income Poverty in Seven Countries', in Smeeding et al. (1990).

SMEEDING, TIMOTHY, O'HIGGINS, MICHAEL, AND RAINWATER, LEE (eds) (1990), *Poverty, Inequality and Income Distribution in Comparative Perspective: The Luxembourg Income Study*, Washington, DC, and London: The Urban Institute and Harvester Wheatsheaf.

SMITH, ADAM (1776), *An Inquiry into the Nature and Causes of the Wealth of Nations*, Oxford: Clarendon Press, reprinted 1976.

SMITH, L., ROSEN, C., and FALLIS, G. (1988), 'Recent Developments in Economic Models of Housing Markets', *Journal of Economic Literature*, Vol. 26, pp. 29–44.

SMITH, STEPHEN (1991), 'Distributional Issues in Local Taxation', *Economic Journal*, Vol. 101, No. 406, May, pp. 585–99.

SOLTOW, L. (1968), 'Long-Run Changes in British Income Inequality', *Economic History Review*, second series, Vol. 21, No. 1, pp. 17–29, reprinted in Atkinson (1980).

SPENCE, MICHAEL (1973), 'Job Market Signalling', *Quarterly Journal of Economics*, Vol. 87, August, pp. 355–74, reprinted in Diamond and Rothschild (1978).

SPENCER, HERBERT (1884), *The Man versus the State*, New York: Appleton.

SPICKER, P. (1986), 'The Case for Supplementary Benefit', *Fiscal Studies*, Vol. 7, No. 4, pp. 28–44.

STEEL, D., and HEALD, D. (eds) (1984), *Privatizing Public Enterprises*, London: Royal Institute of Public Administration.

STEPHENSON, GEOFFREY (1980), 'Taxes, Benefits and the Redistribution of Incomes', in Sandford *et al.* (1980).

STERN, NICHOLAS H. (1982), 'Optimum Taxation with Errors in Administration', *Journal of Public Economics*, Vol. 17, pp. 181–211.

STEVENS, R. B. (ed.) (1970), *Statutory History of the United States: Income Security*, New York: McGraw-Hill.

STIGLER, GEORGE (1971), 'The Theory of Economic Regulation', *Bell Journal of Economics and Management Science*, Vol. 2, Spring, pp. 137–46.

STIGLITZ, JOSEPH E. (1987), 'The Causes and Consequences of the Dependence of Quality on Price', *Journal of Economic Literature*, Vol. 25, No. 1, pp. 1–48.

STIGLITZ, JOSEPH E. (1988), *The Economics of the Public Sector*, 2nd edn, New York and London: Norton.

STOCK, JAMES H., and WISE, DAVID A. (1988), 'The Pension Inducement to Retire: An Option Value Analysis', Working Paper No. 2660, Cambridge, Mass.: NBER.

STRACHEY, JOHN (1936), *The Theory and Practice of Socialism*, London: Gollancz.

SUGDEN, ROBERT (1982), 'On the Economics of Philanthropy', *Economic Journal*, Vol. 92, No. 366, June, pp. 341–50.

SUGDEN, ROBERT (1983a), 'On the Economics of Philanthropy: Reply', *Economic Journal*, Vol. 93, No. 371, September, p. 639.

SUGDEN, ROBERT (1983b), *Who Cares? An Economic and Ethical Analysis of Private Charity and the Welfare State*, Occasional Paper 67, London: Institute of Economic Affairs.

SUGDEN, ROBERT (1984), 'Reciprocity: The Supply of Public Goods Through Voluntary Contributions', *Economic Journal*, Vol. 94, No. 376, December, pp. 772–87.

SUMMERS, LAWRENCE H. (1989), 'Some Simple Economics of Mandated Benefits', *American Economic Review*, Vol. 79, No. 2, May, pp. 177–83.

SURREY, STANLEY S. (1948), 'Federal Taxation of the Family – The Revenue Act of 1948', *Harvard Law Review*, Vol. 61, July, pp. 1097–164.

SURREY, STANLEY S. (1958), 'The Federal Income Tax Base for Individuals', *Columbia Law Review*, Vol. 58, June, pp. 815–30.

URREY, S. S., and MCDANIEL, P. R. (1985), *Tax Expenditures*, Cambridge, Mass.: Harvard University Press.

SWEEZY, PAUL (1942), *The Theory of Capitalist Development*, London: Dennis Dobson.

SWENARTON, MARK (1981), *Homes Fit for Heroes: The Politics and Architecture of Early State Housing in Britain*, London: Heinemann.

TAWNEY, R. H. (1921), *The Acquisitive Society*, London: Fontana, reprinted 1961.

TAWNEY, R. H. (1953), *The Attack and Other Papers*, London: Allen and Unwin.

TAWNEY, R. H. (1964), *Equality*, 4th edn, London: George Allen and Unwin.

TAYLOR, ALAN J. (1972), *Laissez-faire and State Intervention in Nineteenth-century Britain*, London: Macmillan.

THANE, PAT (1982), *The Foundations of the Welfare State*, London: Longman.

THEIL, HENRI (1967), *Economics and Information Theory*, Amsterdam: North Holland.

THUROW, LESTER C. (1971), 'The Income Distribution as a Pure Public Good', *Quarterly Journal of Economics*, May.

TIEBOUT, CHARLES (1956), 'A Pure Theory of Local Expenditures', *Journal of Political Economy*, October.

TITMUSS, RICHARD M. (1956), *The Social Division of Welfare*, Liverpool University Press, reprinted in Titmuss (1958).

TITMUSS, RICHARD M. (1958), *Essays on 'The Welfare State'*, London: Allen and Unwin, 3rd edn, 1976.

TITMUSS, RICHARD M. (1968), *Commitment to Welfare*, London: Allen and Unwin, 2nd edn, 1976.

TITMUSS, RICHARD M. (1970), *The Gift Relationship*, London: Penguin.

TOBIN, JAMES (1968), 'Raising the Incomes of the Poor', in Gordon, K. (ed.), *Agenda for the Nation*, Washington, DC: The Brookings Institution.

TOBIN, J., PECHMAN, J., and MIESZKOWSKI, P. (1967), 'Is a Negative Income Tax Practical?', *Yale Law Journal*, Vol. 77.

TOLLEY (1991), *Social Security and State Benefits, 1991–92*, ed. by Matthewman, J., Croydon, Surrey: Tolley Publishing Company.

TOWNSEND, PETER (1979), *Poverty in the United Kingdom*, London: Penguin.

TOWNSEND, P., and DAVIDSON, N. (1982), *Inequalities in Health*, London: Penguin.

TULLOCK, GORDON (1970), *Private Wants, Public Means*, New York: Basic Books.

TULLOCK, GORDON (1971), 'The Charity of the Uncharitable', *Western Economic Journal*, Vol. 9, pp. 379–92, reprinted in Letwin (1983).

TULLOCK, GORDON (1976), *The Vote Motive*, Hobart Paperback No. 9, London: Institute of Economic Affairs.

UK (1842), *Inquiry into the Sanitary Condition of the Labouring Population of Great Britain*, London: HMSO.

UK (1885), *Report of the Royal Commission on the Housing of the Working Classes*, London: HMSO.

UK (1914), *The Land, Vol II: Urban*, Report of the Land Enquiry Committee, London: HMSO.

UK (1942), *Social Insurance and Allied Services* (The Beveridge Report), Cmd 6404, London: HMSO.

UK (1943), *Educational Reconstruction*, Cmd 6458, London: HMSO.

UK (1944a), *A National Health Service*, Cmd 6502, London: HMSO.

UK (1944b), *Employment Policy*, Cmd 6527, London: HMSO.

UK (1944c), *Social Insurance*, Pt I, Cmd 6550, and Pt II (Workmen's Compensation), Cmd 6551, London: HMSO.

UK (1960), *Grants for Students* (The Anderson Report), Report of the Committee Appointed by the Minister of Education and the Secretary of State for Scotland, Cmnd 1051, London: HMSO.

UK (1962), *A Review of the Medical Services in Great Britain*, London: HMSO.

UK (1963), *Higher Education* (The Robbins Report), Cmnd 2154, London: HMSO.

UK (1966), *A Plan for Polytechnics and Other Colleges*, London: HMSO.

UK (1968), *The Administrative Structure of the Medical and Related Services in England and Wales*, London: HMSO.

UK (1970), *The Future Structure of the National Health Service*, London: HMSO.

UK (1972a), *Proposals for a Tax-Credit System*, Cmnd 5116, London: HMSO.

UK (1972b), *National Health Reorganisation: England*, London: HMSO.

UK (1972c), *Public Expenditure White Papers: Handbook on Methodology*, London: HMSO.

UK (1973), *Report and Proceedings*, Select Committee on Tax-Credit, Session 1972–73, HC 341-I, 341-II, 341-III, London: HMSO.

UK (1974), *Better Pensions Fully Protected Against Inflation*, Cmnd 5713, London: HMSO.

UK (1975), *Minutes of Evidence*, Select Committee on a Wealth Tax, Volume II, Session 1974–75, HC 696-II, London: HMSO.

UK (1977), *A New Partnership for Our Schools*, London: HMSO.

UK (1978a), *The Financing of Occupational Pension Schemes*, Evidence of the Government Actuary's Department to the Committee to Review the Functioning of Financial Institutions, London: HMSO.

UK (1978b), *Royal Commission on Civil Liability and Compensation for Personal Injury*, Cmnd 7054, London: HMSO.

UK (1979a), Royal Commission on the Distribution of Income and Wealth, *Report No. 7: Fourth Report on the Standing Reference*, Cmnd 7595, London: HMSO.

UK (1979b), *Report of the Royal Commission on the National Health Service*, London: HMSO.

UK (1983a), *The Structure of Personal Income Taxation and Income Support*, Third Special Report from the Treasury and Civil Service Committee, Session 1982–83, HC 386, London: HMSO.

UK (1983b), *The Structure of Personal Income Taxation and Income Support, Minutes of Evidence*, Treasury and Civil Service Committee Sub-Committee, Session 1982–83, HC 20-I, London: HMSO.

UK (1983c), *The Structure of Personal Income Taxation and Income Support, Appendices*, Treasury and Civil Service Committee Sub-Committee, Session 1982–83, HC 20-II, London: HMSO.

UK (1985a), *Employment: The Challenge for the Nation*, Cmnd 9474, London: HMSO.

UK (1985b), *Reform of Social Security*, Cmnd 9517, London: HMSO.

UK (1985c), *Reform of Social Security: Programme for Change*, Cmnd 9518, London: HMSO.

UK (1985d), *Reform of Social Security: Background Papers*, Cmnd 9519, London: HMSO.

UK (1985e), *Housing Benefit Review*, Cmnd 9520, London: HMSO.

UK (1985f), *The Government's Green Paper 'Reform of Social Security'*, Seventh Report from the Social Services Committee, Session 1984–85, HC 451, London: HMSO.

UK (1985g), 'The Effects of Taxes and Benefits on Household Income 1984', *Economic Trends*, No. 386, December, pp. 99–115.

UK (1985h), *Reform of Social Security: Programme for Action*, Cmnd 9691, London: HMSO.

UK (1986a), *The Reform of Personal Taxation*, Cmnd 9756, London: HMSO.

UK (1986b), *Report of the Committee of Inquiry into Unnecessary Dental Treatment*, London: HMSO.

UK (1991), *Report of the Government Actuary on the Drafts of the Social Security Benefits Uprating (No. 2) Order 1991 and the Social Security (Contributions) (Rerating) (No. 2) Order, 1991*, Cm 1779, London: HMSO.

UK (1992a), *Financial Statement and Budget Report, 1992–93*, London: HMSO.

UK (1992b), *The Government's Expenditure Plans, 1992–93 to 1994–95: Department of the Environment: Annual Report*, Cm 1908, London: HMSO.

UK (1992c), *The Government's Expenditure Plans, 1992–93 to 1994–95: Department of Health and Office of Population Censuses and Surveys: Departmental Report*, Cm 1913, London: HMSO.

UK (1992d), *The Government's Expenditure Plans, 1992–93 to 1994–95: Department of Education and Science: Departmental Report*, Cm 1911, London: HMSO.

UK (1992e), *The Government's Expenditure Plans, 1992–93 to 1994–95: Department of Social Security: Departmental Report*, Cm 1914, London: HMSO.

UK (1992f), *The Government's Expenditure Plans, 1992–93 to 1994–95: Serving Scotland's Needs*, Cm 1915, London: HMSO.

UK (1992g), *The Government's Expenditure Plans, 1992–93 to 1994–95: A Report by the Welsh Office*, Cm 1916, London: HMSO.

UK (1992h), *The Government's Expenditure Plans, 1992–93 to 1994–95: Northern Ireland*, Cm 1917, London: HMSO.

UK (1992j), *Public Expenditure Analyses to 1994–95: Statistical Supplement to the 1991 Autumn Statement*, Cm 1920, London: HMSO.

UK AUDIT COMMISSION (1986), *Managing the Crisis in Council Housing*, London: HMSO.

UK BOARD OF INLAND REVENUE (1983), *Cost of Tax Reliefs for Pensions Schemes: Appropriate Statistical Approach*, London: HMSO.

UK CENTRAL ADVISORY COUNCIL FOR EDUCATION (ENGLAND) (1963), *Half our Future* (The Newsom Report), London: HMSO.

UK DEPARTMENT OF EDUCATION AND SCIENCE (1986), *Report by Her Majesty's Inspectors on the Effects of Local Authority Expenditure Policies on Education Provision in England, 1985*, London: HMSO.

UK DEPARTMENT OF EDUCATION AND SCIENCE (1988), *Top-Up Loans for Students*, Cm 520, London: HMSO.

UK DEPARTMENT OF EDUCATION AND SCIENCE (1991), *Higher Education: A New Framework*, Cm 1541, London: HMSO.

UK DEPARTMENT OF HEALTH (1989a), *Working for Patients*, Cm 555, London: HMSO.

UK DEPARTMENT OF HEALTH (1989b), *Caring for People: Community Care in the Next Decade and Beyond*, Cm 849, London: HMSO.

UK DEPARTMENT OF HEALTH (1992), *Report of the Inquiry into London's Health Service, Medical Education and Research*, London: HMSO.

UK DEPARTMENT OF HEALTH AND SOCIAL SECURITY (1976), *Sharing Resources for Health in England: Report of the Joint Resource Allocation Working Party*, London: HMSO.

UK DEPARTMENT OF HEALTH AND SOCIAL SECURITY (1979), *Patients First*, London: HMSO.

UK DEPARTMENT OF HEALTH AND SOCIAL SECURITY (1983), *Report of the NHS Management Enquiry*, London: HMSO.

UK DEPARTMENT OF SOCIAL SECURITY (1991), *Options for Equality in State Pension Age*, Cm 1723, London: HMSO.

UK DEPARTMENT OF THE ENVIRONMENT (1971), *Fair Deal for Housing*, Cmnd 4728, London: HMSO.

UK DEPARTMENT OF THE ENVIRONMENT (1977a), *Housing Policy: A Consultative Document*, Cmnd 6851, London: HMSO.

UK DEPARTMENT OF THE ENVIRONMENT (1977b), *Housing Policy: Technical Volume, Part I*, London: HMSO.

UK DEPARTMENT OF THE ENVIRONMENT (1977c), *Housing Policy: Technical Volume, Part II*, London: HMSO.

UK DEPARTMENT OF THE ENVIRONMENT (1977d), *Housing Policy: Technical Volume, Part III*, London: HMSO.

UK DEPARTMENT OF THE ENVIRONMENT (1985a), *Homeless Households Reported by Local Authorities in England*, May, London: HMSO.

UK DEPARTMENT OF THE ENVIRONMENT (1985b), *Home Improvement – A New Approach*, Cmnd 9513, London: HMSO.

UK DEPARTMENT OF THE ENVIRONMENT (1987a), *Housing: The Government's Proposals*, Cm 214, London: HMSO.

UK DEPARTMENT OF THE ENVIRONMENT (1987b), *Finance for Housing Associations: The Government's Proposals*, London: Department of the Environment.

UK DEPARTMENT OF THE ENVIRONMENT (1987c), *Home Improvement Policy: The Government's Proposals*, London: Department of the Environment.

UK HOUSE OF COMMONS SOCIAL SERVICES COMMITTEE (1988a), *Fifth Report: The Future of the National Health Service*, Session 1987–88, HC 613, London: HMSO.

UK HOUSE OF COMMONS SOCIAL SERVICES COMMITTEE (1988b), *Public Expenditure on the Social Services*, London: HMSO.

UK NATIONAL AUDIT OFFICE (1985), *National Health Service: Control of Nursing Manpower*, Report by the Comptroller and Auditor General, London: HMSO.

UK PENSION LAW REVIEW COMMITTEE (1992), *Consultation Document on the Law and Regulation of Occupational Pension Schemes*, London: HMSO.

UNIVERSITIES CENTRAL COUNCIL ON ADMISSIONS (1985), *Statistical Supplement to the Twenty-Second Report, 1983–84*, London: Universities Central Council on Admissions.

US (1969), *Poverty Amid Plenty: The American Paradox*, Report of the President's Commission on Income Maintenance Programs, Washington, DC: US Government Printing Office.

US ADVISORY COUNCIL ON SOCIAL SECURITY (1938), *Final Report*, S. Doc. 4, 76 Cong. 1 sess. (1939).

US DEPARTMENT OF HEALTH AND HUMAN SERVICES (1989), *Social Security Programs Throughout the World 1989*, Research Report No. 62, Washington, DC.

US FEDERAL EMERGENCY RELIEF ADMINISTRATION (1942), *Final Statistical Report of the Federal Emergency Relief Administration*, Washington, DC.

US HCFA (1989), *Health Care Financing Review*, Annual Supplement, Office of Research and Demonstrations, Health Care Financing Administration, Washington DC: Government Printing Office, December (also published as OECD (1990)).

US NATIONAL RESOURCES AND PLANNING BOARD (1942), *Long Range Work and Relief Policies: Report of the Committee on Long Range Work and Relief to the National Resources Planning Board*, Washington, DC.

US SUPREME COURT (1978), *City of Los Angeles, Department of Water and Power et al. v. Manhart et al.*, Case No. 76–1810.

VARIAN, HAL R. (1984), *Microeconomic Analysis*, 2nd edn, New York: Norton.

VENTI, S. F., and WISE, D. A. (1984), 'Moving and Housing Expenditure: Transactions Costs and Disequilibrium', *Journal of Public Economics*, Vol. 23, No. 1/2, February/March, pp. 207–43.

WAGSTAFF, ADAM (1991), 'QALYS and the Equity–Efficiency Tradeoff', *Journal of Health Economics*, Vol. 10, pp. 21–43.

WAGSTAFF, ADAM, VAN DOORSLAER, EDDY, and PACI, PIERELLA (1991), 'On the Measurement of Horizontal Inequity in the Delivery of Health Care', *Journal of Health Economics*, Vol. 10, pp. 169–206.

WALKER, ALAN, and TOWNSEND, PETER (eds) (1981), *Disability in Britain*, Oxford: Martin Robertson.

WARLICK, JENNIFER L. (1981), 'Participation of the Aged in SSI', *Journal of Human Resources*, Vol. 17, pp. 236–60.

WEALE, ALBERT (1978), *Equality and Social Policy*, London: Routledge and Kegan Paul.

WEAVER, CAROLINE L. (1982), *The Crisis in Social Security: Economic and Political Origins*, Durham, North Carolina: Duke University Press.

WEBB, M. (1984), 'Privatisation of the Electricity and Gas Industries', in Steel and Heald (1984).

WEBB, SIDNEY, and WEBB, BEATRICE (1909), *The Break Up of the Poor Law*, Minority Report of the Poor Law Commission, Part I, London: Longman.

WEISBROD, BURTON A. (1969), 'Collective Action and the Distribution of Income: A Conceptual Approach', in Joint Economic Committee, *The Analysis and Evaluation of Public Expenditures*, Washington, DC: US Government Printing Office.

WEISBROD, BURTON A. (1983), 'Competition in Health Care: A Cautionary View', in Meyer, Jack (ed.), *Market Reforms in Health Care*, Washington, DC, and London: American Enterprise Institute for Public Policy Research.

WEITZMAN, MARTIN L. (1977), 'Is the Price System or Rationing More Effective in Getting a Commodity to Those Who Need It Most?', *Bell Journal of Economics*, Vol. 8, pp. 517–24.

WEITZMAN, MARTIN L. (1984), *The Share Economy*, Cambridge, Mass.: Harvard University Press.

WEST, EDWARD G. (1970), *Education and the State*, 2nd edn, London: Institute of Economic Affairs.

WHITEHEAD, CHRISTINE M. E. (1974), *The UK Housing Market: An Econometric Model*, Farnborough, Hants: Saxon House.

WHITEHEAD, CHRISTINE M. E. (1980), 'Fiscal Aspects of Housing', in Sandford *et al.* (1980).

WHITEHEAD, CHRISTINE M. E. (1983), 'Possible Effects of the Removal of Mortgage Interest Tax Relief', in UK (1983c).

WILENSKY, HAROLD L., and LEBEAUX, CHARLES N. (1965), *Industrial Society and Social Welfare*, New York and London: Free Press and Collier-Macmillan.

WILES, PETER J. D. (1974), *Distribution of Income: East and West*, Amsterdam: North Holland.

WILLETTS, DAVID (1992), *Modern Conservatism*, London: Penguin.

WILLIAMS, ALAN (1985), 'Economics of Coronary Artery Bypass Grafting', *British Medical Journal*, 3 August, pp. 326–9.

WILLIAMSON, J., *et al.* (1964), 'Old People at Home: Their Unreported Needs', *Lancet*, 23 May, pp. 1117–20.

WILLIAMSON, J. G. (1980), 'Earnings Inequality in Nineteenth-Century Britain', *Journal of Economic History*, Vol. XL, No. 3, pp. 457–76.

WILLIS, J. R. M., and HARDWICK, P. J. W. (1978), *Tax Expenditures in the United Kingdom*, London: Heinemann, for the Institute for Fiscal Studies.

WILSON, CHARLES (1977), 'A Model of Insurance Markets with Incomplete Information', *Journal of Economic Theory*, Vol. 16, No. 2, December, pp. 167–207.

WILSON, THOMAS (1991), 'The Poll Tax – Origin, Errors and Remedies', *Economic Journal*, Vol. 101, No. 406, May, pp. 577–84.

WINCH, DONALD M. (1971), *Analytical Welfare Economics*, London: Penguin.

WISE, DAVID A. (ed.) (1986), *Pensions, Labor and Individual Behavior*, Chicago: University of Chicago Press.

WITTE, E. E. (1962), *The Development of the Social Security Act*, Madison: University of Wisconsin Press.

WOODHALL, MAUREEN (1983), *Student Loans as a Means of Financing Higher Education: Lessons from International Experience*, Washington, DC: The World Bank.

ZABALZA, ANTONIO, and PIACHAUD, DAVID (1981), 'Social Security and the Elderly: A Simulation of Policy Changes', *Journal of Public Economics*, Vol. 16, pp. 145–69.

ZECKHAUSER, RICHARD J., and PATEL, JAYENDU (1987), 'Treasury Bill Futures as Hedges against Inflation Risk', Working Paper No. 2322, Cambridge, Mass.: NBER.

Subject Index

Author index